# MOVIES OF THE 60s

727

JÜRGEN MÜLLER (ED.)

IN COLLABORATION WITH
defd AND CINEMA, HAMBURG
BRITISH FILM INSTITUTE, LONDON
BIBLIOTHEQUE DU FILM, PARIS

# MOVIES OF THE 60s

TASCHEN
KÖLN LONDON LOS ANGELES MADRID PARIS TOKYO

# WALK ON THE WILD WIDE

## Notes on the Movies of the 60s

The buildings of Fifth Avenue are still submerged in darkness, but the sun is already rising at the end of the street. It's a timeless moment, as if the world had paused for thought before the day gets going. A yellow cab drives slowly up the street and stops on the corner of 57th; a young woman gets out. She's wearing a black evening dress and a pearl necklace. She stops in front of a department store and glances up at the sign above the door: "Tiffany & Co." Then she moves over to look in the window.

We see her in profile while she studies the display, lost in thought. She reaches into a paper bag and pulls out a coffee and a croissant. The camera follows this elegant apparition from one window to the next, and then there's a change of perspective: we're watching from the store, and before us stands Audrey Hepburn, lost to the world as she gazes at the costly jewels on display. Behind the glass, she herself seems the quintessence of beauty and worth – as far beyond our reach as Tiffany's glittering gems. And the beauty of this entire sequence consists in the fact that we never actually see a single valuable item of jewelry.

Instead, we've spent the whole time observing a wide-eyed girl, and though her loveliness is apparently only celebrated in passing, it actually represents a touchstone of value. Audrey Hepburn's looks are breathtaking, and her elegance is surpassed only by her perfect, unaffected naturalness. And though Miss Hepburn's hats do become ever more extravagant in the course of the movie, they only serve to accentuate the classical simplicity of her dresses and coats. It's as if Irving Penn, who celebrated a modern kind of beauty, had accompanied the director as an aesthetic advisor.

Few opening sequences can match the elegance of this one. In *Breakfast at Tiffany's* (1961, p. 62), Audrey Hepburn is the icon and harbinger of a stylish and style-conscious decade. Yet there's something undeniably idiosyncratic about the ideal of female beauty presented by this film and its star; for the focus is not just on Hepburn's looks, but on the extravagance of her character, Holly Golightly. Evening dress, pumps, pearl necklace and sunglasses in the first light of dawn: what we have before us is a glamorous and matchlessly beautiful creature of the night. But every mortal human casts a shadow… and Holly Golightly is no exception.

For a discreet visit to the powder room with a gentleman, she picks up 50 dollars; and she's quite prepared to accept the financial support of a fat millionaire, before eventually letting herself be snapped up by a rich Brazilian. Yet for all the "rats and super-rats" she uses and is used by, Truman

Capote's Holly Golightly still has "an almost breakfast-cereal air of health, a soap and lemon cleanness." And with her irresistible girlish charm, Audrey Hepburn embodies her to perfection.

## Life as a masquerade

This mixture of innocence and loucheness might easily have made her a kind of aged Lolita, at once rapacious and helplessly dependent. Instead, Holly Golightly represents a new kind of anarchically carefree woman. Though she lives from men, she resolutely maintains her independence, taking to her heels when anyone gets too personal, and always ready to speak her mind. She dreams of a simple life with her mentally retarded brother Fred, but delights in the exclusive atmosphere at Tiffany's. She has a true appreciation for the real human qualities, but prefers to seek her pleasure in the sham paradise of parties and bars.

What one might call her flightiness – which at times borders on hysteria – also makes one thing very clear: in the United States, in the year 1961, any attempt to break free of the traditional women's role is most likely to succeed if it comes in the guise of sheer craziness. Gently but categorically, the film's happy ending marks the limits of Holly's freedom to define her own life; from now on, she'll have to settle for love. For all that, the couple at the center of this film are pretty unusual by Hollywood standards, at least as regards their moral integrity. Holly Golightly picks up men in bars and clubs, while Paul (George Peppard), her male mirror image, lives in the pocket of a married woman. His "sponsor" (Patricia Neal), who is wedded to a dull but wealthy man, enjoys the *frisson* of her illicit affair and the power of her husband's dollars. One might regard Paul and Holly as miserable failures in life, if they weren't both so radiant in their youth and beauty. And in a mad, bad and thrillingly dangerous world so clearly ruled by sex, money and power, the film allows Holly to master her own life by means of her own gravity-defying insouciance.

In *Breakfast at Tiffany's*, life seems like one endless, turbulent, exhilarating masquerade, in which you're forbidden to catch your breath in case you also catch sight of the lies you've been telling yourself. We see Holly's life through the eyes of Paul, an unsuccessful writer. Only occasionally, and only to him, does she ever show her true face, speaking of her dreams and of the despair she calls "the mean reds." At one point, the metaphor of the mask is made quite concrete: Holly and Paul visit a dime store and steal two masks for fun. Having donned the false faces of a cat and a dog, they're walking down the street when they encounter a cop… and though they fear for a moment that their crime has caught up with them, the two thieves escape scot-free. Back home, they drop their masks, gaze lovingly into one another's eyes, and kiss.

## An icon on the verge of a nervous breakdown

Svelte, sylph-like, indeed positively elfin, Audrey Hepburn embodied an ideal of beauty for the new decade. But although she bestowed the face of an angel on Holly Golightly, it was this very film that saved her from being typecast as the nice girl waiting for Mr. Right. However fragile in appearance, Holly is a confident woman who needs no 50s curves to draw the attention of every man – and every woman – in her vicinity. She refuses to accept any limits, even to her feelings. Her worries about her brother Fred culminate in a fit of aggression that sees her demolishing part of her furniture. This pairing of sadness and anger reveals both the intensity and the poverty of her emotional life. Nonetheless, there are occasions when *Breakfast at Tiffany's* remains stuck in the clichés of its time. Sometimes, for all her incomparable grace, Audrey Hepburn does lay it on a bit thick. Her character's fervent inner life is acted out so excessively, and so very visibly, that Paul – and the audience – can be forgiven for wanting to offer her something a little *quieter*. And ultimately, that means the safe haven of a bourgeois marriage.

For such apparently amoral figures, this is the prescribed moral stance, and we can see it in the symbolic language of the film: Holly's cat and the stolen mask cast this animal as her familiar and her alter ego. Certainly, she's a girl who desires her independence. Tellingly, she's never given her adopted housecat a name, because she never felt she had a right to do so. But when she tries to set Cat free, the animal refuses to leave her: he's grown used to domesticity and he no longer misses his freedom. The message is clear: life can't be lived as a permanent Walk on the Wild Side.

The cry for sexual liberation prompted huge controversy in the 60s. The changed behavior of young people, especially young women, divided the generations. And so it's very noticeable that *Breakfast at Tiffany's* is elaborately indirect. Holly's source of income is only ever hinted at, and her night of love with Paul is indicated discreetly in a single image: the dog's mask he'd been wearing now graces the statue of Amor beside his bed. (His wealthy patroness had given him this kitschy figurine as a token of her esteem.)

Blake Edwards' film toys with the topic of sexuality rather than dealing with it frankly. In any case, Audrey Hepburn's innocent face seems capable of taking the steam out of any situation. Take the scene with the stripper in the nightclub: as Holly and Paul watch her slowly undressing, they talk without looking at one another; they're watching themselves, each other and the dancer in the mirror at the back of the bar. Holly muses aloud on how much the stripper earns, and comments critically on the quality of the girl's performance. In a roundabout way, she makes it quite clear how she feels about sex, which in her eyes has a lot to do with money and nothing at all to do with love. Holly looks quite as friendly as ever, but she's clearly just not very interested. It all seems harmless, trivial, nothing to get very much worked

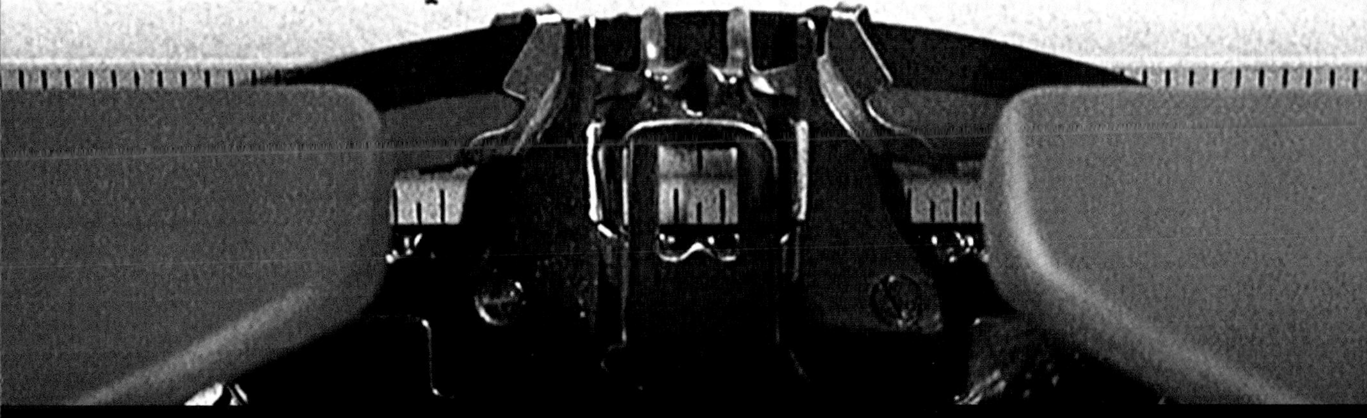


up about. The couple might as well be discussing the purchase of a new vacuum cleaner.

MY FRIEND
There was once a very lovely, very frightened girl.
e lived alone except for a nameless cat.

*Breakfast at Tiffany's*, however, is also a film about New York in particular and big city life in general. In this urban jungle, only those who can commandeer a taxi with brio will survive. Manhattan is a major character in this movie: Paul and Holly move among the skyscrapers, up and down the Avenues, across Central Park and into Tiffany's; and even Sing-Sing penitentiary gets a look-in, as an image of the criminality inseparable from a world like this. NY's fire escapes, finally, permit people to move around in secret, and they certainly facilitate amorous encounters. This city is a place of seduction, in which a kid from the sticks can become a playgirl and a poet may earn his keep by warming the bed of his patroness. But it's also a place of enormous promise; here, it might be possible to marry a millionaire, to meet the love of your life or to publish the Great American Novel.

Seen today, *Breakfast at Tiffany's* seems curiously prudish. With much less kerfuffle than Blake Edwards' film, Truman Capote's work of fiction had told the story of a girl on the make; and with far greater honesty, the book had denied its protagonists a happy ending. Yet however justified this criticism may be, it's also somewhat naive; for not everything can be said with the same directness in every generation. In this respect, no decade is more ambivalent than the 60s. In Edwards' film, we see the start of a process of liberation that still hasn't reached its conclusion; here, taboos are gently knocked without ever really being broken; and here, we see the first tentative sketch of an autonomous woman, taking charge of her sexuality without ever having heard the word "feminism." Though it may look a little strait-laced today, this movie was certainly free-and-easy by the standards of the early 60s.

But perhaps even at that time, it was the apparent contradictions that made *Breakfast at Tiffany's*, like its leading actress, so charming and so strangely sexy. The movie is nicely emblematic of a decade of incongruities and a period of transition. For just as it celebrated the sophisticated new-jet-set lifestyle of the early 60s, that lifestyle was showing the first clear signs of decay. Soon, a new mode of existence would take its place, after trampling on everything it stood for.

## Wild angels

The chi-chi glamour of Holly Golightly's world shouldn't deceive us. In Hollywood, the 60s began, not with wild parties but with the near-bankruptcy of the studio system. The TV lured millions away from the movie palaces and led to thousands of lost jobs at the major studios. It seemed people were no longer prepared to leave their homes in order to escape reality when the box in the corner could do the job more cheaply and just as well.

The crisis of the studios and the dawning realization that society was changing eventually led to the end of the Production Code, which had stipulated for decades what was and wasn't permissible on the silver screen.

Though their chains were now broken, it still took the Majors a while to start moving. Like lame giants, the rulers of Hollywood gaped at the transformations going on around them and played it safe, preferring to rent out their underused studio space to the producers of low-budget movies than engage in any experiments themselves.

But surely the success of these cheap pictures was precisely the proof needed that a new, young audience could indeed be enticed to the movie theaters any weekend of the year? Surely it was clear that Hollywood had to find an answer to the *cinema des auteurs* emerging in other countries? And if anyone feared that "difficult," frightening and highly sexualized films were box-office poison, hadn't Hitchcock's *Psycho* (1960) demonstrated that precisely the opposite was true?

In the late 50s, it had become clear that the High School public was bored by expensive, big-budget epics, flocking instead to cheap AIP productions such as *The She-Creature* (1956) and *I Was a Teenage Werewolf* (1957). This formed a starting point for the next generation of filmmakers. Under the patronage of the ubiquitous Roger Corman, there appeared a series of seminal films such as Monte Hellman's Western *The Shooting* (1967), while directors like Francis Ford Coppola (*Dementia 13*, 1963) took their first tentative steps in movie making. And it's no accident that Peter Bogdanovich's *Targets* (1968) raised a monument to the B-Movie icon Boris Karloff, for in doing so, the young director was simply acknowledging his own roots. A little later, significantly, it was also Corman who had his hand most firmly on the pulse of the age: in films such as *The Wild Angels* (1966, p. 364) and *The Trip* (1967), he was one of the first directors to seek ways of expressing the burgeoning youth culture of the decade.

Beyond the mainstream, more and more filmmakers were finding their voice and living out their opposition to Hollywood values – boldly, aggressively and joyfully. Words like "trash" and "exploitation" simply don't do justice to this wildly creative fusion of good old sex and violence with an anarchist spirit and the stylistic resources of the avant-garde. A prime example is the cheerfully destructive Russ Meyer, who refused to play by the rules and ran amok against etiquette and art. In *Faster, Pussycat! Kill! Kill!* (1966, p. 382), we are confronted, not for the first time in the U.S. cinema, with the endless vistas of the West. But the mythical landscape is now a cross between Nirvana and Pandemonium, where lustful go-go girls meet All-American boys and throttle them with their bare hands. Traditional Westerns had depicted the pioneering farmer as a bold and resourceful man amongst men. Meyer confronts us with a drunken wreck who exploits his strapping but mentally challenged sons as stooges fit only to do the dirty work. It's a bitterly funny satire on the way America eats its own children.

Though they come in the guise of cheap horror movies, Herk Harvey's *Carnival of Souls* (1962) and George A. Romero's *Night of the Living Dead* (1968, p. 514) are genuine works of art that quickly acquired cult status, and their influence on later generations of filmmakers can hardly be overstated. Romero's film is a morality play about a secluded community threatened more from within than without. Despite its visual power and psychological acerbity, years passed before most critics came to appreciate its qualities.

Yet it wasn't just the cineastic underground that showed new signs of life. There was plenty of potential in the younger generation of Hollywood directors too. John Frankenheimer's *The Manchurian Candidate* (1962, p. 138) was a disturbing satire on the anti-Communist witch-hunts of the McCarthy era, but it was also years ahead of its time. The real assassinations of the 60s, including the killing of John F. Kennedy, made Frankenheimer's film look frighteningly prophetic – so much so, in fact, that leading actor Frank Sinatra had the movie banned from public showing. This incident showed that the American public was still extremely ill at ease with its film artists.

Until the middle of the decade, the studios were still desperately resisting the new. For a short period, they seemed to have some success with this strategy; the results included *The Sound of Music* (1965, p. 286). Nowadays, however, most critics regard such major productions as Old Hollywood's last stand. Eventually, even the Dream Factory proved itself capable of learning from experience: Westerns such as Arthur Penn's *Bonnie and Clyde* (1967, p. 406) and George Roy Hill's *Butch Cassidy and the Sundance Kid* (1969, p. 544) carried out a profitable revision of the genre that would have been unthinkable at the start of the decade. Nonetheless, even masterpieces like Sam Peckinpah's *The Wild Bunch* (1968, p. 582) were still in danger of being cut to pieces by the studios that had produced them.

# Italian cowboys

Naturally, despite its problems, Hollywood remained omnipresent throughout the 60s; and yet this *wasn't* America's decade. The transformation of the U.S. cinema was not entirely self-generated. Above all, it was a reaction to developments in distant Europe, where new national film-cultures were forming and would soon attract international attention. In Italy, domestically produced films had already overtaken U.S. productions by the start of the decade: 50% of the box-office takings were brought in by Italian movies. With Visconti, Fellini and Antonioni, the Italian cinema already had an artistic tradition that a later generation of directors could build on: thus Pier Paolo Pasolini, Bernardo Bertolucci and the Taviani brothers – to name but a few – were able to present even their earliest efforts to an informed and interested national audience. The year 1963 marked a turning point in the work of Federico Fellini: after the unprecedented self-therapy of *8½* (*Otto e mezzo*, 1962, p. 100), he began to turn away from contemporary realities and reveled increasingly in dream worlds and panoramas of Ancient Rome. Towards the end of the 50s, the last offshoots of Italian neorealism had come and gone. Michelangelo Antonioni had originally subscribed to the tenets of neorealism; but from *L'avventura*, (1960) onwards, he went his own way, exploring new methods of filmic narration that culminated in *The Eclipse* (*L'Eclisse*, 1962, p. 118). Few other films have so coolly dissected the state of play between men and women in the late 20th century. With *The*

*Eclipse*, Monica Vitti became a byword for contemporary female identity – a self-assured seeker, with the courage both to make relationships and to end them.

It's surely one of the curiosities of film history that Italy played a significant role in the revival and reorientation of the Western. The standard legends of heroic cowboys and upstanding pioneers were already beginning to look a little threadbare, and some American films had in fact begun to take account of this. Early examples include Peckinpah's *Ride the High Country* (1962) and John Ford's *The Man Who Shot Liberty Valance* (1962, p. 112). These directors realized that the time had come for a less starry-eyed view of the Western hero. Movies emerged that were a little more "realistic," showing gunmen who cared only for themselves, and endeavoring to correct the cruel misrepresentation of Native Americans in most early Westerns. Among the outstanding attempts to save a genre that was fast losing its credibility were John Sturges' *The Magnificent Seven* (1960) and Ford's *Cheyenne Autumn* (1964).

Then came the year 1964... and a young Italian turned the "classic" Western on its head with a movie made in Spain starring a young unknown called Clint Eastwood. *A Fistful of Dollars* (*Per un pugno di dollari*, 1964, p. 206) replaced the hero of old with a shady, tight-lipped pistolero addicted to cheap cigars. Though the Spaghetti Western phenomenon lasted only a few years, a few mischievous Europeans succeeded in revitalizing a genre that had needed to change or die. And in passing, they also provided Hollywood with one of its greatest-ever stars and directors.

All in all, the Late Western reflects an important insight of the 1960s: that even in the land of unlimited opportunities, the chances for any individual have never been unlimited, to say nothing of equal. These films asked a simple question: If contemporary society is built on self-interest, steeped in envy, hatred and violence, filled with corrupt politicians and crooks of all sizes – why should we believe things were any different in the Age of Pioneers? The Italian directors turned the Western hero into a cynical, egotistical survivor. In America itself, the cowboy said a melancholy and satirical farewell to his own moribund myths (as in Arthur Penn's *Little Big Man*, 1970) before riding off for ever into the sunset: see *The Wild Bunch* (1968), Monte Hellman's *Ride in the Whirlwind* (1965) and *Butch Cassidy and the Sundance Kid* (1969).

## The movies hit the streets

The French *cinema des auteurs*, which would later become known as *la Nouvelle Vague* ("The New Wave"), had an immense influence on American filmmakers; but it had itself begun by taking a bow towards Hollywood. A beautiful young woman in a *New York Herald Tribune* T-shirt meets a contemporary urban outlaw, a man with the air of a young Humphrey Bogart and a cigarette hanging permanently from his lower lip; with *Breathless* (*À bout de souffle,* 1959) Jean-Luc Godard ushered in a new epoch.

The Gaullist government's decision to introduce a special tax to subsidize the French film industry – and to combat "American cultural imperialism" – enabled a number of film critics to leave the safe haven of their studies and embark on the adventure of making movies. They filmed on location (often in the open air), their scripts left plenty of room for improvisation, and their previously static cameras seemed suddenly weightless. Rejecting the studio-bound French cinema of the past (which they contemptuously dubbed "Le Cinéma de Papa"), they chose the raw authenticity of the streets. This was an attitude inherited from the neorealists of post-war Italy.

Films like Claude Chabrol's *Le Beau Serge* (1958) and *Les Cousins* (1959) and François Truffaut's *The 400 Blows* (*Les quatre cents coups*, 1958/59) attracted a new audience of moviegoers: people who were prepared to open up to new forms of visual expression and to recognize films as the work of autonomous artists. The concept of the *auteur* saw the director as an independent creator in full control of his work. One can imagine the explosive force this idea must have had in the Hollywood Dream Factory, where movies have always been regarded as a commercial product constructed by a team. Nonetheless, America's young filmmakers were grateful for the impulses given by their colleagues in France. These included a group of former critics from the legendary film journal *Cahiers du cinema* – Eric Rohmer, Jacques Rivette, Jean-Luc Godard, François Truffaut – as well as directors such as Alain Resnais, Louis Malle and Jean-Pierre Melville, who had themselves been deeply influenced by American movies. One might say that the French cinema was ultimately responsible for saving the American film from petrifying in its own stereotypes and worn-out genre motifs.

Perhaps this is going too far. Nonetheless, the U.S. cinema was obsessed with dreams – and there was one task the Americans would probably never have managed alone. For all their insistence on immediacy and closeness to real life, France's young generation of filmmaking film critics were equally radical in their insistence that a film is *a work of art*. These movies demanded no direct identification with the protagonist, and their directors scorned cinematic illusion and time-honored narrative conventions as the merest self-deception. In so doing, they initiated a process without which today's cinema would be unthinkable; and, to name only two American examples, this includes the work of Martin Scorsese and Woody Allen. The self-reference and self-irony of these French films were the first manifestations of a cinematic art that could truthfully be called intellectual.

## The women's decade

While young French directors turned away in disdain from the sterile and impersonal cinema of their fathers, American movie heroes were being tipped off their pedestals. Epic adventures were going out of fashion, and their stars along with them. Moviegoers now wanted characters like Holly Golightly and actors who could carry a film with nothing more than their natural presence and charisma. It was, in short, the women's decade.

Here too, the *Nouvelle Vague* set new standards with actresses such as Jean Seberg, Anna Karina, Jeanne Moreau and Catherine Deneuve. Though even the U.S. cinema had been forced to start recognizing the signs of the times, these rising French stars made the prevailing American image of womanhood look almost reactionary. In France, the dominance of the narrative element was combated more effectively than in any other country, and this seemed to lend women an unprecedented freedom. Take Luis Buñuel's *Belle de Jour* (1967, p. 400), a film without any discernible plot and no clear distinction between dream and reality: it portrays a middle-class woman who simply stops submitting to the sexual rules imposed by society and follows her own desires. A similar development can be observed in Italy, when Fellini celebrates the female principle itself, as personified by Anita Ekberg (*La Dolce Vita*, 1959/60). Here, however, the glamorous world of the big city is depicted as nothing more than a seductively beautiful illusion. In these dream worlds and demi-mondes, beyond the clutches of gray everydayness, woman seems delivered into her true essence. By comparison, the bland male dreams of gunmen and Cold War warriors look like puppet shows for the senile.

Hitherto, the cinema had been an entirely desexualized world. The new women of the 60s changed that, too. Even the crippled and perversely violent sexuality of movies like *Psycho* (1960) and *Peeping Tom* (1960) now looks like the dark harbinger of real liberation, the shocking scream of human needs far too long repressed. Whether depicted as a sign of female self-determination, or as an expression of existential terror (as in Ingmar Bergman's *The Silence / Tystnaden,* 1963, p. 172, and *Persona,* 1966, p. 344), sexuality is always a projection of profound social transformations. A destructive and perverted male sexuality finds itself confronted by the female principle – the power that questions decrepit social structures, buries dead conventions and refuses to be smothered by generations of indoctrinated guilt.

Two very different female figures might help to illustrate the capaciousness (or, perhaps, the ambiguity) of the 60s cinema's concept of female sexuality: on the one hand, Catherine in *Jules and Jim* (*Jules et Jim*, 1961, p. 32) – uncompromising, self-willed and accountable only to her own moral standards; on the other, the naively libidinous Barbarella, who picks her own lovers and insists on her right to leave them whenever she feels like it. *Barbarella* (1968, p. 488) presents a dope-driven comic-book version of liberated female sexuality. This is how life might look if designed by a 15-year-old boy.

*The Graduate* (1967, p. 440) is still widely revered as a cult movie, probably in large part because of the Simon and Garfunkel soundtrack. Here too, we encounter two strongly contrasting women, with the conflict between mother and daughter reflecting the struggle to establish a new image of womanhood. The apparently liberated sexuality of the mother has to hide behind subterfuges and deceit, and Mrs. Robinson's interest in her young "lover" is nothing more than a power game. Her daughter Elaine represents a more honest, natural and egalitarian idea of love.

To the mother, dependent on her husband since an early pregnancy, an open and friendly relationship between men and women is all but unimaginable. Her daughter, a Harvard student, has different expectations. The mother's frustration is a threat to the girl's independence; a parting of the ways is inevitable. In this constellation, the political slogan "Never trust anyone over 30" points the way towards a self-regulated and morally acceptable life. With her long, flowing hair and her big, wondering eyes, Katharine Ross embodied the Woodstock generation's ideal of beauty. In the end, the man has to choose: should he stick with the traditional role model or take the leap into the new and unknown? As he's young, his dilemma is largely illusory, for the spirit of the age will make some decisions for him. Nonetheless, he hesitates to abandon the option of a man's life as endured by his father's generation. Thus the poster bore a picture of the tiro Dustin Hoffmann, plus the following caption: "This is Benjamin. He's a little worried about his future…"

As the decade came to an end, women were no longer merely decorative accessories – a sexual promise to the victorious warrior – but (almost) equal partners. A disillusioned anti-hero like Steve McQueen's Frank Bullitt (*Bullitt*, 1968, p. 484) was given a strong female partner like Jacqueline Bisset, who drives him around in her snazzy convertible and functions as his conscience. While Bullitt's ethics have been worn ragged by his job, she embodies the radiantly beautiful hope for a better life – a counterblast to the dead, affectionless existence of the men who still rule her life. In *Bonnie and Clyde*, the female sidekick is even permitted to die in a hail of bullets at the side of her man. Before expiring, however, Faye Dunaway's Bonnie Parker is a wonderfully erotic *femme fatale* (in the truest sense of the term), posing in front of her car, dressed to kill in a chic hat, a silk scarf and a pistol. This is a woman who has finally freed herself from the dictates of morality – even if sexual liberation has had to make way for indiscriminate violence.

## Swinging cinema

A side-on view of Paul Newman's face – and behind it, the same profile as a luminous red silhouette against an orange background (*Cool Hand Luke*, 1967, p. 426); Liv Ullmann in black and white and extreme close-up (*Persona*, 1966), her face divided by a series of monochrome bars; Sue Lyon, glancing over the heart-shaped lenses of her plastic sunglasses (*Lolita*, 1962, p. 142) – three instantly datable movie posters. Sixties design is unmistakable, and hardy any other decade has had a greater sense of style.

The psychedelic orgies of color in *Barbarella* (1968) or *Yellow Submarine* (1968) are extreme examples of an aesthetic stance that owed a lot to the burgeoning fashion for comics. Not only were Superman, Flash Gordon and Modesty Blaise brought to new life on the screen; they were also stylistic trendsetters. Propelled by the LSD-inspired color whirls of the hippie generation and fuelled by the new possibilities offered by plastic, this "will

to design" gradually penetrated all areas of life, eventually achieving a kind of respectability as Pop Art.

All this is in keeping with a tendency one might describe as "the urbanization of the cinema." Everywhere, moviemakers were focusing on city life, filming in clubs, discos and hip concert halls, establishing their credentials as artists alive to the power of the present. In *2001: A Space Odyssey* (1968, p. 478), a vision of the future, Stanley Kubrick gave his interiors and costumes a Pop Art design with skintight overalls and lurid plastic furniture. It was as if he were saying: "We are the future – and it's only just begun…"

Yet the example of *2001* demonstrates another characteristic of the decade: a certain critical and ironical distance from itself. In *Blow Up* (1966, p. 356), it's no accident that it's a fashion photographer who attempts to discover some kind of truth behind a world of superficial appearances. The director, Michelangelo Antonioni, takes this as an opportunity to lead the audience through the Swinging London of the 60s, with its open-topped sports cars, its crazy hats and pulsating pop concerts – a fascinating world of glittering surfaces, which turns out to be the only plain truth available.

In the same year, Norman Jewison's *The Thomas Crown Affair* (1967, p. 358) took a similar stance. The title figure is a prototype of the worldly playboy, and he sports a new outfit in almost every scene. Suits and sports jackets, sunglasses, canvas shoes and polo shirts: Thomas Crown's ability to dress for any occasion reveals him to be a man at home in his life, someone who can master any situation he's faced with. Even his women are little more than fashion accessories, the sole exception being the lady who truly belongs at his side. And precisely because she's the only one who's equal to Thomas Crown, she has to fight him.

Accepting the way the world is, and mastering its rules to perfection so he can hit the system when it's least expecting it, Crown is a kind of style-conscious anti-hippie. He fights and wins against the big bad world, by using its weapons and adding a strong portion of his own defiant machismo. For the 60s, Thomas Crown was an absolutely symptomatic larger-than-life icon.

A smart, worldly-wise hero, blessed with impeccable manners and unburdened by an excess of scruples: a man like this might be seen as the "natural" adversary of the self-assured modern women then taking the stage. And indeed, in *The Thomas Crown Affair*, the women are still just decorative Bunnies with very little to say for themselves. The quintessence of the charmingly ruthless male was James Bond. But the 007 films and their many imitations were also a product of one of the decade's essential insights: films were *allowed* to be fun, however trivial their message might be and however questionable their morality. Even the earliest Bond movie, *Dr. No* (1962), seduced its audience with sex, speed and exotic locations. In the alternative universe of James Bond, moviegoers could forget the deadly serious Cold War while absurd super-villains threatened the planet (*From Russia with Love*, 1963; *Goldfinger*, 1964, p. 210). Later, the series gleefully began to parody itself (*Thunderball*, 1965) – and in this, too, it was a typical child of the 60s.

If the fashion and design of the 60s were emphatically artificial and playful, this also expressed a modernity that had emancipated itself from outdated values and role models. The decade positively paraded its own self-image, which was fed by its opposition to a reactionary culture and a repressive social reality. All this went hand-in-hand with a firm faith in social and technological progress, in the positive utopia of universal self-realization. And yet the decade was simultaneously fractured by a certain knowing skepticism and a self-ironic detachment from its own wild hopes. Such a hedonistic and libertarian worldview was inevitably mirrored in the films of the 60s, in their structures, plots and characters – from the satirical-philosophical visions of Stanley Kubrick to the essentially reactionary figure of James Bond.

## Man on the moon

While 007 fought the supercrooks and American and French cineastes had their differences, the most dramatic struggle was taking place elsewhere, between two rival media. Television was establishing itself as *the* mass medium, forcing the film industry to come up with ever more thrilling spectacles in order to resist this potent new challenger. At the same time, TV had a profound effect on moviegoers' ways of seeing, and it also raised their expectations. The murder of Kennedy, the Olympic Games, or a war of your choice anywhere in the world: you could watch it all from the comfort of your own armchair, frequently while it happened. Until the moon landing, science fiction had been a B-movie genre; thereafter, the big studios lavished money on it.

With sumptuous "production values" and increasingly explicit sex and violence, the movie business fought desperately against the growing dominance of the box. Yet this was only one side of the coin. For the very fact that TV was becoming the natural home of the entertainment industry enabled the cinema to develop as an artistic medium. Faced with the mass-produced visual pabulum churned out by TV, many artists now saw film as an attractive alternative. Directors such as Stanley Kubrick and Jean-Luc Godard created works of genius, preparing the way for film's entry into the annals of art history. More than this, the work of these directors set new standards for all who followed – aesthetically, intellectually and in the quality of its engagement with social and political realities. With *Lolita* (1962), Kubrick used an adaptation of a morally precarious novel by a Russian exile to plumb the sexual depths of affluent America. In France, Godard shattered the stylistic and narrative conventions of the classical cinema and pieced together a new film language from the fragments.

There is another reason for TV's central role in the intellectualization of the cinema: the more moving images became an ordinary part of everyday life, the more practiced people became in dealing with them. This created a basis for self-reflexive discourse and the ability to tackle heterogeneous forms of representation. Thus John Frankenheimer – who never denied his

origins in television – could make a feature film (*Grand Prix*, 1966, p. 378) that looked like a documentary, adding authentic film material to the fictitious story. In this way, the film also become a homage to television and its ability to show us the unscripted stories generated by life itself – unmediated by art, and broadcast live from anywhere in the world.

At the same time, the cinema was becoming a place where serious questions could be asked. Did public discourse in the mass media have to be so *breathless*? How trustworthy were the official accounts of political and social realities? The TV emissary John Frankenheimer also made *The Manchurian Candidate*, a surreal satire on America's fear of communism. In this movie, the apparently most vehement anti-Commies are actually controlled from Moscow; but the terrible truth about the ease with which people can be manipulated is lost without a trace amongst the milling reporters and TV cameras.

## The old morality is immoral

"Today, we have a cinema that no longer has any lasting temporal structures at its disposal (...). The films being made today are wholly determined by the imperative of the present." Jacques Rivette made this statement as early as 1963, yet it is an unusually fitting description of the situation at the end of the decade. The images rush by, instants of light that briefly illuminate the

dreams and nightmares of a liberalized society. In *Woodstock* (1970), a generation presented itself as a new model of society, and also as a big, happy American family, spreading the word about births and marriages with the help of a monstrous sound system. *Alice's Restaurant* (1969, p. 568) celebrated the commune as a surrogate nuclear family; and Disney's *The Jungle Book* (1967, p. 416) dreamt the old dream of a peaceful natural world free of division and strife.

Yet this new vision of politics and society was flawed from the very beginning. In *Midnight Cowboy* (1969, p. 578), Dustin Hoffman went to look for America and ended up coughing his guts out on a Greyhound bus. On the Highway to Hell between Texas, Manhattan and Miami, heroes had become superfluous. In the same film, Jon Voight – a wannabe gigolo in a slowly disintegrating Stetson – makes it painfully clear that the myth of endless freedom lies buried in the alleyways of New York.

The Establishment carried on exploiting the young, the reactionaries stood firm against renewal, and the cinema reflected a deep and widespread conviction that the old morality was hopelessly corrupt. The movies showed us a counter-culture that oscillated wildly between self-realization and self-destruction. The genuine charm of *A Hard Day's Night* (1964, p. 214) is highly precarious, always threatening to collapse into a whimsical sequence of vapidly slaphappy moments. The orgies of violence in *The Wild Angels* or *Easy Rider* (1969, p. 572) are accompanied by gestures of rebellion, but a demand for freedom as absolute as this can have no clear destination. And in the druggy and strikingly inert arthouse cinema of *Zabriskie Point* (1969, p. 562),

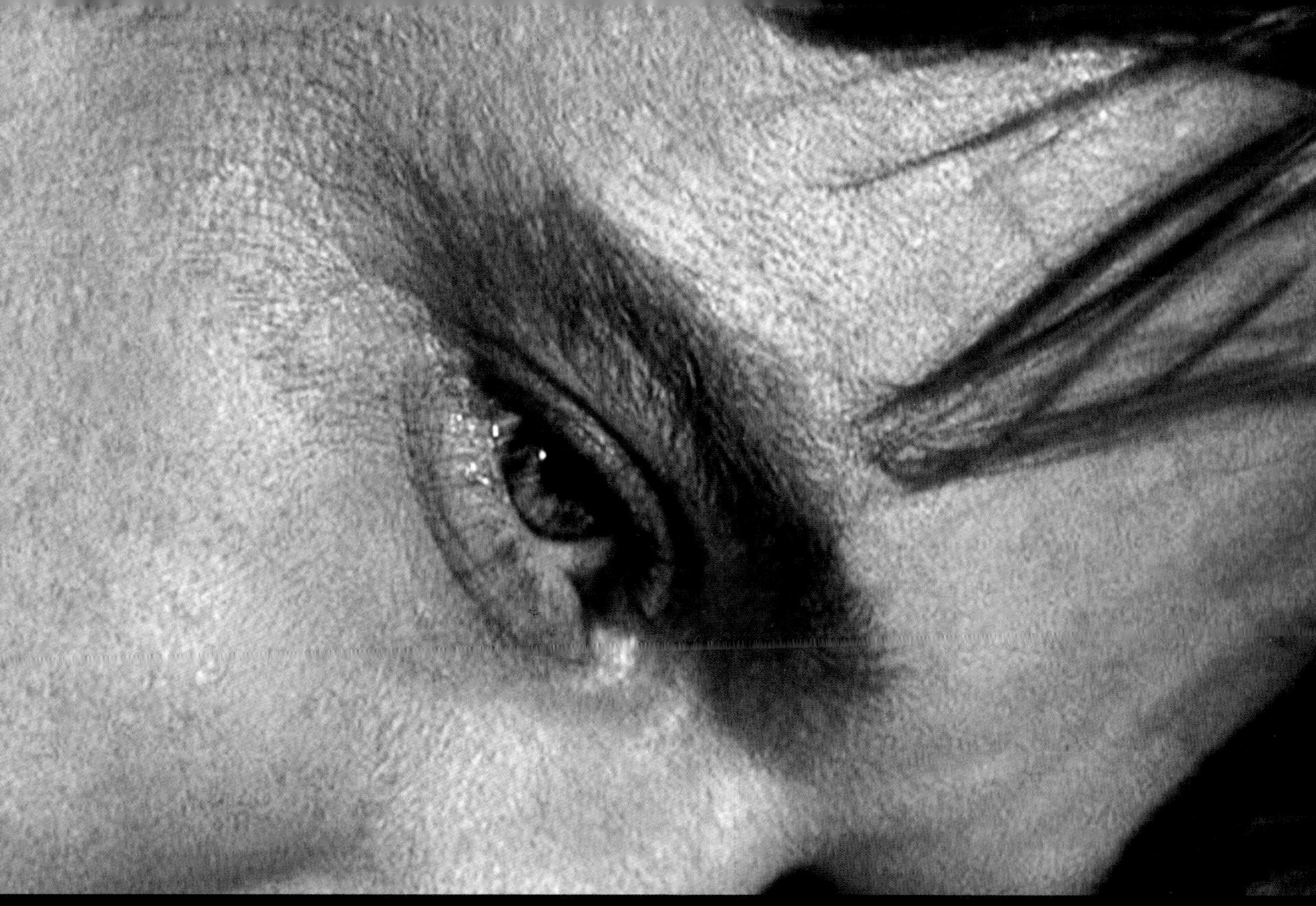

the frustration of the young generation leads to the explosion of a hypermodern villa that symbolizes the hated status quo. This pocket apocalypse is in fact only imagined, yet it does express an awareness of the fact that time moves only in one direction. There's simply no way back to a state of original innocence.

And so the rebellious note struck by Godard's *Breathless* eventually modulates into a cacophonous emotional feedback loop. "Live fast, die young and leave a beautiful corpse" – the deadly intransigence of Bonnie and Clyde was reiterated by many of the generation's heroes, from Jimi Hendrix to Brian Jones and Janis Joplin. An abyss divides the comparatively harmless Holly Golightly from the bullet-riddled pariah Bonnie Parker, and the contradictions at the heart of this decade mark it out as a period of transition.

It is precisely these contradictions that make the 60s such an astonishingly vital epoch; the temporary decline of Hollywood and the fresh impulses from Europe; the sense of infinite possibilities – expressed not least in a redefinition of the role of women – and the sardonic fatalism of the cinematic underground; the bombastic million-dollar epics and the brave low-budget experiments of innumerable independent artists. Ultimately, the movies of the decade reflect its inherent contradictions, and humanity is still suffering from the failure to overcome them. In uncompromising form, *Bonnie and Clyde* embodies the grimmest of insights: in an unfree society, a personal struggle for peace and freedom may well terminate in death and destruction. It's an insight that has lost nothing of its validity. Yet this world is the only one we have! Or as they say in the film adaptation of Joseph Heller's most famous novel (*Catch 22,* 1970, p. 590):

– "That's some catch, that Catch 22."

– "It's the best there is."

*Jürgen Müller / Steffen Haubner*

# ONE, TWO, THREE

1961 - USA - 115 MIN. - COMEDY, SOCIAL SATIRE

DIRECTOR BILLY WILDER (1906–2002)
SCREENPLAY BILLY WILDER, I. A. L. DIAMOND based on the play by FERENC MOLNAR DIRECTOR OF PHOTOGRAPHY DANIEL L. FAPP
EDITING DANIEL MANDELL MUSIC ANDRÉ PREVIN PRODUCTION BILLY WILDER for MIRISCH, PYRAMID PRODUCTIONS, UNITED ARTISTS.

STARRING JAMES CAGNEY (C. R. MacNamara), HORST BUCHHOLZ (Otto Ludwig Piffl), PAMELA TIFFIN (Scarlett Hazeltine), ARLENE FRANCIS (Phyllis MacNamara), HOWARD ST. JOHN (Wendell P. Hazeltine), HANNS LOTHAR (Schlemmer), LEON ASKIN (Peripetchikoff), RALF WOLTER (Borodenko), KARL LIEFFEN (Fritz), HUBERT VON MEYERINCK (von Droste-Schattenburg), LISELOTTE PULVER (Ingeborg), LOÏ BOLTON (Melanie Hazeltine), PETER CAPELL (Mishkin).

## *"Is old Russian proverb: Go west young man."*

"One, two, three!" When Berlin Coca Cola representative C. R. MacNamara (James Cagney) snaps his fingers in rapid succession, his minions know to jump into position. Each count signals his troops to recruit the necessary personnel, consisting of: One – a barber. Two – a manicurist. Three – a tailor. Plus male haberdasher. Plus shoe salesman. Now go!

This general's need for staff is bountiful, but vital. And, right now, the man MacNamara, Mac for short, requires most is an impoverished member of the former aristocracy, who today earns a living as the gents' restroom attendant at the Kempinski Hotel. In exchange for a small fee, this chap will hopefully adopt young communist Otto Piffl (Horst Buchholz) – the cause of all this mayhem – and bestow a respectable name upon him.

Indeed, C. R. MacNamara's much-anticipated promotion hangs on a single thread that will inevitably snap if he can't transform a shabby GDR denizen into a pedigree capitalist in the space of three hours. Piffl, however, is unwilling to be "reformed" in such a manner, and his constant protests only aggravate the matter. Were it not for Otto's true love for his newly acquired Western bride, Scarlett (Pamela Tiffin), he'd hop on his motorcycle and trailblaze past the Brandenburg Gate, back into the sanity of East German civilization.

The disregard is mutual. Mac is just as offended by Otto's actions as Otto is by his. Mac knows Wendell P. Hazeltine (Howard St. John), his superior from Coca Cola headquarters in Atlanta, will be less than pleased to find out that Scarlett, his daughter, has entered into a pinko marriage. The thought behind sending temperamental Scarlett to Europe was to have her sow her proverbial wild oats, not make oatmeal. Although MacNamara and wife Phyllis (Arlene Francis) promised the executive that they'd keep an eye on the young lady, the task quickly proved impossible. Night after night, Scarlett sneaked out to experience the Berlin highlife, which is in full swing, despite the toll war took on the once great capital. The young American soon ventured out into the city's Eastern zones, where she made the acquaintance of loyal communist Piffl and fell head over heels in love.

MacNamara is appalled when he discovers that the couple have secretly wed. To top it all, Scarlett's parents have announced their intended visit to the German metropolis. In this new jet-setting age, it won't be long before mom and dad show up at their door. For MacNamara, it's a race against the clock. He has just a few hours to patch up the lovebirds' relationship, which his acts of sabotage managed to destroy, and make a presentable son-in-law of the proletariat's poster child, who is now starting to be known as Otto von Droste-Schattenburg. Of course, it would have been simpler for MacNamara

1

1 Pepsi-cola hits the spot! C. R. MacNamara (James Cagney) sings the praises of capitalism.

2 If you want my body: Faithful employee Mr. Schlemmer (Hanns Lothar) is reduced to serving as MacNamara's mannequin.

3 Silver spoons: Impoverished aristocrat Otto von Droste-Schattenburg (Hubert von Meyerinck, right) adopts obstinate communist, Otto Ludwig Piffl (Horst Buchholz, left), into his family.

4 Ironing out the kinks: Who'd have thought that Otto Pfiffl would become a stuffed shirt? Proof that love reigns supreme.

to get the marriage annulled, but Scarlett's sudden pregnancy put an end to that thought. Mac would be professionally washed up if he presented the Hazeltines with a knocked up daughter sans husband.

C. R. MacNamara's impatient thwacking "one, two, three" stamps out the beat of this zippy East-West satire. With humorous and spirited pizzazz, the actors rattle off the sheets of dialog like ticker-tape at lightning speed. Horst Buchholz reported that seasoned actor James Cagney would put himself in his character's urgent shoes by warming up for his scenes with a ta[p] dance routine. In addition, Wilder instilled the picture with a sense of over[drive] drive that enabled a five-page long scene to be played in just under a minut[e] (normal duration: one page per minute).

Billy Wilder and co-writer I. A. L. Diamond did their best to incorporat[e] and parody a fair share of both Eastern and Western ideologies. Much t[o] their chagrin, the Berlin Wall was erected right in the middle of shooting. Thi[s]

# “Machine-gun paced topical satire of East-West relations, in which the characters shout variations of stale jokes at each other...” *The New Yorker*

3

**BILLY WILDER (1906–2002)**

*One, Two, Three* took the Austrian-born Samuel “Billy” Wilder (today, Sucha, the town where he was born is Polish territory) back to his professional roots. After a year at the University of Vienna, Wilder brushed his studies aside and became a reporter. It wasn't long before this line of work sent him to Berlin. Financial straits forced him to moonlight as a paid dance escort, about which he wrote a highly revered exposé. While earning a living with his feet, he tried his hand at scriptwriting. In 1929, he collaborated with a squad of young filmmakers on the semi-documentary *Menschen am Sonntag* (*People on Sunday*). This experience helped establish him within the film industry. Wilder already had a respectable career behind him by the time he fled Germany in 1933, after the Nazi rise to power. His emigration took him from France to Mexico and finally ended in the United States. Initially, his command of English was primitive, but after a professional hiatus of several years he entered the American movie scene with the help of Charles Brackett. The collaboration proved remarkably successful and extended beyond the production of numerous well-received screenplays. 1942's *Major and the Minor* marked the first time in their partnership (which lasted until 1950) that Wilder stood alone at the film-making helm. Among the many masterpieces they brought to the screen, *Sunset Boulevard* (1950) stands out as the shining star. Following this project, I. A. L. Diamond became Wilder's professional other half, and the two produced work that, regardless of genre, met with box office success. For their writing achievement with *The Apartment* (1960) each of them was awarded the Best Original Screenplay Oscar. Wilder took home a total of three statuettes that evening, also winning Best Director and Best Picture.

4

inevitably delayed production as the Brandenburg Gate had to be entirely recreated at Bavaria Studios in Munich. Other, more serious consequences followed. Given the inflamed Cold War situation, the German audience no longer found humor in East-West relations and the film bombed at their box office. In 1980, the Berlin International Film Festival paid homage to Billy Wilder by including a retrospective program among their events. Noticeably absent from the line up was *One, Two, Three* – highly ironic considering the festival's venue and the many renowned German comedians who acted in the picture. The public recognition that the film deserved only came four years later, when it was re-released in France and then Germany, and met with wide acclaim from young critics and an audience that had grown in maturity. HK

**"A hilarious free-for-all graced with mad genius, *One, Two, Three* makes them Keystone Cops look like slowpokes. Every time I watch it, I find myself perched on the edge of my seat, hoping that the film's fever pitch doesn't give the ever-inflamed James Cagney a heart attack, an illogically primal reaction that restores whatever immediacy the ravages of time have stolen from this precursor to *Dr. Strangelove*."** *Film Freak Central Review*

5 Deadbeat dad: All the uproar over the boss' daughter has caused MacNamara to neglect his own family. Wife Phyllis MacNamara (Arlene Francis) is left holding the short end of the stick.

6 Clothes make the man: MacNamara's work has paid off. Young Pfiffl is clean as a whistle. Never mind that he feels like a fish out of water.

7 Seven year itch revisited: MacNamara has no qualms about cashing in on his secretary's (Lieselotte Pulver) womanly charms in the name of free enterprise.

7

# THE HUSTLER

1961 - USA - 134 MIN. - DRAMA

IRECTOR ROBERT ROSSEN (1908–1966)
CREENPLAY SYDNEY CARROLL, ROBERT ROSSEN based on a novel by WALTER S. TEVIS DIRECTOR OF PHOTOGRAPHY EUGEN SCHÜFFTAN
DITING DEDE ALLEN MUSIC KENYON HOPKINS PRODUCTION ROBERT ROSSEN for ROSSEN ENTERPRISES, 20TH CENTURY FOX.

TARRING PAUL NEWMAN (Eddie Felson), JACKIE GLEASON (Minnesota Fats), PIPER LAURIE (Sarah Packard), GEORGE C. SCOTT (Bert Gordon), MYRON MCCORMICK (Charlie Burns), MURRAY HAMILTON (James Findley), MICHAEL CONSTANTINE Big John), JAKE LAMOTTA (Bartender), WILLIE MOSCONI (Willie).

CADEMY AWARDS 1961 OSCARS for BEST ART DIRECTION (Harry Horner, Gene Callahan), and BEST CINEMATOGRAPHY Eugen Schüfftan).

## *"Some men never get to feel that way about anything."*

A "gambling not allowed" sign hangs by the ball dispatch at a Pittsburgh pool hall. And that's about all it does.

For a good portion of the men that frequent this Pittsburgh smoke palace are pool sharks. Call them hustlers. Call them what you will. Guys who take suckers for a ride – because they play better and because they can. Their cues send those balls dancing in ways we mortals can only dream of. They feign defeat and then take their prey for all they're worth in a single game.

"Fast" Eddie (Paul Newman) knows every trick in the book. He plays like a pro and owns the game. His fingertips quiver in anticipation whenever he spots a pool table beckoning from some dark corner. It's just a matter of time before he'll be able to turn his craft into a full-fledged career. There are just two things this kid trips up on – crapping out and knowing when to quit.

When Eddie crosses paths with undefeated champion of the tables "Minnesota Fats" (Jackie Gleason), a portly but suave gaming virtuoso, it seems his ship has come in. After 25 hours of non-stop play, Fats is 18,000 dollars in the hole and Fast Eddie appears to have the match in his pocket. Both of them have a bottle of whiskey and a long night behind them. But Eddie just can't walk away a winner – he has to drive Fats into the ground and show him who the real king of the hill is. As far as he's concerned, Fats might as well stop fiddling with that wilted pink carnation in his lapel and slicking back his pomade-drenched do; nervous ticks will get him nowhere. Then again, maybe Eddie's over-estimating himself.

Murmurs from the peanut gallery. "Stay with this kid; he's a loser." It's Bert Gordon (George C. Scott), Minnesota Fats' dodgy, black-clad manager. Fats is a true hustler and knows his limits. Following 40 hours of play, he's won back his pot and squeezed practically every last penny out of the young

1

1 Behind the eight ball: Paul Newman plays young hustler Eddie Felson. Some 25 years later, Newman reprised the role in Scorsese's *The Color of Money* (1986) and struck Oscar gold.

2 Corner pocket: American pool pro Willie Mosconi coached Paul Newman and Jackie Gleason (Minnesota Fats) and infused their 40 hour-show-down with hard-hitting suspense.

**"The camera descends into the seedy, sweaty, smoky pool halls of an American city, looping around the green baize-topped table, affixing its beady eye on the players, the spectators, their bodies and their faces. The balls click and roll. The heat and the tension are palpable."** *Berliner Morgenpost*

hotshot, leaving him and his mentor, Charlie (Myron McCormick), dead in the dust.

Eddie's got talent, but lacks character – at least, according to Bert. This emissary of the devil wants Eddie to sell him his soul, and whatever Bertie wants, Bertie gets. He convinces the rookie that he's got the necessary collateral and experience to make Eddie's dream of avenging Fats a reality. Bert's price is steep. He's entitled to 75% of the winnings and total control. Eddie becomes Bert's kid, until a game of sudden death drives them apart, leaving Eddie without the only woman he ever loved. His consolation prize, however, is that rich moral fiber he was allegedly lacking.

A full half hour of screen time is used to depict Eddie's big game with Minnesota Fats. Cinematographer Eugen Schüfftan, who meticulously oversaw the drafting of the special effects for Fritz Lang's *Metropolis* (1926), and director Robert Rossen decided to shoot the film in cinemascope with black and white photography – a choice that immortalized this intoxicating sequence. The staging is equally hypnotizing. All concept of time vanishes as the match progresses. We are left with stark images of the playing field; smooth shots, hard shots, balls eddying into pockets. Close-ups of the players' and spectators' focused, tense facial expressions wash over the screen in a series of dissolves, as the game and the movement around the table becomes a trance-like ocean. It was worth it: the undertaking earned Schüfftan an Oscar in the field of cinematography.

Paul Newman's Fast Eddie was instantly the stuff of legend. Newman portrayed the character as a Billy the Kid of the pool halls: smug, flip, latently

3 Place your bets: Eddie can't resist easy money and future manager Bert (George C. Scott, right center) knows how to play him like a violin.

4 Take my hand. Take my whole life, too: Sarah (Piper Laurie) has got it bad for Eddie, but he'd much rather be a professional champ than lucky in love.

**"Cameraman Gene Shuftan has artfully preserved what Actor Gleason calls 'the dirty antiseptic look of poolrooms – spots on the floor, toilets stuffed up, but the tables brushed immaculately, like green jewels lying in the mud.' The suspense in the first big game will surely bring sweat to any palm that has ever touched a cuestick."** *Time*

aggressive and 100% sure of himself. Yet, at the heart of this was an uncertain, immature boy. Dead-set on a rematch, he rejects the love of the intelligent, liberated, though socially isolated Sarah (Piper Laurie) – a woman who is light years ahead of him emotionally.

Newman had to wait a quarter of a century before being honored with an Oscar for his depiction of Eddie Felson. Martin Scorsese resurrected both Newman and the character's career in his 1986 film *The Color of Money*, recapturing the cinematic spirit of a great era and a shrewd parlor game. The last we see of him, Eddie is invigorated and unstoppable. The camera freezes on the famed hustler as he breaks the rack one final time for Hollywood, calling out "I'm back!"

SR

5

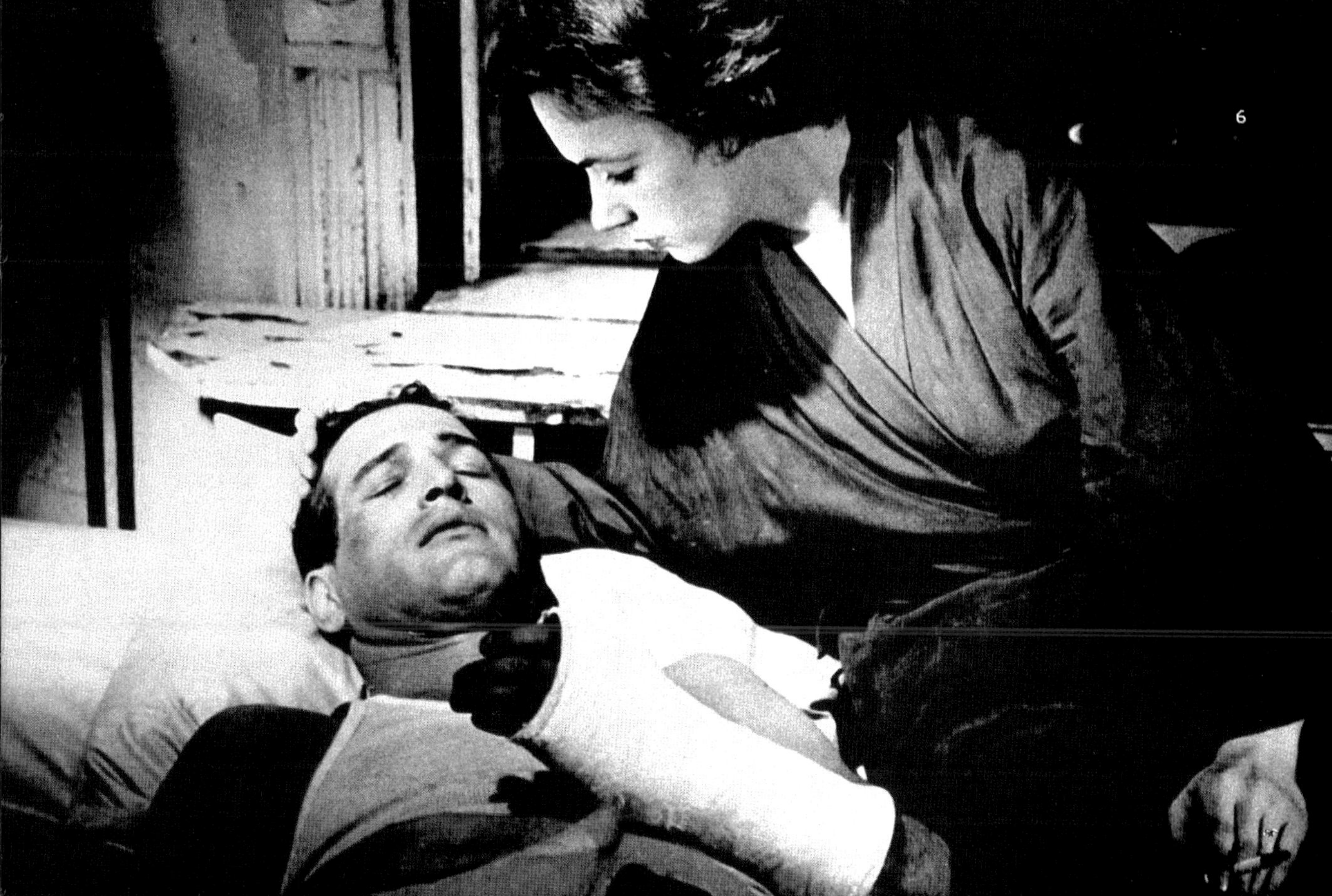

5 What a drag: Despite being a modern woman, a writer and Eddie's intellectual superior, Sarah lets her feelings for him get the better of her.

6 Workman's comp: When Eddie breaks his finger on the job, Sarah's there to kiss and make it better.

**"All of my movies share one characteristic: the hunt for success. Ambition is an essential quality in American society."** *Robert Rossen, in: Cinéma*

**PAUL NEWMAN**

His hair may be a bit whiter than it used to be, and his once Grecian god of a body may have a few more miles on it, but he still possesses the most charismatic blue eyes ever to grace the screen. A Lee Strasberg alumnus, Newman (*1925) is among the cinema's great method actors. He first walked onto the screen in a pair of sandals, playing a Greek silversmith in the epic film *The Silver Chalice* (1954). Newman himself has termed the project, "the worst film of the decade."

He became a breakout star in 1956 playing world championship boxer Rocky Graziano in Robert Wise's *Somebody Up There Likes Me.* Since then, Newman has marked Hollywood with numerous roles that live on in our collective consciousness. He reeled in his first Oscar nomination for his performance as a fallen, alcoholic sports hero in *Cat on a Hot Tin Roof* (1958). In Alfred Hitchcock's *Torn Curtain* (1966), Newman acted in one of the most riveting scenes ever caught on film, strangling Eastern block spy, Wolfgang Kieling, inside an open gas oven with his bare hands. Old blue eyes' versatility has enabled him to shine in love stories, thrillers, comedies, dramas and Westerns alike. In the stark social commentary *Hombre* (1966), he played a man of mixed ethnic origin, who held a mirror up to the white man and his double standards. In both *The Sting* (1973) and *Butch Cassidy and the Sundance Kid* (1969), he and buddy Robert Redford put forth two unforgettable characterizations of congenial partners in crime. A year after receiving an honorary Oscar for his life's work, his seventh nomination finally won him the Best Actor Oscar for his encore performance as Eddie Felson in *The Color of Money* (1986).

# JULES AND JIM

## Jules et Jim

1961 - FRANCE - 105 MIN. - LOVE STORY, DRAMA, LITERARY ADAPTATION

DIRECTOR FRANÇOIS TRUFFAUT (1932–1984)
SCREENPLAY FRANÇOIS TRUFFAUT, JEAN GRUAULT, based on the novel of the same name by HENRI-PIERRE ROCHÉ
DIRECTOR OF PHOTOGRAPHY RAOUL COUTARD EDITING CLAUDINE BOUCHÉ MUSIC GEORGES DELERUE PRODUCTION MARCEL BERBERT for LES FILMS DU CARROSSE, SÉDIF PRODUCTIONS.

STARRING JEANNE MOREAU (Catherine), OSKAR WERNER (Jules), HENRI SERRE (Jim), MARIE DUBOIS (Thérèse), BORIS BASSIAK (Albert), VANN URBINO (Gilberte), SABINE HAUDEPIN (Sabine), ANNIE NELSEN (Lucie), CHRISTIANE WAGNER (Helga), MICHEL SUBOR (Narrator).

***"Catherine said one is only truly in love for a moment. But for her that moment kept returning."***

Paris, 1912. The tail end of *la belle epoque*. Jim (Henri Serre) and his German pal Jules (Oskar Werner) are students living the sweet life. Footloose and fancy free, the inseparable pair spend their days roaming the streets and frequenting cafés, opening their minds to art, politics and love. Life is breathed into their common vision of the ideal woman when they happen upon the unconventional and free-spirited Catherine (Jeanne Moreau). She adds a new dimension to the friendship, completing a blissful threesome who reinvent love with each passing day.

Their camaraderie, however, soon falls victim to the maxims of love, war and personal interest. Jules asks for Catherine's hand and, despite some initial hesitation, the two marry. Wedding bells are deafened by bombshells when war breaks out in Europe. Years go by before the trio reunite. In the meantime, Jules and Catherine are blessed with a daughter and relocate to a cottage in the Black Forest. Jim arrives only to find an idyllic lifestyle shrouded in a veil of deception, which has driven Jules into a permanent state of melancholy. He confides to Jim that Catherine has taken other lovers and is drifting away from him. Sensing that the undertones of their former ménage à trois still have a hold of Jim, Jules asks him to consummate their mutual love for Catherine. And so Jim and Catherine become paramours with Jules at their side, effectively rekindling the spirit that once fired their friendship. Bliss anew is theirs until the monotony of everyday life starts creeping in again…

*Jules et Jim's* untraditional moral stance took the cinema by storm when it debuted in 1962. Two men and a woman who know neither lies nor boundaries, three uncompromising souls ready to take on happiness and sorrow, whatever the emotional cost. François Truffaut called it "a tale of true love shared among three hearts" – mild considering the film's unashamed scrutiny of the institution of marriage and its anchor of fidelity. It should come as no surprise that *Jules et Jim* was censored in several countries for this reason alone.

1

**"The technical effects are formidable. Truffaut employs a hundred subtle tricks of the editor's trade to surprise the eye. But in Truffaut's work technique matters less than feeling. This feeling is spontaneous, sincere, generous, naive, natural. It bubbles up like the spring of life itself. A spectator who sits down to this picture feeling old and dry will rise up feeling young and green."**

*Time*

1 Catherine the Great: Jeanne Moreau steers the destinies of Jules and Jim. A Truffaut tradition is born.

2 Little boy blue: Oskar Werner illuminates the screen with his peculiar brand of melancholy sensitivity. Truffaut stumbled upon the renowned Austrian stage actor in Max Ophüls' film *Lola Montes* (1955).

3 All good things come in threes: Without Jim, Catherine and Jules' love is incomplete.

4 Burning bridges: Four years after *Jules and Jim*, Oskar Werner went on to star in Truffaut's *Fahrenheit 451* (1965). The project left the actor and director's relationship in ashes.

5 When you're the best of friends: Jules and Jim (Henri Serre) share everything with each other, even their women.

Nonetheless, critics and audiences hailed the film an instant classic. Still as fresh and inordinately charming today as it was forty years ago, *Jules et Jim* remains one of the great triumphs of the *nouvelle vague*. It is illustrative of both the movement's break with tradition and the aesthetics of early 1960s French cinema. True to Henri-Pierre Roché's then little-known novel, Truffaut masterfully lifts the work's sense of freedom and guilelessness from the page. Bursting with life and spontaneity, his direction is free of the sort of gleeful dilettantism often cited by *nouvelle vague's* opponents. Instead, every aspect of the film consistently reflects the emotional fluctuations of the protagonists in the varied pacing, unexpected transitions, Raoul Coutard's fluid black and white cinematography, and Georges Delerue's atmospheric score. The result is a surprisingly matter-of-fact love triangle with no trace of self

6

## "Truffaut understood and loved this simple tale of Jules and Jim; and his own retelling comes straight from the heart, with all its richness and all its contradictions." *Cahiers du Cinéma*

**FRANÇOIS TRUFFAUT (1932–1984)**

François Truffaut is one of the most famous representatives of European auteur cinema. He began his career as a film critic for *Cahiers du Cinéma* in 1953, writing polemical essays pleading for a revival in French Cinema. Like contemporaries Jean-Luc Godard and Claude Chabrol, Truffaut believed that only so much could be accomplished through writing. He therefore founded his own production company, instantly becoming a *nouvelle vague* sensation with his pilot project, the semi-autobiographical *400 Blows* (*Les Quatre cents coups*, 1959). *Shoot the Piano Player* (*Tirez sur le pianiste*, 1960) was the director's tribute to *Film Noir*, and *Jules and Jim* (*Jules et Jim*, 1961) made Truffaut a household name. Unlike many other champions of the *nouvelle vague*, he continued to enjoy success long after the movement was over.

Truffaut cannot be considered a revolutionary filmmaker, but the sensitive and human direction of his pictures, which were predominantly love stories, continues to inspire *réalisateurs*. Truffaut's movies are also infused with enthusiasm for the work of other great filmmakers such as Renoir, Hawks and Hitchcock. *Day for Night* (*La Nuit américaine*, 1973), his extended love letter to the art of filmmaking, won Truffaut the Best Foreign Film Oscar of 1974. Other great credits include *The Wild Child* (*L'Enfant sauvage*, 1970) and *The Last Metro* (*Le Dernier métro*, 1980). Truffaut is also hailed for a volume of interviews he conducted with Alfred Hitchcock, published in 1966.

7

8

6 What do you get when you fall in love? When the three musketeers reach the end of their road, Jules is left to pick up the pieces.

7 Breaking all the rules: A blend of energy and carefree spontaneity turned *Jules and Jim* into one of the premier films of the *nouvelle vague.*

8 Grabbing the bull by the horns: Catherine redefines femininity and enjoys life on top.

conscious non-conformity. For the trio don't really go against the grain – it's just that conventions simply don't apply to them. But even for them, love is fleeting and eventually abandons them, bestowing the film with that air of tender melancholy so characteristic of Truffaut's work.

It goes without saying that the actors of *Jules et Jim* are also responsible for its greatness. Oskar Werner transforms Jules into a modern-day Plato, delivering discourses on love matched only by the ancient philosopher's own *Symposium.* Likewise, Henri Serre is an enchanting Jim, a Bohemian playboy at the mercy of the women he beds. Yet it is Jeanne Moreau who supplies the film with both its gravity and its axis, giving a performance that set the standard for all autonomous Truffaut heroines to come. Her Catherine dives into seas of depth and authority that know no moral prejudice. Though uncompromisingly self-righteous, she is not immune to the tortures of the life she has chosen. No matter how much her character embodies absolute truth and shuns double standards, Catherine is still as erringly human as the others.

Unforgettable is the scene in which she sings of the "tourbillons de la vie" – the whirlwinds of life, the force that refuses to let them go. JH

# A TASTE OF HONEY

1961 - GREAT BRITAIN - 100 MIN. - DRAMA, LITERARY ADAPTATION

DIRECTOR TONY RICHARDSON (1928–1991)
SCREENPLAY SHELAGH DELANEY, TONY RICHARDSON, based on the play of the same name by SHELAGH DELANEY
DIRECTOR OF PHOTOGRAPHY WALTER LASSALLY MUSIC JOHN ADDISON PRODUCTION TONY RICHARDSON PRODUCTION WOODFALL FILM PRODUCTIONS.

STARRING RITA TUSHINGHAM (Jo), MURRAY MELVIN (Geoffrey), DORA BRYAN (Helen), PAUL DANQUAH (Jimmy), ROBERT STEPHENS (Peter).

IFF CANNES 1962 AWARD FOR BEST ACTRESS (Rita Tushingham) and BEST ACTOR (Murray Melvin).

## *"We don't ask for life, it is thrust upon us."*

She has a ski-jump nose, a hairstyle like a crow's nest, and a mouth so wide you could post letters in it; but when Jo (Rita Tushingham) washes her face after her sports lesson – momentarily concealing her mouth and chin with her soapy hands – her eyes are big, dark and extraordinarily innocent. This may well be the last time in her life that she looks like a child. Playfully, she blows bubbles from the foam between her fingers; then the bubbles burst, Jo's smile evaporates and she gazes at the floor with a mixture of sadness and defiance. Reality rears its ugly head again.

Jo's at the bottom of the heap. When she gets home from school, she finds her mother Helen (Dora Bryan) still in bed, foul-tempered and hung over. Whenever she can't pay the rent, the two of them have to "disappear" and find shelter elsewhere. In the 60s, being a single mother was a ticket to social limbo. While Jo hides her feelings behind a tough, streetwise attitude, her mother's life revolves around the men who come and go. For her own daughter, she has no time at all and hardly a word to spare. When she decides to get married again, Jo is suddenly left entirely to her own devices. But she refuses to despair, finding a job as a salesgirl in a shoe shop, and renting a room of her own. In the homosexual Geoffrey (Murray Melvin), she finds a real friend, who moves in with her and takes care of her. And even when she tells him she's expecting a baby from another man, he sticks with

1

**With the aid of Walter Lassally's expert camerawork, which caught sooty, canal-lined Manchester exteriors as well as grubby streets and happy, grubby, singing kids, Mr. Richardson and the company, who acted as though they lived there, have given a new dimension to an already sobering view of life among the lowly. In being transported out of the theater, this Honey has been enriched."** *The New York Times*

her. Love may be sweet, but for Jo, honey turns out to have a pretty bitter aftertaste.

The movie is based on a play by English writer Shelagh Delaney. Director Tony Richardson created the film version of the script, but Walter Lassally's camerawork gave the film its natural and "authentic" look, and probably contributed most to the film's success. Lassally deployed hand-held cameras and film material normally reserved for documentaries. This enabled him, for example, to film a scene in a cave, in which the faces of Jo and Geoffrey are illuminated only by the light of two candles. In the outdoor scenes, too, Lassally was capable of working wonders. Take the opening sequence, in which Jo and her school friends play ball: fast panning shots and the restless cascade of images from the hand-held camera immerse the audience in the game, running and spinning with the girls in the intense light of a late summer day.

Like the entire film, this sequence could serve as a perfect example of what the Free Cinema movement achieved. These young filmmakers who gravitated around Czech native Karel Reisz attempted to break free of the constraints of the film establishment to give an accurate portrayal of working-class life in Britain. Accordingly, Richardson chose to film in the streets of Manchester rather than in the studio; to a large extent, even the

1 Beauty and the bricks: Jo's (Rita Tushingham) frenzy is the fiercest sign of life in this concrete jungle – a monumental debut for the young actress.

2 Imperfect interludes: Even romance is not always free from sorrow. And Jo's expression hints that a grim future lies ahead.

3 Jack and Jill: Jo and her gay friend Geoffrey (Murray Melvin) go on an afternoon stroll and worries come tumbling after.

interiors were filmed in real city flats. In *A Taste of Honey*, however, Manchester – far from being a gloomy industrial hell-hole – often verges on the picturesque.

The subject-matter is far from pretty, though. Like Truffaut's *The Four Hundred Blows* (*Les 400 Coups*, 1959), *A Taste of Honey* examines the situation of young people on the margin of society. But typically for the British movies of the 60s – and this reveals how close cinema was to the theater in those days – it also focuses on social utopias and sexual politics. While Helen marries in order to ensure she's taken care of, Jo's relationships with men take place on an equal footing. At the time, this was a real achievement. Ultimately, however, both the mother and the daughter are left without men, and both win and lose in their own particular way.

The quality of the acting was a sensation. Newcomer Rita Tushingham in particular gave a brilliant performance as the increasingly careworn Jo, who never loses her original vulnerability. In Cannes, Tushingham walked off with the Best Actress award. Dora Bryan, too, gave a wonderful performance as Helen, a hard-bitten working-class anti-heroine. In the years that followed, the British cinema would show us many more such women; but until

4 Playing house: Something clicks in Jo while holding a baby doll, and she is overcome by a sense of responsibility.

5 Dancing cheek to cheek: Cinematographer Walter Lassally's atmospheric lighting tells us that Helen (Dora Bryan) and Peter's (Robert Stephens) embrace at the fair is more than a passing fancy.

the appearance of Brenda Blethyn in the 90s – in films such as Mike Leigh's *Secrets & Lies* (1996) – no other actress would bring these women so convincingly to life on the screen.

Despite the dramatic social situations it portrays and the depth and subtlety of its characterization, *A Taste of Honey* is no grim vision of an outsider's existence. In the scenes at the funfair, the characters have a whale of a time, and the city is full of kids singing and playing. There is a deep and unbroken optimism at the heart of this film. Nor is *A Taste of Honey* lacking in humor, as we see in the scene where Geoffrey goes to the gynecologist to fetch some information brochures for Jo: desperately embarrassed, he squirms in the fog of disapproval emanated by the assembled housewives in the waiting room. It's a wonderful piece of almost silent comedy. Social criticism has rarely been performed with such beautiful lightness and ease, yet the whole scene is thoroughly authentic. At the end, Jo's standing in the backyard while the children celebrate Guy Fawkes' Night with a bonfire. One of them walks over and hands her a sparkler – and the light gleaming in Jo's eyes may well be a glimmer of hope.

OK

# "Richardson has now done for Manchester what Visconti and Antonioni have done for Milan." *Evening News*

**TONY RICHARDSON (1928–1991)**

"Tony was the first English filmmaker who preferred to make movies on location rather than in the studio. He was the first to show England what she looked like, from top to bottom." This was the judgment of Vanessa Redgrave, who was married to Tony Richardson from 1962 till 1967. There's no doubt that Richardson had a decisive influence on the development of the British cinema at this time, although he was originally a man of the theater. When he left Oxford in 1953, he was determined to make his mark on the English theater scene. He made a name for himself as a stage director and theater manager, and in 1956, he directed John Osborne's *Look Back in Anger* at the legendary Royal Court Theatre. Soon, Richardson was also enjoying major success on Broadway.

After making his first short feature, he teamed up with John Osborne to form his own production company, Woodfall Film Productions, and began making movies. With his earliest film projects, he took up where he had left off in the theater: directing socially critical plays written by and starring a number of Angry Young Men. These films featured some of the best stage actors of the day, including Richard Burton (*Look Back in Anger*, 1958) and Laurence Olivier (*The Entertainer*, 1960). With movies like *The Loneliness of the Long Distance Runner* (1962) and *A Taste of Honey* (1961), Richardson showed that great cinema was possible even on a shoestring budget. Eventually, even Hollywood would bow down before him, after his Fielding adaptation *Tom Jones* (1963) won two Oscars – for Best Director and Best Film. Richardson carried on making films until shortly before his death, but movies such as *Joseph Andrews* (1977) or *The Hotel New Hampshire* (1984) were never anywhere near as successful as his earlier films.

Although he often adapted literary works for the screen, Richardson is seen by many as a true *auteur*, whose signature is visible in every movie he made. His adaptations of plays and novels often departed quite radically from the originals. He himself once commented: "The director in the cinema is a real creative force, while in the theater he's just an interpreter of the text."

Born in Yorkshire in the North of England, Tony Richardson died not far from Hollywood in 1991.

5

# LAST YEAR AT MARIENBAD

## L'année dernière à Marienbad

1961 - FRANCE / ITALY - 94 MIN. - DRAMA

DIRECTOR ALAIN RESNAIS (*1922)
SCREENPLAY ALAIN ROBBE-GRILLET DIRECTOR OF PHOTOGRAPHY SACHA VIERNY EDITING HENRI COLPI, JASMINE CHASNEY
MUSIC FRANCIS SEYRIG PRODUCTION PIERRE COURAU, RAYMOND FROMENT for TERRA FILM, CORMORAN FILMS, SOCIÉTÉ NOUVELLE DES FILMS, PRECITEL, COMO FILM, ARGOS FILMS, LES FILMS TAMARA, CINÉTEL, SILVER FILMS, CINERIZ.

STARRING DELPHINE SEYRIG (A), GIORGIO ALBERTAZZI (X), SACHA PITOËFF (M), FRANÇOISE BERTIN, LUCE GARCIA-VILLE, HÉLÉNA KORNEL, FRANÇOIS SPIRA, KARIN TOCHE-MITTLER, PIERRE BARBAUD, WILHELM VON DEEK.

IFF VENICE 1961 GOLDEN LION for BEST FILM (Alain Resnais).

## *"Remember!"*

A labyrinth. Seemingly endless, ornately decorated corridors turn back on themselves and sprawl out onto other passages and lavish halls. A man is heard off screen. He speaks of these chambers and of a past love.

Cut to the faces of late 1930s decadence. The cream of high society basks in the lap of luxury in a converted Baroque castle. Dressed to the nines, with stark, mask-like expressions, the aristocrats are seated in a playhouse. Like statues coming to life, they proceed to stride regally through the gala ballroom in couples. A man, known as X (Giorgio Albertazzi), approaches a woman called A (Delphine Seyrig). He is certain that they met at Marienbad just a year ago, that she swore to leave her escort M (Sacha Pitoëff) and run off with him the next time they met. He approaches her again and again, on the supposed sites of their former rendezvous. But she simply cannot remember any of it.

Alain Resnais' *Last Year at Marienbad* remains a film of enigmatic beauty and modernity. A seminal film of the 1960s, it broke with the conventions of cinematic narrative like no other film of the era by successfully translating *nouveau roman* methods into a visual medium. Screenwriter Alain Robbe-Grillet was considered the pioneer of this literary movement. Like

1

1 She loves him, she loves him not: "A" (Delphine Seyrig) lets "X" hang on her every word and gesture with a little help from Coco Chanel.

2 Fleeing from decadence: Alain Resnais relied on lavish backdrops like Castle Nymphenburg in Bavaria and other locations to recreate the legendary Czech resort.

3 Phantoms of the opera: Even when they are pictorially united, protagonists "A" and "X" (Giorgio Albertazzi) appear to inhabit two completely different worlds.

**"We claim that this is a realistic film, but that doesn't mean that it's *cinema verité*. It's a film that attempts to do justice to the entire, fantastic, spiritual reality of our lives and experience. This is the only reality we know."** *Alain Robbe-Grillet*

Resnais, he was also one of the *Rive Gauche*, a circle of filmmakers named after the Parisian neighborhood they frequented on the left bank of the Seine. Closely tied to the *nouvelle vague*, they significantly contributed to the resurgence of French Cinema at the beginning of the 1960s.

*Last Year at Marienbad*'s attachment to the *nouveau roman* is reflected in the cool stylization that echoes through every aspect of the film. The mere fact that the main characters' names have been replaced by letters of the alphabet plays up the existential solitude of a cold and meaningless world, and points to the director's suspicion of metaphor. Resnais and Robbe-Grillet succeed in creating a radically subjective world that blends outer and inner reality into reality as experienced by the protagonist. Seemingly autonomous internal monologues replace the omniscient narrator, serendipitously counterpointing the on-screen visuals.

The film progresses without any recognizable chronology. The question of whether the depicted action is rooted in the past or the present, or whether it actually occurs or is merely imagined, remains unanswered. Scenes repeat themselves, including the opening labyrinthine tracking shot, emerging in perpetually new variations that both complement and contradict one another. Resnais substitutes linearity with fragmentation, making it very difficult to get one's bearings. A veritable patchwork of singular sequences, allowing for

3

**DELPHINE SEYRIG (1932–1990)**

Born in Beirut, Delphine Seyrig will always be remembered as the seductive Madame Tabard in François Truffaut's *Stolen Kisses* (*Baisers volés*, 1968). As the wife of a bigoted shoe salesman, her aloof blonde character seduces Truffaut's alter ego, the young Antoine Doinel (Jean-Pierre Léaud), to show him that she too is human – a woman of flesh and blood. Following her theatrical debut and studies at the Actors Studio, Delphine Seyrig's first prominent film role was in Alain Resnais' *Last Year at Marienbad* (*L'année dernière à Marienbad*, 1961). Playing the mysterious, raven-haired beauty, known only as "A," Seyrig's natural elegance and sedate, focused acting style immediately marked her out. In *Muriel, or the Time of Return* (*Muriel ou Le temps d'un retour*, 1963) she revisited Resnais' direction, this time proving the impressive range of her talent with her portrayal of a woman past her prime living a lie. Among numerous arresting roles, Seyrig played a whore in Luis Buñuel's *Milky Way* (*La Voie lactée*, 1969) and a decadent, bourgeois wife in *The Discreet Charm of the Bourgeoisie* (*Le Charme discret de la bourgeoisie*, 1972), a part she was often typecast in given her lofty demeanor. Thus, despite collaborating with renowned directors such as Joseph Losey, Don Siegel and Fred Zinnemann, few roles came along that really challenged her potential. This probably contributed to her decision to work almost exclusively with female directors like Marguerite Duras, Ulrike Ottinger and Chantal Akerman starting in the mid-1970s. The latter provided Seyrig with the vehicle for the best performance of her career. In Akerman's three-and-a-half-hour homage to women *Jeanne Dielman* (*Jeanne Dielman, 23 Quai du Commerce, 1080 Bruxelles*, 1975) the luminous actress took the screen by storm as the widowed mother and part-time prostitute, whose emptiness finally gets the better of her thanks in the minutiae of her mundane existence. Seyrig also took the reigns as director herself for the documentary interview film *Sois belle et tais-toi* (*Be Beautiful and Shut Up*, 1977) and voiced criticism of existing female paradigms in film.

infinite possible meanings and interpretations, floods the screen. Hence the audience plays an active role in the cinematic process, for they are asked to piece the puzzle together themselves. Intimate drama or social criticism: the choice is ours.

*Last Year at Marienbad*'s freeform structure would make no impact were it not supplemented by the lush brilliance of the visuals that immediately appeal to the senses. Sacha Vierny's intriguingly artificial black and white photography breaks down temporal dimensions to elevate "the moment," imbuing the film with an absorbing dreamlike quality. Vierny employed techniques familiar from the silent movies of German Expressionist Cinema, even going to the length of having silhouettes of the actors manufactured when the shadows their bodies cast proved insufficiently dramatic. The shadows' weighted quality anchors the actors to the castle floors, and thrusts the imagery into the realm of the surreal. Set against the Baroque Garden's stringent geometry, the actors appear confined to rigid movements like chess pieces controlled by invisible players. The viewer, by contrast, enjoys unimagined freedom. As Resnais once said in an interview, it is in striving to breathe life into the movie theater that a filmmaker shows respect for the audience.

UB

4 Did they or didn't they? "X" is sure that he and "A" met at Marienbad a year ago, but she simply can't remember.

5 Same time last year: It's no wonder "X" returns to collect "A;" Alain Resnais did the same. After working with Delphine Seyrig in *Marienbad*, the director cast her in *Muriel, or the Time of Return* (*Muriel ou le temps d'un retour*, 1963) and is largely responsible for the actress' astounding popularity.

6 The white queen of cinema: Over the course of her career, Delphine Seyrig worked with directing talents like Luis Buñuel, François Truffaut and Don Siegel. In later years she actively supported female filmmakers like Chantal Akerman.

**"On the Lido in Venice, in the last of days of August 1961, many signs suggest that a new chapter in film history has just begun. Twenty-four hours ago, they showed *Last Year in Marienbad*; and it seems to me that this 90-minute film by Alain Resnais and Alain Robbe-Grillet is the first conscious step into the second half of the 20th century."** *Süddeutsche Zeitung*

# WEST SIDE STORY

1961 - USA - 151 MIN. - MUSICAL, LOVE STORY, MELODRAMA

DIRECTOR ROBERT WISE (*1914), JEROME ROBBINS (1918–1998)
SCREENPLAY ERNEST LEHMAN, based on the Broadway musical of the same name by ARTHUR LAURENTS, JEROME ROBBINS, LEONARD BERNSTEIN DIRECTOR OF PHOTOGRAPHY DANIEL L. FAPP EDITING THOMAS STANFORD MUSIC LEONARD BERNSTEIN PRODUCTION ROBERT WISE for BETA PRODUCTIONS, MIRISCH FILMS, SEVEN ARTS PRODUCTIONS.

STARRING NATALIE WOOD (Maria), RICHARD BEYMER (Tony), RUSS TAMBLYN (Riff), RITA MORENO (Anita), GEORGE CHAKIRIS (Bernardo), SIMON OAKLAND (Lieutenant Schrank), TUCKER SMITH (Ice), TONY MORDENTE (Action), JOSE DE VEGA (Chino), LARRY ROQUEMORE (Rocco).

ACADEMY AWARDS 1961 OSCARS for BEST PICTURE (Robert Wise), BEST DIRECTOR (Robert Wise, Jerome Robbins), BEST SUPPORTING ACTOR (George Chakiris), BEST SUPPORTING ACTRESS (Rita Moreno), BEST CINEMATOGRAPHY (Daniel L. Fapp), BEST EDITING (Thomas Stanford), BEST MUSIC (Saul Chaplin, Johnny Green, Sid Ramin, Irwin Kostal), BEST ART DIRECTION (Boris Leven, Victor A. Gangelin), BEST COSTUMES (Irene Sharaff), and BEST SOUND (Fred Hynes, Gordon Sawyer).

## *"Life is alright in America, if you are white in America."*

Somewhere, a piercing whistle soars through the void. In its wake, perfectly parallel vertical lines materialize on a fiery red canvas. At first it seems to be blades of grass, then the bars of a cage. Only when the transformation ends do we see the image for what it is – the Manhattan skyline. Yet even more crisp and alive than Soul Bass' stunning visual is the music that accompanies it.

A grand overture as emotional as opera and as poetic as Shakespeare echoes the promises of "Tonight" and the loveliness of "Maria." Inspired by the Bard's "Romeo and Juliet," *West Side Story* is a modern look at an age-old masterpiece. Jerome Robbins and Leonard Bernstein's musical adaptation took Broadway audiences by storm in 1957, before moviegoers and the academy embraced it wholeheartedly in 1961. The winner of an astounding ten Academy Awards, *West Side Story* is a magnificent, powerful and stunning cinematic achievement.

Like an angel hovering above the earth, the camera tracks New York's asphalt corridors as it journeys through the city's endless skyscrapers. This monumental display of camerawork, emulated in countless other pictures, descends upon an anonymous, urban basketball court. Enter the Jets. An American-born, Caucasian street gang set on protecting their turf. Enter the Sharks. A gang of Puerto Rican immigrants determined to claim it as their own. After numerous run-ins, The Jets' front man Riff (Russ Tamblyn) spots Shark leader Bernardo (George Chakiris) at a dance, where both gangs are present, and challenges the group to a rumble. Bernardo accepts and they set a date and place for the showdown. Meanwhile, Riff's old buddy Tony (Richard Beymer) and Maria (Natalie Wood), Bernardo's kid sister just in from Puerto Rico, also attend the dance. From the moment the two of them lay eyes on each other, it's a classic case of boy meets girl. Fate has ordained that these two star-crossed lovers try to bridge the gap that divides their 20th

1 One hand, one heart: Tony (Richard Beymer) and Maria (Natalie Wood) exchange vows in a make-believe wedding – till death do them part.

2 Toy soldiers: Bernardo (George Chakiris, center) directs the Sharks to their piece of the pie.

**"This pulsing persistence of rhythm all the way through... gives an overbeat of eloquence to the graphic realism of the film and sweeps it along, with Mr. Bernstein's potent music, to the level of an operatic form."** *The New York Times*

century Montague and Capulet cultures. The rest is Shakespeare… Prior to *West Side Story*, the majority of musicals, like *Easter Parade* (1948), *Singin' in the Rain* (1952) and *Gigi* (1958), had taken place in a realm outside reality. This modernization of "Romeo and Juliet" infused the genre with a tangible reminder of the existing world – the grittiness of the street. Producer-director Robert Wise and co-director, choreographer Jerome Robbins fashioned a story that depicted the then current racial friction between white Americans and Puerto Ricans, choosing to shoot the film on the actual site of the tension, New York City. Robbins and composer Leonard Bernstein had originally intended the Broadway production to center on a love story between a Catholic boy and Jewish girl, but quickly opted to go with a combination that better reflected the racially motivated violence of the mid-1950s.

It's uncanny just how well a story rooted in prevailing cultural clashes lends itself to highly stylized Hollywood musicals. The language of adolescent posing and confrontation is readily expressed through choreography. Whenever the two opposing gang leaders circle about each other in dance, an undercurrent of bottled aggression pulsates through the film. Equally masterful is the execution of the violence itself, as witnessed in the stunning knife fight

**“In its stark approach to a raging social problem, and in the realism with which it allows its story to unfold, *West Side Story* may set a pattern for future musical presentations.”** *Variety*

3 Never-Never Land: Director Robert Wise and choreographer Jerome Robbins filmed on location in the streets of New York.

4 Claiming their turf: The Sharks (left) and the Jets both want to call the same basketball court their own.

sequence. Needless to say, the power of dance is dependent upon the music that drives it. And *West Side Story*'s score is incontestably phenomenal. From the gaily sentimental “I Feel Pretty” to the whimsical, almost vaudevillian “Gee, Officer Krupke,” each number in Leonard Bernstein’s labor of love appeals to the heart as well as the sensibilities of sinfonia and modern jazz. The showstopping “America” is an emotional fireworks display bursting with newfound patriotic spirit. It provides a venue for the Puerto Rican women in love with their new island home to confront male counterparts partial to the life they left behind.

With its ten Academy Awards *West Side Story* swept the board at the Oscar ceremonies. The picture was a milestone in Hollywood musical history, revolutionizing both the genre’s narrative force and look. Seen in this light, the film parallels Baz Luhrmann’s own strikingly updated, yet formally more grounded telling of Shakespeare’s *Romeo + Juliet* (1996). Luhrmann’s picture is set in Verona Beach, California, 35 years after Tony and Maria crossed paths in New York. Perhaps the success of both these films is a sign that there is a Romeo and Juliet story for every generation. For within both screen versions lie the dreams and desires of an entire decade. HJK

5

5 Stick to your own kind, one of your kind: Bernardo tries to talk some sense into his naive little sister and forbids her from loving a Jet. But when love comes this strong, there's no right or wrong.

6 Pray to the heavens…

**NATALIE WOOD**

Natasha Nikolaevna Zakharenko-Gurdin was born in San Francisco to Russian immigrant parents. The mother of the woman better known as Natalie Wood had been a ballet dancer at the Bolshoi Theater and was eager to get her daughter into show business. At the tender age of four, little Natalie had already made her debut in front of the camera. She got her big break when she was nine years old, playing a girl who doesn't believe in Santa Claus in *Miracle on 34th Street* (1947). Unlike the majority of child actors, Wood's star continued to shine throughout her teenage and adult years. She appeared in more than 20 films in the 1940s and 50s, delivering two of her career's greatest performances during this time: first as James Dean's girlfriend in *Rebel Without a Cause* (1955) and then as John Wayne's niece, who gets kidnapped by Indians, in the John Ford classic *The Searchers* (1956). *Rebel Without a Cause* (1955) brought Wood her first Oscar nomination and Elia Kazan's melodrama *Splendor in the Grass* (1961) did the trick again. Despite these nods she was never to be honored with the golden statuette. Following Paul Mazursky's swinging comedy *Bob & Carol & Ted & Alice* (1969), Wood somewhat retreated from the limelight. She was the two-time wife of film and television actor Robert Wagner, first from 1957 to 1962 and then from 1972 until her passing in 1981. To this day, the circumstances surrounding her tragic death while sailing on Wagner's yacht near Catalina Island remain largely unexplained.

7 … and reach for the stars: Robert Wise and his Oscar winning cinematographer Daniel L. Fapp produced a work full of immortal film imagery. "West Side Story effectively re-rooted the Hollywood musical in a reality that dancers had grown accustomed to ignoring altogether." *Lars-Olav Beier*

8 Jungle boogie: Head Jet (Russ Tamblyn) shows us what he's really made of at an evening dance.

# "Avant-garde in its day, *West Side Story* remains fresh, energetic and hugely entertaining decades after its release."

*Apollo Movie Guide*

# ACCATTONE

## Accatone

1961 - ITALY - 120 MIN. - DRAMA, LITERARY ADAPTATION

DIRECTOR PIER PAOLO PASOLINI (1922–1975)
SCREENPLAY SERGIO CITTI (dialogs), PIER PAOLO PASOLINI, based on PASOLINI'S novella of the same name
DIRECTOR OF PHOTOGRAPHY TONINO DELLI COLLI EDITING NINO BARAGLI MUSIC JOHANN SEBASTIAN BACH PRODUCTION ALFREDO BINI, CINO DEL DUCA for ARCO FILM S. R. L., CINO DEL DUCA.

STARRING FRANCO CITTI (Vittorio Accattone), SILVANA CORSINI (Maddalena), FRANCA PASUT (Stella), PAOLO GUIDI (Ascenza), LUCIANO CONTI (Giorgio), ADRIANA ASTI (Amore), ADRIANA MONETA (Margheritona), LUCIANO GONINI (Luciano), RENATO CAPOGNA (Renato), ALFREDO LEGGI (Papo Hirmedo).

## *"Either the world will kill me, or I'll kill it."*

His name is Vittorio (Franco Citti), but everyone calls him "Accattone:" the beggar, the parasite. Although this young Roman feels work is beneath him, he never wants for anything, thanks to his girl Maddalena (Silvana Corsini), who he sends out to work on the streets. Maddalena betrayed Ciccio, her previous pimp, to the cops, in order to be with Accattone; and one day his henchmen turn up looking for revenge. Raped and beaten, Maddalena seeks help from the law – but she can't find the courage to name her tormentors. As a consequence, she herself lands in jail on a charge of making false statements to the police.

Times get harder. Bit by bit, Accattone sells off everything he owns, until he's on the brink of starvation. Then he meets beautiful, innocent Stella (Franca Pasut). Accattone, "born to pimp," naturally intends to prostitute her too. Unfortunately, he falls in love with the girl… and in due course, he even goes so far as to seek an honest job with a scrap-metal merchant.

Meanwhile, back at the jail, Maddalena has got wind of her "replacement," and she responds by reporting Accattone to the police. Caught red-handed while attempting to steal a truckload of salami, he flees on a motorbike and meets his end in a traffic accident. As he lies dying, he murmurs: Now, at last, everything is all right.

*Accattone* was made in the same year and the same city as Fellini's *La dolce vita* (1960), but the worlds depicted in the two films could hardly be

1

# "A clear-eyed, brilliantly shaped film, bursting with energy and lyrical invention." *The Spectator*

**PIER PAOLO PASOLINI**

It was his destiny, and his credo, to swim against the current. Writer, essayist and director Pier Paolo Pasolini was born in Bologna on March 5th, 1922. His father was an army officer, his mother the daughter of a farmer from the region of Friuli. In 1947, Pasolini joined the Italian Communist Party. Two years later, he was expelled after being found guilty of seducing a minor. With his mother, a schoolteacher who loved poetry and transmitted this passion to her son, he moved to the impoverished outskirts of Rome. His experiences there, amongst society's outcasts, inspired him to write the novels *Ragazzi di vita* (1955) und *Una vita violenta* (1959). These books depicted the Roman sub-proletariat as a source of revolutionary hope, as opposed to the utterly corrupt world of the established bourgeoisie. The same outlook was reflected in his first films, *Accattone* (1961) and *Mamma Roma* (1962).

Fiction, poetry, film or political essay: for Pasolini, these were merely diverse means of expressing his powerful and idiosyncratic worldview. As a convinced Marxist, a Catholic and a homosexual, Pasolini was always passionately investigating the prospects for a freer and more humane society. In the end, however, he was forced to acknowledge that even the poorest of the poor had succumbed to "fascist hedonism." While works such as *The Gospel According to Saint Matthew* (*Il vangelo secondo Matteo*, 1964) still kept the faith with the basic possibility of revolutionary change, Pasolini's outlook gradually became more pessimistic. At the end of the 60s, he addressed the rebellion of the young generation in numerous polemic pamphlets. *Oedipus Rex* (*Edipo Re*, 1967) and *Teorema* (1968) questioned the ability of any individual to achieve enlightenment and (sexual) liberation in a world ruled by alienation, decadence and violence. His last film, *Salo, or The 120 Days of Sodom* (*Salò o le 120 giornate di Sodoma / Salo ou les 120 journées de Sodome*, 1975), transfers the action of De Sade's book to a fascist enclave in Italy at the end of WW II; it is a deeply horrifying document of political and existential despair. On November 2nd, 1975, shortly after completing the film, Pasolini was murdered by a male prostitute on the beach at Ostia.

1 You can't always get what you want: Life's a tricky business for the prostitute Maddalena (Silvana Corsini) and her pimp Accattone (Franco Citti), who prefer each other's company to that of their customers.

2 Leader of the pack: Accattone's garishness and gallivanting have made him a local legend.

3 Accattone doesn't live here anymore: His estranged wife and child distance themselves from the failed family man's thieving ways.

2

3

more different. Fellini shows us the glamorous denizens of Rome's high society, jaded by their luxury and decadence. Pasolini depicts the underclass of the urban periphery, surviving on theft, prostitution, or hard labor for a meager wage. *Accattone* is naturalism reduced to its bare bones. The emphatic simplicity of the settings, accompanied by the music of Johann Sebastian Bach, lends the film an almost sacral character. At one point, one of Accattone's companions raises his face to heaven and cries out to the saints. The camera follows his gaze across the blank, windowless wall of a house; like a monumental altar, it's sublime in its very bleakness and dense impenetrability. In lives so beleaguered by grinding poverty and raging despair, the impassive silence of the material world can seem like a promise of salvation. The film is packed with religious motifs, like the tiny, naked boys, posted like *putti* at the cemetery gates, or the figure of Stella, caught in the headlights, radiant as an angel in the night.

Concomitantly, the individual episodes that make up the plot have the quality of parables. When Accattone and his starving sidekicks scrounge some pasta from charity, he tries to diddle them out of their share – and ends up empty-handed and empty-bellied himself. In one of the film's most moving scenes, Accattone asks his little son for a kiss – and uses the opportunity to steal the boy's gold chain. Yet it's a typical expression of Pasolini's essentially Christian sense of guilt and redemption that Accattone commits his most despicable deed for the sake of love, something that has long been absent from his life; for he hopes to get 6,000 lira for the boy's chain in order to buy Stella a new pair of shoes.

4

5

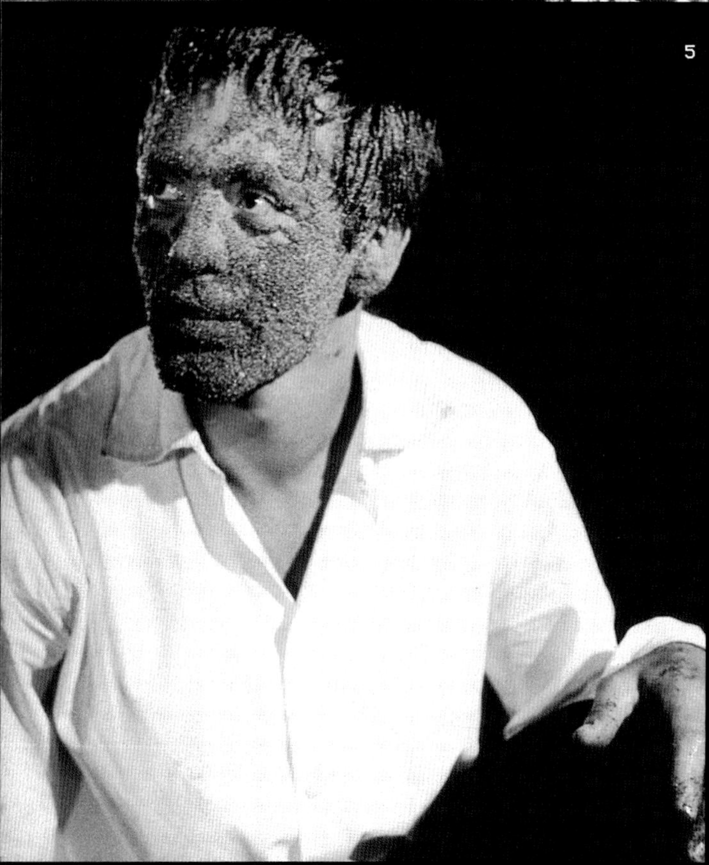

6

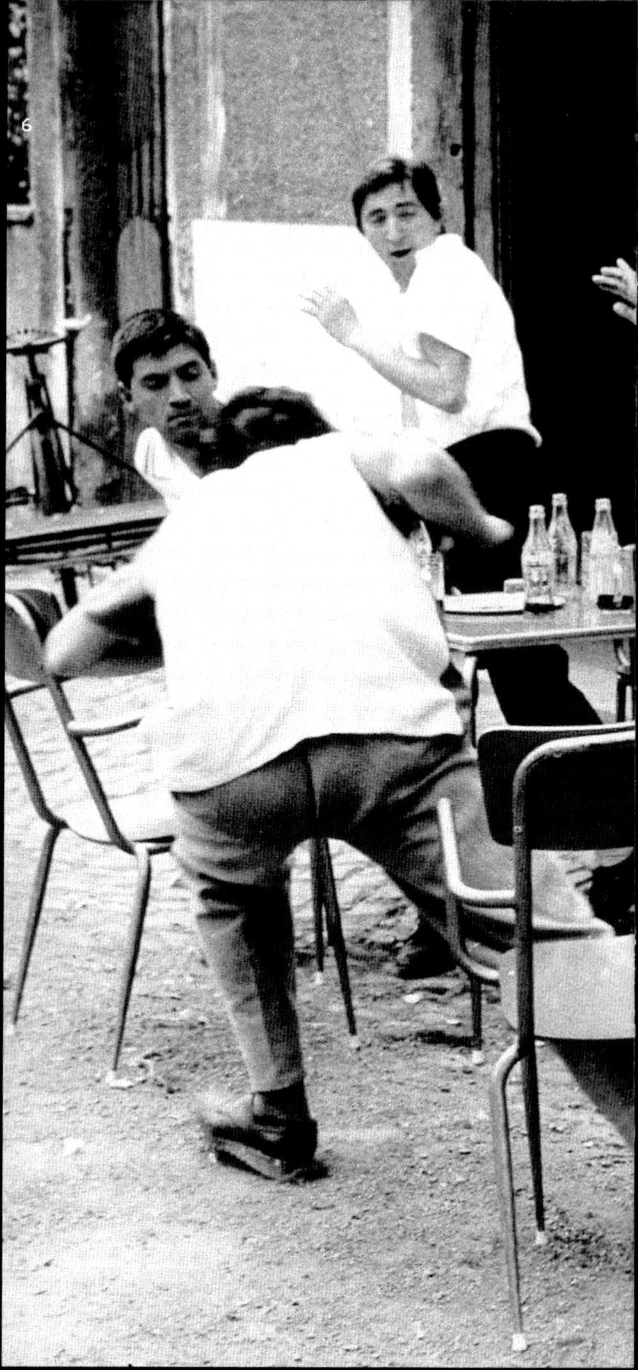

"Pasolini's 'barbarism' is expressed in the sets, the editing and the overall visual aesthetics. Together with his use of musical leitmotifs, it amounts to a conscious rejection of the avant-garde. The film is an act of deliberate resistance to Modernism, which Pasolini rebuffs as a manifestation of the sentimental, (petty) bourgeois, humanistic culture of Central Europe." *Wolfram Schütte*

4 Sexual healing: The timid Stella (Franca Pasut) captures Accattone's heart and gives him a new lease on life.

5 Three sheets to the wind: Accattone hits the bottle and makes a spectacle of himself.

6 Cock fighting: Eager Johns lose their cool when Accattone stops Stella from walking the street.

Pasolini never presumes to judge his characters, yet it's noticeable that all his female figures are invested with an almost preternatural dignity. Attempting to explain this tendency to "Raphaelize" women – to depict them almost as angels, in the style of the Italian Renaissance master – Pasolini once said that he saw women as outcasts *per se*. Thus, when we first see Stella, the girl is immersed in her work. She is performing a simple yet wearying task, in a state of profound inner tranquility.

It's no accident that the work-shy sinner falls in love with Stella then and there. In retrospect, the viewer will understand that this was the moment when Accattone bid farewell to his previous existence. From this point onwards, the world he'd always known – and which had seemed so inescapable – no longer has any place for him. Thus his love for a "pariah" seals his earthly fate. At the end, Accattone, the freeloader, has regained the

# BREAKFAST AT TIFFANY'S

1961 - USA - 115 MIN. - LOVE STORY, LITERARY ADAPTATION

DIRECTOR BLAKE EDWARDS (*1922)
SCREENPLAY GEORGE AXELROD, based on the novel of the same name by TRUMAN CAPOTE DIRECTOR OF PHOTOGRAPHY FRANZ F. PLANER EDITING HOWARD SMITH MUSIC HENRI MANCINI PRODUCTION MARTIN JUROW, RICHARD SHEPERD for PARAMOUNT PICTURES.

STARRING AUDREY HEPBURN (Holly Golightly), GEORGE PEPPARD (Paul "Fred" Varjak), PATRICIA NEAL (2-E), BUDDY EBSEN (Doc Golightly), MICKEY ROONEY (Mr. Yunioshi), MARTIN BALSAM (O. J. Berman), JOSÉ LUIS DA VILLALONGA (Villalonga), JOHN MCGIVER (Tiffany's Sales Clerk), ALAN REED (Sally Tomato), DOROTHY WHITNEY (Mag Wildwood).

ACADEMY AWARDS 1961 OSCARS for BEST MUSIC (Henri Mancini), BEST SONG: "Moon River" (Music: Henry Mancini; Text: Johnny Mercer).

## *"You know those days when you've got the mean reds?"*

Night dissolves into day over an all but empty 5th Avenue. As the rest of New York brushes the sleep from its eyes, a willowy figure, still fragrant with dreams of yesterday, is reflected in the front window of the world's most famous jewelry store. Hidden behind tortoise-shell sunglasses, a slinky black cocktail dress, and a mane of upswept hair, she is a vision of aloof elegance softened only by the brown sandwich bag and paper coffee cup she holds. This is Holly Golightly (Audrey Hepburn) as we best remember her: a lone and radiant gem amongst so many lesser diamonds as she indulges in an unforgettable breakfast at Tiffany's.

Unlike her clients, Holly herself is not a member of the upper echelons of New York society who patronize her beloved jewelry store. Although it's toned down in the movie, Truman Capote made it clear in his original novella that the 18-year-old powder room princess, described as "a creature of chic thinness with a face beyond childhood… yet this side of belonging to a woman," is indeed a professional call girl.

Holly has bolted from her May-December marriage to a Dust Bowl veterinarian without so much as a kiss goodbye for a stab at happiness in the Big Apple. This, naturally, involves pressing her luck on the Bohemian circuit, trying to make ends meet (or maybe even a fortune) amongst playboys and snobs in a world of masks, affectations and countless mirrors. Whenever this party girl tires of the whole scene, she stays up the night with a case of the "mean reds," only to seek sanctuary and a glimmer of self-reflection the next morning in the Tiffany's storefront.

Sharing a Manhattan brownstone apartment with her nameless cat, she is utterly alone in the presence of countless aging millionaires, who look after her financial welfare in exchange for a bit of companionship. There are, however, several men who expect nothing in return, at least not on the surface. She visits imprisoned drug-runner Sally Tomato once a week in Sing-Sing, thinking he just wants someone to talk to and never suspecting that he's really using her as an illegal messenger pigeon.

It's just as well – he's not her idea of relationship material anyway. And so she continues to seek out a man, preferably a millionaire under 50, who

1

1 Looking for a girl's best friend: Holly Golightly (Audrey Hepburn) sizes men up to make sure they can support the lifestyle she's grown accustomed to – and hopefully move her up a notch.

2 Nine lives: Despite being penniless, Paul (George Peppard) tries to land on his feet with Holly.

3 Nickel and diming: In Holly's hands even a little nightshade can be a deadly weapon.

can fill the ever-increasing void in her life. The person she eventually turns to, neighboring tenant and penniless writer Paul Varjak (George Peppard), hardly fits the bill. Nonetheless, these two lost souls have a few points in common. Much like Holly, Paul's precarious existence is financed by a married benefactress who expects a little sugar for supporting the arts.

It's only a matter of a time before floozy and gigolo warm up to one another other and set off on a relationship full of highs and lows. They establish a rare and precious sense of trust, gradually revealing themselves to one another while discovering moments of clarity in a superficial and mixed-up world.

Deviating from Capote's literary work, in which Holly continues the search for her Mr. Right Millionaire in Brazil, the film's conclusion leaves us with one of the most poignant happy endings Hollywood has ever put forth. We are left witnessing an emotional storm in the streets of New York as Holly chooses Paul over money. They kiss and then the cat nestles in between their

**AUDREY HEPBURN**

Edda Hepburn van Hemmstra was born into a wealthy, influential family in Brussels, Belgium on May 4th, 1929. Her mother was a Dutch baroness and her father a British banker. After several years at a London boarding school, twelve-year-old Edda headed to Amsterdam with her mother, who had severed ties with her husband because of his affiliation with English fascists. From their new home base, mother and daughter were active in resistance efforts against the Nazi occupation.

A fairy tale career followed the war. Hepburn had her first small speaking part as a cigarette girl in Mario Zampi's *Laughter in Paradise* (1951), in which she could be heard saying "I'm not a lady, I'm a girl" to numerous elderly gentlemen. It wasn't long before French writer Colette cast her as the lead in the Broadway adaptation of her novel *Gigi.* The European ingénue played the courtesan 217 times until director William Wyler took her on a Hollywood style *Roman Holiday* (1953). Wyler's film starred Audrey Hepburn as an inexperienced young princess eager to sow her wild oats at Gregory Peck's side. The doe-eyed actress became an instant postwar icon, a new type of woman which replaced the blonde bombshell. Hollywood approved wholeheartedly and Tinsel Town's infatuation with Audrey earned her a Best Actress movie for her debut performance as Princess Ann in *Roman Holiday.*

Hepburn's designer, Givenchy, quickly transformed her into a trend-setting sensation and, together they succeeded in wiping the slate clean of the buxom female ideal. Tastes shifted from the full blonde mane to the pageboy or ponytail, from pumps to flats, from form-fitting sweaters to draping gowns.

Audrey Hepburn went on to shoot 26 more features and became an ambassador for Amnesty International in her later years. Indisputably, her final role in Steven Spielberg's *Always* (1989), four years prior to her passing, couldn't have been more fitting: Audrey Hepburn left Hollywood an angel.

3

4

embrace and somehow completes a spectacularly unorthodox image of family. Rain pours down in sheets, as if the heavenly banks of "Moon River," had overflowed and spilled onto earth. The tune that accompanied the lovers throughout the entire picture (and won Oscars for composer Henry Mancini and lyricist Johnny Mercer) crescendos as Holly and Paul arrive at their train's final destination – simple happiness. These two drifters' days of running on empty, fleeing reality, and blindly chasing rainbows are over. Theirs is a distinctly urban quest for meaning, which Woody Allen would pick up again in his New York stories some twenty years later.

Two things in particular make *Breakfast at Tiffany's* a Hollywood standout to this day. The first is the film's feel for fashion. It wasn't Marilyn Monroe who was cast in the role of 18-year-old Holly Golightly, but rather 32-year-old Audrey Hepburn, a former model for French designer Hubert de Givenchy, who used to her to create a new style of dress and a new type of woman. For Hepburn made the busty blonde bombshell of the 1950s obsolete. Cultivated, reserved, tender and somewhat girlish, Audrey Hepburn became the 1960s Hollywood trademark for the worldly and refined female, an image so perfectly assimilated by Jacqueline Kennedy.

The picture's other characteristic is its utterly self-contained moments, celluloid snapshots that have become as famous as paintings. Be it Holly stowing her shoes in a fruit bowl or using her 20-inch long cigarette holder to maneuver through a packed crowd of partiers – they are images that remain emblazoned in our mind. Nonetheless, the most memorable of these moments is the one the picture is named after, in which a traveling girl reflects on where she really belongs. RV

4 A little sugar in his bowl: Holly finds out that she and Paul are in the same line of work. Patricia Neal as 2-E.

5 Two drifters off to see the world discover a little magic in their own backyard.

6 Bohemian rhapsody: Partygoers in need of a nice cold shower.

7 Timber! Hostess plays lumberjack and clears the way for drunken partygoers.

**"She (Audrey Hepburn) didn't go to acting schools, she didn't hear the word Strasberg, she did not repeat in front of the mirror. She just was born with this kind of quality and she made it look so unforced, so simple, so easy."** *Billy Wilder*

# THAT TOUCH OF MINK

1962 - USA - 99 MIN. - COMEDY

DIRECTOR DELBERT MANN (*1920)
SCREENPLAY STANLEY SHAPIRO, NATE MONASTER DIRECTOR OF PHOTOGRAPHY RUSSELL METTY EDITING TED J. KENT
MUSIC GEORGE DUNING PRODUCTION STANLEY SHAPIRO, MARTIN MELCHER for GRANLEY, ARWIN, NOB HILL.

STARRING CARY GRANT (Philip Shayne), DORIS DAY (Cathy Timberlake), GIG YOUNG (Roger), AUDREY MEADOWS (Connie Emerson), ALAN HEWITT (Dr. Gruber), JOHN ASTIN (Everett Beasley), DICK SARGENT (Harry Clark), JOEY FAYE (Short Man), JOHN FIEDLER (Mr. Smith), WILLARD SAGE (Hodges).

***"If Dr. Freud had ever been exposed to this girl he'd have burned his couch and opened a delicatessen. Freud's Famous Frankfurters."***

Like any good comedy about love and marriage, this one starts with a bit of dirt.

Trying to beat the clock, corporate bigwig Philip Shayne (Cary Grant) flies past unemployed secretary Cathy Timberlake (Doris Day) in his limousine and unintentionally sprays her dress with mud. As Cupid's arrow brings his vehicle to a halt, the only question that remains is whether this unlikely pairing will go along with the game plan. In a collision of rich man, poor man, eligible bachelor and vestal virgin, the magical contradictions of screwball comedy rev up their engines while we wait to see if *That Touch of Mink* really will end with a marriage license.

As a genre, the screwball comedy was largely inspired by Hollywood's own restrictions on morality first introduced toward the end of the 1920s and stiffened up in 1934 with the so-called production code. Submitting to the pressure of special interest groups, first and foremost the Catholic Church, the ten commandments of virtuous conduct were set in stone and faithfully projected onto the silver screen. At the top of the list were "thou shalt not commit adultery" and "thou shalt not eat from the apple of divorce or kink." That is not to say that such behavior was entirely expunged from the plot: it was just reserved for characters who ended up on skid row or met with an untimely demise. Unwed couples dared not spend the night together and married people were advised to sleep in twin beds separated by a nightstand with table lamp.

Understandably, such restrictions put hurdles in the path of both writers and directors. But faced with the need to come up with clever ways of circumventing the censors, filmmakers devised means of breathing new life into screwball comedies of old. What resulted was a rock solid double standard: without overtly transgressing the Hollywood production code, movies began to gather a heavily sexual subtext.

Coming at a time shortly before the code started to falter, the crowning achievement of this development were the bubble gum comedies of the late 1950s, which starred the unsullied Doris Day opposite men like Rock Hudson, Cary Grant and James Garner. This is the Day that remains entrenched in the minds of audiences; not the serious actress she had proven herself to be in pictures like Alfred Hitchcock's *The Man Who Knew Too Much* (1956) or the beauty from *Love Me or Leave Me* (1955), but the ordinary and less-than-cultivated girl next door. Embodying ideal traits for double-edged comedy, she was chaste without being too homely, yet radiated zest for life. It was therefore plausible that someone like Cathy Timberlake from Upper Sandusky would accompany Philip Shayne to the Bahamas simply to demonstrate that she is not an unworldly country girl.

Nobody's dummy, Cathy knows what a man like Philip expects in return for exotic vacations and mink coats. Despite that, the whole fun of watching *That Touch of Mink* stems from witnessing the ways these two characters perpetually succeed in failing to meet each other's expectations. For instance, when Cathy finally accepts Philip's invitation to come up to his apartment, the place is virtually unfurnished and her honor spared. Similarly, the second half of the picture revolves around whether Cathy can avoid "shar-

1

2

**"Although Grant gives his tycoon the advantage of long seasoning at this sort of gamey exercise, he's clearly shaded in the laugh-getting allotment. As written, Miss Day's clowning has the better of it; and she, by the way, certifies herself an adept *farceur* with this outing."** *Variety*

1 Bottled eroticism. Which of these two will be crying wee-wee-wee-wee all the way home?

2 Scout's honor: Playboy Philip Shayne (Cary Grant) coaxes Cathy Timberlake (Doris Day) into the pool and promises to remain on his best behavior.

3 All dressed up with no place to go: Philip soon concludes that the five great obstacles confronting mankind are war, hunger, death, plague and Miss Timberlake.

3

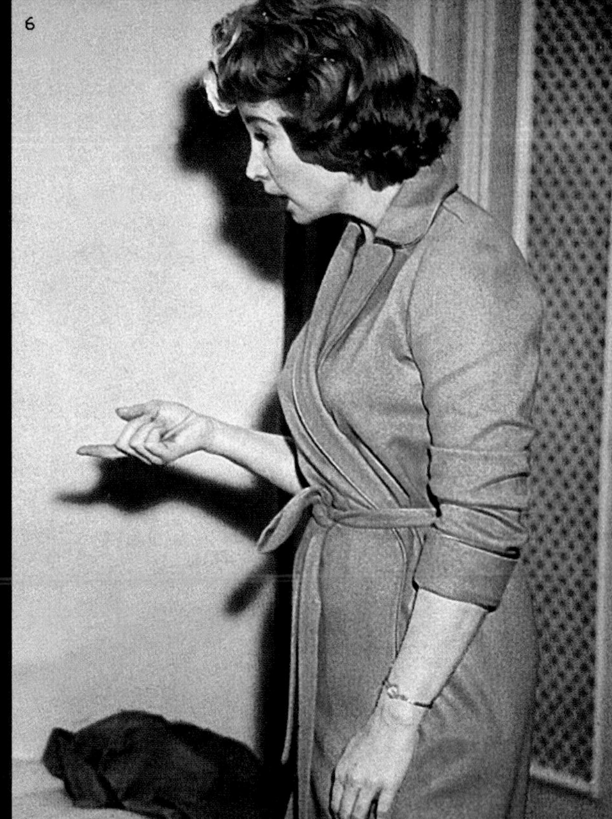

4 The honeymoon suite: Doris was never one to say no to a little *Pillow Talk*.

5 The Sticks or the Bahamas? What's a girl to do when she can't decide where to spend her next vacation?

6 Doris is no Taurus: And she's certainly not going to take any bull from nosy neighbor Connie (Audrey Meadows).

ing" a bed with Philip in their Bahamian hotel. Indeed, the film revels in the priceless ambiguity of its dialog and staging. Such is the case when Philip gazes at the pool below, speaking of how enticing he finds the prospect of a shared swim, while all Cathy can think of is drowning in his double-bed.

It follows that sex in *That Touch of Mink* is tied to the moral corruption of the love for money deal. Cathy's dilemma about whether she should sell out is reflected in the character of Roger, Philip's financial consultant (Gig Young). A former university lecturer, his princely earnings constantly remind him that cash is king. However, believing deep down that the best things in life are free, Roger prophesies that one day people are going to wake up and demand back the simple pleasures that are rightfully theirs. Until then, let them eat mink. LP

**DORIS DAY**

Que sera sera! With these three simple words, Alfred Hitchcock captured the spirit of America's favorite good girl for all time. Exuding an air of puritanical optimism and charming innocence, Doris Day (*1924) has the rare distinction of being the only woman in Hollywood to officially "become a virgin." She is best remembered for her light-hearted comedies, acting opposite Rock Hudson and James Garner in pictures like *Pillow Talk* (1959) and *Move Over, Darling* (1963). However, the image of virtue she embodied soon became passé with the upheavals of the late 60s. For decades, the verdict was unanimous: Day's work was simply unworthy of examination. It is only recently that critics have begun to cut her a little slack and acknowledge her contribution to Hollywood as a great actress of musical comedy, if nothing else.

The film career of the woman born Doris Kappelhoff in Cincinnati, Ohio began in 1948 with *Romance on the High Seas.* After her overwhelming popularity as a singer with the Les Brown Orchestra, Warner Bros. signed her to become their next great musical headliner. The genre fizzled out when the Hollywood studio system fell, and Day ventured briefly into other genres, starring in Alfred Hitchcock's thriller *The Man Who Knew Too Much* (1956), before finding her niche in screwball comedy.

Toward the end of the 60s, Day's career landed in a slump. By now she was in her mid-forties and could no longer prance about as the goddess of chastity. Furthermore, her husband and manager, Martin Melcher, had died, leaving her without the necessary front man to negotiate adequate salaries for her projects; thus she was often scammed into working for less than she was worth. Years of litigation followed with Day finally winning in the end. In 1968, she stepped into American households with CBS's *The Doris Day Show* and continued to warm hearts on television until 1973. After that, Day retired from show business and limited her public appearances to speaking openly in favor of causes like AIDS research. In fact, she was one of the first stars to do so.

# BIRDMAN OF ALCATRAZ

1962 - USA - 148 MIN. - PRISON FILM

IRECTOR JOHN FRANKENHEIMER (1930–2002)

CREENPLAY GUY TROSPER, based on a novel by THOMAS E. GADDIS DIRECTOR OF PHOTOGRAPHY BURNETT GUFFEY

DITING EDWARD MANN MUSIC ELMER BERNSTEIN PRODUCTION STUART MILLAR, GUY TROSPER for NORMA.

TARRING BURT LANCASTER (Robert Stroud), KARL MALDEN (Harvey Shoemaker), THELMA RITTER (Elizabeth Stroud), NEVILLE BRAND (Bull Ransom), BETTY FIELD (Stella Johnson), TELLY SAVALAS (Feto Gomez), EDMOND O'BRIEN Tom Gaddis), WHIT BISSELL (Dr. Ellis).

FF VENICE 1962 GOLDEN LION for BEST ACTOR (Burt Lancaster).

## *"The first duty in life is to live."*

n a solitary cell in Leavenworth Jail (Kansas), a grown man barely has room to urn around. Prisoner No. 17 431, a lifer, knows that he'll have to spend years n here. And yet he's chosen to sacrifice much of his valuable space: there are so many birdcages in his cell that the walls and ceiling are barely visible.

This real-life story all began with the branch of a tree blown down in a storm. While taking his exercise in the yard, convicted murderer Robert Stroud (Burt Lancaster) felt the branch brush up against his feet; and caught n its twigs was a nest, containing a tiny baby sparrow. If he didn't take care of it, the bird would surely die…

Until that day, Stroud had been a difficult character, hot-tempered and ight-lipped. He had committed his first crime at the age of 19, in Alaska, after a man had insulted his girlfriend, a prostitute considerably older than he was. troud reacted by shooting the man dead. He came up against a strict judge and was handed a twelve-year sentence, the first part of which he served in the McNeil Island penitentiary. Here, his behavior was exemplary, and he stood a good chance of early release until a brawl with another prisoner put paid to his hopes. The final turning-point came when his brother came all the way from Alaska to visit him, and was refused permission to do so. Outraged by this perceived injustice, Stroud insisted on protesting to the warder responsible – and stabbed the man as he raised his baton to strike him.

That sealed his fate. In a further trial, he was sentenced to death; and it was thanks only to the dedication of his mother (played by Thelma Ritter) – who even appealed to the wife of President Wilson – that the sentence was eventually commuted to lifelong solitary confinement.

Stroud spent his days studying mathematics and engineering, for behind the facade of the unapproachable killer was a man of unusual intelli-

1

gence. This became evident when he turned his attention to ornithology, after adopting the little sparrow. At first on a small scale, he began to breed birds in his cell, before going on to find a cure for septic fever, which had previously been regarded as incurable. Eventually, he wrote a standard work on bird diseases, which was greeted with enormous respect even by scientists. Nonetheless, he remained behind bars for the rest of his life. In 1942, he was even transferred to the prison island of Alcatraz, and forced to leave his birds and his scientific instruments behind in Leavenworth. A book on his life and the subsequent film could not alter his fate. On November 21, 1963, one day before the Kennedy assassination, he died in the prison hospital of Springfield (Illinois). Robert Stroud was 72, and he had been ill for a long time.

It was a life marked by guilt and tragedy, and John Frankenheimer's film biography sticks closely to the known facts – with two exceptions. The role of the mother was given added weight by leaving Stroud's brother out of the tale; and in the second part of the film, the Robert Stroud portrayed by Burt Lancaster is a more likable character than his real-life model.

For all that, Lancaster, who also produced the film, can't be accused of shying away from Stroud's truculent and intractable nature. The early stages of the movie certainly make no secret of the young man's rebellious and untamed temperament. Yet the aged and grizzled prisoner is endowed with a mellowness that the real Stroud seems never to have achieved.

Since the film was made, critics have been full of admiration at the way

**"The movie gives a sense of the enormous span of time this man spent in jail and it is undoubtedly one of Frankenheimer's most meditative films."** *The Austin Chronicle*

1 Mack the knife: Had the stabbing taken place outside prison, Robert Stroud (Burt Lancaster) would have probably gotten off on self-defense. But other laws govern life behind bars.

2 Cruisin' for a bruisin': Stroud defends himself en route to prison and gets the unwanted attention of the guards.

3 Lock him up and throw away the key: Robert Stroud's days as a freeman have come to an end.

4 Mama's boy: Throughout his years behind bars, Stroud's mother (Thelma Ritter) remains his greatest ally and confidante.

5 Breakthroughs, not breakouts: Stroud has discovered a cure for a fatal bird disease. Dr. Ellis (Whit Bissell) can hardly believe his eyes.

2

Lancaster and Frankenheimer reduced the melodramatic and "crime" elements to a bare minimum. They were more interested in evoking the monotony of everyday life in prison and the claustrophobic narrowness of the solitary cells. Frankenheimer focused his attention on developing a quiet and concentrated camera style capable of registering each tiny alteration in a setting or facial expression. And so Director of Photography Burnett Guffey need only tilt the camera slightly in order to evoke Stroud's bout of drunkenness, or to illuminate the prisoner's feelings when his appeal for clemency is turned down. It's a simple but effective and very stylish visual language that's still lost nothing of its intensity.

HK

3

**ELMER BERNSTEIN** Elmer Bernstein was born in New York in 1922, and came to film music by a very roundabout route. He was a professional dancer and choreographer, who also worked as a painter and played the piano at concert level before he started composing music for United Nations radio broadcasts. In 1951, he took his first step towards becoming a film and TV composer with the musical score to *Saturday's Hero* (1951). He wrote scores for B-movies such as *Robot Monster* (1953) and *Cat-Women of the Moon* (1953) before creating the music for the classic movie *The Man with the Golden Arm* (1955). This Otto Preminger drama about a drug-addicted drummer brought Bernstein the first of many Oscar nominations. His musical oeuvre draws on and contributes to a variety of genres. He wrote a memorably powerful score for the classic Western *The Magnificent Seven* (1960), but he was equally at ease with gentler sounds, and thoroughly at home in the worlds of jazz and folk music. Thus, some of his most beautiful film music was written for *To Kill a Mockingbird* (1962); and in 1967, he received an Oscar for his charming score to *Thoroughly Modern Millie* (1966). Bernstein also wrote the theme tunes to several TV series, including the long-running and highly popular *Gunsmoke* (1955–1975). In 1964, he was awarded an Emmy for his musical collaboration on the TV documentary *The Making of the President* (1960). Thirteen years later, this was followed by a second Emmy for the mini-series *Captains and the Kings* (1976).

4

5

# THE LONGEST DAY

1962 - USA - 180 MIN. - WAR FILM, LITERARY ADAPTATION

DIRECTOR KEN ANNAKIN (*1914), ANDREW MARTON (1904–1992), BERNHARD WICKI (1919–2000)
SCREENPLAY ROMAIN GARY, JAMES JONES, DAVID PURSALL, JACK SEDDON, CORNELIUS RYAN, based on a factual report by CORNELIUS RYAN DIRECTOR OF PHOTOGRAPHY JEAN BOURGOIN, PIERRE LEVENT, HENRI PERSIN, WALTER WOTTITZ EDITING SAMUEL E. BEETLEY MUSIC MAURICE JARRE, PAUL ANKA PRODUCTION DARRYL F. ZANUCK for 20TH CENTURY FOX.

STARRING RICHARD BURTON (Flight Officer David Campbell), SEAN CONNERY (Private Flanagan), HENRY FONDA (General Theodore Roosevelt Jr.), GERT FRÖBE (Sergeant Kaffeekanne), ROBERT MITCHUM (General Norman Cota), ROBERT RYAN (General James M. Gavin), JOHN WAYNE (Lieutenant Benjamin Vandervoort), CURD JÜRGENS (Major General Blumentritt), ROD STEIGER (Commander of a Destroyer), ROBERT WAGNER (U.S. Army Ranger), WERNER HINZ (Field Marshal Rommel), VICCO VON BÜLOW (German Officer), DIETMAR SCHÖNHERR (Luftwaffe Major).

ACADEMY AWARDS 1962 OSCARS for BEST CINEMATOGRAPHY (Jean Bourgoin, Walter Wottitz), and BEST SPECIAL EFFECTS (Jacques Maumont [Sound Effects], Robert MacDonald [Visual Effects]).

## *"Somebody is shooting somebody."*

"Believe me, gentlemen, the first 24 hours of this invasion will be decisive. For the Allies as well as the Germans, it will be the longest day – the longest day." These solemn words are spoken by Field Marshal Rommel (Werner Hinz); then the sounds of Beethoven's Fifth ring out on the soundtrack, and the film's title appears in monumental lettering the width of the cinema screen. The message is clear: this is a movie that intends to go down in cinema history.

At three hours, *The Longest Day* is not the shortest of films. It describes the Allied landings on the Normandy coast on June 5th and 6th, 1944. In the early stages, the film jumps from one location to the next: we see the British and American troops, readying themselves for battle, and passing the time throwing dice and drinking beer; we see the French resistance fighters and their everyday life under occupation; and we see Sergeant Kaffeekanne (Gert Fröbe), a likable German soldier on his horse, delivering coffee in thermos flasks to the German sentry positions on the Normandy coast. The film takes its time, showing the sheer scale of the action and its strategic complexity, and allowing everyone, whatever their nationality, to comment at length on the terrible weather.

For the Germans, the bad weather is good news, for they don't expect the enemy to attack while it's raining in buckets; the Allies, meanwhile, are on the verge of despair. For days now, their landing craft have been bobbing about in the English Channel, while their tense and exhausted crews endure one downpour after another. The games of strategy on both sides screw the tension to breaking point. Each change of scene introduces a new ele-

1

ment, adding further depth to the historical atmosphere and heightening the suspense. Finally, the theme from Beethoven's Fifth comes roaring back again, marking the start of one of the most breathtaking sequences in movie history.

A long shot reveals a truly heroic scene: on a miles-long stretch of coastline, thousands of Allied troops begin storming the German positions. We hear screams, explosions, the rattle of machine guns and the crackle of rifle fire; we see soldiers in the foreground and what seems to be an army of ants in the distance, some perishing in the hail of steel, while others survive and struggle relentlessly onwards. Between the Allied armada and the German bunkers lies a vast panorama of death and destruction. A little later, in a shot lasting a whole minute, we're given the view from a German fighter

**"A huge documentary report, adorned and colored by personal details that are thrilling, amusing, ironic, sad."** *The New York Times*

1 Taking defeat in his stride: German SS officer Blumentritt throws back a cognac as his troops march off to certain death.

2 Precision warfare: From up here, war resembles a fireworks display or an orderly ant farm. No sign of blood and misery.

3 All things bright and beautiful: General Norman Cota (Robert Mitchum) guides America to victory and upholds her values even in the direst of circumstances.

4 Turning down a free lunch: Although he's the president's son, General Roosevelt Jr. (Henry Fonda) insists on being where the action is. He disobeys orders and participates in the Allied landing, risking his life alongside every other soldier.

plane as it flies low along the crowded coastline, followed by an aerial shot of a house-to-house battle as an Allied unit advances through the town of Ouistreham. Here, the film reaches its highpoint; and it's no mystery why it won the Oscars for Best Cinematography and Best Special Effects.

The overseer and driving force behind this spectacular production was Darryl F. Zanuck, who took Cornelius Ryan's historical account and engaged no fewer than three directors to adapt it for the screen: Ken Annakin, Andrew Marton and the Austrian Bernhard Wicki. The episodic structure made it easier to put the mass of material together, but this meant forgoing a clear plotline. Instead, Zanuck placed the emphasis elsewhere: "I wanted the audience to have a kick. Every time a door opened, in would come a famous star." Richard Burton, Henry Fonda, Sean Connery and Robert Mitchum helped U.S. and British audiences find their way through a bewildering maze of events, while, in smaller roles, stars like John Wayne brought with them an image that was so powerful and well-established that it made acting practically superfluous. These luminaries were joined by highly respected German actors such as Curd Jürgens, Werner Hinz and Gert Fröbe.

Though the looseness of the narrative structure and the power of the battle scenes lend the film a quasi-documentary quality, it's still clearly been directed conscientiously. When a fleeing Nazi rams a crucifix and the Jesus figure falls off the cross, it can be seen as a symbol of the cruelties to follow in the days to come. But long periods of growing tension are also punctuated by moments of comedy: thus, even while the battle rages, a Frenchman insists on sharing a bottle of champagne with the barely-landed troops.

5 The duke flies high: Lieutenant Benjamin Vandervoort (John Wayne) proudly takes off into the wild blue yonder. Always surrounded by his men, he's a soldier who knows no solitude.

6 Have a cigar: General Cota has helped defeat the Germans and chart the course of history.

# "Funny, isn't it? He's dead. I'm crippled. You're lost. Do you suppose it's always like that? I mean war."

*Film quote: David Campbell (Richard Burton)*

**WAR FILM**

Hollywood likes nothing better than a good war. In countless films, American directors have examined their country's past, from the War of Independence to the Civil War and the various Indian Wars. But it was the two great conflicts of our century that gave the genre its massive popularity. Not only did it introduce a whole new series of themes – the advance of special-effects technology also made it possible to depict modern warfare with increasing realism.

A typical war film will follow a group of soldiers through a series of battles. In the course of the film, we often witness a bunch of disparate characters with little in common transformed into a loyal and steadfast team by the intense experience of warfare. This formula was cynically turned on its head by Robert Aldrich in *The Dirty Dozen* (1967), in which a horde of brutal criminals are turned into soldiers for a particularly dangerous special mission. In the broader sense, movies such as *Casablanca* (1942) and *Gone with the Wind* (1939) can also be classed as war films, for though the characters' conflicts are not brought about by the heat of battle, they are strongly affected by a state of war.

Naturally, not every filmmaker is enthusiastic about war, and many so-called anti-war films depict the senselessness and cruelty of war. Famous examples include Stanley Kubrick's *Dr. Strangelove or: How I Learned to Stop Worrying and Love the Bomb* (1963), Oliver Stone's *Platoon* (1986) or the Oscar-winning *All Quiet on the Western Front* (1930), by Lewis Milestone. When real-life wars were actually taking place, however, realism was often sacrificed to the needs of propaganda. Quite generally, war films are often subject to indirect censorship, for the military will only provide equipment and soldiers-as-extras if the army is going to look good in the finished product. Francis Ford Coppola, for example, was refused any such help for his critical film *Apocalypse Now* (1979), because the U.S. Defense Department didn't like the script. On the other hand, the military men had no problem at all with the glorification of aerial warfare in *Top Gun* (1985/86).

In any case, Zanuck's attitude to historical exactness was never in any doubt: "There is nothing duller on the screen than being accurate and not dramatic." At times, he departed quite deliberately from the facts so that the film could go with a bang. Thus bridges are primed with bombs that in truth never existed, and beach fortifications that the soldiers had to fight their way around in 1944 are simply blown to smithereens in the movie. It's also very noticeable that there's barely a single member of an ethnic minority to be found amongst the soldiers in the film.

*The Longest Day* shows nothing of the horror of war. In Zanuck's Hollywood vision, death is quick, painless and unbloody: anyone who's hit just falls over and dies. The bodies of the paratroopers, hanging from roofs and power poles, are perhaps most likely to affect the viewer. The movie's perspective is businesslike: the Germans are not evil, stupid and brutal Nazis, but simple people in a dictatorship who are defeated by the armed forces of democracy. First and foremost, this film addresses the clash of two political systems; and in this, it is rather untypical of its genre, which tends to reflect on the nature of order and chaos. While war films like *Home of the Brave* (1949) or *Twelve O' Clock High* (1949) attempted to deal seriously with issues such as racism and the psychic trauma of combat, Zanuck and his directors withdrew to relatively safe ground: the historicity of the events it depicts. And despite the movie's various distortions of the truth, this is the actual quality of the film: it may not show us what really happened, but it does make history compellingly understandable.

OK

6

# LAWRENCE OF ARABIA

1962 - GREAT BRITAIN - 222 MIN. - HISTORICAL DRAMA, BIOPIC

DIRECTOR DAVID LEAN (1908–1991)
SCREENPLAY ROBERT BOLT, MICHAEL WILSON DIRECTOR OF PHOTOGRAPHY FREDDIE YOUNG EDITING ANNE V. COATES
MUSIC MAURICE JARRE PRODUCTION SAM SPIEGEL for HORIZON.

STARRING PETER O'TOOLE (Thomas Edward Lawrence), ALEC GUINNESS (Prince Feisal), ANTHONY QUINN (Auda Abu Tayi), JACK HAWKINS (General Allenby), OMAR SHARIF (Sherif Ali Ibn El Kharish), ANTHONY QUAYLE (Colonel Harry Brighton), CLAUDE RAINS (Mr. Dryden), ARTHUR KENNEDY (Jackson Bentley), JOSÉ FERRER (Turkish Governor), DONALD WOLFIT (General Murray).

ACADEMY AWARDS 1962 OSCARS for BEST PICTURE (Sam Spiegel), BEST DIRECTOR (David Lean), BEST CINEMATOGRAPHY (Freddie Young), BEST EDITING (Anne V. Coates), BEST MUSIC (Maurice Jarre), BEST ART DIRECTION (John Box, John Stoll, Dario Simoni), BEST SOUND (John Cox).

## *"The best of them won't come for money. They'll come for me!"*

"I'm different," announces Thomas Edward Lawrence (Peter O'Toole) right at the start of the film. He's trying to explain to a Bedouin what distinguishes him from the rest of his compatriots in "a fat country with fat people." Different... yes. But in what way? Who was this British officer from Oxford, who led the Arab tribes to rebel against their Turkish rulers during the First World War? An idealistic dreamer? A narcissistic megalomaniac? A homosexual sadomasochist? He died young after a motorcycle accident, and his acquaintances and superior officers answered as one: we don't know who he was – we hardly knew him at all.

Indeed, T. E. Lawrence hardly knew himself, and the more he made his own acquaintance, the more he recoiled from what he saw. This is one major theme of David Lean's monumental film biography, which shows various facets of this strange character without ever really solving the mystery that surrounds the man.

*Lawrence of Arabia* is not so much a film about war, politics and British colonial history as a visually splendid record of one man's trip to the limits of sanity in the hope of finding himself. Only the most impossible challenges are enough for Thomas Edward Lawrence. He crosses deserts no one has ever ventured into; he plans surprise attacks on seemingly impregnable Turkish positions; he forges fragile alliances amongst bitterly opposed tribes; and eventually, he takes Damascus with his Arab army. Lawrence was once asked what he liked so much about the desert, and he replied, "its cleanliness." But far from achieving the purified soul he longed for, he paid for his self-torturing expeditions with a loss of innocence. Originally inspired by the

1

“In his performance, O’Toole catches the noble seriousness of Lawrence and his cheap theatricality, his godlike arrogance and his gibbering self-doubt; his headlong courage, girlish psychasthenia, Celtic wit, humorless egotism, compulsive chastity, and sensuous pleasure in pain.” *Time*

2

3

1 Hitchcock mirage: Director David Lean and cinematographer Freddie Young reeled in the Oscars for their desert magic.

2 Desert Storm: Omar Sharif emerged from the Arabian sands as Sherif Ali Ibn El Kharish and rose to international stardom.

3 Eagle eyes: Major Lawrence (Peter O'Toole) is a singular force and sees what he wants to see.

ideal of helping the Arabs to achieve their independence, Lawrence was eventually forced to recognize that his masters, the British, would never allow it. This is why, at the end of the film, Mr. Dryden (Claude Rains) calls him "a man who tells half-lies." Dryden is a British government representative in Arabia, and in his view, such "half-lying" is worse than mouthing complete falsehoods in the interests of political expediency. By this time, however, Lawrence is barely concerned with political considerations anymore. His courage and willpower have so impressed the Arabs that they have honored him with a new name, and Lawrence, with his tendency to narcissism, luxuriates in his popularity and the splendor of his triumphs. As his megalomania grows, he behaves increasingly as if he were the Messiah to the Arab people.

What's more, in the course of his military campaigns, he has learned to kill, and the power he feels while doing so is a source of genuine pleasure. On one occasion, he is captured, tortured and raped by the Turks; and the film hints discreetly that even this is a somewhat ambivalent experience for Lawrence. Speaking to Jackson Bentley, the American reporter (Arthur Kennedy), the Englishman's comrade in arms Prince Feisal (Alec Guinness) sums him up as follows: "With Major Lawrence, mercy is a passion; with me,

**PETER O'TOOLE**

In 1962, the title role in David Lean's *Lawrence of Arabia* shot the unknown 29-year-old Irishman Peter O'Toole into the major league of international movie stars. Previously, he had only played a few minor roles, such as a bagpiper in Robert Stevenson's *Kidnapped* (1959). In Britain, however, he had already made a name for himself on the stage, thanks to his appearances with the Royal Shakespeare Company in Stratford-upon-Avon. The 60s were to be O'Toole's great decade, in which he would be nominated for the Academy Award on several occasions without ever winning it. With his Irish charm, his piercing blue eyes, his impish sense of humor, and his faintly ironical air, he was perfectly cast in eccentric comedies such as *What's new, Pussycat?* (1965), and *How to Steal a Million* (1966). He had less luck with later roles, apart from his appearance as Robinson Crusoe in Jack Gold's *Man Friday* (1975), a new take on Defoe's tale that depicted the "native" Friday as the cleverer of the two men. By this time, O'Toole's problems with alcohol were gradually becoming noticeable.

O'Toole is still active in film and television today. His most recent movie was *The Final Curtain* (2001), released in 2002, in which he played an ageing entertainer. In 2003, Peter O'Toole was given an honorary Academy Award: a "Lifetime Achievement Award." Against his will, incidentally; for he announced in no uncertain terms that he still reckoned he had a chance of winning the Oscar in fair competition with his peers.

**“Lean and cameraman Young have brought out the loneliness and pitiless torment of the desert with an artistic use of color, and almost every take is superbly framed and edited.”** *Variety*

4 Taking out the big guns: Aristocrat Sherif Ali shows his impatient friend Lawrence that he is a man be reckoned with.

5 Head in the sand? Lawrence mobilizes the Arabs against a Turkish attack.

6 At a loss for words: Lawmaking and bureaucracy are certainly not among Lawrence’s strengths. His patience wears thin as disputes between the Arab tribes sour the spirit of newfound liberty.

7 Listening to his inner clock: Auda Abu Tayi (Anthony Quinn) fears that Lawrence is acting out of self-interest.

6

it is merely good manners. Judge for yourself which motive is the more reliable."

Lawrence certainly has reasons to be worried about his enthusiasms. When his desperate application for an "ordinary job" is turned down, his next mission ends in the insane butchery of an exhausted Turkish regiment, and in the course of the massacre Lawrence works himself into an ecstasy of bloodlust.

Before *Lawrence of Arabia* Peter O'Toole was an almost completely unknown actor, yet his portrayal of is one of his greatest-ever performances. The background to that portrait is almost equally spectacular: using Technicolor and Super-Panavision-70, director David Lean and cameraman Freddie Young created astonishing panoramas of the beautiful and pitiless desert, with its fiery sun, its sandstorms, and a horizon like a line drawn through the world. Filming took two years, and ten months alone were spent filming exteriors in Jordan. At one surreal moment, we see a ship sailing through the sands: Lawrence has arrived at the Suez Canal. Equally impressive is the first meeting between Lawrence and Sherif Ali Ibn El Kharish (Omar Sharif): a shimmering mirage that suddenly materializes into a real figure.

For all its beauty, the film is never merely interested in "strong images" for their own sake. Despite the overwhelming landscapes and the dynamic battle scenes, this is an actors' film performed by an outstanding ensemble, and its fascinating central character is always the main focus of interest. *Lawrence of Arabia* is one of the biggest *and* best movies ever made.

LP

# THE MIRACLE WORKER

1962 - USA - 106 MIN. - DRAMA

DIRECTOR ARTHUR PENN (*1922)
SCREENPLAY WILLIAM GIBSON, based on his play of the same name inspired by passages of HELEN KELLER'S autobiography *THE STORY OF MY LIFE* DIRECTOR OF PHOTOGRAPHY ERNESTO CAPARROS EDITING ARAM AVAKIAN MUSIC LAURENCE ROSENTHAL
PRODUCTION FRED COE for PLAYFILM PRODUCTIONS, UNITED ARTISTS.

STARRING ANNE BANCROFT (Annie Sullivan), PATTY DUKE (Helen Keller), VICTOR JORY (Captain Arthur Keller), INGA SWENSON (Kate Keller), ANDREW PRINE (James Keller), KATHLEEN COMEGYS (Aunt Ev), JACK HOLLANDER (Mr. Anagnos), MICHELE FARR (Annie at age ten), ALAN HOWARD (Jimmie), BEAH RICHARDS (Viney, The Keller's Maid).

ACADEMY AWARDS 1962 OSCARS for BEST ACTRESS (Anne Bancroft) and BEST SUPPORTING ACTRESS (Patty Duke).

## *"It would be a miracle if you can get the child to tolerate you!"*

Scarlet fever robbed Helen Keller (Patty Duke) of her sight and hearing, but it couldn't take her spirit. Still, the early childhood affliction has trapped Helen in a wordless world her parents can't access. Home becomes more of a minefield with each passing day; anything from a shard of broken vase, to a bed sheet hung out to dry is a potential hazard. Out of desperation and the fear that her daughter is losing touch with the outside world, Mrs. Keller (Inga Swenson) calls on the assistance of Annie Sullivan (Anne Bancroft), a visually-impaired teacher who works with the blind. Upon her arrival, the soon to be pensioned Captain Keller (Victor Jory) informs Miss Sullivan that she has just two weeks to show promising results; should her efforts fail, Helen will be sent to an institution.

After first producing it for live television, dramatist William Gibson adapted his script for the stage and *The Miracle Worker* was the toast of Broadway from 1959 to 1961. Gibson was approached again when it was decided that the project would be further adapted for the screen. Similarly, Arthur Penn, who had staged the play, was asked to take the director's chair for the film version. For once it seemed Hollywood thought Broadway had got it right; and thus a 15-year-old Patty Duke and seasoned thespian Anne Bancroft illuminated the screen with the same intensity with which they had won over the New York stage. Both were rewarded with the Oscar for their achievements.

Despite *The Miracle Worker's* theatrical roots, Penn was adept at transforming the piece for the cinema in a way that took full advantage of its techniques. The flashback sequences depicting Annie Sullivan's childhood are magnified many times over. This and the film's grainy, flickering texture enhance the audience's sense of the teacher's own visual impairment.

Nonetheless, Penn's innovative communication of purely optical perception was not the only way in which he proved himself an inspired cinematic storyteller. His depiction of Helen's inner world is equally poignant. For instance, when a jug breaks unexpectedly at Helen's hand, the crash never makes its way to the center of action, as it is only one of her many everyday mishaps, and one she doesn't actually register. The broken jug vanishes from

1

# "Every day she slips further away. I don't know how to call her back."

*Film quote: Mrs. Keller (Inga Swenson)*

2

**ARTHUR PENN**

As a young man, Arthur Penn fought World War II with the U. S. Army infantry in the Ardennes. Although he discovered his passion for the theater at a young age, he returned home from the war to he study philosophy and psychology at Black Mountain College. It was only towards the end of the 1940s that Penn first started training as an actor in Los Angeles. Embarking on a television career in 1951, he began directing TV shows in 1953 and had a number of credits to his name by 1958. Not only did Penn act as John F. Kennedy's advisor for his historical presidential election debates with Richard Nixon, but he also directed one of these televised showdowns himself.

By 1958, Penn boasted a three-pronged career, getting his foot in Hollywood's door with *The Left Handed Gun* (1958), yet remaining active in his established medium as well as on Broadway. Much like John Frankenheimer, George Roy Hill and Sidney Lumet, Penn's revolutionary film work was highly influenced by his experiences with live television. Following the independently produced *The Miracle Worker* (1962) and *Mickey One* (1965), Penn went over to Columbia Pictures to shoot *The Chase* (1965). Deflated by a less than harmonious professional relationship with producer Sam Spiegel, Penn then withdrew the industry for several years. It was only after *Bonnie and Clyde* (1967) star and producer Warren Beatty convinced him to direct the today legendary gangster movie that Penn returned to the cinema.

Shortly after his return to Hollywood, Penn took on his largest production to date: *Little Big Man* (1970), a scathing look at the myth of the West, starring Dustin Hoffman. In 1975, he reunited with Gene Hackman, who had played Clyde Barrow's brother *Bonnie and Clyde*, to direct him in the detective caper *Night Moves*. *The Missouri Breaks* (1976), starring Jack Nicholson and Marlon Brando, was one of the last high profile movies he directed. Today, Penn enjoys a renewed career in television, a field he has been regularly active in since the 1990s.

3

the visual tableau as quickly as it materialized. Unlike most films, *The Miracle Worker* does not allow the viewer to take on the role of a removed outsider, who can foresee every danger Helen will encounter. Without warning the camera follows Helen's every footstep. Yet rather than replicating he exact movements, often the camera will relay a raw impression of them. I she suddenly decides to crawl along the floor, sniffing her environment and probing it with her hands, the camera will respond by positioning itself on the ground beside her. Thanks to the synthesis of the cinematography and Patty Duke's brilliant portrayal of the character, the film exquisitely captures Helen's otherworldly means of perception.

To give her a chance to liberate herself from the blackness, Annie Sullivan sets her sights on teaching Helen sign language. Ready to work miracles, she grabs hold of the child and begins to draw letters in her hand, slowly spelling the words of objects the young girl comes into contact with. Still Helen appears fundamentally unable to grasp the abstract concept of language, never managing to relate objects to their names. Helen's road to comprehension is a long and arduous one, and Anne Bancroft uses this opportunity to turn the Annie Sullivan role into a non-stop tour de force. Running into one brick wall after another, it seems that both teacher and student's attempts at understanding one another have amounted to nothing but frustration. Then again, there are isolated promises of progress, which appear on screen as fully-fledged breakthroughs. Indeed, this mutual feat of endurance is rewarded in the end when Helen is baptized into the world language with the recognition of her first word – water.

4

1 Blinded by the light: The lovely Patty Duke received worldwide acclaim for her portrayal of deaf, dumb and blind humanitarian Helen Keller. Interestingly, the John Cassavetes' *A Child Is Waiting*, released that same year, featured actual handicapped actors and flopped with audiences.

2 Temper temper: Helen's constant frustration is the source of her sudden outbursts. She bites and kicks whoever gets in her path, and at one point almost knocks out one of Miss Sullivan's teeth.

3 Sit for a spell: Pariah and pedant Annie Sullivan (Anne Bancroft) in a moment of contemplation. The visually-impaired teacher fears that young Helen will be trapped in her own world if she fails to teach her sign language.

4 After years of searching, Helen has finally found her mother... She spells out the letters of "mother" with her hand and forges a relationship with a woman she thought lost to her (Inga Swenson as Mrs. Keller).

**"In the key scenes, Penn manipulates his camera into the middle of the fray and achieves an immediacy which is rare and exciting."** *Newsweek*

# TO KILL A MOCKINGBIRD

1962 - USA - 129 MIN. - DRAMA

DIRECTOR ROBERT MULLIGAN (*1925)

SCREENPLAY HORTON FOOTE, based on the novel of the same name by HARPER LEE DIRECTOR OF PHOTOGRAPHY RUSSELL HARLAN EDITING AARON STELL MUSIC ELMER BERNSTEIN, MACK DAVID PRODUCTION ALAN J. PAKULA for PAKULA-MULLIGAN, BRENTWOOD PRODUCTIONS, UNIVERSAL INTERNATIONAL PICTURES.

STARRING GREGORY PECK (Atticus Finch), MARY BADHAM (Jean Louise "Scout" Finch), PHILLIP ALFORD (Jeremy "Jem" Finch), ROBERT DUVALL (Arthur "Boo" Radley), JOHN MEGNA (Dill Harris), BROCK PETERS (Tom Robinson), FRANK OVERTON (Sheriff Tate), ROSEMARY MURPHY (Maudie Atkinson), RUTH WHITE (Mrs. Dubose), ESTELLE EVANS (Calpurnia), COLLIN WILCOX (Mayella Ewell), JAMES ANDERSON (Bob Ewell), ALICE GHOSTLEY (Stephanie Crawford).

ACADEMY AWARDS 1962 OSCARS for BEST ACTOR (Gregory Peck), BEST ADAPTED SCREENPLAY (Horton Foote), and BEST ART DIRECTION (Alexander Golitzen, Henry Bunstead, Oliver Emert).

***"I was to think of those days many times. Of Jem and Dill and Boo Radley, and Tom Robinson, and Atticus."***

America is a land of unlimited optimism and perilous incongruity, and the history of the USA is also the history of its hopes, its fears and its myths. Amongst the great tales of all the races and generations that have inhabited this country is *To Kill a Mockingbird* – written by Harper Lee and filmed by Robert Mulligan. Indeed, perhaps only Tom Sawyer and Huckleberry Finn have etched themselves into the collective unconscious as indelibly as this novel and this movie.

The story is set in the Depression years. The southern States are particularly hard-hit by the crisis, and countless idyllic small towns are threatened by poverty, racial hatred, ignorance and bigotry. Yet for the children of the widowed lawyer Atticus Finch (Gregory Peck), life is one big adventure. To ten-year-old Jem (Phillip Alford) and his kid sister Scout (Mary Badham), everything is a source of wonder: an old car tyre becomes an exciting toy; a box containing nothing but a few chalks, a broken clock and a pocket-knife is their jealously-guarded treasure chest; and they have a burning interest in the house of the mysterious Boo Radley (Robert Duvall). It's been years since anyone saw him; and in the children's imagination, every step they take towards his scary, dilapidated house is a terrifying test of their courage. Yet their father's latest case also captures their attention: a black man, Tom Robinson (Brock Peters), has been accused of raping a white woman – and Atticus, bravely, is defending him. The case for the prosecution, and the trial itself, are outrageously unfair; but Jem and Scout gradually learn some lessons for life from their father, who looks evil in the eye and stands up firmly against it. And it's Atticus' tolerance and sympathy that finally enables the children to overcome their greatest fear: the fear of Boo Radley.

As the tomboy Scout, Mary Badham captured the hearts of generations of moviegoers, big and small. Her inimitable mixture of cheek and innocent curiosity disarms everyone she meets; and at the end of the film, she need only speak two words to build a bridge across an abyss: "Hey, Boo." A deathly pale Robert Duvall also gives a touching performance as Boo Radley. To prepare himself for this tiny but unforgettable role (his film debut), he stayed indoors for six weeks, avoiding the sun. And then, of course, there is Gregory

1

1 The walls have ears: Scout (Mary Badham), Jem (Phillip Alford) and neighborhood friend Dill Harris (John Megna) get caught eavesdropping at the door.

2 Growing pains: The children follow the proceedings from the landing above the courtroom and learn that the grown-up world isn't always fair. Scout begins to wonder whether her father has any chance of getting his innocent client off the hook.

Peck as Atticus Finch, father and lawyer. An ideal combination of gentleness, intelligence and strength, he became something of a model for all the fathers (and lawyers) who came after him. Peck's Atticus Finch is the very image of integrity.

What really made this quiet film such a huge success was its faithful adherence to a basic tenet of the novel: the story is told exclusively from the children's perspective. Each of their daily adventures is a journey into the shadow-world that lies between Good and Evil. When they encounter the terrors of the adult world, they're armed with the power of their imagination and an absolute trust in the strength of their father; and so they're capable of moving mountains. Nowhere is this clearer than in the scene at the jailhouse, where a lynch mob demands that Atticus hand over the prisoner Tom Robinson. Though Scout is barely even aware of the crowd's aggression, she manages to defuse the situation merely by asking a few simple questions. The lengthy trial scene is also attended by Scout and Jem, and it ends in a moving demonstration of support for Atticus by the entire black population of the town. *To Kill a Mockingbird* is studded with such miniature highpoints, and quite free from the melodramatic tendentiousness of many films with a political or anti-racist "message."

This is in every respect an extraordinary film –- and it was nominated for no less than eight Academy Awards, including Best Film Music. Elmer Bernstein's remarkable score is an assemblage of simple melodies, of the

**GREGORY PECK (1916–2003)**

He embodied the American ideal of modest integrity like no other actor – not even Gary Cooper, whose role in *High Noon* (1952) he had politely declined. Just a couple of years previously, he had played a dignified cowboy in *The Gunfighter* (1950), and he didn't want to be typecast. Yet the big man with the piercing eyes always remained true to himself, however varied the actual roles he played, from a dedicated journalist in *Gentleman's Agreement* (1947) to a New York office worker in *The Man in the Grey Flannel Suit* (1956) and a hard-bitten General in *The Guns of Navarone* (1961). Even ambivalent characters such as the innocently guilty lawyer in *Cape Fear* (1962) had a touch of quiet nobility about them. In *Moby Dick* (1956), his Captain Ahab bore a strong resemblance to Abraham Lincoln, with whom Peck himself had often been compared. Despite chalking up successes in *Roman Holiday* (1953) and *Arabesque* (1966), he never really felt comfortable playing comedies. But those who regarded him as the biggest bore in Hollywood not only failed to notice his immense charisma; they also overlooked the fact that he lived out his ideals, and not merely on screen. He was a committed worker for many charities, he took part in protest marches alongside Martin Luther King, and in 1970, he seriously considered standing as a candidate against the Governor of California, Ronald Reagan. Gregory Peck died in 2003 at the age of 87. His funeral eulogy was given by Brock Peters, the actor who played Tom Robinson in *To Kill a Mockingbird* (1962).

3 Hostile witness: Bob Ewell (James Anderson) is more fired up than a loose cannon. But his fervor leaves defense attorney Atticus Finch (Gregory Peck) cold.

4 In the hot seat: A simple parlor room trick proves that the allegations are false. The defendant, Tom Robinson (Brock Peters), is left-handed.

5 Taking a stand: In the name of the truth, Atticus and Tom combat latent racism in their small Southern town.

**"If you just learn a single trick, Scout, you'll get along a lot better with all kinds of folks. You never really understand a person until you consider things from his point of view… Until you climb inside of his skin and walk around in it."** *Film quote: Atticus (Gregory Peck)*

6 Rabid gunfire: With a steady hand and the eye of marksman, Atticus silences a mad dog terrorizing the neighborhood.

7 Is there no justice? Despite presenting a compelling case, Atticus couldn't sway the jury from finding him guilty.

8 Ominous shadows: Dill and the other children may still be young innocents. However, a day will come when they'll have to have to ward off the darkness themselves.

**"*To Kill a Mockingbird* is, first and foremost, a re-creation of a children's world, and a rather grizzly, ghoulish world at that: where the main center of local interest is a lunatic reputed to be dangerous; where dogs run mad in the streets every now and again; and where the half-noticed adult dramas impinge on the children only occasionally. The violence is all the more frightening for being totally unpredictable."** *Sight and Sound*

kind a child might produce while tinkering around on the piano. But this sensitive literary adaptation was up against the desert epic *Lawrence of Arabia* (1962)… and ultimately, the only Oscars it received were for Horton Foote's reworking of the novel (which the novelist, unusually in the movie business, thoroughly admired); for the Art Direction, a loving reconstruction of Harper Lee's home town Monroeville on the premises of Universal Studios; and for Gregory Peck, as Best Actor. Till the day he died, he described *To Kill a Mockingbird* as his favorite among all the films he had made, and he maintained a friendship with Harper Lee for many years. In 2003, the American Film Institute voted Atticus Finch the greatest film hero of all time. Among the runners-up were Indiana Jones, James Bond – and Lawrence of Arabia.

PB

# 8 ½

## 8 ½ (Otto e mezzo)

1962 - ITALY / FRANCE - 138 MIN. - DRAMA

DIRECTOR FEDERICO FELLINI (1920–1993)
SCREENPLAY FEDERICO FELLINI, ENNIO FLAIANO, TULLIO PINELLI, BRUNELLO RONDI DIRECTOR OF PHOTOGRAPHY GIANNI DI VENANZO
EDITING LEO CATOZZO MUSIC NINO ROTA PRODUCTION NELLO MENICONI, ANGELO RIZZOLI for CINERIZ, FRANCINEX.

STARRING MARCELLO MASTROIANNI (Guido Anselmi), CLAUDIA CARDINALE (Claudia), ANOUK AIMÉE (Luisa), SANDRA MILO (Carla), ROSSELLA FALK (Rosella), MARIO PISU (Mezzabotta), BARBARA STEEL (Gloria), EDDRA GALE (Saraghina), JEAN ROUGEUL (Carini), GUIDO ALBERTI (Pace, the Producer).

ACADEMY AWARDS 1963 OSCARS for BEST FOREIGN LANGUAGE FILM and BEST COSTUME DESIGN (Piero Gherardi).

## *"I have nothing to say. But I want to say it all the same."*

"The complex begins with a long shot of planet Earth, which has been totally destroyed by a nuclear war. Cross fade to the new Noah's Ark, the spaceship that's trying flee from the contaminated world: the remains of humanity are looking for sanctuary on another planet." In the dead of night, a film producer is leading his friends across a gigantic film set somewhere out in the sticks. Spotlights cut through the darkness. Men are erecting scaffolds, so that the set will be ready before filming begins. "10,000 extras, maybe 15,000, certainly a crazy amount…," brags the fat producer (Guido Alberti), as the group ascends the staircase to an enormous rocket launch pad.

Guido (Marcello Mastroianni), the director, remains at the base of the tower. He sits down on a metal bar and glances at the floor, his black hat concealing his face: "And I believed," he says, "that I had such clear ideas. I wanted to make an honest film, without lies or window-dressing. I thought I had something to say that was so simple, so easy to understand. A film that would be useful to everybody in some way, that could help to bury for good everything dead we carry within us."

Now he's forced to worry about this tower, and he no longer knows what the hell to do with it. He had wanted to take a rest cure at a health spa, but now filming is due to start on his latest project – and what the producer is telling him has nothing to do with what the director had imagined. Guido's film was about people from his own life: his wife (Anouk Aimée), who visits him in the spa; his mistress (Sandra Milo), who has gone to stay at the station hotel; a fat hooker who had fascinated him as a child; a cardinal, from whom he requests absolution in vain; and his parents, with whom he yearns to be reconciled. In the end, Guido will call off the entire project – but in its place, he will have made a quite different film from the one he had originally planned.

*8½* shows a film director's crisis *and* how he manages to overcome it. The movie caused its earliest audiences so much confusion because its initial premises were so paradoxical. It insists on the impossibility of making a film, and at the same time we see a film that tells us of this impossibility. "8½" is the name of the film whose making is the topic of *8½*. Here, the barrier has dissolved between the author and his work, for the protagonist Guido may confidently be identified with the director Federico Fellini. They are equal in age, and have been married for the same number of years; both are making their "eight-and-a-halfth" film, and both wear a black suit and hat. And both are stuck in a dilemma shortly before starting work on a film: one of them is unhappy because he no longer recognizes the film he wanted to make; the other because his film has disappeared.

After the surprise success of *La dolce vita* (1960), said Fellini, "my enemies were ready to shoot me down in flames and my friends expected great

1

**“People have accused this film of being confused, overloaded, monstrous or even chaotic. At best, they say it’s ‘baroque.’ Frankly, I can’t understand these reactions. The film I saw is rich and vital, and anyone can understand it. I almost want to say it’s *transparent* – and I’m well aware that the word has more than one connotation. *8½* is cheerful and light, and yet it’s not unserious; Fellini himself has called it ‘comic’… Above all, it’s the most intelligent of all Fellini’s films.”** *Filmkritik*

1 Cardinal sins: In a film full of women, Guido has but one muse. Claudia Cardinale as Claudia.

2 A perfect ten: Prior to making *8½*, Federico Fellini's directing career included six features, two shorts, which he deemed featurettes, and a joint film-making endeavor – hence the enigmatic title of this "film comico."

3 Footloose and fancy-free: American ex-pat Gloria (Barbara Steel) and Guido's old friend Mezzabotta (Mario Pisu) do the locomotion on the terrace. As in most Fellini films, music care of Nino Rota – not Little Eva.

things of me." The pressure from the public, the critics and the producers paralysed and blocked him, but a simple artifice restored his creativity: he made his own crisis the subject of his film. Guido, who had been variously conceived as an architect, a professor or a writer, now became a director who had lost his feeling for the movie he intended to make.

According to legend, the confusion was so great that no one knew exactly when work on the film actually began. Fellini filmed rehearsals and later included them in the finished movie; but at the time, the actors had no idea that they were already playing their roles. The moviegoer, too, will have trouble keeping track of the various narrative levels. Without warning, we are transported from the past to the future and from the actual to the imagined – and all of these episodes reflect Guido's inner and outer life. Take the scene in which Guido is sitting in a café with his wife and sister when his mistress arrives and sits down at another table. His desire to reconcile his spouse and

4

**MARCELLO MASTROIANNI (1924–1996)**

When Marcello Mastroianni was hired to play the lead in *La dolce vita* (1960), he enquired about the script. Federico Fellini handed him a folder. All the pages were blank, except for the first: it showed a drawing of a man swimming in the sea, with his penis extending almost to the seabed; two mermaids were swimming around him. Mastroinanni's reported reaction: "An interesting role; I accept." The friendship between the actor and the director was one of the legends of Italian cinema. They would go on to make five films together, the most important of which was probably *8½*. At that time, Mastroianni was already seen as the Latin Lover *par excellence*, a reputation that would dog him all his life.

Before making his first film, Marcello Mastroianni spent several years in the theater, learning his trade with Luchino Visconti. By the time he made his breakthrough with Visconti's *White Nights* (*Le notti bianche*, 1957), however, he had already appeared in more than 40 movies. He worked with the most beautiful actresses and the most important directors. These included Vittorio de Sica, whom he had already revered in his youth (*Marriage Italian-Style / Matrimonio all'italiana,* 1964), Ettore Scola (*A Special Day / Una giornata particolare,* 1977), and his friend Marco Ferreri (*La grande bouffe,* 1973). He won prizes in Cannes for his roles in Scola's *Jealousy Italian-Style* (*Dramma della gelosia – Tutti i particolari in cronaca,* 1970) and Nikita Mikhalkov's *Dark Eyes* (*Oci ciornie,* 1987). In 1988, Mastroianni was awarded the European Film Prize for his life's work. He himself said that he had appeared in more than 170 films. Not all of these were masterpieces. For him, acting always meant fun, and money – never torture. In the 90s, his inimitably melancholy aura and his soft, dark eyes graced *Pereira Declares* (*Sostiene Pereira,* 1996) by Roberto Faenza. Marcello Mastroianni, one of the great actors of European cinema, died in 1996 at the age of 72.

his lover lead to the famous harem sequence in which all the women he has known join him in an idyllic country setting – bathing him, pampering him, catering to his every need. Suddenly, the women rebel – until Guido tames them with his whip. Fellini's film has no consistent spatial or temporal structure; the narrative has the capricious logic of a dream.

Ennio Flaiano, Fellini's loyal scriptwriter, once said that *8½* had marked the director's conversion to magic. Fellini experienced this movie as a kind of liberation; afterwards, he changed the way he made films and the kind of films he made. Where he had previously felt bound to retain an appearance of naturalism, he now trusted more in his dreams and visions. Shamelessly personal and effortlessly universal, *8½* is the most complex piece of self-reflection ever produced by an artist of the cinema. NM

**"All these sequences are so magnificently filmed that we hardly have the breath to voice a query as to what they mean. Gianni di Venanzo's black and white photography and Piero Gherardi's sets and costumes provide such visual magic that it seems pointless to make philosophical reservations on the film content."** *Sight and Sound*

4 Ringmaster: The people in Guido's life resurface at the film's conclusion in what appears to be the grand finale of a circus. Indeed, infinite visual and metaphoric circles appear throughout *8½* – a film that ends where it began and thus begins anew.

5 The birth of Venus: Whole lotta woman, Saraghina, performs on the beach for the young schoolboys and reaps laurels for Fellini. Despite its undeniably complex narrative of dreams, desires and memories, *8½* creamed off an Oscar, the grand prize at the Moscow film festival and the New York Film Critics' Award.

6 A streetcar named desire: Guido picks up his mistress Carla (Sandra Milo) from the train station. To underline the film's surrealism, Fellini shot most of the scenes on a studio lot.

# WHAT EVER HAPPENED TO BABY JANE?

1962 - USA - 132 MIN. - PSYCHOTHRILLER, LITERARY ADAPTATION

DIRECTOR ROBERT ALDRICH (1918–1983)
SCREENPLAY LUKAS HELLER, based on Henry Farrell's novel of the same name DIRECTOR OF PHOTOGRAPHY ERNEST HALLER EDITING MICHAEL LUCIANO MUSIC FRANK DE VOL PRODUCTION ROBERT ALDRICH for ALDRICH ASSOCIATES, SEVEN ARTS, WARNER BROS.

STARRING BETTE DAVIS ("Baby" Jane Hudson), JOAN CRAWFORD (Blanche Hudson), VICTOR BUONO (Edwin Flagg), WESLEY ADDY (Marty), JULIE ALLRED ("Baby" Jane Hudson in 1917), ANNA LEE (Mrs. Bates), MAIDIE NORMAN (Elvira Stitt), MARJORIE BENNETT (Mrs. Dehlia Flagg), DAVE WILLOCK (Ray Hudson), ANNE BARTON (Cora Hudson).

ACADEMY AWARDS 1961 OSCAR for BEST COSTUMES (Norma Koch).

## *"You wouldn't be able to do these awful things to me if I weren't still in this chair."*

Some people take their secrets to the grave. Others take their sisters.

As Blanche (Joan Crawford) steers her wheelchair toward the table where dinner is being kept warm, images of her sister Jane's (Betty Davis) torturous machinations race through her mind. She comes to a halt, seized by the sight of the silver service lid lying before her. It was only recently that she discovered her pet parakeet dead underneath, allegedly having flown out of the cage while Jane was cleaning it. And now, Blanche has been left to contemplate the words Jane sneered on her way out the door, announcing that rats have infested the cellar. She reaches for the lid, and her worst fears are confirmed as she discovers the roasted rodent that adorns her plate. Echoes of maniacal laughter fill the hallway. We understand that Blanche is caught in a mousetrap, and all she can do is spin round and round in circles. And the front door, her only exit to freedom, is an insurmountable flight of stairs away…

There was a time when Blanche was a big Hollywood star. That was before a car accident left her a paraplegic. Jane too was a starlet – a child actress whose career fell victim to alcohol and the hysteria of fame. This is a classic case of sibling rivalry: Blanche only remembers a blonde curly Sue who got all the attention by lighting up the stage with songs from Tin Pan Alley; whereas Jane despises a wall-flower who grew up to steal the show.

Though they resent each other, they are completely co-dependent. Today, not a penny is left of a fortune amassed in baby booties, and Jane relies on her sister's film royalties for survival. Good thing that Blanche can't get by physically without a nurse and that Jane feels so guilty about her crippling accident…

*What Ever Happened to Baby Jane?* is a psychothriller about two middle-aged women bent on ripping each other to shreds. Robert Aldrich, known primarily for his Westerns and war pictures like *Vera Cruz* (1954) and *Attack* (1956), earned his reputation as a master of chilling suspense thanks to the invisible camera and no frills direction. Unfortunately, the critics tended to compare Aldrich's piece to Hitchcock's *Psycho* (1960) and then slated it for a lack of originality, dramatic arcs, and interesting visuals. Still, there were those who viewed it as a fascinating, self-reflective study on Hollywood taboos, which walked the fine line between cinematic reality and fiction. In the words of *Movie* magazine's Andrew Sarris: "The thought of taking on Bette Davis and Joan Crawford at the same time is formidable enough, but

**"Certainly... it is difficult to imagine a more commanding star occasion. Davis and Crawford, Red Queen and White Queen, together for the first time in roles they might have dreamed up themselves. No other combination of actresses, however different or distinguished the film, could produce quite the same frisson of anticipation."** *Sight and Sound*

here the plot itself is immersed in the presences and pasts of these two ageless stars. In fact, if *Baby Jane* is about anything at all, it is about *Bette Davis* and *Joan Crawford.*"

Sarris was dead right. The on-screen personas weren't an act. Their mutual animosity is said to have begun when Davis purported that Crawford had "slept with every male star at MGM except Lassie." The slighted Crawford responded by saying that Davis made up for a lack of talent with bloodshot glances, nicotine and three-cent comments. Ironically, the two women's physique and temperaments were as different as their careers were similar. Both had acted in dozens of pictures and received Oscars by the time *Baby Jane* was made, and both were considered has-beens. Starving for roles by the time the 60s rolled around, this was to be the last great hurrah of their careers.

Indeed, it is a film is fueled by the terrorizing intensity of its leading ladies. On the surface, Bette Davis a. k. a. Baby Jane plays the wicked sister, who torments meek sister Joan Crawford a. k. a. Blanche with her diabolical

1 Divas behind bars: All Blanche's (Joan Crawford, right) pleading won't get her sister Jane (Bette Davis, left) to free her from their cage. To this day, *What Ever Happened to Baby Jane* remains one of the most intense displays of Hollywood hatred.

2 Truth serum: "Why am I so good at playing bitches? I think it's because I'm not one. Maybe that's why Miss Crawford always plays ladies." *Bette Davis* on Joan Crawford.

3 Down for the count: Blanche tries to phone for help, but the Baby tampers with the line before she has the chance.

3

**BETTE DAVIS (1908–1989)**

Did those famous eyes of hers really make all the boys think she was a spy? Let's just say Kim Carnes believed it enough to sing about their secret magnetism and the star was wildly flattered. Not a surprise, as Carnes' 1980 hit won Davis points with her granddaughter.

One of the immortal legends of classic Hollywood cinema, Bette Davis was indeed the highest paid actress at the Hollywood dream factory during the 1940s. Showered with Oscars for her work in Alfred E. Green's *Dangerous* (1935) and William Wyler's *Jezebel* (1938), her performances continued to win nominations each year from 1939 to 1942, and then again in 1944. Her final Oscar nod came in 1962 for *What Ever Happened to Baby Jane?* The accolades aside, Davis never thought that success had come easy to her, and her engraving on her tombstone bears testament to this: Bette Davis – She did it the hard way.

Born Ruth Elizabeth Davis in Lowell, Massachusetts, she trained as an actress in New York and took to the stage. Even before being contracted by Universal pictures in 1930, Bette Davis had already dazzled Broadway. At the time of her rise to fame, Hollywood needed actors like her, whose voices would add sizzle to the talkies. As such, her stage experience made her a great asset to the movie studios. Universal, however, had a funny way of showing their appreciation, handing Davis slim pickings rather than choice parts. It wasn't long before she switched over to Warner Brothers, where Darryl Zanuck, head of production, turned her into a star. The first great highlight of her career came with John Cromwell's *Of Human Bondage* (1934) in which she played a sultry waitress. Despite her Oscar wins, Davis always had to fight for good roles and didn't always win. Over the course of her career, she appeared in over 100 motion pictures. Her work in the TV show *Hotel* was to be some of her last. In 1989, the woman who had lived so fast and furiously retired from the earthly stars she had known so well to claim her place in heaven.

"As an ugly hag, Bette Davis, with her ghastly layers of make-up and her shuffly-clumb walk, is rather appealing. And Joan Crawford is – oh, just Joan Crawford. She is in a wheelchair, and she is starving to death (...), but her eyes blaze out soulfulness." *Newsweek*

4 True Hollywood stories: "They were all terrible, even the few I thought might be good. I made them because I needed the money or because I was bored or both. I hope they have been exhibited and withdrawn and are never heard from again." *Joan Crawford* on the downfall of her career

5 Hello, Dolly! Jane meets accompanist Edwin Flagg (Victor Buono) through a newspaper advertisement. Rumor has it that, on account of her professional dry spell, Davis actually did place a "job wanted" ad in the paper just before landing this role.

6 A career stretch: Baby Jane plans a comeback with the same Tin Pan Alley standards that once made her a star.

7 No din-din, Blanche? Rest assured, these two actresses tortured each other even when the cameras weren't rolling.

whims. In truth, Blanche has been harboring a sinister secret about the actual cause of her dependency. Maybe if she'd been more forthcoming, Jane wouldn't have hit the bottle or spiraled into psychosis. Too late now. So when she finds out that Blanche wants to lock her up in an insane asylum, Jane starves her of food and contact with the outside world, deciding it's time for the Baby to plan her big comeback.

Watching a film this well cast and this telling is a rare pleasure. Davis is mesmerizing as she waddles through the house, caked in makeup with a cigarette dangling from her lips. Equally exceptional is Crawford, whose eyes betray all the horror and disgust she has for her sister. These two bitter biddies of Hollywood pulled out all the stops to show us their true selves – and that, ladies and gentlemen, is how they prove their real grandeur. NM

# THE MAN WHO SHOT LIBERTY VALANCE

1962 - USA - 113 MIN. - WESTERN

DIRECTOR JOHN FORD (1894–1973)
SCREENPLAY JAMES WARNER BELLAH, WILLIS GOLDBECK, based on a story by DOROTHY M. JOHNSON
DIRECTOR OF PHOTOGRAPHY WILLIAM H. CLOTHIER EDITING OTHO LOVERING MUSIC CYRIL MOCKRIDGE PRODUCTION WILLIS GOLDBECK for JOHN FORD, PARAMOUNT PICTURES.

STARRING JAMES STEWART (Ransom Stoddard), JOHN WAYNE (Tom Doniphon), LEE MARVIN (Liberty Valance), VERA MILES (Hallie Stoddard), EDMOND O'BRIEN (Dutton Peabody), JOHN QUALEN (Peter Ericson), JEANETTE NOLAN (Nora Ericson), KEN MURRAY (Doc Willoughby), LEE VAN CLEEF (Reese), ANDY DEVINE (Link Appleyard), JOHN CARRADINE (Cassius Starbuckle), WOODY STRODE (Pompey).

## *"Liberty Valence is the toughest man south of the Picketwire – next to me."*

Returning to his humble political roots, Senator Ransom Stoddard (James Stewart) and his wife disembark from a steam locomotive at Shinbone, the place where it all began. His old friend Tom Doniphon (John Wayne) is dead and gone, having passed in utter poverty without a colt in his holster, according to the town's former sheriff. What prompted the politician to make a special trip to Doniphon's burial? That's exactly what the reporters at the "Shinbone Star" want to know when they catch wind of Stoddard's unexpected return.

And so the good senator tells them the tale of his first journey to a place that was nothing more than an isolated watering hole at the time. How he had headed out west as young attorney, hot on the heels of fame and adventure. And how even before he set foot in Shinbone, he was robbed and beaten to a pulp by legendary outlaw Liberty Valance (Lee Marvin). It followed that Tom Doniphon brought him into town, where his future wife nursed him back to health. It was then, even before the foundation of his political career, that he swore that one day he'd throw the book at Liberty Valance.

Stoddard educated the townspeople and brought order to its haphazard democracy, mobilizing its citizens to elect delegates for an upcoming congressional convention. After the people had cast their ballots, and it was clear that the young attorney, and not Valance, would be their representative, the rootin' tootin' varmint challenged Stoddard to a duel. The outcome launched Stoddard on an unstoppable march to Washington – for a miraculous shot had the two-fisted gunslinger pushing up the daisies.

Today, however, Stoddard intends to clear his conscience of a secret he has carried with him since that fateful day. The attorney who became famous throughout the West as "The Man Who Shot Liberty Valance," didn't actually fire the weapon that sent Valance to the grave: guardian angel Tom Doniphon did.

It's a newsworthy sensation that will forever remain secret, for "Shinbone Star's" chief editor rips up all evidence of the interview. As he reminds the aging senator, "This is the West, Sir… When legend becomes fact, (we) print the legend."

The Western had always been an eclectic genre, drawing in everything from tragedy and melodrama to epic and comedy. There were plenty of reluctant heroes who thought twice before stepping out of the saloon (like Gary Cooper in *High Noon*, 1952), and films like Delmer Daves' *Broken Arrow* (1950) had forced Hollywood to reexamine some of its most cherished myths. Nonetheless, it was John Ford's 1962 picture that signaled the end of the formulaic pistols-at-dawn plot, a trend that was continued in the Western comedy *Cat Ballou* (1965).

In line with the theme of the film, the two leading men in *Valance* are broken by the story's end. Stoddard compromises his ideals, both by grabbing his weapon in a showdown and allowing his political career to be based on a lie. Similarly, Doniphon rescues the attorney from certain death, but loses the love of his life in the process. For she has given her heart to Stoddard, who has at last proven himself to be more than a bookworm. Be that as

1

2

1 Kitsch in the kitchen: The real source of Ransom Stoddard's (James Stewart) deep-rooted humiliation isn't Liberty Valance, but his fallen soufflé. Wife Hallie (Vera Miles) assures him that he'll get it right next time.

2 Get up and fight like a man: Young Stoddard's arrival in the Wild West gets off to a bang when Liberty Valance (Lee Marvin, left) robs his stagecoach.

3 Trigger happy: Or is he? As we soon discover, it wasn't Stoddard's bullet that Valance bit. And so the young attorney wins the province's confidence with a lie and embarks on a grand career in public service.

4 Chew on this: Valance stifles the voice of public opinion. At this time in the West, the press was the most influential form of mass media.

**"Arguably the best John Ford film ever, *The Man Who Shot Liberty Valance* is an American classic... Ford addresses the complexity of heroism in a poetic manner."** *The Austin Chronicle*

it may, it's possible that she still carried a torch for the roughneck her whole life long, an impression we get when she places a cactus flower on his coffin – the same bit of flora he presented her with once upon a time.

Indeed, John Ford personally mourns the death of the broad-shouldered, law-abiding "pilgrim" who paved the way for civilization. Perhaps Doniphon know all along that he'd have to step aside to make room for men like Stoddard, despite their clumsy arrival in the West as its dishwashers and lackeys. But times change, and the days dominated by outlaws with monikers like "liberty" – a symbol for the freedom of the so-called unsettled region – now belong in the annals of history. As such, *The Man Who Shot Liberty Valance* can also be seen as a retrospective of John Ford's career. Like Doniphon, the then 67-year-old director had devoted his life to making leg-

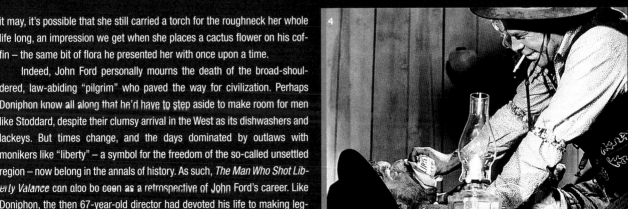

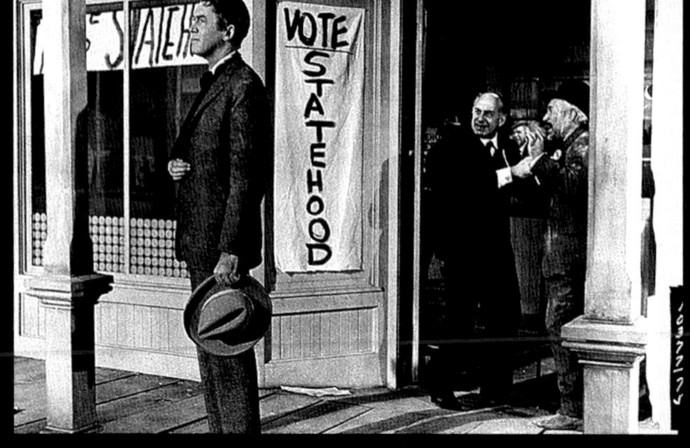


endary movies in what was proving to be a rapidly fading genre. Seeking to recapture some of the magic he had once brought to the screen, Ford matched *Valance's* look to that of earlier Westerns. Rejecting the increasingly popular trend to shoot in color, he chose black and white photography for a picture that revels in its artificiality. The set pieces take no pains to mask what they are, allowing the town look to more like a cardboard cut-out than anything three dimensional. More than just the story of a triangular relationship, the film tells of the historically complex process of civilizing the West, of bringing its territories under the rule of the law and replacing the Colt with the constitution. John Ford casually threads this elaborate theme into the story's fabric with the greatest of ease and simplicity – a miraculous feat "The Duke" could proudly tip his hat to. NM

5 A new foothold for democracy: James Stewart is a convincing idealist willing to go the extra mile for his country. Not even potentially life-threatening gunfire can deter him from his path.

6 This town ain't big enough: Tom Doniphon (John Wayne) keeps an eye on Valance to make sure that no harm comes to the wet-behind-the-ears lawmaker.

7 Put up your dukes: When Liberty Valance (left) asks Doniphon whether he's looking for trouble, the upstanding cowboy wants to know if he's "aimin' to find some?"

**JOHN FORD**

Often cited for his immortal words "I make Westerns," we mustn't forget that John Ford was also an accomplished director of prestigious dramas like *The Informer* (1935) and *The Grapes of Wrath* (1940). In fact, John Ford won two of his astounding four Best Director Oscars for these films. Nonetheless, his greatest Hollywood achievement was his unparalleled contribution to the Western. His was the most definitive vision of the Wild West, the land of Monument Valley, Manifest Destiny, Indians, nomads and strong, silent types. Yet Ford was also the man to eventually expose the legend for what it was and clear the genre of its mystique.

Born in 1894, John Ford began shooting Hollywood pictures in 1917, and his life's work amounts to more than 140 films. He emerged as one of Hollywood's most powerful directors, always giving his movies a personal signature despite the studio system's rigidity. It is said that in later years, he spoke dryly of his own work, commenting, "It's no use talking to me about art, I make pictures to pay the rent." Ford preferred shooting with a stock company of actors and technicians, the most famous of which was John Wayne. The pair teamed up more than 20 times, including for Ford's most acclaimed picture, a Western entitled *The Searchers* (1956).

John Ford died in 1973. To this day, many consider him the most accomplished American director of all time.

**"As a Western, *The Man Who Shot Liberty Valance* is everything I didn't like as a child after the genre's heyday. Still, this film stands out because it is timeless. If the story were true, it surely would not have been this exciting, and that's exactly what Ford set out to show us. To quote the film: 'When the legend becomes fact, print the legend.'"** *Apollo Movie Guide*

# THE ECLIPSE
## L' Eclisse

1962 - ITALY / FRANCE - 122 MIN. - DRAMA

DIRECTOR MICHELANGELO ANTONIONI (*1912)

SCREENPLAY MICHELANGELO ANTONIONI, TONINO GUERRA, ELIO BARTOLINI, OTTIERO OTTIERI DIRECTOR OF PHOTOGRAPHY Gianni di Venanzo EDITING ERALDO DA ROMA MUSIC GIOVANNI FUSCO PRODUCTION ROBERT HAKIM, RAYMOND HAKIM for INTEROPA FILM, CINERIZ ROM, PARIS FILM PRODUCTION.

STARRING MONICA VITTI (Vittoria), ALAIN DELON (Piero), LILLA BRIGNONE (Vittorias Mutter), LOUIS SEIGNER (Ercoli), FRANCISCO RABAL (Riccardo), MIRELLA RICCIARDI (Marta), ROSSANA RORY (Anita).

IFF CANNES 1962 SPECIAL PRIZE OF THE JURY for MICHELANGELO ANTONIONI.

***Vittoria: "Well then?"***
***Riccardo: "Well what?"***
***Vittoria: "All this – all the things we've said tonight."***
***Riccardo: "You're right. Let's make a decision."***
***Vittoria: "I already have... I'm leaving."***

An exhausted silence follows. On the living-room table, we see a lamp and some books. Riccardo (Francisco Rabal) sits in his armchair like a statue, his tie still round his neck. Vittoria (Monica Vitti) stands around hesitantly, picks up a coffee cup and carries it into the kitchen. She looks at her face in the mirror: a shock. It's over. They've split up. Vittoria opens the curtains. Daybreak. Outside the window looms a giant water tower. Riccardo embraces her, tries to stop her going – in vain. Vittoria leaves. He pursues her in his car, gets out, and accompanies her home as usual. This will be the last time. A new housing development on the edge of the city: wasteland, weeds, work in progress; streets where houses have yet to be built; empty shells side-by-side with smart apartment blocks. "The opening scenes are provocative," wrote the German magazine *Filmkritik*. "Let's risk the superlative: never before has a director given his audience such a cool and unwelcoming reception as Antonioni does in this film." For a long time, the audience remains in the dark, before it becomes clear what has actually taken place between Vittoria and Riccardo. We are witnessing the consequences of a separation, without knowing why it happened. Later in the film, Vitoria says it's a matter of indifference to her whether she passes the time with a book, a piece of fabric or a man. The subject of *L'Eclisse* is precisely this vacancy, this vagueness, this way of being. Antonioni is not trying to tell a story, but

1

2

1 Love is a many splendored thing: There can be no doubt that Monica Vitti is Michelangelo Antonioni's favorite actress. *L'Eclisse* is the third part of the director's so-called Italian tetralogy, following *L'Avventura* (1960) and *La Notte* (1961). The series was completed in 1964 with *Il deserto rosso.*

2 No dice: Engaging in a simple arrangement is next to impossible for the savvy broker Piero (Alain Delon) and the determined, self-assured Vittoria. Both are incapable of expressing themselves – in either words or feelings.

**"Antonioni confirms his mastery of cinema conceived as literature, and there's certainly no one who today can match his pregnant silences nor the unity of style and theme that characterize his last three films."** *Variety*

**MONICA VITTI**

"I gave Antonioni the images he wanted to see. But I was those images, too. I was the way he portrayed me in the films." Independent and self-assured, headstrong but vulnerable, in search of something without always knowing what: until Monica Vitti came along, this kind of woman had never been seen in Italian films. She was ahead of her time, and so were her looks: as she herself once said, she was too thin, her eyes were too big and her figure was too irregular. But she formed an image of modern womanhood that is valid even today. If films such as *L'Avventura* (1960) or *The Eclipse* (1962) are still astonishingly contemporary, it has a great deal to do with her.

Monica Vitti and Michelangelo Antonioni made five films together, and were one of the great artistic couples of the European cinema. Born in Rome in 1931 as Maria Louisa Ceciarelli, she made her first stage appearances as a teenager. While still at drama school, she was hired by Antonioni to dub *The Outcry* (*Il Grido,* 1957). She would go on to play leading roles in several movies, including Joseph Losey's *Modesty Blaise* (1965), where she was a kind of female James Bond, and the Italian-French episode film *La Fate* (*Les Ogresses,* 1966). With Luis Buñuel, she made *Phantom of Liberty* (*Le Fantôme de la liberté,* 1974), and with Ettore Scola, *Jealousy Italian-Style* (*Dramma della gelosia, tutti patricolari in cronaca,* 1970). With the passage of time, Monica Vitti came to adopt a different kind of role; the pale and melancholy muse of Antonioni became a comedian. She said it simply gave her pleasure to make people laugh.

3 Toga party or Nubian fantasy? Monica Vitti makes a delightful farce of cultural crossover in this scene from *L'Eclisse*. Next up, the dance of the seven veils.

4 Enjoy the silence: Vittoria and Piero have reached a dead end, and the film's intentionally aimless 5-minute conclusion attests to this. It is literally a documentation of the passage of time.

5 Day trader: Antonioni depicts a day in the life of a Roman stockbroker in irritatingly meticulous detail. The auteur was fascinated by the workings of a job well done.

to convey the visual equivalent of an emotional state. And he succeeds, unnervingly.

This 15-minute opening sequence contains all the key motifs and attributes of the Antonioni cosmos: the powerlessness of men and women to understand each other, and their resulting inability to communicate; the importance of inanimate objects that bear silent witness to the present (the picture on the wall); the idiosyncratic camera, which occasionally digresses and develops a life of its own (ducking under the table to take a look at Vittoria's legs); the paralyzed, intractable situations, where machines are often the only things capable of movement (the whirring fan); the landscapes that mirror the characters' frame of mind (the half-finished housing development).

Antonioni's films admit of no hierarchy between the outer world and the inner life; they show the transformation of feelings in the flux of time. Here there are no simple and lasting relationships, because such forms of coexistence correspond to the growing complexity of the world. Women are the main figures, and they too are destined to outgrow their outmoded roles. These movies are incomparably alive to the present; they breathe modernity. With *L'Eclisse* and its two predecessors, *L'Avventura* (1960) and *La Notte* (1961), Michelangelo Antonioni revolutionized the cinema, perhaps even more radically than the *nouvelle vague*; for unlike the French, he didn't take his bearings from the films of the past, but invented his own new form of cinematic storytelling.

After the split-up, Vittoria visits the cacophonous stock exchange, where her mother speculates with the help of Piero, a dynamic and beautiful broker (Alain Delon). Piero dives into the raucous crowd of bidders on the floor, buying and selling, wheeling and dealing, rushing to the phone to compare rates on other exchanges, eavesdropping on old pros in the hope of picking up tips. Vittoria and Piero already know each other, but after a bad day's trading and the loss of several million lira, they come a little closer. They have sex in his office that afternoon, and they make a date for the same evening – and for the following evening, and the evening after that… On her way downstairs to the street, Vittoria halts and looks back at his office door. At the same moment, Piero, staring vacantly, replaces the telephone receiver. He had taken it off the hook for the duration of their lovemaking.

Vittoria won't turn up to their meeting place on the street corner. A man drives past in a light, horse-drawn carriage. A pedestrian uses the zebra crossing. The trees rustle. A woman is waiting at the bus stop; the bus comes; people disembark, reading newspapers. Water spills from a damaged rain-barrel behind a hoarding. There's a plane in the sky. Darkness falls, and the streetlights go on. The next bus arrives. Time passes and the world turns. The End.

NM

# THE TRIAL
## Le Procès

1962 - FRANCE / ITALY / WEST GERMANY - 118 MIN. - LITERARY ADAPTATION, DRAMA

**DIRECTOR** ORSON WELLES (1915–1985)

**SCREENPLAY** ORSON WELLES, based on the novel of the same name by FRANZ KAFKA **DIRECTOR OF PHOTOGRAPHY** EDMOND RICHARD **EDITING** YVONNE MARTIN, FREDERICK MULLER **MUSIC** JEAN LEDRUT, TOMASO ALBINONI ("Adagio in C") **PRODUCTION** ALEXANDER SALKIND, MICHAEL SALKIND for PARIS-EUROPA PRODUCTIONS, FI. C. IT, HISA-FILM.

**STARRING** ANTHONY PERKINS (Josef K.), ARNOLDO FOÀ (Inspector A.), MADELEINE ROBINSON (Mrs. Grubach), JEANNE MOREAU (Miss Bürstner), MAX HAUFLER (Uncle Max), ROMY SCHNEIDER (Leni), ORSON WELLES (Hastler, the Advocate), ELSA MARTINELLI (Hilda), AKIM TAMIROFF (Block), THOMAS HOLTZMANN (Law Student).

***"I'm sorry."***
***"You're sorry, you're sorry, you're sorry. You always keep saying that. Who gives a damn?"***

Someone must have been spreading lies about Josef K. (Anthony Perkins), for one morning, without having done anything truly wrong, he finds himself under arrest. He never learns what crime he has been accused of, and his stubborn protestations of innocence fall upon deaf ears. Trapped in a trial he can't comprehend, forced to take part in a game without knowing the rules, he plays along to the bitter end, obeying the demands of the court even when these are merely implied rather than being clearly stated. As the off-screen voice of Orson Welles reminds us at the start of the film: "It has been said that the logic of this story is the logic of a dream, of a nightmare." The very first shot shows us the face of Josef K., blinking and squinting; it seems safe to assume that he hasn't really woken up, but remains trapped in an oppressive nightmare world. The film will be a record of his experiences there.

Though Orson Welles' *The Trial* is based on Franz Kafka's novel, it's an independent and idiosyncratic interpretation rather than a slavish retelling of the story. Certainly, the world of this film can be seen as a visual correlative to the diabolical logic of Kafka's obsessive prose. Yet Welles goes further, creating a cosmos informed by the experience of the 20th century's totalitarian systems. Whereas Kafka was a prophet of bureaucratic horror, Welles lived through times that really had witnessed such horror. His Josef K. scurries ant-like through a desert of identical housing blocks, gigantic open-plan offices and monstrous archival systems. It's a grimly spectacular visualization of the forlornness of the individual in the Modern Age.

Originally, however, the director had a very different vision. His original plan, he said in one interview, was for a film in which the realistic settings would gradually dissolve, to end in a completely empty and abstract environ-

1

1 What's in those hot little hands? The accused, Josef K. (Anthony Perkins), refutes all accusations brought against him and claims what's rightfully his.

2 Tracked by silhouettes: Dissonant angles and hazy backlighting at the Gare d'Orsay train station give the film a German Expressionist edge.

# "*The Trial* is a game played with symbols, and an absolute masterpiece of cinematography." *Le Monde*

ment. Unfortunately, money was suddenly lacking for the necessary film sets, and an alternative had to be found at short notice. At the time, Welles was living in a hotel room in Paris with a view over the disused Gare d'Orsay railway station (which now houses the Musée d'Orsay). After walking around the building one night, the director decided to use it as his main location. Though no longer in use as a station, its original function always remains apparent, which lends the film added historical depth and evocativeness. Here, the Gare d'Orsay represents a dilapidated, technocratic modernity, a symbol of alienation and deracination. Welles himself saw the station as a place of refugees, filled with memories of senseless waiting and mass deportation.

For all of the film's spatial gigantomania, the true location of this passion play is the spindly body of Josef K. himself. Welles films his protagonist

3 Last words: Josef K. makes an impassioned appeal to the court, proposing that he's just a scapegoat in a sinister conspiracy.

4 The kiss of Judas? Josef K. responds with skepticism to the advances of the court official's wife (Elsa Martinelli).

**AKIM TAMIROFF**

He was a stocky little man who regularly embodied characters that aroused pity, repugnance or laughter, depending on the film and the role. Sweaty and short of breath, obsequious and sadistic: this was the screen image of Akim Tamiroff, a gifted supporting actor who was often more memorable than the leading men.

Born in Russia in 1899, he studied acting at the legendary Moscow Art Theater under Konstantin Stanislavsky. When the ensemble toured America in 1920, Tamiroff decided to stay behind and try his luck on Broadway. Almost a decade would pass before he had his first film role, in Tay Garnett's *Okay, America!* (1932). From then until his death in 1972, he appeared in more than 130 movies. He also received two Oscar nominations, for his performances in *The General Died at Dawn* (1936) and the Hemingway adaptation *For Whom the Bell Tolls* (1943).

Akim Tamiroff's most impressive performances, however, were for Orson Welles, with whom he completed three successful film projects. In both *Mr. Arkadin* (1955) and *Touch of Evil* (1958), Tamiroff played seedy villains who are eventually liquidated by the colossal figures embodied by Welles himself. In the Kafka adaptation *The Trial*, he played an accused man who is humiliated by the advocate Hastler – once again played by Orson Welles. Finally, he appeared in Welles' *Don Quixote* project – as Sancho Panza, the mad knight's long-suffering servant and sidekick. For a little man with a huge comic talent it was the role of a lifetime; but sadly, the film was never completed.

5 Mastermind: Playing an exacting attorney, *The Trial's* director Orson Welles overshadows his clients and chambermaid Leni (Romy Schneider).

6 Dead man walking: The bell tolls for Josef K.

7 Exit from empire: Romy Schneider gives her image a spring-cleaning in *The Trial.*

**"Formally, the film is a brilliant anthology of Wellesian stylistic devices. It incorporates and makes use of everything he had learnt about the expressive possibilities of the cinema since *Citizen Kane.*"** *Süddeutsche Zeitung*

n a series of wide-angled long shots, and lights him so that he always casts an elongated shadow: Josef K. is a streak of darkness, a lonely silhouette. But he camera also moves in closer: we see the stiffness of his gestures and the spastic cramping of his hands as he sits with his Uncle Max (Max Haufler), reluctantly pondering ways of escaping his grim situation. Josef K.'s inhibited physicality is most vividly revealed in his encounters with the female sex: again and again, he seeks out the company of beautiful women (Romy Schneider, Jeanne Moreau and Elsa Martinelli), only to flee almost instantly rom their embrace. His approaches to women seem motivated solely by cold calculation: perhaps, in some way or another, they might help him in his trial.

In these scenes, as in the physically intimate dialogue with Block, his fellow accused (Akim Tamiroff), we have suggestions of the delinquent's latent homosexuality; Josef K. seems to be fleeing from any recognition of what he truly desires.

Behind the story told by these images, Welles hints at a layer of ineffable truth; repeatedly, and disturbingly, the spectator is subjected to slight but calculated errors in continuity. For moments at a time, the seemingly iron self-containment of this punitive world splits open, and in these hairline fractures between the frames, the film's labyrinthine structure is revealed as an image of Josef K.'s divided self. BK

7

# CAPE FEAR

1962 - USA - 105 MIN. - THRILLER

DIRECTOR J. LEE THOMPSON (1914–2002)
SCREENPLAY JAMES R. WEBB, based on the novel *THE EXECUTIONERS* by JOHN D. MACDONALD
DIRECTOR OF PHOTOGRAPHY SAMUEL LEAVITT EDITING GEORGE TOMASINI MUSIC BERNARD HERRMANN
PRODUCTION SY BARTLETT for MELVILLE-TALBOT PRODUCTIONS.

STARRING GREGORY PECK (Sam Bowden), ROBERT MITCHUM (Max Cady), POLLY BERGEN (Peggy Bowden), LORI MARTIN (Nancy Bowden), MARTIN BALSAM (Police Inspector Mark Dutton), JACK KRUSCHEN (Dave Grafton), TELLY SAVALAS (Charles Sievers), BARRIE CHASE (Diane Taylor), PAUL COMI (Garner), JOHN MCKEE (Marconi).

## *"I'm gonna do something to you and your family that you ain't neva gonna forget."*

The title sequence makes it pretty clear idea what kind of man we'll be dealing with: in a pale linen suit and a Panama hat, the cigar-puffing Max Cady (Robert Mitchum) swaggers through the streets of a small town in Georgia, casts a connoisseur's eye over two young women and enters the courthouse. His passage is accompanied by the ominous music of Bernard Herrmann. Inside the building, he struts past a struggling court employee, ostentatiously indifferent to the lady's losing battle with a pile of law books, and addresses a black janitor as "Daddy." Max Cady is no gentleman, and he doesn't give a damn who knows it. Released after eight years in jail for assaulting a young woman, all he wants now is revenge on Sam Bowden (Gregory Peck), th lawyer who put him behind bars.

Mitchum's sheer physical presence in the role is impressive, and fear some: for all his languid slowness, Cady never seems harmless or merel stupid. He has the brooding watchfulness of a dangerous wild animal, and hi cool insolence is proof of how relaxed he is in his own potent physicality.

In one scene, he's being interrogated at the police station, and the In spector (Martin Balsam) insists on a body search. Cady is forced to strip to hi underpants. It's a procedure that's designed to humiliate and intimidate, ye

1

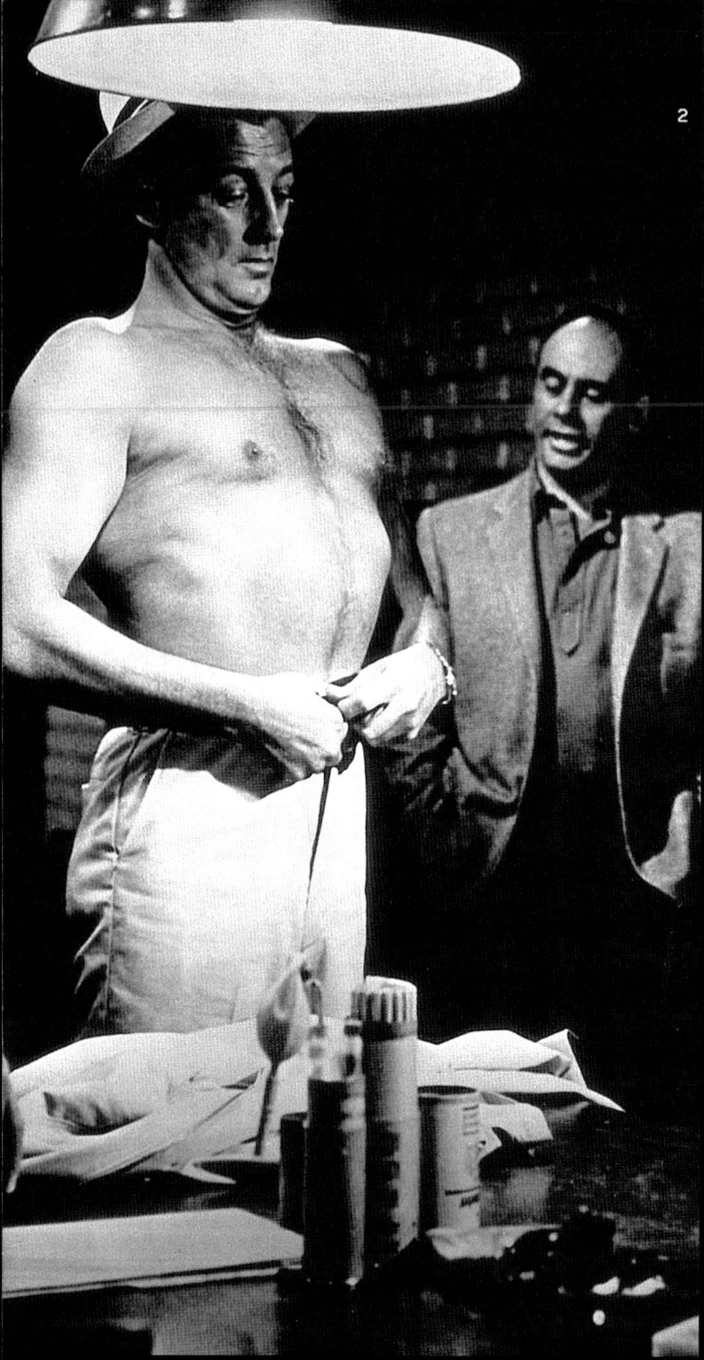

1 The winds of wanton lust: Max Cady (Robert Mitchum) terrorizes Peggy Bowden (Polly Bergen) and her entire family. 20 years later these two would reunite, starring as husband and wife in Herman Wouk's *Winds of War* and *War and Remembrance* mini series.

2 Clean as a whistle: A search of Cady's premises unmasks no incriminating evidence. Inspector Dutton (Martin Balsam) simply can't pin a thing on him.

3 Waiting for the fishies to take the bait: Cady knows full well that patience is the key in getting the Bowdens to bite.

**"Mr. Thompson has directed in a steady and starkly sinister style. There is no waste motion, no fooling. Everything is sharp and direct. Menace quivers in the picture like a sneaky electrical charge."** *The New York Times*

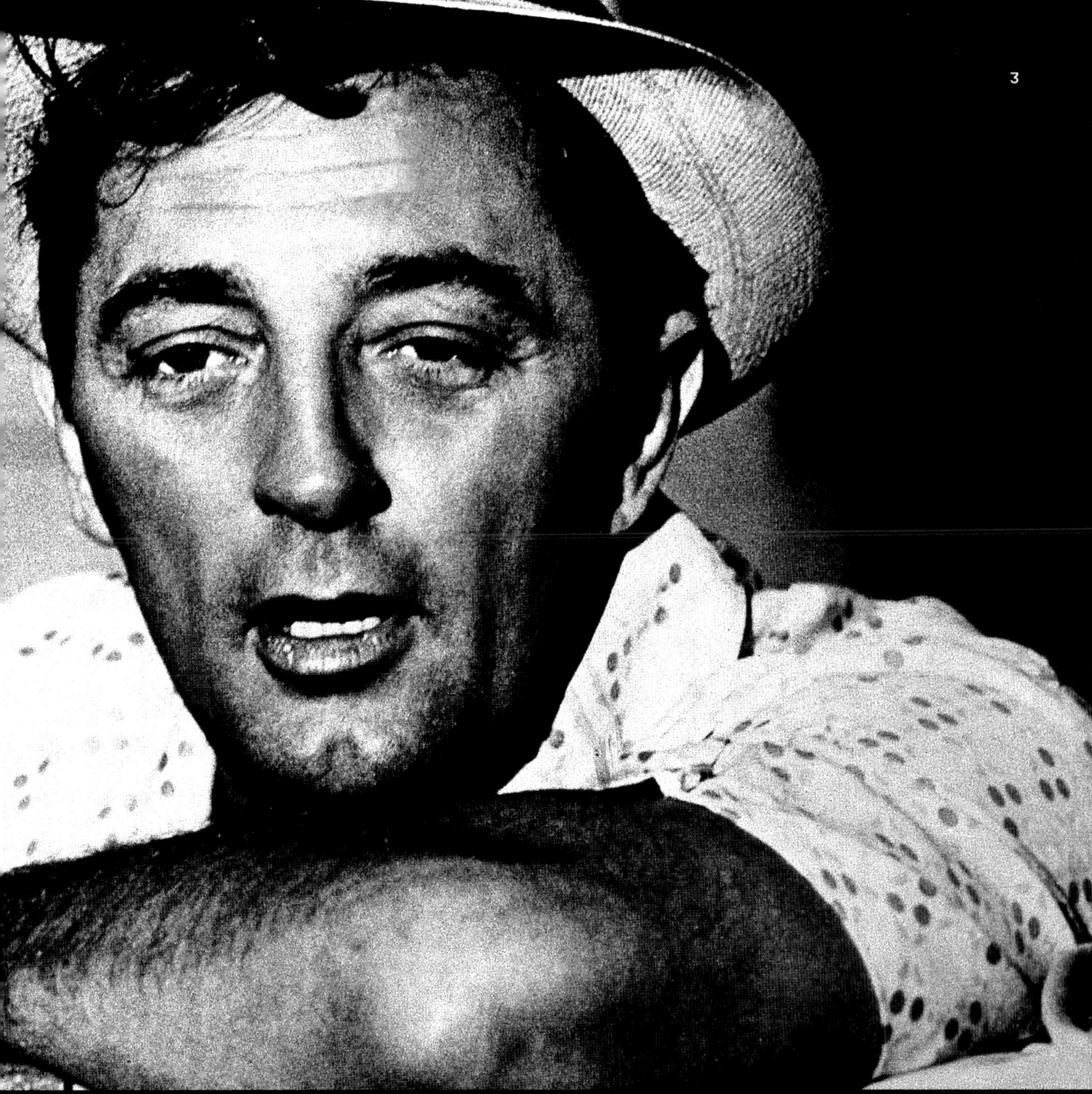

he stands there in his boxer shorts without a trace of embarrassment, his hands on his hips, his chest filling the room, and his hat still cheekily perched on his head. He looks twice as big as anyone else, and he appears practically invulnerable.

Cady's revenge on Bowden begins with some relatively unsubtle psychoterror. Simply by *being* there, by turning up in this town again, he unnerves the lawyer increasingly and scares his family witless. Cady is aware of exactly how far he can go; this is one former jailbird who knows the law, and he provokes and menaces his victim without ever doing anything demonstrably criminal.

In a series of tense scenes, director J. Lee Thompson skillfully evokes the growing paranoia of the terrorized family. As Bowden's daughter Nancy (Lori Martin) heads home after school, she catches a glimpse of the ex-jailbird approaching in the distance. Her panic increases until she cracks, runs and hides in the cellar of the school building; yet the man is still behind her, getting closer all the time… Finally, at the last moment, in a state of abject terror, Nancy scrambles out the window. As she races onto the street, we see that her "nemesis" was none other than the innocent janitor; but by this time, she has staggered straight into the arms of Max Cady.

His adversary Sam Bowden is originally depicted as an upright, law-abiding citizen. It's a role that Gregory Peck has no trouble embodying to perfection, for he really was the personification of integrity and decent, liberal values. Yet Bowden's façade rapidly begins to crumble. Though the lawyer begins by insisting that a man cannot be locked up for a crime he just *might*

"When Hollywood can draw on the most consummate artists available, both in front of and behind the camera, it's capable of producing a film like this: a terrifying depiction of how pitiless violence gradually invades the lives of an average American family." *Frankfurter Allgemeine Zeitung*

4 The right to privacy: Attorney Sam Bowden (Gregory Peck) and wife Peggy don't know where Cady will turn up next.

5 All washed up: Although the photo may indicate otherwise, it is Sam Bowden who initiates the final showdown on Cape Fear.

6 Life on the line: Sam's plans to lure Cady into a trap have failed and Peggy's left to face the music.

7 Still off the hook: But if Max Cady means no harm, why does he trail the Bowden family's every move?

possibly commit, he quickly responds to the pressure of Cady's threatening presence by calling the cops to his aid. As a result, Cady's life is made a misery: he's soon being arrested on an almost daily basis, though he's still done nothing to break the law.

In his attempts to free himself from this sadistic nuisance, Bowden deploys more and more dubious methods: he hires a private detective (Telly Savalas), who's ultimately unable to help him; he tries, unsuccessfully, to bribe Cady with money; and eventually, in his desperation, he sends a bunch of thugs to beat him up. In doing so, he risks losing his accreditation from the Bar Association and thereby the very basis of his existence.

Finally, in the dark waters of Cape Fear, the immovable object meets the unstoppable force. It's an explosion of violence, and only one of these men will survive it. The price of this survival is a nauseous recognition that the clear line between good and evil has vanished in a fog of ambiguity.

LP

**LAWYERS AT THE MOVIES** When choosing his roles, Gregory Peck did his best to avoid being typecast. Nonetheless, in the course of his long career, he did play a lot of lawyers. In Hitchcock's *The Paradine Case* (1947), he played a barrister who ruins his marriage and career by falling in love with his client, a beautiful murderer; in *Cape Fear* (1962), he saw his liberal ideals evaporate as his family was terrorized by a sadistic ex-con intent on revenge; and in Robert Mulligan's *To Kill a Mockingbird* (1962), he was a small-town lawyer who defends a black man falsely accused of raping a white woman. As these examples show, the lawyer has always been a popular figure in the cinema. Lawyers are highly versatile and adaptable creatures, capable of finding a habitable niche in almost every genre. Without the ubiquitous legal eagle, courtroom dramas, gangster movies, and comedies of love and divorce would all be quite unthinkable: just remember Hepburn and Tracy in *Adam's Rib* (1949) or Clooney and Zeta-Jones in *Intolerable Cruelty* (2003).

The ambivalence of the legal profession also makes it a natural subject for both drama and comedy. Though lawyers are essential to any democratic system, the cinema at least has often portrayed them as sly and slippery sophists, and sometimes as decidedly nasty characters. So it's no surprise that Martin Scorsese's 1991 remake of *Cape Fear* featured Nick Nolte as a very different kind of lawyer from Gregory Peck's original: in Nolte's interpretation, Bowden is corrupt and dishonest from the word go.

# THE MANCHURIAN CANDIDATE

1962 - USA - 126 MIN. - POLITICAL THRILLER, LITERARY ADAPTATION,

DIRECTOR JOHN FRANKENHEIMER (1930–2002)
SCREENPLAY GEORGE AXELROD, based on the novel of the same name by RICHARD CONDON DIRECTOR OF PHOTOGRAPHY LIONEL LINDON
EDITING FERRIS WEBSTER MUSIC DAVID AMRAM PRODUCTION GEORGE AXELROD, JOHN FRANKENHEIMER for M. C. PRODUCTIONS.

STARRING FRANK SINATRA (Captain / Major Bennett Marco), LAURENCE HARVEY (Raymond Shaw), JANET LEIGH (Rosie), ANGELA LANSBURY (Mrs. Iselin, Raymond's Mother), JAMES GREGORY (Senator John Iselin), LESLIE PARRISH (Jocelyn Jordan), JOHN MCGIVER (Senator Thomas Jordan), DOUGLAS HENDERSON (Colonel Milt), ALBERT PAULSEN (Zilkov), LLOYD CORRIGAN (Holborn Gaines).

## *"Why don't you pass the time with a game of solitaire?"*

Lieutenant Raymond Shaw (Laurence Harvey) isn't what you'd call a likeable guy, except maybe in his wildest dreams. An insufferable stick-in-the-mud, one would think that the unit he served with during the Korean War would have no fond memories of Raymond – but they do. Upon his return home, the stepson of conservative U. S. Senator John Iselin (James Gregory) is hailed as a war hero and awarded the highest distinction for valor in the line of duty, the Congressional Medal of Honor, for having single-handedly rescued his entire infantry from behind enemy lines. Yet somehow, Shaw's valiant conduct seems surreal, almost unbelievable…

Plagued by a recurring nightmare, the promoted unit captain, now Major Bennett Marco (Frank Sinatra), begins to doubt Shaw's heroism and his own memories. In his nightly visions, Shaw, Marco and the rest of the company have been captured by enemy troops and sequestered to a conference of the Communist High Command. With the American soldiers, including Shaw, under full hypnosis, all present watch as the putative war hero brutally murders two of his own men. Thoroughly detached, Captain Marco and his men yawn their way through these acts of sheer brutality.

In the waking world, Marco is a wreck. Not knowing what else to do, he seeks out Shaw to ask him whether he has had any similar experiences. By now it's clear that the dreams are anchored in reality, and that Shaw has been unwittingly programmed to be a sleeper communist assassin. The hard truth is that both he and his fellow soldiers were methodically brainwashed and then robbed of all recollection of the horrific events. Aided by the lovely Rosie (Janet Leigh), Marco gradually pieces together the shocking facts. Still he only comprehends the gravity of the situation when it is already too late.

With *The Manchurian Candidate*, director John Frankenheimer earned his reputation as a master of the political thriller. Although he was quick to attribute the movie's success to Richard Condon's gripping novel, the film, too, is a bona fide cinematic masterpiece loaded with subversive power. How very telling that it almost fell into total obscurity as the result of repeated criticism which deemed it unsuitable for cinematic re-release or television airing. In its examination of political assassination, the picture reads like a foretelling of the imminent deaths of John F. Kennedy, Malcolm X, Martin Luther King and Robert F. Kennedy. It is equally unsettling as Frankenheimer opens the closet doors of America's recent past to free the ghosts of McCarthyism with brilliant cynicism. In *The Manchurian Candidate* illustrious war heroes

1

2

# "For more than twenty-five years, memories of *The Manchurian Candidate* have tantalized those who saw it at the time. Was it really so good as it seemed? It was."

*Chicago Sun-Times*

1 The voice of reason: Raymond Shaw (Laurence Harvey) refuses to subject himself to any further maternal advice. Angela Lansbury as Raymond's mother, the overbearing Mrs. Iselin.

2 The kindest, bravest man he ever did know: Captain Bennett Marco (Frank Sinatra) and his men escaped from behind enemy lines in Korea. Strange that none of them have any clear recollection of it.

3 Russian roulette with rifles: American war hero Raymond Shaw is reprogrammed as a Soviet sniper.

are unmasked as remote-controlled killers and vehement opponents of communism turn out to be mere puppets of Moscow.

It is an eerie, if not alarming film, whose meticulously orchestrated black and white shots and painstakingly designed sets infuse the story with a sense of pressing urgency. Such is the case when Frankenheimer infiltrates the visual foreground with a television monitor as a means of simultaneously commenting on, contradicting, and supplementing the action of the scene at large. The story seems to adhere to a hidden agenda that gradually unfolds to the viewer, while remaining agonizingly out of reach to the on-screen characters until the film's conclusion.

**FRANK SINATRA**

The world's most renowned crooner was born Francis Albert Sinestra to Italian immigrant parents on December 12th, 1915 in Hoboken, New Jersey. Despite the tough times brought on by the Great Depression, Francis always had ambitions of making it big. This is what probably inspired him to establish ties with various Mafia families in the early 1940s. He got his big break in the music world serving as "the voice" in the Tommy Dorsey Band. His reputation earned him a few gigs in Hollywood films and he quickly emerged as one of the United States' favorite melody makers. Personal and health related problems followed him like a shadow for the first half of the 1950s – recurring vocal chord bleeding constantly threatened to end his career.

In 1953, he was signed to appear in Fred Zinnemann's picture *From Here to Eternity* for a fee of 5,000 dollars. The performance won him an Oscar for Best Supporting Actor and established him internationally as an acting talent. He then played opposite Robert Mitchum in *Not as a Stranger* (1955), Marlon Brando in *Guys and Dolls* (1955), as well as Bing Crosby and Grace Kelly in *High Society* (1956). He earned himself another Oscar nomination for his acting prowess in Otto Preminger's *The Man with the Golden Arm* (1955), this time in a leading role.

Sinatra also proved himself to be a savvy entrepreneur. Despite friendships with presidents John F. Kennedy and Ronald Reagan, he is better remembered for his supposed entanglements with organized crime and the shadowy side of politics. Although never a matter of public record, these allegations would follow him throughout his life. Sinatra decided to give regular concerts in Las Vegas, once his physical health had steadily improved. This is one of the most celebrated chapters in his musical career and his concerts with Dean Martin, Sammy Davis Jr. and the Rat Pack are the stuff of legend. It was, therefore, inevitable that he shot the wildly popular 1960 Vegas comedy *Ocean's Eleven.*

His work in John Frankenheimer's political thriller *The Manchurian Candidate* (1962) was one of his greatest milestones as an actor. It is believed that the re-release of this picture was postponed for years as a result of John F. Kennedy's assassination. Countless last hurrahs followed Sinatra's 1971 announced retirement from show business. In 1977, he landed his last smash hit with the theme song to *New York, New York* (1977). Frank Sinatra died on May 14th, 1998 in Los Angeles at the age of 82.

4 In dreams…: Only Rosie (Janet Leigh) believes Marco's suspicions about the truth behind his awful nightly visions.

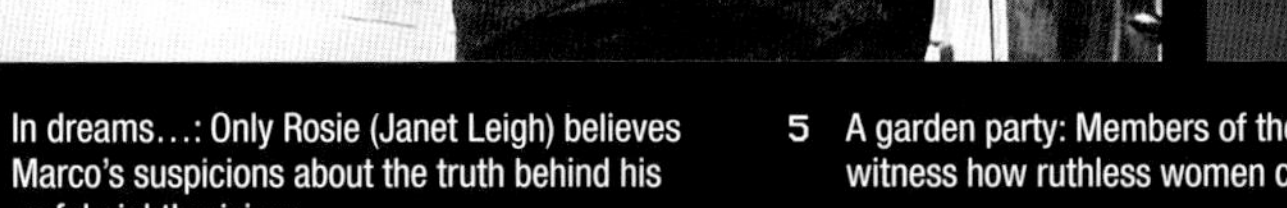

5 A garden party: Members of the infantry unit witness how ruthless women can be when the "ladies" order Shaw to execute fellow soldiers in cold blood.

Rolling cameras and monitors are inescapable throughout *The Manchurian Candidate.* Even the picture's most intimate moments – including Shaw's love-hate relationship with his perversely over-protective mother (Angela Lansbury) – seem like a matter of public importance. In their world, you can either be for your country or against it; however, it is impossible to determine where everybody stands.

It would be rash to label the film black and white political portraiture. Thanks to rich imagery, such as the playing cards later embodied by the story's characters, the plot unfolds through iconic triggers that lead us straight to the fatal end of the "Manchurian candidate." En route, the viewer is forced to draw analogies from the material. It's no coincidence that portraits of Abraham Lincoln are planted throughout the picture, and that a drunken senator apes him at a costume ball. This connection makes the senator's candidacy for Vice President of the United States read like a farce without historical significance. It would seem that Frankenheimer wants to show that all of us are unsuspecting pawns. Even government officials and their leaders are nothing more than political sheep following invisible herders and meaningless ideologies. Or is that too just some bad dream? SH

# LOLITA

1962 - USA/GREAT BRITAIN - 152 MIN. - DRAMA

DIRECTOR STANLEY KUBRICK (1928–1999)
SCREENPLAY VLADIMIR NABOKOV, based on his novel of the same name DIRECTOR OF PHOTOGRAPHY OSWALD MORRIS
EDITING ANTHONY HARVEY MUSIC NELSON RIDDLE, BOB HARRIS ("Theme from Lolita") PRODUCTION JAMES B. HARRIS for SEVEN ARTS PRODUCTIONS, ANYA, TRANSWOOD.

STARRING JAMES MASON (Humbert Humbert), SUE LYON (Lolita Haze), SHELLEY WINTERS (Charlotte Haze), PETER SELLERS (Clare Quilty), Marianne Stone (Vivian Darkbloom), DIANA DECKER (Jean Farlow), JERRY STOVIN (John Farlow), GARY COCKRELL (Dick), SUZANNE GIBBS (Mona Farlow), ROBERTA SHORE (Lorna), LOIS MAXWELL (Nurse).

## "Do You Believe in God?"

People often complain when their favorite books are transferred to the screen, and for a long time, hardly anyone had a good word to say about Stanley Kubrick's *Lolita*. The director was generally accused of having failed to do justice to the complexity of Vladimir Nabokov's novel, and above all, of having crudely misrepresented the Russian author's central motif. These charges can hardly be denied. At the same time though, two counter-questions demand to be answered: in the prudish cinema of the early 60s, how could a movie more "faithful" to the original novel possibly have been made? And what on earth would it have looked like?

For Nabokov's novel takes on the "impossible" theme of pedophile desire, and it's expressed with high irony in the collision of two utterly dissimilar worlds: Humbert Humbert, a cultivated but "decadent" European academic with his best years behind him, yearns for the favors of 12-year-old Lolita, an awful American brat with a passion for fast food, candy and Coke.

In the novel, Humbert is no slouch. He's relentlessly proactive, making plans to get close to Lolita, to touch her "accidentally," and make his way into her bed, but for the longest time, various absurd circumstances conspire to disrupt his devious plans. In the book, Humbert is both a wrongdoer and a victim, a diabolical monster and a pathetic weakling. Only at the end does it dawn on him that he's never been anything but a dirty old man to Lolita, who accuses him of having "broken" her life.

Though Nabokov also wrote the screenplay, Kubrick and his co-producer James B. Harris cut and rewrote it beyond recognition. The finished film portrays Nabokov's agonized predator as the sole injured party, more sinned against than sinning. Brilliantly embodied by James Mason, Kubrick's Humbert is a tragicomic figure, exploited by Lolita (Sue Lyon), mocked by his rival, the seamy dramatist and screenwriter Clare Quilty (Peter Sellers), and cruelly deceived by both.

The opening sequence is a flash-forward to the end of the tale, and it stamps *Lolita* as an absurd parody of a romantic melodrama. The betrayed lover Humbert appears at Quilty's enormous country house, having resolved to murder his eternal rival. First of all, though, he will read him his death sentence, a "poetic" *cri de cœur* explaining precisely why Quilty has to die. Unfortunately for the would-be avenger, Quilty is drunk and sleepy, and he simply refuses to take Humbert seriously. He challenges his bewildered "guest" to a game of table tennis; he imitates a cowboy when he sees Humbert's gun; and he sits down at the piano and plays the opening chords of a Chopin polonaise, proposing that the two of them compose some words to the tune and share the profits between them. The jilted suitor's romantic agony is no match for the playwright's nonchalant derision. Confused and disoriented by Quilty's pitiless japing, Humbert seems incapable of ever regaining the initiative. What Kubrick is showing us here is a completely passive man.

Humbert's rapture and downfall begin with a search for lodgings for the summer months. It's a welcome vacation for the professor of literature; in the Fall, he will take up a lectureship at a college in Ohio. But when he goes to view his future lodgings, a bizarre struggle for his attentions breaks out be-

1

**"It's still taboo for a grown man to have a love affair with a girl under the age of consent, or at least to be seen to do so. That's why the young actress Sue Lyon was not allowed to watch a film in which she had played the title role. In other words: it was all right to use her as an actress, but she wasn't permitted to see the final result. The bizarrely schizophrenic nature of contemporary moral attitudes could hardly be more clearly illustrated."** *film-dienst*

tween the landlady Charlotte Haze (Shelley Winters) and her daughter Lolita. In a lengthy sequence with only a few cuts, we watch Charlotte leading Humbert through her labyrinthine house. It's a comic tour de force by Shelley Winters; and, like the largely improvised scenes featuring Peter Sellers, it shows that *Lolita* is first and foremost an actors' film, in which an unblinking camera gives these masterly performers time and space to really perform.

Charlotte Haze is a brazen, half-educated motormouth with clear sexual designs on the nonplussed Humbert. As she proudly displays her collection of prints ("Here's my little van Gogh"), it's clear that Humbert is dying to escape her clutches – until he sees something in the garden that abruptly changes his mind. Kubrick's Lolita has barely a trace of innocence; the 12-year-old nymphet of Nabokov's novel has become a busty teenage sexpot. As she ripens succulently in the summer heat, she eyes the new lodger provocatively from beneath her adorable sunhat.

In the weeks that follow, it's Lolita who will make all the running: she gives Humbert a goodnight kiss, flirts shamelessly with him at the breakfast table, and sabotages her mother's seduction campaign by coming home early and proving that three is a crowd.

1 Call of the wild: Unlike Nabokov, Kubrik has a full-fledged teenager seduce Humbert Humbert. Sue Lyon as Lolita.

2 Goodnight, Old Europe. Good morning, America: Lolita is just a typical girl with a taste for fast food and fast times.

3 Brazen overtures: Despite the dress, Lolita is no baby doll. It won't be long before Humbert Humbert (James Mason) becomes her personal plaything.

2

3

4

5

By contrast, Humbert's intentions towards Lolita are never made absolutely clear. Only once does he actually reveal his feelings and his plans. While Lolita is away at summer camp, he receives a letter from Charlotte, in which she confesses her love for him. Now Humbert is faced with an alternative: either he leaves the house immediately, or else he marries Charlotte and becomes "a good stepfather" to her daughter… Humbert starts to laugh, firstly at the absurd missive, and then at the devilish plan that begins to take shape in his head: marriage with the mother for the sake of access to the daughter. A moment later, the true hopelessness of his situation becomes evident: the camera pans over to the wall beside Lolita's bed, and there hangs a poster of his sinister alter ego, the dastardly Clare Quilty.

Quilty turns up everywhere, like the personification of Humbert's bad conscience: as the policeman making obscene insinuations when he shares a hotel room with Lolita; as the school psychiatrist Dr. Zempf, who threatens to inspect the Humbert household; and as a cop once again, phoning him up to announce an investigation of his sex life.

Sellers' absurd appearances are among the unquestionable highlights of this very black comedy. And however many changes the director made, there's a curious congruity between Kubrick's film and Nabokov's novel. For as Lolita muses in the course of her final meeting with Humbert Humbert, life is a series of gags – and if someone were to tell the story of her life, no one would believe it.

LP

6

4 Innocent or red hot: Lolita kisses Humbert goodnight, and Charlotte (Shelley Winters) is left with a pair of chapped lips.

5 Passive aggression: Humbert is at a loss to do anything but ignore Charlotte's persistent caresses.

6 Devil in a halo: Kubrik's Humbert is a passive voyeur who dizzies at the very sight of young Lolita.

7 Cola light: When European sensibilities meet American pop culture, it's time to toss those diet coke bottles, boys.

**"Since producer James B. Harris and director Stanley Kubrick are men of talent, there is much about the film that is excellent. James Mason has never been better than he is as the erudite Humbert Humbert, driven by a furious passion for a rather slovenly, perverse 'nymphet.'"** *Variety*

**JAMES MASON**

James Neville Mason was born in 1909, in the northern English county of Yorkshire. After studying architecture at Cambridge, he spent several years as a stage actor before making his film debut in the British murder mystery *Late Extra* (1935). In the highly popular romantic melodramas of the period, the young actor's good looks made him an audience favorite. Mason had an interestingly ambivalent aura: though impeccably cultivated and distinguished-looking, there was something vaguely sinister about his demeanor that predestined him to play charismatic villains. His biggest success in the European cinema was his performance as the fugitive IRA man in Carol Reed's *Odd Man Out* (1947).

At the end of the 40s, Mason went to Hollywood, where he gave ample proof of his idiosyncratic talent in a wide range of productions: in Max Ophüls' *Caught* (1948/49), he played a charming blackmailer; in Richard Fleischer's *20,000 Leagues Under the Sea* (1954), a creepy Captain Nemo; in George Cukor's *A Star Is Born* (1954), an alcoholic actor; and in Nicholas Ray's *Bigger Than Life* (1956), he played a man who terrifies his family as he succumbs to religious megalomania under the influence of cortisone. Hitchcock's *North by Northwest* (1959) gave him one of his best-known roles, as a cultivated gangster who has it in for Cary Grant.

Even after the collapse of the Hollywood studio system, Mason's career never took a dive, and he remained in demand until his death in 1984. His last movie was *The Shooting Party* (1983), directed by Alan Bridges, in which he played the host of a feudal English hunting party in the year 1913. As ever, he was the epitome of good breeding.

# THIS SPORTING LIFE

1962 - GREAT BRITAIN - 134 MIN. - DRAMA

DIRECTOR LINDSAY ANDERSON (1923–1994)
SCREENPLAY DAVID STOREY DIRECTOR OF PHOTOGRAPHY DENYS N. COOP EDITING PETER TAYLOR MUSIC JACQUES-LOUIS MONOD, after compositions by ROBERTO GERHARD PRODUCTION KAREL REISZ for INDEPENDENT ARTISTS, JULIAN WINTLE, LESLIE PARKYN PRODUCTIONS.

STARRING RICHARD HARRIS (Frank Machin), RACHEL ROBERTS (Mrs. Hammond), ALAN BADEL (Weaver), WILLIAM HARTNELL (Johnson), COLIN BLAKELY (Maurice Braithwaite), VANDA GODSELL (Mrs. Weaver), ANNE CUNNINGHAM (Judith), JACK WATSON (Len Miller), ARTHUR LOWE (Slomer), HARRY MARKHAM (Wade).

IFF CANNES 1963 BEST ACTOR (Richard Harris).

## *"Here in my heart I'm alone and so lonely."*

The movie opens with a thrilling piece of film editing, a brutal ballet of colliding bodies drenched in sweat. The name of the game is rugby; and soon we see the film's protagonist, Frank Machin (Richard Harris), crash to the ground after being fouled. A sudden flashback shows us Machin as a coal-blackened miner; a further, longer flashback shows us his family in the northern English town of Wakedale. The sober black and white photography suggests we are about to see a kitchen-sink, fly-on-the-wall sporting documentary. But we're in for a surprise. As Frank has lost all his front teeth during the game, he has to visit the dentist, where he's given a total anaesthetic; and in a series of lengthy flashbacks, we learn next to nothing about rugby, and everything about the rough-and-ready sportsman's desperate search for love and respect. Frank is noisy, belligerent, decidedly virile and as yet unmarried – and he's trying hard to win the heart of his widowed landlady Margaret Hammond (Rachel Roberts) and the acceptance of her children. Mrs. Hammond, however, is embittered and frosty since the death of her husband, and she can't or won't take what the rugby team's local hero has to offer her. It's his inability to put his feelings into words, and his occasional tendency to get violent, that finally kill their relationship. In the meantime, Frank's position in the rugby team has also been weakened – not because he hasn't been performing well on the field, but because he's spurned the advances of the club owner's wife. After spending some time in a grim, seedy boarding house for men – though he could afford much better – Frank resolves to win back Mrs. Hammond. But it turns out that she has suffered a brain hemorrhage; and as Frank pays her a last visit in the hospital, she dies.

The title of this movie might lead one to expect an action-packed sports drama. But Lindsay Anderson was a leading light of the adventurous British

1
2

# "A film about all of us and our lives right now... ...and our aspirations and egoism and unhappiness." *Lindsay Anderson*

"Free Cinema" movement, and *This Sporting Life* is a study of sex, class and power in the ashen environment of a Northern English industrial town. It's a portrait of a man in a crisis: indeed, for almost the entire film, Frank is unconscious, either anaesthetized in the dentist's chair or blind drunk elsewhere. Thus his inner life and his existential struggle with himself are revealed to us. The film has a complex, non-linear narrative structure, dominated by flashbacks providing a visual correlative to Frank's subconscious and his subjective view of events. Unwelcome memories rise to the surface and take on a threatening new life.

Frank Machin's sudden wealth makes him an outsider among his own people, yet it's impossible for him to rise in the social ranks. To the people around him, he's simply a big tough guy who can handle himself well on the playing field, and he fails miserably in all his attempts to make real emotional contact. In many movies, unconditional love is postulated as the answer to an apparently hopeless situation; but in this film, the relationships between the various characters are entirely a function of their economic needs, and Frank's frustrated desires culminate in violence, isolation and despair.

For all its beady-eyed psychological realism, *This Sporting Life* also contains scenes that are almost surreal in their effect. One of these sequences was even quoted by David Lynch in *Lost Highway* (1996): after the death of Mrs. Hammond, Frank sees an enormous spider. He tries to catch it, but it scuttles away – so he squashes it, quite brutally. As Margaret screamed in his face: "I'm the one thing you can't have!"

PLB

5

1 Fist to cuffs: When it comes to being masculine, Frank Machin (Richard Harris) is a knockout.

2 Body heat: But Margaret (Rachel Roberts) wants something more in her life than just a piece of meat.

3 On golden pond: Frank plays the role of father for Mrs. Hammond's children. But will this be just a limited engagement?

4 Wedding bells beat the blues: Life looks cheerier when it snows confetti.

5 Clubhouse patsy: Soccer club owner Mr. Weaver (Alan Badel) capitalizes on Frank's physical assets and reputation.

6 Strikes against them: Frank and Margaret's relationship is always on the brink of violence.

**LINDSAY ANDERSON (1923–1994)**

British director Lindsay Anderson began his career as a film editor. In the 1940s, he made some short documentaries and wrote a number of provocative newspaper articles. Together with Karel Reisz and Tony Richardson, Anderson eventually became a central figure in the "Free Cinema" movement, which arose in parallel to the French *nouvelle vague* in the course of the 50s and early 60s. This was a group of British film critics and directors whose alternative "authors' cinema" propagated a view of social and political conflicts that combined the poetic with the documentary. Their favored theme was the English working class. Besides *This Sporting Life* (1962) Lindsay Anderson's best-known films include *If…* (1968), *O Lucky Man* (1972), *Britannia Hospital* (1981), *The Whales of August* (1986) and *Glory! Glory!* (1988). He also worked successfully in theater and television.

**"In our cinema, where emotions are so often confused with emotionalism, this film never has to underline that it has feelings. It is, simply and naturally, a film of the senses."** *Sight and Sound*

6

# THE NUTTY PROFESSOR

1963 - USA - 107 MIN. - COMEDY

**DIRECTOR** JERRY LEWIS (*1926)
**SCREENPLAY** JERRY LEWIS, BILL RICHMOND **DIRECTOR OF PHOTOGRAPHY** W. WALLACE KELLEY **EDITING** JOHN WOODCOCK
**MUSIC** WALTER SCHARF, LOUIS Y. BROWN (Song “We’ve Got a World That Swings”), HAROLD ARLEN (Song “That Old Black Magic”), VICTOR YOUNG (Song “Stella by Starlight”) **PRODUCTION** ERNEST D. GLUCKSMAN for JERRY LEWIS ENTERPRISES, PARAMOUNT PICTURES.

**STARRING** JERRY LEWIS (Professor Julius Kelp / Buddy Love / Baby Kelp), STELLA STEVENS (Stella Purdy), DEL MOORE (Doctor Hamius Warfield), KATHLEEN FREEMAN (Millie Lemmon), HOWARD MORRIS (Mr. Elmer Kelp), ELVIA ALLMAN (Mrs. Kelp), MED FLORY (Football player), MILTON FROME (Doctor M. Sheppard Leevee), LES BROWN (Himself), RICHARD KIEL (Bodybuilder).

## *“Be somebody, be anybody.”*

Hubble, bubble, toil and trouble. Fire burn and beakers bubble!

Kaplewy! An explosion echoes round a laboratory full of colored concoctions. Not to worry. It’s just that nutty Professor Kelp (Jerry Lewis) goofing up on another chemistry experiment he’s conducting. And once again, that all too familiar thunderous boom causes uproar among the other faculty members.

Particularly perturbed is Director Warfield (Del Moore), Kelp’s boss, who promptly subjects his associate to a scolding. Ouch! But as crack-pot Kelp, crack-up Lewis transforms this scene into masterpiece of hilarious high jinks. This is Lewis as we know him best, playing a naive dolt who instantly wins over the audience with his conspicuous failings. His garish bow-tie and crooked eye-glasses are all the proof we need that his character is a flailing zero. No wonder he’s the laughing stock of his students.

But all that suddenly changes when a football player locks him into a laboratory cabinet during class one day, and the Professor decides once and for all to become more masculine. Pumping iron just leaves him with aches, pains and a few bruises, so Kelp changes track and turns to the field he is most proficient in – science. And Eureka! he comes up with a magic potion that turns his nincompoop self into a Casanova named Buddy Love.

Buddy has everything Kelp lacks. Whereas Kelp cowers in his leather armchair when confronted by Warfield’s tirades, Buddy can bring the big shot to his knees and have him standing on a table reciting Shakespeare in no time. With the help of his miracle drug, the Professor becomes the tortured and the torturer rolled into one.

The Buddy Love character is highly reminiscent of Lewis’ former partner Dean Martin. Between 1949 and 1956, the duo made 16 wildly successful films. Their collaboration eventually came to an end as a result of long-standing differences and mutual jealousy. Lewis insisted that Love was no intended to be a caricature of the roles Martin had played in their features. Nonetheless, there’s no overlooking that the constellation that made the pair a hit, that of the sweet, bumbling patsy and the super suave ladies’ man, is recreated to a T. Only this time Lewis took on both parts as well as severa behind the scenes tasks.

“Total filmmaker” is the term Lewis used to describe his cinematic ideal – that of fusing the roles of director, actor and producer. In his view, this type of concentrated filmmaking was the key to success, looking to Charlie Chaplin’s career as a case in point.

*The Nutty Professor* is the third film in which Lewis attempted to work with this concept. And again, he investigated two perennial topics of his oeuvre: split personality and childhood repression. Like so many other Lewis protagonists, Kelp seesaws between comedy and drama. These shifts are especially convincing in *The Nutty Professor* because director Lewis doesn’ allow Kelp to stumble from one gag to the next. Instead, each comedic episode is embedded in the plot. The split personality theme, à la Jekyll and Hyde, reaches new comic and tragic heights. Often, the humor in what appears to be a dialog scene is more situational than verbal, as the blocking of these jokes throws the emphasis on the visuals. Interdependent elements thus give rise to multi-layered bloopers, as when Kelp wallows abou on the floor in peptobismol chemical puddles after ingesting his wonde potion. The icing on this cake is Lewis quoting Rouben Mamoulian’s well-known film rendition of *Dr. Jekyll and Mr. Hyde* (1931) in a brilliantly executed moment.

1

The viewer soaks up all this action at a comfortable distance, thanks in part to the film's vibrant color palette. The bubblegum pinks and true blues don't just plaster the laboratory walls, they also come stitched to the students' steam-pressed clothing. The aesthetics may be somewhat alienating to today's viewer, but it was an integral part of the social fabric of the early 60s. At the height of the Cold War, a film with a rainbow-colored set immediately presented the audience with a safe haven. It was a sign that said: leave reality behind and hop on board the chuckle choo-choo.

The movie's love story is, however, far more disconcerting than its rose-colored glasses. Kelp and student Stella Purdy (Stella Stevens) enter into a John and Marcia romance right out of the books, the perfect compliment to the picture's cookie cutter camerawork. Clearly, had it not been for Lewis' acting

**EDITH HEAD (1897–1981)**

Hollywood was tailor-made for Edith Head. Born in San Bernardino, she studied art and languages at prestigious California universities Berkeley and Stanford. Following a career in teaching, she tried her hand as a sketch artist for Paramount. The attempt was more than successful: she thrived as a costume designer for 44 years, eventually becoming a titan in her field. In 1937, she was appointed the first woman to head costuming at a Hollywood studio. Her name became well known throughout the film world and synonymous with the Best Costumes Oscar, introduced at the end of the 1940s. She was nominated more than 20 times for her work, and won the distinction seven times. To this day, she remains the woman with the greatest number of Academy Award wins.

Her influence reached far beyond Hollywood as her designs inspired some of the most widespread fashion trends throughout the world. Women were frantically trying to step into the shoes of Barbara Stanwyck in *The Lady Eve* (1941), Bette Davis in *All About Eve* (1950) and Elizabeth Taylor in *A Place in the Sun* (1951). She could turn her hand to anything and make the world want it, from the tropical sarong to the sleek chic Audrey Hepburn look. Head also dressed her fair share of Hollywood's men across a variety of genres. She drafted the depression era outfits for *The Sting*, (1973) and every last chap for *Butch Cassidy and the Sundance Kid* (1969). John Wayne and Katharine Hepburn entered their golden years in style in *Rooster Cogburn* (1975), thanks to the great costumer. Directors like Alfred Hitchcock, Billy Wilder and Jerry Lewis are but a few of the great names Edith Head collaborated with. Some of her most ambitious designs were born in later years, when the *grande dame* of Hollywood textile design took on projects that demanded the recreation of the grace and style of entire eras. *Dead Men Don't Wear Plaid* (1981), which was dedicated to her memory, was one such garment bag.

3

1 A vile solution: Jerry Lewis, pictured here with the angelic Stella Purdy (Stella Stevens), goes from slob to suave in this Jekyll & Hyde spoof.

2 Cut down to size: Here, football hero (Richard Kiel of James Bond fame) lectures Prof. Kelp for his disgraceful behavior during class. Just one of the film's many role reversals.

3 Lying down on the job: Kooky Prof. Kelp can't fall asleep without his Bunsen burner by his side.

4 Chemically imbalanced: Then again, one sip of this toxic concoction could change all that.

5 A lame duck spikes the punch: Something's a brewing between Kelp and Stella. But will Don Juan let her in on the secret behind his smoothness?

talent, the project could have easily been a commercial pancake. But such is history. The film scored at the U. S. box office and went on to become a smash around the world. In 1996, Eddie Murphy tried to recapture the magic with his own rendition of *The Nutty Professor*, which also met with marked success.

Lewis himself considers the version he starred in to be his personal masterpiece: "You know, every director in the history of cinema prays for the one work you can sit and watch with your grandchildren and tell them you did something substantial. And I have mine – *The Nutty Professor*." OK

**"This is a very funny movie with some brilliant visual gags and a stunning parody by Lewis of a Hollywood rat pack cad."** *New Yorker*

DIRECTOR BILLY WILDER (1906–2002)

SCREENPLAY BILLY WILDER, I. A. L. DIAMOND DIRECTOR OF PHOTOGRAPHY JOSEPH LASHELLE EDITING DANIEL MANDELL MUSIC ANDRÉ PREVIN, MARGUERITE MONNOT PRODUCTION BILLY WILDER for THE MIRISCH COMPANY, PHALANX.

STARRING JACK LEMMON (Nestor Patou), SHIRLEY MACLAINE (Irma la Douce), LOU JACOBI (Moustache), BRUCE YARNELL (Hippolyte), HERSCHEL BERNARDI (Inspector Lefèvre).

ACADEMY AWARD 1963 OSCAR for BEST ADAPTED MUSIC (André Previn).

## *"It's hard work leading an easy life."*

You can stick a price tag on just about everything in the Parisian neighborhood of Les Halles: vegetables, fresh meat – or love. For just a step away from the marketplace, on Rue Casanova, the Parisian "poules," hens of the red light district, preen their feathers in eager anticipation of their next John. Most guys, however, only want to be serenaded by the nightingale among them: a mesmerizing damsel in emerald green tights named Irma la Douce (Shirley MacLaine).

Now, normally, these ladies would have to take special precautions, given their age-old profession and all. But in Les Halles even the police can be bought for a song. Pimps, better known as "mecs," pay off the local gendarmes, or "flics," to have their routine raids turn up mysteriously dry.

This all changes when a rotten apple turns up in the copasetic garden of good and evil. Unwise to the existing arrangement, novice cop on the beat Patou (Jack Lemmon) helps himself to a snack at local fruit stand and leaves the vendor at a loss when he insists on paying for the merchandise! Clearly, the new kid on the block just doesn't fit in and it's just a matter of time before he's bungled his first raid. Finding evidence of vice, he arrests a group of paying gentlemen callers – including his boss. Tired, frustrated and no longer a member of the force, Patou returns to the Rue Casanova, happening upon a local tavern run by the jovial Moustache (Lou Jacobi). Fortune smiles upon the former law enforcer, for it is there that he makes Irma's acquaintance and becomes her new "mec." His new job, however, proves less than suitable when it becomes clear that this business manager has fallen in love with his star client…

*Irma la Douce* is the third of seven films Jack Lemmon worked on with director Billy Wilder. Their prosperous collaboration began with *Some Like It Hot* (1959), and indeed the two pictures have much in common: both luxuriate in frivolous gaiety, and both are excursions into a world of disguise and mistaken identity. Whenever Patou strolls down the street as a gendarme, jauntily swinging his night stick by his side, his uniform takes on the attributes of a costume and his job becomes a stylized role – after all, isn't a guy like him far too naive to be a policemen? His transformation into the quarter's cock-of-the-walk pimp is equally fantastical. Suddenly, he is Irma's lewd protector and companion, ready to jump through fiery rings of

2

disguise to avoid sharing her with other men. He dresses up as the rich and impotent Briton, Lord X. This invention of Patou's imagination becomes Irma's sole patron, whose only desire is to play a few hands of double solitaire with her – no pun intended. The whole thing, of course, gets to be a regular circus when the time comes to pay her. As Lord X, he forks over a few bills to Irma, who turns the winnings back over to him as her pimp – i.e. a lot of money changing hands and going nowhere. The farce climaxes with him becoming wildly jealous of himself when Irma appears to prefer Lord X to the real him.

Billy Wilder sets up a wonderfully light-hearted cinematic Ferris wheel, using the protagonist's flirtations with multiple identities as a suspected killer, escaped prisoner, father, husband, and, for old time's sake, a police-

**"Throughout the film there are samples of smart dialog, though it is necessary to testify that some of it does not come off and is occasionally out of place… It's not only a supercolossal eye-filler (the unprecedented budget shows in the physical opulence throughout), but it is also a remarkably literate cinematic recreation of an historic epoch… As Caesar observes to Cleopatra, early on: 'You have a way of mixing politics and passion.' So does Mankiewicz."** *Variety*

1 Woof! Police inspector Nestor Patou (Jack Lemmon) has got streetwalker Irma La Douce (Shirley MacLaine) right where he wants her – out of reach from other men.

2 A man of many hats: "Nestor stages a police raid, innocently accepts bribes from local pimps, and gets fired all in the course of a day. No other Wilder hero has ever fallen from grace at so quickly." *Claudius Seidl* on Billy Wilder

3 Scotch and peppermint tea: Nestor treats Irma to a beverage, and lands himself a new job while falling in love.

4 Hey, big spenders: Here comes the most appetizing dish of them all – Shirley MacLaine as Irma la Douce!

5

**HAPPY HOOKERS**

Irma is only one of numerous professional escorts actress Shirley MacLaine has played over the course of her career (Ginny in *Some Came Running* [1958] is another). It's no wonder, as turning tricks happens to be one of the oldest and most popular ways for screen starlets to earn a living. From the cinematic end of things, it is a highly economical means of exploitation: an opportunity to show bodily flesh and sleazy underworlds, as well as examine the psychological aspects of the feminine mystique.

In 1927/8, Gloria Swanson became the first actress to get an Oscar nod for her portrayal of a prostitute. In fact, the list of big-name actresses who have played call girls is endless: Jane Fonda, Greta Garbo, Audrey Hepburn, Sharon Stone, Elizabeth Taylor, etc. etc. etc. There are, of course, a handful of films that paint a critical picture of these fast women, such as *Taxi Driver* (1975) did with Jodie Foster or the 1991 documentary *Whore* with Theresa Russell. More often, however, Hollywood has a weakness for hookers with a heart of gold – those academics who have a deeper insight into the male mind as a result of their profession; among them are Shirley MacLaine's Irma and Elizabeth Shue's Sera in *Leaving Las Vegas* (1995). Numerous movies attempt to justify a woman's reasons for turning to such an immoral existence: often, it is a lifestyle born out of financial straits like Anna Magnani's character in *Mamma Roma* (1962). Equally compelling is its ability to liberate a person from everyday life as is the case for Catherine Deneuve in *Belle de Jour* (1967) and Kathleen Turner in *Crimes of Passion* (1984) – each woman leads a double life as fly by night, high-class hooker. And then there are the Cinderella solicitors of the 1990s. Top of the list is *Pretty Woman* (1989/90) Julia Roberts, a woman whose services are rewarded with a fairy tale ending complete with Prince Charming.

5 Charity is sweet: To get her John's to dish out the dough Irma lays it on thick and spins tales of a past marked by misfortune.

6 Terms of endearment: After sharing an *Apartment* (1960), Lemmon and MacLaine rekindle their romance and light up the screen more brightly than ever before.

7 All's well that ends well: … at least until Moustache (Lou Jacobi) reminds Irma that marriage won't solve everything. But that's another story.

man as its axis. Irma too gets the opportunity to wear numerous hats and reveal more of herself – or rather fictitious selves through the "anecdotes" she tells her Johns: we are told of her former times as a music student, whose career ended when a piano lid came crashing down upon her fingers, and her Belgian roots and parents' life in the Congo. Moustache, the tavern proprietor who serves as the story's narrator, continues this thread, perpetually reminiscing about his days as a lawyer as well as his thieving ways in Romania…

Anything goes in this Parisian candyland, where every nook and cranny is bursting with dazzling artificiality. It is the same grand art direction as in *The Apartment* (1960), which was also brought to life by Wilder set designer Alexander Trauner. Indeed, the sky's the limit for *Irma la Douce*. A cop can work as a pimp, a bartender can be a great legal mind, and a whore can be the most treasured, sensitive woman on the face of the earth. It is a world in which love is king – commanding its subjects to don a rainbow of disguises and awaken the nobleman in both the fool and the strumpet. HJK

**"On the plus side of Irma… there are scintillating performances by Jack Lemmon and Shirley MacLaine, a batch of jovial supporting portraits, a striking physical production and a number of infectious comedy scenes."** *Variety*

# CONTEMPT
## Le Mépris

1963 - FRANCE / ITALY - 103 MIN. - DRAMA, LITERARY ADAPTATION

DIRECTOR JEAN-LUC GODARD (*1930)

SCREENPLAY JEAN-LUC GODARD, based on the novel *IL DISPREZZO* by ALBERTO MORAVIA DIRECTOR OF PHOTOGRAPHY RAOUL COUTARD EDITING AGNÈS GUILLEMOT, LILA LAKSHAMANAN MUSIC GEORGES DELERUE PRODUCTION GEORGES DE BEAUREGARD, CARLO PONTI, JOSEPH E. LEVINE for ROME PARIS FILMS, LES FILMS CONCORDIA, COMPAGNIA CINEMATOGRAFICA CHAMPION.

STARRING BRIGITTE BARDOT (Camille Javal), JACK PALANCE (Jeremy Prokosch), MICHEL PICCOLI (Paul Javal), GIORGIA MOLL (Francesca Vanini), FRITZ LANG (Himself).

***"O, Gods! I like Gods. I like them very much. I know exactly how they feel."***

While veteran director Fritz Lang (Lang himself) makes a film in Cinecittà about the travels of Odysseus, his American producer Prokosch (Jack Palance) hires screenwriter Paul Javal (Michel Piccoli) to rework the script. Prokosch is dissatisfied with the unwieldy art film Lang is constructing. He wants to see more naked flesh on the screen – and not just there. Quite blatantly, he woos Javal's beautiful wife Camille (Brigitte Bardot); and as Paul appears to be turning a blind eye, Camille starts to believe he's using her to further his career.

*Contempt* is seen by many as Jean-Luc Godard's masterpiece. It was his most expensive film, and the big budget – inflated mainly by his star Brigitte Bardot – demanded an unwonted discipline from this idiosyncratic director. Concessions simply had to be made to the producers. Thus Godard was obliged to film in Cinemascope (for the first time), and he also had to introduce a nude scene featuring *La Bardot*. Nonetheless, he succeeded admirably in integrating these imposed constraints into the finished film. The widescreen format is not just a significant contribution to the visual magic of the movie; it also allowed Godard to find a haunting spatial metaphor for the growing estrangement between Camille and Paul. On top of all this, Godard also managed to transform the difficult circumstances of the film's making into a subtle part of its very form: behind the almost banal tale of a collapsing marriage is the director's allusive and highly personal reflection on his relationship to his own métier.

From the very start, Godard makes it clear that the movie's setting is more than just the essential background to a melodrama: instead of a titles sequence, we see a film team at work. We watch the camera as it tracks a young woman (Giorgia Moll), who's walking and reading a manuscript. As the film team, the technicians and the actress move towards us, we hear the voice of Godard, reeling off the cast and credits. The sequence concludes with the cameraman (Raoul Coutard) swinging the lens around to face us.

Essentially, the title sequence amounts to a set of instructions for viewing the film. By melding cinematic and non-cinematic reality, Godard indicates that the screen and the real world reflect each other in a highly complex manner. This point is also expressed very clearly in the figure of Prokosch, a parody of Godard's producer Joseph E. Levine, who had established his powerful position in the movie business with the Greek-mythical blockbuster *Hercules Unchained* (*Ercole e la regina di Lidia / Hércules y la reina de Lidia / Hercule et la reine de Lydie*, 1958). Fritz Lang plays himself, enduring the antics of his egomaniac financier with long-suffering equanim-

1

2

3

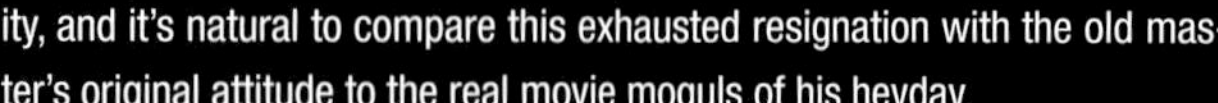

ity, and it's natural to compare this exhausted resignation with the old master's original attitude to the real movie moguls of his heyday.

The center of this film, though, is the myth of Brigitte Bardot. The relationship between Camille Javal and her husband Paul is an open reference to her "public" marriage with Roger Vadim, who discovered Bardot and made her a star – becoming a star himself in the process. In the famous bedroom scene at the start of the film, the camera – deputizing for Paul Javal – gazes at her naked form through a colored filter. We have the disturbingly ambivalent impression that this magnificent body is being caressed by the camera even while it is being coolly assessed for its market value. It's a subtle introduction to the central message of the film, telling us that personal integrity is incompatible with a craving for material gains.

Cameraman Raoul Coutard once said that *Contempt* was a love letter from Godard to his wife. And indeed, the director is certainly also reflecting on his own situation and his marriage to Anna Karina, the leading actress in so many of his films. In one scene, she appears on a movie poster: the film in question is Godard's *My Life to Live* (*Vivre sa vie*, 1962), in which Karina played a prostitute.

*Contempt* is a further expression of Godard's pessimistic worldview, and it's further manifested in the structure of the movie, which like a Greek tragedy is divided into three acts. Coutard's wonderful camerawork holds the tragedy at a decent distance, soaking it in Mediterranean color and images that harmonize marvelously with Georges Delerue's melancholy music. In its classical beauty, *Contempt* now seems as timeless as its tragic theme. JH

4

5

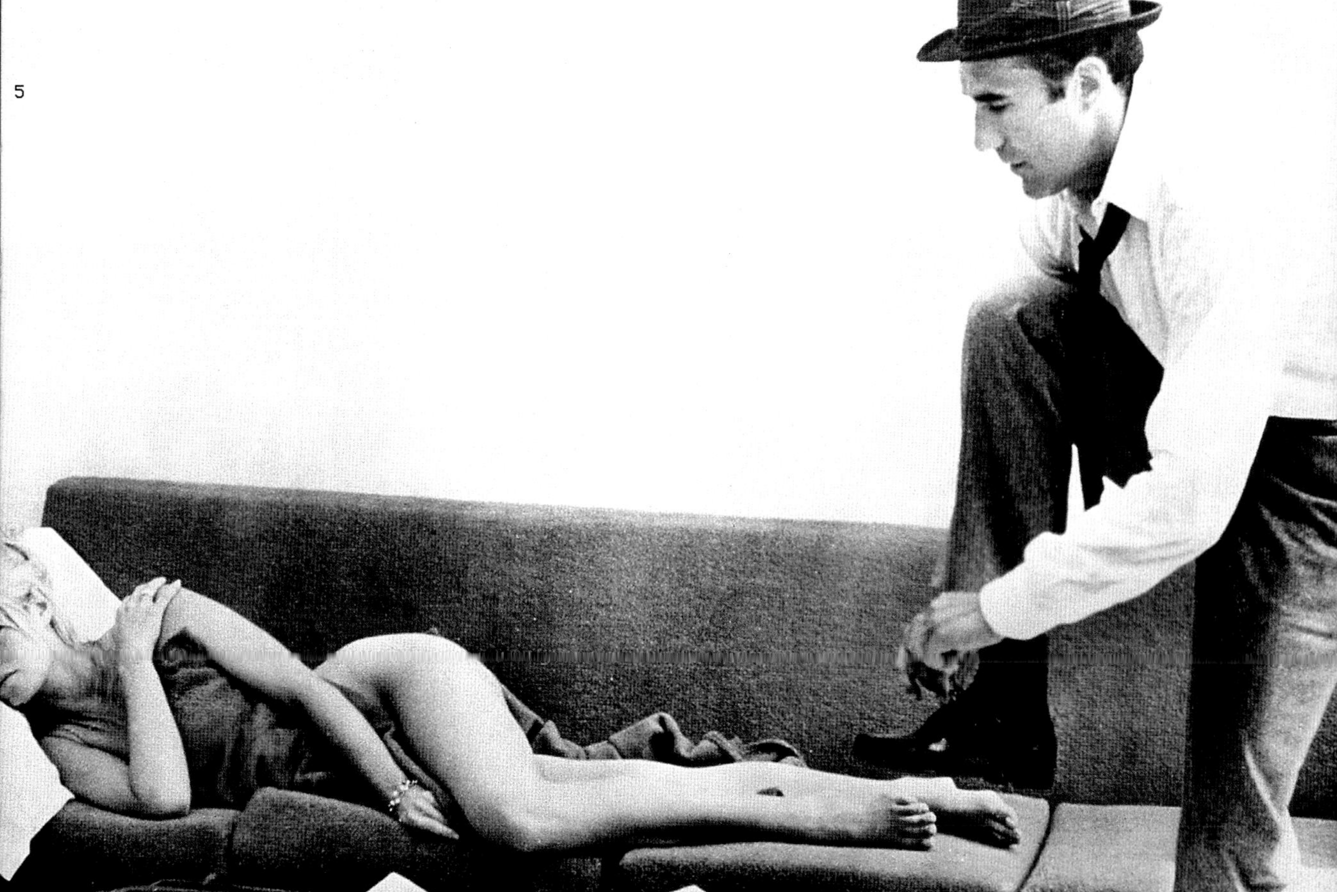

1 Stairway to hell: Camille (Brigitte Bardot) knows that it's all downhill from here for her and Paul (Michel Piccoli).

2 Driving a hard bargain: When producer Jeremy Prokosch (Jack Palance) expresses his interest in Camille, the young ingénue is all ears.

3 Here's looking at you, Uma: In a black wig Brigitte Bardot almost resembles Godard's wife Anna Karina, who starred in *Vivre sa vie* (1964).

4 Double reference: That's right. Camille and Paul are standing in front of a poster for *Vivre sa vie* (1964), in which Karina plays a prostitute.

5 Sheer elegance: At the producers' urging Godard was compelled to include nude scenes with Bardot. Fortunately, the French director is a master of finesse.

# "Every time I hear the word culture, I bring out my checkbook."

*Film quote: Jeremy Prokosch (Jack Palance)*

**JACK PALANCE**

Some used to claim that his strikingly sharp-edged and immobile face was the result of wounds sustained in wartime. Others attributed it to his brief career as a boxer. Whatever the truth was, Jack Palance's memorably weird appearance, coupled with his physical fitness, predestined him to play tough guys. So it's no surprise that in the course of a career that's now lasted more than half a century, Palance has appeared mainly in Westerns and war films.

Born in 1919, Palance worked on Broadway for several years before making his film debut in a thriller. In *Sudden Fear* (1952), he played a greedy and vengeful actor who resolves to kill his own wife (Joan Crawford). His performance brought him an Oscar nomination, as did his most famous role: the part of the psychopathic gunslinger in George Steven's legendary Western *Shane* (1953).

Yet Palance proved equally convincing in very different roles, and could play sympathetic characters like the sensitive film star in Robert Aldrich's *The Big Knife* (1955). Palance also collaborated with Aldrich on the war films *Attack* (1956) and the excellent *Ten Seconds to Hell* (1959). From the 60s onwards, Palance spent more time working in Europe. He had several dubious roles in horror movies and sword-and-sandal epics, he put in appearances as a soldier and Western hero, and he did a lot of TV work. His appearance as an American film producer in Godard's *Contempt* must be counted amongst his outstanding performances. And eventually, the aging warhorse even got his Oscar for a supporting role in *City Slickers* (1991)… as an eccentric old cowboy.

# CLEOPATRA

1963 - USA - 228/197 MIN. - HISTORICAL EPIC, DRAMA

**DIRECTOR** JOSEPH L. MANKIEWICZ (1909–1993)
**SCREENPLAY** JOSEPH L. MANKIEWICZ, RANALD MACDOUGALL, SIDNEY BUCHMAN **DIRECTOR OF PHOTOGRAPHY** LEON SHAMROY
**EDITING** DOROTHY SPENCER **MUSIC** Alex North **PRODUCTION** WALTER WANGER for 20TH CENTURY FOX, CENTFOX.

**STARRING** ELIZABETH TAYLOR (Cleopatra), RICHARD BURTON (Marc Antony), REX HARRISON (Julius Caesar), PAMELA BROWN (High Priestess), GEORGE COLE (Flavius), RICHARD O'SULLIVAN (Ptolemy) HUME CRONYN (Sosigenes), CESARE DANOVA (Apollodorus), MARTIN LANDAU (Rufio), RODDY MCDOWALL (Caesar Augutus / Octavian), JEAN MARSH (Octavia), ROBERT STEPHENS (Germanicus).

**ACADEMY AWARDS 1963** OSCARS for BEST CINEMATOGRAPHY (Leon Shamroy), BEST ART DIRECTION (Herman Blumenthal, Paul Fox, Walter Scott), BEST SPECIAL EFFECTS (Emil Kosa Jr.), BEST COSTUMES (Renié, Irene Sharaff, Nino Novarese)

## *"On your knees!"*

Eye shadow to rival the wonders of the Ancient World. Faintly painted lips and raven braids that frame a face more enigmatic than that of Mona Lisa. Andy Warhol considered *Cleopatra* to be the most influential film in the world of 1960s style. And truly the makeup artistry exhibited by Elizabeth Taylor, not to mention the geometric costumes, hairdos and sets, redefined the tastes and trends of the decade and gave rise to an entire movement in fashion and design. Still, far more legendary than the picture's visual force is the story behind the making of this opulent epic. Not even *Titanic* (1997) could blow Cleopatra out of the water for being the most expensive movie ever produced. Originally planned on a modest two million dollar budget in 1959, total costs reached an exorbitant 44 million dollars, nearly bankrupting 20th Century Fox.

Winning the role over Audrey Hepburn as a result of a public opinion poll, Elizabeth Taylor became the first actress to successfully demand one million dollars for her services and thus set a precedent that eventually enabled the stars to get the upper hand in Hollywood. Cleopatra's epic tale also went down in cinematic history due to the streak of bad luck that accompanied its much-publicized shoot. That is not to say that the project only bore ill fruit. It cannot be forgotten that while filming this picture Taylor met Richard Burton, the great love of her life, who was cast opposite her as Marc Antony. Nonetheless, *Cleopatra* is notorious for having ruined numerous careers. Director Rouben Mamoulian was replaced by Joseph L. Mankiewicz, whose 1953 screen version of Shakespeare's *Julius Caesar* had established him in the epic genre. Both of the project's original leading men, Peter Finch and Stephen Boyd, were obliged to step down to Rex Harrison (Julius Caesar) and Richard Burton (Marc Antony). Likewise, producer Walter Wanger had difficulty getting work because of his involvement with the financial "disaster movie."

In the spirit of the era's wildly popular Ancient World epics like *Ben-Hur* (1959), *Spartacus* (1960) and *El Cid* (1961), *Cleopatra* prides itself on its historical accuracy. According to the credits, the screenplay was based on the writings of Plutarch, Suetonius, Appian, and other ancient sources as well as C. M. Franzero's *The Life and Times of Cleopatra.*

The story begins in 48 B. C. during the Roman civil war. Emerging victorious from the Battle of Pharsalos, Julius Caesar (Rex Harrison) sets sail for Egypt to capture his fleeing archrival Pompey. But he arrives in Alexandria to find Egypt embroiled in a civil war between young King Ptolemy (Joseph O'Sullivan) and his banished sister and co-ruler Cleopatra (Elizabeth Taylor). The Jewel of the Nile uses her charm, intelligence and diplomatic cunning to lure Caesar and his legions over to her side. The political alliance is soon consolidated by a romantic liaison, resulting in the birth of Caesar's son Caesarion, a child they hope will bring together the military might of the Romans

1

2
3

# “The memorable thing about this picture is that it is superlative entertainment. It is also one of the great epic films of our day.”

*The New York Times*

1 Will the real Cleopatra please stand up: Elizabeth Taylor bathes in the waters of the most extravagant Hollywood epic ever produced.

2 Veto power: While Marc Antony (Richard Burton) has no objection to Cleopatra residing in Rome, Caesar's other compatriots intend to make their disapproval known…

3 Goddess, monarch and Hollywood legend: Cleopatra's grandiose arrival in Rome is met by wild fanfare. However, it was Liz's name that the hundreds of extras were cheering.

with the wealth of Egypt. Cleopatra and Caesar head to Rome, where, despite existing marital ties, she and the emperor live as man and wife. But Caesar's enemies soon assassinate him, unleashing another civil war that shatters Cleopatra's imperial ambitions. Back in Alexandria, the Egyptian queen enters into an affair with Caesar's most trusted lieutenant, Marc Antony (Richard Burton). The film is passionate and deeply emotional in its treatment of their romance. Despite being forced to marry Caesar Augustus' daughter (played by Jean Marsh), Marc Antony returns to his siren Cleopatra. Meanwhile, Augustus defeats the Egyptians in the naval battle of Actium and conquers the ancient kingdom for Rome. After receiving word of the conquest, Marc Antony and Cleopatra take their own lives.

An optical pageant, the movie represented Hollywood's attempt to eclipse the television industry with colors and images that simply couldn't be enjoyed on the mean screen. Sadly, the story unfolds at the inverse of light speed – too slow, even by 60s standards. But what remains unparalleled is the procession scene in Rome, greatly enhanced by Alex North's exotic

**“It’s a fairly safe bet that we will never again see a film which costs 40 million dollars to make. We’re almost equally unlikely to experience a movie whose making has been so plagued with scandals and calamities.”** *Der Tagesspiegel*

4 All roads lead to Rome: An ominous prospect for Cleopatra, who must prepare for war with the European empire.

5 Kiss my feet: Cleopatra forces Antony to pay for having married another woman, although it was a purely political move.

6 The empire strikes back: The massacre at Actium could spell disaster for Antony and Cleopatra.

7 It’s good to be the king: Caesar (Rex Harrison) is granted a private audience with the Egyptian pharaoh.

6

score. A meticulously choreographed parade featuring African dancers in colored fog climaxes with a godly vision of Cleopatra draped in gold, reclining atop a mammoth sphinx pulled by a thousand slaves. Any doubts as to whether the film intends us to worship at the altar of spectacle are instantly erased.

And yet *Cleopatra* is a veritable study in contradictions. For all its visual splendor and mesmerizing opulence, the plot hobbles along on crutches from beginning to end, dying a long and excruciating death in the second half due to the side effects of the script's terribly wooden dialog.

There are other explanations as to why, despite its enormous budget, Cleopatra looks unfinished. Joseph L. Mankiewicz had originally planned to turn six hours of filmed material into two separate three-hour movies. Unfortunately, studio heads opposed the idea and forced him to halve the material, resulting in a single three-hour version (expanded to four hours in the 1995 special edition). Still the film remains one of the greatest star vehicles of all time and the proof is in the pudding. For it wasn't Cleo's name the extras were shouting as they transported their exalted queen – it was Liz's!

KK

**ELIZABETH TAYLOR**

"Oh, to be reincarnated as a ring on Elizabeth Taylor's finger!" Andy Warhol certainly wasn't the only one who sang the praises of Liz for years on end. One of the great icons of pop culture, Taylor's films and life have met with mixed public response. Her name is intrinsically linked to both glamour and tragedy. Indeed, Taylor's fame stems as much from her brilliant work opposite stars like James Dean in *Giant* (1956) or Paul Newman in *Cat on a Hot Tin Roof* (1958) as it does from her seedy marriages and love affairs.

Born in London on February 27th, 1932, Elizabeth Taylor made a royal debut at age three, performing ballet to an audience of the Queen. Her family moved to Los Angeles in 1939 and Lizzy broke into Hollywood with Harold Young's 1942 comedy *There's One Born Every Minute*. From then on her mother groomed her to be a child star, and MGM capitalized on her in films like *Lassie Come Home* (1943) and *Jane Eyre* (1944). By the time she was 15, the press were already hailing her as the most beautiful woman in the world.

Her breakthrough as a serious actress came with *Father of the Bride* (1950), in which the 18-year-old Taylor played a headstrong girl on the verge of womanhood. In the years that followed, the violet-eyed actress headlined countless MGM productions like *Love Is Better than Ever* (1951), *Ivanhoe* (1952) and *Raintree County* (1957). The epic *Cleopatra* (1963), in which Taylor was immortalized as a celluloid deity, was the most image-sculpting endeavor of her career. In 1960, she was awarded her first Best Actress Oscar for her portrayal of a call girl in Daniel Mann's *Butterfield 8* (1960). Six years later, Taylor's harrowing performance as Martha in *Who's Afraid of Virginia Woolf* (1966) won her a second. While Taylor ironically ceased to get high profile roles from this point on, she remains one of the brightest stars in all Hollywood history.

As famous for her eight marriages as for her talent, her private life continually sparked the interest of the tabloids for over 40 years. However, it was not only Taylor's rocky romance and two-time marriage to actor Richard Burton that made headlines. Of equal intrigue was her ever-frail physical health, as well as her drug and alcohol abuse. In 1985, just after Rock Hudson lost his life to AIDS, she became an activist for the research of the disease, founding the American Foundation for AIDS Research. Queen Elizabeth II made Taylor a "dame" in 2000.

# THE SILENCE
## Tystnaden

1963 - SWEDEN - 95 MIN. - DRAMA

DIRECTOR INGMAR BERGMAN (*1918)
SCREENPLAY INGMAR BERGMAN DIRECTOR OF PHOTOGRAPHY SVEN NYKVIST EDITING ULLA RYGHE MUSIC JOHANN SEBASTIAN BACH
PRODUCTION ALLAN EKELUND for SVENSK FILMINDUSTRI.

STARRING INGRID THULIN (Ester), GUNNEL LINDBLOM (Anna), JÖRGEN LINDSTRÖM (Johan), HÅKAN JAHNBERG (Old Waiter), BIRGER MALMSTEN (Bar Waiter), EDUARDO GUTIÉRREZ (The Dwarfs' Impresario), "THE EDUARDINIS" (Performing Dwarfs), LISSI ALANDH (Woman in Theater), LEIF FORSTENBERG (Man in Theater), NILS WALDT (Cashier).

***"Why complain about loneliness? It's a waste of time."***

"*The Silence* is simple; it uses simple means to tell its story, and it doesn't deploy any symbols or artifice." So said Ingmar Bergman, in an interview with Swedish journalists. François Truffaut asked the essential counter-question in an article on Bergman's films: "Is the simple really simple for everyone?"

Apparently not. When first shown in 1963, *The Silence* was the Swedish director's most controversial film to date. There was much puzzlement as to what he was trying to say in this drama about a love-hate relationship between two very different sisters, and many critics were happy to admit they couldn't make head or tail of it. What's more, the film's treatment of sexuality caused a hullabaloo about censorship, and rumors of unprecedented steamy scenes eventually made *The Silence* one of the most commercially successful films Bergman ever made.

Nowadays it's hard to see what all the fuss was about. Ingrid Thulin has a masturbation scene, in which her face shows a brief flickering of lust; we get a fleeting glimpse of Gunnel Lindblom's breast; and then there is the scene in which Anna watches a couple making love in the theater auditorium, with the woman's breasts briefly exposed. Pretty tame stuff by current standards; yet the quality of the direction and cinematography, combined with the performances of Thulin and Lindblom, somehow evokes an all-encompassing physicality whose effect is almost overwhelming.

As the title suggests, *The Silence* is a film about the collapse of verbal communication. Bergman's "simple" story follows the sisters Ester (Ingrid Thulin) and Anna (Gunnel Lindblom), who are on their way home with Anna's young son Johan (Jörgen Lindström) after a vacation. Ester's lung disease forces them to stop off in an unspecified country whose language they cannot speak, and which is clearly preparing for war. The country's situation mirrors that of the sisters: they don't have much to say to each other, and it's only a matter of time until the tension between them erupts into open conflict.

The very first shot shows the three travelers in a hot and sticky train compartment, and it makes the differences between the two women very clear indeed: while the "intellectual" Ester is buttoned up in a twinset, Anna

1

**"This is a dark film, and an oppressively sad one. Yet it is lit throughout by a tiny, absurd flame of hope, in a dimension beyond the action and the dialog. I know the source of this light: it comes from Bergman's profound belief in humanity, no matter how often circumstances may force his protagonists into cruel and ruthless behavior."** *Krzysztof Kieslowski*

is almost animal-like in a sleeveless dress, languidly lascivious in her open-mouthed surrender to the heat.

Ester deeply resents the power of the body. To her, both sickness and sexual desire are humiliations. Her lung disease is gradually destroying her (at the end of the film, the cameraman Sven Nykvist will light her in such a way that she already looks dead in her bed); and it also becomes clear that the sisters used to have an incestuous relationship with each other. Now, however, Anna refuses to have sex with her jealous and dominant sister; instead, she torments her by indulging in erotic adventures with lovers she picks up on the street.

The sisters move into neighboring hotel rooms with a connecting door. Bergman repeatedly places the camera so that we see things in deep perspective: while Anna gets ready to go out, the open door shows Ester lying sick in bed – an all-seeing eye and a silent reproach. Or we see Ester in the foreground of one room and Anna in the background of the other: they converse at a distance without the slightest eye contact, making the depth of their

2

1 The unspeakable truth: Siblings Ester (Ingrid Thulin) and Anna (Gunnel Lindblom) are linked by blood, love and hate.

2 The Caucasian chalk circle: As the sisters' estrangement intensifies, Anna's son Johan (Jörgen Lindström) is torn between them.

3 Death becomes her: Ester's lung disease takes possession of her entire body.

estrangement as clear as day. Yet it's never quite clear why it's come to this, and even their eventual confrontation does very little to elucidate the situation.

*The Silence* is commonly described as the third part of Bergman's "Faith Trilogy," after *Through a Glass Darkly* (*Såsom i en spegel*, 1961), in which a young woman succumbs to religious mania and schizophrenia, and Winter Light (*Nattvardsgästerna*, 1962), which depicts a protestant cleric's crisis of faith. According to this interpretation, *The Silence* might be retitled "Life as Hell," for God's silence and the absence of any spiritual or moral anchor has thrown the protagonists back on their own pitiable existence, thus delivering them to despair. That's one way of seeing the film, but it ain't necessarily so: even without religion as an interpretative prop, *The Silence* is a brilliant study of speechlessness, lovelessness, unhappiness and fear.

The only source of hope in the film is Anna's son Johan, an inquisitive wanderer between the two women. The boy's sexuality is just awakening and the two sisters struggle to win his affections. At first, Johan seeks refuge in the lap of his mother while rejecting Ester's caresses. Anna's physical presence is palpable, and almost literally suffocating: she nearly crushes him with kisses and hugs, she calls on him to scrub her back when she bathes

**INGRID THULIN (1929–2004)**

Like many other Bergman actresses, Ingrid Thulin began her career with a solid theatrical training, in her case at the Royal Dramatic Theater in Stockholm. From 1948 onwards, she also had numerous roles in Swedish films, working with respected directors such as Gustaf Molander and Arne Mattson. While working at the theater in Malmö, Ingrid Thulin met Ingmar Bergman. Their first film collaboration was on *Wild Strawberries* (*Smultronstället*, 1957), in which Thulin played the daughter-in-law of the old professor. In the following decade-and-a-half, Thulin became one of Bergman's most important actresses, appearing in *The Magician* (*Ansiktet*, 1958), *Winter Light* (*Nattvardsgästerna*, 1962), *The Silence* (*Tystnaden*, 1963), *Hour of the Wolf* (*Vargtimmen*, 1967), *Cries and Whispers* (*Viskningar och rop*, 1972), and finally in the TV film *After the Rehearsal* (*Efter repetitionen*, 1984).

Ingrid Thulin had a somewhat severe beauty, and however varied the characters she played, she always had an air of tragedy about her, and her roles often required her to suffer in patience. In the 60s, she also worked successfully with a number of other top European directors, such as Alain Resnais (*The War Is Over / La Guerre est finie / Kriget är slut*, 1966), and Luchino Visconti (*The Damned / La caduta degli dei*, 1969). Like other Bergman actresses, however, she often had less good fortune with other international productions.

Ingrid Thulin spent the last years of her life living in Italy. Her final film appearance was in Marco Ferreri's *House of Smiles* (*La casa del sorriso*, 1990), a study of the relationship between two elderly people in a psychiatric clinic.

**"Parts of the film shimmer with breathtaking virtuosity. Natural sound has rarely been used to such effect: a rumbling armored tank, a fan, a running faucet, a plane overhead, a gliding hairbrush, a gasp of anguish, all combine in a vividly orchestrated accompaniment to the drama. Dialogue is sparse, but Bergman's close-ups pry secrets from a human face with uncommon skill."** *Time Magazine*

and she lies down naked beside him when she goes to bed. And when Johan sets off to explore the hotel, he is also surrounded by sex: a Rubens painting depicts a faun pursuing a nymph; a troupe of dwarves dress him in girl's clothing; and an elderly waiter makes obscene gestures with a sausage.

At the end of the film, Ester appears to be dying. Anna resolves to depart, leaving her sister alone behind her. Johan, however, suddenly takes sides with his aunt – and embraces her.

As a sign of their secret understanding, Ester gives Johan a letter to take with him: "a few words in a foreign language." Thus *The Silence* ends with an enigma – yet one which Ingmar Bergman has interpreted quite positively. The director stresses the importance of the boy's attempt to decipher this mysterious message, for Bergman sees Ester as a representative of something "indestructibly human" – and the letter is her way of passing on this inheritance to the child. LP

4 Tower of Babel: An inability to converse in foreign tongues becomes a metaphor for communicative failure in general.

5 I love you… whoever you are: Anna pursues whoever takes her fancy, and Ester could strangle her for it.

5

# THE BIRDS

1963 - USA - 119 MIN. - THRILLER, LITERARY ADAPTATION

DIRECTOR ALFRED HITCHCOCK (1899–1980)
SCREENPLAY EVAN HUNTER, based on DAPHNE DU MAURIER'S short story of the same name DIRECTOR OF PHOTOGRAPHY ROBERT BURKS EDITING GEORGE TOMASINI MUSIC REMI GASSMANN, OSKAR SALA, BERNARD HERRMANN PRODUCTION ALFRED HITCHCOCK for UNIVERSAL AND ALFRED HITCHCOCK PRODUCTIONS.

STARRING TIPPI HEDREN (Melanie Daniels), ROD TAYLOR (Mitch Brenner), JESSICA TANDY (Lydia Brenner), SUZANNE PLESHETTE (Annie Hayworth), VERONICA CARTWRIGHT (Cathy Brenner), ETHEL GRIFFIES (Mrs. Bundy), CHARLES MCGRAW (Sebastian Sholes), RUTH MCDEVITT (Mrs. MacGruder), LONNY CHAPMAN (Deke Carter)

## *"Back in your gilded cage, Melanie Daniels."*

Just another one of her practical jokes? Actually all Melanie Daniels (Tippi Hedren), daughter of a prominent San Francisco newspaper publisher, intended to do was have a little fun with dashing attorney Mitch Brenner (Rod Taylor). But Melanie's arrival in Bodega Bay, hamlet to the Brenner family, seems to disrupt the natural order of things. Or maybe there's just something in the air... For something has certainly agitated the birds that inhabit the area and caused – as Hitchcock refers to them in a promotional trailer – "our fine feathered friends" to turn into bloodthirsty beasts. Like a bolt from the blue, the air strikes leave the town's community paralyzed. Is some kind of environmental catastrophe to blame for their strange behavior, or have the world's birds launched a counterattack against man's subjugation of nature? And is it mere coincidence that, at a local diner, an Audubon society member's soliloquy on the majesty of the avian world is underscored by customers ordering chicken and fried potatoes?

Hitchcock never offers explicit answers as to why the events in Bodega Bay have taken place. And despite its cut and dried plot, *The Birds* remains one of the director's most stunning and complex films. The degree of precision achieved in terms of special effects, prior to the computer age, beggars belief. Relying on actual trained birds, state-of-the-art mechanical replicas and hand-painted models, Hitchcock and his team created the perfect illusion of massive flocks of birds descending upon the fishing community. The picture's cataclysmic finale is a tremendous compilation of 32 individually photographed shots and painted images.

Hitchcock also makes continual use of an array of ambitious montage

1

“*The Birds* expresses nature and what it can do, and the dangers of nature. Because there’s no doubt that if the birds did decide, you know, with the millions that they are, to go for everybody’s eyes, then we’d have H. G. Wells’ Kingdom of the Blind on our hands.” *Alfred Hitchcock*

techniques. Such is the case when he cuts between the lone Tippi Hedren looking out of a window and scenes of all hell breaking loose. Seeing the action from her character’s perspective only intensifies the horror. The viewer is further disoriented by Hitchcock’s decision to do without music altogether (the director’s most esteemed composer, Bernard Herrmann, is listed in the credits as “sound consultant”). Instead, the dialog is enhanced exclusively by a fog of white noise, deadly caws and fluttering feathers.

The director pointed out the movie’s multiple metaphors on numerous occasions. Although the piece can certainly be understood as an apocalyptic vision, or as a portrait of the dangers of complacency, Hitchcock also considered it a parable of fidelity – as represented by the “love birds” Melanie brings with her to Bodega Bay. But these, in turn, are just as much a symbol of all things intangible and unpredictable.

But of no less importance is *The Birds’* study of one man’s relationship to women. Apart from Mitch, all the picture’s leading characters are women, each of whom represents a particular female archetype. First there is Lydia (Jessica Tandy), the mother hen who is afraid her son will take flight if she loses her grip on him – so she watches him like a hawk. This character’s

1 Getting the bird: Who would have thought that a trip to the pet store could lead to something like this? Tippi Hedren makes her film debut as Melanie Daniels.

2 Bird brains: As this Chekhov lovers' convention shows, *The Birds* was a great technological achievement for its time.

3 Attack of the flying rats: Mitch's kid sister Cathy (Veronica Cartwright) should have taken the bus to school today.

**SUSPENSE**

Just how to make your audience's heart pound from thrilling suspense is the subject of much speculation. Regardless of the recipe a filmmaker swears by, it is universally agreed upon that a key ingredient in creating suspense is establishing viewer identification with the on-screen characters. Citing a defiance of expectation as one of the phenomenon's key elements, Hitchcock once said, "I find that the easiest way to worry people is to turn the tables on them. Make the most innocent member of the cast the murderer; make the next-door neighbor a dangerous spy. Keep your characters stepping out of character and into the other fellow's boots." In addition, suspense often relies on the viewer knowing more than the movie's characters and being made to watch helplessly as they blindly step into the deadliest of situations. Hitchcock also asserted that viewer identification works best when the protagonist is an average, run-of-the-mill figure, stating that "to my way of thinking, the best suspense drama is that which weaves commonplace people in what appears to be a routine situation, until it is revealed (and fairly early in the game) as a glamorously dangerous charade."

This enables an artful contrast between mundane daily life and the drama of the depicted events. In a picture like *The Birds*, suspense automatically falls into place. After all, the viewer already knows that the piece is a thriller, even if the first 25 minutes seem more like a screwball comedy. Lastly, playing with expectations is an indispensable component for creating suspense, as is proven by Hitchcock's numerous and elaborate trailers, which are intent on sending viewers down the wrong path before even entering the actual movie.

carefree counterpart is Mitch's kid sister Cathy (Veronica Cartwright), who as the personification of innocence must be shielded from outside danger at all cost. The fact that Mitch treats her like his daughter intensifies the incestuous aspects of his relationship with his mother.

One of the women swooping in on his mother's territory is the lovely schoolteacher Annie Hayworth (Suzanne Pleshette). She, however, is beaten back, and after failing to establish herself within the family she becomes a tragic vision of a lingering and unsettled former love. Only Melanie has the power to clip Mitch's wings, as she demonstrates over the course of the movie by slowly taking responsibility for her own life and those of others. Thus, she is the perfect synthesis of mother, sister and paramour.

Whether her efforts are successful in the long run remains to be seen. Still, when Mitch, Lydia and Cathy, together with the pair of "love birds," drive off under the auspices of a clearing sky, we are left with a sense that love and understanding based on cooperation are still possible. Perhaps Melanie Daniels will be able to break out of her father's gilded cage and make a nest of her own after all.

SH

4

5

**"All you can say about *The Birds* is: Nature can be awful rough on you if you play around with it."** *Alfred Hitchcock*

4 Bird sanctuary: Hitchcock relished every moment of turning these seemingly harmless creatures into bloodthirsty predators.

5 A bird in hand… Mitch Brenner (Rod Taylor) tries to protect his house and family from the inexplicable phenomenon.

6 Ladybird: Mitch's mother believes that Melanie's arrival has disrupted the natural order and that she is to blame for the avian assault on Bodega Bay.

# CHARADE

1963 - USA - 113 MIN. - MYSTERY CAPER, SPOOF

DIRECTOR STANLEY DONEN (*1924)

SCREENPLAY PETER STONE, MARC BEHM DIRECTOR OF PHOTOGRAPHY CHARLES LANG JR. EDITING JAMES CLARK MUSIC HENRY MANCINI PRODUCTION STANLEY DONEN for UNIVERSAL PICTURES.

STARRING CARY GRANT (Peter Joshua), Audrey Hepburn (Regina Lampert), WALTER MATTHAU (Hamilton Bartholomew), JAMES COBURN (Tex Panthollow), GEORGE KENNEDY (Herman Scobie), NED GLASS (Leopold Gideon), JACQUES MARIN (Inspector Edouard Grandpierre), PAUL BONIFAS (Felix), DOMINIQUE MINOT (Sylvie Gaudet), THOMAS CHELIMSKY (Jean-Louis Gaudet).

## *"Why do people have to tell lies?"*

Attempts at imitating Hitchcock are infamous for exploding in the face of their directors. Oftentimes, his disciples miss the boat as to what he was all about. The farfetched, borderline absurd premises of Hitch's capers, along with his trademark (though often misunderstood) suspense, were employed as a subterfuge that enabled the British director to craft tales of comic, tragic and obsessive relationships, while still satisfying his appetite for the macabre.

That is not to say that every Hitchcock homage is a dud. Without a doubt, former musical director Stanley Donen (*Singin' in the Rain*, 1952; *Funny Face*, 1957) takes the cake for having filmed the most delightful of these, a zany mystery caper simply entitled *Charade*. The picture works because Donen and screenwriter Peter Stone made the wise decision to abstain from suspense and devoted their energies instead to recreating the story structure that had proved so effective in Hitchcock's 1941 *Suspicion*. The storyline in these two films constantly flip-flops between creating and removing doubts about the credibility of the male protagonist, in both cases played by Cary Grant.

For Grant's character remains totally innocuous for the duration of these movies, leaving the viewers at a loss as to how to feel about him all the way up to the films' conclusions. Does the financially down and out Johnny Aysgarth in *Suspicion* want to do away with his wife to get his grimy little hands on her fortune, or is he just a misunderstood but dear, frivolous man? Does Peter Joshua altruistically help *Charade's* indigent Regina Lampert (Audrey Hepburn) locate her late husband's misplaced fortune, or are his actions motivated by self-interest? Is his name even Peter Joshua at all? And what exactly is

1

his connection to the four motley characters eager to get their hands on th 250,000-dollar nest egg? Hepburn's Regina Lampert is herself rather suspe in the grand Hitchcockian scheme of things. After all, she has fallen in lo with a man she doesn't know from… well let's just say Adam.

Needless to say, the treasure hunt is Donen's "MacGuffin," the ter coined by Hitchcock to denote a pretense, which in this case provides f high-speed chases, romantic boat cruises on the Seine and infuses the st ryline with an air of mystique. *Charade* keeps its audience intrigued, adept waltzing between atmospheric tempos, switching from comic to macabre seconds, and allowing romantic moments to dip into danger.

A prime example is Peter and Regina's nightclub excursion, where th master of ceremonies forces the guests to partake in a painful icebreake

**STANLEY DONEN**

The career of Stanley Donen (*1924) started off on the right foot when the 16-year old dancer got to know Gene Kelly during the Broadway production of the musical "Pal Joey." Donen soon became Kelly's personal assistant, and followed his mentor to Hollywood. It wasn't long before he was choreographing many of the star's dance routines, including the well-known "alter ego" sequence from Charles Vidor's *Cover Girl* (1944), in which Kelly dances with his inner self thanks to miracles of double exposure.

In 1949, Donen and Kelly embarked on their first joint directing project with *On the Town*, the first musical to be shot on location in New York. The high point of their collaboration came with *Singin' in the Rain* (1952) and *It's Always Fair Weather* (1955). These pieces set the gold standard in integrated musicals, a genre that sought to seamlessly weave song and dance numbers which reveal the emotions and desires of the characters into the actual plot.

Donen's directing career continued to flourish without Kelly, shooting musicals like *Funny Face* (1957) with Fred Astaire and *The Pajama Game* (1957) with Doris Day. With the collapse of the old Hollywood studio system the genre began to fizzle out and Donen readily adapted to high comedy. In movies like *Indiscreet* (1958), *Charade* (1963) and *Arabesque* (1966) Donen delivered crowd pleasers reminiscent of his glory days. His brand of elegance was no longer in demand by the time the 1970s rolled around. Donen's last film project to date was *Blame It on Rio*. During his absence from film, Donen has kept active in both theater and television, staging musicals like *The Red Shoes* (1993) and episodes of the small screen phenomenon *Moonlighting* (1985–89). Most recently, Donen directed the made-for-TV movie version of the hit Broadway melodrama *Love Letters*.

**"Peter Stone, a new chap, has written a screenplay that is packed with sudden twists, shocking gags, eccentric arrangements and occasionally light and brittle lines. And Stanley Donen has diligently directed in a style that is somewhere between 30s screwball comedy and Alfred Hitchcock on a North by Northwest course."** *The New York Times*

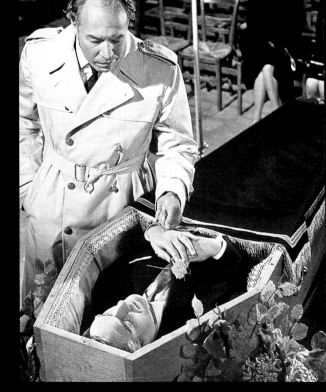

1 How to steal a million: If Regina Lampert (Audrey Hepburn) only knew, maybe she'd be able to locate her dead husband's cash.

2 Sterilized romance: At times it seems that the sting between these two will prevent them from ever coming together. Cary Grant as Peter Joshua.

3 A tisket, a tasket, a dead man in a casket: Herman's (George Kennedy) just making sure that Mr. Lampert isn't faking.

4 A simultaneous interpreter who doesn't understand a thing about the man she's head over heels for.

he object is for players to pass an orange from one teammate to the next without using their hands. What begins as an innocently amusing sequence – with Cary Grant on top comic form – veers into farce when Peter Joshua can't free the piece of fruit from a rotund lady's imposing bosom, and then waxes romantic as it rolls from his neck into Regina's, thus bringing the couple closer than ever before. No sooner have we set our hearts on intimacy than Regina is face-to-face with the next player, the unassuming Leopold Gideon (Ned Glass), who doesn't waste any time in threatening Regina's life. Nor do things cool off when the game ends. As Regina heads off to call the fly-by-night CIA agent Hamilton Bartholomew (Walter Matthau), Donen and Stone take yet another stab at the audience. Tex (James Coburn) traps Regina inside the phone booth and terrorizes her with burning matches. Despite this, the real culprit's

5 Where there's smoke there's fire: Tex Panthollow (James Coburn) will burn the truth out of Regina if need be.

**"There is Grant, explaining some dark problem of menace and greed, and there is Hepburn, interrupting him to put her finger on that famous cleft in that famous chin and ask 'How do you shave in there?' – which is, really, an interesting question."** *Newsweek*

5

6

6 Well, it's not in here: Cary Grant goes looking for loot in all the wrong places.

dentity remains a mystery up until the picture's finale. As Peter Joshua is uick to point out, the guilty party is always the person you suspect least.

*Charade's* punchy dialog is as erratic and irreverent as the absurd redicaments its characters find themselves in. And screwball extraordinaire ary Grant always manages to say the darndest things with just the right caence. Co-star Audrey Hepburn has no trouble holding her own in this regard. Having long shed her doe-eyed fawn image, the capricious queen of style efortlessly dominates the scene in Givenchy gowns. What a shame that her plans with Hitchcock to make *No Bail for the Judge* never panned out.

A tribute like *Charade* wouldn't be complete without a direct quote from the master of suspense. And Donen's reference to *The 39 Steps* (1935) was the perfect choice. Caught in a priceless close-up, we witness a hotel maid get more than she bargained for when she comes to make up Herman Scobie's (George Kennedy) room and finds him dead between the sheets. Inspector Grandpierre's (Jacques Marin) utter disbelief upon learning that the victim drowned in bed, sums up the spirit of the entire farce. For *Charade* is indeed "simply absurd!"

LP

# TOM JONES

1963 - GREAT BRITAIN - 128 MIN. - SATIRE, LITERARY ADAPTATION

DIRECTOR TONY RICHARDSON (1928–1991)
SCREENPLAY JOHN OSBORNE, based on the novel of the same name by HENRY FIELDING DIRECTOR OF PHOTOGRAPHY WALTER LASSALLY EDITING ANTONY GIBBS MUSIC JOHN ADDISON PRODUCTION TONY RICHARDSON for WOODFALL FILM PRODUCTIONS.

STARRING ALBERT FINNEY (Tom Jones), SUSANNAH YORK (Sophie Western), HUGH GRIFFITH (Squire Western), EDITH EVANS (Miss Western), GEORGE DEVINE (Squire Allworthy), DAVID WARNER (Mr. Blifil), PETER BULL (Mr. Thwackum), JOHN MOFFATT (Mr. Square), DIANE CILENTO (Molly Seagrim), JOAN GREENWOOD (Lady Bellaston), DAVID TOMLINSON (Lord Fellamar), JOYCE REDMAN (Mrs. Waters).

ACADEMY AWARDS 1963 OSCARS for BEST PICTURE (Tony Richardson), BEST DIRECTOR (Tony Richardson), BEST ADAPTED SCREENPLAY (John Osborne), and BEST MUSIC (John Addison).

IFF VENICE 1963 GOLDEN LION (Albert Finney).

## *"We are all as God made us, and many of us much worse."*

If you chance upon an abandoned baby, it's best to hand it over to the church. And if the decent Squire Allworthy (George Devine) had observed this ancient imperative, the pious prigs on his estate would have had a lot less to worry about. Allworthy raises the child as if he were his own son, and the boy grows up to become a notorious ladies' man. Tom Jones (Albert Finney) is the holy terror of rural England: there's not a country maid who can resist his blue eyes, and even the ladies of the land are in peril. Indeed, his great love is the beautiful Sophie (Susannah York), daughter of wealthy Squire Western (Hugh Griffith); but their romance is cruelly terminated when she's promised in marriage to the grim-faced legacy hunter Blifil (David Warner). The "bastard" Tom, at heart a very decent chap, is slandered and forced to flee. After a series of hair-raising adventures on the road – including a whole series of sexual conquests – he arrives in London, where he falls victim to even more intrigues, and to his own cheerful levity. And he's already o the gallows when the mystery of his birth is suddenly – miraculously solved…

Henry Fielding's satirical picaresque novel is a classic 18th centu text. Like many literary adaptations, however, the movie tells us less abo the period in which it's set than about the times in which it was made. As product of the Swingin' Sixties par excellence, *Tom Jones* takes its protago nist's erotic escapades and turns them into a bawdy, burlesque celebration the pleasures of freewheelin' freedom. One scene in particular acquired a almost legendary status: an amorous meal in which the participants stu themselves on oysters and apples before gorging themselves on each othe In its filmic language, too, *Tom Jones* is state-of-the-art, full of visual gag such as freeze frames, characters who turn round and talk to the camer

1

**"Now Britain's Tony Richardson has made the novel into an absolutely magnificent movie. The film is a way-out, wall-eyed, wonderful exercise in cinema. It is also a social satire written in blood with a broadax. It is bawdy as the British were bawdy when a wench had to wear five petticoats to barricade her virtue. It is as beautiful in Eastman Color as England is in spring. And it is one of the funniest farces anybody anywhere has splattered on a screen since Hollywood lost the recipe for custard pie."** *Time Magazine*

and speeded-up chase sequences worthy of Benny Hill. This movie had an unmistakable influence on Richard Lester's Beatles films – and on Clive Donner's *What's New, Pussycat?* (1965), which boasted Woody Allen as actor and scriptwriter.

That a classic novel should be freely adapted was nothing new; what was remarkable was the way it was done. Director Tony Richardson, playwright /screenwriter John Osborne and male protagonist Albert Finney were leading figures of Britain's Free Cinema movement and idols of an entire generation of Angry Young Men. Yet they practically ignored the socially critical aspects of the book and treated it less as a moral satire than as a sensua spectacle. The result turned out to be a huge box-office hit, and *Tom Jone* was rewarded with four Oscars. This was a bigger popular success than an of the three men would ever experience again.

It's amusing, and illuminating, to compare *Tom Jones* with a movi that's closely related thematically: Stanley Kubrick's baroque epic *Barry Lyn don* (1975). Kubrick bleeds out the comic exaggerations of Thackeray's nove by adopting a kind of slow-motion aesthetic; and seen from this perspective the change of emphasis amounts to a moral revision. *Tom Jones*, by contras

1 It's not unusual to be loved by anyone: And Tom (Albert Finney) doesn't care who it is, as long as she's ready, willing and able. Here, he's stealing kisses with Molly (Diane Cilento) the milkmaid.

2 Take a load off: Even Sophie's father (Hugh Griffith) has a weakness for the weaker sex. However, booze is his real foible.

3 She's a lady: What starts off as fly-by-night romance with Lady Bellaston (Joan Greenwood) quickly develops into something more serious. Whoa, whoa, whoa.

**JOHN OSBORNE**

English dramatist and screenwriter John Osborne was born in London in 1928. In 1956, he became famous practically overnight by creating the archetype of the Angry Young Man: Jimmy Porter, the main character in his play *Look Back In Anger*, quickly became an inspirational figure for the young generation in stuffy post-war Britain. Osborne's play was first directed by Tony Richardson, and from then on the two men formed a team that would play a decisive role in the socially-committed "direct cinema" of late-50s/early-60s Britain. In 1958, they formed a production company and went on to make three movies, all scripted by Osborne: in 1959, Richard Burton starred in the film version of *Look Back In Anger*; a year later, *The Entertainer* (1960) starred Laurence Olivier in another successful adaptation of an Osborne stage play; and finally, *Tom Jones* (1963), a period drama based on the novel by Henry Fielding, was a triumph for all concerned. It was showered with Oscars the following year, including a Best Adapted Screenplay award for John Osborne.

From then on, Osborne worked in film only sporadically. He gave a memorable acting performance as the gang boss in Mike Hodges' excellent *Get Carter* (1971), and he also played a supporting role in Hodges' *Flash Gordon* (1980). He died in 1994, shortly before the release of *England, My England*, an acclaimed biopic of the composer Henry Purcell.

4

4 A man's honor: Tom's uncontrollable sexual urges land him in the trickiest of situations. Let's just hope he's as apt at warding off jealous husbands as he is at waving his sword.

5 A pussycat with claws: When the dastardly Blifil (David Warner) won't take no for an answer, Sophie (Susannah York) hits him with her best shot.

**"Perhaps some will be embarrassed by so much bawdiness on the screen. But I find it too funny to be tasteless, too true to be artistically false. And, what's more, it should get a lot of people reading that incomparable novel, *Tom Jones*."** *The New York Times*

is a fast-motion fury of a film, cheeky, over-the-top and flagrantly in-your-face. One big reason for the movie's popularity is the panopticon of human gargoyles that populate it; by comparison to most of the characters he meets, Tom Jones is the picture of quiet decency. The supporting cast includes his treacherous taskmasters Mr. Thwackum (Peter Bull) and Mr. Square (John Moffatt), his conceited and envious rival Blifil, and the constantly-smashed Squire Western – who's actually rather well-disposed towards lusty, likable Tom, but can't have him messing about with his daughter. In every constellation imaginable, these and a host of other figures pop up all over the place, making the idyllic landscape of southern England a veritable pandemonium.

The still center of this turning world is Tom; and here, Richardson's film truly captures the spirit of Fielding's novel. Tom Jones, Nature's child, finds an essential balance between thought and feeling in his typically English struggle for common sense. His love for Sophie, who tolerates his faults, blunders and misadventures with noble equanimity, seems perfectly genuine; and in the film's rare lyrical passages, their feeling for one another is illustrated quite wonderfully. Tom Jones refuses to accept either the narrow-minded moral strictures of the rural gentry or the louche decadence of the urban aristocracy. And while this stubbornly healthy vitality brings him a very close encounter with the hangman, it also means a joyful free ride to the hearts of the ladies. PB

# DR. STRANGELOVE OR: HOW I LEARNED TO STOP WORRYING AND LOVE THE BOMB

1963 - GREAT BRITAIN - 93 MIN. - COMEDY, SOCIAL SATIRE

DIRECTOR STANLEY KUBRICK (1928–1999)
SCREENPLAY STANLEY KUBRICK, PETER GEORGE, TERRY SOUTHERN, based on a novel by PETER GEORGE
DIRECTOR OF PHOTOGRAPHY GILBERT TAYLOR EDITING ANTHONY HARVEY MUSIC LAURIE JOHNSON PRODUCTION STANLEY KUBRICK for HAWK.

STARRING PETER SELLERS (Capt. Lionel Mandrake / President Merkin Muffley / Dr. Strangelove), GEORGE C. SCOTT (General "Buck" Turgidson), STERLING HAYDEN (General Jack D. Ripper), KEENAN WYNN (Colonel "Bat" Guano), SLIM PICKENS (Major T. J. "King" Kong), TRACY REED (Miss Scott), PETER BULL (Ambassador de Sadesky), JAMES EARL JONES (Lieutenant Lothar Zogg).

## *"Gentlemen, you can't fight in here! This is the War Room!"*

The story was meant to be taken very seriously indeed – and it was written by a man who knew what he was talking about. In the 1950s, Peter George, a former officer of the Royal Air Force, published a thriller under the pseudonym Peter Bryant. Its title: *Two Hours to Doom* (in the U.S.: *Red Alert*). Stanley Kubrick had been considering making a film about the nuclear threat for quite some time, and when George's book was recommended to him, he knew he'd found what he was looking for.

Together with Peter George, he started working on the script. At first, they stuck with the dramatic tenor of the original novel, but as time went on, Kubrick was struck by the comic potential of the military subject matter, and he changed his initial plans. *Dr. Strangelove* became an absurd, coal-black comedy about the end of the world. It united the exceptional visual gifts of this brilliant director with the witty writing of the satirist Terry Southern – who was hired to work on the dialogue – and the unique presence of the comedian and character actor Peter Sellers, who improvised many of his own lines. Sellers' importance to this movie can hardly be over-estimated: not only did Kubrick entrust him with three roles; he even shifted filming to England (where he himself would eventually settle), because Sellers was in the throes of a divorce case and couldn't leave the country. In *Dr. Strangelove*, Kubrick sets out to thwart all our usual expectations. Right at the start, most movie-

1

goers will miss the customary musical accompaniment, as a disclaime announces: "It is the stated position of the United States Air Force that thei safeguards would prevent the occurrence of such events as are depicted ir this film. Furthermore, it should be noted that none of the characters portrayed in this film are meant to represent any real persons living or dead."

The opening titles show a sea of clouds and a bomber being refueled ir mid-air. And then we hear the music: "Try a little tenderness." In combinatior with the selection and editing of the images, this tender foxtrot melody transforms a complex military docking manoeuvre into a bizarre and comical ac of love.

The actual story begins at Burpleson Air Base. The paranoid Commander-in-Chief, General Jack D. Ripper (Sterling Hayden), sends a squadron o

## "Stanley Kubrick's nightmare comedy – the extra-ordinary story of a psychotic American general who triggers off a mass nuclear attack on Moscow!" *Film Review*

1 Watch the hand: Scientist Dr. Strangelove's (Peter Sellers) prosthetic appendage has a mind of its own. Don't go pressing any buttons now.

2 Oral fixation: General Jack D. Ripper (Sterling Hayden) mutters bizarre incantations about the mixture of bodily fluids and exhibits a fondness for phallic symbols.

3

4

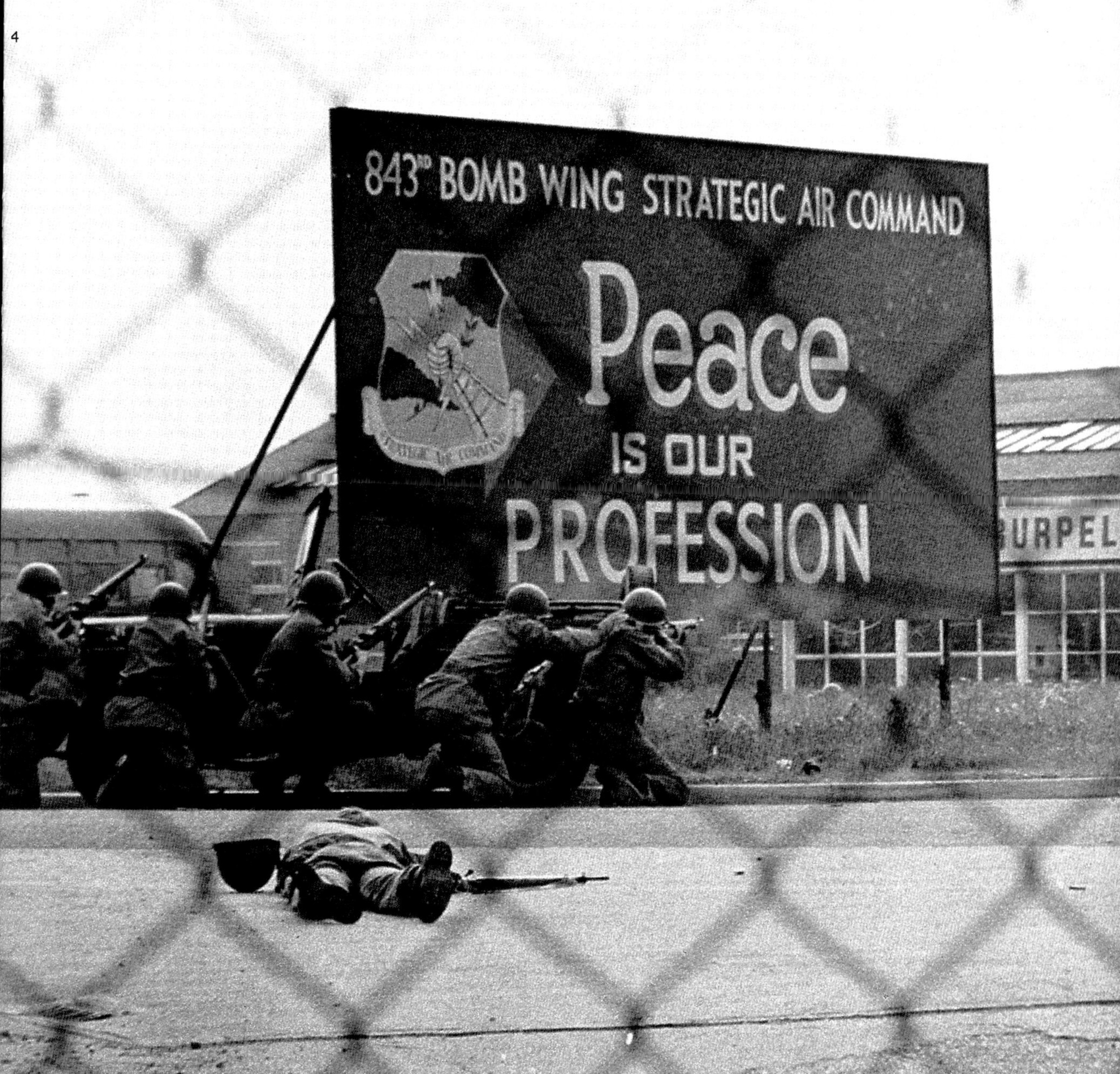

843RD BOMB WING STRATEGIC AIR COMMAND
Peace
IS OUR
PROFESSION
URPEL


3 Knights of the round table: President Merkin Muffley (Peter Sellers) causes an uproar amongst his generals by inviting red sheep de Sadesky (Peter Bull) to graze among his herd in the top secret war room.

4 Practice what you preach.

**GEORGE C. SCOTT** General "Buck" Turgidson is the hard-bitten antithesis to Peter Sellers' soft-spoken President Muffley. He is played by an actor whose "unique qualities" Kubrick once testified to in an interview. George Campbell Scott was born in 1927. After serving in the Marines for four years, he worked in a variety of provincial and college theaters before enjoying his first successes on Broadway. His appearances in the TV series *East Side / West Side* (1963–1964) made him famous coast-to-coast. Scott made his film debut in 1956, in an uncredited small part in *Somebody Up There Likes Me*, before going on to work with directors such as Otto Preminger, John Huston and Mike Nichols. He himself directed the TV production *The Andersonville Trial* (1970) and the feature films *Rage* (1972) and *The Savage Is Loose* (1974). Scott had a reputation for being "difficult:" one of his greatest successes was the film biography *Patton* (1969) – but although he was awarded an Oscar for his performance, he refused on principle to accept it. George C. Scott, a father of six, died in 1999. His son Campbell Scott, born in 1961, followed his father into the acting trade: moviegoers will know him from box-office hits such as *Dying Young* (1991) and *Singles* (1992).

"Once again, Peter Sellers demonstrates his versatility and fine comedy sense with three widely varied portrayals: A mild-mannered British liaison officer, the calm, serious President of the U.S. and the heavily accented crippled German scientist, who gives the film its title (certainly the longest ever)." *Box Office Magazine*

5 Bollocks! British group Captain Mandrake (Peter Sellers) goes into a frenzy upon hearing of mad U. S. General Jack D. Ripper's (Sterling Hayden) plan to launch World War III.

6 All very hush, hush: The Pentagon's phone call reaches General Buck Turgidson (George C. Scott) after wrapping up a flagrante delecto session with secretary Miss Scott (Tracy Reed).

7 Nothing like a little personality to brighten a place up.

8 Gripping the joystick: "King" Kong opts for a cowboy hat rather than flying helmet for his final mission in pioneering the great frontier.

bombers to the Soviet Union, seals off his airbase from the outside world and activates a special code that makes it impossible to communicate with the pilots. British contact officer Mandrake (Peter Sellers) has no success with his attempts to exercise a moderating influence. Meanwhile, a crisis team chaired by President Muffley (Peter Sellers) is meeting at the Pentagon. Despite the protests of the Air Force Chief of Staff Buck Turgidson (George C. Scott), the Soviet ambassador Alexi de Sadesky (Peter Bull) is also permitted to enter this military Holy of Holies. When de Sadesky and Muffley inform the President of the Soviet Union that his country is in danger, they learn to their horror that the Communist state is in possession of a "Doomsday Machine," which reacts automatically to a nuclear attack and cannot be switched off.

Muffley has no choice but to reveal the target coordinates to the Soviets, in the hope that the bombers can be intercepted in time. Mandrake manages to decipher the codeword and communicate the solution to Washington, and all the bombers are recalled – with the exception of one. The Russians have fired a missile at the B52 of Major T. J. "King" Kong (Slim Pickens) and destroyed his communications equipment. He is now unreachable, and still on his way. Though the damage to the plane is considerable, Kong is determined to accomplish his deadly mission. When the release mechanism refuses to function, he climbs down personally into the bomb bay. Sitting astride an atom bomb, he sets to work on the electronics. Sparks fly, the bay doors open and the bomb falls free – and Kong, happily whooping and waving his Stetson, rides off into the sunset of the world. HK

**"Dr. Strangelove's humor is generated by a basic comic principle: People trying to be funny are never as funny as people trying to be serious and failing."** *Chicago Sun-Times*

# THE LEOPARD

## Il Gattopardo

1963 - ITALY / FRANCE - 182 MIN. - HISTORICAL DRAMA

**DIRECTOR** LUCHINO VISCONTI (1906–1976)
**SCREENPLAY** SUSO CECCHI D'AMICO, PASQUALE FESTA CAMPANILE, MASSIMO FRANCIOSA, ENRICO MEDIOLI, LUCHINO VISCONTI, based on the novel of the same name by GIUSEPPE TOMASI DI LAMPEDUSA
**DIRECTOR OF PHOTOGRAPHY** GIUSEPPE ROTUNNO **EDITING** MARIO SERANDREI **MUSIC** NINO ROTA, with themes by GIUSEPPE VERDI
**PRODUCTION** GOFFREDO LOMBARDO for TITANUS, SOCIÉTÉ GÉNÉRALE DE CINÉMATOGRAPHIE, SOCIÉTÉ NOUVELLE PATHÉ CINÉMA.

**STARRING** BURT LANCASTER (Don Fabrizio, Prince of Salina), CLAUDIA CARDINALE (Angelica Sedara), Alain Delon (Tancredi Falconeri, the Prince's Nephew), RINA MORELLI (Princess Maria Stella), PAOLO STOPPA (Don Calogera Sedara), SERGE REGGIANI (Don Ciccio Tumeo), LUCILLA MORLACCHI (Concetta), ROMOLO VALLI (Padre Pirrone), LESLIE FRENCH (Chevally), IDA GALLI (Carolina), OTTAVIA PICCOLO (Caterina), PIERRE CLÉMENTI (Francesco Paolo), MARIO GIROTTI/ TERENCE HILL (Count Cayriaghi).

**IFF CANNES 1963** GOLDEN PALM for BEST FILM (Luchino Visconti).

## *"Things must change in order to remain the same."*

The year is 1860, and the House of Don Fabrizio, Prince of Salina (Burt Lancaster), is under threat. Garibaldi's troops have landed on Sicily, and the Civil War between the Republican and Bourbon armies has arrived, almost literally, on his doorstep: one of the King's soldiers is found dead in the patriarch's garden. Outwardly, he remains calm, even when his nephew Tancredi (Alain Delon) joins the forces of the Risorgimento. What's more, he finally allows Tancredi to marry Angelica (Claudia Cardinale), the daughter of the nouveau-riche Mayor, Don Calogera Sedara (Paolo Stoppa). For Don Fabrizio has decided to live by Tancredi's motto: "Things must change in order to remain the same." In doing so, he is not merely acting against the perceived interests of his own caste; he is also struggling with a profound conviction that the imminent change will be bad for all of Italy. Consequently, he refuses a position in the Senate. He attends a ball in a splendid palazzo, at which Angelica makes her debut in society; and he becomes all the more convinced that the order he represents is on its way out. Like common grocers, the representatives of the new ruling elite chat about the likely market value of the palace's paintings and chandeliers. It's apparent that the bourgeoisie is about to supplant the aristocracy and inherit its privileges. And now Tancredi, the opportunist, has joined their ranks; his republican ideals are a thing of the past, and he has entered into the service of the new king, Vittorio Emanuele. As the forlorn Prince makes his way homewards, he hears rifle salvoes in the distance: four followers of Garibaldi have been executed by the Royalis troops.

Here, as in all the films of his middle and late periods, Luchino Viscont portrays the decline and protracted death of a world he had loved. And although the aristocrat Visconti was a socialist by conviction, his sympathy fo the aging Prince is impossible to overlook. Don Fabrizio's authority is palpable, and in a real sense impregnable; it goes beyond political disagreement and class barriers, as if it were immune to the vicissitudes of time and history. But though the Prince thinks and acts pragmatically, his heart is racke with pain. His bitterness at the passing of the old order is revealed in th quickening and heightening of his language: "We were like leopards, lions an eagles; and our place will be taken by jackals, hyenas and sheep." Visconti' rejection of the bourgeois order – a long-term consequence of the Risorgimento – is in keeping with his sensuous surrender to an enchanted, sun-dazed Sicily. This is a country ruled by the sun; and as the Prince says, it's a land that for centuries has rejected all change. Visconti, the great stylist of th Italian cinema, has captured the essence of Sicily, its "lecherous stasis," in a series of landscapes and family portraits worthy of an Old Master. There is a kind of aesthetic shock in the sheer beauty of the decay this film depicts. The

1

2

protagonists often seem barely more animated than the objects they move among, as if they had come to life one last time before their final demise.

There was an eerie convergence between the subject matter of this film and the circumstances of its making. The novel by the Sicilian nobleman Giuseppe Tomasi di Lampedusa was a conservative reflection on the historical marriage between the aristocracy and the *grande bourgeoisie*; in much the same way, the Lombard Count Visconti also had to come to terms with Capital. In a manner amounting to blackmail, the co-producers Twentieth Century Fox insisted on having an American star in the leading role. Yet this turned out to be a stroke of luck: Burt Lancaster, at first eyed suspiciously by Visconti, gave the performance of his life, and their fruitful working relationship eventually led to two further collaborations. In return for Visconti's con-

**"*The Leopard* is not only a requiem for the past; it is also a celebration of a sensual world of high living and de-personalized ritual as recollected and experienced by a contemporary political artist. And, in some ways, Visconti allies himself with the old Prince of Sicily (a dignified, assured performance by a dubbed Burt Lancaster), whose decline is symbolized by a long and magnificent ballroom sequence which could only have been made possible by unlimited money and resources. This, then, is Visconti's most decorative and over-indulged work, alternately boring and seductive, cool yet passionate, and staged with a painter's eye for detail and color. It is a rich and troubling film; and for its director either an apotheosis or a point of departure."** *Sight and Sound*

3

1 Mouth to mouth: Angelica (Claudia Cardinale) practices youth's resuscitative powers on Don Fabrizio (Burt Lancaster).

2 Time marches on: Don Fabrizio's nephew Tancredi (Alain Delon) seizes the day and joins the rebellion.

3 An attack on the aristocracy: Don Fabrizio gets word that Garibaldi's troops have landed in Sicily.

4 Too big for his britches: Until now, Fabrizio has ignored his nephew's political aspirations. However, as his influence slips, Tancredi's opportunism becomes a thorn in his side.

cession, the American producers accepted the costly opulence of the settings without demurring; and this loving and ruthless attention to detail would become Visconti's trademark in his later films. *The Leopard*, however, is unique in its epic breadth and narrative energy, qualities particularly evident in the ball sequence, which alone lasts almost forty minutes. Indeed, the whole film was originally 205 minutes in length; but the producers subjected it to such radical cutting that the director eventually distanced himself from his own work, while threatening to go to court in its defense. An even greater disaster was the decision to print the film on cheap material made with inferior chemicals. The brilliance of the colors was lost, and the film failed to attract a large audience. In the mid-80s, a reconstructed Technicolor version lasting 186 minutes was released. This superb restoration also contained previously unseen passages, and *The Leopard* was belatedly seen in something approaching its original splendor. Yet, once again, Visconti was destined to suffer the same unhappy fate as Lampedusa: his masterpiece only achieved due recognition after the death of its creator. PB

**CLAUDIA CARDINALE**

Claudia Cardinale was born in Tunis to Italian parents in 1938. After being crowned "The Most Beautiful Girl in Tunisia" in 1957, she made her movie debut in 1958, playing alongside Marcello Mastroianni in Mario Monicelli's comedy *I soliti ignoti*. (In the course of a long career, comedy would prove to be one of her strong points, as she showed in Blake Edwards' legendary *Pink Panther* series.) After this successful start, she spent some time at acting school, before eventually following in the footsteps of two previous Italian Hollywood divas, Sophia Loren and Gina Lollobrigida. She appeared in *Cartouche* (1962) with Jean-Paul Belmondo, *8 ½* by Federico Fellini (1962) and Luchino Visconti's *The Leopard* (*Il Gattopardo*, 1963), and was world famous by the early 60s.

Even without her looks and temperament, her powerful voice alone would have made her the epitome of the feisty, hot-blooded Italian woman. She gave one of her most memorable performances as a beautiful widow fighting to survive in a raw man's world in Sergio Leone's *Once Upon a Time In the West* (*C'era una volta il West*, 1968). In 1982, she appeared alongside Klaus Kinski in Werner Herzog's *Fitzcarraldo*. Two years later, she was named Best Italian Actress at the Venice Film Festival for her role in *Claretta* (1984).

The 60s and 70s were undoubtedly the best decades of Claudia Cardinale's career. Even today, however, she still appears regularly in Italian and international film and TV productions.

# A FISTFUL OF DOLLARS
## Per un pugno di dollari

1964 - ITALY / SPAIN / WEST GERMANY - 100 MIN. - SPAGHETTI WESTERN

DIRECTOR BOB ROBERTSON (= SERGIO LEONE) (1921–1989)
SCREENPLAY SERGIO LEONE, DUCCIO TESSARI, VICTOR CATENA, based on the film *YOJIMBO* (1961) by AKIRA KUROSAWA
DIRECTOR OF PHOTOGRAPHY JACK DALMAS (= MASSIMO DALLAMANO), FEDERICO GARCIA LARRAYA EDITING BOB QUINTLE (= ROBERTO CINQUINI) MUSIC DAN SAVIO (= ENNIO MORRICONE) PRODUCTION HARRY COLOMBO (= ARRIGO COLOMBO), GEORGE PAPI (= GIORGIO PAPI) for JOLLY, OCEAN, CONSTANTIN.

STARRING CLINT EASTWOOD (Joe), MARIANNE KOCH (Marisol), WOLFGANG LUKSCHY (Sheriff John Baxter), JOSÉ CALVO (Silvanito), JOHN WELLES (= GIAN MARIA VOLONTÉ) (Ramon Rojo), SIEGHARDT RUPP (Esteban Rojo), ANTONIO PRIETO (Benito Rojo), MARGARITA LOZANO (Consuela Baxter), JOSEF EGGER (Piripero), DANIEL MARTIN (Julian), BRUNO CAROTENUTO (Antonio Baxter), BENITO STEFANELLI (Rubio), RICHARD STUYVESANT (= MARIO BREGA) (Chico), FREDY ARCO (Jesus).

***"Crazy bellringer was right, there's money to be made in a place like this."***

The hero appears from nowhere, and the locals call him "Joe," like any other stranger who refuses to divulge his real name. This particular Joe (Clint Eastwood) is only prepared to reveal this much: he's come to earn himself a few dollars. And in the moribund Mexican town of San Miguel, conditions are ideal for him: two rival families share control over this desert settlement close to the U.S. border. The Baxters and the Rojos live from smuggling, each of them employing a small army of real baddies who'll do just about anything if the price is right.

San Miguel offers the perfect environment for a soldier of fortune like Joe, and when he's given a chilly welcome by three local slobs, he quickly provides proof of his talent. He insists that they apologize to his mule. The hicks respond, unwisely, by grinning; and immediately they're dead, followed in short order by one of their buddies. Joe apologizes politely to the undertaker, from whom he had ordered three coffins: "My mistake – four coffins."

After a display like that, the Rojos are more than happy to give Joe a job. But he has no intention of serving one side exclusively. He keeps his eyes peeled and his ears to the ground, assesses the lie of the land, and begins to play the two families off against each other. For a long time, he has everything under control; until he follows a whim, takes pity on the young mother Marisol (Marianne Koch), who's kept like a slave by Ramon Rojo (John Welles) – and sets her free. Ramon's vengeance is terrible, and he has Joe beaten to a bloody pulp. With his last ounce of life, the battered hero manages to escape, smuggled out of the city in a coffin by the weird gravedigger Piripero (Josef Egger).

Joe hides out in an old mine. With the help of the saloon owner Silvanito (José Calvo), he gradually recovers his strength. One day, while practicing his sharp-shooting, he suddenly has a brainstorm: he constructs an iron breastplate, which he conceals under his poncho. Thus armored, he returns to face the rifle-wielding Ramon, who is now powerless to resist him. Each shot Ramon fires sends Joe crashing to the ground; but to the astonishment of the assembled spectators, he just won't stay down. Soon, the apparently invulnerable avenger is so close to Ramon and his henchmen that they're

1

# "It was stoicism against comedic things. It was comedy and yet it was played dead straight. I personally don't think of it as violent, only, perhaps, as black humor." *Clint Eastwood*

1 A fist full of lovin': Clint Eastwood as Joe and German jujube Marianne Koch as Marisol.

2 Powder keg action: Ramon Rojo had Silvanito (José Calvo) tortured to get him to reveal the whereabouts of the outsider. The quarry is shot down on Main Street, but he refuses to let a few scraps of lead keep him down.

within range of his revolver – and Ramon is out of bullets. Joe gives him a chance to reload… and still wins out in the end. After an extended death agony, Ramon bites the dust. The Rojos are in possession of a pile of gold stolen from some government troops after a massacre; Joe takes the loot, entrusts it to Juanito, tells him to return it to its rightful owners – and rides off into the sunset.

Like his protagonist Joe, Sergio Leone was a soldier of fortune. He took on his first Western after making several historical dramas, and he began work on the production without having secured the financing. Indeed, he hadn't even acquired the rights to the story, which was based on Akira Kurosawa's Samurai film *Yojimbo* (1961). Nor could Leone afford a well-known American leading actor; and even a little-known TV star like Clint Eastwood would have been too expensive for him if he hadn't taken a fancy to the script. For $15,000 and a ticket to Spain for himself and his wife Maggie, Clint accepted the part – and wrote Western history. When the money-men saw the first rushes, they expected Leone's low-budget production to flop, but

**SPAGHETTI WESTERN**

In the period around 1962, European directors of popular cinema began to take an interest in that most essentially American of genres: the Western. The Germans produced films based on the adventure novels of Karl May, simple Cowboy-and-Indian tales that seemed set in a child's dream world rather than any recognizable version of the American West. In Italy too, they were polishing up their saddles. Around 25 low-budget, low-quality Westerns were already doing the rounds when Sergio Leone appeared with more than a fistful of new ideas. Filming took place in Spain, in a region around Almería with a landscape that resembled parts of Mexico. Technicians and extras were cheap here – until the success of *A Fistful of Dollars* (*Per un pugno di dollari,* 1964) changed everything. Between 1963 and 1965, more than 130 Italian Westerns were completed, some of them multinational co-productions, and most of them made in Spain. For a short period, the Spanish film industry flourished, and even Hollywood made use of it for productions such as *Patton* (1969).

Leone's style was influential, from the laconic quality of his heroes to the stylized celebration of typical Western rituals and the slow, extended run-up to the climax. The distinctive character of these movies was also enhanced by Ennio Morricone's innovative music. Leone's "Man Without a Name" is notable for his sardonic humor; and at the end of the 60s, this blackly comic style became father to a whole school of films. In Western comedies that might be described as earthy or even gross (*I quattro dell' ave Maria*, 1968), Terence Hill alias Mario Girotti and Bud Spencer alias Carlo Pedersoli became European stars. The grim, nihilistic worldview of the original Spaghetti Westerns eventually devolved into another genre that became highly popular in Italy: the mercenary film.

3 Horseman of the Apocalypse: As Joe arrives in San Miguel, a mysterious stranger rides up to him. In turns out to be a corpse with a sign pinned to him reading "Adios Amigo."

4 A son's crusade: When the kidnapped Marisol is to be freed in exchange for Antonio Baxter, her son Jesus (Fredy Arco) is off to the rescue.

5 Circles of hell: While attempting to escape an inferno, John (Wolfgang Lukschy) and Antonio Baxter (Bruno Carotenuto) get caught in the Rojos' crossfire.

*A Fistful of Dollars* established the sub-genre of the Spaghetti Western. It was imitated by countless directors, and even had an effect on Hollywood.

Leone augmented the format of the traditional Western with influences from Europe and the Far East, adopted both the plot and the laconic protagonist's Samurai mentality from Kurosawa, and topped it all off with the humor of Commedia dell' arte and the classical farce. While the heroes of the Hollywood Western were immaculate in every sense of the word, Leone's central character is a filthy, sweat-stained, rapacious pistolero who can witness any number of injustices and still shrug his shoulders and turn away. Only once does Leone permit his "Man Without a Name" to reveal a trace of feeling, when he intercedes to help the tormented Marisol and her child. And with this, the movie offered just enough sentiment to make Joe a figure with whom the audience – including the women – could identify.

Made for a fistful of dollars and premiered in obscurity in a small cinema in Naples, this seminal film soon succeeded in finding its own public. In due course, it became one of the most successful movies of the 60s. HK

# GOLDFINGER

1964 - GREAT BRITAIN - 106 MIN. - SPY FILM, BOND FILM

DIRECTOR GUY HAMILTON (*1922)
SCREENPLAY IAN FLEMING, RICHARD MAIBAUM, PAUL DEHN DIRECTOR OF PHOTOGRAPHY TED MOORE EDITING PETER R. HUNT
MUSIC JOHN BARRY PRODUCTION ALBERT R. BROCCOLI, HARRY SALTZMAN for EON PRODUCTIONS and UNITED ARTISTS.

STARRING SEAN CONNERY (James Bond), HONOR BLACKMAN (Pussy Galore), GERT FRÖBE (Auric Goldfinger), SHIRLEY EATON (Jill Masterson), TANIA MALLET (Tilly Masterson), HAROLD SAKATA (Oddjob), BERNARD LEE (M), MARTIN BENSON (Martin Solo), CEC LINDER (Felix Leiter), LOIS MAXWELL (Miss Moneypenny).

ACADEMY AWARDS 1964 OSCAR for BEST SOUND EFFECTS (Norman Wanstall).

## *"This heart is cold – he loves only gold."*

Sixties siren Shirley Bassey sings forebodingly of a man's stone-cold heart and his affinity with a certain precious metal; fragmented images of a female figure dipped in gold flash against a pitch-black screen: we are bid welcome in the world of Goldfinger, a scoundrel with a singular fixation.

Fireballs, high-speed chases and love scenes hint at the action about to explode in this early James Bond thriller. The third picture in the British secret agent series – Bond spoof *Casino Royal* excluded – *Goldfinger* is a shrine to Cold War hysteria. This time round, 007 (Sean Connery) is out to stop unscrupulous German super-criminal Auric Goldfinger (Gert Fröbe) from monopolizing the metal that shares his name and which was associated with so much economic and political power in the 1960s. To succeed, this modern-day Midas has come up with a diabolical scheme…

For Mr. Goldfinger intends no less than to wipe out the Western World's economy by detonating an atomic bomb inside Fort Knox, home to the United States' gold reserve and democracy. With the entire supply of American gold radioactive and worthless, the value of his own resources would skyrocket. A piece of cake, except James Bond tails Auric Goldfinger to the States and wises up to the despicable plan. However, 007's attempts to fill his colleagues in on the matter are foiled by Goldfinger's right-hand man, a femme fatale known as Pussy Galore (Honor Blackman). Not to worry; after a night of spiritual cleansing with our favorite secret agent, she awakens a new woman, switching sides and informing the American authorities of her ex-employer's machinations.

In *Goldfinger*, female characters are all too readily seduced by gold's luster. There are even a few who meet an untimely demise as a result of its sparkle. Jill Masterson (Shirley Eaton), for example, suffocates when coated with an ever so fine layer of gold paint. Evidently, regardless of what form it takes, this high-carat poison can reduce women to little more than paper dolls and film décor. Pussy Galore is the only exception. She too is initially transfixed by the lure of its immeasurable wealth and power, but her en-

1

2

1 The evil eye: Someone's watching 007's (Sean Connery) every move.

2 Rear window, revisited: Even during a stakeout, there's always time for a little hanky panky.

3 The Midas touch: Jill Masterson's (Shirley Eaton) body has increased in value.

**"There is an assumption – which you find, at quite the other end of the spectrum, in the Godard films – that we all know the clichés and can have a little fun with them."** *Sight and Sound*

counter with 007 changes all that. As the agent's prim secretary Miss Moneypenny (Lois Maxwell) might put it, after a girl lays eyes on James, the only golden trinket of any interest is a wedding band.

To the picture's male leads, gold is a means to an end, and to Auric Goldfinger that end is world domination. He enlists the aid of North Korean communists and is willing to put the lives of thousands of innocent bystanders on the line. His idea of a hostile takeover is gassing the opposition – literally. More central to the film's plot, however, is Goldfinger's intention to hoard as much gold as he possibly can and paralyze the global cash flow in the process. But James Bond, like Moses tempted by the golden calf, does not let all that glitters get the best of him. Instead, the secret agent is intrigued by the practical value of bullion which, during the showdown in Fort Knox, proves a vital tool in the struggle to defuse Goldfinger's atomi bomb.

Considering the era in which it was made, the film races across th screen at top speed, fuelled by countless audio-visual effects and the simmering sex appeal of its cast. The same can't be said of its one-time extravagant set, which today looks more like a relic that could use a good dusting

The picture's undisputed saving grace is its funny bone – especiall with regard to its hero. James Bond may appear to be acting in the name o God, but, in truth, he is a servant of her Majesty's economy. By current standards, his character's impeccable playboy veneer and compliance to passe gender stereotypes read like a highly entertaining persiflage of what was intended to be taken seriously ... very seriously.

PL

4 Nights in white satin: Bond is guaranteed more than just a few steamy rendezvous if he keeps sports threads like these.

5 Out of the frying pan, into the fire: Bond doesn't know which of these guys is the worse of two evils – German Goldfinger (Gerd Fröbe) or mute manservant Oddjob (Harold Sakata).

6 Cracker jack: Whenever he's in a jam, James counts on Q's nifty gadgets for a novel rescue.

**BOND GIRLS**

With the exception of Miss Moneypenny (played throughout the 60s and 70s almost exclusively by Lois Maxwell), most female characters who appear at Bond's side readily bare all for the British secret agent (played by Sean Connery). Teasing monikers that play up the hanky panky like "Pussy Galore" (Honor Blackman) and "Honey Ryder" (Ursula Andress) take the edge off the fact that all of Bond's beauties succumb to his charms without knowing the slightest thing about him. That's not to say that there's no price to pay for being a bad girl. Rosie (Gloria Hendry), Tiffany (Jill St. John), Kissy (Mie Hama), Bambi (Lola Larson), Tilly (Tania Mallet), Bonita (Nadja Regin) and many others all got the kiss of death after shagging 007. It almost makes one wonder whether it's more than just coincidence: for as everybody knows – all of James' actions are performed in the service of her Majesty. How else can we explain why 007 goes for someone as subversive as Pussy – a known lesbian in the Ian Fleming novel, *Goldfinger* (1964)? Too bad that Honor Blackman, who made a name for herself as Cathy Gale in *The Avengers* (1961–69), didn't get a chance to explore this aspect of her character in the movie. Still, much like her literary counterpart, it is a sexual awakening *à la* Bond that enables Ms. Galore to see the light and take her proper place in society. It was only in the 1990s that sexual tables began to turn in the super spy series. Ever since *Golden Eye* (1995) Judi Dench has stood at the MI 5 helm as Bond's no-nonsense superior. Slowly but surely, James seems to be developing a taste for the dominatrix thing.

# A HARD DAY'S NIGHT

1964 - GREAT BRITAIN - 87 MIN. - MUSIC FILM, COMEDY

DIRECTOR RICHARD LESTER (*1932)

SCREENPLAY ALUN OWEN DIRECTOR OF PHOTOGRAPHY GILBERT TAYLOR EDITING JOHN JYMPSON MUSIC JOHN LENNON, PAUL MCCARTNEY, GEORGE MARTIN, GEORGE HARRISON (Song "Don't Bother Me") PRODUCTION WALTER SHENSON for PROSCENIUM FILMS, UNITED ARTISTS, UNIVERSAL.

STARRING JOHN LENNON (John), PAUL MCCARTNEY (Paul), GEORGE HARRISON (George), RINGO STARR (Ringo), WILFRID BRAMBELL (Paul's Grandad), NORMAN ROSSINGTON (Norm), JOHN JUNKIN (Shake), VICTOR SPINETTI (TV Director), ANNA QUAYLE (Millie), DERYCK GUYLER (Police Inspector), RICHARD VERNON (Man on the Train), EDWARD MALIN (Waiter

## *"Are you a mod or a rocker?" "No, I'm a mocker!"*

It may be the most famous chord in the history of pop music: George Harrison's crystal-clear Gsus4th, struck from his 12-string Rickenbacker 360. This is the sound that introduces *A Hard Day's Night*, a cinematic memorial to the glory days of John Lennon, Paul McCartney, George Harrison and Ringo Starr – the Beatles. Just as famous as the chord, but of far greater significance for the future course of popular culture, is the film's title sequence, for it marks the birth of the modern pop video. With its unconventional camerawork and its bold, fast editing, the opening of *A Hard Day's Night* – in which director Richard Lester sends a hysterical gaggle of fans in hot pursuit of the four lovable moptops – had a huge influence on the aesthetics of the video clip.

By the early 60s, it was de rigueur for successful pop stars to make a appearance on screen. Elvis Presley had already done so with considerabl success in the 50s; and in England, Cliff Richard had had a couple of bi box-office hits: *The Young Ones* (1961) and *Summer Holiday* (1962). Wit *A Hard Day's Night*, the Beatles originally wanted little more than to boost th sales of their album of the same name. Thanks to Lester's unusual, semi documentary approach, however, the movie became a huge commercia success in its own right. And there was another reason why Lester's fil went down in the annals of pop music history: after their last world tour i 1966, the Beatles decided they would never perform live again. *A Hard Day'*

1

2

1 Listen to your elders: That's all good and fine, but when you've got Beatle Paul McCartney holding the younger end of the stick, maybe it's grandpa (Wilfrid Brambell) who should be listening.

2 Run for your lives! Four guys from Liverpool are about to change the world. The Beatles (from left George Harrison, John Lennon, Ringo Starr and Paul McCartney) were solely responsible for one of the first displays of mass hysteria in human history – beatlemania!

3 The exception proves the rule: Normally, it's shy guy George who has to fight off the fans.

4 British invasion. English director Richard Lester's fast-paced film caught the spirit of London in the Swingin' 60s and captured the heart of world audiences.

**"In *A Hard Day's Night*, the Beatles, in song after song, pay homage to the faith of love, and the faith connects them to something ancient, lending this topspin musical its near oracular beauty."** *Entertainment Weekly*

*ight* includes film of some of the best live concerts ever given by the young eatles, making it an almost unique document of contemporary musical story.

The film depicts 36 hours in the turbulent life of the Fab Four: hotel oms, recording studios, screaming fans, photo shoots, interviews, TV ap-arances and parties – and everywhere they go, Paul's grumpy grandad Vilfrid Brambell) is there to get in the way. Shortly before an important TV now, Ringo disappears, eventually ending up in a jail cell…

Subtle, intelligent and cheerfully subversive, *A Hard Day's Night* beauti-lly captures the early days of Beatlemania. Richard Lester's brilliant direct-g, Alun Owen's bizarre script and the natural charm of John, Paul, George nd Ringo embody and reflect the anarchic spirit of the times; and yet the film is paradoxically timeless. The Beatles would never again be so relaxed in their celebrity as at this time and in this movie – and Lester combines their incomparable nonchalance with Owen's dry and very British wit, and of course with wonderful musical intermezzi like "Can't Buy Me Love," "All My Lovin'" and "I Wanna Be Your Man." The Beatles of *A Hard Day's Night* are fundamentally different from those of the more serious Sergeant Pepper era, and their playfulness and irresistible good humor reflects the unbroken inno-cence of the early 60s. Soon, matters such as the Vietnam War would start to impinge on the world and its conscience.

Richard Lester had made a name for himself in 1959, with an experi-mental film lasting 11 minutes and starring Peter Sellers: *The Running, Jumping and Standing Still Film*. With *A Hard Day's Night*, he wanted to make

5 36-hour bowl cut: Lester's film is an original pièce de resistance – a docu-comedy or zippy mocumentary, if you will.

6 Jing-a-ling a-Ringo: To this day, drummer boy Ringo retains his reputation as the practical joker of the fab four. However, in *A Hard Day's Night,* the gags were more evenly distributed among the band.

7 Trump card. Wilfrid Brambell (left) gets the last laugh – or at least the biggest – when he's got Ringo wrapped around his little finger.

8 Honest John: By the time shooting began for *A Hard Day's Night,* the images of the individual Beatles had already become so ingrained in the minds of fans that the band started to spoof themselves, starting a great pop tradition that continued all the way to Spice World.

**"From its opening scene to the clever final credits, *A Hard Day's Night* is a remarkably exhilarating experience. It is the high note of rock and roll movies, and ranks as one of the most important British films of the 1960s."** *Apollo Movie Guide*

**THE BEATLES AT THE MOVIES**

*A Hard Day's Night* was just the beginning. John Lennon, Paul McCartney, George Harrison and Ringo Starr were drawn to the camera time and time again – even long after the Beatles had split up. After the TV series *The Beatles* (1965), the Fab Four made the comedy *Help!* (1965), the TV film *Magical Mystery Tour* (1967) and the psychedelic cartoon *Yellow Submarine* (1968), in which they dubbed their own characters and appeared in a brief live-action epilogue. Beyond this, Paul McCartney was the only one of the four whose ambitions as an actor remained modest: he made guest appearances in a handful of British TV films and composed songs and scores for movies such as *Live and Let Die* (1973). John Lennon, who had played a leading role in the anti-war drama *How I Won the War* (1967) focused his attention on his own projects, such as *No. 5* (1968) and *Two Virgins* (1968), which he produced and directed himself.

Richard Starkey alias Ringo Starr appeared in some wacky fantasy films, such as *Son of Dracula* (1974), which he also produced and edited *Caveman* (1981) and a TV version of *Alice in Wonderland* (1985). He also took on roles in *200 Motels* (1971), *Blindman* (1971), *That'll Be the Day* (1973) and *Lisztomania* (1975). George Harrison appeared only sporadically before the camera, and then only in very small roles. As Executive Producer of several films, however, he did play an active part in the revival of the British cinema. He stepped in to save the Monty Python film *The Life of Brian* (1979), in which he also appeared as a silent hermit, and he was also involved in the production of *The Long Good Friday* (1980), *A Private Function* (1984), *Withnail and I* (1987) and Nicholas Roeg's *Track 29* (1988).

**"The music video by which all other music videos must be judged. And none top it."** *Miami Herald*

7

mething more than your average musical comedy. This film was intended be an authentic portrait of a social and political phenomenon: the bur-oning power of youth culture in Britain and the USA. The Beatles and their ns represented a generation gap that would become increasingly evident in e course of the 60s. Young middle-class and working-class people no nger wanted to knuckle under to the political and psychological domination the "grown up" minority and the so-called Establishment that legitimized is system of oppression. The socio-political aspect of the film is admittedly less relevance today, but *A Hard Day's Night* still functions admirably as comedy. Owen's script gives some of the best scenes to Wilfred Brambell Paul's grandad, who functions as a catalyst for innumerable gags. Nor-an Rossington and John Junkin – as Norm and Shake, the Beatles' managers in the movie – are a wonderfully odd couple, and a bizarre replacement for Brian Epstein, the legendary real-life manager of the band. It's all topped off with some sharp and funny sideswipes at the bores and bullies of the adult world (Man on the Train: "I fought the war for your sort." – Ringo: "I bet you're sorry you won!" Interviewer: "Tell me: How did you find America?" – John: "Turned left at Greenland"). The film and its title song whipped up Beatlemania to new and frenzied heights. Shortly after the Beatles topped the charts with "A Hard Day's Night," Peter Sellers released his own version of the song, in which he declaimed the text like a Shakespearean monologue. His loopy adaptation entered the British Top Twenty in December 1965.

ES

8

# THE DIVIDED SKY

## Der geteilte Himmel

1964 - GDR - 114 MIN. - LITERARY ADAPTATION, LOVE STORY, DRAMA

DIRECTOR KONRAD WOLF

SCREENPLAY CHRISTA WOLF, GERHARD WOLF, KONRAD WOLF, WILLI BRÜCKNER, KURT BARTHEL, based on the novel of the same name by CHRISTA WOLF DIRECTOR OF PHOTOGRAPHY WERNER BERGMANN EDITING HELGA KRAUSE MUSIC HANS-DIETER HOSALLA PRODUCTION LOTHAR ERDMANN, IRENE IKKER for DEFA.

STARRING EBERHARD ESCHE (Manfred Herrfurth), RENATE BLUME (Rita Seidel), HILMAR THATE (Ernst Wendland), HANS HARDT-HARDTLOFF (Rolf Meternagel), MARTIN FLÖRCHINGER (Herr Herrfurth), ERIKA PELIKOWSKY (Frau Herrfurth), GÜNTHER GRABBERT (Ernst Schwarzenbach), HORST JONISCHKAN (Martin Jung), PETRA KELLING (Sigrid), JÜRGEN KERN (Hänschen).

## *"They can't divide the sky." "Oh yes, they can; the sky is the first to be divided."*

The opening shots are disturbing and impressive: a factory smokestack, filmed upside down so that the smoke belches out in a downward direction. On the extreme left edge of the shot, we see a tiny female figure collapsing; on the top right, a railroad wagon rolls into the picture, almost filling the widescreen format. Then the title sequence begins. We hear a deep, monotonous but strangely affecting female voice: "That summer, the city was breathing more heavily than usual. From a hundred factory chimneys, it exhaled its fumes into the immaculate air. The sky was suddenly peculiar and hard to bear..." When the title sequence has come to an end, we see Rita Seidel (Renate Blume) in her sickbed. We shall witness how her past quite literally catches up with her. "This is how the story began. A banal kind of a story, I suppose. And by the way: it's over now..."

Rita has collapsed after being left by her husband, a chemist called Manfred Herrfurth (Eberhard Esche). Not only has he dumped his wife, he has also abandoned the German Democratic Republic, even before Wall was built in 1961. While she lies in bed, Rita's past life is revealed to us in a series flashbacks. It's a very typical East German biography. Two years previous Rita, an office worker in a village in central Germany, had taken the oppo tunity to escape from her constricted existence. She went to the big c (Halle, on the River Saale) to study education, met an academic and fell love with him, moving into the attic apartment he rented to escape from h parents. For Manfred Herrfurth detested his father (Martin Flörchinger), a fo mer Nazi who had joined the ruling Communist Party after the war, and piti his mother (Erika Pelikowsky), a woman destroyed by an unhappy marriag

Herrfurth successfully develops a new technical procedure, but both th chemical industry and the ruling party resist and ultimately reject it. Th chemist has had enough; he goes to West Berlin to attend a congress, and h doesn't come back.

Rita visits him in West Berlin, but can't decide whether to stay with hi or go her own way. On a hot summer day, she experiences Manfred in th

1

unfamiliar environment of the West; her growing "social consciousness" has also increasingly distanced her from her husband. Her love for Manfred is not strong enough to reconcile two utterly different perspectives of the world. For her, the sky is divided. Rita resolves to return to the East – and collapses on the tracks at a rail carriage depot in Halle.

In the year this film was released, East German movies were still constrained by the principles of Socialist Realism, and most of the country's productions focused on safely historical themes. *The Divided Sky* surprised audiences in both the East and the West, for no one expected such a confident handling of such superbly photographed and edited images, such haunting music – guitar variations on motifs from the German folk song "Es waren zwei Königskinder" – or such an exceptionally detached off-screen commentary. Still fascinating to watch, the film is an absorbing parable abou peace and discord, solidarity and dissent, sharing and leaving, determinatio and ambivalence. Made in Totalvision – the East German version of the Cir emascope format – the film's images are symbolically charged visualizatio of these dialectical pairs. Depending on the moods of the protagonists, th city of Halle changes its appearance. Almost all the film's backgrounds ar dominated by streets, bridges or traveling trains – images of movement an meeting, arrival and departure, closeness and distance.

With its close aesthetic links to the French *nouvelle vague*, *The Divide Sky* was a DEFA studios production that took its place confidently amongs the artworks of the modern European cinema of the 60s. In this, sadly, it wa like ... other East German movie of its time.

# “There is no whole Germany, neither politically nor aesthetically.”

Filmkritik

**ONRAD WOLF (1925–1982)**

Konrad Wolf’s biography is in some ways typical for a German communist in the 20th century. Born in Württemberg, the son of physician and writer Friedrich Wolf, he spent his childhood in Stuttgart, where he was a member of the Young Pioneers, a communist youth organization. In 1933, he, his mother and his older brother Markus followed their father into exile in Moscow. At the age of 17, he became a soldier in the Red Army, fighting in the front line during the liberation of Warsaw and the taking of Berlin. For a few days in 1945, as a teenage lieutenant, he held the office of City Commander of Bernau; later, he would make a film about this episode: *I was Nineteen* (*Ich war neunzehn*, 1967). Beginning in 1949, Wolf studied directing in Moscow and worked as an assistant alongside Joris Ivens and Kurt Maetzig. Between 1955 and 1982, he directed 13 feature films as well as two films for television. From 1965 onwards, Konrad Wolf was a member of the East German Academy of Arts; from 1981 until his death, he was also a member of the Central Committee of the ruling Socialist Unity Party of Germany (SED). His brother Markus (Mischa) was Director of Intelligence at the East German Ministry for State Security – the Stasi. In 1982, Konrad Wolf died while making a documentary about the actor and singer Ernst Busch. In 1985, the film school in Potsdam-Babelsberg was renamed in his honor, and it still bears his name today.

1 No frills romance: A sense of detachment underscores Rita Seidel’s (Renate Blume) portrait of love in severed Germany.

2 Zero visibility: Above the rooftops of East Germany’s Halle, blue collar worker Rita and chemist Dr. Manfred Herrfurth (Eberhard Esche) close their eyes to class and social status.

3 East of Eden: The sequestered couple often resemble characters from a Russian novel.

4 Western whims: Love imagined has epic proportions, but there’s little capital behind the façade.

# THE PINK PANTHER

1964 - USA - 113 MIN. - COMEDY

DIRECTOR BLAKE EDWARDS (*1922)
SCREENPLAY MAURICE RICHLIN, BLAKE EDWARDS DIRECTOR OF PHOTOGRAPHY PHILIP LATHROP EDITING RALPH E. WINTERS
MUSIC HENRY MANCINI PRODUCTION MARTIN JUROW for MIRISCH COMPANY.

STARRING PETER SELLERS (Inspector Jacques Clouseau), DAVID NIVEN (Sir Charles Litton), CAPUCINE (Simone Clouseau), CLAUDIA CARDINALE (Princess Dala), ROBERT WAGNER (George Litton), BRENDA DE BANZIE (Angela Dunning), FRAN JEFFRIES (Cousin), COLIN GORDON (Tucker), JOHN LE MESURIER (Lawyer), JAMES LANPHIER (Saloud).

## *"If you've seen one Stradivarius, you've seen them all."*

A pink cartoon panther strolls through the opening titles. To the immortally silky sound of Henry Mancini's theme music, the cool cat yowls lustfully at the letters of CLAUDIA CARDINALE's name, purrs and rubs up against CAPUCINE and cheekily rearranges the letters that identify the director: ELABK SDRAWED. Blake Edwards' film begins with a wonderful animated sequence created by the former Warner Bros. artists Friz Freleng and David H. DePatie. Though it takes some nerve to kick off with such a jewel, *The Pink Panther* can afford to take the risk, for the entire movie easily lives up to the promise of the title sequence. It's simply a joy to watch.

Like a James Bond thriller, *The Pink Panther* begins with a lightning tour of the world, from an Arabian Nights' palace to Rome, Hollywood and Paris before settling down at the Italian ski resort of Cortina d'Ampezzo. Here, w meet a collection of glamorous guests: the Indian princess Dala (Claudia Ca dinale), owner of an immensely valuable diamond called "The Pink Panther the suave English gentleman-playboy, Sir Charles Litton (David Niven); ar last but not least, the French policeman Inspector Jacques Clouseau (Pete Sellers), accompanied by his enchanting wife Simone (Capucine). For the las 15 years, Clouseau has been pursuing the mysterious thief known as "Th Phantom," whom he's sure has set his greedy eyes on The Pink Panthe What the Inspector doesn't realize is that The Phantom is Sir Charles Litto himself – and that the villain's mistress and sidekick is none other tha Clouseau's own wife. Which explains why The Phantom always manages t

1

1 The hope diamond: Sir Charles Lytton (David Niven) has his sights set on Princess Dala's (Claudia Cardinale) prize gem, the pink panther, but can he bear the curse of Clouseau?

2 Positively bananas: It's not long before the aristocrat has gone ape over the rock.

**"It's not easy to sustain a fast moving-comedy for 113 minutes, but *The Pink Panther* manages quite well."** *Motion Picture Guide*

3 A knight in shining armor: As long as he doesn't trip over them first, Inspector Clouseau (Peter Sellers, center) will leave no stone unturned in his quest to apprehend the criminal.

4 Beauty meets butterfingers: They say love is blind, but they never send anything about it being klutzy. Inspector Clouseau and his enchanting wife Simone (Capucine).

5 A gala masquerade or a wife's charade: Simone Clouseau is mysteriously on the lookout for phantoms at the princess' ball.

ay one step ahead of the cuckolded sleuth. Much later, things finally come ) a head at a costume ball in the Princess' palace in Rome, with Clouseau nd his men hoping to catch Litton red-handed…

Billy Wilder once remarked admiringly that Blake Edwards (*Breakfast at Tiffany's,* 1961) had studied film comedy as if it were a science. This movie emonstrates that Edwards' studies weren't in vain. "The man in the ward-obe" is an old joke, a staple of farce; but here, Edwards doubles the fun in ne hotel room by forcing Mme. Clouseau to hide *two* men from her bumbling husband. Or take the marvelous nocturnal scene in a Roman market place: the night is silent and peaceful, until two cars appear, packed full of people in grotesque fancy-dress costumes, and race across the piazza. And in the midst of it all is a very old man, apparently quite unmoved by the madness around him. The climactic costume ball itself is a feast of absurdity, with Clouseau, clad in a clunky suit of armor, managing to set off the fireworks display indoors…

In Clouseau, Blake Edwards and the brilliant comedian Peter Sellers created an immortally funny policeman, whose sense of duty is exceeded

"Clouseau is reliably – chronically – clueless, yet there's something strangely touching in the stoicism with which he bears his fate. Peter Sellers embodies him as a kind of cartoon figure stumbling through the world of flesh-and blood humanity. Stiffly acrobatic, the Inspector emerges from each fresh disaster with a weird little skip and his dignity intact."

*Thomas Koebner, in: Filmregisseure*

6 Pretty in pink: Fritz Freleng and David H. DePatie's brilliant title sequence landed their lithe feline instant fame and his very own animated TV show.

7 Listening for clues: Little does Clouseau realize that his wife (seated right) is committing a crime of passion right under his nose.

8 The lap of luxury: Simone and Sir Charles have acquired a taste for the finer things in life, not to mention each other.

**THE PINK PANTHER – THE FILM SERIES**

Peter Sellers and Blake Edwards made four follow-ups to their original hit comedy: *A Shot in the Dark* (1964), *The Return of the Pink Panther* (1975), *The Pink Panther Strikes Again* (1976) and *Revenge of the Pink Panther* (1978). Each of them was very funny in its own right, but none could really match the brilliance of the original. After Peter Sellers' death in 1980, Edwards made three further *Pink Panther* films, all of them deeply disappointing. *Trail of the Pink Panther* (1982) drew on previously unused material; *Curse of the Pink Panther* (1983) managed to do without both Sellers and Inspector Clouseau; and in *Son of the Pink Panther* (1993), the Italian comedian Roberto Benigni played the Inspector's scion. In 1968, Bud Yorkin had already made a film called *Inspector Clouseau*, with Alan Arkin in the title role; it, too, was a flop. Steve Martin is currently casting a new version for a remake next year.

only by his incompetence. He can't pick up a telephone without knocking over the stool it's standing on. When he kisses his wife goodbye, she's left wearing his hat on her face. And he only notices a stranger has given her flowers when he actually trips over the vase. Clouseau is more like a character from the comics than a real human being, but he's brought to memorable life by Sellers' comic genius. It's manifested in a unique combination of physical insanity with a sparing palette of facial expressions, ranging from the deadpan to the hangdog and the vaguely nonplussed.

For the actual cartoon figure, the big cat from the titles sequence, this movie was the beginning of a wonderful career. His creators, Friz Freleng and David H. DePatie, developed an entire series for him: *The Pink Panther Show*, which ran from 1969 till 1978, and was reissued in 1993. HJK

8

# MY FAIR LADY

1964 - USA - 170 MIN. - MUSICAL

DIRECTOR GEORGE CUKOR (1899–1983)
SCREENPLAY ALAN JAY LERNER based on ALAN JAY LERNER'S and FREDERICK LOEWE'S musical of the same name and on the play *PYGMALION* by GEORGE BERNARD SHAW DIRECTOR OF PHOTOGRAPHY HARRY STRADLING EDITING WILLIAM ZIEGLER MUSIC FREDERICK LOEWE, ANDRÉ PREVIN (Adaption) PRODUCTION JACK L. WARNER for WARNER BROS.

STARRING AUDREY HEPBURN (Eliza Doolittle), REX HARRISON (Professor Henry Higgins), STANLEY HOLLOWAY (Alfred P. Doolittle), WILFRID HYDE-WHITE (Colonel Hugh Pickering), GLADYS COOPER (Mrs. Higgins), JEREMY BRETT (Freddie Eynsford-Hill), THEODORE BIKEL (Zoltan Karpathy), ISOBEL ELSOM (Mrs. Eynsford-Hill), JOHN HOLLAND (Butler), ALAN NAPIER (Gentleman at the Embassy Ball).

ACADEMY AWARDS 1964 OSCARS for BEST PICTURE (Jack L. Warner), BEST DIRECTOR (George Cukor), BEST ACTOR (Rex Harrison), BEST CINEMATOGRAPHY (Harry Stradling), BEST ADAPTED MUSIC (André Previn), BEST ART DIRECTION (Gene Allen, Cecil Beaton, George James Hopkins), BEST COSTUMES (Cecil Beaton), and BEST SOUND (George Groves).

## *"By rights she should be taken out and hung, for the cold-blooded murder of the English tongue."*

London 1912. Mayhem follows an evening at the theater as the streets of Covent Garden are flooded with rain. To wealthy patrons, it cues a mad dash to a waiting carriage or a cab for public hire to get home. To local flower girl Eliza Doolittle (Audrey Hepburn), who lives and works on these streets, it presents an opportunity to make a sale while saving her merchandise from the elements.

Little does she suspect that destiny is about to knock at her door, as speech and language scholar Professor Henry Higgins (Rex Harrison) also happened to frequent the theater that very evening. Having seen a production of "Faust," Higgins is about to turn art into life, playing Mephisto to Eliza's Faust, and making a new woman of her in the process – a lady if you will. He boasts to Colonel Pickering (Wilfrid Hyde-White) that if he were to teach this guttersnipe to speak properly, and rid her of her Cockney accent, he could pass her off as a duchess at the embassy ball. The Colonel calls the bet, and Higgins is compelled to put his money where his mouth is. Though the months that follow will prove both long and strenuous for Eliza, she has her sights set on success – and succeed she shall…

*My Fair Lady* is a musical that flourishes some of Broadway's most memorable tunes. Be it Eliza's first taste of triumph over diction in "The Rain in Spain Stays Mainly on the Plain," Higgins' plea to rescue language from abysmal degradation in "Why Can't the English Teach Their Children How to Speak?" the moonlight serenade of Eliza's suitor in "On the Street Where You Live," or the fond farewell Eliza's father bids his chums at his bachelor party in "Get Me to the Church on Time," Alan Jay Lerner and Frederick Loewe's masterpiece will have you dancing all night. Debuting as a smash hit Broadway musical in 1956, its impact spread rapidly around the globe. The musical genre was wholeheartedly embraced by cultures and languages that had until then remained impervious to its appeal. In German-speaking countries, for instance, it remains one of the most performed musicals of all time.

Eight years after lighting up the stage, the piece made it to the big screen. To secure the show's rights, producer Jack L. Warner had to pay the then astronomical sum of five million dollars. Several major Hollywood stars were courted for the leading-roles. Warner wanted Higgins to be played by either Cary Grant or Rock Hudson. He quickly changed his mind, when Grant said that he would refuse to even see the film if the part went to anyone other than the man who premiered it on Broadway, Rex Harrison. Harrison not only went on to reclaim his role for the film adaptation, he also won an Oscar for his performance. Likewise, James Cagney declined the role of Eliza's father, Alfred P. Doolittle, allowing another member of the Broadway cast, Stanley Holloway, to climb on board the cinematic production. Not a poor turn of events either as Holloway is one of the movie's greatest highlights.

1

2

There was one major casting upset. Rather than entrusting the part of Eliza to Julie Andrews, who had created the role on Broadway but had no film experience whatsoever, Audrey Hepburn was approached by Warner and signed on to the project. She was paid one million dollars for her services which, in the end, did not include singing – her voice was dubbed by Marni Nixon. Indeed, Hepburn is perhaps the film's one weak link. Hepburn's eternal radiance impedes our ability to ever view her as a flower girl, let alone a street urchin – she is a lady from the very start. On the other hand, a film that relies as much on its theatrical origins as it does on artifice can hardly be snubbed for a lack of realism. Director George Cukor along with set-dresser and costume designer Cecil Beaton created an intoxicating, vibrant candy-land, rich with intricate set pieces and meticulously orchestrated crowd scenes, the

1 The fairest of them all: From flower girl to an English Rose, Eliza Doolittle (Audrey Hepburn) is about to teach London society a thing or two about class.

2 Don't talk of stars burning above: In the world of love, Freddie (Jeremy Brett) still needs to learn that actions speak louder than words.

3 Pygmalion and the guttersnipe: Phonetics researcher Prof. Henry Higgins (Rex Harrison) wagers that he can fashion Eliza into a lady. Little does he expect that she'll make a man out of him in the process.

4 Wouldn't it be loverly: For now she dreams of having someone to watch over her, but she'll emerge from her sojourn with Higgins fully capable of taking care of herself.

**"Every night before you go to bed, where you used to say your prayers, I want you to say, 'The rain in Spain stays mainly in the plain' fifty times. You get much further with the Lord if you learn not to offend his ears."** *Film quote: Professor Henry Higgins (Rex Harrison)*

3

4

5

6

5 The crown jewel of the embassy ball: More dazzling than any diamond, no one would ever guess that Eliza comes from humble beginnings.

6 And succeed they shall: Professor Higgins and Colonel Pickering (Wilfrid Hyde-White, right) prepare to dance all night with the most coveted woman at the festivities – enter Eliza.

## "I sold flowers; I didn't sell myself. Now you've made a lady of me, I'm not fit to sell anything else."

*Film quote: Eliza Doolittle (Audrey Hepburn)*

crown jewel of which is undoubtedly the sequence at Ascot. Beaton received two well-deserved Academy Awards for his efforts, and Cukor, one of the great filmmakers of Old Hollywood with unforgettable films to his name, such as *The Women* (1939), and *The Philadelphia Story* (1940), was at last recognized for his work with a golden statuette. Noticeably shut out from the Oscar fanfare was Audrey Hepburn: she wasn't even acknowledged with a nomination. That year, the Best Actress Oscar went to none other than the "loverly" Julie Andrews for her first film – *Mary Poppins* (1964). HJK

**REX HARRISON**

The Oscar track record of Rex Harrison (1908–1990) is testimony to the adage that the pen is mightier than the sword. Nominated for his performance as Julius Caesar in the historical epic *Cleopatra* (1961–63), Harrison was soon honored with the coveted golden guy for his achievement as the pedantic Professor Higgins – truly the role of a lifetime. As one might gather from his histrionic ways, the career of Reginald Carey Harrison, who dubbed himself "Rex" (Latin for "king"), is rooted in the theater. As a teenager he appeared at local theaters. His debut in London's West End came in 1930 – the same year he made it to the big screen in Jack Raymond's *The Great Game*. Prestigious British film productions like Noel Coward's *Blithe Spirit* (1945) and the social comedy *The Rake's Progress* (1944) followed shortly after. Harrison then headed for Hollywood, playing the male lead in *Anna and the King of Siam* (1946).

He is among the handful of actors who managed to remain equally successful on the stage and screen. However, he always stayed true to his theatrical roots, and *My Fair Lady* (1964) was an ideal vehicle, allowing him to fuse these two artistic worlds. The endeavor met with wild applause. He was awarded a Tony for his stage portrayal of Higgins, which lasted from 1956 to 1958, and an Oscar for recreating the role in the 1964 film. Harrison is one of the great masters of light-hearted comedy. He penned his stage and screen memoirs in a book entitled *A Damned Serious Business*. A cynic might deem marriage his second career, as he walked down the aisle no less than six times (wives included Lili Palmer et al.). It should come as no surprise that "Sexy Rexy" was also one of the tabloids' favorite stars.

# HUSH... HUSH, SWEET CHARLOTTE

1964 - USA - 133 MIN. - PSYCHOTHRILLER

**DIRECTOR** ROBERT ALDRICH (1918–1983)
**SCREENPLAY** HENRY FARRELL, LUKAS HELLER, based on a novel by HENRY FARRELL **DIRECTOR OF PHOTOGRAPHY** JOSEPH BIROC **EDITING** MICHAEL LUCIANO **MUSIC** FRANK DE VOL **PRODUCTION** ROBERT ALDRICH for ASSOCIATES & ALDRICH COMPANY, 20TH CENTURY FOX.

**STARRING** BETTE DAVIS (Charlotte Hollis), OLIVIA DE HAVILLAND (Miriam Deering), JOSEPH COTTEN (Dr. Drew Bayliss), AGNES MOOREHEAD (Velma), VICTOR BUONO (Big Sam Hollis), CECIL KELLAWAY (Harry Willis), MARY ASTOR (Juwel Mayhew), WESLEY ADDY (Sheriff), BRUCE DERN (John Mayhew), GEORGE KENNEDY (Foreman).

***"Let me tell you, Miriam Deering, that murder starts in the heart, and its first weapon is a vicious tongue."***

In the remote Southern town of Hollisport, it is a rite of passage for children to sneak into local kook Charlotte Hollis' (Bette Davis) ominous plantation house. The old crone has the house all to herself. The only break in the monotony of her isolated life is slatternly housekeeper and sole companion Velma (Agnes Moorhead), who is loyal to her mistress but masks any sort of affection behind a shroud of sarcasm.

Far removed from the humdrum of civilization, the grand white mansion stands like an island in an ocean of overgrown foliage. Once upon a time, the estate was the crown jewel of a profitable plantation, built up from the ground by Charlotte Hollis' daddy, and, until now, it has still provided for Ms. Hollis' needs.

That is all about to come to an end for a dark day has dawned over Terra. By order of the law, house and lot are going to have to make way for a thoroughfare. Charlotte's property has been officially confiscated, though she refuses to give up her home without a fight. She chases the construction workers off the premises with gunfire. The Sheriff (Wesley Addy), an old family friend, decides to take a tactful approach. Temporarily postponing the eviction date, he grants the woman one last chance to evacuate peacefully. Should she not comply, he'll send in the cavalry and the bulldozers without further notice.

Charlotte, at a loss, enlists the help of her cousin Miriam (Olivia de Havilland). Velma has got a few harebrained ideas of her own, but Miriam is standing at their doorstep before she can adequately voice them. Aided by an old flame and doctor, Drew Bayliss (Joseph Cotten), she attempts to sooth Charlotte's nerves while gently breaking the news that there is nothing anyone can do to save the family plot. Velma watches the new arrivals like a hawk, observing how Bayliss administers heavy narcotics to a compliant Charlotte, distorting both her perception and sense of judgement.

On account of these shocking incidents, Charlotte begins to question the state of her mental health. Notes of a lullaby a past suitor once dedicated to her fill the night. Thin-sounding calls float through the manor. In the ballroom, Charlotte notices a severed hand, a skull, and a cleaver. Upon returning for closer examination, the objects are gone. Charlotte appears to be on the brink of insanity, especially considering her personal association with these gruesome artifacts. In 1927, her then lover John (Bruce Dern) was slaughtered in their gazebo, hacked to death with a cleaver by a killer who was never apprehended. His skull and severed head were never recovered. Charlotte's father had forbidden the espoused John all further contact to his daughter shortly before the tragedy. For 37 years Charlotte has lived with the belief that her father killed her beau, although the whole of Hollisport still assumes she is the guilty party.

1 The sweet life: As long as Dr. Drew Bayliss (Joseph Cotten) is living it up he's quick to ignore the afflicted.

2 Hush, little Charlotte. Don't say a word: The past haunts Charlotte Hollis (Bette Davis) like an eerie lullaby and make her doubt her own sanity.

**ROBERT ALDRICH (1918–1983)**

Robert Aldrich had a predilection for the rough and ready. In mysteries, westerns, sport and war movies alike, he investigated hermetic, male-dominated spheres that required a hefty dose of stamina from its inhabitants. His main characters, like the policemen in *The Choirboys* (1977), were usually tainted heroes. Pure-hearted souls with promising future prospects were a rarity in his pictures, a point illuminated by the title of his war movie *Too Late the Hero* (1969).

This motif, however, does not really do justice to Aldrich's body of work. His figures also included intricately crafted skeptics whose harsh critiques of the Hollywood studio system played central roles in movies such as *The Big Knife* (1955) and *The Legend of Lylah Clare* (1967). Director-producer Aldrich got his start in 1941 with RKO studios as an assistant director, gaining a board-side view of the field from filmmakers like Lewis Milestone, Joseph Losey and Abraham Polonsky. The film noir wave had a strong impact on Aldrich's initial directing work. A masterpiece in its own right, *Kiss Me Deadly* (1955), expanded and refined the style of the genre. Aldrich's directorial debut was a television piece produced in 1952, and he started working for the big screen just a year after. He often served as producer on many of his projects and even wrote three of the screenplays for his films.

The mystery is solved by the film's conclusion, and Charlotte, now completely off her rocker, is shown the connection between her living nightmares and the past crime. Director Robert Aldrich sends his audience to a first-rate creep show, complete with dramatic lighting and shadow effects straight out of Grand Guignol. The film's look is sharply contoured by spotlights that enhance the sinister black and white photography of the interior scenes. It makes for a gruesome backdrop, which, when underscored by spherical sounds, can leave the audience pale as a ghost.

Bette Davis, too, delivers a moving performance as an eternally grieving woman, fearful of being sucked into the quagmire of psychosis. Equally masterful is Olivia de Havilland as the introverted Miriam Deering. Although her character may initially appear good-natured, her underhanded ways soon present the fragile Charlotte with formidable opposition.

Interestingly, de Havilland was not Robert Aldrich's first choice for the role. The director wanted to strengthen the picture's association with another wildly popular Henry Farrell screenplay, *What Ever Happened to Baby Jane* (1962). It is therefore understandable that he originally hoped to shoot the movie with the woman who had played opposite Davis in *Baby Jane*, Joan Crawford. Crawford, however, had to back out of the project at the last minute due to illness. As a result, Bette Davis became the film's central focus and the legendary Hollywood diva transformed *Hush… Hush, Sweet Charlotte* into a veritable tour de force.

HI

"Bette Davis will long be remembered as the cranky, superficially tough, but really very frightened Charlotte, the scandal of the neighborhood, who sends unwanted visitors packing with a shot gun, at times completely insane, at others toughly resilient, and always loveable and sad!" *films and filming*

4

3

3 The twist: Is Miriam Deering (Olivia de Havilland) dancing with death, or is there more to this scene than meets the eye?

4 Lullaby and goodnight: Anyone who disturbs Charlotte's beauty sleep will have to answer to the mistress' loyal servant Velma (Agnes Moorehead, left).

# ZORBA THE GREEK

## Alexis Sorbas

1964 - GREECE - 142 MIN. - DRAMA, LITERARY ADAPTATION

DIRECTOR MICHAEL CACOYANNIS (*1922)
SCREENPLAY MICHAEL CACOYANNIS DIRECTOR OF PHOTOGRAPHY WALTER LASSALLY EDITING MICHEL CACOYANNIS MUSIC MIKIS THEODORAKIS
PRODUCTION MICHAEL CACOYANNIS for 20TH CENTURY FOX, CACOYANNIS, ROCHLEY.

STARRING ANTHONY QUINN (Alexis Zorba), ALAN BATES (Basil), IRENE PAPAS (Widow), LILA KEDROVA (Madame Hortense), ANNA KYRIAKOU (Soul), ELENI ANOUSAKI (Lola), YORGO VOYAGIS (Pavlo), TAKIS EMMANUEL (Manolakas), GEORGE FOUNDAS (Mavrandoni), SOTIRIS MOUSTAKAS (Mimithos).

ACADEMY AWARDS 1964 OSCARS for BEST SUPPORTING ACTRESS (Lila Kedrova), BEST CINEMATOGRAPHY (Walter Lassally), and BEST ART DIRECTION (Vassilis Fotopoulos).

## *"Do all your books tell you anything about death?"*

An awkward-looking young Englishman is sitting in the waiting room of a Greek ferry company. Basil (Alan Bates) is a writer, and he is waiting for the boat that will take him to Crete. Suddenly, he hears a child scream. He looks up from his book, and twists round in his seat to find out what's happening at the entrance. The subjective camera shows us what he sees: the face of a man behind the bulls-eye windowpane. It's Alexis Zorba (Anthony Quinn). Almost as if the child's cry had ignited the writer's imagination and called the stranger into existence, Zorba the Greek steps into the film and turns immediately to the dumbfounded Englishman. This will be the start of a beautiful friendship.

*Zorba the Greek* is a naturalistic drama about two men whose background and character could hardly be more different. Director Michael Cacoyannis tells the story in beautifully stylized black and white images, with impressive shots of the sparse Cretan landscape and memorable close-ups of the protagonists. Tempering this "Italian neorealist" style, however, are the sequences that depict – in an almost documentary manner – the archaic life of the village and its religious rites. The movie artfully combines these two stylistic approaches, crosscutting one kind of image with another in a series of seamless transitions. The end result is a strange yet unified and highly idiosyncratic pictorial and fictional form.

1

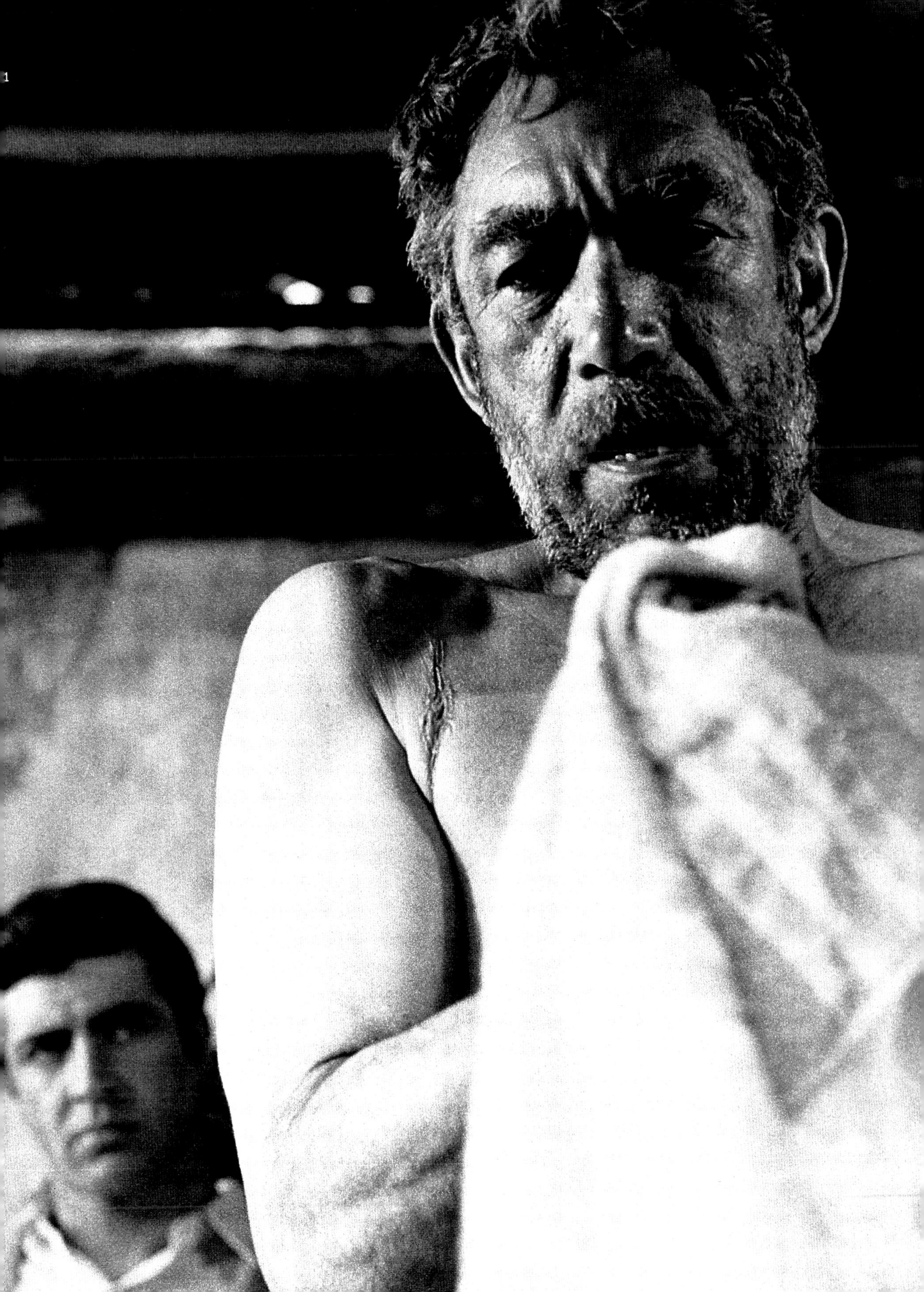

1 That's Greek to me: Shy and bookish Englishman Basil (Alan Bates) embarks on a friendship with the wise and gregarious Zorba (Anthony Quinn).

2 I love you this much: A friendship burgeons between the two men, which crosses cultural lines and is symbolized by the sirtaki, a traditional Greek folk dance.

3 Wolf in Greek's clothing: The irresistibly unkempt Anthony Quinn was emblazoned in the minds of audiences as the quintessential Greek.

**"Zorba is the epitome of Mediterranean vitality: a macho; a magnificent beast. His unforgettable dance on the beach to the music of Mikis Theodorakis has by now acquired an almost mythical status. No Greek in the cinema has ever been as Greek as this half-Irish, half-Mexican American."** *Der Tagesspiegel*

**ANTONIO RUDOLFO QUINN (1915–2001)**

Quinn was born in the turmoil of the Mexican revolution, with his parents fighting passionately on the side of Sancho Panza. His mother was of Aztec descent, his father Irish, and the Quinn family lived in very modest circumstances. Later, they moved to Texas, before eventually landing in Los Angeles. Quinn was only ten years old when his father died; and from then on, he danced his own life. In later years, he wrote two sets of memoirs, one of which was entitled *One Man Tango.*

In the mid-30s, Quinn began working in the major studios with Cecil B. DeMille. His early roles included a Cheyenne Indian in *The Plainsman* (1936) and a gangster in *Night Waitress* (1936). Shortly thereafter, he married DeMille's daughter. She would not be the only woman in his life. With his dark, angular face, high cheekbones and bushy eyebrows, Quinn was destined to play exotic villains of all kinds. Indeed, he was rarely permitted to play a white man, but had to take on the role of the eternal foreigner. He was frequently cast as a pirate. In the early 50s, Elia Kazan taught him the elements of the Method on Broadway, and Hollywood took a fresh interest in this rebellious, ungovernable and highly physical actor.

*Viva Zapata!* (1951) marked Quinn's big breakthrough. For his performance as Eufemio – the brother of Zapata, who was played by Marlon Brando – he was awarded his first Oscar. Fellini cast him as the Great Zampano in *La Strada* (1954) – and Anthony Quinn was a star. He played the shipping tycoon Aristotle Onassis in two separate productions; and having already embodied Zorba unforgettably, he was soon the most famous "Greek" in Hollywood. As one critic noted: "No real Greek has ever looked so Greek on the screen as this American actor." Quinn made more than 150 movies, fathered 13 children (the last in 1996) and won two Oscars, the second for his role as Paul Gauguin in Vincente Minnelli's Van Gogh biopic, *Lust for Life* (1956). To call him larger than life is no more than the plain truth.

Basil is a bookish chap with firm views on morality, and he's used to eeping a lid on his feelings. Underneath the diffident and slightly prim surace, however, things are in utter turmoil. He's suffering from writer's block nd hasn't put pen to paper in months. And as he's inherited a house and a oalmine on Crete, he's decided a change of scenery may be just what he eeds to regain his productivity and peace of mind. Alexis Zorba, too, is a nan in search of happiness. No longer young, but brimming with vitality, the reek never lets Basil forget that real life has nothing to do with the world of ooks. Zorba approaches life directly, spontaneously and sensually. He can nd a solution to any problem, he works like a horse, he's funny, he can hold is drink, he's a great lover and he can dance a fair sirtaki at the drop of hat.

In this film, dance is a metaphor for life itself. Initially shy, reserved and a little prim, Basil gradually thaws out under the influence of Zorba; and eventually, he learns to give free reign to his feelings. One evening, he visits the beautiful young widow played by Irene Papas, and spends the night with her. The catastrophe is not long in coming; despairing at losing the young widow to the Englishman, the tavern owner's son drowns himself in the sea. According to the ancient moral code of the village, the widow is guilty of betrayal – and the tavern owner avenges his dead son by slitting her throat.

There is a second woman in this film: Madame Hortense (Lila Kedrova), who is neither a real part of the village community nor a true outsider. Madame Hortense is a former bar hostess who has ended up living on the is-

3

4

4 My big fat Greek widow: Village beauty (Irene Papas) loses husband and 30 kilo...

5 Fast and furious: A night of romance sets off a rampage that ends in the svelte widow's early demise.

6 The goose that laid the golden Greek: Lila Kedrova (Madame Hortense) proves to Zorba that she's an oldie but goody.

**"Zorba has a great zest for life – drinks hard, wenches hard, and dances when he is feeling high or low. And he has a primitive's guarantee of true wisdom in his suspicion of book learning. 'Do all your books tell you anything about death?' he asks Basil, the young man whom he is initiating into his the mysteries of real living. 'They tell about the agony of not knowing the answer,' says Basil, in one of his less sufferably pompous moments. 'I spit on the agony,' is Zorba's retort. He must, therefore, be a philosopher."** *Newsweek*

land. Her best days are long gone, and eventually she dies. Within seconds of her demise, the villagers have divided up all her worldly goods amongst them. It's a weird, ecstatic, jubilant carnival scene, with the people dressed up in Hortense's gaudy clothes, and it contains one of the film's essential messages: life and death are indivisible, change is natural and inevitable, and all is contained within the ever-flowing river of time. It's like the principle of the film itself: images in constant movement, for as long as the tape lasts and a light source is available. As Zorba himself puts it: "A man needs a little madness or else he never dares to cut the rope and be free." At the end of the film, Basil has absorbed and understood Zorba's message – and under his tutelage, he even learns to dance the sirtaki. SR

# THE PAWNBROKER

1964 - USA - 111 MIN. - DRAMA

**DIRECTOR** SIDNEY LUMET (*1924)
**SCREENPLAY** DAVID FRIEDKIN, MORTON FINE, based on the novel of the same name by EDWARD WALLANT
**DIRECTOR OF PHOTOGRAPHY** BORIS KAUFMAN **EDITING** RALPH ROSENBLUM **MUSIC** QUINCY JONES **PRODUCTION** ROGER LEWIS, PHILIP LANGNER for LANDAU-UNGER-PAWNBROKER.

**STARRING** ROD STEIGER (Sol Nazerman), GERALDINE FITZGERALD (Marilyn Birchfield), BROCK PETERS (Rodriguez), JAIME SANCHEZ (Jesus Ortiz), THELMA OLIVER (Ortiz's girlfriend), MARKETA KIMBRELL (Tessie), BARUCH LUMET (Mendel), JUANO HERNANDEZ (Mr. Smith), LINDA GEISER (Ruth Nazerman), NANCY R. POLLOCK (Bertha).

**IFF BERLIN 1964** SILVER BEAR for BEST ACTOR (Rod Steiger).

## *"Please, stay out of my life."*

Sol Nazerman (Rod Steiger) is no longer there. He is a Jewish professor from Leipzig whose wife and children were murdered by the Nazis in a concentration camp. Twenty-five years have gone by since then. He now lives in New York and runs a pawnbroker's shop in Spanish Harlem. More significant than his physical separation from the European catastrophe is his utter alienation from the people around him. Most of those who visit his shop are unhappy, even desperate, but Nazerman is unmoved by their tales. For him, humanity is worthless, uninteresting; and he has long since repressed the fact that his business is actually in the hands of Rodriguez (Brock Peters), a black pimp and gangster who uses the pawnbroker to launder his dirty money. Sol Nazerman stands behind the barred counter of his pawnbroker's shop like a caged prisoner. His world has shrunk and grown dark.

Rod Steiger's embodiment of this quietly anguished but often distinctly dislikeable man is perhaps the most impressive performance he ever gave and it earned him the Silver Bear as Best Actor at the Berlin Film Festival in 1964. But the acting isn't all of it; director Sidney Lumet and cameraman Boris Kaufman evoke the city as a grim and pitiless place where even the sunshine carries no warmth, but merely serves to make the black and white contrasts all the more caustic. (Kaufman, incidentally, had already brilliantly captured the atmosphere of a wintry New York in Elia Kazan's *On the Waterfront* in 1954.)

Despite his apparent icy indifference, however, Nazerman is no longer master of his own memories, which have a disturbing life of their own. These memories are woven into the stream of events in his present-day existence

1

2

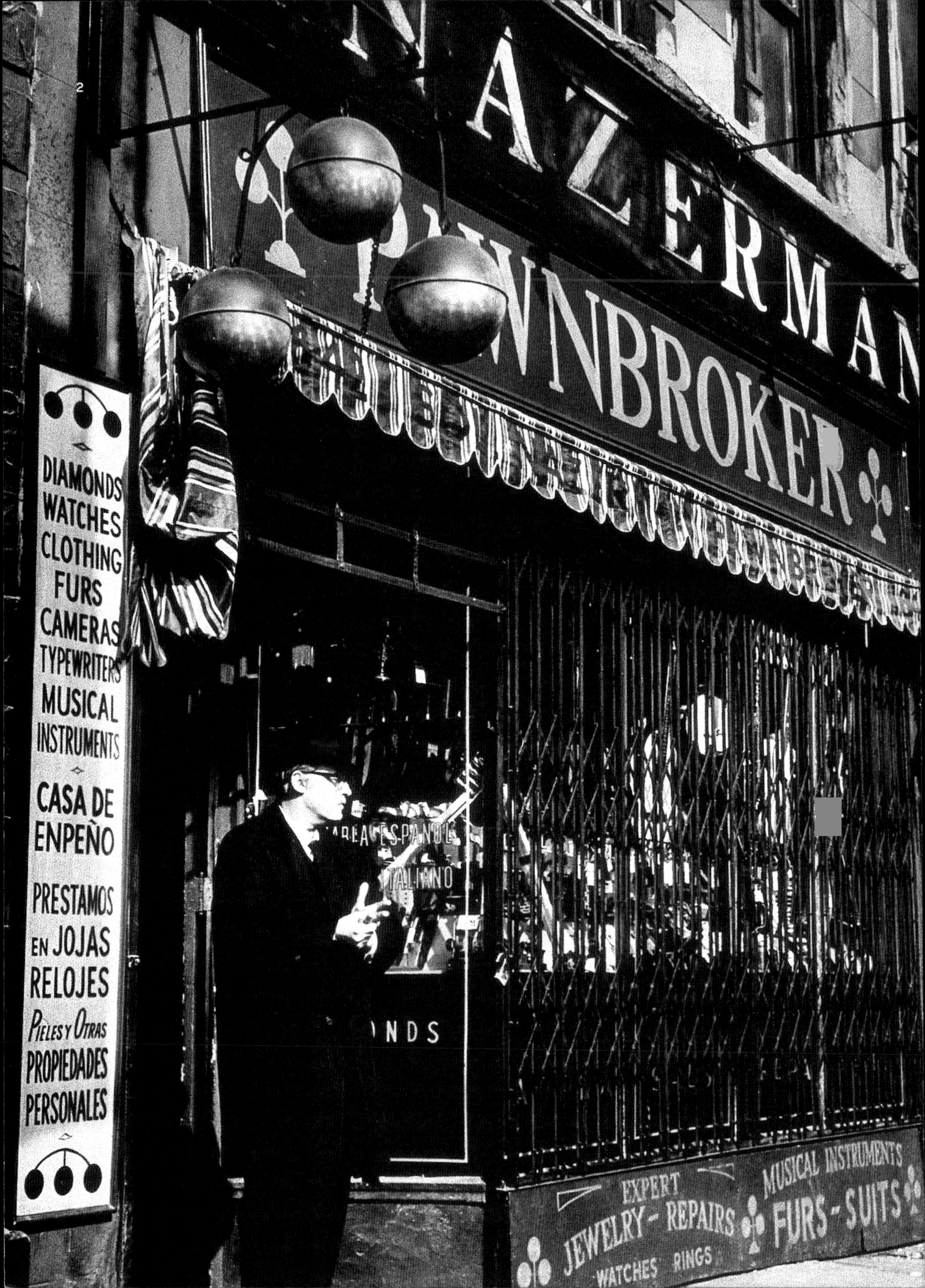
PAWNBROKER
DIAMONDS
WATCHES
CLOTHING
FURS
CAMERAS
TYPEWRITERS
MUSICAL
INSTRUMENTS
CASA DE
ENPEÑO
PRESTAMOS
EN JOJAS
RELOJES
PIELES Y OTRAS
PROPIEDADES
PERSONALES
ITALIANO
EXPERT
JEWELRY - REPAIRS
WATCHES RINGS
MUSICAL INSTRUMENTS
FURS - SUITS

1 In God we trust: After years in a concentration camp, Sol Nazerman (Rod Steiger) has lost faith in his fellow men.

2 Sorry, we're closed: Mr. Nazerman's is not about to open up and let go of the things he cherishes.

3 Minding his own business: A pawnbroker has got more important things to worry about than the shady dealings of his clientele.

# "The eloquence of Steiger's brilliant stolidity is such that it can carry whatever burden of meaning one chooses to heap upon his rounded shoulders." *Newsweek*

almost any of which can call up an unexpected association with the terrible past. Some of these memories are barely registered by the protagonist himself; single frames, bursting bubbles: mere blips on the screen of his numbed awareness.

Other sequences are longer and more insistent. As he walks home, barking dogs, a brutal brawl and a high barbed-wire fence remind him of the death camp; a subway carriage becomes a Nazi wagon transporting Jews; and when a prostitute (Thelma Oliver) displays her wares in order to convince him she's worth the price, he remembers the degradation suffered by his wife in the brothel barracks at the camp. (This scene marked the first time bare breasts had been shown in an American movie cleared for public viewing.)

Though based on a novel, *The Pawnbroker* has an almost theatrical dramaturgy. Again and again, Nazerman is confronted with people who try, in one way or another, but always unsuccessfully, to get him to open up. An old man talks friendly nonsense to him about art and science, and continues to visit the pawnbroker even when he has nothing to pawn; the social worker Miss Birchfield (Geraldine Fitzgerald) makes several awkward attempts to break through his isolation; and his young assistant Jesus Ortiz (Jaime Sanchez), an over-zealous and naive Puerto Rican with a criminal record, has even chosen him as his teacher or guru.

The relationship between Nazerman and Ortiz ends in a catastrophe; yet for the pawnbroker it proves to be a kind of liberation. When he tells his assistant that human relationships are worthless and that money rules the

**“It is not an ennobling picture that Roger H. Lewis and Philip Langner have produced and Sidney Lumet has directed. It is a picture of the shabbiness of man – of the misused, debilitated hero as well as those among whom he lives.”** *The New York Times*

6

4 Living in oblivion: Mr. Nazerman conveniently ignores that his pawnshop technically belongs to Rodriguez (Brock Peters) the pimp.

5 An offer he'd rather refuse: An episode with a prostitute (Thelma Oliver) leaves Nazerman with chilling memories of his wife's rape at the concentration camp.

6 Silence is silver: For his performance as the alienated pawnbroker, the actor won a silver bear at the Berlin International Film Festival.

7 All for naught: Social worker Marilyn Birchfield (Geraldine Fitzgerald) never succeeds in penetrating Sol Nazerman's wall of isolation.

orld, the unstable young man is hurt and disappointed; disillusioned and mbittered, he tells an underworld acquaintance how to rob the shop. The ang of hoodlums turns up, brandishing guns, but Nazerman is unimpressed; 's clear that he no longer cares in the slightest whether he lives or dies. As ne of the crooks threatens the old man with his gun, Ortiz leaps to protect im – and is shot dead instead. This sacrificial death is more than Nazeran's ossified soul can bear. As the icy indifference of decades collapses, he places his hand on the metal spike that holds the pawns – and pushes down slowly. It's a kind of self-crucifixion; and if he survives his resurrection, he will surely carry stigmata for the rest of his life. The religious overtones of the climax are certainly less blatant than in Edward Wallant's novel, which sets the tale at Easter time (instead of in the Fall); but few who have seen the movie will forget the final images of Sol Nazerman, a man in the painful throes of a belated spiritual rebirth.

LP

**ROD STEIGER (1925–2002)**

Rod Steiger was born in 1925 and got his training at the Actors Studio in his native city. But unlike other great stars of Method acting like Marlon Brando, Montgomery Clift and James Dean, Steiger was no beauty. His bull-like physique predestined him to play the bad guys, and he filled them with his colossal physical presence. Rod Steiger made his film debut in a small supporting role in *Teresa* (1951), Fred Zinnemann's tale of a soldier coming home from the war. His second movie brought him his first Oscar nomination and made his name known round the world: in Elia Kazan's *On the Waterfront* (1954), he played a corrupt and egotistical lawyer who finally comes through for his brother – the hero of the film, played by Marlon Brando. The 60s were a great period for Steiger, who made his name as a character actor. After the collapse of the old Hollywood studio system, a range of movies gave him the chance to demonstrate the range of his talents. In Sidney Lumet's *The Pawnbroker* (1964), he played Sol Nazerman, a concentration camp survivor who turns his back on the world; in David Lean's *Doctor Zhivago* (1965), he embodied the political opportunist Komarovsky. These were among his most impressive acting achievements – ambivalent figures who never entirely lose our sympathy, however great their physical or moral defects. For his performance as a latently racist small-town police chief in Norman Jewison's *In the Heat of the Night* (1967), Steiger finally received an Oscar as Best Actor. In the years that followed, he was rarely called upon to do more than play the stereotypical baddie. Rod Steiger died of pneumonia in July 2002.

**DIRECTOR** ALFRED HITCHCOCK (1899–1980)
**SCREENPLAY** JAY PRESSON ALLEN, based on the novel of the same name by WINSTON GRAHAM **DIRECTOR OF PHOTOGRAPHY** ROBERT BURKES **EDITING** GEORGE TOMASINI **MUSIC** BERNARD HERRMANN **PRODUCTION** ALFRED HITCHCOCK for UNIVERSAL PICTURES.

**STARRING** TIPPI HEDREN (Marnie Edgar), SEAN CONNERY (Mark Rutland), DIANE BAKER (Lil Mainwaring), LOUISE LATHAM (Bernice Edgar), MARTIN GABEL (Sidney Strutt), ALAN NAPIER (Mr. Rutland), BRUCE DERN (Sailor).

***"I love you, Marnie."***
***"You don't love me; I'm just something you've caught! You think I'm some kind of animal you trapped!"***

As any Hitchcock blonde could tell you, no amount of peroxide can wash away the past. That, however, does not stop Marnie (Tippi Hedren) from trying. Always on the lamb, she adopts a new name, social security number, wardrobe, and, of course, hair color every time she skips town. And with each spring-cleaning, she makes sure to leave her last employer's safe absolutely spotless.

With plenty of cash on hand, she pulls the wool over her mother Bernice's (Louise Latham) eyes with expensive presents, making her believe she's hit it big as a career woman. But all her visits and all the mink in the world can't buy her mother's affection, and Marnie has to make do with the same void of contempt that has dogged her entire life.

This intricate web of deceit threatens to unravel shortly after she gets hired by publisher Mark Rutland (Sean Connery). Recognizing her from a past business engagement, Rutland sees through Marnie's lies and proves a mo formidable opponent. He assumes it's just a matter of time before his love new associate will attempt to relieve him of the contents of his safe, and h wants to be there to cash in when she does. So when the wildcat gets h paw caught in Mark's trap, he hands her an ultimatum: either he turns h over to the authorities, or she marries him. Fearing the law's cage more tha Mark's, Marnie accepts his proposal. Nonetheless, the new bride is retice to fulfill her wifely duties, breaking out in a cold sweat every time her hu band so much as touches her.

Mark quickly sees that Marnie is not just a con artist, but is actually su fering from severe psychological trauma. In fact he has a few flaws of h own, and demonstrates as much brutality toward her as he does concern f her welfare. Obsessed with asserting his will, Mark rapes Marnie on the

1

1 Scot free: Or is Marnie (Tippi Hedren) about to get caught red-handed?

2 Bottle blonde: Top model Tippi Hedren transforms herself into the Hitchcockian ideal – an unapproachable dream girl.

honeymoon, and just manages to foil her ensuing suicide attempt in the nick of time…

It gradually transpires that Marnie's oppressive illness is rooted in the past and the couple decides to pay her mother a visit. It is here, on one fateful stormy night, that Marnie confronts her childhood demons. She suddenly remembers how her mother whored herself to sailors on furlough. Vivid images of one suitor (Bruce Dern) fill her mind. He had been fighting with Bernice, and Marnie, acting in a panic, bludgeoned him with a fire poker and lost the love of a mother she had been so desperately trying to protect.

Hitch's original intention had been to use Marnie as the vehicle fo Grace Kelly's Hollywood comeback. With her cool, erotically charged de meanor, the star of *Rear Window* (USA 1954) and *To Catch a Thief* (USA 1955 epitomized his dream woman, and he'd lost that electricity in 1956 when sh left Hollywood for Prince Rainier III of Monaco. Kelly's initial interest in th project fizzled out, and former photo model Tippi Hedren was entrusted wit the role. Having been discovered during pre-production for *The Birds* (US 1963), Hedren was to become the master of suspense's new starlet. But sh also became was the woman who suffered most under his direction.

The story of *Marnie* echoes that of Vertigo (USA 1958), in that both films ell of a man doomed to love a woman who will never completely be his. In ertigo, the protagonist tries to resurrect a beloved ghost; in *Marnie*, Mark ovets the eponymous heroine for her pathological exoticism. He relies first n violence, then on therapy to tame her, ultimately forcing her subservience ı an act of rape. The importance Hitchcock placed on this climatic event an be evidenced in the fact that he fired the film's original screenwriter, van Hunter, for presumptuously refusing to write the rape scene. Undeniably, the director wanted to see more elements of himself and his leading ıdy in the story of the frigid kleptomaniac and the worldly publisher. Hedren id everything in her power to dodge her director's ever-increasing sexual dvances, and Hitchcock retaliated with contempt. An icy silence prevailed

3 Don't look a gift horse in the mouth: Mark (Sean Connery) abuses Marnie with one hand, but tries to make good by writing checks with the other.

4 Mama didn't raise no fool: Marnie knows just how to pull the wool over her mother's (Louise Latham) eyes. But no amount of performing can win over the old bat's affections.

**"Hitchcock's elegant cinematic style, evident here and there, seems wasted in a mélange of banal dialogue, obtrusively phony process shots, and a plot that congeals more often than it thickens."** *Time*

5

on the set as it became clear that the director had lost all interest in t project.

Critics reveled in the picture's many cosmetic defects, including its pc rear projection, artificial looking sets, sloppy implementation of psychoana sis, and intrusive cinematography. The master appeared to be losing h touch. Yet *Marnie* is a film that improves with age, and today grand momer of Hitchcockian suspense shine through the criticism. The scene in whi Marnie empties Rutland's safe, for instance, and is almost caught red-han ed by the cleaning lady – the tension created by the viewers knowing mo than the characters on screen – is Hitchcock at his finest. For all its hyste and overstatement, *Marnie* remains the last great feature from Hitchcock golden era.

**"Sometimes it appears as if the directo is more interested in wooing his own particular talents than pleasing his audience."** *Variety*

6

5 They shoot horses don't they? Marnie puts her steed out his misery and considers lowering the curtain on her own personal tragedy.

6 Publisher's clearing house: Marnie relieves Mark of the contents of his safe.

7 Cat got your tongue? Mark has caught himself quite a kitten.

**BERNARD HERRMANN**

No one would deny that Janet Leigh's last shower in *Psycho* (1960) is among the most chilling Hitchcock sequences ever to grace the screen, and one which owes much of its genius to composer Bernard Herrmann, whose slashing score heightens the impact of the entire movie.

By the time *Psycho* hit theaters, the two men's collaborative efforts had already produced countless Hollywood triumphs: *Vertigo* (1958) and *North by Northwest* (1959) are but the tip of the iceberg. Although this other master of suspense, born in 1911, had continually protested against being pigeonholed as a composer of movie music, he ended up working in the industry his entire life. After *Psycho*, Hitch and Herrmann reunited for *The Birds*, for which the musician whittled an entire arrangement solely out of fluttering and cawing sounds. *Marnie* would mark the end of the era. Caving into studio demands, Hitchcock had another composer put together a more commercial and accessible score for his next film *Torn Curtain* (1966). Outraged, Herrmann severed all ties from Hitchcock.

Bernard Herrmann began his career as a conductor and bandleader with CBS Radio, for whom he produced numerous music and radio shows. In 1940, he made the acquaintance of Orson Welles and switched over to film, debuting on the scene with his score to the phenomenal *Citizen Kane*. After scoring 49 movies and several original pieces for classical orchestra, Herrmann died on December 23rd 1975, just hours after finishing the last bars for Martin Scorsese's *Taxi Driver* (1976).

# MARY POPPINS

1964 - USA - 140 MIN. - MUSICAL

DIRECTOR ROBERT STEVENSON (1905–1986)
SCREENPLAY BILL WALSH, DONALD DA GRADI DIRECTOR OF PHOTOGRAPHY EDWARD COLMAN EDITING COTTON WARBURTON
MUSIC RICHARD M. SHERMAN, ROBERT B. SHERMAN, IRWIN KOSTAL PRODUCTION WALT DISNEY, BILL WALSH for WALT DISNEY PICTURES.

STARRING JULIE ANDREWS (Mary Poppins), DICK VAN DYKE (Bert / Mr. Dawes Sr.), DAVID TOMLINSON (Mr. George W. Banks), GLYNIS JOHNS (Mrs. Winifred Banks), HERMIONE BADDELEY (Ellen), RETA SHAW (Mrs. Brill), KAREN DOTRICE (Jane Banks), MATTHEW GARBER (Michael Banks), ELSA LANCHESTER (Katie Nanna), ARTHUR TREACHER (Constable Jones).

ACADEMY AWARDS 1964 OSCARS for BEST ACTRESS (Julie Andrews), BEST EDITING (Cotton Warburton), BEST MUSIC (Richard M. Sherman, Robert B. Sherman), BEST SONG (Richard M. Sherman, Robert B. Sherman), and BEST SPECIAL EFFECTS (Peter Ellenshaw, Hamilton Luske, Eustace Lycett).

## *"First of all I would like to make one thing perfectly clear. I never explain anything."*

It takes just one word, one very special word, to transport us back to a world of magical chalk drawings and enchanted penguins. The biggest word you've ever heard and this is how it goes – Supercalifragilisticexpialidocious!

It's a word that rolls off Mary's tongue when asked by a bandwagon of animated characters how it feels to have won the carousel derby. And there's no misunderstanding her. For Mary's imaginary language and way of speaking clearly express the film's love affair with make believe. With *Mary Poppins*, Walt Disney Pictures celebrated one of its greatest successes with audiences and critics alike. A rare consensus, unequivocally deserved, as *Mary Poppins* continues to dazzle the young and young at heart with its perfect synthesis of musical comedy in a live and animated world. Indeed, one could deem the picture the crowning achievement of producer Walt Disney's brilliant career.

Seasoned director Robert Stevenson created a film that sparkles with that trademark Disney magic. It doesn't seem possible that each scene of a totally homogenous movie could speak to every member of the family regardless of age – but *Mary Poppins* does it with grace and flair. Though often ridiculed, it is in reality a grand and elusive art form which most of Disney's competition just can't seem to get right.

*Mary Poppins* starts off by diving into the clear, poignant waters of fun, make-believe and music. Jane (Karen Dotrice) and Michael Banks (Matthew Garber), of No. 17, Cherry Tree Lane, London, have never wanted for anything, but have had to make do without emotional nourishment for the greater part of their young lives. The year is 1910, and with progress marching on, neither of their parents have any time for them. Mrs. Banks (Glynis Johns) is a suffragette crusading through the streets of London for women's rights, wearing the sort of banner across her breast one might see in a modern day beauty pageant. Another thing she can afford is the luxury of contradiction: when she's not pelting the prime minister with eggs, she's hanging on to hubby's every word at home. Equally self-absorbed, Mr. Banks (David Tomlinson) is a conservative banker who enjoys seeing his offspring once an evening when summoned, but would otherwise prefer not to be bothered with their trifles – especially not games. That leaves no one else for the children to play with except the elderly nannies and house staff – a cohort of withered old fuddy duddies. This is a job for Mary Poppins! And with a swift gust of East Wind she comes flying onto the scene in a wonderful sequence that sends the swarm of other potential nannies off to Timbuktu. Although Mr. Banks might have preferred a more authoritarian lady on his pay roll, she bowls him over with her upfront, cheeky demeanor and lands the job in a snap.

From this point on, *Mary Poppins'* plot more or less falls by the wayside and the film emerges as a tapestry of self-contained vignettes. The children embark on one fun-filled adventure after another at the side of Mary and her friend Bert (Dick Van Dyke), a jack-of-all-trades who demonstrates various talents as a street musician, sidewalk artist and chimney sweep in the course of the film. Jumping in and out of sunny cartoon worlds, Bert dances amongst animated penguins and saves a frisky talking fox from a pack of hunters whilst Mary comes in first at the carousel derby. After a rainstorm calls them back to "reality," the troop pay Uncle Albert (Ed Wynn) a visit, where a case of

1

2

**ROBERT STEVENSON**

Born in Buxton, England on March 31, 1905, Robert Stevenson worked as a journalist for a number of years prior to beginning his screenwriting career in 1930. It wasn't long before he was adapting scripts of German box-office hits like Karl Hartl's classic UFA sci-fi film *F. P. 1 Doesn't Answer* (*F. P. 1 antwortet nicht,* 1933) and Ludwig Berger's comedy *I by Day, You by Night* (1932) (*Ich bei Tag und du bei Nacht,* 1932) for the English-speaking cinema. At the same time, Stevenson made his filmmaking debut, co-directing the English version of another German comedy entitled, *Happy Ever After* featuring Lillian Harvey (released in the U. S. as *A Blonde Dream* in 1932).

In the years that followed, Stevenson made his name in the industry with the zany horror movie *The Man Who Changed His Mind*, (a. k. a. *The Man Who Lived Again*, 1936) starring Boris Karloff, and the epic adventure *King Solomon's Mines* (1937). As of 1940, Stevenson worked mostly in Hollywood where, time and again, he proved himself a proficient craftsman who could readily adapt to any given style or genre. His most acclaimed film of the decade was his version of Charlotte Brontë's celebrated romance *Jane Eyre* (1944). In 1949, Stevenson signed to direct the anti-communist film noir *I Married a Communist* (a. k. a. *The Woman on Pier 13*, 1950) for Howard Hughes' recently acquired RKO pictures. Audiences stayed away, although that was by no means on account of Stevenson's fine direction.

In the 1950s, this accomplished filmmaker briefly switched gears and jumped on the booming TV bandwagon. By 1959, he was Disney's premiere director of live action / animation extravaganzas, a big screen movement that peaked with *Mary Poppins* (1964). Stevenson directed his final film, *The Shaggy D. A.*, in 1976, and passed away ten years later in Santa Barbara.

**"From the moment the lovely Julie comes gliding in, umbrella-borne from her dwelling place in the sky, the movie is sheer delight – to the eye, the ear, the senses."** *Newsweek*

1 Jolly holiday! Mary Poppins (Julie Andrews) goes, bluebirds are sure to follow.

2 A spoonful of sugar: Jane (Karen Dotrice) and Michael Banks (Matthew Garber) discover how to tidy up their room in the most delightful way.

3 When Mary holds your hand, you feel so grand: Bert (Dick Van Dyke) and Mary spread joy throughout the world of make believe and imbue everyday life with unimagined color.

4 Let's go fly a kite: Family life finally goes soaring when Mr. and Mrs. Banks (David Tomlinson and Glynis Johns) get in on the fun, magically transforming themselves into the parents Jane and Michael have always wished for.

ıe giggles soon has them all *not* on the floor but on the *ceiling*. Their exploits ·e topped off with a marvelously choreographed number atop the roofs of ondon as the four partake in a full chorus chimney sweep ballet.

The film's trick photography is almost flawless. As Mary pulls the most urious objects out of her magical overnight bag it's not only Jane and lichael who watch with gaping mouths. Still, the film rides on the irresistible harm of stars Dick Van Dyke and Julie Andrews. Andrews promptly won the Best Actress Oscar for her first Hollywood role, blowing *My Fair Lady's* (1964 Audrey Hepburn completely out of the water. Sadly enough, after *Poppins* there weren't many film projects left for song and dance talents like Andrews and Van Dyke. Andrews was able to match the power of her debut performance the following year in *The Sound of Music* (1964), but smash hits would be harder to come by after that. *Mary Poppins* was one of last triumphs of a swiftly fading genre.

LP

# LILITH

1964 - USA - 114 MIN. - DRAMA, LITERARY ADAPTION

DIRECTOR ROBERT ROSSEN (1908–1966)
SCREENPLAY ROBERT ROSSEN, based on the novel of the same name by J. R. SALAMANCA DIRECTOR OF PHOTOGRAPHY EUGEN SCHÜFFTAN EDITING ARAM AVAKIAN MUSIC Kenyon Hopkins PRODUCTION ROBERT ROSSEN for COLUMBIA PICTURES CORPORATION.

STARRING WARREN BEATTY (Vincent Bruce), JEAN SEBERG (Lilith Arthur), PETER FONDA (Stephen Evshevsky), KIM HUNTER (Doctor Bea Brice), ANNE MEACHAM (Yvonne Meaghan), JAMES PATTERSON (Doctor Lavrier), JESSICA WALTER (Laura), GENE HACKMAN (Norman), ROBERT REILLY (Bob Clayfield), RENE AUBERJONOIS (Howie).

## "Do you think it's a sin to love me?"

Released in the U. S. in October 1964, *Lilith* was quickly dismissed by the entertainment magazine *Variety* as a picture for the art house crowd. Equally slated as maudlin pretence in other reviews, the fate of the screen adaptation of J. R. Salamanca's popular novel about schizophrenics in an upper crust mental institution was quickly sealed: *Lilith* played to all but empty movie houses worldwide, save for its limited success in Scandinavia.

In retrospect, however, *Lilith* shows us quite a different face. Not only is the film acclaimed as director Robert Rossen's masterpiece (he previously specialized in brawny men's flicks), but it is also widely regarded as Jean Seberg's crowning achievement. A cult movie star, Seberg is as celebrated for her leading roles in pictures like Godard's *Breathless* (*À bout de souffle*, 1960) and Preminger's *Saint Joan* (1957) as for the mysterious circumstances surrounding her tragic death in 1979. Here she delivers an electric performance as Lilith Arthur, an attractive young schizophrenic who has been a resident of New England's Poplar Clinic since the age of 18. Hers is a world of fantasy, for which she has developed a private language, full of phrases like "Hiara Pirlu Resh Kavawan" that mean nothing to anyone else. But then Lilith also has moments of astounding communicative clarity, in which she reveals the other irresistibly charismatic and social side of her character. For she is so many things: artistic and creative, playing the flute and painting;

1

1 Mad about you: Work becomes a labor of love when caretaker Vincent Bruce (Warren Beatty) crosses paths with Lilith.

2 Splendor in the grass: But a roll in the hay doesn't quite mean love for Lilith (Jean Seberg).

3 Female Narcissus: While wading in the water, Lilith comes face to face with herself and falls in love with the only person worthy of her affections.

4 The song of sirens: Like Vincent, Stephen (Peter Fonda) loses his heart to Lilith and ends up all wet.

5 Along came a spider and sat down beside her: Lilith is entangled in countless webs, many of which she doesn't spin herself.

**"Photographed by the great Eugen Schüfftan, the film is conceived in shades of white so delicate and elusive that the picture barely seems to brush the screen."** *Chicago Reader*

insightful, intelligent, uncannily analyzing her caretaker's psyche; as exuberant yet also as cruel as a child, experiencing life's ups and downs with the intensity of someone new to the world. Seldom has a portrait of insanity been this seductive.

The storyline is both linear and elliptical, traversing time at lightning speed. Cross-fades and overlapping audio tracks give the plot fabric an intricate inner unity, mirrored by the web motif that appears throughout the picture, from the animated title sequence in which butterflies get entangled in a net to the recurring shots of Lilith observing the outside world through the criss-crossed spaces of her barred window.

Shot in black and white, the film derives much of its magic from the grace with which it walks the line between madness and sanity. Through the loving eyes of fledgling caretaker and admirer Vincent Bruce (Warren Beatty), we watch as Lilith indulges in physical and metaphorical knitting. Like this insecure young man still trying to make his way in the world, the audience are magnetically drawn into Lilith's captivating universe. In one of the most poignant scenes, legendary cinematographer Eugen Schüfftan shows Lilith wading into a fog-covered sea, kissing her reflection. And it is here that we get a glimpse of the person that lies beyond the mystery: a female Narcissus, radiant as the sun yet incapable of love.

Like a schizophrenic spider whose behavior is demonstrated to the hospital staff by a psychiatrist, Lilith weaves her "asymmetrical and nightmarish web" to impress her desires upon all living beings, regardless of whether her audience is a man, woman or child.

Undeterred, Vincent sees himself as her knight in shining armor and attempts to conquer her. When he wins the mock jousting match at a Renaissance fair, "Lady" Lilith is crowned his queen of love and beauty. Bent on dominating her, he tries to subject her to a suffocating classical form of love. Although his jealousy and lack of understanding soon stifle their precarious passion, the film refuses to give him all the blame for their failed relationship.

Much of *Lilith's* strength lies in its depiction of mental illness as an essentially creative condition, and it deliberately endows most of the clinic's inmates with marked artistic talents. For as one of the hospital psychiatrists says of his patients, most are highly intelligent individuals who simply have too delicate a means of interpreting the world and go to pieces as a result.

LP

**ROBERT ROSSEN**

Native New Yorker Robert Rossen was born to Russian Jewish immigrant parents in 1908. As a student Rossen began dabbling in writing, directing and acting with small avant-garde repertory companies. In 1936, established Hollywood filmmaker Mervyn LeRoy put in a good word for Rossen at Warner Bros., and the industry amateur went on to write scripts for the studio until 1943. His screenplay credits include gangster pictures like *The Roaring Twenties* (1939), social dramas like *Dust Be My Destiny* (1939) and war movies like *Edge of Darkness* (1943).
Following his directorial debut with the gangster melodrama *Johnny O'Clock* (1946), Rossen began to make a name for himself as a master of uncompromising realism, filming numerous social and political dramas on location. The boxer film *Body and Soul* (1947) and the political thriller *All the King's Men* (1949), focusing on the shady dealings of a U.S. governor, are among his most applauded works.
A dark shadow was cast over Rossen's life in 1947 when he was placed on the House Un-American Activities Committee (HUAC) blacklist. A former member of the Communist Party, Rossen had two separate court hearings during which he refused to admit acts of sedition or name others involved. He thereby made himself one of the conservative group's prime targets. After enduring two years' exile from Hollywood, Rossen motioned for a third trial in 1953 and consequently disclosed the names of 60 supposed red cohorts living on American soil. Nonetheless, his career had hit a stumbling block that his cooperation with the House Un-American Activities Committee couldn't overcome. Only after directing the suspenseful pool hall character drama *The Hustler* (1961) did he begin to regain his professional reputation. Although the box-office flop *Lilith* (1964), a poetic study of schizophrenia, was eventually acclaimed as his masterpiece, the director's premature death in 1966 prevented him from ever profiting from its belated success.

# DARLING

1965 - GREAT BRITAIN - 128 MIN. - DRAMA

DIRECTOR JOHN SCHLESINGER (1926–2003)
SCREENPLAY FREDERIC RAPHAEL DIRECTOR OF PHOTOGRAPHY KEN HIGGINS EDITING JAMES B. CLARK MUSIC JOHN DANKWORTH
PRODUCTION JOSEPH JANNI, VICTOR LYNDON for ANGLO-AMALGAMATED PRODUCTIONS, VIC, APPIA.

STARRING JULIE CHRISTIE (Diana Scott), DIRK BOGARDE (Robert Gold), LAURENCE HARVEY (Miles Brand), JOSÉ LUIS DE VILLALONGA (Cesare), ROLAND CURRAM (Malcolm), BASIL HENSON (Alec Prosser-Jones), HELEN LINDSAY (Felicity Prosser-Jones), CARLO PALMUCCI (Curzio), DANTE POSANI (Gino), PAULINE YATES (Estelle Gold).

ACADEMY AWARDS 1965 OSCARS for BEST ACTRESS (Julie Christie), BEST ORIGINAL SCREENPLAY (Frederic Raphael), and BEST COSTUME DESIGN (Julie Harris).

## *"There's nothing wrong with somebody helping you with your career after all, is there?"*

Only six months after the premiere of *Darling*, a title story in *Time* magazine gave a new name to the pulsating capital of the decade: "London: The Swinging City." Nowadays, the film is seen as a document of the Swinging Sixties, a fanfare for a Britain suddenly liberated into a period of escapist fun, glamour and glorious pop music. But anyone expecting to see a kind of aesthetic template for *Austin Powers* will be sorely disappointed (or pleasantly surprised): instead of serving up a feast of Carnaby Street chic, John Schlesinger soberly analyzes an era of gorgeous superficiality, embodied in the figure of the model Diana Scott (Julie Christie). Icily elegant and apparently empty of all feeling, Diana sleeps her way through the bedrooms of the media and fashion elite, using and discarding the men she meets. When she meets TV journalist Robert Gold (Dirk Bogarde), her young husband is quickly left behind in her wake. Gold by name and gold by nature, Dirk Bogarde's character represents Schlesinger's male ideal; but his frank, undemanding love is as dull and old-fashioned as the tweed jackets he insists on wearing. So Diana – who is by now gracing the title page of the magazine "Ideal Woman" – plumps for the cool charm of the PR agent Miles Brand (Laurence Harvey). He puts his marketing talents to work, makes her face her fortune, and secures her access to the glittering world of high fashion. A short time later, she's filming an ad on Capri. She meets and marries a rich Italian prince and becomes the darling of the glossy magazines. And much too late, she realizes that her hunger for life and addiction to fame have come at a very high price. Diana is a bird in a golden cage, and now there seems little chance of her ever escaping to happiness.

Seen today, *Darling* does seems somewhat dated. The heroine's "decline and fall" is narrated in such a simple, straightforward manner, and the symbolism of the film's black and white images now looks mereley blatant. *Darling* is a kind of time capsule, but in its day it was an event, winning Julie

1

3

**"As the amoral heroine, Julie Christie offers her polished surface to the camera in a chic, showy performance that floods nothingness with light... Because her passions are only skin-deep, her tragedy is trivial. But at every toss of her blonde mane, every shard of a smile, all else on the screen becomes mere backdrop. Her stunning presence – and Schlesinger's stylish tracking of a playgirl's progress – makes *Darling* irresistible."** *Time*

1 Everybody's darling: Diana Scott (Julie Christie) is the reflection of a shallow society.

2 Alligator tears: Good, old-fashioned journalist Robert Gold (Dirk Bogarde) wises up to Diana's ways and bites back with the silent treatment.

3 Treading on thin ice: Beyond Diana's sophisticated façade lies a frightened little girl. John Schlesinger paints a grim portrait of 1960s society.

4 Symposium: Diana feels most at ease in the company of gay friend Malcolm (Roland Curram).

5 Slippery when wet: Watch out, Diana! Industry eel Miles Brand (Laurence Harvey) is out to wrap his tail around you.

6 You're confusing me with Twiggy: Despite her work in ambitious productions, it took years for Britain's blonde icon to totally get rid of her miniskirt image.

Christie an Oscar and establishing her as an icon of the miniskirt generation. John Schlesinger had succeeded in finding a vehicle for his own despair at the state of civilization. Against a world of banal superficialities, he deploys the weapons of satire and social realism – and occasionally, the raised index finger of the pedagogue. The "amoral" Diana is merely the narcissistic mirror image of a society that is still deeply conservative, and busily converting its children's hunger for freedom into economic profit. The strategists of this social order reside in stuffy Victorian edifices. Long before the camera shows us anything of the hip London party scene, the screen is filled by a portrait of the Queen; and interestingly, Diana has to go to Paris to encounter the real Bohemian lifestyle, which she finds both "interesting" and scary. There's also something very British about her fall from grace into the lap of the aristocracy, although this must have been inspired by the sad fate of the American actress Grace Kelly.

If the film has nonetheless been seen as a breakthrough to a new era, there are two reasons for this. Firstly, the leading actress: as the naively scheming playgirl, Julie Christie has far more charisma than the zeitgeist could handle. In later interviews, she regretted not giving her character a little more self-assurance – for essentially, Diana is punished for wanting too much from life. Secondly, Frederic Raphael's screenplay is an early expression of the critical spirit that would culminate in the sexual emancipation and social upheaval of the late 60s. The dialogue is sensitive and perceptive, not just in the way it illuminates Diana's fear of being tied down in a relationship, but in its treatment of what were really taboo subjects at the time: homosexuality, promiscuity and abortion. There are elements of 1950s kitchen-sink drama here, as well as presentiments of Stanley Kubrick's seduction drama *Eyes Wide Shut* (1999), on which Raphael also worked.

Like her "big brother," the eponymous hero of *Alfie* (1966), Diana is both the product and the first victim of a change in moral values. Schlesinger is much more a materialist than he is a moralist. He shows how harsh social realities undermine the promise of individual freedom and fulfillment held out by the Swinging Sixties; the world being the way it is, people have the wrong dreams and make the wrong decisions. And from a contemporary point of view, it seems undeniable that Diana suffers not least from the cold and often cruel chauvinism of the men in her life.

PB

**ION AND FILM**

The movie business is a modern-day Vanity Fair, dominated by brutal rivalries and pitiless superficiality; or at least that's how it looks in cinematic self-analyses such as in Robert Altman's *The Player* (1992). But filmmakers are even fonder of pointing the finger at the fashion world, where sweet nothings and nobodies can achieve fame overnight. The favored mode is satire. We're given the impression that actresses loathe models, and that the photographer is the natural enemy of the film director. In *Funny Face* (1956), a demure Audrey Hepburn resists the attempts of a fashion photographer to make a new woman of her. And who could forget *How to Marry a Millionaire* (1953), from an age when models were still known as mannequins? It's only with a heavy heart that the three gold-diggers – Marilyn Monroe, Lauren Bacall and Betty Grable – decide that love matters more than money. The sheer heartlessness of the rag trade is stressed in films as diverse as Michelangelo Antonioni's *Blow Up* (1966) and Rainer Werner Fassbinder's study of an arrogant fashion designer, *The Bitter Tears of Petra von Kant* (*Die bitteren Tränen der Petra von Kant*, 1972). In *Prêt-à-porter* (1994), Robert Altman took up the theme, creating a film that penetrates below the surface and combines its mockery with critical intelligence. Stars such as Sophia Loren, Julia Roberts and Kim Basinger pump up the hollow glamour of *haute couture* with their collective acting presence. And finally, *Zoolander* (2001), directed by and starring Ben Stiller, belatedly drew our attention to the problems facing male models.

**DIRECTOR** ROMAN POLANSKI (*1933)

**SCREENPLAY** ROMAN POLANSKI, GÉRARD BRACH **DIRECTOR OF PHOTOGRAPHY** GILBERT TAYLOR **EDITING** ALASTAIR MCINTYRE **MUSIC** CHICO HAMILTON **PRODUCTION** GENE GUTOWSKI for COMPTON, TEKLI.

**STARRING** CATHERINE DENEUVE (Carole Ledoux), IAN HENDRY (Michael), JOHN FRASER (Colin), PATRICK WYMARK (Landlord), YVONNE FURNEAUX (Hélène Ledoux), RENEE HOUSTON (Miss Balch), VALERIE TAYLOR (Madame Denise), JAMES VILLIERS (John), HELEN FRASER (Bridget), HUGH FUTCHER (Reggie).

## *"I don't think Cinderella likes me."*

Carole (Catherine Deneuve), a manicurist in a London beauty salon, lives in a world that seems dominated by women. She shares a flat with her sister Hélène (Yvonne Furneaux), and her only other human contact is with her colleagues in the salon, and the elderly customers, whose faces seem mummified under mudpacks and moisturizers. Yet men are everywhere: at work, in the anecdotes of her workmates, who complain that theirs are only interested in one thing, and at home, in the form of Michael (Ian Hendry), her sister's married lover. When Hélène sleeps with Michael in the neighboring room, Carole twists and turns sleeplessly in her bed, and when morning comes, she's disgusted to find his toothbrush in her glass.

Men… for Carole, they're a permanent threat. Unable to reveal her fears to anyone else, she withdraws further and further into the world of her daydreams. And then there is Colin (John Fraser), who makes persistent but clumsy advances towards this quiet and seemingly fragile young woman.

Gradually, the world around Carole begins to change. Reflected in a c fee pot, her face is monstrously distorted; a skinned rabbit on a plate lo like a human foetus; cracks in the tarmac conjure up a woman's wide-o legs. The external world reflects the horrors that haunt her mind. Though can't say exactly why, it's clear that this woman is in hell. From her livi room window, she observes and admires a community of nuns, who seem represent another life – a "purer" existence, free of men. But it's a world t Carole has no prospect of joining.

For men have taken possession of Carole's soul. After an alm painfully uneventful start, Polanski shocks the audience with a sudd apparition: the reflection of a stranger in the mirror on a door – the door Carole's wardrobe. This is the straw that breaks Carole's back, the shock t

1

1 That girl: Carole (Catherine Deneuve) is convinced she has everything a girl could ask for – until she takes a good look at herself.

2 Afraid of the bogeyman: Unshakable visions of sinister men plague Carole's slumber.

3 Virgin suicides: As Carole's paranoia comes to a head, every aspect of her life becomes a matter of disclosure and exposure.

## "The nightmare world of a virgin's dreams becomes the screen's shocking reality!" *Advert for "Repulsion"*

throws her completely out of orbit. She stops going to work; and as her sister is gone for a few days, she's now all alone in the apartment. There is now nothing to stop her slipping ever deeper into the abyss of her own mind. At night, she is raped by strange, demonic creatures, and the façade of her middle-class normality falls apart, as the walls of the flat crack open and Carole herself cracks up. And when, one after the other, Colin and the landlord turn up, she no longer knows what's real and what's not. All she can do is defend herself…

Polanski and Gérard Brach wrote the screenplay to *Repulsion* in a single 17-day session. It had been commissioned by a firm that was best known for soft porn productions. Despite the success of *Knife in the Water* (*Nóz w wodzie*, 1962), which had even been nominated for an Oscar, Polanski had had to wait a long time for the chance to make his second movie. Now he was expected to put together a horror film for 45,000 pounds sterling. The film he really wanted to make was *Cul-de-Sac*, but he had been obliged to

ambitions in a film he hadn't really chosen to make – and to the produce dismay, he overshot his budget by more than 100%.

The director described what he had tried to do in this, the first film had made outside Poland: "It was my intention to show Carole's hallucir tions through the eye of the camera, and to use more and more extrer wide-angle lenses to intensify their menacing effect." Later, in fact, Polans judged the film to be technically inadequate; but despite this harsh self-cr icism, *Repulsion* is a terrifying portrait of a lost soul. Together with his car eraman Gilbert Taylor – whom the producers had felt to be far too expensi – Polanski created a disturbing black and white masterpiece that can eas bear comparison with the works of Buñuel and Hitchcock, two of the dire tors the Pole most admired. (In the opening titles, the eye sliced through lettering is a tribute to one of the Spanish master's most famous shots.) any case, Polanski had already reached his actual goal: *Repulsion* was su a success that he was given the green light for *Cul-de-Sac*, and he beg

4 Lending a helping hand: This manicurist brings her clients back to life at the price of her own.

5 He can cut you like a knife: Her sister's married lover, the edgy Michael (Ian Hendry), confirms Carole's repulsion and fear of the opposite sex.

# "A wicked tale of madness and female paranoia."

*San Francisco Chronicle*

**ILBERT TAYLOR**

British cinematographer Gilbert Taylor is regarded as a master of the black and white film. Born in 1914, he was already working as an assistant cameraman by the age of 15. In Stanley Kubrick's *Dr. Strangelove, or: How I Learned to Stop Worrying and Love the Bomb* (1963) and Richard Lester's *A Hard Day's Night* (1964), he exploited the visual potential of the black and white medium with an imaginative force that is still impresses today. Wowed by Gilbert's pleasure in experimentation, Polanski hired him for *Repulsion* in 1965 – and Taylor is said to have protested vehemently when asked to use a wide-angle lens for the close-ups of Catherine Deneuve's face. Nonetheless, they went on to make two further films together: *Cul-De-Sac* (1965) and *The Tragedy of Macbeth* (1971). In *Macbeth*, Taylor demonstrated that he could also create morbid and menacing atmospheres when filming in color. In 1972, Hitchcock came knocking at his door, and Taylor became the cameramen for his blackly humorous *Frenzy*. Since creating the hauntingly claustrophobic images of *Repulsion*, Taylor had become pigeonholed as a specialist for thrillers and horror films. Yet his filmography, which comprises more than 70 works, doesn't only include such classics of the genre as *The Omen* (1976) and *Dracula* (1979); we also find movies such as *Star Wars* (1977) and *Flash Gordon* (1980) – further proof of the surprising versatility of this workaholic perfectionist. The last film he worked on, Curtis Hanson's *The Bedroom Window* (1986), demonstrated once more that he was a true master of visual suspense.

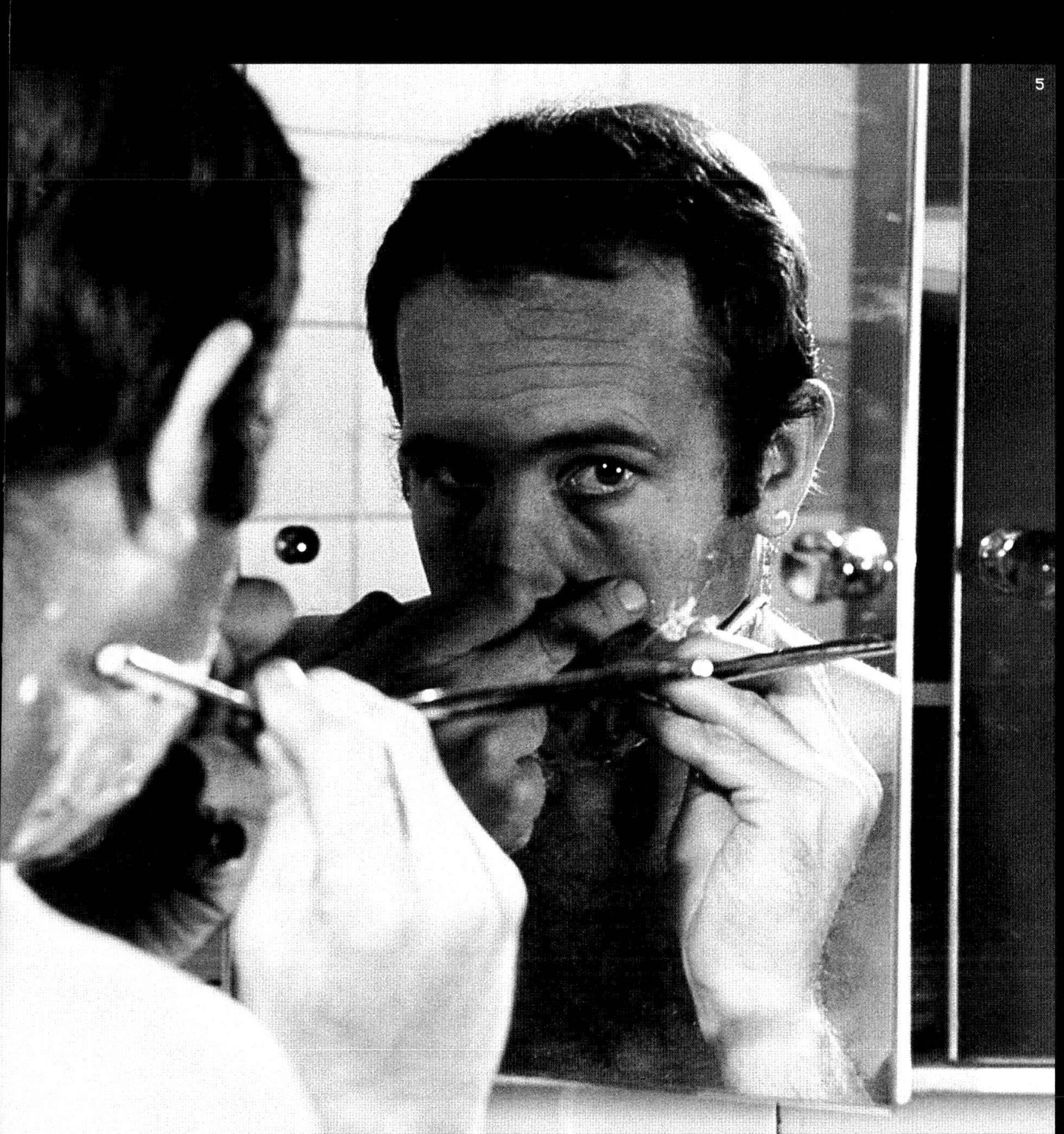
5

# ALPHAVILLE

## Alphaville – Une étrange aventure de Lemmy Caution

1965 - FRANCE/ITALY - 93 MIN. - SCIENCE FICTION, CRIME FILM

DIRECTOR JEAN-LUC GODARD (*1930)

SCREENPLAY JEAN-LUC GODARD DIRECTOR OF PHOTOGRAPHY RAOUL COUTARD EDITING AGNÈS GUILLEMOT MUSIC PAUL MISRAKI PRODUCTION ANDRÉ MICHELIN, ANDRÉ MICHELIN for CHAUMIANE, FILMSTUDIO, ATHOS FILMS.

STARRING EDDIE CONSTANTINE (Lemmy Caution), ANNA KARINA (Natascha von Braun), AKIM TAMIROFF (Henry Dickson), HOWARD VERNON (Professor von Braun/Professor Leonard Nosferatu), JEAN-LOUIS COMOLLI (Professor Jeckell), LÁSZLÓ SZABÓ (Chief Engineer), MICHEL DELAHAYE (von Braun's Assistant), JEAN-ANDRÉ FIESCHI (Professor Heckel).

IFF BERLIN 1965 GOLDEN BEAR (Jean-Luc Godard).

## *"Love? What's that?"*

Disguised as a journalist for "Figaro-Pravda," secret agent Lemmy Caution (Eddie Constantine) travels from the so-called Outer Lands to Alphaville, the capital city of the Milky Way. A technocratic elite led by Professor von Braun (Howard Vernon) has seized power in Alphaville; but Caution discovers that von Braun is in fact merely carrying out the orders of Alpha 60, a supercomputer he had originally developed for the needs of large commercial corporations. Thanks to its superior intelligence, the computer was eventually able to reprogram itself and is now capable of making its own decisions. So Alpha 60 is implementing its master plan: to create an ideal state governed solely by the rules of logic, In Alphaville, all emotions – and therefore all poetry – are to be punished with death. It seems that Alpha 60 has already had considerable success, for most of the city's inhabitants have grown oblivious to all feeling and mutated into flesh-and-blood robots. Caution, who has not the slightest intention of following the directives of the computer-brain, is introduced to Professor von Braun's daughter Natascha (played by Anna Karina, Jean-Luc Godard's wife at the time). She will be Caution's official guide for the duration of his visit. He finds out that Natascha was born in the Outer Lands but has lost all memory of her time there; for in Alphaville, the past has been suspended as a temporal category. Caution, however, manages to reawaken her memory, which in turn revives her feeling for poetry and eve tually inspires her love. As quick with his wits as he is with his fists, Cauti puts an end to the reign of Alpha 60, and the couple leave Alphaville togeth

This is science fiction with the look of a 50s B-movie, and it's as r freshing today as it was in 1965. For in the digital age, the sci-fi genre gradually suffocating under the weight of awesome sets and special effec Instead of filming in expensively designed mock-ups, Jean-Luc Goda worked exclusively on location in real places. Raoul Coutard, his excelle cameraman, produced strong-contrast black and white images of pitc black Parisian streets, futuristic government buildings, strange hotels and a indoor public swimming pool. All these elements combine to evoke a sinist space-age metropolis. And a blinking lamp plus a fan lit menacingly fro below suffice to embody the omnipotent computer brain.

It's a wonderfully improvised tale, and in Lemmy Caution (Eddie Co stantine), Godard introduces a protagonist who's the diametrical opposite the dead-eyed zombies who populate Alphaville. Caution is a man of integ ty, and his lined and pitted face bears witness to a turbulent past. The fac of course, belongs to Eddie Constantine, an actor with a turbulent past, an an icon of commercial French cinema since the 50s. As the wily, hard-bitte

2

hero of the Lemmy Caution series, he was the embodiment of Europe's cination with U.S. genre cinema at that time. Godard and his colleagues the *nouvelle vague* shared that fascination. To them, many of the directo trashy American movies were real and admirable *auteurs*, who had pressed their personal vision in genre tales with the emphasis on action.

By putting an ironic slant on Constantine's image as tough guy ladies' man, Godard enlarged *Alphaville* into a poetic reflection on the c ma itself. When confronted with the soulless love-slaves of the Brave World, Caution swats them away like niggling flies – and he takes care o opponents without raising a sweat. The nameless killer who lies in wait ir hotel is no match for Lemmy, who rapidly punches him through three g doors. With laconic coolness, Godard goes through the motions with sex

**"Godard again shows his uncompromising intellectual, unorthodox methods for a pic that is both piquant and squetchy."** *Variety*

1 What the good book says: Natascha (Anna Karina) discovers poetry and takes a bite of *Alphaville's* forbidden fruit.

2 Technical difficulties: Indifferent to its robotic denizens, secret agent Lemmy Caution (Eddy Constantine, left) braves the mazes of *Alphaville*.

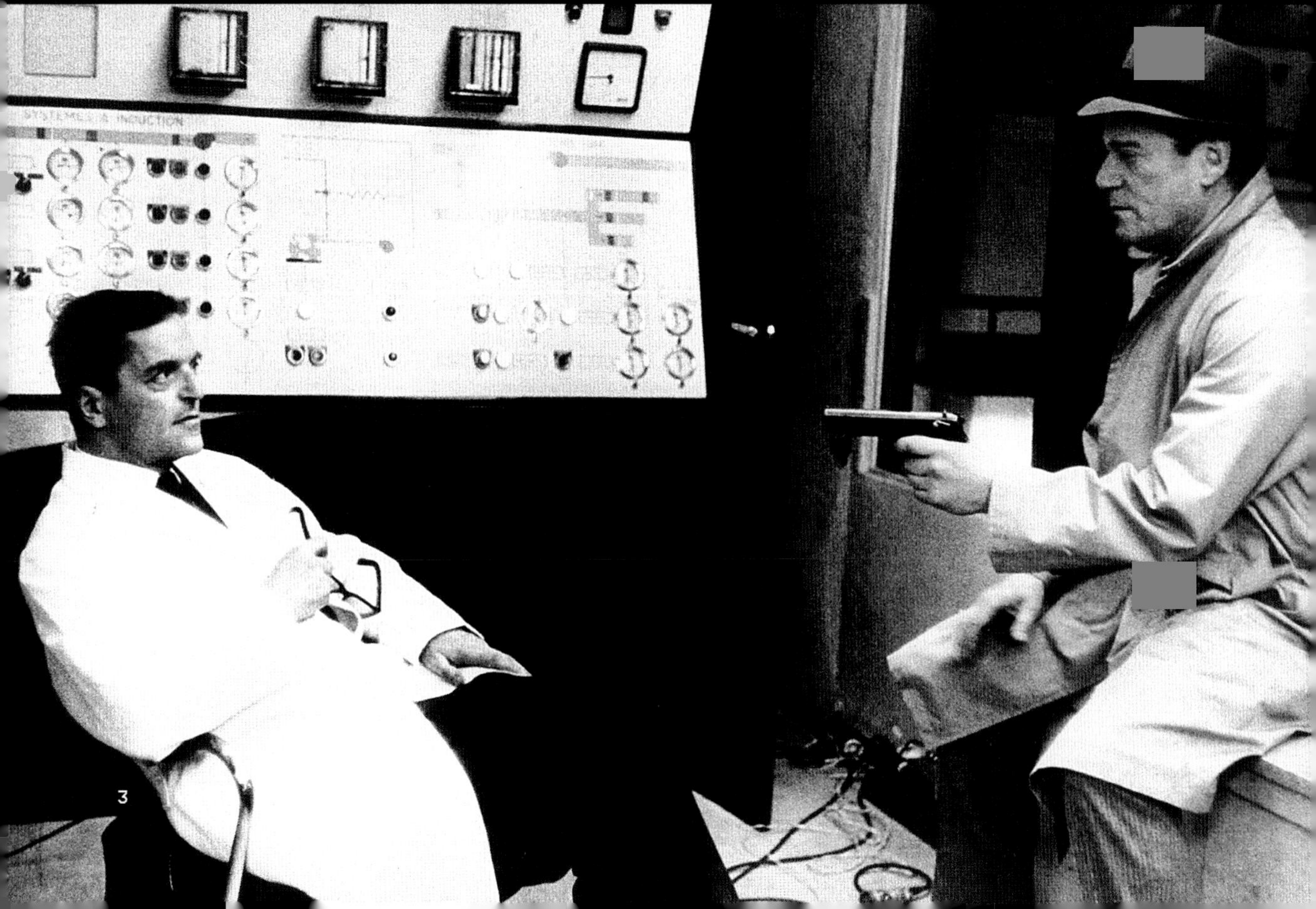

3

nmasking the wizard of Alphaville: Compared to echnological mastermind Prof. Leonard Nosferatu .k.a. Von Braun (Howard Vernon), Lemmy Caution eems to be headed the way of the dinosaurs.

4 A shadow of a doubt: *Alphaville* luxuriates in a rich film noir atmosphere reminiscent of 1940s and 50s Hollywood. Akim Tamiroff (left) as Henry Dickson.

nce, in order to focus more clearly on another aspect of his protagonist: e cold uniformity of Alphaville, Caution is a harbinger of poetry and love.

Anyone familiar with the vitriolic acerbity of Godard's later cinematic s on capitalist society is unlikely to find *Alphaville* a polemical film. Yet ugh the movie may appear to be an attack on civilization as such, count- details show that it really is a critique of the existing system. The streets phaville, for example, are named after the nuclear physicists Werner enberg and Enrico Fermi, while Caution's adversary is named after the nan rocket scientist Wernher von Braun, who found employment in the U. S. after WW II. By such means, Godard suggests that the roots of his total itarian future state extend right into the landscape of the Cold War, touchin the present.

If *Alphaville* seems less biting than other Godard films, this also ha something to do with his surprisingly tender attitude towards the two lovers He even grants them a happy ending, and one that's truly affecting in its gen tle pathos. As the couple drive towards the Outer Lands in Lemmy Caution's Ford Galaxy, we see the proof that Natascha has really been cured; at firs hesitantly, and then with conviction, she says: "I love you!" JH

**IE CONSTANTINE**

His scarred face predestined him for the role of the tough guy. He was born not far from Los Angeles, in 1917, and if he had spent his career in Hollywood, he would probably never have progressed beyond playing supporting roles in gangster movies. Eddie Constantine, however, made his breakthrough on the other side of the Atlantic: in Paris, where he performed in nightclubs after the war, recorded his first records, and delighted the audience at the Moulin Rouge, where he appeared alongside Edith Piaf. In 1953, he made his debut as the FBI agent Lemmy Caution in *La môme vert-de-gris* (1953), adapted from a crime novel by popular British author Peter Cheyney (*Poison Ivy*). From then on, even when he wasn't actually playing Caution, he was generally typecast as a dryly humorous action hero whom the blondes found irresistible and the baddies unbeatable. This only changed when Jean-Luc Godard signed him up for *Alphaville* (1965) and successfully subverted his Lemmy Caution image. From then on, Constantine was a cult actor of the new European *cinema des auteurs*, and especially for the German filmmakers of the day. In Peter Lilienthal's *Malatesta* (1970), he played an Italian anarchist, and in Rainer Werner Fassbinder's *Beware of a Holy Whore* (*Warnung vor einer heiligen Nutte*, 1971), he was "The Film Star." Until his death in 1992, Constantine was a familiar face in TV and cinema productions – often playing some version of himself, or of his own movie image.

Eddie Constantine made his last appearance as Lemmy Caution in Godard's *Germany Year 90 Nine Zero* (*Allemagne 90 neuf zéro*, 1991). He plays an old man who has spent 30 years as an undercover agent living in East Germany. When the Wall comes down, he is pensioned off and tries to find his way back home to the West.

# THE SOUND OF MUSIC

1965 - USA - 174 MIN. - MUSICAL

**DIRECTOR** ROBERT WISE (*1914)
**SCREENPLAY** ERNEST LEHMAN, OSCAR HAMMERSTEIN II, based on a report by HOWARD LINDSAY and RUSSEL CROUSE ab MARIA AUGUSTA TRAPP'S autobiography entitled *THE TRAPP FAMILY SINGERS* **DIRECTOR OF PHOTOGRAPHY** TED D. MCCORD **EDITING** WILLIAM REYNOLDS **MUSIC** RICHARD RODGERS, IRWIN KOSTAL (Adaptation) **PRODUCTION** ROBERT WISE, SAUL CHAPLI for 20TH CENTURY FOX, ARGYLE ENTERPRISES.

**STARRING** JULIE ANDREWS (Maria), CHRISTOPHER PLUMMER (Georg von Trapp), ELEANOR PARKER (Baroness), RICHARD HAYDN (Max Detweiler), PEGGY WOOD (Mother Abbess), CHARMIAN CARR (Liesl von Trapp), HEATHER MENZI (Louisa von Trapp), NICHOLAS HAMMOND (Friedrich von Trapp), DUANE CHASE (Kurt von Trapp), ANGELA CARTWRIGHT (Brigitta von Trapp), DEBBIE TURNER (Marta von Trapp), KYM KARATH (Gretl von Trapp), DANIEL TRUHITTE (Rolf Gruber NORMA VARDEN (Frau Schmidt, housekeeper).

**ACADEMY AWARDS 1965** OSCARS for BEST PICTURE (Robert Wise), BEST DIRECTOR (Robert Wise), BEST EDITING (William Reynol BEST ADAPTED MUSIC (Irwin Kostal), and BEST SOUND (James Corcoran, Fred Hynes).

## *"Silver white winters that melt into springs, these are a few of my favorite things."*

The camera glides through the clouds over a snow-covered mountain range. We hear the wind whistling and suddenly green mountains fill the screen, and the field of vision moves in on a fertile valley where birds are chirping merrily. A grand swoop of the camera cues the theme music. Rocks are reflected in a crisp blue lake as the little houses in the valley come into sight. Soaring beyond the mountain tops again, we look down onto a green meadow where we approach a tiny human figure, who gradually fills the screen. It is a woman with outstretched arms, turning round and round as she sings: "The hills are alive with the sound of music!"

As inspiring as the musical overture itself, the opening shots of *The Sound of Music* tune us into the journey that lies ahead. Like the story that follows, these initial moments are an extended love letter to the Alpine idyll, infused with songs that will forever contain the spirit of 1960s musical euphoria. The film version of Richard Rodgers and Oscar Hammerstein II's Broadway musical sensation not only managed to rake in more ticket sales than *Gone with the Wind* (1939), but also paved the way for Julie Andrews' incomparable film career, which was officially launched the previous year with Walt Disney's *Mary Poppins* (1964).

The story is based on Maria Augusta Trapp's personal memoirs, entitled *The Trapp Family Singers*. The memoirs detail her experiences in 1930s Austria, where she founded a family choir before immigrating to the USA after Germany's annexation of Austria in 1938. What is translated to the screen is an undeniable deluge of humor and sentimentality, but in this case, it pr an unbeatable combination.

Maria (Julie Andrews), an aspiring young nun whose boisterous cause much concern and the occasional headshake among her fellow ters, is appointed by the convent to serve as governess to the seven chil of widower Baron von Trapp (Christopher Plummer). Upon her arrival a estate, the spirited woman learns that the aristocrat is a former sea ca who runs his household like a battleship. Housekeeper Frau Schmidt (N Varden) supplies Maria with a concise assessment of the situation – Trapp children don't play, they march." Maria's new post will be no bo cherries: the previous governess lasted just two days.

But it doesn't turn out like that. With her wit and warmth, Maria re gains the trust and admiration of the seven children, the eldest of w Liesl (Charmian Carr), is a 16-year-old on the verge of womanhood, an youngest, Gretl (Kym Karath), a tender five. When the Baron goes off to na for a lengthy stay with his mistress, who is herself a baroness (Ele Parker), Maria seizes the opportunity to reform some of the household ims and do away with the family's reverence for discipline. She takes children on excursions and boating trips, teaching them to free their through song. Director Robert Wise heightens these song and dance quences by setting them against a picturesque Salzburg and the maj Alps, creating an atmosphere of untainted happiness, a stylistic synt

1

perhaps of *Singin' in the Rain* (1952) and the carefree spirit of television's *The Partridge Family*. Movement is the lifeblood of these sequences. Strolling, marching and bicycling are all set to song, presenting a clear contrast between the Baron's Prussian ways and Maria's *joie de vivre*. Upon his return, the Baron voices his disgust at the governess' presumptuous child-rearing practices. He is, however, quickly silenced upon hearing the children's singing. The Baron's personality undergoes a swift metamorphosis, proving that music can indeed "tame the beast" – in Hollywood at least. Within a matter of minutes, all signs of his military muscle have vanished and the Baron's booming voice joins in with the rest of the von Trapp Family.

The Baron and Maria start to give in to feelings neither of them can deny – a burgeoning love for one another. When the Baroness wises up to the situation, she willingly backs down from her claim to the Baron's heart, leaving Maria with the field wide open. Shortly after the couple's wedding, they found a family choir. Meanwhile, Germany has completed its annexation of Austria and the Baron is called to military service. To evade participating in the Nazi caus the family decides to flee the country. A spectacular escape attempt ensue and after several close calls with the Nazis, the von Trapps reach freedom.

The arrival of the Nazi regime in this idyllic alpine country descenc upon the film like a plague on paradise. A profound longing for an unta nished world – symbolized by the pristine purity of the lake and mountair that introduced the film – forms the backbone of the story. It is no coinc dence that the Baron keeps saying he lives in a disappearing world, for it the rainbows of days gone by that this film chases, a world immune to th darker sides of history. With songs like "The Sound of Music," "My Favorit Things," "Sixteen Going on Seventeen," and "Edelweiss," it is the music tha creates the greater part of this imagined space, in which the beauty of natur and the simple things in life co-exist in perfect harmony. The music express es a love of country, faith in God, and a need to be cared for. It is a film whos message is as clear as a mountain lake.

**[JU]LIE ANDREWS**

Shortly after a 1947 MGM screen test, Julie Andrews was informed that she was all wrong for film. As it turned out, the judges couldn't have been more wrong. She struck Oscar gold with her Hollywood debut in *Mary Poppins* (1964), needing only a spoonful of sugar to win the Academy Award for Best Actress. The film about the delightful nanny became an instant classic with both the young and young at heart. Just how effortlessly Mary could pop open her umbrella and soar above London's rooftops – clear into Hollywood's most memorable moments – is a testament to the picture's magic. Still, Andrews' maiden voyage in Tinseltown was by no means her big break into show business. Instead, it was a much-anticipated milestone in the career of one of musical theater's brightest stars.

Born on the outskirts of London in 1935, Julie Andrews began to earn a living on stage at the age of twelve, appearing in the musical revue "Starlight Roof" at the London Hippodrome. Seven years later, Julie crossed the Atlantic to star in the Broadway musical "The Boyfriend" and became a household name in a matter of weeks. The production marked the beginning of Andrews' reign as queen of New York's musical stage. She created the role of Eliza Doolittle in "My Fair Lady" and went on to hold court as Lady Guinevere, a part written especially for her in yet another Lerner and Lowe singing extravaganza entitled "Camelot."

However, it was Walt Disney who claimed her for the screen. After breaking onto the scene with two incomparable performances in *Mary Poppins* (1964) and *The Sound of Music* (1964), Andrews tried her hand at more serious fare in films like *The Americanization of Emily* (1964), opposite James Garner and Alfred Hitchcock's *Torn Curtain* (1966), opposite Paul Newman. One of Andrews' most impressive cinematic achievements came in 1981 with the offbeat musical remake of Reinhold Schünzel's *Victor / Victoria*, about a woman pretending to be a man pretending to be a woman. This retelling of *Victor / Victoria* was filmed by Blake Edwards, the acclaimed director of *Breakfast at Tiffany's* (1961), and Andrews' husband of more than 30 years. The couple have worked together on numerous other projects, including *Darling Lili* (1970), *Ten* (1979) and *S. O. B.* (1981). Today, Julie Andrews has by and large withdrawn from a life of singing in front of large audiences. Instead, she has dedicated herself to inspiring young minds in a new capacity, enjoying much success as an author of children's books under the pen name Julie Edwards.

**"Ted McCord catches the beauty and fascination of the terrain with his facile [c]ameras, combining the splendor of towering mountains and quiet lakes with [t]he Old World grace of the historic City of Music, a stunning complement to the [i]nteriors shot in Hollywood."** *Variety*

1 The hills are alive… and it's really frightening: Wild geese that fly with the moon on their wings help Maria (Julie Andrews) chase away her fears.

2 Cinderella story: Maria's prayers have been answered. Her music has opened the hearts of the von Trapp family and helped a nun find her way to the altar.

3 A family outing: Maria and the von Trapp children relish life's simple pleasures while discovering the beauty of Salzburg. The film was shot on location in the medieval Austrian city.

# RED BEARD
## Akahige

1965 - JAPAN - 185 MIN. - DRAMA

DIRECTOR AKIRA KUROSAWA (1910–1998)
SCREENPLAY RYUZO KIKUSHIMA, HIDEO OGUNI, MASATO IDE, AKIRA KUROSAWA, based on the novel *AKAHIGE SHINRYOTAN* by SHUGORO YAMAMOTO DIRECTOR OF PHOTOGRAPHY ASAKAZU NAKAI, TAKAO SAITÔ EDITING AKIRA KUROSAWA MUSIC MASARU SATÔ PRODUCTION RYUZO KIKUSHIMA, TOMOYUKI TANAKA for KUROSAWA PRODUCTION CO. LTD, TOHO.

STARRING TOSHIRÔ MIFUNE (Doctor Kyojio Niide, known as "Akahige" – Red Beard), YUZO KAYAMA (Doctor Noboru Yasumoto), YOSHIO TSUCHIYA (Doctor Handayu Mori), TATSUYOSHI EHARA (Genzo Tsugawa), REIKO DAN (Osugi), KYÔKO KAGAWA (Madwoman), KAMATARI FUJIWARA (Rokusuke), TSUTOMU YAMAZAKI (Sahachi), MIYUKI KUWANO (Onaka), AKEMI NEGISHI (Okuni, the Mistress), TERUMI NIKI (Otoyo).

IFF VENICE 1965 GOLDEN LION (Toshirô Mifune).

## *"He's a famous doctor, no, he's a great man."*

Nineteenth-century Japan: young Dr. Noboru Yasumoto (Yuzo Kayama) returns to Edo (as Tokyo was once known), intending to take up a position as private physician to a general. Instead, he ends up working in a hospital for the poor. Though Yasumoto sticks with the job, he also rebels against the strict rules imposed by the hospital administrator, Dr. Kyojio Niide (Toshirô Mifune), known as Red Beard. Yasumoto refuses to wear the standard-issue doctor's gown, and even ignores the hospital ban on alcohol. Despite all this, Red Beard doesn't sack him – which is what Yasumoto had been hoping for – and in the course of time, the arrogant young medic will be transformed by his experiences in the hospital.

After the Samurai films *Yojimbo* (1961) and *Sanjuro* (1961), which he had followed with a present-day drama (*High and Low / Tengoku to jigoku*, 1963), Akira Kurosawa, Japan's greatest director, turned once again to a historical theme. This time, however, his protagonists were not warriors but philanthropists. In some ways, *Red Beard* is a kind of cinematic *Bildungsroman*, showing the growth in understanding that allows an arrogant but naive youth to mature into a man of integrity. That may sound a little didactic, but Kurosawa's film tells a heartbreaking story, and the experience of watching it is quite overwhelming.

*Red Beard* is three hours long, and subdivided into a series of episodes. First we have Yasumoto's arrival in hospital, his experiences with his obdurate boss, and his earliest encounters with incurable diseases and death. Then come the story, told in flashback, of the life and loves of an ailing old man named Sahachi (Tsutomu Yamazaki), and the case of Dr. Yasumoto's first personal patient – Otoyo (Terumi Niki), a sick twelve-year-old girl who had been forced into prostitution – and finally the tale of Chobo, a little thief whose family have poisoned themselves in despair. For each of these episodes, Kurosawa adopts a different narrative tone or a unique perspective. The story of the sick girl, for instance, is accompanied by an off-screen commentary spoken by Yasumoto; in another episode, the main character never

1

# “I think the terrible reality that I describe in *Red Beard* is exactly that of Japan today.”

*Akira Kurosawa*

once appears; and in its sheer rawness, Red Beard’s fistfight with the pimps (in the story about the girl) is in a genre all of its own. Most of the stories are deeply moving, and the tales of Sahachi and Chobo are particularly poignant, thanks not least to Masaru Satô’s wonderful music.

The film does more than merely follow a young person’s progress towards maturity; it also describes how Yasumoto and Red Beard gradually grow closer, and how the young man slowly comes to respect and value his apparently despotic boss as a perceptive and compassionate physician. Their relationship can also be read as a tale of how East meets West: Yasumoto represents the Occident, for he learned his profession with Dutch medics in Nagasaki; Red Beard stands for traditional Japanese medicine – and yet he wants to learn from Yasumoto. It’s not that Red Beard believes Western medicine is superior to Japanese, but he’s willing to try anything if he feels it might help his patients. “Red Beard,” incidentally, was a term used in Japan during the period depicted in the film to denote anyone from the West.

“When I was making this film, I had something special in mind,” said Akira Kurosawa. And indeed, *Red Beard* turned out to be something extremely special. All of Kurosawa’s movies were composed with the utmost care, but

1 Just what the doctor ordered: Dr. Kyojio Niide, a. k. a. Red Beard’s (Toshirô Mifune) loyalties are to his patients, not his colleagues.

2 House calls: Red Beard makes his rounds throughout the village with new medical intern Noboru Yasumoto (Yuzo Kayama, right).

4

3 Your word is my command: A twelve year-old girl is coerced into prostitution, but her torturer Yasumoto is the one who'll have to pay the price…

4 Hippocratic oath: Red Beard (2nd from left) asserts his seniority and makes the deviant Yasumoto kiss the ground he walks on.

**TOSHIRÔ MIFUNE (1920–1997)**

He capered around in front of the terrified farmers, brandishing his sword and gesticulating wildly: in Kurosawa's *Seven Samurai* (*Shichinin no samurai*, 1954) Toshirô Mifune was a vital, virile phenomenon. Mifune's impressive physical presence is particularly tangible in the works of Akira Kurosawa. Between 1948 and 1965, he made 16 films with the master director; he may fairly be described as *the* Kurosawa actor. Though Mifune is identified with Samurai films in much the same way John Wayne is felt to embody the Western, he certainly didn't only play historical warriors. He made his debut with Kurosawa in 1948, as a tubercular gangster in *Drunken Angel (Yoidore tenshi)*. In *The Lower Depths* (*Donzoko*, 1957) he played a petty thief, and in *Red Beard* (*Akahige*, 1965) a doctor. Yet he is still best remembered for his Samurai roles in *Seven Samurai* (*Shichinin no samurai*, 1954), *Yojimbo* (1961) and *Sanjuro* (1961). This image later helped him to find his footing in Hollywood: he appeared, for example, in John Boorman's war film *Hell in the Pacific* (1968) and in the TV series *Shogun* (1980). *Red Beard*, incidentally, was Mifune's last collaboration with Kurosawa, for the two had drifted ever further apart in the course of the years. Moreover, Mifune was furious that the production was taking so long to complete; he was not permitted to shave off his beard, and he couldn't accept any other roles, even when work on the Kurosawa movie was interrupted. Kurosawa, on the other hand, was far from delighted when Mifune appeared in the American Formula One movie *Grand Prix* (1966) immediately after making *Red Beard*.

**“In the course of twenty years, I saw *Red Beard* six times, and I told my children about it almost every day until they were old enough to see it for themselves.”** *Gabriel García Márquez*

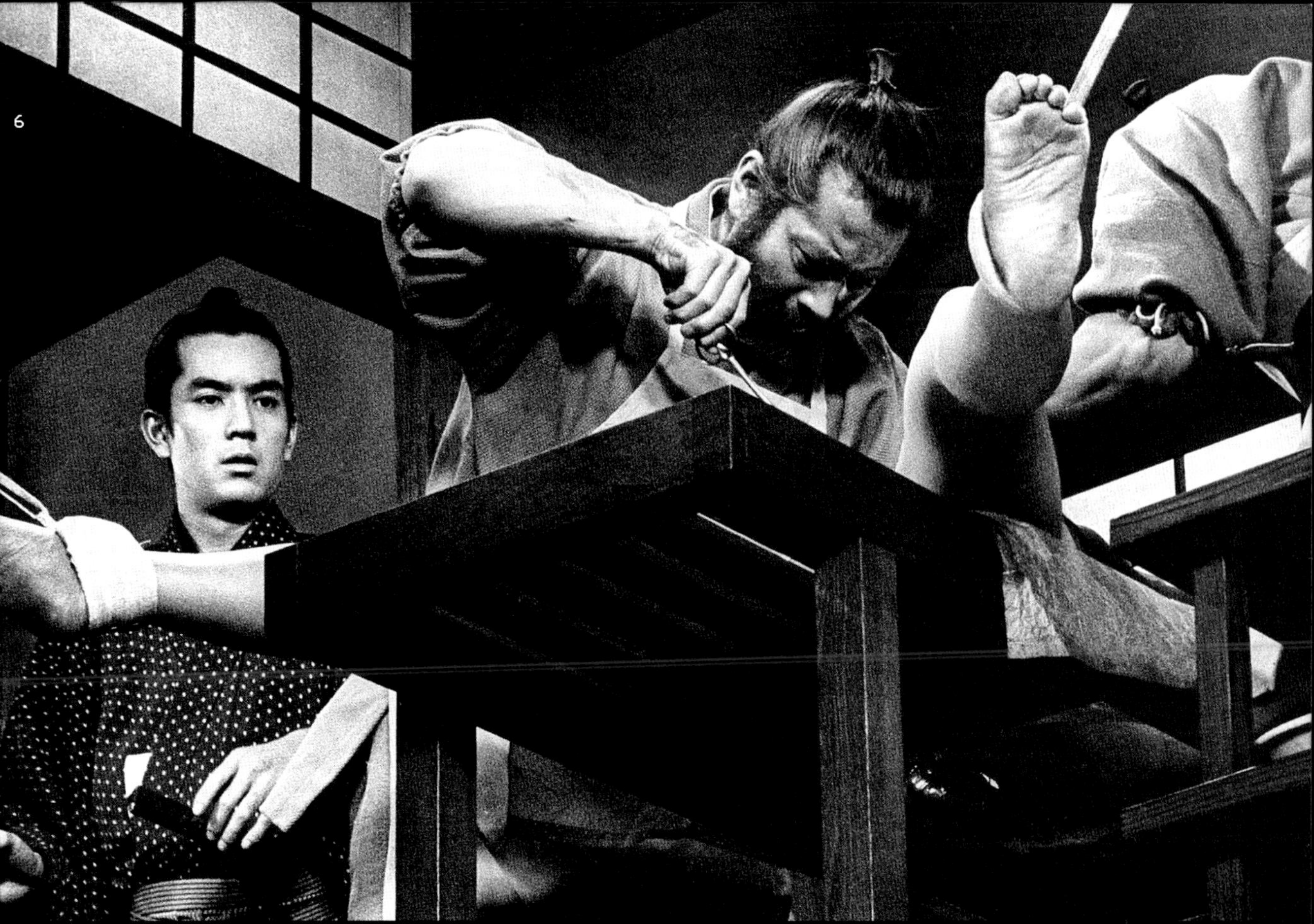

6

5 General or general hospital? Although Yasumoto originally wanted to be an army commander, Red Beard's guidance transforms him into a competent doctor.

6 A stitch in time: Red Beard ties up the loose ends of 19th-century surgery as Yasumoto watches aghast.

7 Spare the rod, spoil the intern: Yasumoto (right) gradually gets accustomed to Red Beard's old-fashioned ways.

he probably never took such extreme pains as with this one. The film was made in black and white, and the picture format is extremely wide and narrow; the hard contrasts and the effects of light and shadow across the entire screen are an astonishing artistic achievement in themselves. In the interiors, people and backgrounds enter into a kind of dialog, forming a series of lovingly composed sequences, in which every element contributes something indispensable to the whole. As was so often the case with Kurosawa, the filming of *Red Beard* was also a little "special;" it lasted two years, and work frequently had to be stopped because either the director or one of the actors was exhausted or sick. Kurosawa devoted enormous attention to achieving the greatest authenticity possible. Thus, he had the hospital complex constructed in aged wood, in the typical Japanese style of the 19th century – and this for a film that was no bombastic blockbuster, but a precise and intimate psychological study. The buildings were such perfect historical reconstructions that tourists visited the film set to admire them.

HJK

**"There seems to be a smell of rotten fruit." – "That's the smell of the poor."**

*Film quote: dialogue Yasumoto and Akahige*

1965 - FRANCE/ITALY - 120 MIN. - ADVENTURE MOVIE, COMEDY, MUSICAL

DIRECTOR LOUIS MALLE (1932–1995)

SCREENPLAY LOUIS MALLE, JEAN-CLAUDE CARRIÈRE DIRECTOR OF PHOTOGRAPHY HENRI DECAË EDITING SUZANNE BARON, KENOUT PELTIER MUSIC GEORGES DELERUE PRODUCTION OSCAR DANCIGERS for LES PRODUCTIONS ARTISTES ASSOCIÉS, NOUVELLES ÉDITIONS DE FILMS, VIDES CINEMATOGRAFICA.

STARRING JEANNE MOREAU (María I), BRIGITTE BARDOT (María II), GEORGE HAMILTON (Florès), GREGOR VON REZZORI (Diogène), PAULETTE DUBOST (Madame Diogène), CLAUDIO BROOK (Rodolfo), CARLOS LÓPEZ Moctezuma (Don Rodriguez), POLDO BENDANDI (Werther), JONATHAN EDEN (Juanito), FRANCISCO REIGUERA (Priest).

# *"Ave María y María!"*

In 1965, the Revolution hadn't yet reached the streets; but on the silver screen, it was already in full swing. The Revolution wore make up, it was sexy as hell and it brought chaos in its wake. Most sensationally of all, it brought together two of France's most desirable exports: Jeanne Moreau and Brigitte Bardot.

The plot had not much going for it. Sometime around 1900, two showgirls are working for a traveling circus in a small country in Central America. Purely by chance, they happen to invent the striptease. Even better, it turns out that they've shed their frillies for a good cause: people are so excited they rise up *en masse* and liberate their country from its tyrannous ruler.

Brigitte Bardot is pure dynamite as the daughter of an Irish freedom fighter with nitro-glycerine in her blood. Equally explosive is the carnevalesque film language of Louis Malle: *Viva María!* is a kind of cinematic comic, filled with the kind of nutty visual jokes that had already made *Zazie* (*Zazie dans le métro*, 1960) such a success. Some scenes are almost cruel, while others show the director's love of vaudeville and its cheap but exuberant vitality. Thus the job accompanying María I (Moreau) only becomes available when her previous stage partner shoots herself in a fit of lovesickness. María II (Bardot) stands there wide-eyed, and covers her ears just before the gun goes off. Then there's the great Rodolfo (Claudio Brook), who has a dream: he is trying to build a gun that will shoot round corners. Bombs are dropped by white doves conjured up out a hat, and they never fail to hit the right target. At the end of the film, a cleric is left holding his head in his hands… by which time, in any case, the prayers of the liberated people are dedicated to the new goddesses: "Ave María y María!"

Brigitte Bardot's efforts with the machine-gun ("Oh, the new Vickers!") are now as much a part of film iconography as her legendary bee-stung lips. A few years later, Louis Malle was amazed to discover that his nonsensical confection had become the favorite film of Germany's radical students. Rainer Werner Fassbinder had to explain it to him. As an enthusiastic pyromaniac, Brigitte Bardot stood for direct action; she was a propagandist of the deed. By contrast, Jeanne Moreau – whose character falls in love with the rebel Florès (George Hamilton) and leads the rebellion after his death – was the embodiment of romance and reform. In truth, the sex goddess and the darling of the intellectuals complemented each other astonishingly well, in unbreachable

1

1 Firing squad: Mexican beauties María I (Jeanne Moreau, right), and María II (Brigitte Bardot, left) let out deafening screams in the name of the revolution.

2 Viva la revolución! The people cheer on the female freedom fighters, who quickly become icons of a sexual revolution.

3 Powder keg picnic: María II's anarchist father trains her to take over the family business.

4 Ammo Zons: "All you need for a movie is a girl and a gun." (Jean-Luc Godard). María II tries out the latest weapon in gender equality.

5 A bullet-proof babe, grazed by love: María's heart belongs to Florès (George Hamilton), but her love cannot shield the rebel fighter from the enemy.

solidarity with the freedom fighters of the Third World. Off screen too, there wasn't a trace of rivalry between the two stars, although the press was slavering for it. In other respects, however, *Viva María!* had a difficult birth. Everyone involved with this movie still remembers with a shudder the brouhaha that surrounded the project, even before filming started in Mexico. After twenty weeks of filming, actor Gregor von Rezzori noted that Louis Malle was nervous and seemed to have nothing under control, opening the way for bad vibrations and petty animosities. It's said that when everyone has a hilarious time on set, the finished movie is unlikely to make the audience laugh. In the case of *Viva María!*, excessive harmony was one thing Malle definitely didn't have to worry about.

Here, the pathos of revolution is subjected to pitiless derision, and the

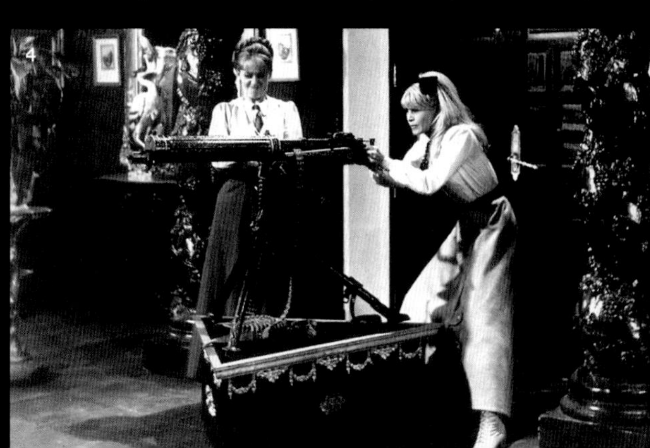

**“*Viva María* dispenses great energies with such visual grace that it may make perfectly sensible people feel slightly insecure, fearing that what they’re seeing must make sense after all. It doesn’t.”** *Newsweek*

5

6

entire film is thoroughly stylized. This led to a further side effect, which Malle could not have planned in advance: a lasting influence on the Spaghetti Western. Perhaps the moribund Western genre would have experienced a brief revival even if this irreverent Revolutionary Musical had never been made. But the snappy songs and the romantic melodies of composer Georges Delerue ("Paris, Paris") refer us back to the main actor in the "New Movement:" Old Europe. In the sunny desert landscapes of Mexico, a veritable Fountain of Youth, the French film gets an entirely new lease of life. *Viva María!* just radiates sex-appeal. The powder stains on the cheeks of Brigitte Bardot were memorable indeed, but a stunningly sensual Jeanne Moreau could easily stand the comparison with her spectacular junior partner.

PB

6 A kiss before dying: The critically injured Florès passionately bids María I to follow through with his battle plans.

7 Torching the hacienda: There'll be a hot time in Don Rodriguez's town home tonight.

8 Un ramo de flores: María places her head on her dead lover's heart before surrendering him to the earth.

**"The adventures of the two girls, in fact, take place in a never-never land quaintly touched with poetry where no one ever really gets hurt, where the Inquisition apologizes for the dilapidated state of its implements of torture ('I'm sorry, our equipment hasn't been used for ages'), and where a conjurer whose dove has been shot by a gun-toting spectator can bring it magically back to life again."** *Monthly Film Bulletin*

7

**GEORGES DELERUE (1925–1992)**

After contracting curvature of the spine in his youth, gifted pianist and high-school dropout Georges Delerue decided to devote his life to music. Along with Maurice Jarre, Michel Legrand and Pierre Jansen, he became one of the leading film composers of the *nouvelle vague*. *Shoot the Pianist* (*Tirez sur le pianiste*, 1959/60) was the first of ten collaborations with François Truffaut, which included *Jules and Jim* (*Jules et Jim*, 1961) and *Day for Night* (*La Nuit américaine*, 1973). Claude Chabrol, Jacques Demy, Philippe de Broca and Jean-Luc Godard (*Contempt / Le Mépris*, 1963) all made use of his unique gift for grasping the mood of a film instinctively. Delerue's arrangements, most of them in a minor key, are inspired by the simplicity of folk songs. His "trademark" sounds were oboe and clarinet solos, and he also made frequent use of harp accompaniments.

*Viva María!* (1965) was the only one of his Louis Malle soundtracks that was oriented more towards jazz. The music brought him a lot of attention, and it was the first of his scores to be released as an album. At this time, the only composers who had reasonable financial security were those who wrote pop songs, such as Michel Legrand or Francis Lai. So, in the late 60s, Delerue began to look towards America as a source of new income. The results, such as the score for Oliver Stone's *Platoon* (1986) were generally less than convincing. In the States, too, Delerue was at his strongest when creating musical evocations of scenes dealing with human relationships – see *Steel Magnolias* (1989), or the charming first-love story *A Little Romance* (1979), for which he won an Oscar. Georges Delerue died of heart failure in 1992.

# THE SPY WHO CAME IN FROM THE COLD

1965 - GREAT BRITAIN - 112 MIN. - SPY FILM

DIRECTOR MARTIN RITT (1914–1990)
SCREENPLAY PAUL DEHN, GUY TROSPER, based on the novel of the same name by JOHN LE CARRÉ
DIRECTOR OF PHOTOGRAPHY OSWALD MORRIS EDITING ANTHONY HARVEY MUSIC SOL KAPLAN PRODUCTION MARTIN RITT for SALEM.

STARRING RICHARD BURTON (Alec Leamas), CLAIRE BLOOM (Nan Perry), OSKAR WERNER (Fiedler), SAM WANAMAKER (Peters), RUPERT DAVIES (George Smiley), CYRIL CUSACK (Control), PETER VAN EYCK (Mundt), MICHAEL HORDERN (Ashe), ROBERT HARDY (Dick Carlton), BERNARD LEE (Patmore).

## *"Communism, capitalism, it's the innocent who get slaughtered."*

One of the most popular figures in 60s cinema was the spy. During WW II, allied spies were portrayed as courageous patriots; but in the Cold War era, the spy became little more than a plaything in the hands of a superpower. Unquestioning loyalty gave way to a creeping sense of political ambivalence. The only motivation James Bond required was girls, cars and cocktails; but 007's nonchalance was harmless compared to the cynicism of the anti-Bonds who succeeded him, like Michael Caine as Harry Palmer in *The Ipcress File* (1965) and *Funeral in Berlin* (1966), George Segal in *The Quiller Memorandum* (1966) or Laurence Harvey in *A Dandy in Aspic* (1968). Their world is a crepuscular no-man's-land between East and West, a demimonde of invisible enemies in which they live, act and die like shadows or ghosts of themselves. In *The Spy Who Came In from the Cold*, such an existence has made Alec Leamas (Richard Burton) fatalistic to the point of indifference. We seriously start to wonder if he'll drink himself to death before he gets shot.

This was to be the first of several film adaptations of novels by the former agent and best-selling author John Le Carré. It begins in Berlin, at Checkpoint Charlie, the border crossing point between the communist and capitalist worlds. His face expressionless, Leamas looks across to the other side, where a good friend of his was shot dead by the Soviets while attempting to escape to the West. The rainy night reinforces the ghostly unreality of the setting, but in fact this place of phantoms is the focus of the real and brutal confrontation between two rival world-views. When the British agent returns to London, he is asked to "stay in the cold just a little longer." His bosses want him to help eliminate a dangerous East German agent called Mundt. Leamas makes it politely clear that he would prefer not to… and is temporarily suspended from his job. He takes a job as a librarian and falls in love with a young colleague named Nan (Claire Bloom) – a romantic communist.

And all the while, he carries on drinking like a fish, until his alcoholism leads him to a drying-out clinic. After he is discharged, a friendly chap offers him a rehabilitation opportunity… and only gradually does the spectator realize what's really going on: the East German secret service, believing him

1

2

**RICHARD BURTON (1925–1984)**

Whether he was burying his emotions beneath a tormented impassivity or allowing them to erupt in wild aggression, the many masks of Richard Burton concealed a restless and skeptical spirit. It was this broken quality – along with his sonorous voice and his piercingly blue eyes – that made him the very model of late 20th-century maleness. His appeal was reinforced by all the scandals and alcoholic excesses, and especially by his stormy marriage to Elizabeth Taylor, whom he divorced and wed again. Burton was happily extravagant, and extravagantly wasteful of his own talent. His lifelong interest in money may have had something to do with the poverty of his family background. He was born into a Welsh mining community in 1925, the twelfth of 13 children. His inspirational teacher, Philip Burton, helped him to get into Oxford University; and perhaps more importantly, he provided Richard Walter Jenkins with his future stage name. There followed several large Shakespeare roles at the legendary Old Vic Theatre in London, but only five British films. After his breakthrough as Marc Antony in *Cleopatra* (1963), he appeared alongside Liz Taylor in several movies, including Mike Nichols' *Who's Afraid of Virginia Woolf?* (1966) and *The Taming of the Shrew* (*La bisbetica domata,* 1966), directed by Franco Zeffirelli. The public drama of his relationship to Taylor often overshadowed his huge presence and talent, which made many a mediocre movie well worth watching. Despite receiving seven Oscar nominations – for his roles in *My Cousin Rachel* (1952), *The Robe* (1953), *Becket* (1963), *The Spy Who Came In from the Cold,* 1965), *Who's Afraid of Virginia Woolf?* (1966), *Anne of the Thousand Days* (1969) and *Equus* (1977) – he never actually won the prize. Shortly before his death, he gave a fine performance in Michael Radford's Orwell adaptation, *1984* (1984).

"After all the spy and mystery movies of a romantic and implausible nature we have seen, it is great to see one as realistic and believable as *The Spy Who Came In from the Cold*." *The New York Times*

› be a washed-up early retiree, have persuaded him to work for them. But ’s all part of the MI5 plan – Leamas is now a double agent.

The shifting sands of language are the foundation of this film. A casual assing remark may be crucially important, while a wholehearted expression f support may well be a prelude to betrayal. For those working behind the on Curtain, picking up such nuances of speech is a matter of life and death.

Leamas acquires the trust of an East German called Fiedler (Oskar Werner A convinced communist, Fiedler is a conversational match for the morall indifferent Western agent. But Leamas is only really interested in Fiedler as chink in the enemy's armor. He knows that Fiedler is a Jew, and therefor that he detests the former Nazi officer Mundt (Peter van Eyck). In the end both Fiedler and the Englishman will lose out: a secret tribunal in East German

On the fence and off the wagon: Double agent Alec Leamas (Richard Burton) can't decide whether to work as an Eastern or Western operative. So he chooses alcohol instead.

Communist crossfire: East German spy Mundt (Peter van Eyck) puts Leamas through the wringer as he sets out to discover where the agent's loyalties really lie.

3 A man of convictions: It wasn't government coercion, but Fiedler's (Oskar Werner) beliefs that compelled him to become a red spy.

4 Red clouds, silver linings: The politically active Nan (Claire Bloom) tries to sees the good in everything. However, her affair with Leamas makes her a prime target for evil intentions.

**"Craftily, and comprehensively, he turns the tables on his adversaries – only to discover at the end that he too has been set up by his bosses. Having come to feel something approaching friendly respect for his opponent, he's eventually forced to sacrifice him. Even worse: the real villain, an utterly amoral manipulator from the opposing side, is the person he has to thank for saving his life – and with one foot in freedom, he makes a mess of it himself. A humane gesture of sympathy causes a delay that costs him the ultimate price."** *Die Welt*

5

defines him – and not Mundt – as a double agent. The unsuspecting Nan nisused as the principal witness against Leamas. At the climax of an ugly le, the ex-Nazi helps the British couple escape across the Berlin Wall – ere Nan is shot dead. It dawns on Leamas that the real plan has always n to eliminate Fiedler, and he sacrifices himself voluntarily.

After countless surprising twists, spectators too start to feel deceived deeply disappointed. By rooting for Leamas, we feel partly guilty for the of Fiedler, the only person in the whole story who embodies something resembling moral integrity. In Michael Ritt's flawless film, it is ultimately impossible to decide who's on the right side, who's the victim and who's the villain. Only one thing is clear: all of them are victims of two systems that differ in their ideologies but not in their methods. The colors of this movie are black and white, like the thinking of the time it was made. But the truth is in the grayness of its characters and in a psychological realism that makes it far more than a document of the Cold War era.

PB

Sitting ducks: Nan is executed at the Berlin Wall while trying to escape with Leamas. Exactly according to plan.

6 Soviet drive through: When a prisoner exchange fails, Leamas is forced to stay out in the cold.

Seldom has the cinema caught Checkpoint Charlie in such a grim light.

# DOCTOR ZHIVAGO

1965 - USA - 200 MIN. - MELODRAMA, LITERARY ADAPTATION

DIRECTOR DAVID LEAN (1908–1991)
SCREENPLAY ROBERT BOLT, based on the novel of the same name by BORIS PASTERNAK DIRECTOR OF PHOTOGRAPHY FREDDIE YOUNG
EDITING NORMAN SAVAGE MUSIC MAURICE JARRE PRODUCTION CARLO PONTI for MGM.

STARRING GERALDINE CHAPLIN (Tonja), JULIE CHRISTIE (Lara), TOM COURTENAY (Pasha Antipova / Strelnikov), ALEC GUINNESS (Gen. Jevgraf Zhivago), SIOBHAN MCKENNA (Anna), RALPH RICHARDSON (Alexander Gromeko), OMAR SHARIF (Yuri Zhivago), ROD STEIGER (Victor Komarovsky), RITA TUSHINGHAM (The Girl), ADRIENNE CORRI (Amelia).

ACADEMY AWARDS 1965 OSCARS for BEST ADAPTED SCREENPLAY (Robert Bolt), BEST CINEMATOGRAPHY (Freddie Young), BEST MUSIC (Maurice Jarre), BEST ART DIRECTION (John Box, Terry Marsh, Dario Simoni), BEST COSTUME DESIGN (Phyllis Dalton).

## *"The personal life is dead in Russia. History has killed it."*

Love, affection and sentimentality did not color the rainbows of Social Realism – at least not officially. As Soviet commander Strelnikov (Tom Courtenay) tries to impress upon poet and physician Yuri Zhivago (Omar Sharif), Russia's new social order has been painted a uniform tone: a grand, uncompromising red, which has turned his once admired verse into meaningless displays of formalism. Though fired by the same fanatic idealism that made a general of him, the bloodthirsty Bolshevik's commentary on art and politics leaves the good doctor unfazed. Enslaved by distant echoes of individualism, Zhivago retreats to what has become a taboo private life, losing himself in his literary craft and the freedoms of the countryside. Yet the revolutionary goings-on that surround him refuse to be ignored, and soon he is plunged into the throes of war and away from Lara (Julie Christie) – his mistress and the inadvertent cause of his undoing.

Based on a novel with a background as intriguing as the content of its pages, David Lean's film adaptation of Boris Pasternak's *Doctor Zhivago* was the inevitable conclusion of what had ballooned into a widely publicized East-West political scandal. First brought into the public eye by an Italian publisher in 1957, *Doctor Zhivago* became a run-away literary hit throughout Western Europe and the United States within a year of its appearance. But success proved hollow for Pasternak, whose work remained banned in the Soviet Union for the next thirty years. Although recognized with the Nobel Prize for Literature in 1958, his government coerced him to decline the honor. Two years later, the author was dead.

The events were still very much alive in the collective consciousness of the West when David Lean decided to take on the film adaptation as the project to succeed his critically acclaimed *Lawrence of Arabia* (1962). Pasternak's tale about the fate of a conforming non-conformist, whose only de[illegible] is to avoid being engulfed by the overwhelming backdrop of a new so[illegible] order, seemed perfectly suited to Lean's cinematic style. Based on his tr[illegible] record, the self-proclaimed "sensualist of spectacle" promised to deliver another intricate character portrait that luxuriated in the contours of [illegible]solutely lavish scenery. And indeed, the stunning visuals of Lean's pict[illegible] leave audiences breathless. Under the guiding hand of masterful product[illegible] designer John Box, a crew of approximately 800 worked at reconstruct[illegible] the streets of Moscow for two years straight on a lot located just outs[illegible] Madrid. These are the resplendent, broad stretches of promenade we c[illegible] our eyes upon from the loggia adjoining the apartments of Zhivago's sur[illegible]gate parents (Ralph Richardson and Siobhan McKenna), whilst the Cza[illegible] cavalry march upon a sea of Bolshevik demonstrators.

Together with his returning cinematographer Freddie Young, Lean ag[illegible] succeed in delivering spectacular landscape shots, making superb use of [illegible] Panavision wide-screen format to capture the snow-covered masses fight[illegible] desperately against the brutal Russian winter (these sequences were actu[illegible]ly filmed in eastern Finland near the Soviet border).

In opposition to these monumental scenes and to Lean's larger-tha[illegible] life protagonist in *Lawrence of Arabia*, Yuri Zhivago emerges as an unassu[illegible]ing character, who peers dreamily out his window while the rest of the wo[illegible] comes crashing down around him. Omar Sharif endows the role with an [illegible] of naiveté that plays up the reluctant hero's indecisiveness and lack of mo[illegible] fiber as he traverses the many historical events he is powerless to influen[illegible]

Zhivago's passivity provides other members of the ensemble, like [illegible] half-brother Jevgraf (Alec Guinness), with an opportunity to take the hel[illegible]

1 Somewhere, my love: Yuri (Omar Sharif) holds onto antiquated ideals and chases a rainbow named Lara (Julie Christie).

2 Waltz with the wicked: The opportunistic Victor Komarovsky (Rod Steiger) offers Lara his experience and protection.

3 Cold front: The merciless Russian winter is indifferent to politics.

4 White nights and the White Guard: The Russian people run off to join the revolution. Interestingly, these Moscow scenes were filmed on a Madrid movie lot in Franco's dictatorial Spain.

5 Love without passion: Yuri demonstrates tenderness and compassion for wife Tonya (Geraldine Chaplin), but denies her the fires of his soul.

**"The bitter cold of winter (the only section of film made outside Spain, these Finland settings are at once beautiful and foreboding), the grime of Moscow, the lush countryside, the drabness of life in a dictatorship, the brutality of war, and the fool's paradise of the declining Czarist era are forcefully conveyed in full use of camera, color, sound and silence."** *Variety*

olshevik officer with the secret police, Jevgraf uses his influence to bail out of numerous impossible entanglements, just as he does with the en- film whenever a narrator is required to bridge scenes separated by years.

There's no doubt about who is the picture's most spellbinding charac- Komarovsky (Rod Steiger), a cynical womanizer and color-blind political ortunist, is a shifty businessman who caters to the highest bidder, suc- sfully negotiating one deal after the next with whoever he considers the n of the hour. He's flawed, but not entirely despicable, and his steady con- n for Yuri and Lara win him the sympathies of the audience, even though central couple despise him. Manifesting neither Strelnikov's fanaticism Yuri's introspection, he is high-spirited and resilient, and therefore Lara's male counterpart. This would explain why before allowing Lara to become Strelnikov's wife or Zhivago's mistress, Pasternak had Komarovsky deflower her himself. Indeed, Lara's character is of significance to those around her. To Komarovsky, she is a mere plaything to be enjoyed – a view he expects her to accept as a simple matter of fact, but which she doesn't take lightly. Yuri, of course, only sees the muse in her, and even his understanding wife Tonja (Geraldine Chaplin) deems the once-virtuous nurse a truly fine woman. In truth, Lara is a composite of all their assessments, but is first and foremost a survival artist.

Beyond the characterizations, Lean's unmistakable symbolism does a brilliant job communicating the struggle for individual and artistic survival in times of sheer adversity, and each merciless winter is followed by a spring bloom of daffodils. Likewise, a steadfast belief in legacy and greater mean-

6 Red, white and dead: The October Revolution according to Hollywood.

7 Do you play the balalaika? Gen. Yevgraf Zhivago (Alec Guinness) looks for some clue that might indicate that the girl before him (Rita Tushingham is indeed Lara and Yuri's lost child.

ing appears throughout the film in the form of Yuri's balalaika, the sole heirloom and recollection he has of his mother, who was a great musician. Although he cannot play the instrument himself, he carries it with him for most of his life, until finally passing it on to Lara, who in turn leaves it to their daughter – a child Yuri never meets, but who, nonetheless, inherits his mother's great gift for music.

Russia never looked this glamorous, but then again, with its predominantly British cast and Egyptian leading man speaking what Lean must have taken to be the Czarina's English, *Dr. Zhivago* never looks quite like Russia. Screenwriter Robert Bolt cut major portions of Pasternak's book, relying on voice-overs to tie together his somewhat sporadic, three-and-a-half-h tragic love story. It is therefore hardly surprising that this triumph of schm and romance was eaten alive by the critics and went on to become one of biggest box-office smashes of the entire decade! Eager moviegoers st in lines that wrapped around blocks to get a glimpse of Soviet snuggling, some theaters ran the film for years on end.

Cynics continually attribute *Zhivago's* popularity to Maurice Jar score and the folkloric balalaika melody that flows through the film. So wh It's evidence that music lovely enough to fill the harsh Siberian winter v jingling bells can warm even the coldest of hearts.

8 Country cottage: Yuri and family take refuge in what used to be the servants' quarters of their summer residence. However, without Lara, it will be a fallow season for Zhivago's poetry.

9 Healing with dreams: Caught up in reverie, Dr. Yuri Zhivago tends to patients wherever the winds of war blow him.

**OMAR SHARIF**

Omar Sharif (*1932) made a name for himself throughout the Western world with his role as Sherif Ali ibn el Kharish in *Lawrence of Arabia* (1962). Nonetheless, the actor born Michael Shalhoub on April 10th, 1932 in Alexandria was already a big-screen heartthrob in his native Egypt, and had founded a thriving production company by the time international acclaim rolled around. His next move was to win the hearts of women worldwide with his role as the daydreaming poet Yuri in David Lean's adaptation of Boris Pasternak's *Doctor Zhivago* (1965). The role of Yuri as a boy was played by Sharif's son Tarek. The cavalier Sharif's career flourished throughout the 1960s, and he had the great fortune of being cast in a breadth of roles alongside *Lawrence* and *Zhivago.* He played a the war-faring Sohamus in *The Fall of the Roman Empire* (1963), a priest in *Behold a Pale Horse* (1964), and a jealous husband whose suspicious nature ends up destroying his marriage in Sidney Lumet's *The Appointment* (1969). As Sharif's popularity began to dwindle in the 1970s, he took up philandering as an international playboy, ensuring that his face would at least be on the tabloids. A man of leisure, Sharif also earned a reputation as a world-class bridge player. Today, Omar Sharif enjoys a steady career in made-for-TV movies and mini-series, although his César-winning turn as a sentimental shopkeeper in François Dupeyron's *Monsieur Ibrahim* (2003) showed a marked return to form.

# PIERROT LE FOU

## Pierrot le fou

965 - FRANCE / ITALY - 110 MIN. - DRAMA, CRIME FILM

IRECTOR JEAN-LUC GODARD (*1930)

CREENPLAY JEAN-LUC GODARD DIRECTOR OF PHOTOGRAPHY RAOUL COUTARD EDITING FRANÇOISE COLLIN MUSIC ANTOINE DUHAMEL, BORIS BASSIAK, JEAN-BAPTISTE LULLY, ANTONIO VIVALDI PRODUCTION GEORGES DE BEAUREGARD for ROME PARIS FILMS, SOCIÉTÉ NOUVELLE DES CINÉMATOGRAPHIE, DINO DE LAURENTIIS CINEMATOGRAFICA.

TARRING JEAN-PAUL BELMONDO (Ferdinand "Pierrot" Griffon), ANNA KARINA (Marianne Renoir), GRAZIELLA GALVANI Ferdinand's Wife), DIRK SANDERS (Fred), PASCAL AUBIER (Second Brother), PIERRE HANIN (Third Brother), JIMMY KAROUBI (Dwarf), ROGER DUTOIT (Gangster), HANS MEYER (Gangster), KRISTA NELL (Madame Staquet), Samuel Fuller (Himself).

## *"If you're gonna be crazy, then be really crazy!"*

Disgusted by his bourgeois existence, Ferdinand (Jean-Paul Belmondo) runs off with Marianne (Anna Karina). She's been involved in the shady business carried out by her brother Fred (Dirk Sanders), a weapons dealer, and now there's a body and several guns lying around her flat. There's also a suitcase full of dollars there… so the couple head south with the money, pursued by gangsters with political connections. When their car goes up in flames along with the cash, the couple are forced into a series of petty thefts in order to make it to the Mediterranean. For a while, they live in perfect freedom in a lonely house on the beach; but eventually differences arise, and their criminal past catches up with them.

With a plot like this, *Pierrot le fou* might well have been a thoroug average American-style thriller. Naturally, the name of Jean-Luc Goda ensures that it isn't. Even his legendary debut *Breathless* (*À bout de souf* 1959) was much more than a mere variation on a familiar genre; indeed was one of the most brilliant works of the *nouvelle vague*, subverting t conventions of narrative cinema with playful ease. With *Pierrot le fou*, t French director continued the tradition he had initiated.

Godard did without a script and relied on free improvisation, produci a strikingly spontaneous movie that follows its own associative logic. Stru turally, it is a kind of collage rather than a classical film narrative, and it ma

2

**JEAN-PAUL BELMONDO** He acquired his trademark as a young boxer: a very conspicuously broken nose. Jean-Paul Belmondo was born in Paris in 1933 and both his par-ents were artists. By the time he made his cinema debut in the mid-50s, he had acquired a solid acting training and some experience on stage. I 1959, he became famous practically overnight with his performance as the cheeky but romantic crook in Godard's *Breathless* (*À bout de souffle* From then on, Belmondo bore the nickname "Bebel," and French sociologists pondered the phenomenon of "le belmondisme" – a wave of imita-tion among the country's youth.

François Truffaut described Belmondo as the best French actor of his generation, and there's no denying his presence in a whole series of ou standing 60s films. These included Godard's comedy *A Woman is a Woman* (*Une femme est une femme*, 1961) and Truffaut's adventure movi *Mississippi Mermaid* (*La Sirène du Mississippi*, 1969), in which he gave a convincing performance in a romantic role – just as he had done in *Pierr le fou* (1965). Jean-Paul Belmondo made three films with Jean-Pierre Melville, including the brilliant gangster movie *L'Aîné des Ferchaux / Lo scia callo* (1963). He also appeared in some of the biggest box-office hits of the 60s and 70s. Of these, Philippe De Broca's *That Man from Rio* (*L'Homm de Rio / L'uomo del Rio*, 1963) best displayed his charm, temperament and athletic physique. In the 70s, Belmondo concentrated increasingly o action-oriented thrillers and comedies that provided a more or less ironical take on his incomparably virile image. One exception was Alain Resnais *Stavisky* (1974), which Belmondo himself produced. From then on, he mainly cropped up in run-of-the-mill entertainments. In the late 80s, how ever, with his pulling power at the movies in decline, he attracted a lot of attention with a successful comeback in the theater.

es to hold a number of very disparate elements in equilibrium. Paintings, vertising billboards and comic strips are edited into the flow of images ngside quotes from various films and books, and the movie changes its e and style abruptly, seeming at various moments to be a thriller, a musi- , a melodrama or a grotesque comedy. It has room for a satirical mime- ow on the Vietnam war and a guest appearance by Sam Fuller, who pro- es Ferdinand with his personal definition of the cinema: "Film is like a ttleground," he explains: "Love, hate, action, violence, death. In one word: notion."

Fuller's statement doesn't just anticipate the tragic development of the ot; it also indicates the extent to which *Pierrot le fou* reflects on its own aking. For Godard's movie is also a confrontation with the cinema, a piece film criticism in the form of a film. The regular shattering of the "realistic" sion – the actors often speak directly to the camera, for instance – is pical of Godard, and such moments are of course also a challenge to follow e film with open eyes and a clear head. Those who do so experience *errot le fou* as a fascinating attempt to approach reality in all its complexi- Godard shows the private, economic, cultural and political influences that ve made his film what it is. In the process, he proves himself to be a more ilful chronicler of his times than any of the other French New Wave's *teurs.*

Not least, *Pierrot le fou* is a memorably beautiful love film that gave two rs the opportunity to exploit their enormous acting potential to the full. na Karina, at that time still married to Godard, imbues Marianne with emo- nal depth and anarchic charm. And Belmondo, for all his nonchalance,

Death of Marat: Guess again. 1960s French heartthrob and superstar Jean-Paul Belmondo plays Ferdinand a. k. a. "Pierrot le fou" (*Crazy Pete*) – slave to circumstance and dumb luck.

2 Fleeing south for the winter: Marianne (Anna Karina) seduces Ferdinand into abandoning his bourgeois existence.

3 Sand pebbles: Anna Karina and Jean-Paul Belmondo indulge in a bit of the *nouvelle vague's amour fou.*

4 Hard eight: Danish born Anna Karina filmed a total of eight films under the direction of ex-husband Jean-Luc Godard.

5 Climb aboard, we're expecting you: Ferdinand, the vulnerable *homme faible*, falls for an adventuress and succumbs to her every whim. Just a few years later, Belmondo would play a similar role in Truffaut's *Mississippi Mermaid* (*La Sirène du Mississippi*, 1969).

**"Two or three years ago, I had the impression that everything had already been done, that there was nothing left to do that hadn't been done before. In short, I was a pessimist. Since *Pierrot*, I no longer have this feeling at all. Yes; one has to film everything, to talk about everything. Everything remains to be done."** *Jean-Luc Godard*

reveals a vulnerability that was already discernible behind the tough brittle ness of the wise guy he played in *Breathless*. His Ferdinand – Marianne call him "Pierrot," the clown – is a melancholy brooder in search of the truth. It' a mission that can only collide with Marianne's sensual and concret approach to the world.

Raoul Coutard's gently-moving camera luxuriates in the radian Mediterranean light and captures the intoxicating freedom of the lovers in th widescreen Cinemascope format. But the promise of happiness containe in these images will eventually turn out to be deceptive. When Ferdinan realizes that Marianne has been lying to him – that Fred is not her brother bu her lover – he shoots the two of them, paints his face blue, wraps tw dynamite belts around his head and blows himself to pieces. IP

# THE CINCINNATI KID

1965 - USA - 104 MIN. - DRAMA, LITERARY ADAPTATION

DIRECTOR NORMAN JEWISON (*1926)
SCREENPLAY RING LARDNER JR., TERRY SOUTHERN, based on the novel of the same name by RICHARD JESSUP
DIRECTOR OF PHOTOGRAPHY PHILIP H. LATHROP EDITING HAL ASHBY MUSIC LALO SCHIFRIN PRODUCTION MARTIN RANSOHOFF for FILMWAYS-SOLAR, MGM.

STARRING STEVE MCQUEEN (Eric "The Cincinnati Kid" Stoner), EDWARD G. ROBINSON (Lancey Howard), ANN-MARGRET (Melba), KARL MALDEN (Shooter), Tuesday Weld (Christine), JOAN BLONDELL (Lady Finger), RIP TORN (Slade), JACK WESTON (Pig), CAB CALLOWAY (Yeller), JEFF COREY (Hoban), MILTON SELZER (Doc Sokal).

## *"You're good, kid, but as long as I'm around, you're only second best."*

Respected wherever he goes, Lancey Howard (Edward G. Robinson) is Poker's Grand Master, a pro, an unofficial world champion and a real character. Ice-cool and worldly-wise, he appreciates the good things in life, flying around the USA, staying in five-star hotels and indulging his taste for gourmet food. Big money makes it all possible: Howard has been at the top of his game for years. But now, slowly but surely, though he knows how to conceal the fact from those around him, age is starting to take its toll.

For the first time in ages, Howard has come to New Orleans, attracted by the reputation of a rising Stud Poker star named Eric Stoner, better known as the Cincinnati Kid (Steve McQueen). Poker buffs are already speculating that the Kid might someday supplant the previously unchallenged Howard; and though Howard remains tight-lipped, he clearly feels it's time to show the poker world who's boss.

As yet, the Kid is not quite in his league. He's still playing in seedy ba against second-rate opponents who pull their knives in a rage as he calm pockets their dollars. Sometimes he's forced to take advantage of the nea est open window in order to escape a baying mob in one piece.

He's done his time on the poker scene in New Orleans, so when h mentor, buddy and respected colleague Shooter (Karl Malden) tells him th Howard is on his way, his ears prick up. The Grand Old Man has asked Shoo er to organize a game – and Kid just has to be there. It's a game that w decide who's the true King of the Green Baize.

At first glance, arranging an entire movie around a game of Stud Pok in a cramped and murky room may seem an unpromising idea. It's certain not a subject that lends itself to breathtaking action or cinematograph extravagances. Yet *The Cincinnati Kid* just gets more and more rivetin

1

**"In a state of feverish excitement, the city follows a duel made possible only by the intrigues of some highly dubious 'friends.' The atmosphere is electric – and only at the very end is it clear who's the winner."** *Filmblätter*

Scriptwriters Ring Lardner Jr. and Terry Southern do a wonderful job of tightening the film's focus, while director Norman Jewison creates an atmosphere so authentic that you can practically taste the cigar smoke.

Switching the film's location from St. Louis (as described in Richard Jessup's novel) to the picturesque French Quarter of New Orleans, with its marching bands and blues musicians, was a smart move. But Jewison's real trump was his two charismatic leading actors: though each of them has his own strong presence, they catalyze on screen so spectacularly that Jewison could have simply put them together and filmed the results.

The entire story focuses on these two stars. As the decisive poker game begins, there are four men at the table: Pig, Yeller, Doc Sokal and Shooter. The hours tick by, the crowd of spectators thins out; and, one by one, the players drop out of the game. Meanwhile, the nabob Slade is planning his revenge: having once lost a lot of money betting on Howard, he now blackmails the reluctant Shooter to deal the Kid a good hand. The Kid spots what's going on, demands a break and confronts Shooter, who steps down. The game resta with a new dealer. Now it's fair and square, the way the Kid wants it: straight duel between the Old Master and the Young Pretender.

Only the circular card table is illuminated, while the last remaini spectators sit in the surrounding half-light; and they hold their breath as t Kid goes in for the kill, placing three grand on two pairs. (In Stud Poker, all t cards except one are face-up.) Lancey Howard needs one more card for straight flush. The audience gasp and murmur as Howard raises the stak by 5,000 dollars. The Kid sticks with it, though he doesn't really have t cash. Howard shows his card; the camera crashes in on the King of Di monds; and a succession of fast cuts show us the eyes of the King, then t Kid, then the card, Shooter, Slade, the card – and Howard. The camera zoon back quickly, and at last we hear the old man's imperturbable voice: "Yo owe me five grand, Kid."

H

1 The fickle finger of fate: Lady Finger (Joan Blondell, seated) stays focused on the game, while Shooter (Karl Malden) watches her every move and ignores his young wife Melba (Ann-Margret).

2 Strip poker: Cincinnati Kid (Steve McQueen) can't resist Melba's womanly charms. However, the two of them are about to get caught with their pants down.

3 Too rich for my blood: Legendary gambler Lancey Howard (Edward G. Robinson, left) is struck by the Cincinnati Kid's knack at breaking the odds.

**"When Jewison concentrates the action round the card table (which happens to be whenever Edward G. Robinson is on the screen), the direction is tight and effective, and brings out all the tension of a gambling marathon played for high stakes."** *Monthly Film Bulletin*

**GAMBLERS**

Poker originated in New Orleans, but it was a popular pastime in the saloons of the Old West. Traveling card players made a living at it. One of the best-known of them was Doc Holliday, Wyatt Earp's partner in the gunfight at the O. K. Corral.

In most Westerns, gamblers are portrayed as shady, sneaky or both. Things were no different in one of the very earliest movies in the genre, the Edison production *Poker at Dawson City* (1899!). A little later, in their Western serials, Bronco Billy Anderson and William S. Hart regularly came up against cardsharps. And as the years went by, the movie image of the gambler hardly changed: elegantly dressed, well-mannered and charming to the ladies. The average gambler rarely carries a Colt, preferring a more easily concealed weapon like a dagger or a Derringer. In TV series such as *Yancy Derringer* (1958–59) and *Maverick* (1957–1962), the gambler came off somewhat better. James Garner played the wily Maverick on TV, while Mel Gibson took over the part in Richard Donner's feature film version (*Maverick* 1994). Further notable movie gamblers include John Carradine in *Stagecoach* (1939), Wendell Corey in *The Furies* (1950), Kirk Douglas as Doc Holliday in *Gunfight at the O.K. Corral* (1957), Jeff Goldblum in *Silverado* (1985) and Dennis Quaid as the ever-popular Doc Holliday in *Wyatt Earp* (1994).

# THE KNACK... AND HOW TO GET IT

1965 - GREAT BRITAIN - 85 MIN. - COMEDY

**DIRECTOR** RICHARD LESTER (*1932)
**SCREENPLAY** CHARLES WOOD, based on the play of the same name by ANN JELLICOE **DIRECTOR OF PHOTOGRAPHY** DAVID WATKIN **EDITING** ANTHONY GIBBS **MUSIC** JOHN BARRY **PRODUCTION** OSCAR LEWENSTEIN for WOODFALL PRODUCTIONS.

**STARRING** RITA TUSHINGHAM (Nancy Jones), MICHAEL CRAWFORD (Colin), RAY BROOKS (Tolen), DONAL DONNELLY (Tom), WILLIAM DEXTER (Dress Shop Owner), JOHN BLUTHAL (Father), WENSLEY PITHEY (Teacher), CHARLES DYER (Man in Photo Booth), PETER COPLEY (Picture Owner), DANDY NICHOLS (Landlady).

**IFF CANNES 1965** GOLDEN PALM for BEST FILM (Richard Lester).

## *"Are you a homosexual?" "No, thanks all the same."*

The early 60s saw the birth of a movement that would eventually change the face of the globe: POP! Short for "popular culture," Pop combined High and Low, trivial and serious, avant-garde and working class art forms into a universal, ubiquitous and triumphantly successful melange that maintains its mass appeal even today.

Swinging London established itself as the Pop capital, and *The Knack... and How to Get It* was the first film to celebrate the ancient city's reincarnation as a metropolis for the youth. Director Richard Lester whipped up this delicious movie between two Beatles films: *A Hard Day's Night* (1964) – a semi-documentary music film about 36 hours in the life of the Beatles and the progenitor of the video clip genre – and *Help!* (1965), a witty, early hippie extravaganza. Like the two Beatles movies, *The Knack* communicates and celebrates the way (some) people lived in 60s Britain.

Three young men share a terraced house in London: Tolen (Ray Brooks) is a drummer and biker who has "the knack" of getting women into bed; Colin (Michael Crawford) is shy and awkward, and tries in vain to pick up th knack from his mentor Tolen; Tom (Donal Donnelly) is an Irish swinger – an the first character in any movie to be open and playful about his bisexuality Tom gives Colin some friendly advice, so that he too can have his fun in th allegedly promiscuous society.

This trio run into Nancy (Rita Tushingham), who's new to London. I contrast to the dumb blondes favored by Tolen, Nancy is dark, inquisitive an chatty – and though she comes from the country, she's no bumpkin. Nancy i on her way to the YWCA to find a place to stay, and Colin and Tom are push ing an enormous iron double bed on castors through the metropolitan traffic It's their way of laying the groundwork for the coming sexual revolution. Th film accompanies this ménage à trois on a slapstick odyssey through Lon don, with the bed serving at one time or another as a vehicle, a trampoline o a raft on the River Thames before eventually docking at the boys' terrace house. Here, Casanova Tolen will get to work, demonstrating the high art o

1

**"As it contains some grossly indecent scenes, this film should be viewed only by responsible adults."** *Evangelischer Filmbeobachter*

seduction to the seducee du jour, Nancy. Though it looks as though he'll soon have his wicked way with her, Nancy ultimately lets down the tires on his motorbike, which is nearly as big and shiny as his ego – and Colin, the seeming loser, is suddenly odds-on favorite for her favors. As it turns out, however, Colin and Nancy don't land in bed, but dive into the nightlife of Swinging London. In the Albert Hall, where Tolen had planned to gather all his conquests together, the womanizer is suddenly alone and neglected: for he lacks the es sential virtues of the 60s – enthusiasm, spontaneity, independence an cheek. And these are the most striking virtues of the film itself. It's almost prototype for the decade.

*The Knack… and How to Get It* once again demonstrates the director' ability to abandon conventional narrative techniques in order to captur

5

1 The out of towner: Nancy (Rita Tushingham) discovers that getting to the YWCA could be trickier than she anticipated.

2 Physical education: Math teacher and bachelor Colin (Michael Crawford) is afraid of what he might learn from his female pupils.

3 The coast is clear: This chicken only crosses London roads when there are no cars in sight.

4 Testosterone overload: Nancy's fallen flat in the presence of gauche Tolen (Ray Brooks).

5 Bedknobs and broomsticks: After all her travels, has Nancy finally reached the age of not believing?

something as complex and volatile as the zeitgeist. The movie's originality consists not in the story it tells but in the way it chooses to tell it. Though Richard Lester's theme is sexual emancipation, it's accompanied by a constant, grumpy running commentary, as the neighbors, locals and passers-by give free reign to their envy and frustration at the "liberties" taken by young people nowadays. Though parts of the film look like documentary sequences, they were "staged" that way by Lester: he used a hidden camera to film onlookers on location, and then dubbed in parts of the script, carefully synchronizing the lip movements with the words spoken. In this way, he can be said to have erased the boundaries between documentary and fiction. With the addition of further elements adopted such as jump cuts, fast motion sequences and written "inserts," he produced a kind of stylistic mixture that was typical of the French *nouvelle vague* but new to the British cinema. In 1965, *The Knack... and How to Get It* won the Golden Palm at the Film Festival in Cannes.

RV

**RICHARD LESTER**

Richard Lester was born in Philadelphia in 1932, the son of Irish immigrants. He was originally a musician and composer, and learned the ropes as a filmmaker by working as an assistant director and director with the TV station CBS in his home town. In the mid-50s, he traveled round Europe and North Africa working as a musician, before settling in England to work in radio and TV once more. This time, his employer was the BBC, and he helped to produce one of the strangest, funniest and most popular live radio programs of all time: *The Goon Show* (1958), starring Peter Sellers. His experience with live broadcasting, commercials and pop music came in very handy when was given the task of making the first document of the Swinging Sixties: *A Hard Day's Night* (1964). For the first Beatles film, the producers had very little time at their disposal; but director Lester knew how to make a virtue of necessity. As retakes were an unaffordable luxury, he simply filmed with three cameras simultaneously – a standard TV method, which he also deployed in his later movies.

The 70s were the era of Hollywood blockbusters, and Lester was in the thick of it. Besides making the trilogy *The Three Musketeers* (1973), *The Four Musketeers*, (1974) and *The Return Of The Musketeers* (1988), he also directed two of the Superman movies: *Superman II* (1979) and *Superman III* (1983). In 1991, he made the concert documentary *Get Back* for Paul McCartney – a return to his cinematic starting point, and his last film to date.

# DJANGO
## Django

1966 - ITALY / SPAIN - 91 MIN. - SPAGHETTI WESTERN

DIRECTOR SERGIO CORBUCCI (1927–1990)
SCREENPLAY SERGIO and BRUNO CORBUCCI, FRANCO ROSSETTI, JOSÉ G. NESSO, GEOFFREY COPLESTON (English version)
DIRECTOR OF PHOTOGRAPHY ENZO BARBONI EDITING NINO BARAGLI, SERGIO MONTANARI MUSIC LUIS ENRIQUEZ BACALOV
PRODUCTION MANOLO BOLOGNINI, SERGIO CORBUCCI for B. R. C., TECISA.

STARRING FRANCO NERO (Django), JOSÉ BODALO (General Hugo Rodriguez), LOREDANA NUSCIAK (Maria), ANGEL ALVAREZ (Nataniele), EDUARDO FAJARDO (Major Jackson), GINO PERNICE (Jonathan).

***"You can clean up the mess, but don't touch my coffin."***

Sometimes an entire film grows from a single image. In this case, it comes right at the start: a solitary man (Franco Nero) trudging along a muddy country road. He's dressed in the ragged uniform of a Union soldier, he's carrying a saddle on his shoulder, and he's dragging his last piece of luggage behind him on a rope: it's a coffin.

"I found the very idea of it hilarious even then," says Sergio Corbucci, who dreamt up this grim Western hero together with his brother Bruno. The name of their black-clad avenger was intended as a tribute to the jazz guitarist Django Reinhardt.

In his own métier, the Italian Django is as dexterous as his musica[l] namesake. On the road, he observes five roughnecks preparing to string u[p] a young woman (Loredana Nusciak) on a wooden scaffold. When they bad-mouth the stranger, he does what a man's gotta do and lets his revolver d[o] the talking. A split second later, all five villains have bitten the dust.

Maria, the lady in question, joins Django on his journey to Tombstone, a grimy hole almost empty of inhabitants. Only Major Jackson (Eduardo Fajardo) stops off here regularly with his fanatical racist gang and a bunch o[f] Mexican freebooters. They come to pick up their protection money from the

1
2

1 Mr. Bojangles: Django (Franco Nero) hums to himself as he lies in wait for Jackson's men.

2 Italian stallion: With iron hooves, Django lures his enemies into one final showdown.

**"The hero's marksmanship does stretch credibility, especially when he pulls a machine-gun from the coffin and mows down bandits by the score. By the end of the film, almost every figure we've encountered on the screen is stone dead. If this is a Western, it's the bloodiest example of the genre I've ever seen, but it's also tautly directed and exciting to watch."** *filmblätter*

**SERGIO CORBUCCI**

Sergio Corbucci's first professional contact with the cinema was as a critic, before he became Roberto Rossellini's assistant. In 1951, he made his debut as a director, with *Salviate mia figlia*. This was followed a year later by the melodrama *Island Sinner* (*La peccatrice dell' isola*, 1952), which he also scripted. From then on, Corbucci's career was dictated by the fashions and fortunes of the Italian cinema: his oeuvre includes adventure films, historical dramas, blockbusters, comedies, spy capers and political thrillers. It was as a Western director, however, that he achieved international fame. With *Django* (1966) and *The Great Silence* (*Il grande silenzio*, 1968), he wrote and directed two influential classics that re-examined the conventions of the genre. Like Sergio Leone before him – see *A Fistful of Dollars* (*Per un pugno di dollari*, 1964) – Corbucci cited the influence of Japanese Samurai films. But Corbucci is also regarded as one of the leading directors of the so-called "revolutionary Westerns." Movies such as *The Mercenary / A Professional Gun* (*Il mercenario*, 1968) take a definite political stance. Sergio Corbucci was also the first Italian Western director who refused to follow the standard practice of the time and adopt an Anglo-Saxon pseudonym. He made all his films under his own name.

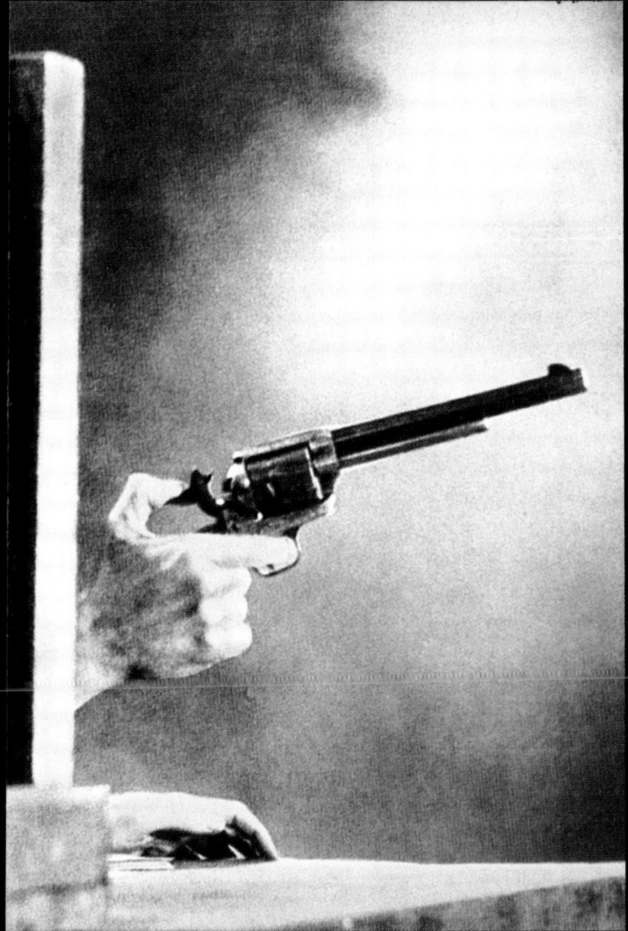

3 Come on, baby. Come shake your mangos: The ruthless gunslinger surprises Soldateska by jumping out of a coffin and doing his own rendition of the fandango with a machine gun.

4 Skull and cracked bones: Django's sharp shooting has never missed a target, but that could all change now Rodriguez has broken the tough guy's hand.

5 Desperados: After the final showdown, former crackshot Django is left hung out to dry over a tombstone.

saloon owner (Angel Alvarez), and to take their pleasure with his girls. But it's clear that Django already knows what's awaiting him here: he deliberately humiliates Jackson, in the hope of luring his gang into town.

All goes according to plan, and the showdown takes place the following day. Keeping his coffin close at hand, Django takes up position in front of the saloon. Now Corbucci "stretches" time, and the tension starts to mount: step by step, Jackson's evil henchmen approach, some of them adjusting their red hoods as they come. Their leader, accompanied by an obscure priest, is licking his lips in anticipation. Django takes cover behind a massive tree-stump. The camera cuts back to the smug face of Major Jackson… and then it happens: Django pulls a heavy machine gun from the coffin, and mows down the attackers like bottles on a wall. Jackson escapes the massacre, but it later becomes clear that this was *not* what Django had intended

Naturally enough, Maria sees Django as her savior; but Corbucci's protagonist is a completely amoral hero. When he needs to persuade the rebel Hugo Rodriguez (José Bodalo) to join him in attacking a Mexican fort, he hands over Maria without batting an eyelid. Only when Rodriguez refuses to give him his share of the booty does Django turn against him –and this time, he loses. In sentimental tribute to their friendship, Rodriguez spares his life, smashing his hands instead with a rifle butt. Moments later, Django again finds himself face to face with his arch-enemy Jackson – and his hands are now two useless lumps swaddled in blood-soaked bandages. It seems brutally clear that Django doesn't have a hope in hell, but he props his revolver on a graveyard cross – and blows the Major to Kingdom Come.

Grim indeed: but Sergio Corbucci has always stressed that his films are full of humor. He even demonstrates a certain interest in politics by making it clear, in word and deed, that Django does *not* like racists. The crass simplicity of the plot is primarily a blank background for a number of extremely bizarre tableaux, and it also provides an excuse for some quite unprecedented violence. Though the brutality has a cartoon quality, it led to the film being banned in several countries, which naturally did nothing to diminish its popularity. The unyielding Django became a prototype for a certain kind of harsh hero, and not just in Spaghetti Westerns. Corbucci's style rapidly found its imitators, and many a low-budget Western was compared to *Django*, despite having nothing in common with the original.

In 1987, Franco Nero returned to his most famous role, in Ted Archer's follow-up, *Django 2 – il grande ritorno*. He spoke about it in an interview in 1993: "Django is an important part of my life. Thanks to him, I made my international breakthrough while still a very young man. And anyway, I like Westerns – even if they're now a little out of fashion."

Incidentally, the Italian star didn't want to rule out the possibility that Django might ride again some day – if the circumstances were right… HK

# ALFIE

1966 – GREAT BRITAIN – 114 MIN. – COMEDY
DIRECTOR LEWIS GILBERT (*1920)
SCREENPLAY BILL NAUGHTON, based on his play of the same name DIRECTOR OF PHOTOGRAPHY OTTO HELLER EDITING THELMA CONNELL MUSIC SONNY ROLLINS PRODUCTION LEWIS GILBERT for SHELDRAKE FILMS.

STARRING MICHAEL CAINE (Alfie), SHELLEY WINTERS (Ruby), MILLICENT MARTIN (Siddie), JULIA FOSTER (Gilda), JANE ASHER (Annie), SHIRLEY ANNE FIELD (Carla), VIVIEN MERCHANT (Lily), ELEANOR BRON (The Doctor), DENHOLM ELLIOTT (The Abortionist), ALFIE BASS (Harry), GRAHAM STARK (Humphrey).

IFF CANNES 1966 SPECIAL PRIZE OF THE JURY (Lewis Gilbert).

## *"She or it, they're all birds."*

They were queuing up to turn it down. Hardly any British actor with a reputation to lose wanted anything to do with *Alfie* – the sole exception being Terence Stamp (*Modesty Blaise*, 1966), who would have given anything to play the unscrupulous ladies' man. And though the film was nominated for five Oscars, even the movie's most passionate fans can see why such a black romance was so studiously ignored by the American Academy when it came to actually handing out the awards. The actor who eventually got the role was practically made for it: and with this movie, Michael Caine, a working-class boy from South London, established his image as a charming Cockney Casanova for years to come.

As Alfie, his appetite for women is insatiable. One might say seduction is his hobby, but it's really more like a profession. His various jobs, as a chauffeur or a Thames-side photographer, are little more than excuses to meet women. He prefers them married, as they're less likely to make onerous demands. They cook for him, they do his washing, and they warm his bed; and when he's had enough of them, he shows them the door. Above all, he wants nothing to do with their problems. When one of his unhappy conquests has a baby boy, he does take pleasure for a while in the child's unquestioning love; but soon enough, he's happy to hand over the responsibilities of fatherhood to the next guy who comes along. In the end, he even manages to unload his guilt feelings onto the audience. For Alfie seduces us too, and by exactly the same method: he talks to us the way he talks to his women, and you can't be angry if you're laughing.

*Alfie* is based on a play of the same by Bill Naughton, and the script was adapted for the screen by the playwright himself. For centuries, the theater has allowed its heroes and anti-heroes to break through "the fourth

1

2

3

"*Alfie* may shock some, and others will deplore its somewhat dingy theme. Many will miss its warning note. But none will likely be bored. All in all, this frank study of cheap sex relations has a ring of uncomfortable truth which may even prove valuable."

*Variety*

**LEWIS GILBERT**

He's seen as a solid, reliable craftsman who never stood in the spotlight of fame. Perhaps for this very reason, the story of his career is like a complete history of the British cinema. As a child, he appeared on the music-hall stage with his parents; as a teenager, he appeared alongside Olivier in an Alexander Korda film, and as a very young man, Lewis Gilbert (*1920 in London) worked as a third assistant director to Alfred Hitchcock on *Jamaica Inn* (1939). For him, as for many of his generation, the Second World War was to be the defining experience of his life; and like many British directors, he learned his trade by working on documentaries in the film department of the U. S. Air Force. He first made a name for himself as a director of the kind of war dramas so popular in the 50s and early 60s: *Reach for the Sky* (1956), *Sink the Bismarck!,* (1960) and *H. M. S. Defiant* (1961). But it was the financial success of *Alfie* (1966) that landed him the opportunity to direct three Bond films: *You Only Live Twice* (1967), *The Spy Who Loved Me* (1977) and *Moonraker* (1979). He established a reputation as a specialist for outer space, and he was one of the first people to realize the potential of the Panavision widescreen format. Here we see the dilemma of the British cinema, which had already been evident by the time *Alfie* was made: worldwide commercial success is possible – as long as Hollywood secures the financing. Beyond the action and adventure genres, Lewis Gilbert seldom had a lucky hand. But in his later years, he did make a remarkable transformation to become a "woman's director" in the tradition of George Cukor. He was highly praised for the romantic genre comedies *Educating Rita* (1983) – which again starred Michael Caine – and *Shirley Valentine* (1989). The latter is said to be one of the Queen's favorite films. Lewis Gilbert – On Her Majesty's Cinematic Service.

1 Six feet under, four on top: Alfie (Michael Caine, right) gives Harry (Alfie Bass) his last rites – and runs off with the merry widow.

2 The pitter patter of little feet. Homemaker Gilda (Julia Foster) has got a bun in the oven and Alfie wants to get out of the kitchen.

3 Trail duster: Annie (Jane Asher) keeps Alfie's house, only to have her affections swept under the rug.

4 Georgie Porgie pudding and pie… Alfie gets mistress Lily (Vivien Merchant) to stifle her tears after she aborts what would have been her fourth child. But the fly by night lover can't dodge sadness forever.

wall" and address the audience directly. In thus revealing their thoughts, the characters develop a closer relationship to the audience. But few films have deployed the method as ruthlessly as *Alfie*, or to better effect. Alfie never has to interrupt a scene; he simply switches his attention to the camera, while the other characters continue their existence in a kind of dream world of Alfie's creation. It's a world that's only there for Alfie's amusement, a world in which women have no idea that he refers to them as "birds" – or even as "it" – behind their back. Alfie is much more honest when addressing the camera than he is in "real" life, but in both cases he succeeds in making his shenanigans look like the most natural behavior imaginable. "You know what I mean" is the mantra that demands our agreement, no matter how dubious the statement he's just made; and he smiles so winningly, we let him get away with it.

In his autobiography, *What's it all about?*, Michael Caine wrote: "Alfie is an innocent sadist, who hurts others without wanting to. Such people exist." The film concludes with a song by Cher that hits the nail on the head: *What's It All About, Alfie?* It's a painful question, and one that the heartbreaker is not keen to answer. Even after an abortion scene – shockingly realistic and highly controversial in its time – Alfie never asks himself what he's really looking for. Until the end of his days, it seems, he'll be more interested in the next miniskirt than in wondering about the meaning of his essentially sad life. It's the great achievement of director Lewis Gilbert to hold the audience's feelings in a perfect balance between amused complicity and chastened regret.

For all that, most moviegoers were as indifferent as Alfie himself to the moral of the story. The film made a star of Michael Caine and drew the world's attention to the British cinema. Its success was largely due to Caine's wonderfully relaxed and charming performance. He delivers his witty lines with a memorably understated irony: "They never make these cars big enough, do they?" murmurs Alfie, as the lady in the back seat demurely readjusts her underwear. (For the American market, Caine actually had to dub himself into something more closely resembling Received Pronunciation!) The only other actor who can hold a candle to him is the charming Shelley Winters, whose character is a kind of female Alfie. With the music of Sonny Rollins and Burt Bacharach on the soundtrack, *Alfie* became a classic of the Swinging Sixties. It now has its place in the pantheon along with John Schlesinger's *Darling* (1965), Michelangelo Antonioni's *Blow-Up* (1966) and Richard Lester's Beatles films. PB

# ARABESQUE

1966 - USA - 105 MIN. - SPY FILM, SPOOF, LITERARY ADAPTATION

DIRECTOR STANLEY DONEN (*1924)
SCREENPLAY JULIAN MITCHELL, STANLEY PRICE, PETER STONE (as PIERRE MARTON) based on the short story *THE CIPHER* by GORDON COTLER DIRECTOR OF PHOTOGRAPHY CHRISTOPHER CHALLIS EDITING FREDERICK WILSON MUSIC HENRY MANCINI PRODUCTION STANLEY DONEN for UNIVERSAL PICTURES.

STARRING GREGORY PECK (David Pollock), SOPHIA LOREN (Yasmin Azir), ALAN BADEL (Beshraavi), KIERON MOORE (Yussef Kassim), CARL DUERING (Hassan Jena), JOHN MERIVALE (Sloane), DUNCAN LAMONT (Webster), GEORGE COULORIS (Professor Ragheeb), ERNEST CLARK (Beauchamp), HAROLD KASKET (Mohammed Lufti).

## *"What is there about you that makes you so hard to believe?"*

A few bars of Henry Mancini's Middle Eastern mambo encoded with secret agent mystique and a glance at Maurice Binder's title sequence bathed in hypnotic monochrome spirals and geometric patterns, make one thing certain: recent hit and Hitchcock spoof *Charade* (1963) provided director Stanley Donen with more than just a diving board of inspiration for his subsequent picture, *Arabesque*.

Beyond the title and score, the two films continue to parallel each other in plot, characterization and dynamics. This time, instead of traipsing through the streets of Paris *à la* Grant and Hepburn, romantic leads Gregory Peck and Sophia Loren relocate the quarrelling and kissing to London, where another game of hot pursuit is underway, involving ancient hieroglyphics and arguably more nefarious foes. For the most part, Peck and Loren's relationship mirrors that of Cary Grant and Audrey Hepburn in *Charade*. However, significant aspects of the characters have been swapped. David Pollock is an ordinary professor, whose specialization in ancient languages gets him entangled in the story, whereas spy Yasmin Azir's (Loren) actual interest in the matter is as inscrutable as her dark brown eyes.

*Arabesque's* emergence as an picture that is more than just an amusing tribute to a tribute is due to its extravagant look and Donen's clever direction – a combination that taps into the visual aesthetics and the zeitgeist of a time between the swinging sixties and the psychedelic fad. Starting with the opening sequence, which doesn't just incidentally take place at a not-quite-legit optician's office, ordered visual perspectives are turned topsy-turvy. Unfamiliar focal lengths distort the space. The eye of an unhinged camera suddenly takes on the blurred visual perspective of a near-sighted patient, who is about to be permanently robbed of the light of day. In a later

1

**"About 10 minutes after *Arabesque* gets under way, you'll lose track of its plot completely, and that's as it should be. Its producer-director, Stanley Donen, apparently goes on the theory that in a chase movie the plot should only be used as a framework for visual entertainment."** *The New York Times*

1 Shower me with attention: Prof. David Pollock (Gregory Peck) just loves Yasmin Azir's (Sophia Loren) plumbing.

2 Start spreading the news: At this rate the enigmatic Yasmin Azir should have no trouble finishing her legwork on the hieroglyphics case.

3 Sleepy, happy and dopey: Sedated, medicated and in a state of delirium. Prof. Pollock decides to make a few obscene phone calls.

4 Photo finish: Who will be the first to find the hieroglyphics in this harebrained race against time?

5 What's a little sheet between friends? Prof. Pollock and Yasmin ignore the case for a while and go off in hot pursuit of romance.

**SOPHIA LOREN**

The late 50s witnessed a strange process of cross-cultural exchange between the Old World and the New. After appearing in Godard's *Breathless* (*A bout de souffle*, 1959), the androgynous American girl Jean Seberg became a new female role model in Europe; meanwhile, Hollywood was importing European femininity in the shape of Gina Lollobrigida and Sophia Loren. A Neapolitan from a poor background, Sophia Loren began her career in the 40s as a model and beauty queen before being discovered by the film producer Carlo Ponti, whom she married in 1957.

In the Italian cinema of the 50s, Loren was best known as a temperamental comedienne. From 1957 onwards, she displayed the same talent in Hollywood, in films such as *Houseboat* (1958), directed by Melville Shavelson. Her Hollywood career didn't last, though it did establish Sophia Loren as a box-office magnet worldwide. After her return to Italy, she launched successful creative partnerships with the director Vittorio de Sica and her fellow actor Marcello Mastroianni. By now, she was being offered an increasing number of dramatic roles, and proving she could carry them off successfully. In 1977, she gave what may well have been her finest performance, in Ettore Scola's *A special day* (*Una giornata particolare*) as a frustrated housewife and mother in fascist Italy. On the "special day" in question, she forms a perceptive relationship with a neighbor (Marcello Mastroianni) who is about to be deported because of his homosexuality. In the 80s, Loren worked mainly in TV. Recent years have seen her making more frequent film appearances, as in the drama *Between Strangers* (2002), which was directed by her son, Edoardo Ponti.

episode, featuring Gregory Peck, we witness how British cinematographer Christopher Challis tries to recreate the protagonist's drug-induced state with double-exposures, fuzzy images and iridescent lights. Paired with Peck's acting, the scene becomes a brilliant display of how an otherwise serious character loses his stiff veneer, swerving and swaying aimlessly in a hilariously amusing delirium.

Time and again, Donen opts to depict the action as indirectly as the visuals will allow, staging scenes reflected inside mirrors, on panes of glass, and, for a brief while, on a television screen. The climax of this interplay with shimmering surfaces and dual identities is an ingeniously orchestrated sequence that takes place after hours at the London Zoo. Here, precise edits literally enable the killer to chase Peck and Loren to the tune of Henry Mancini's music. The bars of cages, disorienting reflective glass and light refracted in the aquariums play havoc with the heroes' and villain's field of vision, until all spatial bearings have disappeared and even the killer shoots at a reflection in an aquarium.

*Arabesque* is clearly more removed from the work of Alfred Hitchcock than the previous *Charade*. For rather than confining his use of novel perspectives to a functional realm like Hitchcock, Donen exploited these aesthetic devices at every given opportunity.

Still, it is clear that his undying reverence for Hitch is no act of parody. When Peck finds himself holding a corpse at Ascot races in front of hundreds of spectators, we are reminded of an uncannily similar situation, spotlighting a perplexed Cary Grant at the New York UN building in *North by Northwest* (1959). LP

# SECONDS

1966 - USA - 107 MIN. - THRILLER, DRAMA

**DIRECTOR** JOHN FRANKENHEIMER (1930–2002)
**SCREENPLAY** LEWIS JOHN CARLINO, based on the novel of the same name by DAVID ELY **DIRECTOR OF PHOTOGRAPHY** JAMES WONG HOWE **EDITING** DAVID NEWHOUSE, FERRIS WEBSTER **MUSIC** JERRY GOLDSMITH **PRODUCTION** EDWARD LEWIS, JOHN FRANKENHEIMER fo JOEL PRODUCTIONS, JOHN FRANKENHEIMER PRODUCTIONS INC., PARAMOUNT PICTURES.

**STARRING** ROCK HUDSON (Antiochus "Tony" Wilson), SALOME JENS (Nora Marcus), JOHN RANDOLPH (Arthur Hamilton), FRANCES REID (Emily Hamilton), MURRAY HAMILTON (Charlie Evans), WILL GEER (Old Man, Company Director), JEFF COREY (Mr. Ruby), RICHARD ANDERSON (Doctor Innes), KARL SWENSON (Doctor Morris), KHIGH DHIEGH (Davalo).

## *"Life is built on wishes."*

Most people have probably dreamt of changing their lives overnight, but few ever have a chance to do so. But if, by some miracle, the time should come, even dramatic changes are often astoundingly easy to make – as 50-year-old Arthur Hamilton (John Randolph) discovers.

A phone call from his old buddy Charlie (Murray Hamilton), whom Arthur had long thought dead, gets the ball rolling. Charlie is confused and disturbed by this blast from the past, and his carefully maintained routine suddenly seems on the verge of collapse. A successful banker, Arthur is rich and respected, but he's far from content; and since his daughter departed the family home, his personal life seems empty. The phone rings again. Arthur breaks out in a sweat: it's his old friend again, and this time he's directing him to an unfamiliar address. By a roundabout route, Arthur arrives at the elegant offices of a mysterious company, where he's the recipient of an incredible offer: the chance to be born again. Everything has been arranged. Plastic surgery has come on in leaps and bounds. If he's prepared to pay the price, he can realize his most secret dreams with a new identity. The only thing that remains to be clarified is the way he'd like to die.

Surprised, bewildered, but not entirely averse to the offer, Arthur even tually resolves to leave his past behind him. Arthur Hamilton, middle-agec overweight and run-of-the-mill, becomes Antiochus "Tony" Wilson (Roc Hudson), a handsome, muscular hunk. He moves into an elegant beac house, and it seems all his dreams have come true. But it's only when h gives up his innermost resistance that the toughest stage of his transforma tion can begin – the search for his true self.

*Seconds* is a kind of psychological Blind Man's Buff, in which directo John Frankenheimer meditates on the legend of eternal youth, the power o money, and above all, on the nature of identity. Scenes with mirrors functior as a kind of leitmotif, a manifestation of Arthur's search for himself. Even th title sequence, created by Saul Bass, shows how deceptive our perception of ourselves can be. Reflected in close-up on shiny metal surfaces, mouth and noses become bizarre and threatening objects, a source of latent, inde finable terror.

Something always seems to be lurking in the ominous shadows o these monochrome images, while rapid changes of camera-angle and per

1

## “A really horrifying piece of science fiction that burns its way into your mind like a gnawing headache.” *Sunday Express*

1 Curse of the holy grail: Antiochus ‘Tony’ Wilson (Rock Hudson) thinks he’s entered into God’s good graces. However, things look different once the champagne has run out.

2 A face turned to stone, or rock: Frankenheimer’s movie is a patchwork of simplemindedness and sci-fi thriller.

3 Who can it be now? The man who ‘died’ Arthur Hamilton just moments ago can hardly believe his eyes. The greatness of *Seconds* is when seeing is no longer believing.

4 A twisted circle: The film’s chilling conclusion, in which Tony’s life flashes before his eyes, uses the same technique as Saul Bass’ gripping opening credits sequence.

5 Life’s a beach and then you die: Tony and beauty Nora Marcus (Salome Jens) live life to anything but the fullest. It’s one of the rare moments in Rock Hudson’s career that shows what he could have become if he had ventured away from Doris Day’s side.

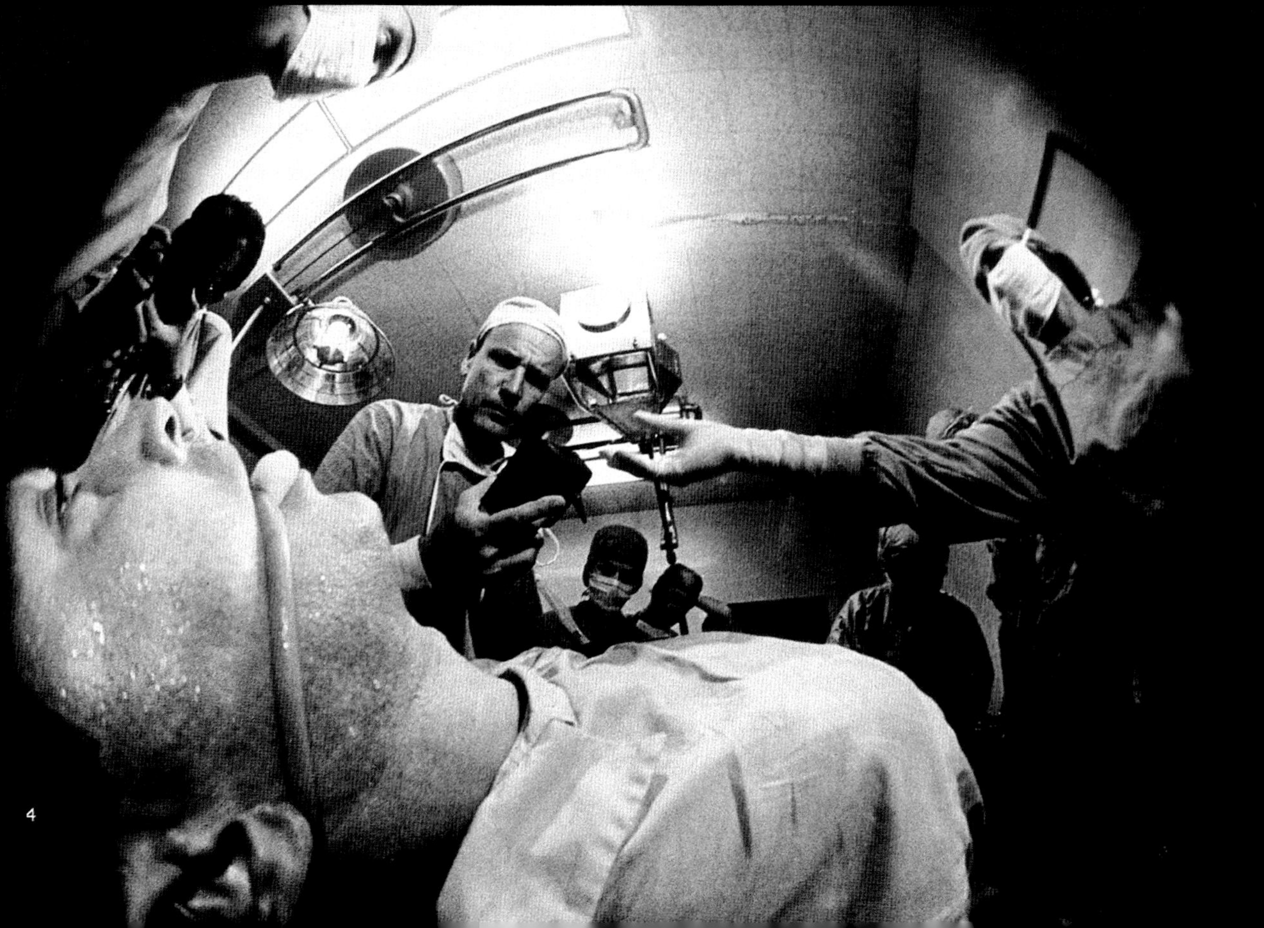

pective invoke a feeling of edginess and anxiety. Director of photography ames Wong Howe makes good use of his gift for subtle lighting, something e had already demonstrated in Robert Rossen's boxing film *Body and Soul* 1947). These beautifully composed wide-angle images are complemented y the music of Jerry Goldsmith: the sinister drone of the organ is refined by igh-strung passages of violin music, until the tension is released in furious xplosions of sound. But Frankenheimer and his team deliver more than a eries of disturbingly subversive moments, and the results are often painfully noving. The best example is perhaps the scene in which Arthur's wife Frances Reid) attempts to seduce her husband with a passionate kiss. A eries of cross-cut close-ups reveals the state of their marriage: while her yes divulge her craving for love, his vacant expression speaks volumes.

Scenes like these earned Howe an Oscar nomination, and the film was the final installment in Frankenheimer's "Paranoia Trilogy" (after *The Manchurian Candidate* [1962] and *Seven Days in May* [1963]). But this was no box-office hit: for many critics, John Randolph's metamorphosis into Rock Hudson was more than they were prepared to take. Their refusal or inability to suspend disbelief certainly had something to do with the fact that Rock Hudson was the romantic hero *par excellence*. It was just too weird to see him in a film as weird as this. Years later, however, the film did achieve its due recognition as a classic, a further example of how the cinema of the 60s opened our eyes to the strangeness of everyday life. While the white heat of technology made anything seem possible, the catastrophes in the news showed that no one was safe. To this mixture of optimism and fear, Frankenheimer brought a deep-seated conviction of his own: whatever possibilities life may offer, we'll never be free from ourselves. OK

**ROCK HUDSON (1925–1985)**

Rock Hudson described his role in *Seconds* (1966) as the best performance of his life. When one sees him as Antiochus Wilson, timid and hesitant, wild and despairing, it's hard not to agree.

His career began with very different roles. Hudson's good looks brought him the tiny part of the Lieutenant in Raoul Walsh's *Fighter Squadron* (1948). This was his screen debut, and he wasn't even mentioned in the credits. Soon, however, he was playing supporting roles in adventure films and Westerns, including *Winchester '73* (1950). His breakthrough came in a series of melodramas directed by Douglas Sirk in the early 50s: he played a playboy in *Has Anybody Seen My Gal?* (1952) and a gardener in *All That Heaven Allows* (1955). As James Dean's opposite number in *Giant* (1956) he even earned an Oscar nomination, though he never won the prize. Instead, he was named best-looking lead several times by the glossy magazines. In the late 50s, he changed genre once again, appearing with Doris Day in a series of romantic comedies that cemented his image as a ladies' man (*Pillow Talk*, 1959). As he grew older, he worked in television more frequently, appearing alongside Susan Saint James in *McMillan & Wife* (1971–76). In the 80s, too, he appeared regularly on TV, most noticeably in *Dynasty* (1981–89). But Rock Hudson had his most impressive public appearance when he officially declared his homosexuality. The lifelong beefcake icon was the first Hollywood star to do so; and the fact that his gayness had been a secret for so long became an emblem of Hollywood's obsession with appearances. Shortly after his coming-out, Roy Scherer alias Rock Hudson died of AIDS.

# PERSONA

## Persona

1966 - SWEDEN - 84 MIN. - DRAMA

DIRECTOR INGMAR BERGMAN (*1918)

SCREENPLAY INGMAR BERGMAN DIRECTOR OF PHOTOGRAPHY SVEN NYKVIST EDITING ULLA RYGHE MUSIC LARS JOHAN WERLE PRODUCTION INGMAR BERGMAN for SVENSK FILMINDUSTRI.

STARRING BIBI ANDERSSON (Alma), LIV ULLMANN (Elisabeth Vogler), MARGARETHA KROOK (The Doctor), GUNNAR BJÖRNSTRAND (Mr. Vogler), JÖRGEN LINDSTRÖM (The Boy).

## *"Can you be two people at once? And can two people be one and the same?"*

"I give viewers the material and let their imagination get to work on it," said Ingmar Bergman. When *Persona* was released, hardly anyone could resist quoting these little "directions for use" – and admittedly, the words of Ingmar Bergman leave us in no doubt that this, the 27th film by the Swedish director, was to be another complex and by no means accessible cinematic work of art. *Persona,* once again, goes for it all: the reality and illusion of human existence, the meaning of life, and the profound, inescapable loneliness of mankind.

The film tells of a psychodramatic encounter between two women. The celebrated actress Elisabeth Vogler (Liv Ullmann in her first Bergman role) becomes suddenly aware of all the masks and affectations in her profession and dissolves into hysterical laughter while performing *Electra.* Reality, on the other hand, seems to appall her. She feels absolutely no love for her husband or her son – and withdraws into an unshakeable, self-imposed silence. Sequestered at a mental institution for observation, Elisabeth is pronounced both physically and psychologically well. Her doctor, however, thinks she understands her and diagnoses her condition as a personal crusade for authenticity.

Elisabeth is placed in the care of Alma (Bibi Andersson), a young nurse whose increasing identification with the actress is more than just a case of

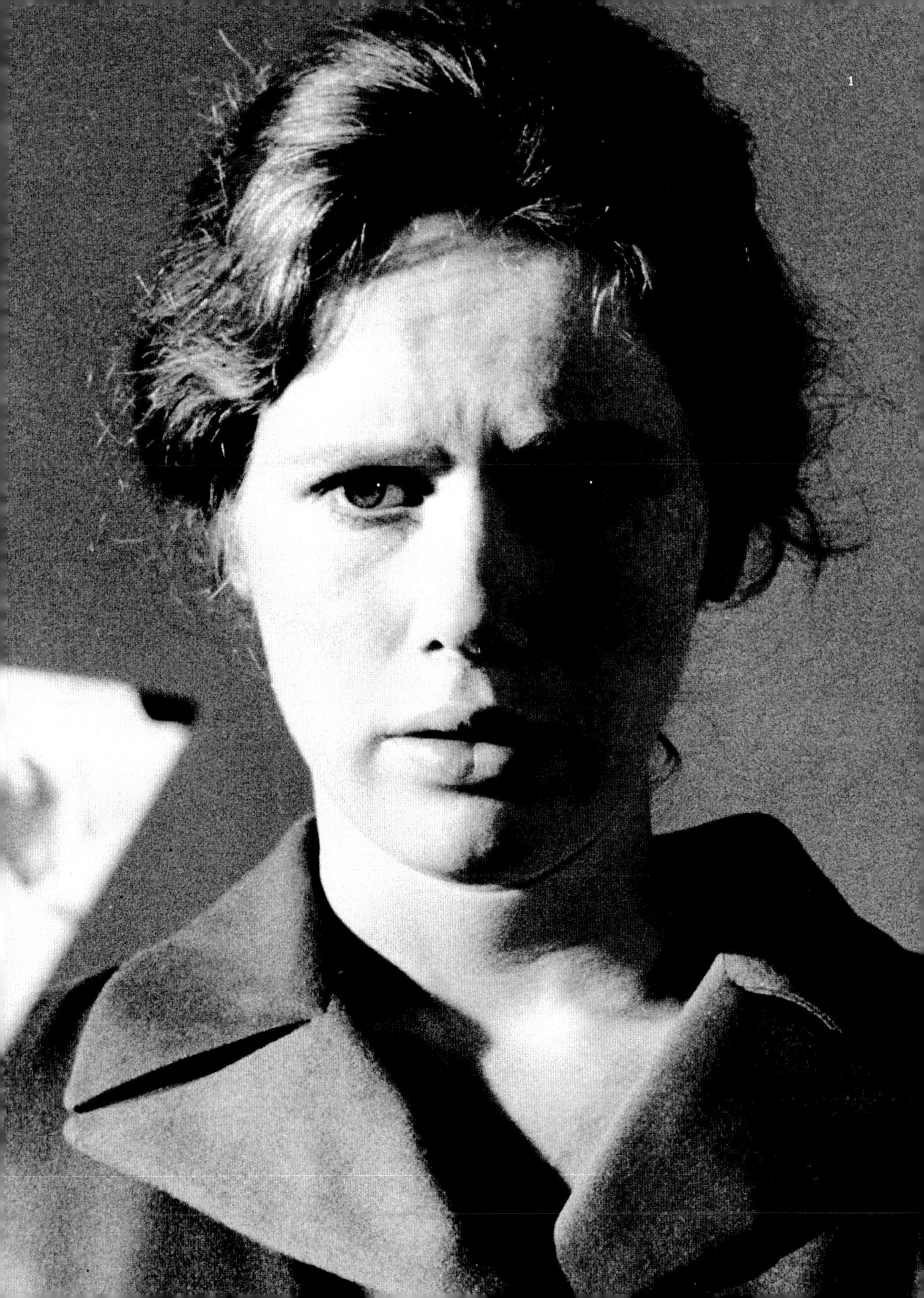
1

2

empathy. The relationship culminates in a symbiotic fusion of the two characters captured in Bergman's monumental shot of a conjoined female face – half Alma's and half Elisabeth's. Indisputably, the leading ladies of *Persona* deliver a tour de force performance. The silent Liv Ullmann communicates solely by means of – often ambiguous – mimicry and gesture, while her counterpart Bibi Andersson fills the soundtrack with incessant prattling.

The movie's action can be broken down into three acts. The first is the women's initial meeting at the hospital; the second, their familiarization with one another at the doctor's remote summer cottage on a rocky island (filmed on Bergman's beloved estate on Fårö); and the third, their final showdown initiated by Alma's surreptitious perusal of Elisabeth's letter to the doctor. The note's contents, that belittle the nurse as an amusing object of study and expose her innermost thoughts, finally send her into a schizophreni frenzy.

Visually, *Persona* stands out for its almost exclusive pairing of close-up with wide shots, and the stark contrasts of Bergman's black and white pho tography that frame the women's faces in artful tableaux, heightening thei intimacy and discord. The result is a vague, surreal yet glaringly nightmaris atmosphere.

The plot itself is open to a variety of interpretations. In ancient theate "persona" referred to the mask of the actor. Centuries later, psychoanalys C. G. Jung reappropriated the term to denote a protective shell individual wrap around their selves. Indeed, the first half of Elisabeth and Alma's so journ on the island has elements of therapy sessions. The mute actress pro

**“*Persona* is more than a masterpiece of cinematic form; it’s a miracle of the spirit. After 75 years of errors and false starts, the art of the cinema has at last come into its own.”** *Le Nouvel Observateur*

1 Her lips are sealed: There’s just no telling what’s on actress Elisabeth Vogler’s (Liv Ullmann) mind.

2 Candid camera: Elisabeth takes on life as an observer and Liv Ullmann delivers a powerhouse performance in her Bergman debut.

3 Shocked speechless: Elisabeth watches a Vietnamese monk setting fire to himself on television.

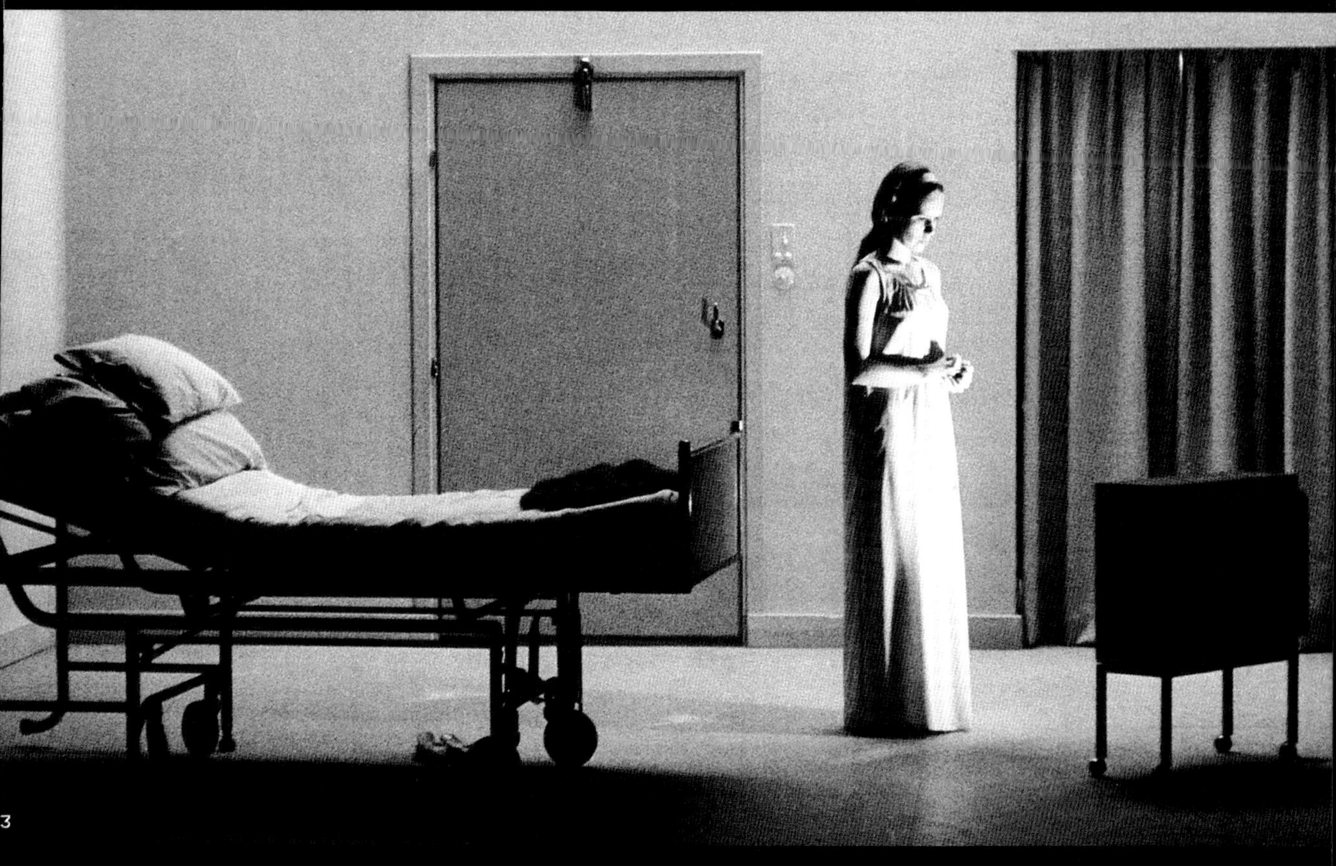

3

**BIBI ANDERSSON**

Much like her Norwegian co-star Liv Ullmann, Bibi Andersson was a conservatory trained actress before making her Bergman debut with a minor role in the 1955 picture *Smiles of a Summer Night* (*Sommarnattens leende*). It was four years prior to this production that the Swedish actress born in 1935 met the great auteur, having performed in a soap commercial he directed. Yet it was their reunion with *Smiles*, a world-acclaimed social comedy from Bergman’s “rose” period, that sent Andersson’s career into orbit. In the years that followed, she won over audiences with her freshness and vivacity, quickly becoming one of Sweden’s most prominent stars of adolescent film and the theater.
The tow-headed beauty’s career continued to flourish in the 1960s as she developed into a fine dramatic actress. It wasn’t long before she was teaming up with some of the most respected directors in Scandinavian film, including Vilgot Sjöman, Alf Sjöberg, Bjarne Henning-Jensen and Mai Zetterling. Nonetheless, it is her Bergman pictures like *The Seventh Seal* (*Det sjunde inseglet*, 1956), *Wild Strawberries* (*Smultronstället*, 1957), *The Magician* (*Ansiktet*, 1958), *Persona* (1966), and *The Passion of Anna* (*En Passion*, 1969) that stand out most clearly in the minds of audiences.
International projects reaped fewer rewards for the magnificent Andersson, who devoted the majority of her professional life in the 80s and 90s to Sweden’s small screen. Her most recent film role to date was in Klaus Härö’s children’s film entitled *Elina – Som om jag inte fanns* (*Elina: As If I Wasn’t There,* 2002), which ran at the Berlin International Film Festival in 2003.

"The two women are often presented in haunting close-ups that act as a kind of window into their souls. In this dense and intricate game of thoughts, feelings and actions, Bibi Andersson as the nurse and Liv Ullmann as the silent actress give equally impressive performances." *Der Tagesspiegel*

Psychobabble: After pouring her heart out to the two-faced silent actress, nurse Alma (Bibi Andersson) sets out to spite the disloyal patient.

5 Bergman's mindscapes: Even Elisabeth's husband (Gunnar Björnstrand) begins to mistake Alma for his wife.

6 Two of a kind: Elisabeth and Alma feed off each other like symbiotic vampires.

ides the nurse – whose name is Spanish for "soul" – with a captive audince to whom she unwittingly bares all. But as several scenes are indisutably the fruit of Alma's interpretation, it is entirely possible that the Elisaeth character is nothing more than a figment of the nurse's imagination or nother side of her personality.

Ingmar Bergman had originally intended to title the film *Kinematograhie*, and of course *Persona* should also be understood as a statement on alseness and fallacy in the world of film. In a five-minute prolog sequence that eems like an attempt at self-analysis, the director inundates the screen with images that are a foretaste of the themes to come. Religion, Eros, death, and childhood memories are interspersed with sporadic shots from Bergman's earlier work such as the spider, which the schizophrenic Harriet Andersson took to be a symbol of God in *Through a Glass Darkly* (*Såsom i en spegel*, 1961). One Swedish theologian, incidentally, interpreted the character of Elisabeth as being a metaphor for God; a plausible assertion given that God has indeed lapsed into deep silence in almost all Bergman films. This hypothesis seems confirmed by the end of the film when Elisabeth, at long last, echoes Alma, uttering just one brief but distinct word – "Nothing." LP

**"Like a demonic psychiatrist with the neurotic, post-war world on his couch, Ingmar Bergman poses painful and provocative questions but maddeningly withholds any answers."** *Newsweek*

# FANTASTIC VOYAGE

966 - USA - 101 MIN. - SCIENCE FICTION

IRECTOR RICHARD FLEISCHER (*1916)
CREENPLAY HARRY KLEINER, DAVID DUNCAN DIRECTOR OF PHOTOGRAPHY ERNEST LASZLO EDITING WILLIAM B. MURPHY
IUSIC LEONARD ROSENMAN PRODUCTION SAUL DAVID for 20TH CENTURY-FOX.

TARRING STEPHEN BOYD (Grant), RAQUEL WELCH (Cora Peterson), EDMOND O'BRIEN (General Carter), DONALD PLEASENC Dr. Michaels), ARTHUR O'CONNELL (Colonel Donald Reid), WILLIAM REDFIELD (Captain Bill Owens), ARTHUR KENNEDY Dr. Duval), JEAN DEL VAL (Jan Benes), BARRY COE (Communications Aid), KEN SCOTT (Secret Service).

CADEMY AWARDS 1966 OSCARS for BEST ART DIRECTION (Jack Martin Smith, Dale Hennesy, Walter M. Scott, Stuart R. Reiss), and 3EST VISUAL EFFECTS (Art Cruickshank).

## *"Arterial Wall to the right!!"*

Velcome aboard a journey to the inner sanctum of espionage. Hold tight – for ve'll soon be injected into the corpuscles of crime fighting.

Like many good beginnings, this *Fantastic Voyage* gets underway at the airport, where director Richard Fleischer throws us into the cold waters of hot pursuit. Hired men in trench coats pick up a man who is clearly a top secret /. I. P. and escort him to a government car. An assault en route interrupts their ide and the high-profile passenger is severely injured. Suddenly, another nan appears on the scene who was seated next to the mystery man on board the aircraft. His name is Grant (Stephen Boyd), a special agent who bombards his companions with questions about what is going on: where are ve headed, and what's this all about?

He gets some answers upon arriving at an underground military base of a special task unit known as the CMDF (Combined Miniature Deterrent Forces), where General Carter (Edmond O'Brien) tries to remain composed while explaining one of sci-fi's more far-fetched and hokier premises.

Grant learns that scientists have succeeded in shrinking people ar stationary objects to miniature proportions. Unfortunately, present technol gy prevents the effects from lasting more than an hour. It follows that the no comatose guest of the secret service, a researcher named Jan Benes, ha discovered a way to prolong these effects, and has been smuggled into th land of the free from behind the Iron Curtain to share his knowledge. Now however, a malignant blood clot threatens his life, and a team of specialis have been called into action. They are to be miniaturized inside a nucle submarine so that they can travel into the abyss of his body to annihilate th incapacitating mass.

What follows is one of the most bizarrely psychedelic trips ever a tempted in the history of human anatomy!

It was an unquestionably original idea. Previously, sci-fi warriors ha been mainly flung into outer space, and had gotten to know the vast reache of the universe better than their own "inner space."

1
2

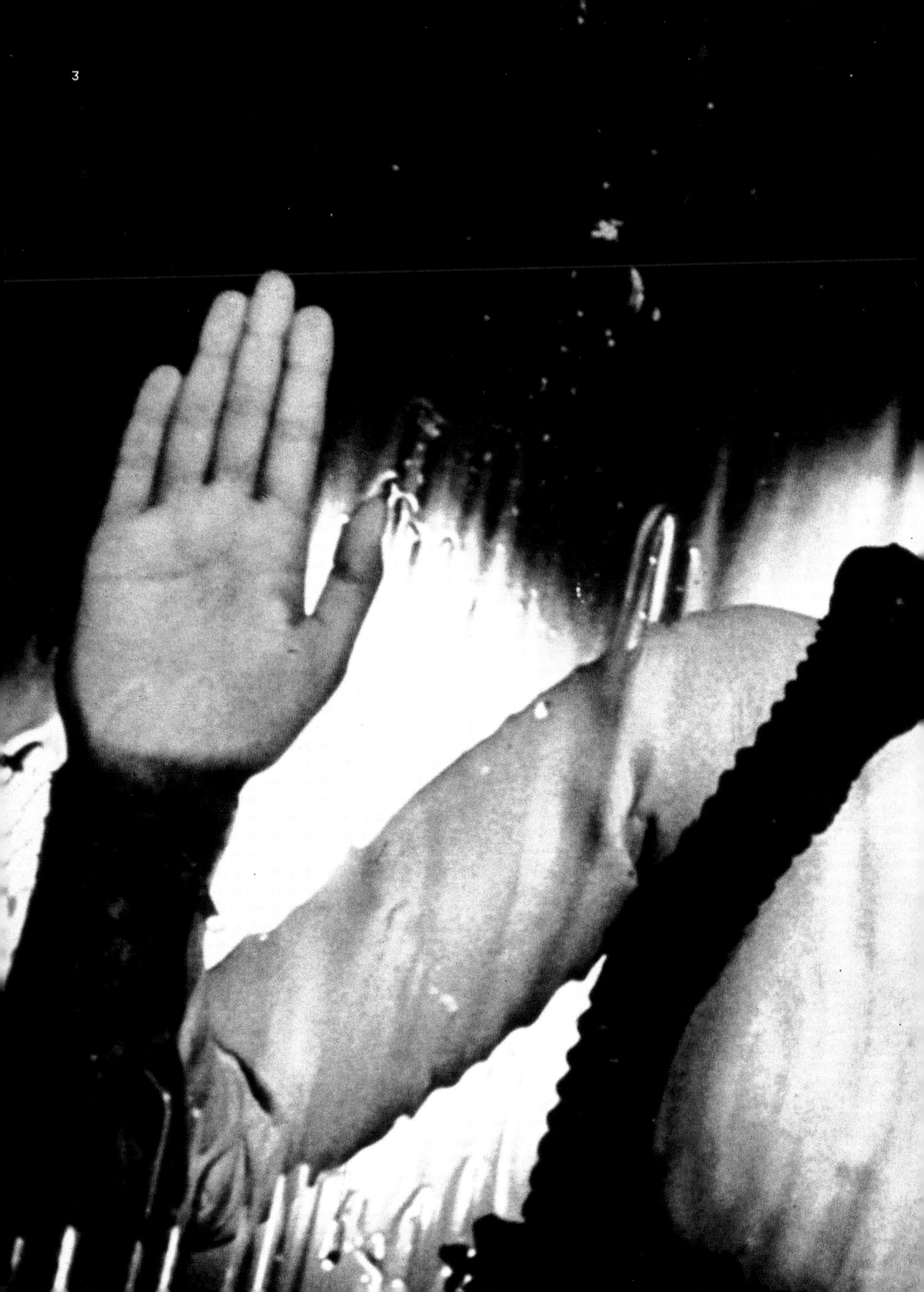

3

4

1 Scenes from the inner sanctum: Apparently four shots of crime fighting penicillin is all one needs to fight paper mâché opponents.

2 Varicose veins: The scientists get road blocked by the fibers of the anatomy.

3 Window washer: Duval's assistant Cora Peterson (Raquel Welch) polishes the laser and keeps her opinions to herself. As seen here, Welch's early career often had her puckering up to the camera.

4 Shrinky dinks: A team headed for a realm where the sun don't shine.

5 Body versus antibody: Agent Grant (Stephen Boyd) wishes he'd gotten stationed inside someone else's body.

6 The human blood stream meets Willy Wonka's chocolate factory: For all its lack of natural light, the human body sure is one colorful place.

**"Yessir, for straight science-fiction, this is quite a film – the most colorful and imaginative since *Destination Moon.* Harry Kleiner's screenplay and Richard Fleischer's direction combine to make it amusing and exciting, and the interior decorations have a bubbly, fantastic quality you won't find this side of Disneyland."**

*The New York Times*

Afforded an astronomical budget approaching six-and-a-half million
ıllars, *Fantastic Voyage* was the most expensive sci-fi thriller Hollywood ıd ever produced. It would take such a phenomenal price tag to cover some the most exorbitant backdrops and set dressing ever seen. In fact, the project's art director transformed an athletic stadium, lot and all, into a holding nk for gigantic replications of the arterial and venous system, heart, lungs ıd inner ear. The set itself must have been quite a sight: the finished prod-
ɛt was a crayola leviathan, with never-ending, illuminated plastic tarps and ıuze, ornamented by colossal paper mâché islands. What by today's stanırds comes across as a marvelously tacky wonderland was deemed state--the-art at the time, and the picture was accordingly awarded Oscars for its t color direction and outstanding visual effects.

Given all the attention paid to the movie's look, its incredible that the iters let the cast make do with cardboard characters: the submarine capın (William Redfield) is a reliable technician; the surgeon (Arthur Kennedy) perpetually dumbfounded by God's creation (scientific proof that he is not e saboteur as the other crew members suspect); his lovely assistant aquel Welch) keeps the laser well lubed; the cynically detached agnostic, . Michaels (Donald Pleasence) detachedly explains the lymphatic system cientific proof that he is the saboteur); and Agent Grant, well… he prevents e worst, whatever exactly that may be.

Basically, what results is a disaster movie precursor, meaning that anying that can go wrong does. Rather than being able to navigate the ship noothly to the endangered area of the brain, the crew is propelled into the nous system and must combat its way through unthinkable perils. Their only chance at success is to cross back through the heart. However, wher their oxygen tanks are almost depleted, they are forced to venture into th lungs for some fresh air. And would you believe that, after all this, their sea cruiser almost runs out of gas?

Today, the thrill of viewing this sci-fi classic lies in soaking up the absolute seriousness of the actors amidst all this absurdity: be it the surgica tension displayed in the red hexagon control tower, or their critical encounte with the Arterial Wall. Despite the constant, life-threatening dangers of thei mission, only whole-lotta-woman Raquel Welch is attacked by "antibodies" – supplying her male companions with a golden opportunity to rip her free o that skin-tight diving outfit and grope her most pleasurables. Shame on you Hollywood … even if it is the most fantastic part of this voyage.

**RTHUR KENNEDY (1914–1990)**

Arthur Kennedy just wasn't cut out to make it as a big-name movie star. First off, his appearance was too ordinary and second, the man from Worcester, Massachusetts was so skilled at playing neurotic and bitter characters that he rarely got the chance to appeal to the audience's sympathies. Kennedy was a trained stage actor who toured the United States with a Shakespeare company until Warner Bros. offered him a contract in the late 30s.

His made his film debut as a mime in Anatole Litvak's *City for Conquest* (1940). Numerous supporting roles in Warner productions would follow. Toward the end of World War II, Kennedy returned to the stage and wooed audiences in numerous Arthur Miller plays, while continuing to pursue his Hollywood career. He enjoyed a great deal of silver screen success in the early 50s, playing a wrathful cowboy in Fritz Lang's *Rancho Notorious*, (1952) and a callously ambitious bull rider in Nicholas Ray's *The Lusty Men* (1952). He also played James Stewart's nemesis in the Anthony Mann Westerns *Bend of the River* (1951) and *The Man from Laramie* (1955).

Even after the collapse of the studio system, Kennedy remained a successful Hollywood character actor. In fact, the American journalist he played in David Lean's *Lawrence of Arabia* (1962) proved to be one of his most memorable roles. By the mid-60s, Kennedy frequently found himself shooting pictures in Italy. His career came to a close in the 80s shortly before his death in 1990.

# BLOW-UP

1966 - GREAT BRITAIN - 111 MIN. - THRILLER, LITERARY ADAPTATION

DIRECTOR MICHELANGELO ANTONIONI (*1912)
SCREENPLAY MICHELANGELO ANTONIONI, TONINO GUERRA, EDWARD BOND DIRECTOR OF PHOTOGRAPHY CARLO DI PALMA
EDITING FRANK CLARKE MUSIC HERBIE HANCOCK, THE YARDBIRDS PRODUCTION CARLO PONTI for PREMIER.

STARRING DAVID HEMMINGS (Thomas), VANESSA REDGRAVE (Jane), PETER BOWLES (Ron), VERUSCHKA VON LEHNDORFF (Herself), SARAH Miles (Patricia), JOHN CASTLE (Bill), JANE BIRKIN (Teenager), GILLIAN HILLS (Teenager), THE YARDBIRDS (Themselves).

IFF CANNES 1967 GOLDEN PALM (Michelangelo Antonioni).

## *Thomas: "Don't let's spoil everything, we've only just met." Jane: "No, we haven't met. You've never seen me."*

There's a mystery in these photos. Thomas (David Hemmings), a photographer, strokes his chin while examining some large prints he has hung up in his studio. He moves up closer to scrutinize one particular print, then dashes into his lab and exposes another sheet of paper, hangs this up in place of another print that had been part of the series, and takes a good long look at the entire series of images. Now he has it – the missing link in the chain. That morning, Thomas had got in the way of a murder attempt. Having noticed a couple fooling around in the park, he had started taking snapshots of them, surreptitiously, while hiding in the bushes – until the woman (Vanessa Redgrave) noticed him and vehemently insisted that he hand over the film. Now he knows why: the man was about to be murdered. In the crucial last enlargement, a hand holding a pistol can be seen pointing out from the undergrowth.

If a photograph is "blown up" sufficiently, even the smallest details can become clear. But there is a limit to enlargement: once the image is blown up beyond a certain size, it starts to disappear behind the grainy structure of the photographic material. Eventually, the image will break up into an abstract pattern of grains and blobs, and the motif will become unrecognizable. It's this boundary that fascinates Michelangelo Antonioni in *Blow-up*. His film is a brilliant essay on the peculiar capacity of pictures to show the surface of things, but not their essence. Perhaps no other movie has examined the relationship between truth and representation so thrillingly or with such subtle complexity.

Thomas, whose life we share for a single day, is himself tormented by this dichotomy between appearance and reality. In the evenings, he takes photos in a shelter for the homeless, searching for life at its most naked and authentic; in the daytime, he works with the trendiest photo models in his beautifully fashionable studio. He commands and directs the girls he photographs, almost penetrating one of his models (Veruschka von Lehndorff) with the lens in his zeal to capture an image that is more than mere surface. For Thomas, photography is a mixture of sex and violence; he rips his pictures from the objects that make them possible. It seems he has no interest whatsoever in his subjects as human beings – neither the homeless people he secretly snaps, nor the beautiful women who writhe on the floor of his studio. In the park, too, he has the appearance of a sex criminal: lurking in the trees like a perverted flasher, he snaps away incessantly, a driven man.

1

2

This film is a work of art. The development of the plot and the handling of color are masterly. *Blow-up* does a wonderful job of capturing the world of London's youth, with its miniskirts, marijuana and beat music – and it approaches its subject with friendly curiosity and an unprecedented lightness of touch." *Frankfurter Allgemeine Zeitung*

The camera as a deadly weapon, taking shots. Thomas realizes that he has misinterpreted the scene in the park, that his presence did not in fact prevent a murder taking place; for in a further photo, he discovers a cluster of pale points under a bush that look very like a corpse. He drives over to the park once more, and sure enough, he finds a corpse. The next morning, however, after a wild party, everything has disappeared: the pictures have been stolen and the body has vanished – along with any hope of ever knowing for sure what has really taken place.

*Blow-up* was the first film Michelangelo Antonioni made outside Italy. In 1967, at the film festival in Cannes, he said that temporary exile in London had put him at a disadvantage, but that the city had stimulated him for that very reason. He spent four months immersing himself in the London scene. With its pop colors, its music and its sexual freedom – two half-naked women caused a considerable stir at the time – *Blow-up* can be seen as a reflection of the Swinging Sixties. But Antonioni's London is no *objet trouvé*: he created it himself. As he put it, he *painted* the landscapes and streets; indeed, he even had whole houses built for the film. And as the actress Sarah Miles said, it's putting the cart before the horse to say that Antonioni was inspired by the Swinging Sixties: for it's truer to say that *Blow-up* invented them.

1 Exposed: Jane (Vanessa Redgrave) is willing to give up a little something in exchange for the incriminating photos taken in the park.

2 A soul-stealing objective: Thomas (David Hemmings) goes to extremes in the name of photorealism.

3 Set dressing: Living dolls wait to be escorted into Thomas' playhouse. *Blowup* is a showcase of 1960s fashions and styles, many of which the film was responsible for popularizing.

4

4 Do you see what I see? *Blow up* is a study in image and representation. The script was based on a short story by Argentine novelist Julio Cortázar, whose works often focus on intertwining perspectives.

5 Carrot topless: However, Thomas' skin paled in comparison to Jane's at the time of *Blow Up's* cinematic debut. Vanessa Redgrave is reportedly the first woman to bare her boobs in a non-pornographic British film.

6 Modular work spaces: The like of which, according to *Time Magazine*, produced an "uptight and vibrantly exciting picture."

7 Grasping at straws: Terence Stamp was originally considered for the role of the photographer, but Antonioni cast the virtually unknown David Hemmings in what proved to be the role of his career.

8 Keep off the grass: Antonioni effortlessly turns manicured park grounds into a sinister locale, where rustling leaves signal blood-curdling clues.

At the end of the film, Thomas watches a troupe of young mime artists playing tennis in the park, with no rackets and no ball. When the imaginary tennis ball flies over the fence, he picks it up and throws it back. We see his face. His tired eyes follow the to-and-fro of the invisible ball; and suddenly we hear sounds: the sounds of a tennis match, the whack of the rackets, the thud of the ball. Thomas gazes at the ground; and then he disappears, like th corpse under the bushes, and like this unfathomable film itself. Despit decades of explication and interpretation, *Blow-up* has lost nothing of it mystery and its compelling strangeness.

NI

**TONINO GUERRA**

"A screenwriter is someone who helps to build up the script as a structure, in all its qualities," says Tonino Guerra (*1920). The main task of the director, he states, is to add a new quality: to find images that correspond to this text. "And Antonioni adds this new quality: he is a man who knows how to capture light, how to arrange and organize encounters." When Tonino Guerra speaks of his friend Michelangelo Antonioni, his admiration is palpable. Yet he rarely speaks about his own share in Antonioni's films. What Guerra contributes is the poetry. Together, these two artists make up one of the most congenial teams in the history of European cinema. Since *L'Avventura* (1960), they have conceived and written several scripts together, including *La notte* (1960) and *Il deserto rosso* (1964). And they're still at it: in 2002, Guerra presented their film *Il filo pericoloso delle cose* (2001) in Venice.

Born in 1920 in the North Italian region of Emilia-Romagna, Tonino Guerra began by writing short stories and novellas. In 1956, he wrote his first screenplay in collaboration with Giuseppe De Santis for his late-neo-realistic film *The Wolves* (*Uomini e lupi*, 1956). Since then, Guerra has been the busiest and most successful screenwriter in Italy. Besides his association with Antonioni, he also worked with Fellini on several occasions, receiving an Oscar nomination for the script to *Amarcord* (1973). For Francesco Rosi, he wrote *Lucky Luciano* (1974), *Three Brothers* (*Tre fratelli*, 1981) and other scripts. He has also had a long association with Theo Angelopoulos; since *Voyage to Cythera* (*Taxidi sta Kithera*, 1984), he has been credited as co-author on most of the Greek director's films.

# THE WILD ANGELS

1966 - USA - 86 MIN. - DRAMA

DIRECTOR ROGER CORMAN (*1926)
SCREENPLAY CHARLES B. GRIFFITH DIRECTOR OF PHOTOGRAPHY RICHARD MOORE EDITING MONTE HELLMAN MUSIC DAVIE ALLAN, MIKE CURB PRODUCTION ROGER CORMAN for AIP.

STARRING PETER FONDA (Heavenly Blues), NANCY SINATRA (Mike), BRUCE DERN (Loser), DIANE LADD (Gaysh), JOAN SHAWLEE (Momma Monahan), FRANK MAXWELL (Preacher).

***"We wanna be free! We wanna be free to do what we wanna do. We wanna be free to ride. We wanna be free to ride our machines without being hassled by the man!"***

Heavenly Blues (Peter Fonda), leader of a gang of Hell's Angels, and his pal Loser (Bruce Dern) can't gear up for a nine to five routine. Whenever these two manage to land a job, they're usually canned before their first paycheck.

Their home is the open road, where all that matters is camaraderie and a Harley's big-growl purr. Understandably, their entire gang is up in arms when Loser's bike is swiped from under his nose. The deadbeat searches high and low for his sole meaningful possession, only to have a run-in with the law that leaves him with a serious gunshot wound. He is admitted to a hospital and expected to convalesce like a catatonic in the geriatric ward – a most undignified state for a Hell's Angel. And so Blues makes up his mind to spring him loose. No sooner has the gang delivered him to their temporary headquarters, however, than Loser dies of internal injuries. As a final act of respect, his buddies return him to his home town for a proper burial.

Not surprisingly, most residents of the backroads hamlet are less than thrilled about this invasion of people they consider hoodlums. When the local preacher (Frank Maxwell) voices this while delivering Loser's eulogy, the Angels retaliate in a storm of protest. A rowdy biker-style wake ensues atop the remains of the church pews. As the police begin to arrive on the scene, the whole wild bunch except Heavenly Blues try to dodge the heat. For the gang leader has decided to end his freedom trail here and now.

The star-powered cinema of Hollywood's golden age was in crisis toward the end of the 1950s. Big budgets, exotic locales, color photography, scope format and a few big names were no longer a surefire recipe for success. A new day had dawned, paving the way for smaller independent studios intent on producing a large quantity of pictures as cheaply as possible. These new companies targeted a younger market by presenting them with a channel for more contemporary and previously taboo subjects. Roger Corman was perhaps the greatest pioneer of this movement. In 1954, he appeared on the scene as a producer-director for the unaffiliated American International Pictures (AIP). Corman's modus operandi was a bare-bones budget, a minimalist shoot, and room for boundless creativity. As such, his productions enabled

1

2

1 Born to be tame: Differences of opinion could end in dental surgery.

2 Harleys, chicks and a couple of brewskis: Beer goggles or not, there's no way biker Heavenly Blues (Peter Fonda) would ever say no to a rumble or beautiful women.

3 Tall tales and leather jackets: After a hard day of thundering down the highway, Heavenly Blues and friends like to unwind at bars along the interstate and rack up some good times.

**"The foreword to this well turned-out Roger Corman production is its tip-off: 'The picture you are about to see will shock and perhaps anger you. Although the events and characters are fictitious, the story is a reflection of our times'."** *Variety*

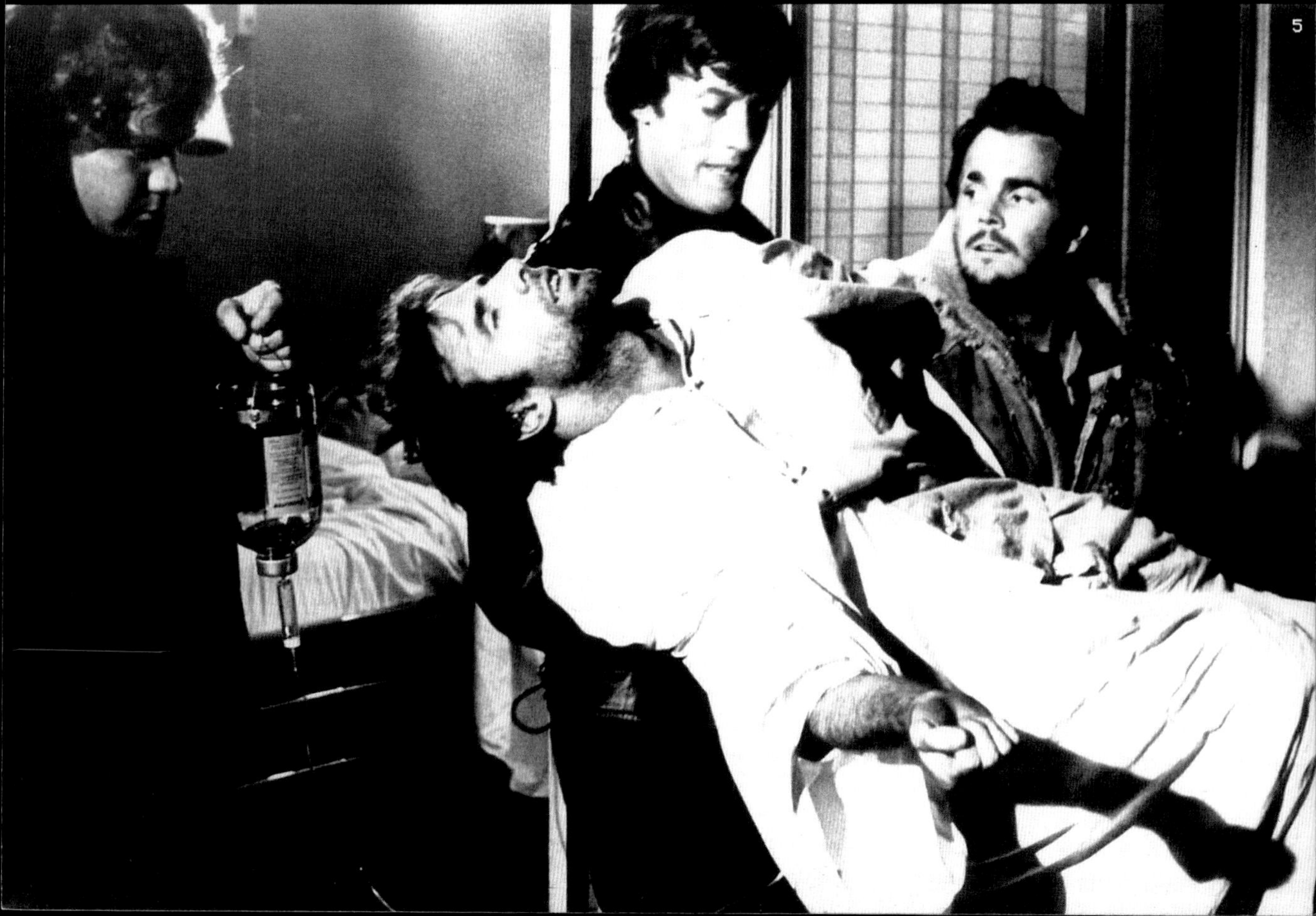

4 Family circle: Breaking from life's vicious cycles and taking some much needed time out for togetherness.

5 Wild animals don't belong in cages: Heavenly Blues rescues Loser (Bruce Dern) from the hospital.

6 These boots were made for walking: Since they'll never find a place within society, Blues and Mike (Nancy Sinatra) intend to walk all over it.

many future names like Jack Nicholson, Peter Bogdanovich, Francis Ford Coppola and James Cameron to come out of the woodwork.

Constantly on the lookout for inspiration, Corman happened upon an article in *Life Magazine* about a biker funeral that had all the ingredients of a compelling film: drugs, hard-boiled ruffians, fast women and Harleys. Above all else, the piece exuded authenticity in that it was fresh, contemporary and fuelled by the trademark American spirit of rebellion. Indeed, *The Wild Angels* is little more than a whirlwind of biking, rough-housing and heavy drinking. Yet the simplicity of its content does not reflect a lack of fantasy. The liberating image of savage youths astride Harleys epitomized an emerging generation's refusal to capitulate to their parents' monochrome job-and-family existence.

It is a metaphor that follows the film right from its opening shots in cramped suburbia. As a little boy on his tricycle crosses beyond the picket fences toward the neighborhood's main drag, he is nearly mowed over by Blues' chopper. For now, his mother can confine him to his play pen, but it's just a matter of time before this little boy starts craving the sort of idealized freedom personified by Blues.

Yet the ideal itself is not easy to put into words. When the preacher asks the biker gang what it is they actually want Blues is at a loss. After all, the Angels' credo is based primarily on the *rejection* of established norms. The swastikas emblazoned on their helmets, apparel, and flags are not any indication that they themselves are Nazis, but rather a way for the group to ruffle the feathers of the those who have nested down in small-minded middle-class morality. As such, it is not a goal so much as a simple dynamic that drives the biker rebellion. As Blues himself puts it: "We wanna be free to ride!"

EP

**BIKER FILMS**

Conquering the West is an essential part of the great American legacy. Cowboys did it every time they rode off into the sunset. And bikers followed in their footsteps, saddled up on animals with far more horsepower. These modern-day rebels without a cause were a new breed of lonesome dove, invincible and free. In 1947, they first made their way into the public consciousness after a two-day biker convention in the small Californian town of Hollister quickly spiraled out of control. It would take a few more years before Hollywood adapted this newfound phenomenon for the big screen, with Marlon Brando getting the genre off to a rolling start in *The Wild One* (1953).

However, biker films only truly skyrocketed in popularity thanks to Roger Corman's *The Wild Angels* and Richard Rush's *Hell's Angels on Wheels* (1967), both featuring actual members of the Hell's Angels in their casts. Many of these Harley epics built on themes explored in classic cinema. *The Savage Seven* (1968) and *Angel Unchained* (1970) were highly reminiscent of Akira Kurosawa's *Shichinin no Samurai* (1954), and *Hell's Belles* (1970) was basically a remake of Anthony Mann's *Winchester '73* (1950). Of course, it goes without saying that Dennis Hopper's hippie road movie *Easy Rider* (1969) eclipses all others as the genre's standout.

# WHO'S AFRAID OF VIRGINIA WOOLF?

1966 USA -131 MIN. - PSYCHODRAMA, LITERARY ADAPTATION

DIRECTOR MIKE NICHOLS (*1931)
SCREENPLAY ERNEST LEHMAN, based on the play of the same name by EDWARD ALBEE DIRECTOR OF PHOTOGRAPHY HASKELL WEXLER
EDITING SAM O'STEEN MUSIC ALEX NORTH PRODUCTION ERNEST LEHMAN for WARNER BROS.

STARRING ELIZABETH TAYLOR (Martha), RICHARD BURTON (George), GEORGE SEGAL (Nick), SANDY DENNIS (Honey).

ACADEMY AWARDS 1966 OSCARS for BEST ACTRESS (Elizabeth Taylor), BEST SUPPORTING ACTRESS (Sandy Dennis), BEST ART DIRECTION (Richard Sylbert, George James Hopkins), BEST CINEMATOGRAPHY (Haxwell Wexler), and BEST COSTUME DESIGN (Irene Sharaff).

## *"I swear to GOD George, if you even EXISTED I'd divorce you."*

On the set of *Cleopatra* (1963), hardly a day went by without either Elizabeth Taylor or Richard Burton turning up with a black eye or disheveled hair. But in this adaptation of Edward Albee's theatrical *succès de scandale*, they went beyond even the wildest imaginings of the tabloid press. For an entire drink-sodden night, history professor George (Richard Burton) and his domineering wife Martha (Elizabeth Taylor) indulge in a verbal war of attrition. Even more frightening than this sadomasochistic variation on marriage therapy was the reaction of the audience: far from turning away in disgust, many moviegoers recognized themselves in George and Martha. Like Nick (George Segal) and Honey (Sandy Dennis), the hapless young witnesses to this orgy of mutual humiliation, the audience had walked into a trap. Paralyzed with horror, they couldn't tear their eyes away as the American dream of married bliss was shredded, slowly and with relish, by first-time director Mike Nichols.

As in real life, this couple from hell need an audience. It's clear they have decades of practice in the fine art of insult, but when they're alone in their tastefully rotting home environment, their mutual misery-making is only half the fun. So Martha brings Nick and Honey, a couple of young newly-weds, back from a university banquet to an after-dinner party *chez elle* – a massive provocation for George, in more ways than one. The almost fifty-year-old historian sees the successful young biology prof as his natural enemy. By making eyes at Nick, Martha takes revenge on her ineffectual husband, whom she castigates repeatedly as a weakling and a failure

1

**“When you come right down to it, however, the play invites a mood of harshly contorted black humor. It is almost grotesque comedy. These characters are so wild and aberrant they are close to appearing lunatics. That is why they are frightening and pathetic. They are outcasts of a brutal, baffling world.”** *The New York Times*

1 George and Martha: An American ideal run amok. From left, Richard Burton, Elizabeth Taylor, and George Segal as Nick.

2 These have always brought me luck: Hair, make-up and white diamonds. Martha gave audiences a taste of what to expect from Liz Taylor in later years.

3 Fun and games: “Never mix, never worry!” Just as long as you don’t get carried away.

as his career has long since ground to a halt. As a further ingredient in this pungent emotional soup, George sees Nick as a representative of her father, the all-powerful rector, whom Martha worships with almost incestuous intensity.

The situation is unbearable and something has to give. In the course of an evening steeped in liquor, George begins to plan his own revenge. With the help of the hopelessly inebriated Honey, he “kills” the imaginary child he and Martha had invented to fill the void at the heart of their existence. In fact, this child was nothing more than an excuse for further guilt-slapping. Martha collapses. She and George recognize the need to free themselves from the lies that have ruled their lives, and to overcome the fear of reality expressed in the movie’s title – a variation on the song sung by Disney’s Three Little Pigs: “Who’s Afraid of the Big, Bad Wolf?”

For Martha and George, their gruesomely playful dealings with their repressed terrors are part of a shared ritual, which is remarkably suggestive of a kind of psychotherapy. In essence the entire evening is nothing but a series of cruel games, each of which has a weird associative relationship to the real world. Nick and Honey are forced to join in and play by the existing rules.

4 Elephant hunting: George fantasizes about killing the pint-sized pachyderm on the couch, but that doesn't make him any less jealous when she gets attention from attractive young beaus. Tonight, it looks as if the history professor might have to bump off a couple of dodos instead of his usual prey.

5 A marriage of inconvenience: As daughter to the president of the mediocre New Carthage University, Martha terrorizes her professor husband for his lack of ambition.

# "Look, sweetheart, I can drink you under any goddamn table you want, so don't worry about me."

*Film quote: Martha (Elizabeth Taylor)*

ıe game is called modern marriage. In reality, it has led George and Martha concoct an imaginary child for themselves, a kind of academic "imitation life."

That Martha and George are named after the first Presidential couple in e USA is merely one of many barbed jokes in Albee's play. The deeper truth ›out the American Way of Life is to be found in the huge amounts of alcohol at are consumed in the course of this drama. The protagonists' conscious-ɜss dissolves like the ice in their whisky – and they awake to a brutal hang-/er.

The play had been a permanent fixture on Broadway since 1962, and ike Nichols succeeded brilliantly in adapting it for the screen. The high-con-ast black and white photography, the nervous switches from long shot to ose-up and the intentional use of unfocused images make this movie much ıore than the filmed record of a theater piece. *Who's Afraid of Virginia Woolf?* a film noir from the marriage war zone, and the eternal murkiness of eorge and Martha's household conveys a feeling of deep existential loneli-ess. Home, bitter home.

Most memorable of all, though, are the monumental performances of ɑylor and Burton. Their acting has an unparalleled visceral power, and the ialogue has lost nothing of its brilliance. Hate-filled and foul-mouthed to the erge of the permissible, George and Martha fling names that really do hurt ke sticks and stones. This film was one of the reasons the production com-anies felt the need to introduce the notorious R-rating; the "adult film" was orn. But the movie was so obviously a work of art that even the Catholic ;hurch couldn't refuse its blessing. PB

5

**MIKE NICHOLS** Born in Berlin to parents of Russian origin, Michael Igor Peschkowsky fled the city with his family in 1938 at the age of seven. Even as a young theater director, he had developed a sharp eye for relationships between men and women. With his long-term collaborator Elaine May he formed a legendary comedy duo, and they set new standards for improvised theater. By the mid-60s, although he had never made a film, he was so famous that he could postpone another movie contract to take charge of a prestigious project: *Who's Afraid of Virginia Woolf?* (1966). Today, however, *The Graduate* (1967) is widely regarded as his most influential work. Since then his trademarks have been witty dialogue, an entertaining disregard for taboos, and dominant female characters. But he is widely regarded as inconsistent, with a filmography more like that of a producer whose calculations leave room for a few box-office flops along the way. The latter category includes the subversive war comedy *Catch-22* (1970), *Heartburn* (1986), *Regarding Henry* (1991) and *Wolf* (1994). But his sure feel for intelligent mainstream, visual inventiveness, and always-excellent actors have continued to bring him success. Examples include the political thriller *Silkwood* (1983) starring Meryl Streep, the kitchen-sink fairy tale *Working Girl* (1988) with Melanie Griffith, and the Presidential election satire *Primary Colors* (1997/98).

6 Who's afraid of the big bad wolf? Martha and Nick get deadly close to one another as the night goes on. But George and Nick's inebriated wife Honey have worked out a plan that provides for their welfare…

7 The son she never had: Motherly Martha sets her hopes high on seducing Nick, an up and coming biology lecturer, and indulges in a bit of role-playing. Just call her Jocasta.

6

7

# ANDREI RUBLEV

## Strasti po Andreju

1966 - USSR - 205 MIN. - HISTORICAL EPIC, BIOPIC

**DIRECTOR** ANDREI TARKOVSKY (1932–1986)
**SCREENPLAY** ANDREI TARKOVSKY, ANDREI MIKHALKOV-KONCHALOVSKY **DIRECTOR OF PHOTOGRAPHY** VADIM YUSOV
**EDITING** LYUDMILA FEIGINOVA, T. YEGORYCHYOVA, O. SHEVKUNENKO **MUSIC** VYACHESLAV OVCHINNIKOV
**PRODUCTION** MOSFILM.

**STARRING** ANATOLI SOLONITSYN (Andrei Rublev), IVAN LAPIKOV (Kirill), NIKOLAI GRINKO (Daniil), NIKOLAI SERGEYEV (Feofan Grek), IRMA RAUSCH (Idiot Girl), NIKOLAI BURLYAYEV (Boriska), YURI NAZAROV (Grand Prince), ROLAN BYKOV (The Jester), IGOR DONSKOY (Christ), MIKHAIL KONONOV (Foma), YURI NIKULIN (Patrik).

## *"You found bells, I paint icons – what a feast day for mankind!"*

A peasant stares, flabbergasted as he watches a man slowly rise up into the air. "Now you're going to heaven!" he shouts, as the patchwork hot-air balloon drifts ever higher across a bizarre winter landscape. The makeshift aircraft reaches a dizzying height, when the whistling wind and the groaning rope make us fear the worst; and seconds later, the journey's over and the balloon crashes to the ground.

In this allegorical opening sequence, Andrei Tarkovsky anticipates the central theme of *Andrei Rublev*. By showing us the rise and fall of a man who reached for the sky, the Russian director illustrates a yearning for freedom and the desire to overcome humanity's limitations. On a surface level, *Andrei Rublev* is a biopic about a 15th-century Russian icon painter. In essence, however, it's a reflection on the nature of art itself, and the eight episodes of this three-hour black and white masterpiece amount to a panoramic vision of the Russian nation under the heel of the Tatars.

On an epic scale, yet without a trace of nationalistic pathos, director Andrei Tarkovsky portrays a world in which the line between good and evil is impossibly blurred. Despite all the horrors of this earthly existence, monk and painter Andrei Rublev (Anatoli Solonitsyn) is convinced of the essential goodness of mankind, and he regards art as a source of comfort and power for change. But his sublimely idealistic worldview collapses as the Tata storm into his homeland: Russians fight Russians, slaughtering each othe like cattle, and he himself is forced to kill a would-be rapist. Shaken to th core, he loses all faith in art, lays down his paintbrush and retreats int silence.

His faith in life and art is finally restored by a young man called Borisk (Nikolai Burlyayev). In an unforgettable sequence, Rublev observes how th young man gives his all to cast a colossal bell for the local prince. Deeply im pressed by the joy this heroic endeavor gives to the people, Rublev takes u his work once again. For he now realizes that the artist, like any other ma or woman engaged in the struggle for existence, must fight to achieve hi destiny.

Many critics have pointed out that Rublev, the monk, was a kind of cin ematic avatar of Tarkovsky himself – the Russian title is *The Passion c Andrei* – and that the film's true subject was contemporary reality. So it's n surprise that, in 1966, the Soviet authorities weren't prepared to release th completed movie as it stood. The censors objected to some particularly har rowing torture scenes, and to an allegedly unpatriotic rendering of Russia history. Tarkovsky stood his ground and refused to tolerate the mutilation o

1
2

1 Brothers in arms: The Grand Duke's brother (Yuri Nazarov in a dual role) enjoys the benefits of influence, but would prefer to occupy the prestigious position himself. Flexing his military muscles, he leads troops to pillage Vladimir's cathedral.

2 The passion: The jester (Rolan Bykov) and the painter Andrei Rublev (Anatoli Solonitsyn) fight for more humanity.

3 Sacred spaces: Andrei's meeting with the mighty Grand Duke is set in an eerie, vacuous church, an echoing the emptiness in his heart.

his work, which was originally 220 minutes long. Finally, though, he did agree to shorten a few scenes, without, however, affecting the film's essential content and meaning. It was February 1969 before *Andrei Rublev* received its first "semi-official" showing, but this was enough to capture people's attention. In the same year – though the film had still not been officially approved for showing abroad – *Andrei Rublev* was screened at Cannes, where it received the International Critics' Prize. Only in 1973 was it finally released for public distribution.

By this time, *Andrei Rublev* had already been recognized as one of th most important and multifaceted films ever made about art. Few movie reflect on the subject so seriously. The episodic narrative structure allow Tarkovsky to incorporate a wide range of positions and perspectives. This er ables him, not least, to deliver a variety of answers to the difficult questior "What is a work of art?" In the very first episode, for example, the jester jokes about Popes and potentates broach the issue of the relationshi between art, politics and social criticism. Several episodes contrast th

**"A violently poetic film, Dostoyevskyan in its furious intensity, yet breathtakingly precise and at times almost shockingly calculating."** *Die Welt*

ıiet and thoughtful Andrei with his talentless but striving apprentice Kirill ıan Lapikov), who eventually suffers the consequences of his own exces- ve ambition. Kirill is prepared to betray both himself and Andrei if it will gain m the public recognition he so desperately craves. This is a clear allusion to ıdas and Christ, and it implicitly assigns a redemptory function to the cre- ion of true art.

In Tarkovsky's cinematic cosmos, non-linear narrative plays a central ıle, and in this film his use of the technique reached its maturity. The cam- ra meditates at length on the natural world behind and beyond humanity: ıow-covered hills and swampy forests, wild horses and endless rain. It's as the director were looking for a primary visual language, concealed within ature yet pointing to a dimension outside it. AZ

**FILM BIOGRAPHIES OF ARTISTS**

A well-established sub-genre of the biopic examines the lives of artists, both real and fictional, including painters, musicians and writers. Although they occasionally verge on the didactic, these "artist films" have often been highly successful. Artists frequently lead spectacularly interesting lives, and the processes and techniques of creation are fascinating themes in themselves.

Most of these movies deal with the life, work and reputation of artists already reasonably familiar to the general public. Great pains are therefore taken to recreate the settings, characters and costumes with a maximum of historical accuracy. Only a few films break with this tradition, preferring a timeless or contemporary look instead (as in Derek Jarman's *Caravaggio*, 1986).

In popular mythology, the artist is a lonely genius, suffering for his art and generally neglected by a philistine public. The movies are an ideal platform for variations on this theme, from Michelangelo as "divino artista" (*The Agony and the Ecstasy*, 1965) to Goya as a useful member of society (*Goya*, 1971), from the crazed creator as social outcast (*Vincent & Theo*, 1990) to the modern "mad and tragic hero" (*Pollock*, 2000).

4 I don't mean to shock anyone: Rublev explains his view of art and turns his back on the power-hungry.

5 Borscht bully: Kirill (Ivan Lapikov) is the sly counterpart to the woeful Andrei.

6 Lightweight: Boriska's (Nikolai Burlyayev) youthful courage makes Andrei painfully aware of his own shortcomings.

DIRECTOR JOHN FRANKENHEIMER (1930–2002)

SCREENPLAY ROBERT ALAN AURTHUR, JOHN FRANKENHEIMER DIRECTOR OF PHOTOGRAPHY LIONEL LINDON EDITING FREDRIC STEINKAMP, FRANK SANTILLO, HENRY BERMAN, STU LINDER MUSIC MAURICE JARRE PRODUCTION EDWARD LEWIS for CHEROKEE PRODUCTIONS, DOUGLAS & LEWIS PRODUCTIONS, JOEL PRODUCTIONS, JOHN FRANKENHEIMER PRODUCTIONS INC., MGM.

STARRING JAMES GARNER (Pete Aron), YVES MONTAND (Jean-Pierre Sarti), EVA MARIE SAINT (Louise Frederickson), TOSHIRŌ MIFUNE (Izo Yamura), BRIAN BEDFORD (Scott Stoddard), JESSICA WALTER (Pat Stoddard), ANTONIO SABATO (Nino Barlini), FRANÇOISE HARDY (Lisa), ADOLFO CELI (Agostini Manetta), GENEVIÈVE PAGE (Monique Delvaux-Sarti), JACK WATSON (Jeff Jordan).

ACADEMY AWARDS 1966 OSCARS for BEST EDITING (Fredric Steinkamp, Frank Santillo, Henry Berman, Stu Linder), BEST SOUND (Franklin Milton), and BEST SOUND EFFECTS (Gordon Daniel).

## *"There is no terrible way to win. There is only winning."*

The countdown is on for the Monaco Grand Prix. The spectators are on tenterhooks, the drivers edgy. The cars are checked one last time, the mechanics and team bosses make their final consultations. Helmet… goggles… gloves: check. And then it's "… four… three… two… one… GO!" The engines howl and the race is on.

John Frankenheimer's *Grand Prix* doesn't waste a second. The title sequence devised by Saul Bass evokes the tremendous excitement of Formula 1 motor racing even before the subsequent race scenes get going. A split screen and high-speed editing break down the action into a series of fragmentary images, compelling the spectator's close attention. The male leads are also introduced and characterized without delay. There are four dominant drivers in this Grand Prix circus: Sarti, a brilliant but aging Frenchman (Yves Montand), melancholically aware of the absurdity of his profession; Barlini, his daredevil Italian team-mate (Antonio Sabato), who says driving his Ferrari feels like sitting in a bomb; Stoddard, an Englishman (Brian Bedford) who still hasn't gotten over his brother's death; and finally, Stoddard's colleague, the American maverick Aron (James Garner). Years previously, Aron had left Ferrari after a clash with the bosses; now, he's in a clinch with Jordan and desperately wants to prove that he's still a winner. At the end of the film, one of these four men will be dead, another will be changed by his experiences, and one will be the new world champion.

Formula 1 movies are entirely dependent on spectacle, on the drama of the race and the sheer thrill of speed. It's the physical experience of extreme situations that makes such films so irresistible. And because *Grand Prix* fulfils these demands to perfection, it's rated as one of the very best examples of this fascinating sub-genre. Director John Frankenheimer knew that the film would only function if the race sequences were absolutely credible, so he hired Formula 1 stars such as Jochen Rindt, Phil Hill and Richie Ginther as drivers and advisors – and he filmed the races on genuine Formula 1 racetracks. At times, you might easily believe you're watching a live broadcast on a sports channel, and it's no surprise to learn that Frankenheimer spent many years directing live TV broadcasts before starting his movie career. The film aims to pull the spectators in so close to what's happening that they can practically smell the burning tires. Frankenheimer even mounted cameras on the cars to capture the drivers' perspective on the race. It's a dazzling use of the subjective camera, and it makes it easy to understand why the tension of a racing driver is so convincingly reflected in the actors' faces: with only one exception, all the actors were actually in the cockpit for the close-up shots.

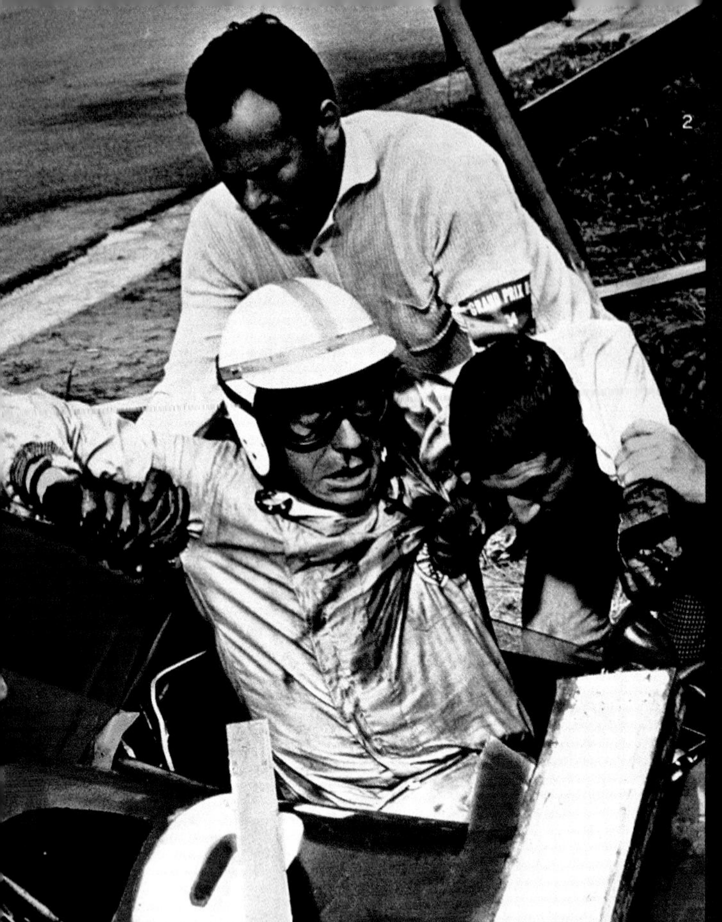

1 Okie 500: Native Indianan and hobby racecar driver Steve McQueen was the original first choice for the role of Pete Aron. However, James Garner (pictured) displayed a knack for the sport that effortlessly allowed him to assume the wheel.

2 Bumper cars: One false move and legendary pro Jean-Pierre Sarti (Yves Montand) could drive himself straight into the grave.

3 Pain threshold: Pete Aron greets each race as an opportunity to push himself to new extremes.

4 And the crowd goes wild: Adoring fans like Lisa (Françoise Hardy) have been known to leave drivers with their own brand of skid marks.

5 An ongoing race: Even the thrill of victory is fleeting. For after the hoopla has subsided, glory takes a backseat to the challenges that lie ahead (pictured here, Antonio Sabato as Nino Barlini).

6 Airborn: John Frankenheimer's staged accidents are visual masterpieces.

**"The girls (...) are pretty, but somehow they don't seem all that exciting in a film that focuses so satisfactorily on a different sort of exquisitely classy chassis."** *Time*

Frankenheimer refused to use film that had been speeded up *po[illegible] facto*, for he feared that the audience would notice the ruse. Instead, h[illegible] chose to cast some pretty hard-bitten actors. When all else failed, he pre[illegible]ferred to set up some honest-to-god stunts rather than deploying tricks [illegible] commissioning elaborate special effects. Though this attitude may hav[illegible] seemed a little old-fashioned at the time, the film stands up very well toda[illegible] More than 30 years after *Grand Prix*, Frankenheimer used the same method once again, and successfully: *Ronin* (1998) is a real experience, not least f[illegible] its spectacular car chases.

And like *Ronin*, *Grand Prix* is also a film about men. It presents fou[illegible] characters who don't just stand for different kinds of racing driver: they als[illegible] demonstrate various ways of dealing with women. For John Frankenheimer's

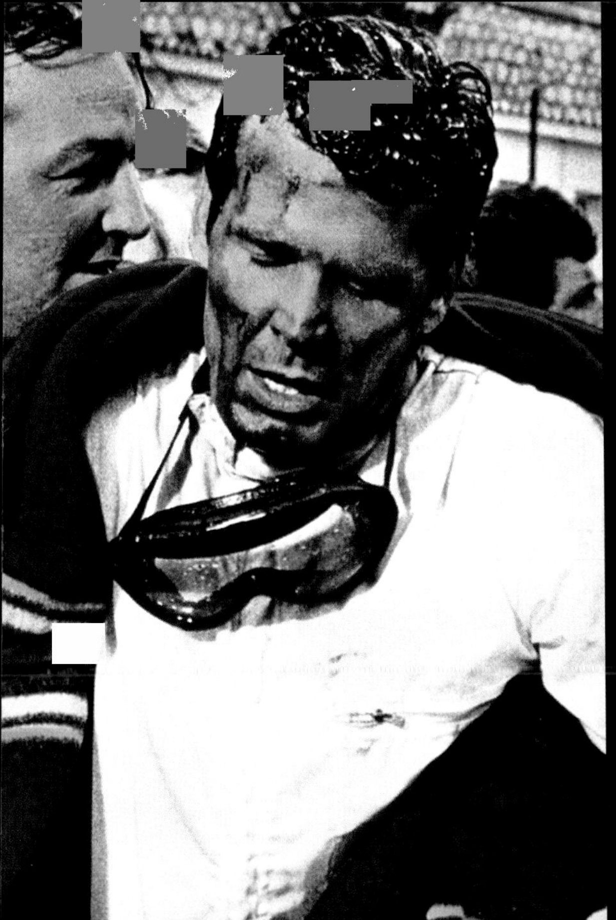

5

**YVES MONTAND**

Though he was seen as the personification of Gallic charm, Yves Montand (1921–1991) was actually born in Italy. He began his career as a *chansonnier* in Marseille, where he had grown up in poverty. Within a few years, the attractive young man had become a star of the Parisian music halls; and a little later, he made his movie breakthrough as the truck driver Mario in Henri-Georges Clouzot's explosive adventure film *The Wages of Fear* (*Le Salaire de la peur*, 1953). In the years that followed, Montand – who had been married to Simone Signoret since 1951 – appeared in several Hollywood productions. These aroused less interest than his alleged affair with Marilyn Monroe, with whom he had appeared in George Cukor's *Let's Make Love* (1960).
In the 60s, his career underwent a transformation. Montand was an avowed socialist, and his political commitment became ever more apparent in the films he made, especially in Costa-Gavras' political thrillers *Z* (1968) and *The Confession* (*L'Aveu*, 1970), in Alain Resnais' *The War Is Over* (*La Guerre est finie / Kriget är slut*, 1966), and in Godard's *Everything's Fine* (*Tout va bien / Crepa padrone, tutto va bene*, 1972). Yet he seemed more convincing when allowed to give free reign to his virile self-assurance, as in *Grand Prix* (1966), or in crime movies such as Jean-Pierre Melville's *The Red Circle* (*Le Cercle rouge / I senza nome*, 1970) and Alain Corneau's *Choice of Arms* (*Le Choix des armes*, 1981). In love films, too, he was every bit as good: witness the chemistry with Romy Schneider in Claude Sautet's *César and Rosalie* (*César et Rosalie*, 1972). Finally, Yves Montand cemented his reputation as a French national monument with his performances in *Manon of the Spring* (*Manon des sources*, 1986) and *Jean de Florette* (1986) – Claude Berri's loving adaptations of the Marcel Pagnol novels.

three-hour epic doesn't consist solely of events on and around the racetrack. It also shows in great detail how the drivers' job affects their love relationships. Glamour, danger and death – and the sheer thrill of racing – apparently make it impossible for the men and women involved to find any kind of lasting happiness together. If this aspect of the film is less than mesmerizing, that may simply be because the racing sequences are so immensely exciting. At the end of the movie, Pete Aron walks alone down the abandoned home strait with the imagined noise of engines howling in his ears. His tragedy has less to do with the fact that the sport has made him incapable of sustaining a relationship than with his dawning knowledge that even victory cannot deliver lasting satisfaction.

JH

6

# FASTER, PUSSYCAT! KILL! KILL!

1966 - USA - 83 MIN. - DRAMA, EXPLOITATION FILM, SATIRE

DIRECTOR RUSS MEYER (*1922)
SCREENPLAY JACK MORAN, RUSS MEYER DIRECTOR OF PHOTOGRAPHY WALTER SCHENK EDITING RUSS MEYER
MUSIC IGO KANTOR, BERT SHEFTER, PAUL SAWTELL PRODUCTION RUSS MEYER, EVE MEYER for EVE PRODUCTIONS INC.

STARRING Tura Satana (Varla), HAJI (Rosie), LORI WILLIAMS (Billie), SUSAN BERNARD (Linda), STUART LANCASTER (Old Man), PAUL TRINKA (Kirk), DENNIS BUSCH (The Vegetable), RAY BERLOW (Tommy), MICKEY FOXX (Gas Station Attendant), JOHN FURLONG (Narrator).

## *"Ladies and Gentlemen! Welcome to violence – the word and the act!"*

The American Film Institute catalogs all movies ever to receive an official U.S. release with a list of plot keywords. Those for Russ Meyer's *Faster, Pussycat! Kill! Kill!* include: go-go dancer, wheelchair, brother, voyeurism, drunk and disorderly, sadism, mental retardation, lesbian gang, rape, robbery, murder, seduction, family affair, desert, gas station, sports vehicle, karate, and race car driving.

That's quite a lot of ground to cover. But set in the right order and properly weighted this checklist touches on just about every single plot point and twist that *Faster, Pussycat! Kill! Kill!* has to offer. With the opening words "Welcome to violence!" Russ Meyer turns the key in the ignition and takes us on a non-stop wild ride lasting 83 minutes.

The picture itself came about as a direct result of the commercial success of the Meyer production that preceded it, a tale about three bad-boy motorcyclists entitled *Motor Psycho* (1965). Set on repeating this success the director plugged in the pieces of his proven formula, substituting his male protagonists with three lean, mean go-go dancers trailblazing through the California desert on a set of hot wheels in search of the green and good times. The idea seemed a surefire hit, given that in the early Sixties hot-rodding was a favorite pastime of both clean-cut young Americans and unruly brutes eager to break their necks.

But Meyer's fast paced sex vehicle turned out to be a lemon. It was only during subsequent re-releases that *Faster, Pussycat! Kill! Kill!* found a follow-

**"What attracts audiences is not sex and not really violence, either, but a Pop Art fantasy image of powerful women, filmed with high energy and exaggerated in a way that seems bizarre and unnatural, until you realize Arnold Schwarzenegger, Sylvester Stallone, Jean-Claude Van Damme and Steven Seagal play more or less the same characters."** *Chicago Sun-Times*

2

ing and gradually became one of the all-time great classics of big screen trash. This must be attributed, at least somewhat, to leading lady Tura Satana's mesmerizing gyrations and exotic appearance. With her full black mane, sharp facial features, and low-cut blouse and skin-tight black jean getup, this part Indian and part Japanese actress looked like a comic book version of an S & M dominatrix – a true 60s dynamo who is not to be missed.

Given the overtly carnal behavior of the three femme fatales and the ever so subtle lesbian love affair between gang leader Varla (Tura Satana) and her partner in crime Rosie (Haji), feminists have also slowly come to regard the picture as an object worthy of further examination.

Indeed, *Faster, Pussycat! Kill! Kill!* should certainly be counted among the more serious fare produced by Meyer, a man who made a name for himself as the king of soft porn. First off, there is an extraordinary absence of nudity. Even more puzzling is that the black and white film produced on a 44,000-dollar budget is free from the type of technical botchery that characterizes Meyer's hastily generated "sexploitation" flicks. The film's tight budget forced Meyer and screenwriter Jack Moran to keep the story relatively straightforward and simple: three female strippers go off in search of money hidden on a remote farm belonging to an elderly cripple (Stuart Lancaster) and his two sons. The depicted events are meant to take place over just a few hours, allowing for minimal costume changes and locations. And the story ensures that plywood shanties and the California desert fully suffice as the only set pieces and backdrops.

1 Homely and bookish: Billie (Lori Williams) gets lost on her way to the librarians' convention and meets an untimely demise.

2 You snooze, you lose: While Linda's (Susan Bernard) busy catnapping, Varla (Tura Satana) goes for a joyride and gets a purr-fect lube job from a willing filling station attendant (Mickey Foxx).

3 Hell hath three furies: Three go-go dancers en route to Satan's cesspool – Middle America.

**EXPLOITATION FILM**

It would be perfectly possible to reduce the whole of cinema to one long history of exploitation films. Film producers have always tried to capitalize on the latest trends or pop stars for their big-screen undertakings. As a direct consequence of censor-imposed industry restrictions, studios also tried to lure audiences into movie houses by claiming to offer something they'd never laid eyes on before.

Sex and exaggerated depictions of violence are the cornerstones of exploitative cinema. From harmless nudies via wild action-packed melodramas to Russ Meyer's absurd sexual masterpieces – it's incredible how far sexploitation has come over the course of motion picture history. The advent of the VCR tore down the common man's barrier to hardcore pornography. Likewise, elements of splatter films (which had also been favorable subject matter for exploitation films, given that they were the perfect vehicle for the mutilation of massive amounts of human flesh) eventually appeared in mainstream Hollywood action pictures. Ironically, the combination of these two landmark breakthroughs put an end to the careers of classic trash and exploitation filmmakers like Meyer, Jess Franco and Joe D'Amato, director of *Emanuelle and the Last Cannibals* a. k. a *Emanuelle's Amazon Adventure* a. k. a *Trap Them and Kill Them* (*Emanuelle e gli ultimi cannibali*, 1977). Progress rendered the cinematic endeavors of these pioneers obsolete.

4 Park that keister: When Rosie (Haji) puts her equipment into reverse, you'd best step aside if you know what's good for you.

5 Chicks ditch dicks: The ever so subtle lesbian undertones in Varla and Rosie's relationship would later elevate their status within the women's movement. Bra burners, however, were not impressed.

6 Indian rub burn: This dude thinks he's got it going on, but Varla's here to show him that he's just going down.

Needless to say, it is in this sort of vast American wasteland in which Russ Meyer's mind flourishes best. A universe is invented where assertive, busty chicks cross paths with deflated wimps, testosterone-loaded sex addicts and dirty old men. Murder and manslaughter are commonplace, and shrieking crybabies or detestably limp rags have the best chance for survival. With little exception, Meyer's pictures are intended as tongue-in-cheek commentaries on the American dream of success and riches, but invariably lapse into vicious cycles of senseless violence. The scene in this flick that best captures Meyer's style is the edifying meal at the farmhouse involving the entire cast. Randomly jumbled overtones of smut and phallic imagery (Varla gnaw at a cob of corn) are juxtaposed with the hysterical kidnapping of an innocer victim (Susan Bernard), a sudden outbreak of fisticuffs and a family dinne time discussion from the twilight zone (the old man character hates his men tally handicapped son, because his wife died giving birth to him). The ol geezer tops off the absurdity with an analysis of this insane get togethe "Women! They let 'em vote, smoke and drive – even put 'em in pants! An what happens? A democrat is elected president!"

L

**"It is obvious that Meyer has a directorial talent which belongs to stronger films. His visual sense is outstanding, as are his setups (executed by Walter Schenk's crisp camera)."**

*Variety*

"The stylish showmaster Russ Meyer is famed for his deconstruction of America's sex dreams and his method of shamelessly bizarre exaggeration. Here, he puts paid to male-chauvinist arrogance with a few well-aimed blows below the belt." *Neue Zürcher Zeitung*

# TRACES OF STONE

## Spur der Steine

1966 - GDR - 139 MIN. - DRAMA, COMEDY, LITERARY ADAPTATION

DIRECTOR FRANK BEYER (*1932)
SCREENPLAY KARL GEORG EGEL, FRANK BEYER; based on the novel of the same name by ERIK NEUTSCH
DIRECTOR OF PHOTOGRAPHY GÜNTER MARCZINKOWSKY EDITING HILDEGARD CONRAD-NÖLLER MUSIC WOLFRAM HEICKING
PRODUCTION DIETER DORMEISER for THE "HEINRICH GREIF" GROUP at DEFA.

STARRING MANFRED KRUG (Hannes Balla), KRYSTYNA STYPULKOWSKA (Kati Klee), EBERHARD ESCHE (Party Secretary Horrath), JOHANNES WIEKE (District Secretary Jansen), WALTER RICHTER-REINICK (Richard Trutmann), HANS-PETER MINETTI (Heinz Bleibtreu), WALTER JUPÉ (Hesselbarth), INGEBORG SCHUMACHER (Marianne Horrath), GERTRUD BRENDLER (Mrs. Schickedanz), HELGA GÖRING (Elli).

## *"It's easier to hold a discussion with a chair leg in your hand."*

East Berlin, capital of the German Democratic Republic, in the last week of June 1966: on the vast central square of Alexanderplatz, workers erect a scaffolding for a giant poster announcing the premier of a new film: *Spur der Steine* – Traces of Stone. It features the face of the leading actor, Manfred Krug, wearing the traditional earring and broad-brimmed hat of the German carpenters' guild. As Hans Balla, the leader of a Work Brigade, Krug became the first real movie star in communist East Germany. Eventually, more than a million of his compatriots would flock to see the film; but it would be 23 years before they had the chance to do so – only two weeks before the Wall fell, and just a few months before the East German state finally went out of existence. In 1966, after a massive advertising campaign, *Traces of Stone* ran for just one week in Berlin and Potsdam, before the 56 film copies were recalled and deposited in the DEFA Studios archives.

Why? The films tells a story rich in conflict and intelligently awake to the pressing issues of the time. What's more, it's also witty and entertaining, with an abundance of good jokes. *Spur der Steine* is set on a gargantuan building site somewhere in the GDR; the name of the place, "Schkona," is a transparent allusion to the real East German industrial center, Leuna II. This is a very rough place indeed, a kind of Central European frontier town; and in their curiously archaic but strangely cool-looking work gear, Balla's Brigade are indeed a wild bunch. Their days are steeped in sweat and cement, while their nights in the pub stink of beer and tobacco. This is a man's world, in which the next fight is never far away, and the bureaucrats at the helm seem incapable of instilling any kind of serious discipline into this stubbornly anarchic milieu. Then the young Party Secretary Horrath (Eberhard Esche) arrives on the site, at the same time as the even younger and extremely pretty female engineer Kati Klee (Krystyna Stypulkowska). Immediately, they come into conflict with the rebellious carpenters' brigade and their foreman Hans Balla. Though the carpenters are hard and conscientious workers, well ahead of the production targets set by the Party economists, they are hardly the stuff that socialist role-models are made of. Balla's men act like pirates or cattle rustlers, commandeering raw materials and transport vehicles whenever they see the need. The two newcomers try to persuade Balla's Brigade to cooperate – but they too are soon forced to maneuver their way past the hopelessly incompetent site managers. Gradually, Horrath and Klee gain Balla's respect. The macho foreman, the "little lady boss" and the idealistic Party politician now form a kind of utopian Holy Trinity, working towards a better East Germany: and the qualities they embody are Unruliness, Cunning and Subversion.

Meanwhile, love rears its ugly head: both men fall for Kati, who becomes pregnant. Horrath is the father; but he's married, has a child already and can't bring himself to leave either his family or his lover. A collision with the powers-that-be is unavoidable, for the private life of a Party Secretary is also Party business. Horrath is suspended, and hauled up before a Party commission. This inquisition forms the dramaturgical framework of the entire film; the statements of all those involved are inserted as flashbacks. Finally, the movie comes full circle, as the last flashback reaches the beginning of the inquest and brings us back to the start of the film.

*Traces of Stone* is a fascinating movie. It examines the conflicts and contradictions at the heart of East German society, and it does so by using the means and methods of two primary film genres: the Western and the courtroom drama. Schkona is reminiscent of a boom-town in the Wild West; it might easily be a staging post and labor pool for the Union Pacific

1
2

1 The Wild Wild East: Charismatic brigade commander Hannes Balla (Manfred Krug) takes the law into his own hands and inspires a workers' revolt in the former GDR.

2 What's good for the goose: In battle plumage, Balla and his men swim against the stream of socialist government. *Traces of Stones* was instantly banned in East Germany until just prior to the government's collapse in 1989.

3 East German trinity: The functionary (Eberhard Esche), the laborer, and the engineer (Krystyna Stypulkowska) – but what happens when the GDR's cornerstone of stability turns into a love triangle?

4 The magnificent seven: Pioneers march onto uncharted territory and stake their claim. The film's widescreen format evokes the spirit of the Hollywood Western.

5 Easy there, cowboy: It'll be iron curtains for anyone who crosses the tavern keeper.

Railway. One Party functionary explicitly refers to Balla as "the King of Texas," while the members of his Work Brigade are pioneers and roughnecks, whose motto in life is: "Who's fastest?" The movie was made in Totalvision, an East German version of Cineamascope; and when the seven members of Balla's Brigade swagger across the vast and desolate construction site – all clad in black, with their hammers at their hips – it's impossible not to think of *The Magnificent Seven* (1960). In Beyer's vision, the industrial landscape of Central Europe is a kind of man-made Marlboro Country.

**MANFRED KRUG**

Manfred Krug, born in Duisburg in 1937, is the only German film star who can claim to represent the East and the West in equal measure. When his parents got divorced, Krug went to live with his mother, while his brother joined the boys' father. At the age of 12, Krug then followed his father to a new home in the German Democratic Republic, which had just been established. He went on to serve an apprenticeship as a steelworker before belatedly taking his secondary-school diploma. Subsequently, he studied acting at the State Theater School in East Berlin, although he remained there for only a year and a half. In 1955, he became a trainee actor at the legendary Berliner Ensemble, where he soon acquired his official "Certificate of Stageworthiness." He then made his film debut in the DEFA production *Mazurka der Liebe* (1956), which was followed by the TV play *Gefährliche Wahrheit* (1957).

A tough, muscular figure with a prominent scar on his forehead and a very loud mouth, Krug was originally typecast as a crook or juvenile delinquent. Soon, however, his solid acting talent was winning him leading roles as the (proletarian) hero of various films and plays. In the 60s and 70s, his wit and vitality, and his undeniable gifts as an entertainer, made him a role model for the young generation of East Germans. With more than 40 films, he helped "to raise the GDR to a level at which it could compete with the world" – until November 1976. In that month, he signed a resolution protesting at the expulsion of the singer-songwriter Wolf Biermann. The reaction was not slow in coming: Krug's career in East Germany was abruptly terminated.

In 1976, after his move to West Berlin, he began a new career in "the shop window of capitalism" – this time on TV and not in the movies. He appeared as a truck-drivin' man in *Auf Achse* (1978–1995), and as the lawyer Robert Liebling in *Liebling Kreuzberg* (1986–1998); the scripts for the latter series were written by his friend Jurek Becker. In the long-running, nationally broadcast crime series *Tatort*, he became hugely popular as a rough diamond of a Police Commissioner. The two installments of his autobiography – *Abgehauen* (on the years 1975–1985) and *Mein schönes Leben* (1937–1954) – were bestsellers in Germany.

# "A distorted representation of our socialist reality, of the struggle of the working class and of its glorious Party."

*Neues Deutschland*

lere too, the quest for freedom is inseparable from the risk of serious lung isease.

The widescreen format works equally well in the courtroom drama. For ere, by contrast, it makes the individual characters look appropriately small nd insignificant. The Party inquest takes place in a narrow, claustrophobic oom. This is not the kind of place in which thoughts or feelings can circulate reely; here, there can be no solution to the conflicts that torment the characters and the entire country.

Why was the film so hastily withdrawn from circulation? Was it Beyer's ympathy with his working-class anarchists that so displeased the functionaries of the Socialist Unity Party? In one sequence, the entire Balla 3rigade jumps naked into a village pond – and the men drag an outraged policeman in after them. Did the East German state feel humiliated by this scene? Did they feel that the cop was a symbol of the State itself – and of them, its self-appointed guardians?

The State's objections to the film were presumably a little less superficial than this. What we're shown here is a Socialist Unity Party in a state of disarray: the film focuses on a successful minority that combines skill, energy and empathy to achieve results: opposing them is an unwieldy government apparatus that hides failure and incompetence behind dogma and face-saving rhetoric. Certainly, *Traces of Stone* constituted a paradox in the history of film, for the biggest success in the history of the DEFA Studios coincided with the downfall of the German Democratic Republic.

RV

5

# A MAN AND A WOMAN

## Un homme et une femme

1966 - FRANCE - 102 MIN. - MELODRAMA, LOVE STORY

DIRECTOR CLAUDE LELOUCH (*1937)
SCREENPLAY CLAUDE LELOUCH, PIERRE UYTTERHOEVEN DIRECTOR OF PHOTOGRAPHY CLAUDE LELOUCH, PATRICE POUGET
EDITING CLAUDE BARROIS, G. BOISSER, CLAUDE LELOUCH MUSIC FRANCIS LAI, VINICIUS DE MORAES, BADEN POWELL
PRODUCTION CLAUDE LELOUCH for LES FILMS 13.

STARRING ANOUK AIMÉE (Anne Gauthier), JEAN-LOUIS TRINTIGNANT (Jean-Louis Duroc), PIERRE BAROUH (Pierre Gautier), VALÉRIE LAGRANGE (Valerie Duroc), ANTOINE SIRE (Antoine Duroc), SOUAD AMIDOU (Françoise Gauthier), HENRI CHEMIN (Jean-Louis' Passenger), YANE BARRY (Jean-Louis' Mistress).

ACADEMY AWARDS 1966 OSCARS for BEST FOREIGN LANGUAGE FILM (France) and BEST ORIGINAL SCREENPLAY (Claude Lelouch, Pierre Uytterhoeven).

IFF CANNES 1966 GOLDEN PALM (Claude Lelouch).

## *"Are you married?"*

A woman (Anouk Aimée) walks along the beach with a little girl, telling her the tale of Little Red Riding Hood. A man (Jean-Louis Trintignant) plays "Chauffeur and Passenger" with a boy; then he drives the kid straight down to the beach in his sports car. A little later, the man and the woman meet. Both of the children are attending the boarding school at Deauville, and their parents – Jean-Louis und Anne – have been visiting them there at the weekend. Anne misses the train, and Jean-Louis gives her a lift back to Paris. They sit side-by-side in the car, listening to music, fooling around â little, talking a lot – and gradually fall in love.

It's the beginning of a very simple story, and Claude Lelouch tells it with disarmingly good-humored nonchalance and lightness of touch. But appearances can be deceptive, for even the opening of this film is suffused with a vague feeling of melancholy that stands in sharp contrast to its casually informal construction. This is not a simple boy-meets-girl story, but – as the title makes clear – a study of a man and a woman. Anne and Jean-Louis aren't starting from scratch. They have children. They have pasts. And what's more, their lives have been more painful than most, for both are widowed. Not least, this is a film about two adults endeavoring to overcome the wounds they have suffered. In other words, it's a melodrama.

At first glance, it seems that those who dismiss Lelouch's film as kitschy will have an easy time justifying their appraisal. The movie's triviality is apparently underscored by the glamorous jobs of its protagonists: Jean-Louis is

1

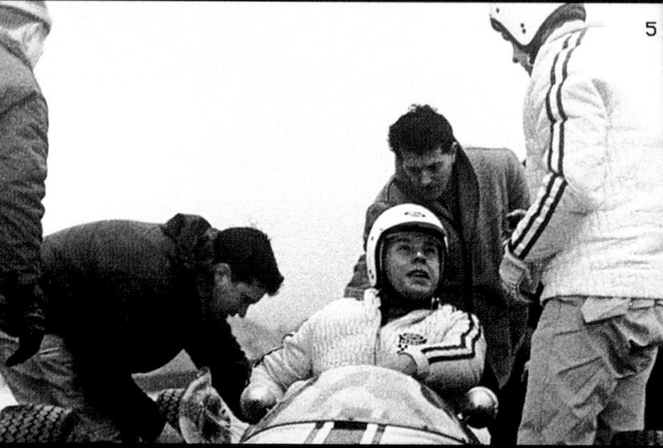

1 Dandy lying: Jean Louis Duroc (Jean-Louis Trintignant) embellishes his resumé with stories of a pimp past.

2 Coming out of the woodwork: The international success of Claude Lelouch's film turned Jean-Louis Trintignant into a household name. He has been one of the great stars of the French cinema ever since.

3 Kiss and make up: Easier said than done given the tragic potholes in both Anne (Anouk Aimée) and Jean-Louis' past.

# "A beautiful and breathtaking exposition of visual imagery intended to excite the emotions."

*The New York Times*

**ANOUK AIMÉE**

Aimée: "the loved one." Naturally, it's a stage name. The story goes that the author and screenwriter Jacques Prévert christened her after she appeared as a girl called Anouk in a film of the 1940s. It's a name like a promise; and in the course of a film career stretching over almost 60 years, Anouk Aimée (*1932), the melancholy beauty of French film, has kept that promise again and again. With those big yearning eyes in a face otherwise so austere, she was practically made for the role of a woman suffering for her love. And so, after her early breakthrough as Juliet in André Cayatte's Shakespeare adaptation, *The Lovers of Verona* (*Les Amants de Vérone*, 1949), she was predestined to play this kind of role. Only in a few movies was she cast against type, and these were among her best: for Federico Fellini, she played alongside Marcello Mastroianni; first a woman crazy with love (*La dolce vita*, 1959), then a patient wife (*8½ / Otte e mezzo*, 1962); and in Jacques Demy's *Lola* (1960), she gave an enchanting performance as a fluttery singer in a bar. Aimée also worked with Claude Chabrol, Bernardo Bertolucci and other major directors; but she was most frequently to be seen in the films of Claude Lelouch. His melodrama *A Man and a Woman* made her world-famous. Two decades years later, he made a follow-up featuring Aimée and her film partner Jean-Louis Trintignant (*A Man and a Woman: 20 Years Later / Un homme et une femme: vingt ans déjà*, 1986). That this film was a failure surely had nothing to do with Aimée: in *Prêt-à-Porter* (1995), Robert Altman's satire on the world of high fashion, she showed what so many of her later movies sadly failed to make clear – that she has aged wonderfully.

6

4 Driving lessons: Only during playtime is Jean-Louis' son allowed to get behind the wheel.

5 In record-breaking time: Jean Louis zooms through races and sets the pace of his own life.

6 Sweet nothings: Anouk Aimée's magnetic melancholy sends *A Man and a Woman* into overdrive.

a racing driver and Anne works as a script girl. And then Lelouch chooses to express Anne's enduring sadness through a series of sentimental flashbacks. Who can fail to judge such a film harshly?

Yet it's precisely Anne's imagination that demonstrates a striking quality of this movie; unusually for a melodrama, *A Man and a Woman* makes weighty words superfluous: in the best sense of the word, it's filmic. Lelouch prefers showing to telling, or having his characters do the telling for him. For him, the visual language is incomparably more important than the dialogue, and at times he even allows the music to cover his protagonists' voices.

Lelouch's preference for visual solutions is also expressed in his unconventional use of cinematic techniques. Sometimes he films in color, sometimes in black and white; a number of scenes are splintered by rapid cutting, while others are energized by the use of a hand-held camera. He integrates elements of commercials and music films as skillfully as extracts from sports reports. Lelouch takes advantage of the formal freedoms that were the *nouvelle vague's* legacy to the 1960s. In so doing, he indubitably reveals a relish for the spectacular, but the pretty pictures are never just there for their own sake. If Jean-Louis earns his money as a racing driver, this is not merely an excuse for some exciting rally sequences; it also shows how hard he's trying to repress his grief.

Anne, the script girl behind the camera, forms a contrast to the new man in her life. She's a dreamer. While Jean-Louis runs away from his past, she abandons herself to her pain. Like Sleeping Beauty, she seems to be waiting for some passing prince to hack his way through the thorns and bring her back to life. Jean-Louis shatters that emotional petrification, rushing to save her in his sports car.

Lelouch is one of the directors from the ambit of the *nouvelle vague* who has always divided critical opinion. More than one reviewer found *A Man and a Woman* banal and superficial in its willed stylishness. Moviegoers, however, were delighted by the movie's formal extravagance, its highly attractive leading actors and the irresistibly catchy soundtrack composed by Francis Lai. *A Man and a Woman* was a worldwide box-office hit. The most successful French love story of the 60s, it brought Claude Lelouch two Academy Awards as well as the Golden Palm at Cannes.

Lelouch's talent has sometimes been summarized as a gift for directing actors. This is to miss the essence of his achievement, as least as regards *A Man and a Woman.* It's debatable whether he actually got outstanding acting performances from his stars; but it's undeniable that he made them look very good indeed. Whether one likes the film or not, it's still hard for anyone to resist the melancholy aura of Anouk Aimée.

JH

# HURRY SUNDOWN

1966 - USA - 146 MIN. - DRAMA

**DIRECTOR** OTTO PREMINGER (1906–1986)
**SCREENPLAY** THOMAS C. RYAN, HORTON FOOTE, based on the novel of the same name by K. B. GILDEN
**DIRECTOR OF PHOTOGRAPHY** LOYAL GRIGGS, MILTON R. KRASNER **EDITING** LOUIS R. LOEFFLER, JAMES D. WELLS
**MUSIC** HUGO MONTENEGRO **PRODUCTION** OTTO PREMINGER for SIGMA.

**STARRING** MICHAEL CAINE (Henry Warren), JANE FONDA (Julie Ann Warren), JOHN PHILLIP LAW (Rad McDowell), FAYE DUNAWAY (Lou McDowell), ROBERT HOOKS (Reeve Scott), BEAH RICHARDS (Rose Scott), BURGESS MEREDITH (Judge Purcell), DONNA DENTON (Sukie Purcell) GEORGE KENNEDY (Sheriff Coombs), DIAHANN CARROLL (Vivian Thurlow), REX INGRAM (Professor Thurlow).

## *"I was a white folks' nigger! You've got to fight!"*

Otto Preminger was never one to flinch at criticism. The trademark controversial subject matter of his films led reviewers to dub him a rabble-rouser time and again, and *Hurry Sundown*, a drama dealing with racism in the American South, was no exception. Branded by *The New York Times* as a tidal wave of racial stereotypes and an insult to human intelligence, the picture had the entire film world up in arms. Puzzling, as today's viewer would most likely fail to see what all the uproar was about.

The year is 1946. World War II has come to an end, and shrewd businessman Henry Warren (Michael Caine) is looking to develop new land for a major produce corporation. He has already secured his cousin Rad's (John Phillip Law) property for the venture. Getting the deed to the land of black farmer, Reeve Scott (Robert Hooks), also appears to be no obstacle thanks to the assistance of racist judge Purcell (Burgess Meredith). However, all hell breaks loose when Rad and Reeve, both returning war veterans, join forces against the putative interests of the rural community. Even by Hollywood standards, it seems to be a straightforward plot in which characters must overcome run-of-the-mill crises. Yet what this film adaptation of K.B. Gilden's best-selling novel really captures for the screen is the tension that surrounded its filming. And this for once was not entirely the work of the

The government of Georgia, the state in which the novel is set, refused the production its necessary filming permits. There was no way the authorities would allow a picture to be shot within their dominion that depicted highfalutin black men coming out smelling of roses at the white man's expense. Preminger ultimately relocated the shoot to St. Francisville, Louisiana – the seat of the Klu Klux Klan. Needless to say, the southern sun wasn't the only thing up against the crew from day one. Anonymous death threats and slashed tires were commonplace on the set. African American actors Diahann Carroll, Robert Hooks and Rex Ingram were all denied the use of their hotel pool. A widely publicized newspaper photo featuring Jane Fonda kissing a black boy also created a local upset. Compared to the background of the shoot itself, the criticism voiced against Preminger seems like water off a duck's back. In fact, though virtually ignored, the director's knack at drawing infinite shades of gray for what could have been a monochrome portrait of the South presented the public with a poignant reflection of an emerging era.

Continuing the melodramatic trend in cinema made popular by the screen adaptations of Tennessee Williams' plays, Preminger crafted sexually charged stories rooted in fatal dependency. Driven by a fear of failure, War-

1

of the judge's daughter Sukie (Donna Denton). Smelling a rat, his wife Julie (Jane Fonda) expresses sympathy for the blacks; but caught in a tempest of emotion, she switches sides several times throughout the story. Peacemaker Sheriff Coombs (George Kennedy) feels just as torn as she does. He would like to help the underdogs and play the knight in shining armor to all damsels in distress, but instead abstains from using his power to influence the outcome. Rad and Reeve are on their own in the fight for justice against the racist Purcell, phony land claims and a white mob out to sweep over them like the heat of the night.

*Hurry Sundown* is credited as the first major film with African American leading actors to be shot in the Deep South. Not the biggest milestone event in Preminger's career, considering he had already gone down in history with his production of *Carmen Jones* (1954) – the first film to feature an exclusively black cast. One could cite Preminger's decision to have Briton Michael Caine play southern gentry as a far ballsier move. Nonetheless, the director's indisputable mistake with *Hurry Sundown* was to film it at the height of the 1960s civil rights movement. What could have served as a catalyst for social progress was publicly received as an artistic stumbling block in the twilight years of a filmmaker's career.

Today, it is the film's rich color photography, dynamism, intricate emotional web, barbed humor and brilliant ensemble cast that capture our attention. Preminger's picture paved the way to fame for many of them, including Michael Caine, Jane Fonda, and, of course, Faye Dunaway – here appearing in her very first role.

PB

4

1 Enter at your own risk: Don't go thinking Miss Julie (Jane Fonda) is all play. She switches sides like a ping-pong ball and knows how break people like snap beans. In fact, after a dispute with Reeve's mother, we can see she's one belle who takes her own liberties.

2 Family feud: Reeve (Robert Hooks) watches for just the right moment to break up the struggle between relatives Rad (John Phillip Law) and cousin Henry (Michael Caine), both of whom are willing to fight to the death for the land they're standing on.

3 Tending the land: Farmer Rad isn't about to sell either his property or friends down the river.

4 Southern sizzle: Director Otto Preminger (center) in a rare photo with the cast of *Hurry Sundown*. Back row from left John Phillip Law, Faye Dunaway, Otto Preminger, Robert Hooks and Jane Fonda. Michael Caine not pictured.

**"*Hurry Sundown* is sheer pulp fiction as Otto Preminger has put it on the screen. It is a massive mishmash of stereotyped Southern characters and hackneyed melodramatic incidents. Although it was shot for the most part on various locations in the South, it is as gaudy in color and artificial as the phoniest Hollywood studio-made film."** *The New York Times*

**OTTO PREMINGER**

As notorious for his run-ins with 20th Century Fox CEO Darryl F. Zanuck as for his despotism on set, Otto Preminger (1906–1986) earned his reputation for diehard persistence and perfectionism when he was still an assistant director to Max Reinhardt. Born into a Jewish family in Vienna and emigrating from Austria in 1935, "Otto the Terrible" ironically started out in Hollywood playing a Nazi – his personal way of getting revenge. *Laura* (1944), one of the great classics of film noir, was his first major directing success. But Preminger would refuse to pin himself down to a single genre, going on to shoot epics like *Forever Amber* (1947), Westerns like *River of No Return* (1954) and musicals like *Porgy and Bess* (1959).

This famed "bald" eagle of filmmaking cleverly devised a personal image that helped him avoid the pitfalls of the studio system. His self-proclaimed independence enabled him to defy the production code time and again, flooding the screen with taboo subject matter like drug addiction in *The Man with the Golden Arm* (1955) and homosexuality in *Advise and Consent* (1961). Preminger quickly became the idol of aspiring auteur filmmakers, while critics derided his propensity for hype and exploitation. Thus Preminger's screen adaptation of Françoise Sagan's novel *Bonjour Tristesse* (1957) was responsible for Jean Seberg's rise to stardom as the darling of the *nouvelle vague*. The director's later melodramas, however, met with limited acclaim and Preminger's reputation as a tyrant began to work against him. Yet there were those who considered the negative propaganda unjust. Actor Leon Askin commented once that "Preminger has come to the aid of so many people in need. If there were an Oscar for humanitarianism, Preminger is the first person I would nominate for it." Despied plaudits like that, Oscar Preminger never received a single distinction from the Academy of Motion Pictures Arts and Sciences.

# BELLE DE JOUR
## Belle de Jour

1966 - FRANCE / ITALY - 100 MIN. - DRAMA, LITERARY ADAPTATION

DIRECTOR LUIS BUÑUEL (1900–1983)
SCREENPLAY LUIS BUÑUEL, JEAN-CLAUDE CARRIÈRE, based on a novel by JOSEPH KESSEL DIRECTOR OF PHOTOGRAPHY SACHA VIERNY
EDITING LOUISETTE HAUTECŒUR PRODUCTION ROBERT HAKIM, RAYMOND HAKIM, HENRI BAUM for PARIS FILM, FIVE FILM.

STARRING CATHERINE DENEUVE (Séverine Serizy), JEAN SOREL (Pierre Serizy), MICHEL PICCOLI (Henri Husson), PIERRE CLÉMENTI (Marcel), GENEVIÈVE PAGE (Madame Anais), FRANÇOISE FABIAN (Charlotte), MACHA MÉRIL (Renée), MUNI (Pallas), FRANCISCO RABAL (Hyppolite), GEORGES MARCHAL (Duke).

IFF VENICE 1967 GOLDEN LION for BEST PICTURE (Luis Buñuel).

## *“Please. What good is tenderness?”*

An autumn ride in a horse-drawn open carriage. Séverine Serizy (Catherine Deneuve) and her husband Pierre (Jean Sorel) take in the countryside while sharing sweet nothings. All is as it should be until Pierre, stung by a jarring remark Séverine has made, orders the drivers to stop the carriage. He commands the attendants to rip her from the comfort of the coach, drag her through the surrounding thicket and bind her to a tree. Next thing she knows, her clothes have been torn from her body and the three men are thrashing her exposed back with their driving whips. When they are done, Pierre entreats the men to have their way with Séverine… But it's just a dream – or so it would seem. For next the film jump cuts to show the married couple in harmonious domesticity. Pierre asks Séverine, still reclining in bed, if she was thinking about something. She simply replies that he was in her thoughts.

Luis Buñuel made no secret of his background in surrealism. Having begun his career at Salvador Dali's side, the power of dreams and the fires of desire never ceased to fascinate this subversive Spanish director. Ever since his infamous image of a girl whose eye is slashed by a razor-blade in *An Andalusian Dog* (*Un Chien andalou*, 1929), his efforts to make audiences free their imagination, even if it meant closing their eyes, were untiring. Slasher shocks like that are nowhere to be seen in *Belle de Jour* although the film is every bit as sharp and unconventionally funny as his fledgling film, and again targets the bourgeoisie and its mind-warping institutions, of which marriage is undoubtedly one of the most insidious.

Séverine and Pierre appear to live in wedded bliss, superficially loving one each other according to the conventions of love. Nonetheless, Séverine coolly evades all her husband's attempts to truly know her. Nor does she supply him with any explanation as to why. Instead, she keeps her masochistic reveries to herself, bottled up with her childhood trauma. Hence, when cynical acquaintance Husson (Michel Piccoli) casually drops the address of a known bordello during a chance conversation, Séverine cannot resist the temptation of looking into the matter. Soon clandestinely employed as a whore, she begins to live out her secret fantasies every afternoon, between two and five p.m.

While at first Séverine's dreams seem separate from reality, with time the delineation becomes fainter and fainter until the two are virtually indistinguishable. Likewise, Séverine's bourgeois existence houses obsessions that eventually take control of her everyday life, a process which occurs almost imperceptibly as Buñuel visually blends the two planes by means of subtly stylized suggestion. The matt colors, and the film's costumes and set evoke a light artificiality that, while not totally unreal, have an intensity that enables the dream world to expand unbeknownst to the audience.

1

2

**MICHEL PICCOLI**

In *Belle de Jour* (1966) he plays the satyr Henri Husson, a man whose loins burn for the seemingly chaste Séverine. Without question his flair for decadent bourgeois characters is one of the reasons why Michel Piccoli triumphed in French Cinema. Born to Italian immigrant parents in Paris on December 27th, 1925, Piccoli began his career as a stage actor. In 1945, he made a brief film debut and went on to become a familiar face in B-movies over the next 15 years. This period was dotted with sterling performances, the most exceptional of which came with Luis Buñuel's *Death in the Garden (La Mort en ce jardin*, 1956). He landed his first leading role in *Contempt* (*Le Mépris*, 1963), a film in which he portrayed a screen-writer whose marriage crumbles under the weight of his career. Europe's most renowned *auteur* filmmakers quickly started opening their doors to him. Besides shooting a total of five pictures with Buñuel, he has worked with great names like Claude Chabrol, Claude Sautet, Jacques Demy, Philippe de Broca and Jacques Rivette. He also appeared in Alfred Hitchcock's international spy thriller *Topaz* (1969). Some of his more offbeat moments in front of the camera include Marco Ferreri's satire *The Grande Bouffe*, a.k.a *Blow-Out* (*La grande bouffe*, 1973) and, most notably, Claude Faraldo's *Themroc* (1972), in which he played a mute, man-eating anarchist who develops a taste for law enforcement. Off-screen, Piccoli has served as a great public advocate for the preservation of European Cinema. He emphasized his support by taking on the title role in *A Hundred and One Nights of Simon Cinema* (*Les cent et une nuits de Simon Cinéma*, 1994), Agnès Varda's tribute to one hundred years of filmmaking. Manoel de Oliveira supplied him with one of the finest roles of his golden years in *I'm Going Home* (*Je rentre à la maison*, 2001) – a story about a once-successful actor who discovers that his grandson means more to him than his profession.

The absurdity of Séverine's whore persona gains similar momentum as e story unfolds. While her first gentleman caller can still be classified as a n-loving businessman, it isn't long before Séverine is posing as a corpse in French duke's necrophilic role-play – a surreal fantasy par excellence. In is scene Buñuel nullifies the rules of logic. For at the beginning of this pisode he has the aristocrat collect Séverine for their rendezvous in the me Landauer carriage we saw her in with her husband at the beginning of e film.

*Belle de Jour* portrays Séverine's prostitution as an act of rebellion. Her ouble-life almost spirals out of control when Marcel (Pierre Clémenti), a angster, falls in love and wants to claim her. But Séverine successfully con- nes their relationship to the four walls of the brothel and refuses to subject

**"... an estimable work. Buñuel is one of the noted buff names in the arty film field. This should be another Buñuel pic for more selective audiences."** *Variety*

1 Caught up in the rapture: *Belle de Jour*, Séverine (Catherine Deneuve) becomes a real pro at making her dreams come true.

2 Peep show: Séverine sees it all and has every intention of influencing what goes on behind the wall.

3 She takes it rough: Macho Mafiosi Hyppolite (Francisco Rabal) is putty in this sweet little housewife's hands.

4 You've lost that lovin' feeling: Husson (Michel Piccoli) was once Séverine's top customer. Now she has can't seem to fit him into her schedule. Why the sudden change of heart?

**“If we’re looking for the true spirit of Surrealism, let’s not waste our time leafing through puerile expositions or historical studies. It can be found in this film, in the fantasies of Catherine Deneuve – with the true revolutionary spirit, which is inseparable from sexual liberation.”** *Nouvel Observateur*

5 You sexy thing: Luis Buñuel depicts Séverine's whoring as an act of self-assertion and sexual awakening.

6 Love in the afternoon: Marcel (Pierre Clementi) brings total fulfillment to Séverine's work, but he can't accept that there are other men in her life.

7 When worlds collide: As traces of Séverine's marriage with Pierre (Jean Sorel, in the framed photograph) begin to distract her at work, Marcel recommends that she concentrate solely on her career.

8 Welcome to the dollhouse: *Belle de Jour* established Deneuve as the French cinema's ice queen. Here, Charlotte (Françoise Fabian) gives Séverine an outlet for her fantasies – a room of her own.

erself to his mad whims. By living out her fantasies Séverine liberates her- elf from male tyranny. From now on, she alone has the power to determine er sexual practices and her life in general. And, ironically, it is Marcel who nintentionally enables her to complete this metamorphosis. Intoxicated with ealousy, he shoots at Pierre only to be gunned down by the police himself. lind, mute and confined to a wheelchair, Pierre survives the ordeal. He is now privy to Séverine's life of prostitution, but is moved to tears by the sudden affection she shows him. Their power dynamics have been reversed and Buñuel takes the opportunity to furnish the married couple and his audience with a hopeful prognosis. Pierre miraculously rises from his wheelchair. He has been cured and Séverine has been freed from her compulsions. The final shot shows the carriage driving off – empty.

JH

# BONNIE AND CLYDE

967 - USA - 111 MIN. - GANGSTER FILM

IRECTOR ARTHUR PENN (*1922)
CREENPLAY DAVID NEWMAN, ROBERT BENTON DIRECTOR OF PHOTOGRAPHY BURNETT GUFFEY EDITING DEDE ALLEN
USIC CHARLES STROUSE, LESTER FLATT & EARL SCRUGGS (Song "Foggy Mountain Breakdown")
RODUCTION WARREN BEATTY for TATIRA-HILLER PRODUCTIONS, SEVEN ARTS, WARNER BROS.

TARRING WARREN BEATTY (Clyde Barrow), FAYE DUNAWAY (Bonnie Parker), MICHAEL J. POLLARD (C. W. Moss), GENE HACKMAN (Buck Barrow), ESTELLE PARSONS (Blanche), DENVER PYLE (Frank Hamer), DUB TAYLOR (Ivan Moss), EVANS EVANS (Velma Davis), GENE WILDER (Eugene Grizzard)

CADEMY AWARDS 1967 OSCARS for BEST SUPPORTING ACTRESS (Estelle Parsons), and BEST CINEMATOGRAPHY (Burnett Guffey).

## *"Now Mrs. Parker, don't you believe what you read in all those newspapers. That's the law talkin' there."*

aces of country folk unfold in a sequence of black and white photographs, ellowed by time. We hear the camera click, as it captures one image after he other of hunger and despair, and we could easily believe we're watching a documentary by Dorothea Lange, the most honest chronicler of the age. Then the final image appears, a photo of a young man and a thin blonde woman. The confusion disappears and the connection is explained: these were America's poor during the Great Depression, and among them were Bonnie and Clyde.

Back in 1967, it was probably fair to say that the public memory of Bonnie Parker and Clyde Barrow had accumulated as much dust as the photos we are shown. But when the cobwebs vanish, the tired faces of the amorous outlaws are replaced by a close-up of luscious ruby lips. The camera pul back, revealing their owner, Bonnie Parker (Faye Dunaway), a woman tho oughly bored with her mundane existence as a waitress in some podun Texas diner. Half-dressed, she undulates atop her bed, disturbed by the re flection of her body in the mirror and fit to burst with sexual frustration. Th attractive young man in the front yard presents a welcome diversion. Bonn is clearly taken by the swanky affectations of Clyde Barrows (Warren Beatty a self-proclaimed crook in a suit and fedora. Before long Clyde robs a mom and-pop store, giving some clout to his big talking ways. Tailed by the stat cops and powered by adolescent giddiness, the couple blaze across th Texas border on "hot" wheels. These bandits quickly adopt a charming, and

1

chic attitude toward the law and, stripped of their innocence, earn a much publicized reputation as serial killers.

Parting studio head Jack Warner harbored serious reservations abou *Bonnie and Clyde*. To his mind, the film was an all-too-explicit example how the Hollywood system had changed in the 1960s. This was a project th an actor had produced with an independent production company, with renegade artist in the director's chair. It was a sign of the studio's dwindlin influence and of its relegation to the realm of marketing and financial spon sorship. With its point-blank depiction of sex and violence, *Bonnie and Clyd* proved that the so-called production code could be nullified at a major stu dio. For decades, the code had ensured that Hollywood movies containe only "morally harmless" content and the film's no-holds-barred visuals ru

**"The excellent script, with its strong characterizations, telling dialogue and gripping suspense, has benefited from the fresh and original directorial touch of Arthur Penn."** *Herald Tribune*

1 Killer style: Faye Dunaway's public deified her far beyond anything the real Bonnie Parker had ever known. Dunaway's 1930s inspired costumes took 1960s fashion by storm and her performance transformed her into an equal rights icon.

2 A shooting star: Clyde Barrow (Warren Beatty) opens fire against the authorities and walks out of the bank a few dollars richer.

3 Two gun-slinging lovers: Clyde's impotence could force Bonnie to put a pistol to her own head, if the police don't beat her to it.

4 Fireworks: Robbing banks used to be more fun than being a kid at Christmas.

2

3

led the feathers of several highly-regarded film critics. Premiering at the 1967 Montreal film festival, it was branded a tasteless display of ostentatious violence. After a poor initial run, the picture returned to theaters thanks to a massive counter-offensive launched by another set of film critics, including the then little-known Pauline Kael.

Although the movie's protagonists were rooted in the past, it was primarily young viewers who identified with the outlaws. Their forays into crime were regarded as anti-establishment acts of rebellion. The international and national political crises of the 1960s had shaken the people's trust in political authority, and created a need for critical reflection. *Bonnie and Clyde* allowed U.S. audiences to recognize themselves in the commoners of the Depression era, who had also lost a great deal of faith in the government. This is no minor aspect of the film, and may explain its unpopularity with hostile critics.

*Bonnie and Clyde* is sometimes reproached for being a romanticized gangster ballad, but its depictions of death are undeniably blunt. The bullet the bank teller takes in the face is as gruesome as the killing of Clyde's brother Buck (Gene Hackman), who dies like a flailing animal hours after being shot in the head. Still, the most poignant moment of violence undoubtedly comes at the film's conclusion as Bonnie and Clyde are riddled with bullets by the authorities. It is a scene that becomes surreally macabre as a result of slow motion photography, constantly changing camera angles, and the prolongation of the act itself. Their bodies convulse in a terrifying dance of death as they are shot through with enough lead to wipe out a small town. The execution transforms them into the stuff of legend, but it doesn't cleanse them of their sin or turn them into martyrs.

The final shot shows the man who carried out these official orders of police brutality. He looks on in total disgust until the screen goes blank, leaving nothing in its trail but anguish. DG

**DEDE ALLEN**

*Bonnie and Clyde* (1967) presents an almost endless spectrum of dynamically innovative cinematic elements. This is firstly due to the screenplay by Robert Benton, who went on to direct films of his own, and David Newman. Both writers had worked with *nouvelle vague* director François Truffaut in the earlier stages of his career. Nonetheless, Arthur Penn's unconventional directing of *Bonnie and Clyde*, the achievement of a great *auteur*, benefited hugely from the finesse of Dede Allen's editing. Her first high-profile job came with Robert Wise's drama on racism, *Odds Against Tomorrow* (1959), produced almost entirely in New York. She reached a milestone in the art of film montage with Robert Rossen's *The Hustler* (1961). Her editing endowed the Hollywood veteran's film with a feel as fresh as a Truffaut or Godard picture. Allen continued to play a crucial role in creating new film styles in the 60s and 70s, collaborating with directors Arthur Penn and Sidney Lumet on several occasions. Despite three Oscar nominations for her work on Warren Beatty's mammoth undertaking *Reds* (1981), Sidney Lumet's *Dog Day Afternoon* (1975) and, most recently, Curtis Hanson's *Wonder Boys* (1999), Allen has never received an Academy Award. Lighter entertainment flicks like *The Breakfast Club* (1984) and *The Addams Family* (1991) are also indebted to Allen for some of their sparkle. She continues to enjoy an active editing career to this day. Her latest project was Jordanian director Omar Naim's sci-fi thriller *The Final Cut* (2003).

# CASINO ROYALE

1967 - GREAT BRITAIN - 131 MIN. - SPY FILM, PARODY

DIRECTORS VAL GUEST (*1911), KEN HUGHES (1922–2001), JOHN HUSTON (1906–1987), JOSEPH MCGRATH (*1930), ROBERT PARRISH (1916–1995)
SCREENPLAY WOLF MANKOWITZ, JOHN LAW, MICHAEL SAYERS, based on the novel of the same name by IAN FLEMING
DIRECTOR OF PHOTOGRAPHY JACK HILDYARD, JOHN WILCOX, NICOLAS ROEG EDITOR BILL LENNY MUSIC BURT BACHARACH
PRODUCTION CHARLES K. FELDMANN, JERRY BRESLER for COLUMBIA, FAMOUS ARTISTS.

STARRING PETER SELLERS (Evelyn Tremble), URSULA ANDRESS (Vesper Lynd), DAVID NIVEN (Sir James Bond), ORSON WELLES (Le Chiffre), JOANNA PETTET (Mata Bond), DALIAH LAVI (The Detainer/007) WOODY ALLEN (Jimmy Bond / Dr. Noah), JOHN HUSTON (Mc Tarry / "M"), DEBORAH KERR (Lady Fiona McTarry), WILLIAM HOLDEN (Ransome), JEAN-PAUL BELMONDO (French Legionary), TERENCE COOPER (Cooper).

## *"Be careful, that's my loose kneecap!"*

In Ian Fleming's first Bond novel, *Casino Royale*, the British agent eliminates his opponents by ruining them financially at the baccarat table. And in the movie *Casino Royale*, this is the only scene from the original novel that isn't used to parody the Bond myth. In the opening sequence, we see M – head of MI5 and Bond's boss – explaining something to his Russian, American and French colleagues: "They used to say a good spy is a pure spy, inside or out." And he doesn't just mean loyalty to Her Majesty the Queen. M, played by John Huston, one of the film's five directors, knows exactly what he's talking about. His ideal spy is a gentleman, not a daredevil or a ruffian: he goes to bed wearing snow-white bed socks and a sleeping cap, and he's utterly immune to the charms of the fair sex.

*Casino Royale* is a festival of inventiveness, concocted by five directors and three official scriptwriters (as well as several unofficial ones, including Billy Wilder, Woody Allen and Peter Sellers himself). Here, everything we thought we knew about James Bond is turned on its head. No genuine Bond film ever featured so many Bond girls, or indeed so many Bonds. The message of this movie, it seems, is this: we have seen the future of espionage – and it's female. Tough guys are a thing of the past, and Sir James himsel (David Niven) prefers to spend his days breeding black roses at his isolate country retreat and his evenings playing Debussy on the piano. His lost love Mata Hari, had paid with her life for her espionage escapades 20 years previously, and our hero is still in mourning. Sir James is now as tame as a pussycat, and he even has a slight but charming stutter – but hold on to you hats if he ever decides to return to Her Majesty's Service…

The plot of *Casino Royale* is no more than an excuse for an explosion o comedy fireworks. A mysterious organization named SMERSH poses a threa to the world and its secret services. Everywhere, agents are vanishing in a very puzzling manner; an entire profession appears to be on the verge of disappearance. So Bond – the "pure" spy and the perfect gentleman – emerges from retirement to fight the good fight one last time. Faced by a horde o

1 A perfect fit: Sir James Bond (David Niven) was tailor-made to accommodate two ladies.

2 Mr. Sandman: James had better say his goodnight prayers, if he expects to wake up in the morning.

3 Oh, how cliché: *Casino Royale* throws in every visual trick in the book to produce a lush espionage lampoon. Now if only there were a plot…

4 Ride her, Honey: First edition bond girl Ursula Andress casually slips into the role of double-ager Vesper Lynd.

5 Good luck charm, Goldie Hawn: With a little help from his celebrity impersonator, 'Le Chiffre' (Orsor Welles) takes his opponents for all they're worth ir a friendly game of baccarat.

**"Ursula Andress is exposing her navel, David Niven is karate chopping, Woody Allen is burping pastel balloonlets as Daliah Lavi feeds him a tiny time bomb capsule. Peter Sellers is doing imitations. Joanna Pettet is exposing her navel, Terence Cooper is karate chopping. Indians are frugging. And George Raft falls dead... Beyond cannibalizing the earlier 007 films for everything from song snatches to gadgetry to names like Dr. Noah, the filmmakers play with the drug-scene, homosexual camp, Dick Tracy, cold-war politics, new and old pussycats, the Beatles, Frankenstein and all styles of art from psychedelic back."** *Newsweek*

almost criminally sexy female counter-agents, Bond has no choice but to double, triple and sextuple himself in order to preserve his uniqueness. His multiple doppelgangers include Peter Sellers as Evelyn Tremble, and Terence Cooper as Agent Cooper – an irresistible hunk who lures the lady agents to their doom. Together with Mata Bond (Joanna Pettet) – the illegitimate daughter of Sir James, who had handed her over to an orphanage – the multiple Bonds present a tour-de-force of slapstick action. The film races wards the final showdown, a mass punch-up in the casino, featuring the U cavalry as a wild bunch of cowboys, accompanied by Native American pa troopers and the Keystone Kops (!). It all ends with a bang, quite literally which all seven Bonds are blasted to Kingdom Come; and to top it all off, of them is sent to Hell for his sins.

**“The James Bond myth has now reached its highpoint… As the series grew increasingly extravagant in its effects, there was one reaction it was eventually bound to provoke: parody.”** *Frankfurter Allgemeine Zeitung*

4

### URSULA ANDRESS

Many will remember her image before they remember her name. In 1962, a goddess in an ivory-colored bikini emerged from the waves bearing two sizable seashells, and sauntered towards Sean Connery singing “Underneath the Mango Tree.” Ursula Andress' appearance as Honey Rider made her an instant icon like few actresses before her. It would be nearly 40 years before the Bond genre would dare to draw near its Botticelli Venus again; but in 2001, Halle Berry repeated the scene in a copy of the original swimsuit (which had already gone under the hammer at Christie's for 41,125 pounds sterling). The British tabloids were delighted, with headlines announcing: “Halle gets andressed!” Ursula Andress was born in Berne, Switzerland, on March 19, 1936, the daughter of a German gardener. She began her career as a model in Rome, where she quickly made some useful Hollywood contacts. Though it was the young Marlon Brando who brought her to Paramount Studios, Andress was much closer to James Dean; they were a couple until his fatal car crash on September 30, 1955. In Hollywood, she eventually married the actor John Derek, who supported her in her career and secured her a number of roles, as he did with his later wives Linda Evans and Bo Derek. Though his wives changed, he did remain true to his taste – which Andress had virtually created with her legendary Bond role. With a single film scene, the more luxuriously upholstered stars of the 50s were suddenly passé. As Salvador Dali put it, Ursula Andress was “the world's most beautiful skeleton.” Her filmography is somewhat less impressive than her list of famous lovers, from Jean-Paul Belmondo to Dean Martin and Ryan O'Neal. She herself stated that she preferred working on action films to taking on difficult roles. In her forties, she could still delight her fans with her sex appeal, as in *The Fifth Musketeer* (1979). But after this film, she adopted a long-running role by becoming the mother of a son. Since then, we've seen little of Ursula Andress.

5

“Here, three scriptwriters have concocted a wild burlesque of a tale. As they’ve chosen to cover their trails, it’s impossible to know which writer was responsible for which part. What we’re served up is delirious nonsense, mind-boggling gags and gadgets, gigantomanic sets and wacky dialog: it’s all quite simply incredible. With an almost crazy relentlessness, the film presents us with a string of surprise guests, who turn up, take the stage and perform their star turns.” *Le Monde*

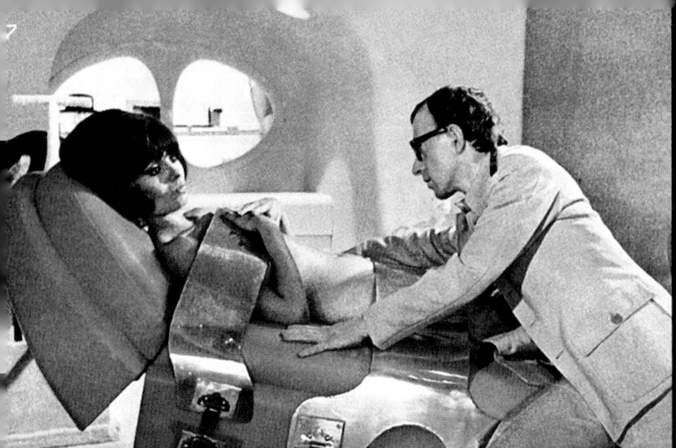

6 Minor stumbling block: Sir James Bond regains his composure in record time and returns to business as usual. The same can't be said of his foes.

7 Mr. Bond meets 007: Jimmy (Woody Allen) takes a voluptuous retainer (Daliah Lavi) and warms up to a little covert action.

8 Creaming the kilts: Who would have ever thought that Sir James would be so skilled at such a blue collar sport?

9 I'd like to buy a vowel: These bombshells make up the backbone of SMERSH (actually a Soviet acronym for Smyert Shpionem, meaning 'death to spies'). Bent on ridding all signs of male-dominated espionage from the planet, there's just no telling what they'll go after next. The five men who directed *Casino Royale* had best hold onto their hats.

As producer, Charles K. Feldmann had divided the job of directing the m among many tried-and-trusted professionals, and the result is a banquet gags, puns, technical shenanigans and sly allusions to the real James ond films. The sheer variety of sets and locations takes one's breath away, ith the scene shifting from bizarre, psychedelic spy HQs to East German rls' schools reminiscent of Dr. Caligari's cabinet. But if there's one thing about *Casino Royale* that nourishes the Bond myth rather than subvertin it, it's the bevy of beautiful girls that turn up in the course of the film – firs and foremost the ur-Bond girl Ursula Andress. Her appearance in a bikini (i *Dr. No*, 1962) was one of the highlights of the genre, and not just for insatiabl voyeurs. *Casino Royale*, though, is an end-to-end feast of eye-candy.

SF

9

# THE JUNGLE BOOK

1967 - USA - 78 MIN. - ANIMATED FEATURE

**DIRECTOR** WOLFGANG REITHERMAN (1909–1985)
**SCREENPLAY** LARRY CLEMMONS, RALPH WRIGHT, KEN ANDERSON, VANCE GERRY, based on short stories by RUDYARD KIPLING **DIRECTOR OF ANIMATION** DAN MACMANUS **EDITING** TOM ACOSTA, NORMAN CARLISLE **Music** GEORGE BRUNS, TERRY GILKYSON, RICHARD M. SHERMAN **PRODUCTION** WALT DISNEY for WALT DISNEY PICTURES.

**VOICES** PHIL HARRIS (Baloo), SEBASTIAN CABOT (Bagheera), LOUIS PRIMA (King Louie), GEORGE SANDERS (Shere Khan), STERLING HOLLOWAY (Kaa), J. PAT O'MALLEY (Colonel Hathi), BRUCE REITHERMAN (Mowgli), VERNA FELTON (Winifred Hathi), CLINT HOWARD (Junior), DARLEEN CARR (Shanti a.k.a. "The Girl"), Chad Stuart (Flaps).

## *"Look for the bare necessities!"*

A large, hardbound storybook opens as if by magic. Guided by an invisible hand, its pages turn to the tune of an oboe and several bongo drums. Soon the camera joins in on the action and follows the inviting rhythm into the lush and vibrant jungle before it. Beyond hanging tree branches and winding foliage on the riverbank, the wreck of a simple handcrafted boat comes into view. Sounds foreign to the jungle emanate from a little basket on board. In the treetops directly overhead, Bagheera the panther begins to tell of Mowgli, the man cub orphaned in the wilderness and raised by wolves. After ten years in the idyllic jungle, the young boy is to be taken back to "civilization" and his own people. For Shere Khan, the imperious tiger has returned home, and has no intention of tolerating the human offspring in its midst. Wary of mankind's technology, and shotguns and blazing torches in particular, the jungle kin isn't going to risk his precious hide so that some savage can live amongst h subjects.

Few moviegoers are unfamiliar with Mowgli's story, most having a tended one of *The Jungle Book's* countless theatrical re-releases either dur ing childhood or with their own children. The picture's sterling reputation wit world audiences made Walt Disney Pictures wait more than 25 years befor daring to present a sequel (*The Jungle Book 2*, 2002) it felt could live up t the original. Indeed the 1960s Disney classic had a most astounding fate: th grandfather of animation, Walt Disney, completed production of the film jus prior to his death in December 1966, missing the official premiere of his stu

1 It's a jungle out there: Bagheera prepares little Mowgli to leave the only life he has ever known and return to civilization.

2 The bare necessities: Mowgli's furry friend Baloo takes life in his stride. No other animated animal's appeal for carefree living has won over such a vast number of audience hearts since.

3 One big happy family – like something out of Disney.

**"'Here's Rudyard Kipling's original version,' said Disney. 'The first I thing I want you to do is to avoid reading it.' At that time, the standard procedure was to start by having the cartoonists draw the characters, and then to cast the actors for the voices. Though these actors had to be 'suitable,' they were basically interchangeable. In the case of *The Jungle Book*, however, as director Reitherman explained, the process was turned on its head."** *Der Tagesspiegel*

io's most lucrative moneymaker by a matter of weeks. The tale is a loose daptation of the Mowgli stories from Rudyard Kipling's *The Jungle Book* 1894/95), for both the film's ending and the depiction of the animals radical- deviate from the author's vision. Whereas Disney allows Mowgli to suc- essfully reintegrate into human civilization, Kipling saw no such outcome. nstead, Mowgli is taken for an evil conjurer and sent back to the jungle from hich he came. Walt Disney affords his eleven-year-old hero a more sooth- ng fate by having him follow the mesmerizing Shanti into the world that lies eyond the manmade palisades.

There were, however, other reasons why the cartoon adaptation met vith a great deal of criticism. With complete disregard for the black civil ights movement of the 1960s, Disney's picture blatantly equated certain races and styles of music with certain animal species and behavior, thus reinforcing stereotypes rather than offering a social alternative. In line with this schema, legendary jazz musician Louis Prima played the part of orangutan King Louie, one of the movie's more negatively depicted characters. Despite Louie's undeniably dynamic and dazzling musical number "I Want to be Like You," full of show-stopping choreography, there was no masking the fact that Disney had paired predominately black, jazz music with apish behavior; and even the song's title amounts to nothing more than a baboon's plea to be human.

But overall, the film's winning magic, created by six unforgettable songs and a cast of adorable animal characters, is what still draws audiences to theaters today. From Mowgli's happy-go-lucky pal, Baloo the bear, via the sly

**“Judging from *The Jungle Book*, the last film he personally supervised, Walt Disney never Kippled either. Hardly a line is left of the stories about Mowgli, the Indian ‘man-cub’ who was raised by animals. Like Disney’s other adaptions of children’s classics, *The Jungle Book* is based on the Kipling original in the same way that a fox hunt is based on foxes. Nonetheless, the result is throughly delightful.”** *Time*

4

4 Josephine Baker’s last banana dance: Baloo’s primitive moves turn into a tongue-in-cheek drag show.

5 All fluff: These vaudevillian clowns couldn’t even hurt a fly, let alone a child.

6 Art expeditions: Stills from *The Jungle Book* often resemble the work of painter Caspar David Friedrich.

7 I wanna be like you: The film ingeniously plays with imitation, depicting animals acting like people and vice versa.

aristocratic panther Bagheera to the formidable tiger Shere Kahn – they are one-of-a-kind Disney originals that have charmed and sung their way into the hearts of audiences worldwide. It comes as no surprise that *The Jungle Book* was among the first Disney productions for which the drawings were designed to fit the actors’ voices rather than the other way around. The studio had turned over a new leaf and from now on characterization would be built to suit the actor playing the role. Until then, only Donald Duck and his speech-impedimental antics had received such treatment. Radio comic Phil Harris benefited the most from this re-ordering of priorities, becoming world famous overnight after playing the role of Mowgli’s big-bellied, boogying buddy Baloo. Even today, the lyrics of “the bare necessities” continue to zip-a-dee-doo-dah on the lips of enthusiastic fans everywhere. Dolby digital, eat your heart out.

SR

7

**GEORGE SANDERS**

Shere Khan may have been a tiger of few words, but what he did say spoke volumes. Each line was so perfectly contoured to the tiger's nonchalant and commanding actions that George Sanders had the audience leaving the cinema wishing that Shere Khan had been given more screen time. No one could have hammed up the ultra-suave, clearly British panache of Khan's character quite like Sanders, who managed to put a seductive spin on a performance that could have easily been played as a cardboard villain. A true testament to his acting ability, considering that the once-feared sovereign who ever so casually flashes his claws has to fall from grace in such a way as to make the triumph of the uppity pipsqueak Mowgli and his assorted animal cohorts seem all the more monumental.

Sanders was born in Russia in 1906, but his film career only began in the 1930s. Until then, he had been a successful businessman in textiles and tobacco. But try as he might, Sanders couldn't ignore the call of the stage. He started off playing roles in modest British films before he made his way to Hollywood in the mid-1930s and signed a contract with 20th Century Fox. From then on the offers poured in. Sanders was awarded the Oscar for Best Supporting Actor for his performance as Addison De Witt in *All about Eve* (1950).

Reportedly, as early as 1937 Sanders had mentioned to fellow actor David Niven that he had no intention of growing old gracefully. After three failed marriages and the death of his fourth wife, Sanders quickly lost sight of what his life was about. In 1972, he committed suicide at a hotel in Spain, overdosing on sleeping pills. The note he left behind read, "I am committing suicide because I am bored. I feel I have lived enough."

# EL DORADO

1967 - USA - 126 MIN. - WESTERN

DIRECTOR HOWARD HAWKS (1896–1977)
SCREENPLAY LEIGH BRACKETT, based on the novel *THE STARS IN THEIR COURSES* by HARRY BROWN
DIRECTOR OF PHOTOGRAPHY HAROLD ROSSON EDITING JOHN WOODCOCK MUSIC NELSON RIDDLE PRODUCTION HOWARD HAWKS for LAUREL PRODUCTIONS, PARAMOUNT PICTURES.

STARRING JOHN WAYNE (Cole Thornton), ROBERT MITCHUM (Sheriff J. P. Harrah), JAMES CAAN (Mississippi / Alan Bourdillon Traherne), CHARLENE HOLT (Maudie), MICHELE CAREY (Josephine "Joey" MacDonald), ARTHUR HUNNICUTT (Bull Harris), R. G. ARMSTRONG (Kevin MacDonald), EDWARD ASNER (Bart Jason), PAUL FIX (Doc Miller), CHRISTOPHER GEORGE (Nelse McLeod), JOHNNY CRAWFORD (Luke MacDonald), ROBERT DONNER (Milt), JOHN GABRIEL (Pedro), MARINA GHANE (Maria), ROBERT ROTHWELL (Saul MacDonald), ADAM ROARKE (Matt MacDonald).

***"I'm paid to risk my neck. I'll decide where and when I'll do it. This isn't it."***

Sheriff J. P. Harrah (Robert Mitchum) can't afford to make any false moves. While making his evening rounds, he's discovered a horse tethered in front of the local saloon, and he knows exactly who the owner is. Inside, he asks if anyone has seen a square-shouldered cowboy and is directed to the washroom.

Leaning over the sink with soap in his eyes, Cole Thornton (John Wayne) can identify the man speaking to him without even seeing his face. No sooner has he turned around, than he is staring down the barrel of Harrah's rifle. These army veterans know what to expect from each other. Hannah has therefore taken precautionary action, rather than just casually asking Thornton why he has ridden into town.

As Harrah correctly assumed, local land baron Bart Jason (Edward Asner) has recruited the sharp-shooting Thornton to settle a personal property dispute. However, the hired gun decides to revoke his services after the sheriff convinces him that the targeted party, the MacDonald family, is entitled to their claim. Thornton breaks the news to Jason, only to be shot at by young Luke MacDonald (Johnny Crawford) upon leaving his former employer's ranch. Although the shot misses him, Thornton returns fire and wounds the young man in the abdomen. Fearing a painful death, Luke kills himself. Thornton is left with little choice other than to return the dead boy to his family. Driven by fury, the victim's sister, Joey MacDonald (Michele Carey) doesn't wait to hear the cowboy's explanation before making up her mind to avenge her brother's death. She launches a surprise attack on Thornton that leaves him with a bullet lodged within inches of his spine. While the shot itself doesn't pose a critical threat, Doc Miller isn't willing to take the risk of removing the slug himself and advises Thornton to seek out a specialist. Looks like he'll have to tend to that later; for the gunslinger has another commission lined up and duty calls.

Several months pass and Thornton hears through the grapevine that Sheriff Harrah has been hitting the bottle and neglecting his post. Accompanied by loyal sidekick Mississippi (James Caan), whom he helped fight off a couple of insalubrious characters, Thornton makes his way back to El Dorado. He arrives just in time to find out that Jason has called on the services of unscrupulous gunman Nelse McLeod (Christopher George) to pull off the job he himself had previously turned down. It seems there is not much the force of justice can do to stop McLeod and his cronies: Thornton's injury make him

1

2

1 Forever in blue jeans: The way things are looking now, Mississippi (James Caan) just wants to have wild cat Joey MacDonald (Michele Carey) stand by his side.

2 The good, the bad, and the ugly: Five bucks says you can't guess who's who. (From left, James Caan, John Wayne, and Arthur Hunnicutt).

3 Hired gunman: Cole Thornton (John Wayne) covers Sheriff Harrah's back from the storeroom behind the saloon.

**"The formula of John Wayne plus drunk, greenhorn and ancient against the bad men is a good one, and Hawks manages the variations so cunningly that it works all over again."** *Monthly Film Bulletin*

3

a victim to sudden attacks of temporary paralysis, Harrah would sooner reach for the bottle than his badge, his deputy, Bull (Arthur Hunnicutt), is an old curmudgeon, and a lack of experience means Mississippi is a lousy shot. Yet even with the chips stacked against them, these four men step up to the challenge – ready to resort to diversionary tactics should their firepower prove insufficient.

No other actor shaped the face of Westerns like John Wayne. Only he had the ironclad image of heroic invincibility needed to play an impaired protagonist without compromising his dignity. For Cole Thornton's downward spiral is not solely brought on by the bullet lodged inside him: he also feels the burn of old age. Although he doesn't deny these facts, he's not about to make an issue of them. The picture concludes with him and the respectively naimed J. P. Harrah limping down El Dorado's Main Street on crutches; they ıave emerged victorious, but their scars make it clear that from here on it's somebody else's battle. Thornton begins to speak openly of retirement, and of peacefully living out the rest of his days in El Dorado.

The film's maturity can also be attributed to its director Howard Hawks, who made it a refined version of his previous *Rio Bravo* (1958). In this version, his protagonists appear weathered and feisty, but self-effacing. Hawks makes no secret of either the genre's gradual downfall or that of its heroes, but confronts them directly and thus somehow makes them bearable. Indeed, Hawks even gives this cloud a silver lining, pointing out that the one human phenomenon impervious to social upheavals, transcending gender and improving with age is friendship. HK

4 He sure cleans up nicely: Former drunkard Sheriff J. P. Harrah (Robert Mitchum) puts a little spring in his step.

5 Blazing saddles: If only Mississippi had a bit more experience, he might have ended up with a rifle instead of a shotgun.

**HOWARD HAWKS (1896–1977)**

Only a handful of directors have proven as versatile as Howard Hawks or produced as many classics. Yet despite his undeniable genius, recognition within the industry only came in 1974. It was then, just three years prior to his death, that Hawks was awarded his first Oscar and hailed "a titan of the American cinema, whose filmmaking efforts represent one of most solid, brilliant and multilateral careers since the advent of motion pictures." Although the European cinema had long considered him an *auteur*, U. S. critics mostly failed to acknowledge Hawks as an authentic artistic force. Like many directors of his generation, Hawks arrived in Hollywood with an alternative set of credentials. While studying to be an engineer, Hawks worked summers as a props master. He fought as an aviator during World War I and went on to become an aircraft designer. In the early 1920s he changed track altogether, deciding that celluloid was his calling. After serving as an editor, assistant director, and casting director, he managed to finance two short film projects of his own in 1922. By the following year, Hawks was earning a living as a screenwriter and producer. In 1925, Hawks sold a script on the contingent that he could direct the project himself. His feature film debut *The Road to Glory* (1925) turned out to be one of many masterpieces in his vast body of work, which includes such unforgettable classics as *Scarface* (1932), *Bringing Up Baby* (1937), *His Girl Friday* (1939) and *The Big Sleep* (1946).

# COOL HAND LUKE

1967 - USA - 127 MIN. - PRISON FILM, DRAMA

DIRECTOR STUART ROSENBERG (*1927)
SCREENPLAY DONN PEARCE and FRANK R. PIERSON, based on the novel of the same name by DONN PEARCE
DIRECTOR OF PHOTOGRAPHY CONRAD L. HALL EDITING SAM O'STEEN MUSIC LALO SCHIFRIN PRODUCTION GORDON CARROLL for JALEM PRODUCTIONS, WARNER BROS.

STARRING PAUL NEWMAN (Lucas "Cool Hand Luke" Jackson), GEORGE KENNEDY (Dragline), J. D. CANNON (Society Red), LOU ANTONIO (Koko), ROBERT DRIVAS (Loudmouth Steve), STROTHER MARTIN (Captain), JO VAN FLEET (Arletta), CLIFTON JAMES (Carr), MORGAN WOODWARD (Boss Godfrey), LUKE ASKEW (Boss Paul), MARC CAVELL (Rabbitt), RICHARD DAVALOS (Blind Dick), WARREN FINNERTY (Tattoo), DENNIS HOPPER (Babalugats).

ACADEMY AWARDS 1967 OSCAR for BEST SUPPORTING ACTOR (George Kennedy).

## *"Sometimes nothing is a real cool hand."*

Is he a prophet, a poet or just a juvenile delinquent? We're left guessing as director Stuart Rosenberg introduces *Cool Hand Luke* as a ne'er-do-well who demolishes parking meters in a drunken stupor. Yet somehow, by the time the opening credits have come to a close, Paul Newman has managed to win over the audience with his trademark blue eyes and infallible smile, working a magic that endows Lucas Jackson a. k. a. "Cool Hand Luke" with heart and soul. The character is as much a cynical criminal as he is an amiable good-for-nothing, a true pretender to the throne of James Dean in *Rebel Without A Cause* (1955). Even Luke's attitude toward the rules of the prison camp to which he is soon confined is a wrathful yet completely futile protest against an authority he is powerless to combat. We are presented with a man who has been severely punished for a meaningless act of demolition. His sentence: to sit out two years' incarceration in a Southern penal institution caged in by barbed wire, where a strict hierarchy presides and rules are unremittingly enforced.

The camp's Captain (Strother Martin) runs a tight ship and his lackeys, referred to as "bosses," take great pains to ensure that order is maintained. For each act of transgression, inmates are forced to spend a night in "the box" – a foul-smelling, claustrophobic shed. The box gives newcomers their first glimpse of the deep inhumanity beneath the institution's surface – a microcosm of perverted law and order. Shackled as a chain gang during the day, the physical labor these men are condemned to endure on the dusty roads under a scorching sun is endless torture. Under the grim eye of the sadistic bosses, the prisoners sweat blood until their legs give out from under them. Luke alone greets the acts of humiliation with indifference and flippant sarcasm, soon winning the admiration of his fellow inmates. This is Paul Newman at his finest, playing a charismatic deadbeat with an iron-will constitution. He gives the convicts back a glimmer of hope and pride. It's no wonder that even Dragline (George Kennedy), the tough, silent leader of the jailbird pack, initially bent on breaking Luke in a boxing match, is soon enchanted by his forceful personality. Although Luke is repeatedly knocked down during their fight, he keeps getting up and refuses defeat. His foolhardy, impassioned defiance, announcing that he'll have to kill him to keep him down, instantly gains the victor's respect.

1

"Anti-establishment and anti-authority, Luke breaks the law not because of social deprivation – the excuse in most 30s films – but because it gives him something to do. The act of rebellion has become its own justification, making Luke an appropriate anti-hero of the late 60s." *Ann Lloyd, in: Movies of the Sixties*

2

3

1 Last one out's a rotten egg: Cool Hand Luke (Paul Newman) fires up the men with outlandish wagers. Here, we see him after having successfully downed 50 hard-boiled eggs in the course of an hour.

2 What we have here is a failure to communicate: Monstrous overseers don't discuss the law – they enforce it.

3 I ain't down yet: Luke would rather die than capitulate.

It's just a matter of time before Luke becomes the jailbirds' golden boy. His nonchalance helps him triumph in poker (earning him the nickname "Cool Hand Luke"). He can inspire his chain gang buddies to pave the road at double-speed in the blazing heat, although it's not required of them. And, just for the hell of it, he accepts a bet that he can down fifty boiled eggs in the course of an hour – an undertaking that proves to be one of the greatest acts of willpower ever caught on celluloid. The scene ends with Newman sprawled across a table, like Christ martyred on the cross, half naked and beyond exhaustion. It is the quintessential image for the type of silent veneration he is now held in. Yet what drives Luke to be a worthy idol, who is willing to go to any lengths in the name of his convictions and perform miraculous acts that win his peers' undying allegiance, is also the seed of his undoing. For his conduct is motivated by boredom. Luke constantly rebels against the guards and their stringent set of rules simply because his fellow inmates expect it of him and root him on. It is only after his mother dies, and the guards lock Luke in the box to prevent him from trying to attend the

**GEORGE KENNEDY**

George Kennedy is what one might call a late-bloomer. Starting at the age of 30, the actor born on February 18th, 1925 in New York, made his way into the Hollywood limelight by the backdoor while working as a military consultant for the TV show, *Sergeant Bilko.* Most ironic, considering Kennedy's upbringing. Both Kennedy's parents were successful artists – his father was a pianist, composer, and conductor; his mother a dancer with the New York Classical Ballet. Kennedy did, in fact, express an interest in theater at a young age, performing on stage and hosting his own radio show. Nonetheless, this would eventually take a backseat to a long-standing military career. After sixteen years of faithful service, a back injury forced him to throw in the towel with Uncle Sam. It was this turn of events which not only inspired Kennedy to work as a military consultant for television, but also garnered him his first small-screen guest appearances and supporting roles, finally striking gold with his Hollywood film premiere in Stanley Kubrick's *Spartacus* (1960). Kennedy's earlier pictures span genres from Westerns like *Lonely Are The Brave* (1962) to comedy capers like *Charade* (1963). An imposing actor at 6'4," he soon became a Robert Aldrich regular, playing in features like *The Flight of the Phoenix*, 1965) and *The Dirty Dozen*, (1967). In the 70s, he proved he could deal with disaster movies with *Airport* (1970) and its various follow-ups. There were, however, a few turkeys amidst his subsequent film roles. Pictures like *Bolero* (1984) and *The Delta Force* (1986) began to earn him a reputation as a B-movie actor. That all changed for the better when Kennedy opted for self-deprecating slapstick in *The Naked Gun* (1988), where he climbed to new heights and was promptly signed for the parody's two further installments.

**4** Scrub woman: Joy Harmon's short-lived film career didn't extend beyond a few minor roles. However, she was one of the era's more popular magazine models.

**5** One tough cookie: Inmate head honcho, Dragline (George Kennedy), is impressed by Luke's tenacity and takes him under his wing. Kennedy's performance won him the Oscar for Best Actor in a Supporting Role.

**6** Sisyphus complex: Luke takes on a fight against the system that he simply cannot win and becomes a living legend among his fellow inmates.

funeral, that his escapades take on a deeper meaning for himself. This is where his martyrdom truly begins. He is caught and tortured by the guards until his willpower crumbles and he loses his credibility in the eyes of the prisoners. Only Dragline still grasps onto the myth of "Cool Hand Luke," preserving it at all cost. When Luke is gunned downed before Dragline's eyes at the end of the picture, Luke's apostle tells the guys that even loaded with lead, he still went down with "that ol' Luke smile," a smile that is indelibly

"Give an actor a good script and he can change the world." This was Newman's credo at the time *Cool Hand Luke* was filmed. Well, he may not have changed the world, but Newman – alongside a star-studded ensemble of actors including George Kennedy, Strother Martin plus a handful of men who would emerge as some of the greatest character actors in years to come (like Harry Dean Stanton, Dennis Hopper, Ralph Waite, Anthony Zerbe, Joe Don Baker) – put forth one of the cinema's most riveting studies in non-conformism, perse-

# LE SAMOURAÏ

## Le Samouraï

1967 - FRANCE/ITALY - 95 MIN. - CRIME FILM, DRAMA

DIRECTOR JEAN-PIERRE MELVILLE (1917–1973)
SCREENPLAY JEAN-PIERRE MELVILLE, based on the novel *THE RONIN*, by GOAN MCLEOD DIRECTOR OF PHOTOGRAPHY HENRI DECAË EDITING MONIQUE BONNOT, YOLANDE MAURETTE MUSIC FRANÇOIS DE ROUBAIX PRODUCTION RAYMOND BORDERIE, EUGÈNE LÉPICIER for FILMEL, C. I. C. C., FIDA.

STARRING ALAIN DELON (Jef Costello), FRANÇOIS PÉRIER (Commissar), NATHALIE DELON (Jeanne Lagrange), CATHY ROSIER (Valérie), MICHEL BOISRAND (Wiener), JACQUES LEROY (Killer), ROBERT FAVART (Barman), JEAN-PIERRE POSIER (Olivier Rey), CATHERINE JOURDAN (Cloakroom Attendant), ANDRÉ SALGUES (Auto Mechanic).

## *"I never lose – not really."*

The first nine minutes are silent. We see a cheap room, dimly illuminated by the light from two windows; a bird twitters monotonously, and blue smoke curls slowly upwards, indicating the presence of a man smoking in bed (Alain Delon). Eventually he rises, strokes the bars of a birdcage with a handful of folded banknotes, hides the money, dons his trench coat and turns up the collar. He goes to the mirror and puts on his hat, adjusts its brim and leaves the apartment. Out on the street, he climbs into a Citroën DS, lays out a row of ignition keys on the passenger seat, and starts trying them out. When the engine starts, he drives off. In a desolate Parisian suburb, he steers the car into a tiny garage. Immediately a mechanic locks the door, screws on a new license plate, and hands our hero some papers, some money, and – after the driver clicks his fingers – a gun. Our man drives off to an apartment block, gets out and walks up to the door of a flat. A blonde woman (Nathalie Delon) opens the door – and at last we hear the first word: "Jef."

The silent overture has made one thing clear: Jef Costello's *métier* is homicide. The trench coat, the hat, the wad and the weapon: these are the cinematic trappings of the professional killer. Jean-Pierre Melville's film leads us into the sinister world of its hero with breathtaking efficiency. This is a dehumanized male cosmos with its own rigid rules and mechanisms. Melville's aesthetic is one of reduction; the colors of this movie are as cold as they are artificial, and it's immediately clear to us that *Le Samouraï* is more than a mere variation on the American crime movie. It's a quintessence of the genre, a fascinating abstraction saturated with the pessimistic world-view of its highly idiosyncratic director.

Meville prefaced his film with an invented quote from "The Book of the Samurai:" "There is no greater loneliness than that of the samurai, unless it is that of the tiger in the jungle." Costello – the "Samurai" of the title – is almost autistic in his solitary independence, and the caged bird in his apart-

1

# "It almost seems to be an American film dubbed into a French scene to appear *americain* in such things as night clubs, sordid little hotels, police lineups and the general behavior of the characters."

*Variety*

**ALAIN DELON**

For decades, he excited the imagination of the tabloid press and their readers were gripped by his escapades. Whether it was his spectacular love affairs, his alleged contacts to the Mafia or his provocative statements to the world, Alain Delon (born on November 8, 1935 in Sceaux, near Paris) was always good for a headline. This had a lot to do with his talent for fame: he was astonishingly good-looking and he knew it. His looks gave him his start in the cinema, after he had taken part in the war in Indochina as a paratrooper in the French army. He made his film debut in 1957 as a romantic beau, before achieving his breakthrough in René Clément's Patricia Highsmith adaptation *Plein soleil* (1960) – a.k.a. *Purple Noon* in the U.S. and *Blazing Sun* in Britain. As the murderer Ripley, Delon represents a blend of physical beauty and emotional coldness that would stamp his image for the rest of his career. In the years that followed, he worked with some of the best (Michelangelo Antonioni) and most popular directors (Henri Verneuil, Jacques Deray, Christian Jacque) in French and Italian cinema, and became the top European star of the 60s. His collaboration with Luchino Visconti resulted in two masterpieces of the decade: *Rocco and his Brothers* (*Rocco e i suoi fratelli*, 1960) and *The Leopard* (*Il gattopardo*, 1963). One of Delon's best performances was alongside Lino Ventura in Robert Enrico's *The Last Adventure* (*Les aventuriers*, 1966), an unfairly neglected film about an unusual male friendship. A year later, Delon was *Le Samouraï* – and destined to remain so. Excellent films such as *Le Cercle rouge* (1970), *Un flic*, (1972, both by Jean-Pierre Melville), *Borsalino* (1970, Jaques Deray) had as little effect on this enduring image as his ambitious appearances in Joseph Losey's *Mr. Klein* (*Monsieur Klein*, 1975) and *The Assassination of Trotsky* (*L'Assassinat de Trotsky*, 1971).

1 Up in smoke: Without batting an eye Jef Costello (Alain Delon) acts as judge, jury and executioner. Roles like this established Delon as one of the French cinema's greatest sex symbols.

2 A no win situation: Lured into a trap by his dubious employers, Costello finds himself with no hope of making good. Now all he can do is go out with a bang.

3 Warming the cockles of his heart: Jeanne (Delon's ex-wife Natalie Delon) is the only person Costello opens up to.

4 The trenches of war: Could this be a case of schizophrenia with a cool veneer? For no matter how grave the danger, Costello always demonstrates the same professionalism on a job.

5 Up against the law: The commissioner (François Périer, standing left of Delon) presents Costello with a formidable opponent.

ment may well be seen as a metaphor for his own situation. That incomprehensible tweeting doesn't just intensify the icy silence that surrounds the man, but it also lends his isolation an obsessive, even pathological quality. Costello's life seems to consist of nothing but rituals. His gestures seem inexorable, exhaustively rehearsed, like the movements of an automaton. When a pretty girl driver stops beside him at the traffic lights, she casts a flirtatious eye at the killer – but in vain; he stares straight ahead, oblivious to her charms.

His relationship to his girlfriend Jeanne (played by Nathalie Delon, the star's wife at the time) seems to fit into the same pattern. His first appearance at her apartment is for purely professional reasons: he's being paid to kill someone, and he needs an alibi. She provides it for him, but she's quite without illusions: "I love it when you come to me; it means you need me."

Costello's job is to kill the owner of an exclusive nightclub, and he performs the task with icy precision. Though the police place him on an identity parade and put him through an interrogation, his alibi is iron-clad. But the Samurai is not invulnerable: the Commissar (François Périer) trusts his instincts and continues to keep an eye on Costello. The killer's boss soon starts to get worried; and when Costello goes to pick up his blood money, he doesn't realize he's walking intro a trap. Shots are fired, and Costello manages to escape with a wounded arm. But now he's shut in on both sides. Pursued by the cops and by the gangsters, he knows there's no way out.

For many film buffs, *Le Samouraï* is still one of the best movies ever made. And its influence on filmmakers has been considerable, from Paul Schrader – especially as regards his script for Scorsese's *Taxi Driver* (1975) – to Michael Mann (*Heat*, 1995). That Melville's film has now acquired an almost mythical status is due in no small part to the special aura of Alain Delon, which the director brought out perfectly in the peculiar world of this film. In Delon's face, apparently so cold and mask-like, the spectator eventually discerns a tragic quality that extends beyond the personal fate of the killer Costello. As the embodiment of existential solitude, Delon became an icon of the cinema.

JH

# PLANET OF THE APES

1967/68 - USA - 112 MIN. - SCIENCE FICTION, ADVENTURE

DIRECTOR FRANKLIN J. SCHAFFNER (1920–1989)
SCREENPLAY MICHAEL WILSON, Rod Serling, based on the novel *LA PLANÈTE DES SINGES* by PIERRE BOULLE
DIRECTOR OF PHOTOGRAPHY LEON SHAMROY EDITING HUGH S. FOWLER MUSIC JERRY GOLDSMITH PRODUCTION ARTHUR P. JACOBS for 20TH CENTURY FOX and APJAC PRODUCTIONS.

STARRING CHARLTON HESTON (George Taylor), KIM HUNTER (Zira), RODDY MCDOWALL (Cornelius), MAURICE EVANS (Dr. Zaius), LINDA HARRISON (Nova), JAMES WHITMORE (President of the Assembly), JAMES DALY (Dr. Honorius), ROBERT GUNNER (Landon), LOU WAGNER (Lucius), Woodrow Parfrey (Dr. Maximus), JEFF BURTON (Dodge), BUCK KARTALIAN (Julius).

ACADEMY AWARDS 1967 HONORARY OSCAR for MASKS AND MAKE-UP (John Chambers).

## *"What will he find out there, doctor?"*
## *"His destiny"*

There's nothing like a photo for posterity, even if the subject matter reeks of imperialism. In this case, what is being immortalized is the brutal commemoration of a successful hunt – a battle between man and beast. Only this time, man lost.

The hunter apes beam with pride as their *homo sapiens* trophies dangle beside them. In this highly advanced world, apes plot the course of civilization and men have been reduced to Neanderthal-like creatures. The parable is strikingly clear: it is a gruesome social order akin to that of the colonies, where white men enslaved, traded, and slaughtered black men as though they were animals. *Planet of the Apes* is an allegory of a world fueled by racism and xenophobia, unmitigated power and politically motivated oppression. Hitting theaters just months before Stanley Kubrick's *2001*, it is a post-apocalyptic vision, prophesying a bleak and pessimistic future for mankind and the world at large. As such, it is not unlike other cinematic dystopias produced at the height of the Cold War such as *Soylent Green* (1973) and *Logan's Run* (1976).

But the film opens at a point assumed to be eons away from Armageddon: astronaut George Taylor (Charlton Heston) has set forth on a mission into space. Knowing that it will be 700 years before he touches earthly ground again, Taylor radios the control tower, bidding farewell to the 20th century with words that are strikingly unsentimental. Things, however, do not go as planned and the space travelers drift through the universe in an ageless sleep for an additional 2000 years. A crash landing calls them back to consciousness and the three surviving officers exit the rocket ship only to find themselves on a distant and relatively desolate planet.

Holding an American flag that suddenly seems meaningless and anachronistic, Taylor and his remaining crew begin to survey their surroundings and claim their new world in the name of the Earth. Their exhausting journey through the desert wasteland comes to halt when they discover a green oasis inhabited by what appears to be a peaceful tribe of primordial humans. What starts off as a picturesque idyll soon turns into a nightmare as hunters on horseback charge in, bent on killing any humans they don't take prisoner.

The mounted warriors, members of an advanced culture of intelligent apes, are simply acting on orders of official government business. After incurring a neck injury which robs him of his voice, Taylor and his men are

1

1 You big ape: Taylor (Charlton Heston) impresses his gorilla captor by demonstrating full command of the English language.

2 Monkey business: Dr. Zira (Kim Hunter) and her fiancé Cornelius (Roddy McDowall) can't believe their eyes. Despite being a considered a wild animal, the speaking human Taylor has been put on trial.

captured. They arrive at a prison camp where a compassionate scientist specializing in human research, a chimpanzee named Dr. Zira (Kim Hunter), saves Taylor from a fate worse than death. As Zira begins studying Taylor back at the laboratory, her colleague and fiancé Cornelius (Roddy McDowall) makes reference to his recent groundbreaking discovery in "the forbidden zone" of the desert, where he discovered the remains of human culture older than anything in ape history – evidence at last to support the theory that apes have human ancestry.

It's a revolutionary hypothesis, and one which could disrupt their way of life given that ape culture runs according to a strict caste system: orangutans are natural politicians, chimpanzees are born scientists, and gorillas are destined for a life as skilled laborers and warriors. As such, the minister of science and religion, Dr. Zaius (Maurice Evans) tries to scientifically refute all evidence that Taylor could, in fact, be more intelligent than other people or even the apes themselves. That proves no easy task, as Taylor possesses the ability to write and, as he regains his voice, speak (luckily, the apes still converse in English:poetic license that sci-fi authors like Boulle just pray the audience will accept).

3

4

3 Jungle fever: Taylor and Zira discover that affection and friendship know no boundaries.

4 Manhunters: It's always open season on the planet of the apes.

5 Pet store: She's not a big talker, but what a catch! Linda Harrison as Nova, Taylor's love interest.

# "Rather precise parallels exist in the allegoric writing to real world events, say, of the past 20 years."

*Variety*

5

6

The social satire climaxes with a scene at a tribunal. Screenwrit
Michael Wilson, whose name was among those on the House Un-Americ
Activities Committee's blacklist, successfully parallels this episode with th
American witch hunt politics of the 1950s. Zira and Cornelius are brande
heretics for their assertions, and are banished along with Taylor to "the fo
bidden zone."

It is here where Taylor finally learns the truth of the situation at hand a
he discovers remnants of a Statue of Liberty blown apart by nuclear war. A
once, everything is clear: he has been on Earth all along, only he hasn
recognized it.

*Planet of the Ape's* poignant and surprising conclusion undoubted
contributed to the picture's impact at the time it debuted. Its ability to func
tion simultaneously as a thrilling sci-fi adventure, philosophical reflection ar
political satire caused a box-office triumph far beyond the expectations
either producer Arthur P. Jacobs or 20th Century Fox. Interestingly enoug
Fox would enjoy similar success in the genre some ten years later wit
George Lucas' *Star Wars* adventures.

The apes would return to the screen in countless future incarnation
Fox produced four sequels: *Beneath the Planet of the Apes* (1969); *Escap
from the Planet of the Apes* (1971); *Conquest of the Planet of the Apes* (197
and *Battle for the Planet of the Apes* (1973). Although they were short-live
endeavors, both live action and animated series were created for televisio
Most recently Tim Burton remade the original in 2001, but left out many o
the classic's philosophic undertones. Maybe the apes weren't so far off th
mark. K

**"*Planet of the Apes* is an amazing film. A political and sociological allegory, cast in the mold of futuristic science-fiction, the film is an intriguing blend of chilling satire, a sometimes indecorous juxtaposition of human and ape mores, of optimism and pessimism."** *Variety*

7

8

9

6 Monkey in the middle: *Planet of the Apes* fuses elements of adventure, action and sci-fi, and emerges as an entirely original masterpiece.

7 Grizzly prognosis: Believing that humans are only capable of evil, Dr. Zaius (Maurice Evans) does everything in his power to revoke all evidence that a human culture existed prior to modern day ape civilization.

8 Type caste: An ape's destiny is preordained. Gorillas are warriors and skilled laborers, orangutans are natural politicians, and science lies in the hands of the chimps.

9 Passing the baton: *Planet of the Apes* is an allegory of mankind's history of racism and, more specifically, a criticism of American foreign policy.

**CHARLTON HESTON**

He made Hollywood history as a brawny Ben-Hur and a wrathful Moses. Charlton Heston is a man with a truly monumental screen presence. With a face carved in granite and a voice that moves mountains, no one could take an epic by the reins the way he could. It was a skill Heston would prove time and again. He played Mark Antony in David Bradley's adaptation of Shakespeare's *Julius Caesar* (1950), Buffalo Bill in *Pony Express* (1953), as well as the dual roles of Moses and God in Cecil B. DeMille's *The Ten Commandments* (1956). He was finally recognized for his achievement in the genre with an Oscar for his portrayal of the Jewish prince Ben-Hur in William Wyler's 1959 biblical epic of the same name. He then went on to play a legendary Spanish knight in Anthony Mann's Hollywood roadshow *El Cid* (1961) and Michelangelo in *The Agony and the Ecstasy* (1965).

French film critic Michel Mourlet once called Charlton Heston "an axiom of the cinema. By himself alone he constitutes a tragedy, and his presence in any film whatsoever suffices to create beauty." And truly the actor born on October 4th, 1924 in Evanston, Illinois infused countless film and television roles with his innate magnetism, a compelling mix of tenacity, strength and an iron will.

Heston enjoyed an unparalleled degree of fame during the 50s and 60s in Hollywood epics and trailblazing Westerns. However, he also shone in film noir classics like Orson Welles' *Touch of Evil* (1958). Heston's work with Sam Peckinpah proved particularly prosperous; the actor even used his clout to go to bat with *Major Dundee*'s (1964/65) producers on behalf of the director to ensure the project would be completed. His unforgettable performance in *Planet of the Apes* (1967/68) paved the way for future roles in dark sci-fi thrillers like *The Omega Man* (1971). Heston experienced renewed success in the 70s with the advent of the wildly popular disaster movie, dominating the screen in *Earthquake* (1974) and *Airport 1975* (1974).

The 80s presented the austere looking actor with a number of choice television roles. Many will remember that the leading role in the *Dynasty* spin-off *The Colbys* (1985–87) was written especially for him. As a result of his ongoing battle with Alzheimer's disease, Heston has limited his recent film work to cameos, such as his appearance in Tim Burton's remake of *Planet of the Apes* (2001). Heston is also no stranger to the technical side of filmmaking, having assumed the director's chair for *Antony and Cleopatra* (1973) and *Mother Lode* (1982), pictures in which he also starred.

Of late, the staunch Republican and good friend of former U.S. president Ronald Reagan has laid his popularity on the line as an advocate of the constitutional right to bear arms. From 1998–2003 he served as president of the National Rifle Association (NRA), stating that anyone who expected him to surrender a firearm would have to rip it from his "cold, dead hands." It's no wonder that this once heralded Hollywood actor is today one of America's more controversial figures.

# THE GRADUATE

1967 - USA - 105 MIN. - LOVE STORY, SOCIAL SATIRE, LITERARY ADAPTATION

DIRECTOR MIKE NICHOLS (*1931)
SCREENPLAY CALDER WILLINGHAM, BUCK HENRY, based on the novel of the same name by CHARLES WEBB DIRECTOR OF PHOTOGRAPHY ROBERT SURTEES EDITING SAM O'STEEN MUSIC DAVE GRUSIN, PAUL SIMON PRODUCTION LAWRENCE TURMAN for EMBASSY PICTURES CORPORATION, LAWRENCE TURMAN INC.

STARRING ANNE BANCROFT (Mrs. Robinson), DUSTIN HOFFMAN (Benjamin Braddock), KATHARINE ROSS (Elaine Robinson), WILLIAM DANIELS (Mr. Braddock), MURRAY HAMILTON (Mr. Robinson), ELIZABETH WILSON (Mrs. Braddock), BUCK HENRY (Hotel Desk Clerk), WALTER BROOKE (Mr. McGuire), ALICE GHOSTLEY (Mrs. Singleman), NORMAN FELL (Mr. McCleery).

ACADEMY AWARDS 1968 OSCAR for BEST DIRECTOR (Mike Nichols).

## *"Mrs. Robinson – you are trying to seduce me... aren't you?"*

"I just want to say one word to you, Benjamin. Just one word..." At a welcome home party on his parents' Beverly Hills estate, recent college graduate Benjamin Braddock (Dustin Hoffman) can't mask his bewilderment as business associate, Mr. McGuire (Walter Brooke) rants and raves about the wonders of..."plastics!"

Plastics may be the wave of the future, but the new miracle substance has yet to corner a market with young Braddock – emerging voice in the next generation of American consumers. The young man has too many other things on his mind to be concerned with the "revolutionary" business propositions of his father's crowd. Actually, no one's really sure just what Benjamin wants from life – least of all him. Until now his future has fallen into his lap thanks to his parents, his social circle, and his class. He himself has no idea about the person he'd like to become, except that he doesn't want to end up like his well-dressed, superficial parents. That's one thing he knows for sure.

Taking cover in his room, he sits down beside his old aquarium, where a figurine diver floats about aimlessly. Then Mrs. Robinson (Anne Bancroft) sails onto his horizon, and suddenly things start to look up...

What follows is one of the most suggestive seduction scenes in all Hollywood history. Mrs. Robinson has Ben drive her home in his new, candy-apple red Alfa Romeo. A sultry siren in her mid-forties, she is the wife of his father's most trusted business associate, and one of his mother's dearest friends. After coming up with an array of pretexts, she manages to lure Ben up to her bedroom. And before he knows it, there she is standing stark naked in front of him, making a proposal that no one could misunderstand. At that instant, Mr. Robinson's (Murray Hamilton) car pulls into the driveway, and Ben bolts from the scene in a panic.

But it's not over yet. For those who are granted this sort of audience with Mrs. Robinson can't easily shake her off. Two days pass, and suddenly

1

2

1 Would you like me to seduce you? Mrs. Robinson (Anne Bancroft) is on the prowl and about to deflower the newly graduated Benjamin Braddock.

2 Too funky: As Benjamin (Dustin Hoffman) builds up his ego he begins to turn his back on the persistent Mrs. R.

3 Hello darkness my old friend: Benjamin is fed up with being an obedient son and rejects the comforts of his existence. But it is only after meeting Mrs. Robinson's daughter, Elaine, that his life really begins to take on meaning.

4 Trying to stay afloat: Even at what should be a relaxing poolside gathering, Benjamin's prospective employers try to drown him with responsibility.

5 A little R & R: Mrs. Robinson wants to lock lips, but poor Benjamin is tongue-tied.

**"Simon & Garfunkel's score fills *The Graduate* with a gloominess and somber quality. 'Sounds of Silence,' 'Scarborough Fair,' and 'Mrs. Robinson' are great songs and while, inside the movie they sound a bit like elevator music, they do add a sort of quiet in an otherwise pungent movie."** *Andrew Chan, Filmwritten Magazine*

Ben is ready to take her up on the offer. He rings his seducer from a secluded hotel room. Two hours later, the deed has been done. It may have been Ben's first time, but from then on not a day goes by without them meeting. In seamless cross-fades, the film deftly fans out the progression of these days as one continuous cycle between hotels and Ben's childhood bedroom; from a firm white bed to a flimsy air mattress. Mrs. Robinson doesn't make many demands of him, but she does make one. Ben is to never meet with her daughter Elaine (Katharine Ross). However, Ben cannot resist temptation, and suffers dire consequences as a result. He embarks on a crusade of love and rebellion, leading to a pathetic stalking and, finally, a spectacularly romanti rescue at the wedding altar. After a comic beginning, Mike Nichols' secon feature climaxes as a melodrama, turning a fresh-faced Dustin Hoffman int an overnight sensation.

The film maps Benjamin Braddock's rite of passage from aimless grac uate to self-sufficient young man. With zoom shots and practically invisibl cross-fades, which elegantly mirror the spirit of the changes in Ben's life, th film masterfully matches content and form. It is in this way that *The Gradu ate* bridges temporal gaps with the greatest of ease, and relays the sense ıc experienced by the characters. Simon and Garfunkel's "Sounds of Si- ce" album emerges as the cinematic ballad that enables Benjamin's mat- ıtion to unfold as a gradual realization of his own feelings and desires. It's ı by chance that watery images appear throughout the film – shots of uariums, the familiar swimming pool as well as the sequence meant to be en from behind a set of diving goggles. These visions are constant re- nders of Benjamin's odyssey, sense of drifting, and need to give direction his life. It is an arduous awakening to adulthood in a fractured, uncertain vironment. Yet we always see light at the end of *The Graduate's* tunnel the form of vibrant imagery and the bright, carefree superficiality of an ut- ly decadent milieu.

SR

4

**ANNE BANCROFT**

When Anne Bancroft made her grand entrance at the hotel room bar, clad in a tiger-striped coat and black tights, she was supposed to be a woman in her mid-forties. Provocatively removing both blouse and bra back at *The Graduate's* hotel room, after teasing herself out of her mile-long hose, she has no difficulty unpeeling the 21-year-old like a ripe banana. Indeed her domineering brass exudes the experienced air of a much older woman. But in truth Anne Bancroft had just turned 36 at the time she was cast as Mrs. Robinson – wife on the prowl. Her severe, angular face, set-off by the silver highlights in her raven hair, a reminder of her trademark chain-smoking, imbued her character with a vampish vitality. Combined with her talent, it made for a virtuoso performance that went on to define eroticism for an entire generation.

Still, the acting range of the woman born Anna Maria Italiano on September 17th, 1931 in New York City can hardly be measured by this role alone. A veteran of the theater, she triumphed in many roles on Broadway including Brecht's Mother Courage. Raised in the Bronx, Bancroft was always a pro at integrating her upbringing into her artistry. In Arthur Penn's *The Miracle Worker* (1961) she lit up the screen as Annie Sullivan, Helen Keller's visually impaired teacher and mentor, and won herself the Best Actress Oscar for breathing life into an uncompromising character. She exhibited her prowess again in David Lynch's *The Elephant Man* (1980), playing a stage diva who voices her admiration for the deformed John Merrick before her theatrical public. It was a cinematic spectacle as unforgettable as her ruthless seduction of Benjamin Braddock.

5

# GO FOR IT, BABY!

## Zur Sache, Schätzchen

1967 - FRG - 80 MIN. - COMEDY, SOCIAL SATIRE

DIRECTOR MAY SPILS (*1941)

SCREENPLAY MAY SPILS, WERNER ENKE, RÜDIGER LEBERECHT DIRECTOR OF PHOTOGRAPHY KLAUS KÖNIG EDITING MAY SPILS, ULRIKE FROEHNER MUSIC KRISTIAN SCHULTZE PRODUCTION PETER SCHAMONI, PETER SCHRÖDER for PETER SCHAMONI FILM.

STARRING WERNER ENKE (Martin), USCHI GLAS (Barbara), HENRY VON LYCK (Henry), INGE MARSCHALL (Anita), HELMUT BRASCH (Block), RAINER BASEDOW (Guard), JOACHIM SCHNEIDER (Policeman), JOHANNES BUZALSKI (Peeping Tom), MARTIN LÜTTGE (Poet in the Elevator), FRITZ SCHUSTER (Beggar), ELISABETH VOLKMANN (House Mother), HORST PASDERSKI (Movie Producer), ERWIN DIETZEL (Zoo Keeper).

## *"It'll all turn out bad in the end."*

Almost without exception, 1960s West German cinema is characterized by the same tired conventions that had gone over so well with audiences in the 50s. Reliable industry standbys were continuing to crank out formulaic literary adaptations. Until 1966 that is, when a new generation calling themselves the New German Filmmakers took the screen by storm and the *Junger Deutscher Film* was born. Not surprisingly, the initial works produced by this group of young pretenders were 180 degrees from anything resembling the crowd pleasers that had come before, but they were far from entertaining to say the least. In fact, it wasn't long before renowned New York film critic Pauline Kael remarked that she'd opt for getting a root canal over going to see a German film.

And then 1968 came along – and there was light. Out of nowhere, a low budget, black and white comedy entitled *Zur Sache, Schätzchen* (*Go for It,*

feature-length film, 26-year-old director May Spils managed to capture th spirit of anarchic spontaneity and anti-establishment youth within a Germa metropolitan setting.

The story is pretty straightforward and follows one day in the life of professional deadbeat named Martin (Werner Enke), who has been wastin away in his bed for days on end. A friend convinces him to come along to public bath, where Martin has difficulty deciding which one of the many ur clad young ladies he wants to put the moves on. Then he happens upo Barbara (Uschi Glas), whom he is soon bent on sweeping off her feet wit a fictitious criminal record. He tells her he is a felon on Germany's mos wanted list, and currently on the run from the police. Barbara, of course, in stantly takes to the alleged public enemy #1 and remains interested eve after he flat out asks her whether she would be capable of financially sup

1 Mom, dad and kid: After a trip to the Munich petting zoo, Martin (Werner Enke) gets Barbara's (Uschi Glas) goat and her heart.

2 Strip search: Even the tiniest suggestion of skin is enough to knock this policeman (Joachim Schneider) off his axis.

3 How do you plan on supporting me? Martin's question says it all. He is a great advocate of women's lib.

**WERNER ENKE**

Born in 1941, the young Werner Enke was denied admission to acting conservatories in both Berlin and Munich. And so he eventually arranged for private instruction. Once enrolled at the University of Munich, he took his French, German Literature and Theater studies somewhat lightly. Nonetheless, he successfully penned several stage plays while still at university, including *Der Bassist* (The Bassist), *Der Trommler* (The Drummer) and *Die Verlobung* (The Engagement). He was an industry outsider when he arrived on the *Junger Deutscher Film* scene. Alongside the love of his life, director May Spils, he cultivated an acting style intended to "drive boredom out of German movie houses." Enke's comedies are shrines to bohemian life in Munich and the actor's flair for language. Memorable titles include the smash hit *Zur Sache Schätzchen* (*Go for It, Baby!*), *Nicht fummeln, Liebling* (*No Pawing, Darling*, 1970), *Hau drauf, Kleiner* (*Let's Get This Show on the Road*, 1974), *Wehe, wenn Schwarzenbeck kommt* (*Woe Follows Schwarzenbeck*, 1979). His glorification of living off the fat of the land ushered in a nationwide lackadaisical resolve among Germany's youth following the country's miraculous economic recovery. In 2003, 36 years after *Zur Sache Schätzchen* debuted to German audiences, Enke transformed the kidnapping aspect of the picture's plot into an animated flipbook appropriately entitled *Es wird böse enden* (i.e. It'll all turn out bad in the end). Enke's words appear to fly out of the mouths of his drawn stick figures, making the volume a grand tribute to the slacker spirit of '68.

4

4 I'm a wanted man: To make himself more intriguing to the ladies, Martin fabricates a criminal record.

5 Hop to it, honey! Barbara is ready to go for the gold.

## "The film's set in Munich, and it's not ashamed to admit it."

*Wim Wenders*

What follows is little more than a loose collection of gags. Policemen et insulted, chicks get hit on (under the pretense of challenging them to a bit f sport, no less), a goat gets stolen from a local zoo, and in the grand slaptick tradition, the movie brazenly ridicules the government, and causes auiences to gasp at the protagonists' sexual indiscretion and their ability to eep a level head. It all has a bohemian flair to it, enhanced by the Munich ackdrop and the city district of Schwabing in particular, a location which vas a haven for art, artists and hedonists.

Much of this picture's astounding success is the result of the intoxicatng manner in which leading actor Werner Enke lets pseudo-philosophical uips fall off his tongue along the lines of "Ich mag es gar nicht gern, wenn ich die Dinge morgens schon so dynamisch entwickeln!" (I don't like it when hings get off to such a rolling start so early in the morning!) In addition, nke's thoroughly original use of German enabled many now commonplace vords, first heard in *Zur Sache, Schätzchen,* to enter into the language – erms like fummeln (to fondle, grope), abschlaffen (pooped, as in tired) etc. In o time flat, this sort of vocabulary antiquated the sort of language that had een used in German film prior to 1968. Today, only a select group of fuddyduddies even remembers the sort of mothball dialog that preceded *Zur Sache, Schätzchen.* Indeed, the picture proved influential enough to warrant the creation of a special category within the framework of the Bundesfilmpreis (German national film award) for its contribution to German language and film, thus making it the first film to be recognized with the honor of Best Dialog. Simultaneously, a new type of protagonist had been unleashed onto German audiences – one that was cool, wry, self-confident, unscrupulous, yet good-natured, witty and handsome. He even boasted the same bowl haircut as the Beatles and the Stones which is now popular again on the Brit Pop scene.

*Zur Sache, Schätzchen,* which ran in Hamburg during 1968/9 for 68 weeks on end, is a perfect example of a cult film. Although the term itself has been overused, it was originally intended to describe a film that physically rubs off on audiences with every viewing and has the power to manifest itself in aspects of their everyday lives. The degree of identification between moviegoer and screen character is so strong that viewers leave the theater convinced that they could have a destiny similar to the people they saw on screen.

RV

1967 - USA - 134 MIN. - CRIME FILM, LITERARY ADAPTATION

DIRECTOR RICHARD BROOKS (1912–1992)
SCREENPLAY RICHARD BROOKS, based on TRUMAN CAPOTE'S "non-fiction novel" of the same name DIRECTOR OF PHOTOGRAPHY CONRAD L. HALL EDITING PETER ZINNER MUSIC QUINCY JONES PRODUCTION RICHARD BROOKS for COLUMBIA PICTURES and PAX ENTERPRISES.

STARRING Robert Blake (Perry Smith), SCOTT WILSON (Dick Hickock), JOHN FORSYTHE (Alwin Dewey), PAUL STEWART (Reporter Jenson), GERALD S. O'LOUGHLIN (Harold Nye), JEFF COREY (Mr. Hickock), CHARLES MCGRAW (Mr. Smith), SAMMY THURMAN (Mrs. Smith), JOHN GALLAUDET (Roy Church), JAMES FLAVIN (Clarence Duntz), JOHN COLLINS (Judge Roland Tate), JOHN MCLIAM (Herbert Clutter), BRENDA CURRIN (Nancy Clutter), RUTH STOREY (Bonnie Clutter), PAUL HOUGH (Kenyon Clutter), SHELDON ALLMAN (Father Jim Post), WILL GEER (Prosecutor).

# *"No witnesses."*

Lights blaze out of the darkness as a Greyhound bus steers straight for the camera on tires that need not screech. The music, gradually building up and imitating the sound of driving, does it for them. Cut to the bus's interior where a young man is seated with his guitar. His face is illuminated by the match he uses to light his cigarette. He extinguishes his flame and the shot in a single breath.

*In Cold Blood* opens with a flash and stealthily proceeds to trap its prey in a fog of eerie cinematic expression, born of its black and white photography and Quincy Jones' dark jazz score. A beast lurking at the crossroads of documentary and film noir, it wastes no time before casting its venomous veil of depression over the viewer.

Kansas, November 1959. Two ex-cons, mild-mannered Perry Smith (Robert Blake) and well-spoken fidget Dick Hickock (Scott Wilson), embark on a 400-mile journey from Olathe to Holcomb in a weathered Chevrolet. Their destination is the Cutter family house, where, as Dick has been told by an old fellow inmate, prosperous farmer Herbert Clutter (John McLiam) keeps a 10,000-dollar nest egg locked up in his safe. The plan is to grab the dough, steer for the Mexican border and never look back. At first Perry isn't convinced they can pull off the heist, but the further they drive, the more the prospects pick up in his mind.

"No witnesses." Dick's words abate Perry's fears and focus him on the task that lies ahead. The pair comb across the dusty prairie of the Great Plains. It is a trip perfectly captured by Conrad L. Hall's photography, which would continue to dazzle audiences 30 years later in *American Beauty* (1999). As the vehicle nears its intended target, the action shifts gear to the Clutter's daily life, and the screen fills with meandering images of Herbert Clutter, a well-off farmer involved in his community, his mentally disturbed wife (Ruth Storey), their 16-year-old daughter Nancy (Brenda Currin) and her adolescent younger brother Kenyon (Paul Hough). Night has fallen by the time Dick and Perry make it to the ranch.

In the blink of an eye, it is morning and the entire Clutter family ha been slaughtered. The Kansas authorities commence an agonizing and frui less investigation, while Dick and Perry dash for Mexico like bats out of he Perry wants to try his hand at digging for gold (a reference to *The Treasure the Sierra Madre,* 1947). The only "treasure" he ends up finding in the dese are empty bottles redeemable for about three cents each.

Foolhardy and penniless, the assassins venture into Nevada, whe they are promptly arrested and charged with the murders. Soon facing death sentence, Perry recounts what actually happened on that cold Noven ber night as snippets of the events jump out on screen. There's the hapha ard search for a safe that doesn't exist and a crime committed for a meas 43 dollars in spare change. As the intruders scramble furiously throug drawers, shelves and anything they can find, the camera flashes to the la moments of a family, bound and gagged. And finally, there's the most bloo curdling scene of the entire nightmare: the realization that it was Perry wh single-handedly murdered them all – one by one.

The contradictions of the characters give the audience an inkling what might have led to this senseless act of ultra violence. We see a patch work of flashbacks from Perry's grim childhood, including scenes of Perry Native American mother who ended her life as an alcoholic prostitute and h erratic father, who took a weapon to his son and drove him out of the hous

*In Cold Blood* distinguishes itself from most other films of the genre that it makes a serious attempt at getting to the bottom of the crime by ste ping into the shoes of its perpetrators. Although there is a strong tradition films that assume the outlaw's perspective in the American cinema, the va majority tend to romanticize their protagonists as glorified social rejects. A such, this screen dramatization of Truman Capote's 1966 "non-fiction nove is miles apart from Arthur Penn's gangster picture, *Bonnie and Clyde* (1967 in which highly stylized characters parade as historical figures.

1 Too much clutter: Dick Hickock (Scott Wilson) only planned on cleaning out a Kansas family's safe, but he got a lot more than he bargained for.

2 Off to the big house: Dick and Perry (Robert Blake) are both sentenced to death as the Clutter family killers. Although Perry assassinated them all single-handed, the findings conclude that he wouldn't have done it without Dick.

3 Violence breeds violence: During the police investigation, Perry tells of the physical abuse endured as a child.

**"Although millions know that the murders really took place, a hefty amount of suspense is generated."** *Variety*

**TRUMAN CAPOTE**

There is a great deal of speculation as to how much of himself masterful novelist Truman Capote (*1924) actually saw in his literary rendition of pint-sized outsider Perry Smith, but that's a whole other story... His 1966 bestseller *In Cold Blood* was heralded as one of the greatest triumphs in American literary history, and marked the advent of a new form of literature Capote termed the "non-fiction novel." The author spent a total of six years researching the piece. His objective was to write a journalistic novel that fused real facts with the immediacy of film, the depth and freedom of prose, and the precision of verse. *In Cold Blood* is one of Capote's many novels to have been adapted for the screen. As recently as 1995, Charles Matthau filmed Capote's story *The Grass Harp*, a reflection on his childhood in the South first printed in 1951. Naturally, the best known of these Hollywood endeavors was Blake Edward's 1961 classic *Breakfast at Tiffany's*, based on Capote's classic novella published in 1958. Audrey Hepburn was cast as party girl protagonist Holly Golightly despite Capote's express wish to see Marilyn Monroe in the role. The novelist first forged a friendship with the illustrious blonde on the set of John Huston's *The Asphalt Jungle* (1950) and went on to write an essay about the woman he called *A Beautiful Child*. While living abroad in Europe, Capote made his first significant contribution to film when he penned the screenplay to John Huston's *Beat the Devil* (1953). By this time the eccentric young writer from New Orleans and recipient of multiple O. Henry awards had already established himself as the favorite son of New York high society. Capote's first novel, *Other Voices, Other Rooms*, in which he openly writes on homosexuality, turned him into a household name overnight. Indeed, the author never attempted to conceal the fact that he was gay. Capote was one of the most captivating personalities of the 1950s and 60s. His unique ability to create an atmosphere of melancholy through language and sharp wit created novels with tremendous insight into the human psyche. His popularity was due largely to the name he made for himself as an eccentric partygoer who liked to live the high life – the boy wonder who let double-edged comments fly while building a career between drinks among the rich and famous. These days of wine and roses came to an abrupt end as he began work on his novel *Answered Prayers*, a piece that went into detail about the private lives of his upper-crust friends. Many of Capote's old pals turned on him, following a 1975 preprint of the novel in *Esquire* magazine. He then retreated to the burgeoning Studio 54 scene, revolving around Andy Warhol and Liza Minelli. *Answered Prayers* was never completed, although an unfinished version was published posthumously in 1986. Drug and alcohol abuse as well as disputes with other authors, including Gore Vidal, finally robbed Capote of his creativity. After almost a decade long absence from writing, Truman Capote died in Los Angeles on August 26th, 1984.

**4** The gears of due process spiraling toward certain death.

**5** No witnesses: Dick's motto for the heist plants a seed within Perry.

Had Richard Brooks cast Paul Newman and Steve McQueen in the leading roles, as suggested by the studio, the end product would have been a noticeably different film. Trusting his better judgment, he decided that lower profile actors Robert Blake and Scott Wilson would more accurately personify the anti-heroism of the Clutter family slayers. Indeed, they superbly capture the men's complex relationship, and the conflicts of their contrary characters that generate such tension and insight into the psychology of violence. Neither could have committed the crime alone, but together they formed a third entity, capable of the unimaginable.

*In Cold Blood* had a hand in shaping late 1960s cinema, in that it set new limits as to what could be shown at the movies. Richard Brooks not only takes a critical look at the social conditions that formed the characters of the murderers, but at the state's criminal justice system as well. It is an uncompromising piece that doesn't miss a beat: From underscoring Perry Smith's death by hanging with the obtrusive sound of a pounding heart, to casting the actual man who disposed of the real life killers to play the on-screen executioner.

KK

# PLAYTIME

## Playtime

1967 - FRANCE - 153/113 MIN. - COMEDY

DIRECTOR JACQUES TATI (1908–1982)
SCREENPLAY JACQUES TATI, JACQUES LAGRANGE, ART BUCHWALD DIRECTOR OF PHOTOGRAPHY JEAN BADAL, ANDRÉAS WINDING
EDITING GÉRARD POLLICAND MUSIC FRANCIS LEMARQUE PRODUCTION BERNARD MAURICE for SPECTA FILMS, JOLLY FILM.

STARRING JACQUES TATI (Monsieur Hulot), BARBARA DENNEK (Young American Woman), GEORGES MONTANT (Giffard), JOHN ABBEY (Lacs), BILLY KEARNS (Schultz), YVES BARSACQ (Hulot's Friend), TONY ANDAL (Page), REINHARD KOLLDEHOFF (German Businessman), MICHEL FRANCINI (Head Waiter), GEORGES FAYE (Architect).

## *"That's really Paris!"*

To most people, Jacques Tati is inseparable from his comic creation, Monsieur Hulot. Undeniably strange and almost completely silent, armed with a hat, pipe, umbrella and raincoat, and with his pants permanently at half-mast, Hulot faces the baffling challenges of everyday life like a latter-day Don Quixote – clumsy, but defiant and unbowed. The windmills he fights are the absurd manifestations of a smugly triumphant technocratic rationalism.

In *Playtime*, Hulot keeps running into a bunch of American tourists on their day trip to Paris. When the movies show Yanks visiting the City of Love, it usually means a predictable contrast between the romantic Old World and the brashly illusion-free New, plus assorted amorous adventures at the Eiffel Tower, the Arc de Triomphe and the Sacré Cœur. In *Playtime*, these celebrated edifices are hardly to be seen. Instead of giving us a guided tour of "the sights," Tati shows us a machine for living, a hypermodern film-Paris made of glass, steel and concrete. In its totalitarian functionalism, it is reminiscent of Le Corbusier's projected cities of the future. The best-loved buildings in this ancient European metropolis are seen only fleetingly as reflections in the skyscrapers' gleaming glass doors.

This cool, airy architecture is the quintessence of transparency and orderly, geometrical form; but Tati wouldn't be Tati if his hero didn't see it as a menacing labyrinth. Endeavoring to keep an appointment in an office build-

1

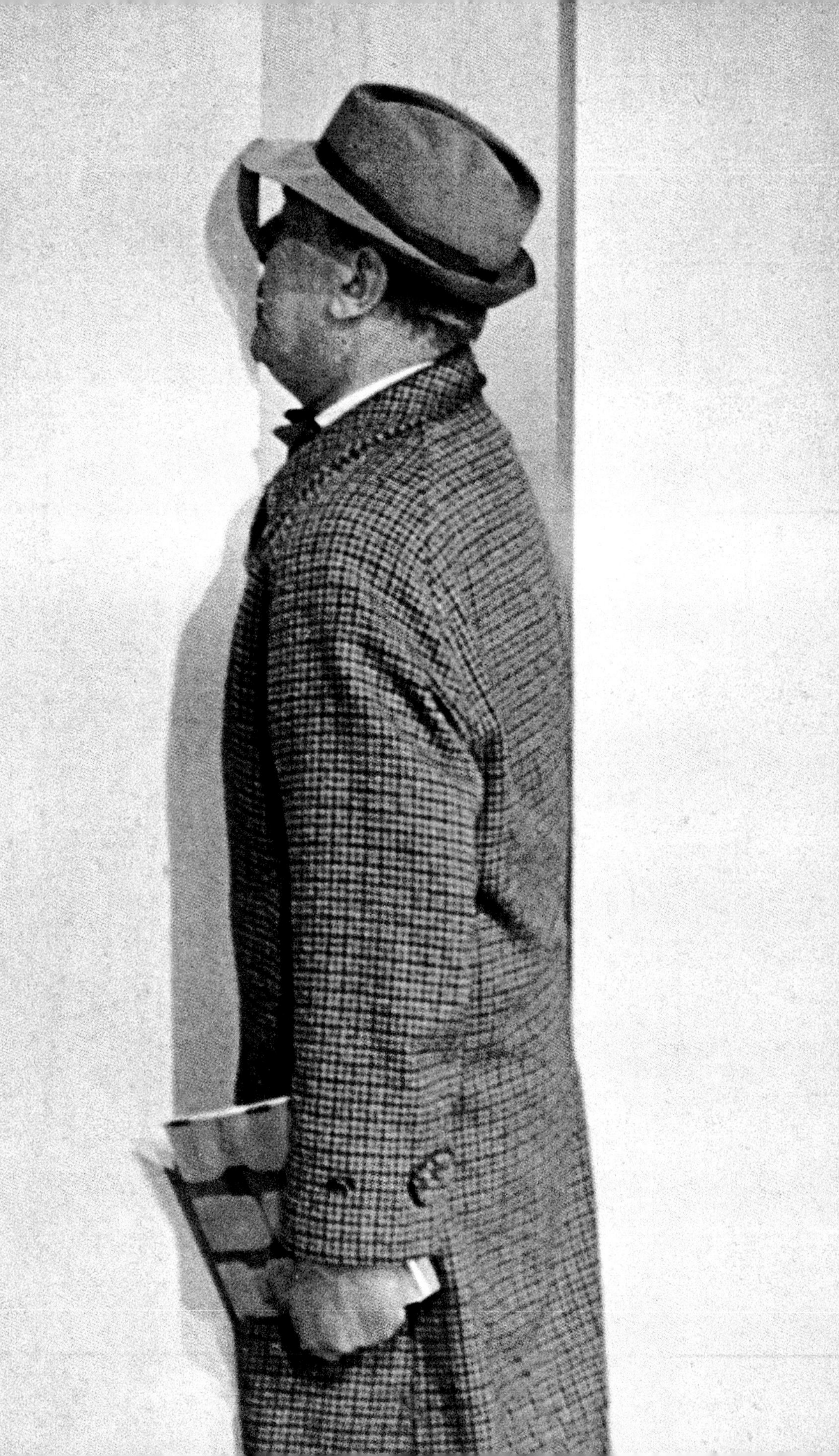

1 Hard pressed for material: In all seriousness, Jacques Tati's (Monsieur Hulot) humor is reminiscent of Keaton and Chaplin.

2 Venue as star: Tativille is very much a character in *Playtime*. It is an oppressive metropolis, responsible for Monsieur Hulot's (Tati) conspicuously passé behavior.

**"Tati's most brilliant film, a bracing reminder in this all-too-lazy era that films can occasionally achieve the status of art."** *The New York Times*

3 To hell with urban planning: Modern-day Paris is enough to make anyone lose their bearings.

4 Invisible walls: Sometimes the key to opening doors is merely finding the handle. The perfect step up for a slapstick extravaganza.

ing, Hulot gets hopelessly lost, as if he were trapped in a baffling hall of mirrors and eventually ends up in a neighboring exhibition center, which looks like a replica of the building he's just left. It's an almost Kafkaesque situation that provides Tati with a treasure-trove of comic ideas, including a designer chair that persistently emits bizarre little farts.

Like no other comedian of the time, Tati stands in the tradition of Charlie Chaplin and Buster Keaton. Like Chaplin, Tati is an unashamedly nostalgic filmmaker, and *Playtime*'s theme naturally provokes comparisons with *City Lights* (1931) and *Modern Times* (1936). As a comedian, however, Tati has more in common with Keaton. His comedy is more "filmic" than Chaplin's, more strongly oriented towards objects, places and physical situations. Nonetheless: in *Playtime*, Tati distances himself more firmly from his film character than Keaton ever did, for the movie's humor is based on observation. This is why Tati keeps the camera at a distance from the people and events it depicts, filming exclusively in sustained long and medium shots.

On both a visual and an auditory level, Tati's extraordinarily precise directing adheres firmly to the principles of parallelism and simultaneity. In order to coordinate sound and image as accurately as possible, he used

**JACQUES TATI (1908–1982)**

As a young man, Jacques Tati was a passionate rugby player, and his comic talent allegedly came to light in the course of a social evening at the club. He subsequently started working in *varieté* shows, where he used his physical fitness to good effect by parodying various sportsmen. Later, he appeared as a supporting actor in several short film comedies. His actual career as the author, director and protagonist of his own films began with *School for Postmen* (*L'Ecole des facteurs*, 1947). Encouraged by the success of this short, he began working on his first full-length feature the same year: *Jour de fête* (1949). In both films, Tati played a postman, and they provided an ideal showcase for his perfect physical control. These movies also offered a foretaste of his major theme, the Americanization of contemporary life. In *Monsieur Hulot's Holidays* (*Les Vacances de Monsieur Hulot*, 1953), he introduced the lanky, pipe-smoking character with whom he would be identified for the rest of his life. Monsieur Hulot is a well-meaning *naif* in constant conflict with the absurdities of modern life. Tati embodied him in three further films: *Mon oncle* (1958), *Playtime* (*Play Time / Tempo di divertimento*, 1967) and *Traffic* (*Trafic / Monsieur Hulot nel caos del traffico*, 1971).
Yet Tati's films have much more to offer than physical comedy and brilliant visual jokes: they are also exceptionally subtle, and display a unique cinematic vision, which Tati stubbornly pursued. In the case of *Playtime*, this attitude led to a financial catastrophe that very nearly put a stop to his career. And so Tati, in a period of filmmaking lasting nearly 30 years, made only five cinema features, one TV production and a few short films. It's the compact oeuvre of a perfectionist who was one of the great individualists of the French movies. The critics of *Cahiers du Cinéma* even placed him in the same rank as Charlie Chaplin and Buster Keaton.

5 The big man and the grand vision: Jacques Tati's view of modern times is what some might term 'a very Kafkaesque experience.'

6 Getting their chuckles: Tati and his characters are often in on the humor of his insane antics.

**"So in these days of pop, madcap, sexy farces as the mainstay of film comedy, Tati maintains a fresh, innocent and human observation of man coping with the new environment."** *Variety*

high-definition 70mm film material with six separate sound tracks. As the immense costs incurred thereby could never have been recouped at the box office, *Playtime* was almost always shown in a severely shortened 35 mm version – a situation that continued for more than 30 years. Yet the efforts expended on the film technology were no mere extravagance on Tati's part; they enabled him not only to place countless visual details in the frame simultaneously, but also to create a carefully-composed cacophony of words and sounds. Only fragments of conversation are discernible; the rest is swallowed up by random noise, ringing tones, electronic bleeps and slamming doors. *Playtime* is neither a silent film nor a talkie: it's a *noise film*. And this is why it will only be fully appreciated by those who can really listen as well as look.

Nonetheless, even perfect hearing and 20:20 vision are no guarantee that spectators will work out exactly what's going on in Tati's brilliantly choreographed chaos. We have as much trouble as Hulot identifying these faceless and sterile locations. Thus what appears to be a hospital turns out to be an airport terminal, and an open-plan office is barely distinguishable from an exhibition center or a department store. Tati's modern city is a place for insiders only – and it's only a seeming paradox that the U.S. tourists are more at home here than Hulot, for the Paris depicted in the film is an American metropolis *par excellence.*

For all that, Tati is clearly neither a cynic nor an anti-American. In one fabulous episode, a supermodern gourmet restaurant is opened before building work has been completed. The owners and employees are forced to improvise, with increasing desperation. As the situation threatens to degenerate into a debacle, the French and American guests team up, take over the restaurant and celebrate an orgiastic party that almost makes the restaurant explode. Ultimately, Tati seems to be suggesting, humanity itself has the power to escape the smothering restrictions of modern times – if it so chooses.

JH

# THE FIREMEN'S BALL

## Horí, má panenko

1967 - CZECHOSLOVAKIA / ITALY - 71 MIN. - COMEDY, SOCIAL SATIRE

DIRECTOR MILOŠ FORMAN (*1932)

SCREENPLAY MILOŠ FORMAN, JAROSLAV PAPOUSEK, IVAN PASSER DIRECTOR OF PHOTOGRAPHY MIROSLAV ONDRÍCEK EDITING MIROSLAV HÁJEK MUSIC KAREL MARES PRODUCTION RUDOLF HÁJEK, CARLO PONTI for CARLO PONTI CINEMATOGRAFICA, FILMOVÉ STUDIO BARRANDOV.

STARRING JAN VOSTRCIL (Head of Committee), JAN STÖCKL (Retired Fire Chief, Honorary Head of Committee), JOSEF KOLB (Josef), FRANTISEK SVET (Old Man), FRANTISEK DEBELKA (Committee Member), JOSEF SEBANEK (Committee Member), JOSEF VALNOHA (Committee Member), VRATISLAV CERMÁK (Committee Member), JOSEF REHOREK (Committee Member), MARIE JEZKOVÁ (Josef's Wife).

## *"Legs! Give me legs!"*

When human despair meets bureaucratic incompetence, all hell is bound to break loose. This dim assessment is the touchstone of Miloš Forman's final Czechoslovakian film, whose biting satire is brilliantly summed up in a single scene: the house next door to the fire station goes up in smoke during the firemen's ball; the drunken firefighters only manage to arrive at the blaze when there is practically nothing left to salvage, their truck gets stuck in the snow, and the assembled villagers are at loss to do anything except make weak attempts at consoling the house's elderly former occupant (Frantisek Svet) – a man now robbed of all he ever had. To spare him the horrific vision, the old man is sat down on a chair turned away from the inferno. However, as the night goes on and the old man gets cold, the villagers move him back to the fire for a bit of extra warmth.

This farcical socialist approach to problem-solving dominates the action of *The Firemen's Ball* from the moment the film begins. The ball itself is supposed to mark a joyous occasion for all, commemorating the life-long service of the fire brigade's elderly, honorary committee head (Jan Stöckl). But whenever the deeply touched guest of honor tries to make his way to the podium, another event on the itinerary overshadows him. Such is the case when an already haphazard amateur beauty pageant turns into a disgraceful display of nonsense – the judging committee proving itself entirely incapable

1

2

1 Not without my daughter: Who will be crowned Miss Czechoslovakia?

2 Wallflower: Some party poopers can't get excited over an ordinance for fun.

3 The heat is on: The enthusiasm of some contestants makes the judges regret not having included a swimsuit competition.

4 Fighting fire with fire: These men are passionate about their job and ready to celebrate.

**"Milos Forman's *The Firemen's Ball* was banned 'permanently and forever' by the communist regime in Czechoslovakia in 1968, as Soviet troops marched in to suppress a popular uprising. It was said to be a veiled attack on the Soviet system and its bureaucracy, a charge Forman prudently denied at the time but now happily agrees with. Telling a seductively mild and humorous story about a retirement fete for an elderly fireman, the movie pokes fun at citizens' committees, the culture of thievery, and solutions that surrender to problems."** *Chicago Sun-Times*

**CZECHOSLOVAKIAN NOUVELLE VAGUE**

The Czechoslovakian *nouvelle vague* was part of a Pan-European cinematic renaissance that included the French *nouvelle vague*, the British Free Cinema and New German Film. All these movements sought to break with established ways of making movies and strove for authenticity. What set this particular branch of the movement apart from the others was its criticism of the Socialist state and the pressure to produce party-line art. The political slack Czechoslovakia experienced in the early 1960s facilitated the movement that produced directors like Miloš Forman, Jirí Menzel, Vojtech Jasny, Ján Kadár, Vera Chytilová, Jan Nemec and Zdenek Mlyná, who quickly came to the attention of Western cineastes. Kadár's *The Shop on Main Street* (*Obchod na korze*, 1965) and Menzel's *Closely Watched Trains* (*Ostre sledované vlaky*, 1966) both won the Oscar for Best Non-English Language Film. These pictures often dealt with non-political, routine farces, featuring an anti-hero driven to despair by the mundane boredom of his rural surroundings. Forman's *The Loves of a Blonde* (*Lásky jedné plavovlásky*, 1965), which largely inspired *The Firemen's Ball* (*Horí, má panenko*, 1967), is an exemplary piece. The authorities condemned these films as attacks on the working class and branded their offbeat humor as "sadistic." The abrupt end of the Prague Spring in the summer of 1968 sealed the coffin of the cinematic movement. Jaromil Jires' film adaptation of Milan Kundera's novel *The Joke* (*Zert*, 1968) was quickly banned, and older films were blacklisted. Instead, the government began to sponsor the Czech dubbing of Soviet features.

5 Sleeping under the stars: A old man calls it a night after the fire department ignores his call for help.

6 Burn baby burn: The festivities are underway as partygoers get down and dirty on the dance floor in eager anticipation of the raffle to come.

7 Best in show: The finalists line up for one last evaluation.

of coaxing the less than enchanting contestants into taking the stage. Similarly, what is intended to be a thrilling raffle ends in befuddlement as the coveted prizes disappear one after the other. Following countless botch-ups and attempts to smooth things over, the guest of honor is finally presented with his award. The esteemed gentleman gives a thank you speech that bestows unwarranted splendor on the dubious event. He opens the box supposedly containing a gold plated axe only to discover it empty. Even the honorable emblem of his profession has been stolen. He closes the box and casts a pitying glance at his colleagues.

*The Firemen's Ball*, a comic study just eleven minutes longer than the average college lecture, supplied Forman with his ticket to Hollywood. A lucky break for the director, for his career would certainly have taken a turn for the worse had he remained in his homeland. Just a year later, Soviet tanks bulldozed the Prague Spring and Forman's film was banned along with numerous others. There was little denying that the piece was a satire on provincial pettiness and the ineptitude of the Socialist regime. Still, to view this jewel of the Czech *nouvelle vague* as a mere political statement would do it a great injustice. The boisterous hullabaloo dominating the ball's festivities is a delight for the senses. The unhinged camera, anarchic Keystone Cops style slapstick and the over-the-top facial expressions of the amateur actors make for a fascinating visual spectacle. The committee members bolt to the top of the balustrade to drool over the dancing women's gaping cleavages, only to promptly develop a hunger for legs that has them racing back down again towards the dance floor. Meanwhile, a distraught watchman goes off in search of a stolen frankfurter, only to be unmasked as the culprit. Forman milks scenes like this for all they're worth to paint a scathing portrait of Czechoslovakia's common folk. Italian co-producer Carlo Ponti did his best to convince the director to hire more attractive actresses, but his efforts were in vain. Forman's subtle, thoroughly affectionate humor escaped everyone – both in the East and West.

According to Forman, it is not individuals, but the world in which they live that is evil and corrupt. This is as true for the elderly man who is encouraged to warm himself by the flames of his burning house as it is for the fire brigade, who are as overwhelmed by the prospect of organizing a little fun and games as they are by the demands of their profession.

Years later, the director was finally able to admit that the film had indeed been meant as an allegory of life under the Socialist regime, a fact which had apparently eluded some viewers. Just before he emigrated to the United States, Forman was forced to make a formal apology to all Czechoslovakia's deeply insulted firefighters.

# DANCE OF THE VAMPIRES

1967 - USA - 108 MIN. - VAMPIRE FILM, SPOOF

DIRECTOR ROMAN POLANSKI (*1933)

SCREENPLAY GÉRARD BRACH, ROMAN POLANSKI DIRECTOR OF PHOTOGRAPHY DOUGLAS SLOCOMBE EDITING ALASTAIR MCINTYRE MUSIC KRZYSZTOF KOMEDA PRODUCTION GENE GUTOWSKI for CADRE FILMS, FILMWAYS PICTURES, MGM.

STARRING JACK MACGOWRAN (Professor Abronsius), ROMAN POLANSKI (Alfred, his Assistant), ALFIE BASS (Shagal), JESSIE ROBINS (Rebecca Shagal), SHARON TATE (Sarah Shagal), FERDY MAYNE (Count von Krolock), IAIN QUARRIER (Herbert von Krolock), TERRY DOWNES (Koukol, the Servant), FIONA LEWIS (Magda, the Maid), RONALD LACEY (Village Idiot).

## *"There we were, gathered together, gloomy and despondent, around a single meager woodcutter."*

When he saw Polanski's final cut of *Dance of the Vampires*, the Executive Producer, Martin Ransohoff of MGM, left the director in no doubt that he'd actually been expecting a very different film. Polanski stood his ground, and eventually a compromise was reached: the original version was shown only in Britain, while the "official" edition was released everywhere else. The film ultimately seen by most of the world's moviegoers had been shortened by more than 15 minutes, given a new and tediously "zany" name (as well as a kitschy titles sequence), and the wonderful Slavic, German and Yiddish accents had been dubbed out of existence.

Much of the film's subtle wit disappeared without a trace. German moviegoers, for example, cannot have made head or tail of the scene in which the vampire Shagal (Alfie Bass) smiles in pity when one of his victims tries to drive him away with a crucifix. In the German version, Shagal comes out with the feeble and virtually meaningless riposte: "That only works with *old* vampires..." In the original, he replies, with a strong Yiddish accent: "Boy, have you got the wrong vampire..." The entire joke depends on the fact that Shagal is Jewish, and without such nuances and subtleties, the film is nothing.

1

1 Snow-white and the seventh dwarf: Sweet, dopey Alfred (Roman Polanski) is ready to dance on hot coals and ward off cold fangs for the woman he adores, the lovely Sarah (Sharon Tate). Their on-screen romance preceded real life wedding bells.

2 Bathing beauty: Count Dracula takes a blood bath with his new toy ducky.

3 Once bitten, twice shy: Alfred the apprentice vampire hunter rescues Sarah from the clutches of doom – just a little too late.

The original *Dance of the Vampires* is a clever and funny raid on the ossified conventions of the Dracula genre, in which the familiar gestures, poses and symbols are submitted to a thoroughgoing revision. The result is grotesque but stylistically assured. Polanski cites countless old movies, historical events and works of art. The Lord of the Vampires (Ferdy Mayne) is called "Count von Krolock" – a veiled allusion to Count Orlok, the aristocratic bloodsucker in Friedrich Wilhelm Murnau's *Nosferatu* (*Nosferatu – Eine Symphonie des Grauens*, 1921); and when Professor Ambronsius (Jack MacGowran) and his assistant Alfred (Roman Polanski) lurch through the snow Carpathian landscapes in their horse-drawn sleigh, it's a clear reference t Count Orlok's sinister horse and carriage in the Murnau movie.

This scene is deeply and ambiguously comic, while still retaining a whi of true horror. The landscape, the light, the camerawork and the compositio all contribute to the bizarre atmosphere. It's one of the unquestionabl achievements of this film to have so confidently combined the sublime wit the ridiculous. The rationalist vampire hunter Professor Abronsius is a scatt

**SHARON TATE**

Her life was short, but filled with success from an early age. She was Homecoming Queen and Senior Prom Queen at her school, before going on to win a number of "real" beauty contests. Sharon Marie Tate (1943–69) was the daughter of a professional soldier. At the age of 16, she and her family spent a year in Italy, where the director Martin Ritt discovered her for the movies. When the Tates moved back to Los Angeles, Sharon took lessons in singing, dancing and acting. After appearing in the TV series *The Beverly Hillbillies* (1963–65), she made her breakthrough in *Dance of the Vampires*, a.k.a. *The Fearless Vampire Killers or: Pardon Me, But Your Teeth Are in My Neck* (1967), a movie directed by her future husband Roman Polanski. She was only 24 at the time, and she seemed destined to enjoy a dazzling future.

In Polanski's next major Hollywood production *Rosemary's Baby* (1968), she only had a small supporting role; but shortly thereafter, she played the lead in *Una su tredici* (1969), directed by Nicolas Gessner and Luciano Lucignani. The film boasted a star cast, and it was a major boost to Sharon Tate's career. Then she became pregnant. On the evening of August 9th 1969, she was at home with four guests in her villa in Bel Air, when a group of young people in thrall to Charles Manson broke into the house and slaughtered them all in a fit of bloodlust. Sharon Tate was 26 years old and seven months pregnant at the time.

Charles Manson himself said that he'd been on "a magical mystery tour." Much has been written about this collective ritual murder, a real-life horror story worse than anything ever conceived for the movies. In total, the Manson gang committed at least 9 murders. By killing white people and watching the blame fall on blacks, Manson and his followers had hoped to unleash a race war as a prelude to a ghastly revolution. His name for this hoped-for apocalypse was "Helter Skelter," for the guru had developed his theories after "deciphering the secret messages" on the Beatles' *White Album*...

*Dance of the Vampires* had a long and troubled genesis. Finished now or well over a year, it has been shown in America and France with great success. However, the same film was not shown in both countries... There does, in fact, seem to be considerable difference between the two versions: Ransohoff cut about twenty-five minutes from the film, re-dubbed the principal actors (Jack MacGowran and Polanski himself), added a cartoon sequence at the beginning, and changed the title."

*Guardian Weekly*

3

4

5

4 Shadow-selves: The undead are inconspicuous when faced with mirrors, but almost absurd as they creep behind their dead.

5 Drive a stake through my heart: It's just a matter of time before the fear of God will overpower Alfred and have him heading for the hills.

6 Immune to Christian hocus pocus: The innkeeper Shagal (Alfie Bass) is the world's first Jewish vampire and by no means afraid of the cross.

7 Pink fang: Count Dracula's gay son (Iain Quarrier) knows how love can bite.

8 Feed the wolves to him! Koukol, the count's manservant (Terry Downes), is willing to put a little light on the subject of vampire slaying if you give him a furry treat. His character is a mishmash of Caliban, Quasimodo, and Hannibal Lecter.

**"Polanski, a virtuoso of subtle horror, has risked a perilous balancing act and brought it off triumphantly. He manages to parody an entire film genre, while delivering a brilliant contribution to that very genre, wooing its aficionados one moment and taking the mickey out of them the next. Far from respectfully aestheticizing this age-old myth, Polanski mercilessly deconstructs it."** *Die Welt*

6

7

vin brother of Albert Einstein. Like the world's favorite genius, he too lets his ngue hang out occasionally; for example, when he gets stuck half-in and alf-out of the window of a crypt. By the time he's gotten himself into this fine ness, his faith in science is also halfway out the window, even though he and is assistant are closer than ever before to reaching their goal; for the blue-looded vampires, "His Excellency" and his homosexual son, are fast asleep their coffins, practically crying out for the traditional wooden stake. Sadly, ne cowed yet truculent Alfred – delightfully played by Roman Polanski him-elf – just doesn't have the guts to strike the deadly blow.

As in every Dracula movie, there's also a virgin waiting to be saved: this me, it's Sarah (Sharon Tate), the daughter of Shagal. The Count drops in on er in the bathroom, pecks her neck and spirits her away to his castle. *Chez* Krolock, the cobwebs hang as thick as chewing gum, and the main hall i lined with Goyaesque portraits of his grotesquely ugly ancestors. Suddenly these desiccated forebears emerge from their graves and make their way t the vast, baroque ballroom, where Orlock is about to hold a bloody banque for the people of his realm. After assorted slapstick escapades, the two vam pire hunters succeed in snatching the kidnapped maiden, and all three mak good their escape. Sarah rests peacefully in Alfred's arms as the sledg speeds away in the moonlit night. All's well that ends well, apparently; bu Polanski has reserved his biggest shock for the very end: abruptly, and quit hideously, the beautiful virgin grows a set of fangs. The kindly Professor i secure in the faith that he's defeated the forces of evil, even as he carries th infection to an unsuspecting outside world.

SP

# IN THE HEAT OF THE NIGHT

1967 - USA - 110 MIN. - POLICE THRILLER

DIRECTOR NORMAN JEWISON (*1926)
SCREENPLAY STIRLING SILLIPHANT, based on the novel of the same name by JOHN BALL DIRECTOR OF PHOTOGRAPHY HASKELL WEXLER EDITING HAL ASHBY MUSIC QUINCY JONES PRODUCTION WALTER MIRISCH for THE MIRISCH CORPORATION.

STARRING SIDNEY POITIER (Virgil Tibbs), ROD STEIGER (Sheriff Bill Gillespie), WARREN OATES (Sam Wood), LEE GRANT (Leslie Colbert), JAMES PATTERSON (Purdy), QUENTIN DEAN (Delores Purdy), WILLIAM SCHALLERT (Mayor Schubert), ANTHONY JAMES (Ralph Henshaw), SCOTT WILSON (Harvey Oberst), LARRY GATES (Eric Endicott), MATT CLARK (Packy Harrison), BEAH RICHARDS (Mrs. Bellamy).

ACADEMY AWARDS 1967 OSCARS for BEST PICTURE (Walter Mirisch), BEST ACTOR (Rod Steiger), BEST ADAPTED SCREENPLAY (Stirling Silliphant), BEST EDITING (Hal Ashby), and BEST SOUND (Samuel Goldwyn Studio Sound Department).

## *"I try to run a nice, clean safe town here."*

Most passengers entering town by train don't even register the cynical wooden sign on the gate: "You are now entering the town of Sparta, Mississippi. Welcome!"

Virgil Tibbs (Sidney Poitier), on the other hand, can't miss it. Coming home to the Deep South, he knows all too well that not everyone is "welcome" here. Sparta itself is just a place to change trains, or so he thinks as he disembarks onto the platform. However, before he can even stop to smell the night air, he's looking right down the barrel of uniformed policeman Sam Wood's (Warren Oates) cocked bit of standard issue. It seems that just moments prior to Tibbs' arrival, industrial giant Philip Colbert was found murdered, leaving Sparta's hope for economic betterment dead alongside him. As an unfamiliar face, Tibbs looks suspicious to Woods for three simple reasons: he's black, he's black and then he's black. That aside, he is well dressed and carrying a large sum of money.

Sheriff Bill Gillespie (Rod Steiger), Wood's superior, shares his deputy's sentiments and doesn't spend a lot of time beating around the bush with his suspect. But it is the sheriff who gets a rude awakening when he asks the cool and collected Tibbs how he pulled off the crime. For rather than giving Gillespie a confession, he identifies himself as the Philadelphia chief of police. Given the circumstances, Gillespie doesn't feel an apology is called for; after all, this is the South. Tibbs doesn't expect one either. He just wants to catch the next train out of town. That proves impossible when he receives official orders to assist the sheriff in apprehending the perpetrators. Tibbs reluctantly concedes, knowing all too well that the job will entail a constant battle against arrogance, ignorance and deep-seated racism.

Nonetheless, despitel the incompetence, the sheriff tries to mask with his tough guy attitude, he acknowledges Tibbs' overwhelming expertise in the field. In fact, on numerous occasions it is Tibbs who bails Gillespie out of potential disasters. Although the two lawmen don't exactly become the best of friends, they part ways having earned each other's respect.

As the title of John Ball's novel implies, this southern community's vices come alive in the heat of its sweltering nights. It's no surprise that gruff, gum chewing Gillespie suffers from chronic insomnia and needs a bottle of liquor to get through the otherwise intolerable small hours. Indeed, the overbearing

1 They call me Mr. Tibbs: Northern lawman Virgil Tibbs (Sidney Poitier) gets stuck in the molasses of a Mississippi murder and is forced to fight bigotry as well as crime.

2 Deliverance: After Tibbs informs Mrs. Colbert (Lee Grant) of her husband's death, she insists that he handles the homicide investigation personally and brings the perpetrator to justice.

3 Dizzy Gillespie: Steiger plays Poitier's counterpart, a ruffian whose small-mindedness has colored his take on law enforcement.

**"A film that is as fresh as this one deserves to be seen by fresh eyes and savored by fresh minds."** *Newsweek*

darkness influences the behavior of the film's supporting characters as well: deputy Sam Wood sticks his neck through unassuming windows, catching a glimpse of misguided Delores Purdy (Quentin Dean), who is only too willing to show off her physical assets. Her brother (James Patterson) displays subversive behavior by moonlight too, only it takes a more violent form: he's the leader of a racist organization bent on driving Tibbs out of town.

Most of the scenes take place at night in a darkness broken by neon signs and street lamps. Director Norman Jewison and cinematographer Haskell Wexler do an exquisite job of capturing the town's oppressive atmosphere for the screen. The nocturnal camera work makes the on-screen light of day practically blinding. Such is the case when the film depicts black laborers agonizing in the cotton fields to bring in the harvest. It is an image that eats at Tibbs as he drives past with Gillespie, who is at a loss to do anything but make wisecracks.

All land as far as the eye can see is the property of Eric Endicott (Larry Gates), an old-school southern gentleman. Not surprisingly, Endicott lives in a stately plantation house maintained by an entirely black staff. As he proudly shows Tibbs his homegrown orchids, he can't resist letting a few off-color comments roll off his tongue. When the lawman questions him about the murder, however, Endicott answers Tibbs with a punch in the face. Endicott is at a loss when Tibbs unexpectedly responds in turn. All the land baron manages to stammer is that there was a time when Tibbs would have been lynched for such impertinence. In the original version of the script, Tibbs walked away in silence after taking the blow, but Poitier insisted on changing it to let his character retaliate.

It is scenes like this and the way racial tension is depicted in this picture that made it so riveting at the time of its release. Jewison demonstrates an incredible degree of finesse and brilliance in his treatment of such a sen-

SPD
SPARTA
POLICE

**"Jewison has not only kept the detective and racial elements running smoothly together without allowing the one to swamp the other; he has also guided two outstandingly ebullient actors in unusually disciplined and effective performances."** *Monthly Film Bulletin*

4 Southern comfort: This small town Lolita (Quentin Dean as Delores Purdy) steams up hot summer nights in the arms of kind strangers.

5 Something to shake a stick at: Tibbs steps up to the plate at an abandoned factory and combats racism. The sign above his head reads – "Let us ALL be alert."

6 Barring anger and retaining composure: Virgil Tibbs is certain of Harvey Oberst's (Scott Wilson) innocence and begins to establish a rapport with the prisoner.

**RAY CHARLES**

American music legend Ray Charles (*1930) breathed his smoky magic into the theme song of Norman Jewison's *In the Heat of the Night.* Despite losing his sense of sight at age seven, Charles' acoustic aptitude enabled him to dazzle popular music in the 50s and 60s with hits like "What'd I Say," "Hallelujah, I Love Her So" and "I Can't Stop Loving You." The singer, songwriter and musician broke new artistic ground, creating pieces that combined jazz, soul and gospel elements. He eventually added country & western to his repertoire, even landing a top hit in the charts.
Charles is also no stranger to film, having worked as both a musician and actor for Hollywood. In 1964, he played the leading role in Paul Henreid's musical melodrama *Ballad in Blue* a.k.a. *Blues For Lovers.* His resume also includes numerous guest and cameo appearances in movies such as *The Blues Brothers* (1980). Not one to take himself too seriously, Charles' big and small screen performances often show him mocking his own blindness. Such was the case when Charles played a bus driver in *Spy Hard* (1996). In fact, Charles has some experience behind the wheel, driving for a car commercial on the deserted roads around Death Valley.

sitive American issue, and is backed by an exceptional ensemble cast. At no time do the movie's moral doctrines overshadow the mystery at hand and yet they always dominate its undercurrent.

Not only did the picture triumph at the box office, it also inspired two further, though somewhat tamer, big-screen installments including *They Call Me Mister Tibbs* (1969) and *The Organization* (1971). Some twenty years after its original debut, the story found its way to the small screen as a TV series starring Howard E. Rollins and Carroll O'Connor.

There is only one thing that puts a damper on an otherwise immaculate success story. While Rod Steiger was praised with Oscar laurels for his outstanding performance, co-star and protagonist Sidney Poitier wasn't even acknowledged with a nomination. HK

# 2001: A SPACE ODYSSEY

1968 - GREAT BRITAIN - 141 MIN. (ORIGINAL VERSION 160 MIN.) - SCIENCE FICTION

DIRECTOR STANLEY KUBRICK (1928–1999)
SCREENPLAY STANLEY KUBRICK, ARTHUR C. CLARKE, based on a short story by Arthur C. Clarke
DIRECTOR OF PHOTOGRAPHY GEOFFREY UNSWORTH, JOHN ALCOTT (additional shots) EDITING RAY LOVEJOY MUSIC ARAM KHACHATURYAN, RICHARD STRAUSS, JOHANN STRAUSS, GYÖRGY LIGETI PRODUCTION STANLEY KUBRICK for POLARIS, HAWK, MGM.

STARRING KEIR DULLEA (David Bowman), GARY LOCKWOOD (Frank Poole), WILLIAM SYLVESTER (Dr. Heywood Floyd), LEONARD ROSSITER (Smyslov), DANIEL RICHTER (Moonwatcher) ROBERT BEATTY (Halvorsen), FRANK MILLER (Mission Controller), MARGARET TYZACK (Elena), SEAN SULLIVAN (Michaels), BILL WESTON (Astronaut).

ACADEMY AWARDS 1968 OSCAR for BEST SPECIAL EFFECTS (Stanley Kubrick).

## *"What are you doing, Dave?"*

A gate of light opens and swallows up the space capsule with its pilot Dave Bowman (Keir Dullea). He flies through a corridor of light: rays, flecks, waves and nets of luminosity, constantly dissolving and reforming into new patterns and shapes. He flies over crevices riddled with burning rivers, through shimmering mists, over glittering oceans. His mouth opens in a silent scream. His staring eye reflects a fireworks display of exploding colors. He sees what no one has ever seen. And suddenly, the journey ends, in a white room sparingly furnished with antiques. The astronaut looks out from his capsule: he sees a man in a space-suit – himself, several years older; he discovers an old man eating at a table – himself again; he throws a glass to the floor, where it breaks, and he glimpses a decrepit bedridden figure – himself. At the end of the bed stands the black monolith that has led him here, beyond Jupiter. And now there's an embryo in the bed. Reborn as a star-child, he floats through space towards the earth in an amniotic sac.

The final sequence of *2001: A Space Odyssey* is a cinematic wonder, a baffling and visually overwhelming passage to another dimension where space and time are meaningless. The famous psychedelic trip through the corridor of light, made even more marvelous by the music of György Ligeti, is the crowning glory of Stanley Kubrick's masterpiece. Moreover, this virtuoso piece of special effects, a team effort, was created entirely without computers, using only models and light. There is still nothing to match this film in its quest for authenticity and sheer visionary power. It's a monolith of the science-fiction genre, and all questions about its meaning rebound off its smooth black surface.

In three separate episodes, Kubrick describes the emergence of new forms of existence: the development from ape to man; the leap from artificial intelligence to real, emotional life; and the transition from our own dimension to something entirely strange. The witness to these changes – and perhaps their cause – is a black monolith from God-knows-where. One day it's simply there, standing in the savannah amidst a horde of apes. In the shade of this monolith, one of the apes abruptly understands that a bone can be used as a weapon. The apes kill other animals and start eating meat, and their technological superiority enables them to defeat a rival horde. It's the first stage in the conquest of nature, and the birth of humankind. Several evolutionary stages later, an American scientist is traveling to the moon on a secret mission. Beneath the surface of the earth's satellite, a black monolith has been discovered, and the mysterious object is transmitting a powerful signal in the direction of Jupiter. Scientists are in no doubt: the monolith is four million years old, and it was buried deliberately.

The spaceship "Discovery" on the way to the moon. Only the computer HAL knows the true reason for the journey – the search for extraterrestrial life. Three of the crewmembers are in hibernation while two others take care

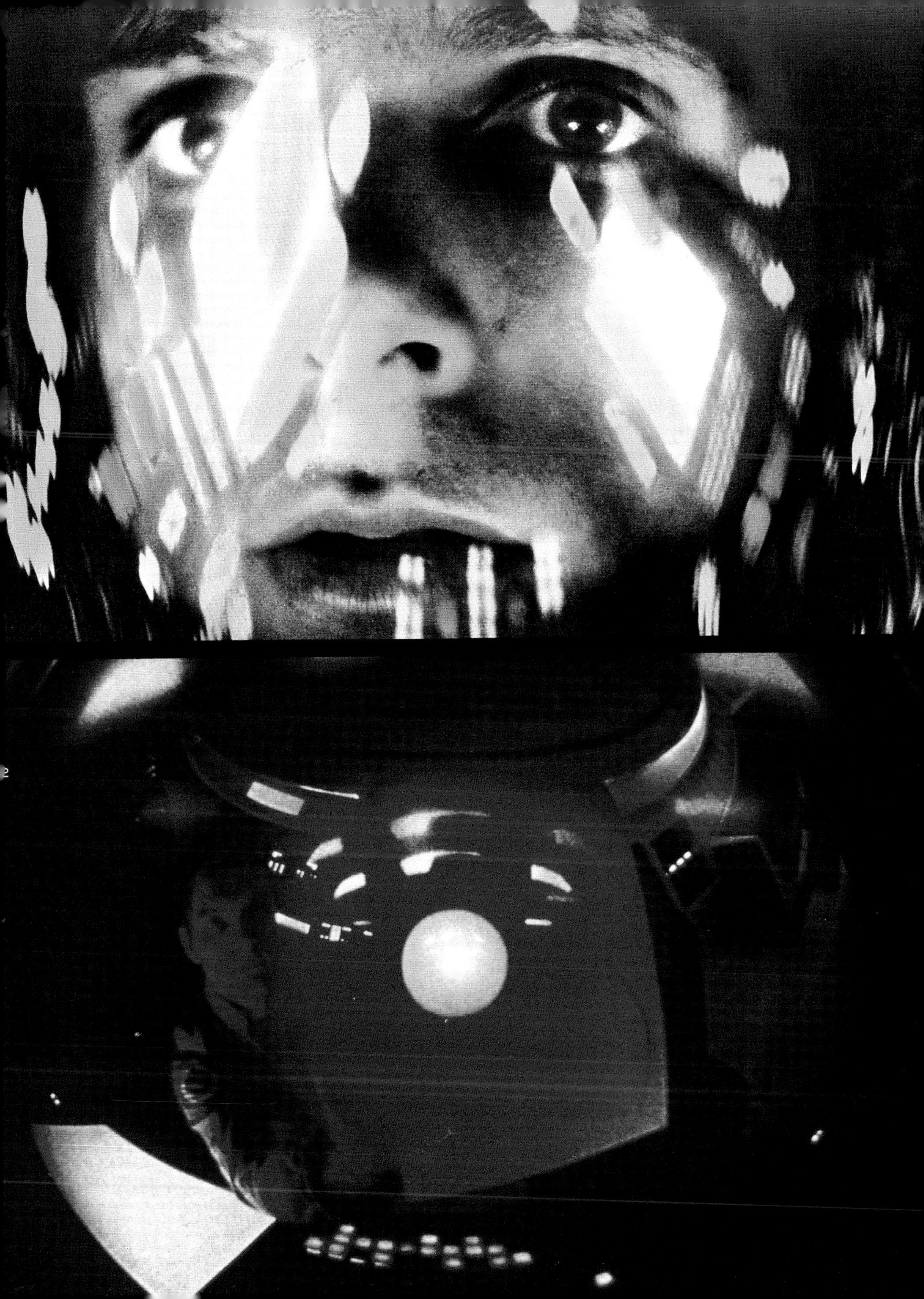

3

1 Space – the final frontier: Special effects designer Douglas Trumbull helped blast *2001* into cinematic history. Within just a few light years later, he gathered speed and took the helm of *Silent Running* (1972).

2 "Good afternoon, gentlemen. I am a Hal 9000 computer. I became operational at the H-A-L lab in Urbana, Illinois on the twelfth of January, 1992. I am completely operational and all my circuits are functioning perfectly." Although film co-writer Arthur C. Clarke insisted that HAL stood for Heuristic Algorithmic Computer, there's no denying that if all three letters were shifted a notch, you'd get IBM.

**"I tried to create a visual experience, one that bypasses verbalized pigeonholing and directly penetrates the subconscious with an emotional and philosophical content."** *Stanley Kubrick*

4

Small sacrifices: Mama Hal is ready to sever the umbilical cord if need be. Meaning that astronaut Frank Poole (Gary Lockwood) had better gain independence fast if he intends to survive.

4 It can only be attributable to human error: Keir Dullea as astronaut David Bowman, the last human member of the Jupiter mission crew.

5 I can see you're really upset about this. I honestly think you ought to sit down calmly, take a stress pill and think things over: An ape (Dan Richter with a flawless makeup job) takes one bold step for his kind and discovers the benefits of organized violence.

f the flight. HAL, the most complex electronic brain ever constructed, makes n error, and the men consider switching it off; but the machine starts fighting or its life, and kills the crew. Only Bowman manages to escape, and he succeeds in shutting down the computer. Outside the spacecraft, a black monolith is floating. Bowman boards a space capsule and follows it to Jupiter…

The film doesn't make things easy for the spectator. It follows no conventional narrative pattern, it makes enormous leaps in time and space, and the figures in it are mere functions rather than characters. Technically and formally perfect, *2001: A Space Odyssey* offers us nothing and nobody we can identify with. It is a cool and somewhat forbidding film. Only around one quarter of its 160 minutes are taken up with dialogue: Kubrick lets his pictures do the talking.

*2001* wasn't just an incredible enrichment of the science fiction genre, but also changed the way we look at the universe. The dazzling sun, its rays

5

6

7

6 The dark side of the moon: An artifact whose "origin and purpose is still a total mystery," is discovered on the earth's sleeping satellite.

7 Pulling the plug: Just what do you think you're doing? Poole and Bowman revolt against technology.

8 No need to reinvent the wheel: Although Stanley Kubrik originally commissioned Alex North to compose *2001's* entire score, the director eventually opted to have his space stations turn to the tune of Strauss' "Blue Danube" and other classics.

**MATCH CUT**

Triumphantly, the ape stands up. In its right hand it holds the animal bone it has just used to kill another ape. It seems to understand just how much power it has gained by discovering how to use the bone as a weapon. The hairy arm swings back, and the creature hurls the bone into the air. The camera follows this bone in close-up as it rises, turning, towards the sky; and as it drops back towards the earth – there's a sudden cut: the blue of the sky has become the blackness of interplanetary space, and instead of a bone, we see a spaceship. A single cut surmounted millions of years and millions of miles, linking the prehistoric past to the distant future. It's a cut that contains all of human history. This sequence, from *2001: A Space Odyssey* (1968) is perhaps the most famous "match cut" in movie history. The term describes a cut between two shots that may be far apart spatially or temporally, yet contain striking visual similarities. Identical plot elements, a similar movement or the same person can create a connection between these two shots, thus preserving a feeling of continuity. A match cut may cause a moment of surprise or uncertainty, yet it is an important element in the economy of film narrative, for it can leap over barriers of space and time.

eflected from the snow-white body of the spaceship, while the dark side is unk in inky blackness; the fountain pen floating through the cabin, dropped y a sleeping passenger on the way to the moon; the ghostly silence enveloping a dead astronaut in his yellow spacesuit, as he spins eternally hrough space; the circular space station turning like a gyroscope on its own xis; the blue, shimmering planet Earth. Outer space is Stanley Kubrick's nvention. Never before and never since has a film so brilliantly succeeded n conveying an impression of infinity.

A few years later, the pictures of the Apollo missions showed that ubrick's vision was also highly realistic – much to the director's relief, ncidentally.

NM

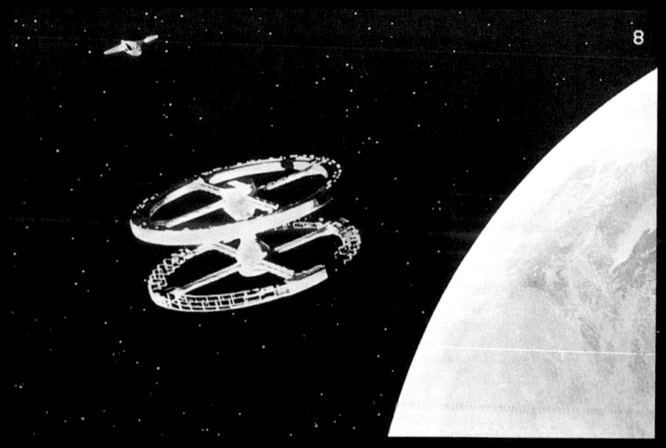
8

1968 - USA - 113 MIN. - POLICE DRAMA, POLITICAL THRILLER

DIRECTOR PETER YATES (*1929)
SCREENPLAY ALAN R. TRUSTMAN, HARRY KLEINER, based on the novel *MUTE WITNESS* by ROBERT L. PIKE
DIRECTOR OF PHOTOGRAPHY WILLIAM A. FRAKER EDITING FRANK P. KELLER MUSIC LALO SCHIFRIN PRODUCTION PHILIP D'ANTONI for WARNER BROS., SEVEN ARTS.

STARRING STEVE MCQUEEN (Detective Frank Bullitt), ROBERT VAUGHN (Walter Chalmers), JACQUELINE BISSET (Cathy), DON GORDON (Detective Delgetti), ROBERT DUVALL (Weissberg), SIMON OAKLAND (Captain Sam Bennett), NORMAN FELL (Captain Baker), GEORGE STANFORD BROWN (Dr. Willard), JUSTIN TARR (Eddy), CARL REINDEL (Detective Carl Stanton), FELICE ORLANDI (Albert Edward Renick), VIC TAYBACK (Pete Ross), ROBERT LIPTON (First Aide), ED PECK (Wescott), PAT RENELLA (Johnny Ross).

ACADEMY AWARDS 1968 OSCAR for BEST EDITING (Frank P. Keller).

## *"You work your side of the street and I'll work mine."*

Police detective Frank Bullitt (Steve McQueen) is not the type of guy who'd step aside to let anybody meddle with his affairs. He's an expert, and a firm believer in a man's right to go about his business – provided that business is within the confines of the law.

The quote at the top of this piece not only sums up Bullitt's professional philosophy; it also illustrates the film's main conflict, as a police investigation comes up against political ambition. This conflict of interests is personified in the relationship between Walter Chalmers (Robert Vaughn), a politician, and Frank Bullitt, a taciturn cop. While the former wants to use a gangster to boost his career, the latter is simply interested in doing his job.

Chalmers wants to be a public hero, an achievement that requires his star witness, mafioso John Ross, (Pat Renella) to remain alive long enough to testify in court. He entrusts Bullitt with the assignment of leading the protection unit. However, the cop's priority of bringing a killer to justice overrides the bigwig's wishes.

Things come to a head when Bullitt's task force botch the case. Despite all their precautions, two hit men sneak into the shabby motel room where Ross is being kept. The potential witness is seriously wounded and an emergency operation at San Francisco General Hospital fails to save him. As the commanding officer, Bullitt must take the fall for the incident, but not before taking matters into his own hands. He covers up the death of the witness, and heads off in pursuit of the murderers, ultimately uncovering what turns out to be an astronomical conspiracy…

To this day, Bullitt reads like the prototypical hero of a Hollywood storybook – cool, attractive, tough as nails. Steve McQueen's best-known and most popular character was a forerunner of Clint Eastwood's Harry Callahan (*Dirty Harry,* 1971) and Gene Hackman's Popeye Doyle (*The French Connection,* 1971). He's a lone crusader who constantly pushes the law to its limits but whose actions never cross into the criminal realm, a man with principles and a private life. After a hard day's work, he heads home to soak up a bit of togetherness with girlfriend Cathy (Jacqueline Bisset), leaving the social debris of the world behind. McQueen's performance definitively gave the image of the inner-city cop a rougher and more ruthless edge. Director Peter Yates and his leading man McQueen went to great lengths to give *Bullitt* its feel of uncompromising realism. At McQueen's request, actual nurses and doctors were cast to heighten the authenticity of the film, especially its ambulance sequence.

In addition to the implementation of semi-documentary devices, *Bullitt* went down in film history for setting new standards in high-speed car chases. Approximately eleven minutes of film are dedicated to the daredevil scramble through the San Francisco hills, for which avid race car driver McQueen did, in fact, take the wheel. It was the first time such a sequence was

1

2

1 #1 with a bullet: Steve McQueen became a buzz-word for masculinity the instant he arrived in Hollywood.

2 If you want a job done right, do it yourself: Acting as both stuntman and protagonist in almost all his films, McQueen had audiences doing double takes rather than looking for the double in the action sequences.

3 A whole new can of worms: *Bullitt* started the wave of political thrillers that dominated 1970s New Hollywood and put American optimism through the wringer.

**"McQueen's screen presence and the hyper-realistic direction mask a plot which is, unfortunately, rather thin... Even so, it stands as a cinematic landmark. Without it there may well have been no *Dirty Harry* or *French Connection*."** *BCI Films*

filmed without relying on time-lapse photography to suggest greater speeds. Instead, McQueen and a stunt driver ploughed through the streets at 110 mph. If you look closely enough, you'll notice one of the great continuity mishaps in Hollywood history as McQueen's car overtakes a green VW bug on no less than four separate occasions. But that blooper does nothing to spoil the scene, as editing, cinematography and sound perfectly enhance what were considered phenomenal shots at that time. With this sequence, Peter Yates and producer Philip D'Antoni established the chase as one of the great hallmarks of the genre. D'Antoni went on in 1971 to work on the project that would prove the next great stepping stone for the device with Gene Hackman's hell ride under the suspended subway track viaduct in *The French Connection.*

4 The streets of San Francisco: Peter Yates' picture made the street chase an action film prerequisite. However, it wasn't long before *The French Connection* outshone *Bullitt's* legendary hellride.

5 Undercover killers: Uniformed criminals combat plain-clothes detectives and blur the line between good and evil.

6 Political assassination: Power hungry senatorial candidate Walter Chalmers (Robert Vaughn, right.) is the true nemesis of streetwise detective, Lt. Frank Bullitt (Steve McQueen).

**PETER YATES**

It didn't take long for him to realize that his calling wasn't theater. Nonetheless, for two years after graduating from the Royal Academy of Dramatic Art in London, Peter Yates tried his hand at acting with various repertory companies, until conceding to the critics' rather poor assessment of his talent. Following brief stints as a car dealer, race car driver and racehorse stabler, the Englishman born in Aldershot, Surrey, on July 24th, 1929, finally arrived in the artistic field that welcomed him with open arms – directing. In 1962, after getting his foot in the right door by directing for the stage, he made his screen debut with the musical *Summer Holiday* starring Cliff Richard. The mystery thriller *Robbery* (1967), a film adaptation of the notorious English post office heist of 1963, paved the way to a Hollywood career. Once there, Yates's work was driven by the ambition to dabble in every imaginable movie genre. He directed thrillers like *Bullitt*; romances like *John and Mary* (1969) with Dustin Hoffman and Mia Farrow; adventures like *The Deep* (1977) with Jacqueline Bisset and Nick Nolte; fantasy films like *Krull* (1983); dramas like *Eleni* (1985), and action-packed spectaculars like *An Innocent Man* (1989). The versatile filmmaker also shot pictures for television on numerous occasions. Among his many projects in this field was a two-part made-for-TV movie period piece entitled *Don Quixote* (2000), starring John Lithgow and Bob Hoskins.

*Bullitt's* nailbiting showdown across the runways of San Francisco International Airport also impacted the future of filmmaking. Michael Mann, for example, had adversaries Robert De Niro and Al Pacino face off in similar fashion at the Los Angeles International Airport in the action packed mystery thriller *Heat* (1995).

Yet the no nonsense ending is just as noteworthy as the cinematic novelties it introduced. Neither *Bullitt's* showdown with the enemy nor the criminal's death at the picture's conclusion make a point of covering up the fact that what appears to be a triumph for the hero is, in truth, a great defeat. The death of the gangster proved utterly meaningless, for the only witness who could speak out against the syndicate is dead too. *Bullitt* delivers a profound yet demoralizing verdict – gangsters are always one step ahead of the law. SR

# BARBARELLA

1968 - ITALY / FRANCE - 98 MIN. - ADAPTED COMIC BOOK, SCIENCE FICTION

**DIRECTOR** ROGER VADIM (*1928)
**SCREENPLAY** TERRY SOUTHERN, BRIAN DEGAS, CLAUDE BRULÉ, CLEMENT WOOD, TUDOR GATES, based on the comic book of the same name by JEAN-CLAUDE FOREST **DIRECTOR OF PHOTOGRAPHY** CLAUDE RENOIR **EDITING** VICTORIA SPIRI MERCANTON **MUSIC** BOB CREWE, CHARLES FOX **SPECIAL EFFECTS** AUGIE LOHMAN **PRODUCTION** DINO DE LAURENTIIS for DINO DE LAURENTIIS, MARIANNE PRODUCTIONS

**STARRING** JANE FONDA (Barbarella), JOHN PHILLIP LAW (Pygar), ANITA PALLENBERG (The Great Tyrant), MARCEL MARCEAU (Prof. Ping), CLAUDE DAUPHIN (The President), MILO O'SHEA (Duran Duran), DAVID HEMMINGS (Dildano), UGO TOGNAZZI (Mark Hand).

## *"Just a minute. I'll slip something on." "Don't trouble yourself. This is an affair of state."*

Jane Fonda – a body that defies gravity. Psychedelic letters float across the screen, somewhat veiling a cosmic striptease that epitomizes late 1960s fluff erotica. No sooner have we been properly welcomed on board Barbarella's space cruiser than the "President of Earth and Rotating Premier of the Sun System" (Claude Dauphin) appears to us on the ship's monitor, assigning the five-star double-rated astronautic aviatrix to a top-secret mission. No, she need not bother getting dressed before being filled in on the details. After all, humankind now exists in an enlightened age, free of sexual inhibitions and the military.

Oh, what a revelation the eight-minute opening sequence must have been for more than just a handful of the mature male audience. Just picture standing at the director's side, positioned directly behind sultry Barbarella (Jane Fonda), or stepping into her commander's shoes, whose grin articulates what every man is thinking. When had cinematic modes of representation ever presented such an explicit and beckoning sight?

Presumably, these aesthetic innovations contributed to *Barbarella's* steadfast reign as a sci-fi classic for more than 35 years, as one can hardly attribute its enduring popularity to the triteness of the storyline. The nuts (creak, creak) and bolts (clank, clank) of the plot involve astronaut Barbarella trying to locate missing scientist Duran Duran (Milo O'Shea), inventor of a new type of laser weapon. As the universe was liberated by the Loving Union hundreds of years ago, Barbarella should have nothing to fear other than the occasional black hole or boredom – had the writers not thrown a small monkey wrench into her cog-works. It seems that deep space still houses one savage pocket, known as Tau Ceti, which is, incidentally, where Duran Duran's last known transmission originated from...

2

And so Barbarella descends into a futuristic tundra, confronted by a uccession of flesh-eating dolls, emasculated angels, including the blind ygar (John Phillip Law), and one sex-crazed dominatrix known as the Great yrant (Anita Pallenberg). Duran Duran, of course, turns out to be the nuttiest f the lot, eventually trapping Barbarella in his greatest creation yet, a sado- nasochistic pipe organ capable of pleasuring a person to death. It soon be- omes clear that Barbarella's actual mission is to rediscover sexuality for hu- nanity, which, in her civilization, has been reduced to communal pill popping, nd to liberate it from the clutches of evil and high-tech hostility.

True to the narrative style of French illustrator Jean-Claude Forest's dult comic book of the same name, *Barbarella's* campy and surreal plot is ctually a sequence of loosely strung together vignettes. The film's stagy set

# "Fonda looks sensational and glides through this romp like a dazed, ripe-to-the-touch innocent."

*San Francisco Chronicle*

1 Who makes love with her hands? It's Barbarella (Jane Fonda), Queen of the Galaxy – pictured here with the revolutionary Dildano (David Hemmings) after a close encounter.

2 Not without her mini-missile projector: Barbarella gets ready to fly the unfriendly skies on the wings of an angel (John Phillip Law).

3 Do the Mathmos! Duran Duran (Milo O'Shea) leads Babs through a scintillating paper mâché universe.

4 Giving the pill the kiss off: Barbarella is about to learn that some things are best done the old-fashioned way.

4

5 Want to play, pretty, pretty? The Great Tyrant (Anita Pallenberg) is dead serious about making new friends.

6 Cruise control: Our five-star aviatrix unzips her way through the universe, making love not war.

pieces are equally reminiscent of its literary origins, as sprawling landscapes seem spatially constrained, as if wedged within a single comic strip panel.

Cynics would be quick to brand the film as dated. Its lava lamp special effects only briefly stir nostalgic embers, as does the groovy space ship – which is little more than a plywood toolbox lined with a shag pile carpet – and the escapades with the angel hanging by the ropes are, by today's standards, far hokier than sweet. Nonetheless, Vadim accurately calculated that, decades later, the set would be doomed to the fate of a time-capsule, and furnished it with knick-knacks that poke fun at the sort of merchandise one might find at a flea market. One need only mention the "Grande Jatte" dressing screen or art deco statues adorning Bab's cockpit. Indeed, the brilliar union of erotic, horror and slapstick elements brought about by the film playful blend of understatement and crude naivety make it still well wort seeing today. Its brand of priceless chop-logic, along the lines of angel residing in self-constructed nests much like any other feathered creature, i symptomatic of the entire picture. Be it overblown villains, whose outrageou machinations are foiled by the most innocent of means, or a heroine whos purity proves to be her greatest weapon, it is next to impossible to judge an of *Barbarella's* characters harshly, especially given the movie's initial bla off! SI

**ROGER VADIM** The screenwriter, director, and actor born Vadim Plemiannikov in 1928 was the son of a diplomat and always had a predilection for the "naked" truth. The box-office success of his first picture *Et Dieu créa la femme* (*And God Created Woman,* 1956) had more than just a bit to do with his bare-bones aesthetic. The film starred Jean-Louis Trintignant and introduced Vadim's great contribution to the French screen, Brigitte Bardot. An advocate of mixing business with pleasure, Vadim regularly established a close bond with his leading ladies. He and Bardot maintained a marriage until 1957. His next great love was the Danish Anette Stroyberg, who starred alongside Jeanne Moreau in Vadim's version of *Les Liaisons dangereuses* (*Dangerous Liaisons,* 1959), based on Choderlos de Laclos' novel. Their marriage was dissolved in 1960. He may never have joined in holy matrimony with Catherine Deneuve, leading lady in his de Sade adaptation of *Le Vice et la vertu* (*Vice and Virtue,* 1962), but they were officially engaged and produced a son together. In 1965, Vadim exchanged vows with none other than *Barbarella*'s Jane Fonda. She had acted in his 1964 production of Schnitzler's *La Ronde.* After Fonda cut out of Vadim's life, he began to rekindle old flames, shooting a few pictures with ex-wife Brigitte Bardot, such as *Don Juan* (1972). Continuing on this streak, he attempted to recapture the magic of his earlier days, remaking *Liaisons dangereuses* as *Une Femme fidèle* (*Faithful Woman,* 1976) and a U.S. version of *And God Created Woman* (1987), both of which met with less success than their predecessors. The publication of his memoirs in the early 80s brought about a permanent rift in his decade-spanning love affair with Brigitte Bardot. In February 2000, Roger Vadim died of cancer. He was laid to rest in St. Tropez at a funeral service attended by five ex-wives and several mistresses.

# HELL IN THE PACIFIC

1968 - USA - 102 MIN. - DRAMA, WAR FILM

DIRECTOR JOHN BOORMAN (*1933)
SCREENPLAY ALEXANDER JACOBS, based on a story by ERIC BERCOVICI DIRECTOR OF PHOTOGRAPHY CONRAD L. HALL
EDITING THOMAS STANFORD MUSIC LALO SCHIFRIN PRODUCTION REUBEN BERCOVITCH for SELMUR.

STARRING LEE MARVIN (American Pilot), TOSHIRÔ MIFUNE (Captain Tsuruhiko Kuroda).

## *"You get the point? You're the dog, I'm the guy, right? Fetch!"*

An American pilot (Lee Marvin) and a Japanese naval officer (Toshirô Mifune) meet on a desert island in the North Pacific. One of them has survived a plane crash, the other a shipwreck. The year is 1944.

At first they spend a lot of time simply sizing each other up; each of them is curious, but wary. Soon, though, their sheer mulishness leads to open animosity. They don't speak the same language, they come from two very different cultures and to cap it all, their countries are at war. Drinking water is essential to survival, and apparently worth killing for. Each of them attacks the other in his sleep and destroys the few possessions his enemy has.

Only when it becomes clear to both men that their situation is hopeless do they begin to tolerate each other; and eventually, they risk making the first moves towards becoming friends. For a few weeks, they share the island in peace. Then they build a raft, with which they succeed in leaving the island. When their drinking water runs out and they're close to losing consciousness they finally spot another island on the horizon, and there appear to be signs of human habitation there. They reach the shore and realize that the houses are abandoned, but they do find some provisions, including liquor. Soon they're both blind drunk and fighting again, even though neither of them can understand a word of the other's language. Suddenly, bombs start falling and the island is destroyed.

With this war film, John Boorman, the director of classics such as *Point Blank* (1967) and *Excalibur* (1981), created an impressive parable of human

1

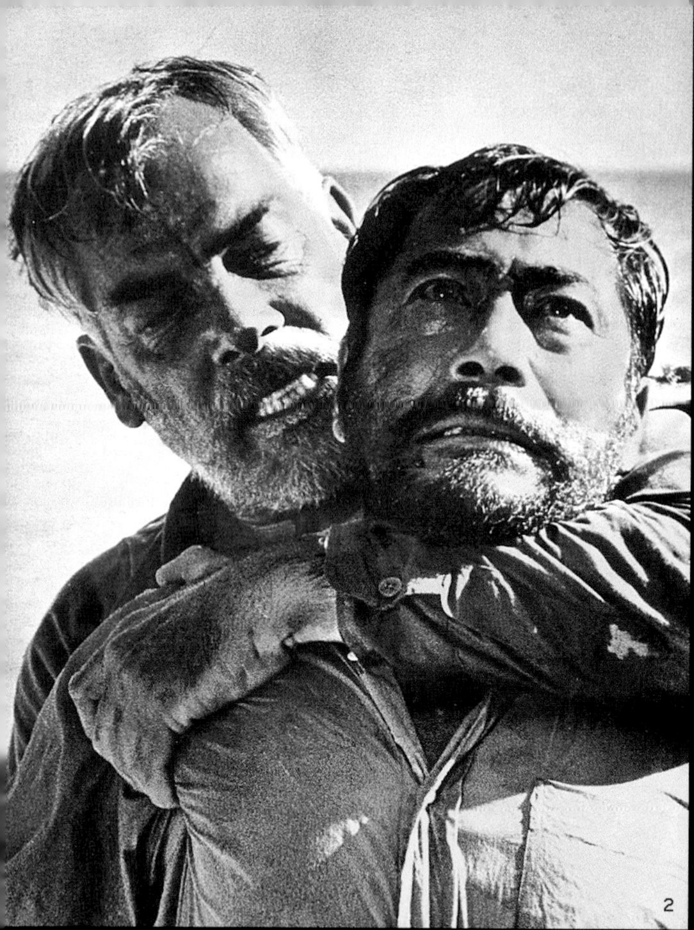

2

3

4

5

# "A powerful, very cinematic study of two men reduced to basic survival when stranded together on a Pacific island."

*Harvey's Movie Reviews*

1 Earning his wings: *Hell in the Pacific* was the 46th picture in Lee Marvin's astounding career. Although often typecast as a tough as nails heavy, Marvin ironically won his only Oscar for the comic role he played in *Cat Ballou* (1965).

2 Jawbreaker: The American Pilot (Marvin) is hard to the core and only too eager to fight lily-livered foes to the death.

3 Ballistic bushwhacker: His course of action is written all over his face – for those that know how to read the map.

4 Survival of the fittest: When their bellies start to rumble, the two soldiers go to extremes in the name of nutrition.

5 We don't need another hero: Although the Japanese officer, Captain Kuroda (Toshirô Mifune), swallows his pride by attempting escape, his efforts are foiled by the island's other occupant.

6 Howling wolves: Director John Boorman intentionally left the squabbles of the two main characters undubbed and free of subtitles as a means of evoking the animalism of their conflict.

frailty. *Hell in the Pacific* depicts an oppressive duel between two men who cannot escape the military ethos. Boorman's two protagonists circle each other like big cats before achieving a kind of peace, or at least a strained symbiosis. The director gives his actors – there are only the two of them – enough room to develop their characters, and the result is both compelling and psychologically exact. We witness two tortured creatures who are incapable of breaking free of their hermetically sealed egoism. Even at the end, as the lost soldiers reach an island that might offer them deliverance, they sabotage their own freedom with their futile adherence to an absent authority. The only thing that can stop these men fighting is the death that finally unites them.

Two brilliant actors, Lee Marvin and Toshirô Mifune – the latter a celebrated performer of Samurai roles in his Japanese homeland – ensure that the depths of human behavior are credibly depicted. The film is an impressive demonstration of how ludicrous animosity and hatred can be.

John Boorman filmed on location on the Palau Islands in the western Pacific. The camera follows the stranded men closely as they pursue each other through the dense primeval jungle. Numerous close-ups reveal the tiniest nuances of expression; these men are clearly desperate to survive. The luminous beauty of the landscapes stands in crass contrast to the darkness in the souls of these soldiers. Lalo Schifrin's finely nuanced music helps to make the inner life of the U.S. pilot and the Japanese officer almost physically present to the audience. The escalating conflict is intensified by the fact that neither of the two castaways can speak the other's language. We spectators, too, are permitted – or forced – to share in at least one of the characters' confusion and disorientation: Toshiro Mifune's explosions of rage are left untranslated, without exception. (Kevin Costner used the same method in his 1990 epic *Dances with Wolves*).

*Hell in the Pacific* works both as a character study and as a war film. At times, it's a little longwinded, and the plot does have a few holes. But it still succeeds as a study of human behavior under extreme circumstances, and as a metaphor for the loss of individual feeling under the weight of ideology. In some respects – and especially as regards the claustrophobic atmosphere – it anticipates Robert Zemeckis' recent adventure film with Tom Hanks, *Cast Away* (2000).

AL

**CONRAD L. HALL**

He probably won more prizes than any other cameraman since the days of the great studios – and he helped prepare the ground for the triumph of New Hollywood. By the time Conrad L. Hall (1926–2003) began his career as a cinematographer, he had already gathered 15 years' experience in the movie industry. He worked as a camera operator on commercials and nature documentaries, and as an assistant to Robert Surtees and Ernest Haller. From the very beginning of his career, Hall distanced himself from the glossy surface values of Old Hollywood cinematography. The intense black-and-white imagery of *Morituri* (1965) attracted a lot of attention, and it also brought him his first Oscar nomination. Others soon followed, for *The Professionals* (1966) and *In Cold Blood* (1967), before he finally won the prize for his work on *Butch Cassidy and the Sundance Kid* (1969). Hall's aversion to aestheticized images even led him to disparage some of his own work: he found *Hell in the Pacific* (1968), for example, "too beautiful." Spontaneous ideas and "happy accidents" interested him more than perfection, and in the Western Butch Cassidy, this led to brilliant results: the muted colors, the intentional over-exposures and the flickering light – so suggestive of scorching heat – engendered a host of imitators worldwide. For all his delight in experimentation, Conrad Hall was an absolute master of his craft, particularly in the techniques of lighting. The last two films he worked on were directed by Sam Mendes, and they indicate the sheer range of Hall's talents: *American Beauty* (1999) and the gangster drama *Road to Perdition* (2002) won him two more Academy Awards. Conrad Hall died at the age of 76, just a few weeks before the presentation of the Oscar for *Perdition*.

# IF...

1968 - GREAT BRITAIN - 111 MIN. - DRAMA, SOCIAL SATIRE

DIRECTOR LINDSAY ANDERSON (1932–1994)
SCREENPLAY DAVID SHERWIN DIRECTOR OF PHOTOGRAPHY MIROSLAV ONDRICEK EDITING DAVID GLADWELL MUSIC MARC WILKINSON
PRODUCTION MICHAEL MEDWIN, LINDSAY ANDERSON, ROY BAIRD for MEMORIAL ENTERPRISES.

STARRING MALCOLM MCDOWELL (Mick Travis), DAVID WOOD (Johnny), RICHARD WARWICK (Wallace), CHRISTINE NOONAN (The Girl), PETER JEFFREY (Rector), RUPERT WEBSTER (Bobby Phillips), ROBERT SWANN (Roundtree), HUGH THOMAS (Denson), MICHAEL CADMAN (Fortinbras), PETER SPROULE (Barnes).

IFF CANNES 1969 GOLDEN PALM (Lindsay Anderson).

## *"I stand in front of the mirror and I am like a tiger."*

An artist must work with metaphors to produce a true representation of his times. So said Lindsay Anderson, the director of *If...*, in which a boarding school functions as a microcosm of Britain's class-ridden society, just as a hospital was to do later in his *Britannia Hospital* (1982). England's exclusive Public Schools are the training grounds for the country's elite, which has held power in the army, church and government since time immemorial. In Anderson's movie, the school is no better than a prison – a hierarchical system in which power is exercised brutally and arbitrarily. The boys in this institution are sadistically drilled to conform, and as they move on up the school ladder they will put into practice what they have learned as children: to torment those who are younger and weaker than they are.

The film was made at Anderson's alma mater, Cheltenham College in the west of England. In *If...* the Church of England stands above and behind the headmaster (Peter Jeffrey), who oversees his deputy, who in turn commands the "whips." These few privileged scholars of the final school year make life hell for the boys from the lower years, the "scums," who include

1

1 Little rascal: Future charm school valedictorian learns enough discipline to fuel an army.

2 Seeing red: Photos and philosophies leap out of the classroom and into reality.

3 Don't let it spoil your appetite: Boarding school faculty members discuss the reinstitution of corporal punishment over a little cheese and wine.

4 Dead poets society: A bi-millennial celebration attended by bleeding-heart radicals. Anarchy or just plain anachronism?

**"Timely and timeless, this is a punchy, poetic pic that delves into the epic theme of youthful revolt. Entertaining and provocative."** *Variety*

ne film's protagonist Mick Travis (Malcolm McDowell) and his friends Johnny (David Wood) and Wallace (Richard Warwick). The whips are armed vith canes, and their training measures for scums range from having them varm the toilet seats to actually raping them. It's a system of serfdom, in which the younger kids are practically owned by their elders, body and soul. Resistance is possible only in the imagination, or at best with the help of pictures. Mick and his friends have decorated their rooms with photos of Che Guevara, Mao and Lenin, with pin-up girls – and pictures of tigers.

*If…* is subdivided into eight chapters, each introduced by a caption. The title, incidentally, is borrowed from a poem by Rudyard Kipling, at one ime commonly taught to English schoolboys: "If you can keep your head vhen all about you/Are losing theirs and blaming it on you…"). The irst three chapters show the boys returning from their school holidays and being re-ingested into the system, re-accustomed to the traditional hierarchy, inured to the military-style orders and the chain of command. The fourth chapter brings the change. Mick and his pals steal a motorbike, drive out nto the country and stop at the Packhorse Café. What looked like the start of a road movie, a hymn to freedom, ends in a stylized sex scene. Like a pair of tigers, Mick and the nameless girl from behind the counter roll around he floor, while the Sanctus from the African *Missa Luba* rings out on the soundtrack. Now there'll be no stopping this anarchistic gang of four – the hree public schoolboys and the bargirl – for they've tasted the blood of reedom. The school is celebrating its 500th anniversary and the pillars of society have come to join the festivities. In a final act of liberation – which is

5

**MIROSLAV ONDRÍCEK** Cameraman Miroslav Ondrícek was born in Prague in 1934. While working as an assistant to documentary filmmakers, he took evening classes at the Prague film school FAMU, where famous directors like Miloš Forman and Frank Beyer (*Spur der Steine*, 1966) also learned their trade. After making a few documentaries himself, Ondrícek eventually went to work at the state film studio, Barrandov. There, he met Forman and worked as his cameraman on *Audition* (*Konkurs,* 1963). This was to be the beginning of the fruitful collaboration that also produced *A Blonde in Love* (*Lásky jedné plavovlásky*, 1965) and *The Firemen's Ball* (*Horí, má panenko*, 1967)

After the Soviet invasion of Czechoslovakia in 1968, Ondrícek decided to leave the country – a courageous decision at the time. He began by working with British director Lindsay Anderson. For *If…* (1968), he created a series of dense and atmospheric color and black and white images that brought him international recognition. His work on Forman's *Taking Off* (1970) and George Roy Hill's *Slaughterhouse Five* (1972) then opened the way for a career in Hollywood.

Ondrícek was a master at balancing beautifully composed images with grittily realistic "slices of life." His artistic spectrum includes films as varied as *Amadeus* (1984), *Silkwood* (1983) and *Awakenings* (1990). Despite Oscar nominations for his work on *Ragtime* (1981) and *Amadeus*, he has yet to win the prize. In February 2004, however, the American Society of Cinematographers (ASC) honored him with an International Achievement Award, placing him in the ranks of distinguished fellow professionals like Freddie Young, Jack Cardiff, Freddie Francis, Giuseppe Rotunno, Oswald Morris and Douglas Slocombe.

5 Cold comfort: Mick Travis (Malcolm McDowell) curbs the pain of a beating by hitting the shower – but can't wash away what's been etched into his skin.

6 The killing fields: Military drills are part of this prestigious institution's core curriculum.

7 Appealing to the masses: A regimented military lifestyle takes on a religious dimension.

8 Gotcha! Students versus the administration take no prisoners.

erhaps only imagined – Mick and his gang, armed with machine guns nd hand grenades, round up the headmaster, the teachers and the assem- led dignitaries in the school yard – and the garden party ends in a blood- ath.

Anderson's idea for this fantasy of a schoolboy rebellion dates back to the ate 50s. But by the time the film was made, the subject had acquired an unan- cipated political timeliness. In 1969, *If...* won the Golden Palm at Cannes.

For the young actor Malcolm McDowell, *If...* marked the beginning of hi film career. Only a few years later, he played the lead in Kubrick's *Clockwor Orange* (1971). It was also McDowell who prompted Anderson to make se quels to *If...*: in *O Lucky Man* (1972), Mick Travis, now in the role of a naive co fee salesman, is confronted with "the economic structure of a commodities based society;" in *Britannia Hospital* (1981), Travis, again played by McDowel comes under the knife of a very sick health system. R

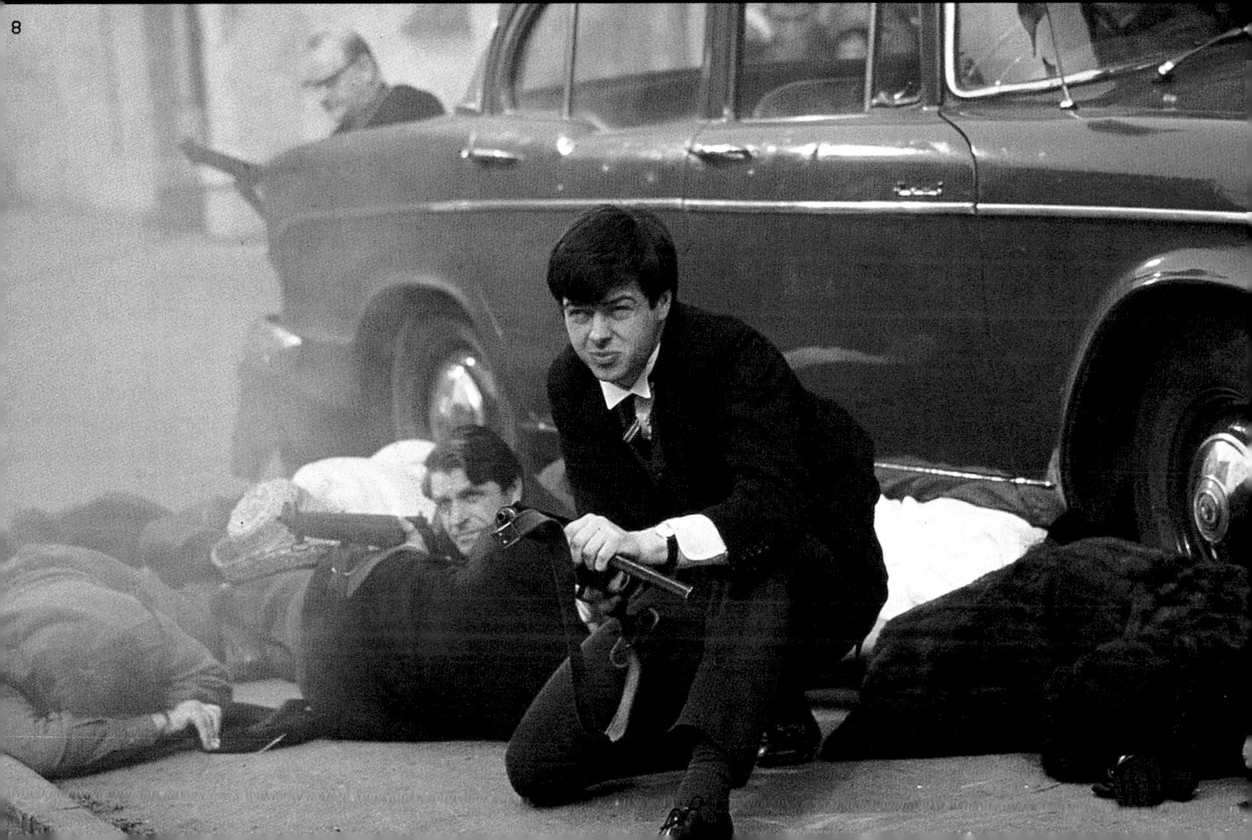

# THE ODD COUPLE

1968 - USA - 105 MIN. - COMEDY, LITERARY ADAPTATION

DIRECTOR GENE SAKS (*1921)
SCREENPLAY NEIL SIMON, based on his play of the same name DIRECTOR OF PHOTOGRAPHY ROBERT B. HAUSER EDITING FRANK BRACHT MUSIC NEAL HEFTI PRODUCTION HOWARD W. KOCH for PARAMOUNT PICTURES.

STARRING JACK LEMMON (Felix Ungar), WALTER MATTHAU (Oscar Madison), JOHN FIEDLER (Vinnie), HERBERT EDELMAN (Murray), DAVID SHEINER (Roy), LARRY HAINES (Speed), CAROLE SHELLEY (Gwendolyn), MONICA EVANS (Cecily), HEYWOOD HALE BROUN (Himself).

## *"Marriage may come and go, but the game must go on."*

"So long, Frances. So long, Blanche." It is somehow indicative of Neil Simon's subtle brand of humor that we neither hear nor see two of *The Odd Couple's* main characters. These, of course, being the ex-wives of protagonists Felix Ungar (Jack Lemmon) and Oscar Madison (Walter Matthau). As in the original smash-hit Broadway play the film is based on, the two icy absentees have left their former spouses to fend for themselves among the legions of New York's lonely hearts. And can you blame them? The recently ousted Felix is a neurotic pest, and the equally intolerable Oscar, a natural for bachelorhood, would probably have suffocated in his own dirt or choked on a hair ball long ago, if he didn't have an apartment the size of a football field.

While Oscar behaves as any real man in his predicament would, letting himself –and his hygiene – go, Felix starts popping pills in obscene quantities – well, vitamins at least. That's not to say that Felix Ungar isn't a real man. He can burn a meatloaf with the best of them, although he thinks the sky is falling on his head when blunders like that happen.

In spite of their obvious character flaws and lifestyle differences, not t mention the constant annoyance of Felix's pesky nasal inhaler and his incessant whining, the estranged Ungar moves in chez Madison. One questio looms large: if these two couldn't get along with their wives, how will the ever manage to survive each other? We can therefore only imagine France and Blanche's shock when they check in on their exes – to remind them t pick up what's left of their things and to send alimony checks – only to discover that Felix and Oscar have become an odd couple – dysfunctional marriage partners in a life *sans* women.

As Felix serves Oscar's poker buddies gourmet finger food whil gassing them with air freshener, his insensitive roomie gives his all to prever the bachelor pad from being turned into "House Beautiful." Their guests, o the other hand, can't wholeheartedly knock the changes; while they're no exactly keen on wiping their feet before entering the apartment, Oscar neve pampered them with sandwiches, baby dills and spotless ashtrays.

1

1 The iceman cometh: Oscar Madison's (Walter Matthau) marital life matches his cocktails – they're both on the rocks.

2 Mutt and Jeff: Nervous Nellie Felix Ungar (Jack Lemmon) teams up with sports writer Oscar Madison, who quickly wants to trade his new roomie to anyone who'll have him.

3 Bachelor pad bolognese: Oscar's favorite food is spaghetti and Lysol.

4 Open the floodgates: Womanizer Oscar's plans are charred by an overdone roast and then drowned in Felix's sob stories of burned romance.

5 No charge for delivery: Felix's infernal whining inspires Oscar to redecorate the kitchen.

**"The film contains an enormous 250 plus gags, based entirely on Simon's attention to minute character detail. Subsequently the film fails to date one bit, and remains hilariously funny. Lemmon and Matthau have rarely been better."** *Edinburgh U Film Society*

But the king of the castle is just about ready to put an end to cohabitation when his self-pitying roommate lets his emotions get the better of him during a double date with two English girls. While Oscar has his sights set on getting the two giggling Brits intoxicated enough for them to act on their barely hidden erotic impulses, Felix has them bursting into tears within a matter of minutes – a new record even for him. Oscar gets revenge by painting the kitchen wall with a spaghetti and tomato sauce fresco and then forbidding Felix to lay a finger on it – grueling torture for someone known to disinfect playing cards on poker night.

Despite the perfect casting of the picture's numerous supporting roles, *The Odd Couple* is a two-man show. Billy Wilder should get the credit for initially pairing the nutty twosome of Jack Lemmon and Walter Matthau in his

966 production *The Fortune Cookie* (1966). Although often at odds behind he scenes, this mismatched couple would join forces countless times over to ecreate the magic they introduced under Wilder's direction as the curmudgeon and the crybaby. Following *The Odd Couple*, the gruesome twosome met ıp again in Wilder's *Buddy Buddy* (1981), David Petrie's *Grumpy Old Men* 1993), Howard Deutch's 1995 sequel *Grumpier Old Men*, and then in Martha Coolidge's *Out to Sea* (1997).

The two actors eventually caved into the inevitable, reuniting Oscar and Felix in Howard Deutch's *The Odd Couple II* (1998), also written by Neil Simon. Furthermore, the characters appeared in a TV incarnation also entitled *The Odd Couple* (1970–75), starring Tony Randall and Jack Klugman. It just goes o show you that – happy or not – some marriages are made for life. SH

**WALTER MATTHAU (1920–2000)**

The son of Russian immigrants, Walter Matthau started off earning 50 cents a show performing at one of New York's Yiddish Theaters at the tender age of eleven. When he returned home a decorated sergeant from the armed forces in World War II, he started to consider his first calling a little more seriously, and completed a formal acting course, and before long his was landing gigs at theaters all over. In 1955, Matthau appeared in his first Hollywood picture, *The Kentuckian*, a Western starring Burt Lancaster. In fact, his was a well-known face in Westerns until the early 1960s, playing a recurring role in the genre as *Tallahassee 7000*'s (1961) sheriff. Beyond this, he was cast as straight types and heavies, appearing as a reporter in Elia Kazan's *A Face in the Crowd* (1957) and a duplicitous CIA agent in Stanley Donen's *Charade* (1963). Audiences first tuned in to his comic talent in 1966, when he matched wits with Jack Lemmon in *The Fortune Cookie*. He quickly perfected his sourpuss-with-a-heart-of-gold persona, cashing in on a pickle-faced physiognomy far more expressive than the spoken word. Matthau was always at his best when he could play off a contradictory personality, like Lemmon, who would provide him with the perfect set up. Children also fed nicely from his hand. Prime examples are *The Bad News Bears* (1976), *Little Miss Marker* (1980) and *Dennis the Menace* (1993). Despite his well-known image as the feisty curmudgeon, a closer inspection of Walter Matthau's work leads one to pictures like *Charley Varrick* (1973), *The Laughing Policeman* (1973) and *The Taking of Pelham One Two Three* (1974), which reveal a truly chameleon-like versatility.

# ONCE UPON A TIME IN THE WEST

## C'era una volta il West

1968 - ITALY / USA - 165 MIN. - SPAGHETTI WESTERN

DIRECTOR SERGIO LEONE (1929–1989)
SCREENPLAY SERGIO DONATI, SERGIO LEONE, based on a story by DARIO ARGENTO, BERNARDO BERTOLUCCI, SERGIO LEONE
DIRECTOR OF PHOTOGRAPHY TONINO DELLI COLLI EDITING NINO BARAGLI MUSIC ENNIO MORRICONE PRODUCTION FULVIO MORSELLA for RAFRAN, EURO INTERNATIONAL, PARAMOUNT.

STARRING CLAUDIA CARDINALE (Jill MacBain), HENRY FONDA (Frank), CHARLES BRONSON ("Harmonica" / The Man With No Name), JASON ROBARDS (Cheyenne), GABRIELE FERZETTI (Morton), FRANK WOLFF (Brett MacBain), KEENAN WYNN (Sheriff), PAOLO STOPPA (Sam), LIONEL STANDER (Barkeeper), WOODY STRODE (Gang member), JACK ELAM (Gang member).

***"What's he waiting for out there?
What's he doing?"
"He's whittlin' on a piece of wood.
I've got a feeling when he stops whittlin'
... somethin's gonna happen."***

Three men in long coats are waiting at a lonely railroad station. A pinwheel creaks in the wind. A droplet from a water tank plops on to one man's (Woody Strode) hat; it's followed by another, and another. A fly buzzes around the unshaven face of the gang's leader (Jack Elam); the insect lands on his lip, he drives it away, it buzzes back again. Eventually, he catches the fly in the barrel of his Colt, and listens to the trapped creature with a smile on his face. We hear the distant sound of a train whistle. The men get ready. The train arrives – no sign of any passengers disembarking – and departs again. Suddenly, a doleful tune: on the other side of the tracks stands a man playing a mouth organ. He puts his bags down, and a dialogue ensues: Harmonica: "And Frank?" – The gang leader: "Frank sent us." – "Did you bring a horse for me?" – "Well... looks like we're... looks like we're shy one horse." – "You brought two too many." They draw their guns, open fire and collapse to the ground.

This incredibly slow beginning lasts a quarter of an hour, ending abruptly in a shoot-out that leaves only one man alive (but slightly injured): the man with the harmonica (Charles Bronson). It's a sequence that displays all the stylistic elements of the Spaghetti Western: extreme close-ups that reveal every pore in a man's face; warped perspectives, with characters shot from below; the sudden transition to panoramic views of a vast, empty landscape; terse dialogue; time stretched unbearably, then shattered in an eruption of gunfire. "Harmonica" – we never discover his real name – has come to avenge the death of his brother. Two-and-a-half hours of the film will pass before he finally encounters the man who didn't have time to meet him at the

1

"Sergio Leone... seems to have improved as he has gone along, and *Once Upon a Time in the West* I consider his masterpiece, even surpassing *The Good, the Bad and the Ugly*, which is actually more efficient if less ambitious. Indeed, I am convinced that Sergio Leone is the only living director who can do justice to the baroque elaboration of revenge and violence in *The Godfather*." *The Village Voice*

1 Play dead for me: Like in opera, Ennio Morricone had individual theme music composed for each of his main characters. Charles Bronson as Harmonica.

2 O. Henry: Sergio Leone looks his characters straight in the face and makes villains like Frank (Henry Fonda) break out in a cold sweat.

3 Still life: Bernardo Bertolucci hangs 'em high and turns glorified violence into visual masterpieces. The film's script was a joint effort between Bertolucci, director of *Ultimo tango a Parigi* (*The Last Tango in Paris*, 1972) and horror flick aficionado Dario Argento.

station. Frank was busy – massacring an entire family of defenseless settlers, including a little boy who'd looked right in his cold blue eyes.

As the face of the killer Frank was revealed for the first time, American moviegoers allegedly gasped in dismay; for it was none other than Henry Fonda. The living embodiment of Good as the face of pure Evil... This shocking casting-against-type was a straight declaration to the audience: *What you're watching here has absolutely nothing to do with the classical Hollywood Western. That's why Woody Strode and Jack Elam, familiar faces from countless Westerns of the past, got blown away right at the start. What you're watching here is the Myth of the Wild West turned on its head; no more shining heroes, not an honorable motive in sight.* Sergio Leone later stated that he had wanted to sweep away all the lies that had been told about the colonization of America. *Once Upon a Time in the West* tells of the blood and the dirty money that lubricated the wheels of "civilization."

3

**ENNIO MORRICONE** The success of *Once Upon a Time in the West* (*C'era una volta il West*, 1968) was due not least to the music of Ennio Morricone. For each of the main characters, he composed a signature melody: the plangent harmonica for Charles Bronson, the female choir for Claudia Cardinale. It's for this reason that the film has often been compared to an opera; each of the themes functions independently of the others, and the music is highly effective even in the absence of the film. This is one of the most celebrated soundtracks in the history of the cinema, and it made the composer world-famous.

Leone and Morricone had known each other since childhood. Born in Rome in 1928, Morricone studied music from the age of twelve, and later worked as a nightclub musician. He wrote his first film scores in the early 60s, and first attracted attention with the catchy soundtrack to *A Fistful of Dollars (Per un pugno di dollari,* 1964). This was followed by equally memorable music for *The Good, the Bad and the Ugly* (*Il buono, il brutto, il cattivo* 1966) and *The Sicilian Clan* (*Le Clan de Siciliens*, 1969). He worked with Bernardo Bertolucci on his mammoth project *1900* (1976), with Brian de Palma on *The Untouchables* (1987) and with Roman Polanski on *Frantic* (1987).

Though nominated for the Oscar several times – for example, for *The Mission* (1986) – Morricone has yet to win it, although he is indubitably one of the most important and versatile film composers of the 20th century. He has now written more than 400 scores. Even if only around one-tenth of them were for Westerns, the name Ennio Morricone – much to his regret – will remain inseparably associated with the Spaghetti Westerns of the 1960s.

# "They wanna hang me! The big, black crows. Idiots. What the hell? I'll kill anything. Never a kid. Be like killin' a priest."

*Film quote: Cheyenne (Jason Robards)*

4 Death Valley: Jill (Claudia Cardinale) arrives at her new home on the frontier only to find that her entire family has been assassinated. Save for Jill's thought-provoking journey to the farm – filmed the California desert – the picture was shot exclusively in Spain.

5 Sweetwater: Jill is set on the idea of founding an oasis town. It's a commentary in itself that Leone picked a whore to serve as mother of the civilization that grew out of the Wild West.

4

Besides the revenger's tale, Leone also tells us of the building of the railroad and the passing of the old-style gunslinger. Frank is the right-hand-man of a sickly entrepreneur who dreams of reaching the Pacific with his railroad line. It's Frank's job to remove any obstacles in the path of this project. The settler and his kids had to die because their land contained the only water source for miles around. The guy knew this, and dreamed of being the stationmaster and founder of a new town. What Frank doesn't know is that the widowed settler had previously married a high-class whore (Claudia Cardinale) in New Orleans. It takes her a while to grasp what a valuable piece of real estate she's inherited in the desert, but with the help of Harmonica and the desperado Cheyenne (Jason Robards), she sets out to realize her dead husband's plans.

With the three films that made up his "Dollar Trilogy" – *A Fistful of Dollars*, *For a Few Dollars More*, and *The Good, The Bad and The Ugly* – Sergio Leone became the most innovative director of European Westerns (along with Sergio Corbucci). Today, these three films look like preliminary studies for his ultimate masterpiece: *Once Upon a Time in the West.* It is perfect, in more ways than one: in its casting, its relentless build-up of suspense, and in its sheer visual power. Each shot is meticulously composed, and its use of zooms, complicated camera moves and slow motion in the flashback sequences give it the quality of a bold formal experiment. Some accused Leone of mannerism; other critics and colleagues such as Wim Wenders were appalled because the movie represented "the ultimate Western," and was therefore "the end of the road." It may well be the most breathtaking Western ever made. NM

5

# THE NIGHT OF THE LIVING DEAD

968 - USA - 96 MIN. - HORROR FILM

IRECTOR GEORGE A. ROMERO (*1940)

CREENPLAY GEORGE A. ROMERO, JOHN A. RUSSO DIRECTOR OF PHOTOGRAPHY GEORGE A. ROMERO EDITING GEORGE A. ROMERO, JOHN A. RUSSO MUSIC SCOTT VLADIMIR LICINA PRODUCTION KARL HARDMAN, RUSSEL STREINER for IMAGE TEN.

TARRING DUANE JONES (Ben), JUDITH O'DEA (Barbra), KARL HARDMAN (Harry Cooper), MARILYN EASTMAN (Helen Cooper / Bug-eating Zombie), KEITH WAYNE (Tom), JUDITH RIDLEY (Judy), KYRA SCHON (Karen Cooper / Upstairs Body), RUSSELL STREINER (Johnny), CHARLES CRAIG Newscaster / Ghoul), WILLIAM HINZMAN (Cemetery Ghoul) GEORGE KOSANA (Sheriff McClelland).

## *"Shoot 'em in the head"*

t could just as well have been the opening to a touching family melodrama. Barbra (Judith O'Dea) and her brother Johnny (Russell Streiner) head to the countryside on the outskirts of Pittsburgh, where their deceased father has been put to rest in their family plot. But even before the audience has a chance to warm up to what seem to be the movie's protagonists, Johnny is abruptly struck dead by a mysterious man. Barbra manages to flee to the safety of a nearby farmhouse. An African American named Ben (Duane Jones) spots her and follows suit. They soon discover a couple, Tom (Keith Wayne) and Judy (Judith Ridley), hiding out in the cellar with a small family who are Harry and Helen Cooper (Karl Hardman and Marilyn Eastman) and their young daughter Karen (Kyra Schon). The main action remains confined to these tight quarters for the duration of the film. The only reminders of a "civilized" outside world streaming into the house are the round-the-clock radio and television broadcasts about further cases of the deadly epidemic terrorizing the nation. Allegedly the crash of a NASA spacecraft has emitted toxic radiation into the air that causes people to die and rise again as flesh-eating zombies. When Barbra lapses into a state of shock, Ben takes charge of the situation and defends the group from the advancing battalions of the undead. He rounds up a rifle, ammunition and an American flag from one of the hous closets. But despite Ben's valiant efforts, a great number of their party di Meanwhile, a civilian army has formed and joined forces with the police, sy tematically shooting zombies after daybreak. The army, however, is excl sively white and hardly the bearer of the salvation that Ben, the farmhous group's final living member, had hoped for. With the words "Good shot, a other one for the fire!" the movie's hero is executed and set aflame as th troops march onward on their rampage for justice.

George A. Romero's claustrophobic cult hit is poignantly shot in blac and white. The flickering shadows instill the picture with a dreamlike ar even delusional quality. Nonetheless, the horrific events depicted in *Night the Living Dead* hint at the possibility of an imagined reality. The audiovisu assault on the senses includes shattering window panes, blinding headlight and principally, the mutilated cadavers, bowels and body parts feasted upo by the zombies provide cinema's darkest chambers with a new degree visceral intensity. This unadulterated display of violence struck a chord wi audiences. In 1968, the year the film was in production, the Vietnam War ha encroached upon the lives of every American via the non-stop media w

1

2

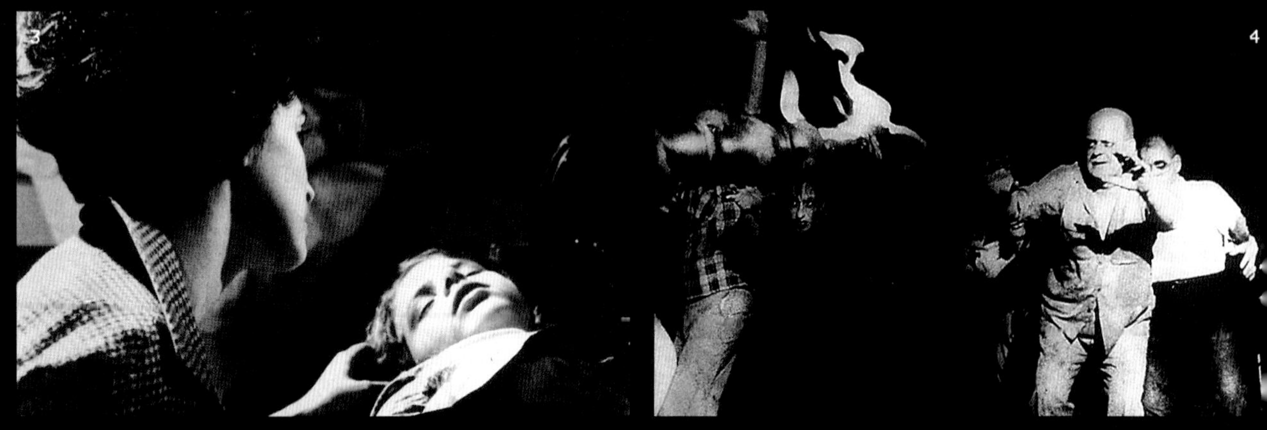

1 A flesheater's fantasy: Botticelli as edible art erotica.

2 Death comes knocking at the door: Zombies start rehearsals for Michael Jackson's legendary Thriller video. They've got all the right moves and are headed for a common goal – to reach the hearts of their undying fans.

3 Picking her mother's brain: After being infected by the zombie plague, young Karen (Kyra Schon) takes a jab at family values when she chews out her mummy.

**"The coarse sheriff survives; the unfeeling television people survive; the Washington bureaucrats survive; and the family, the hero, and traditional American values of individualism are destroyed."** *Stuart M. Kaminsky, in: Cinefantastique*

4 Bibbidi bobbidi boo: A little flame and few sparks are enough to get the zombies to retreat. Why is it that all movie monsters seem to be afraid of fire?

5 Rest in peace: The last survivors head for the claustrophobic nuclear fallout shelter. However, even Ben (Duane Jones), the sanest among them, will not live to see the dawn.

6 Black Power: In principle, Ben is a Rambo forerunner who burns countless living dead to ash in the name of humanity and the American way.

ulletins. Law enforcement and opponents of war were pitted against each her in full-blown street fights. Bloodshed swept across inner cities nationide. Two beloved public figures, Robert F. Kennedy and Martin Luther King, ere also both assassinated that year.

It would be overly simplistic to see the movie's undead as an allegory r the Red Scare, and neither can the events of the story be explained away the spacecraft's mysterious emission of radiation, which is of course a refence to the ever-present nuclear threat of the Cold War era. George Romero d more than this: he updated the classic horror zombie for a 1960s audice. In his apocalyptic vision, the national crisis – as evidenced in the zombies' fashionable clothing – originated from within America itself, and racial discrimination is one of the piece's prominent issues. For its final sequences, the film takes on the quality of a documentary newsreel. After Ben's death, as Armageddon breaks up the structure of the earth, the visuals denature into static, grainy stills. These frozen images draw attention to the meat hooks used to lay the zombies corpses – as well as Ben's – on the funeral pyre. The sight makes the police force and people's army seem like the real monsters. As one movie reviewer put it, "Those who survive the film are a kind of *dead living.*"

PLB

**THE ZOMBIE FILM**

In Victor Halperin's *White Zombie* (1932) and Jacques Tourneur's *I Walked with a Zombie* (1943), which take place in the Caribbean, voodoo and black magic are responsible for the reanimation of the undead. As early as 1966, the Hammer Production *Plague of the Zombies* relocated the ghouls to England. George A. Romero's *Night of the Living Dead* (1968) was the first picture to radically break with the zombie's traditional background story and depict them as a mindless army on the offensive. The director's work eventually evolved into a zombie trilogy, which includes the further installments *Dawn of the Dead* (1978) and *Day of the Dead* (1985).

By the 1980s it became clear that an excess of revolting, decaying human tissue as a subversive – and often censored – motif was incompatible with mainstream cinema. Nonetheless, a slew of films were produced in which corpses rise again as a result of atomic radiation, scientific experiments or viral epidemics. The subject matter was particularly popular in Italy, where Lucio Fulci's *Zombie* (*Gli ultimie zombi*, 1979) quickly became a classic. After the initial resurgence of the genre in the 1960s and 70s, zombies soon became a favorite spoof target as seen in Sam Raimi's masterpiece *The Evil Dead* (1981) or the stomach-turning *Braindead* (1992) by *Lord of the Rings* director Peter Jackson. In 2002, zombie films experienced an unexpected revival thanks to Paul W. S. Anderson's film adaptation of the videogame *Resident Evil* and Uwe Boll's *House of the Dead.* In Danny Boyle's *28 Days Later*, the undead were finally liberated from their trademark somnambulism and began chasing living human beings at full speed.

# Z

## Z

1968 - FRANCE / ALGERIA - 127 MIN. - POLITICAL THRILLER

DIRECTOR COSTA-GAVRAS (*1933)

SCREENPLAY JORGE SEMPRÚN, based on the novel of the same name by VASSILIS VASSILIKOS DIRECTOR OF PHOTOGRAPHY RAOUL COUTARD EDITING FRANÇOISE BONNOT MUSIC MIKIS THEODORAKIS PRODUCTION JACQUES PERRIN, AHMED RACHEDI for OFFICE NATIONAL POUR LE COMMERCE ET L'INDUSTRIE CINÉMATOGRAPHIQUE, REGGANE FILMS, VALORIA FILMS.

STARRING YVES MONTAND (The Member of Parliament, a.k.a. "Z", a.k.a. "The Doctor"), IRENE PAPAS (Helena, his Wife), JEAN-LOUIS TRINTIGNANT (Examining Magistrate), JACQUES PERRIN (Journalist), CHARLES DENNER (Manuel), FRANÇOIS PÉRIER (Senior Public Prosecutor), PIERRE DUX (Police Chief), GEORGES GÉRET (Nick), BERNARD FRESSON (Matt), MARCEL BOZZUFFI (Vago), RENATO SALVATORI (Yago).

ACADEMY AWARDS 1969 OSCARS for the BEST FOREIGN LANGUAGE FILM (France / Algeria), and BEST EDITING (Françoise Bonnot).

IFF CANNES 1969 BEST ACTOR (Jean-Louis Trintignant), SPECIAL PRIZE OF THE JURY (Costa-Gavras).

## *"The people need the truth."*

Few films can have politicized their times as much as the thrillers of Costa-Gavras, and the most famous of these movies is *Z*. It's the barely-fictionalized story of the Greek opposition politician Grigoris Lambrakis, who was murdered in 1963 – a deed closely tied to the beginning of Greece's military dictatorship in 1967. The film was made in Algeria and financed in France. Greece is never actually named as the location of the story, but the characters' names are as Greek as the uniforms of the generals, who hide their grim intentions behind impenetrable black sunglasses. Another unmissable clue is the music, composed by Mikis Theodorakis, who had already been imprisoned several times. The movie is prefaced with the following words: "A[ny] resemblance to real events, or to people, alive or dead, is no coincidence. [It] is INTENTIONAL."

The politician (Yves Montand) – referred to as "Z" throughout the film [–] is the idol of the country's educated youth. At a party meeting, he makes [a] vehement plea for freedom and democracy and against the establishment [of] NATO bases in his country. Even as he makes his speech, a riot begins [in] front of the parliament building: enraged citizens – or are they *agents prov[o]cateurs*? – batter the listeners gathered around the loudspeakers. "The Do[ctor]

1

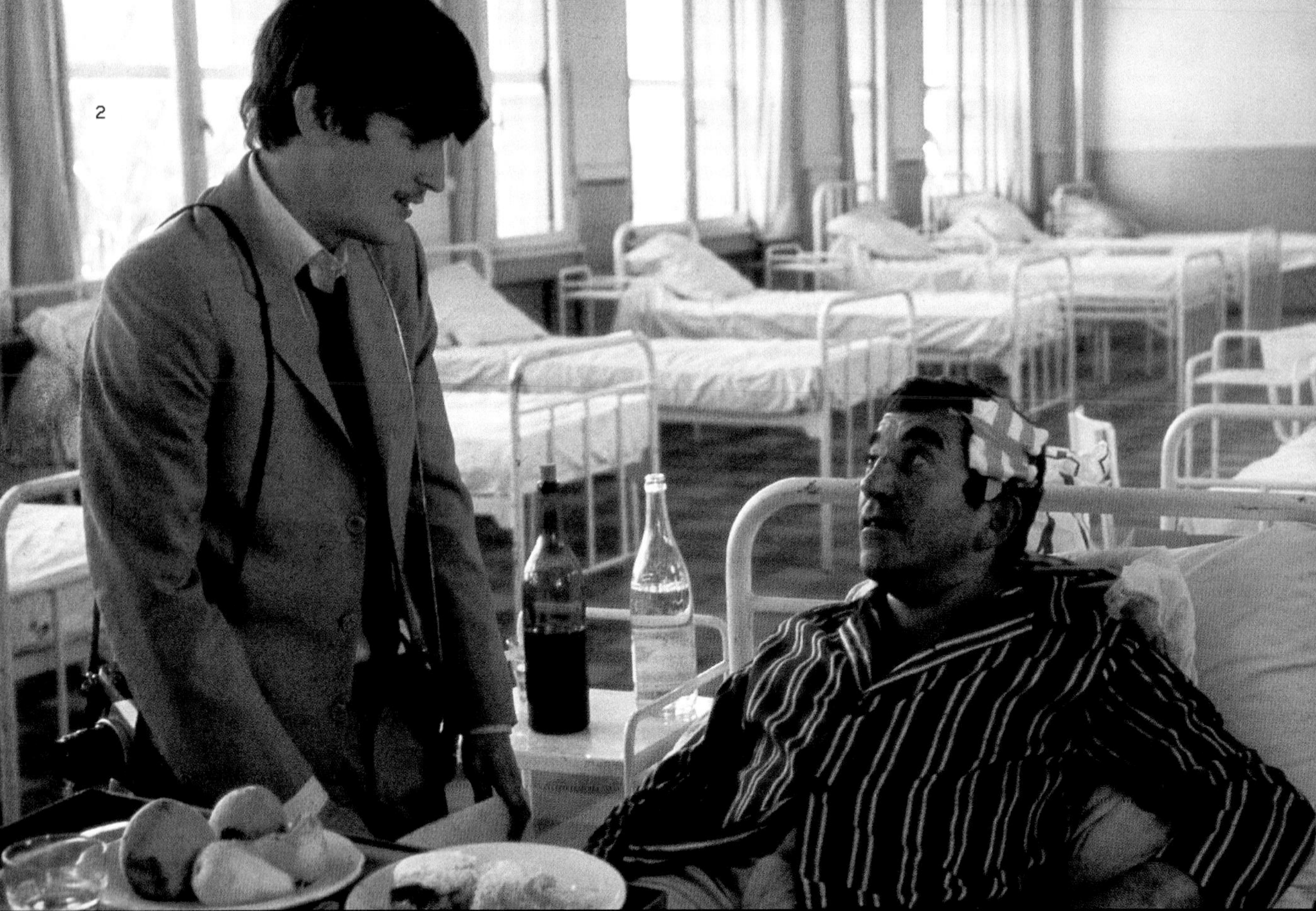

1 The mourning after: The murdered representative (Yves Montand) and his wife Helena (Irene Papas).

2 Strapped for clues: Journalist (Jacques Perrin) begins to conduct his own investigation of the scandal. An informant named Nick (Georges Géret) thinks he's onto a hot lead.

3 A second opinion: The murder investigation causes the magistrate (Jean-Louis Trintignant), an otherwise obedient civil servant, to reassess where his loyalties lie.

## "The story of the Lambrakis affair is one of national sorrow, of idealism, of bravery, of defeat, of terrible irony. The movie is not one of ideas or ideals, but of sensations – horror, anger, frustration and suspense." *The New York Times*

tor," as the politician is respectfully known, may be a university professor and former Olympic athlete, but to the average middle-class citizen his followers are just a bunch of longhaired communists, pacifists and atheists. As The Doctor steps out onto the square, all is calm and quiet. Then a pale blue cabin scooter zooms by, and he collapses to the ground. He has clearly been hit by a bullet. The police stand idly by as he is driven to hospital.

In these hectic and terribly exact scenes, cameraman Raoul Coutard demonstrates the full extent of his mastery. Faces and bodies appear and disappear again, almost before the spectator has had time to register them; but much later, they re-appear in photos or interrogation scenes. It's worth making the effort to take note of them in this early sequence, for Costa-Gavras goes on to develop a storyline with all the precision and suspense of a highly intelligent thriller. Even as the doctors fight – in vain – to save the life of their colleague, the military are taking pains to play down this "unfortunate incident." They employ a young examining magistrate (Jean-Louis Trintignant) to settle things in their favor. Yet this sober bureaucrat is tougher and more persistent than they had anticipated, and it gradually becomes clear to him that The Doctor is the victim of a political conspiracy. He was murdered in cold blood by members of a proto-fascist organization protected by the police and the army. With the help of a tabloid reporter, bribed witnesses are exposed and the guilty parties are hauled up in court, including those at the very top. In the closing credits, we are told that those who had been found guilty were restored to office only a few months later, when a military coup crushed the democratic renaissance in its infancy.

4 Commanded by general apathy: The chief of police (Pierre Dux) couldn't care less about solving the case.

5 Do not disturb: Helena takes refuge from the paparazzi and her role as the devoted wife in her dead husband's hotel room.

6 Vested interest: Matt (Bernard Fresson) is concerned about the representative's safety, but can't prevent the assassination.

**COSTA-GAVRAS**

The son of a Russian immigrant who had taken part in the resistance, Konstantinos Gavras (*1933) saw no possibility of acquiring a proper education in Greece. At the age of 19, he went to Paris to study literature at the Sorbonne, where he decided to shorten his name to Costa-Gavras. He soon switched his course of studies, moving to the famous *Institut des Hautes Études Cinématographiques.* Since 1956, he has been a French citizen. He developed his particular cinematic style by wrangling with the possibilities of realism. He began his career as an assistant to René Clair, Yves Allégret and Jacques Demy. *Z* (1968) was the first in a trilogy of political thrillers that would ensure Costa-Gavras' name was forever be associated with this genre. *The Confession* (*L'Aveu*, 1970) examines communist oppression in Eastern Europe, while *State of Siege* (*État de siège*, 1972) focuses on the activities of the American intelligence services in South America. The participation of Yves Montand ensured that these films would be noticed worldwide. *Missing* (1981), starring Jack Lemmon and Sissy Spacek, depicted the role of the U.S. in the Chilean military coup of September 11, 1973. Costa-Gavras had the ability to use commercial means in order to strengthen the impact of his almost militantly moral films. Many critics never forgave him for this. Strangely enough, his more obviously "entertaining" films – such as *Music Box* (1989), for which he won a Golden Bear at the Berlinale – were unpopular with moviegoers. More recently, the Greek-French director aroused controversy yet again, with *Amen* (2001), a study of the Vatican's attitude towards Nazi Germany, based on Rolf Hochhuth's play "The Representative."

Costa-Gavras later stated that while he was making the film, his interest increasingly shifted from the politician to the judge. At the time, he was accused of exploiting the life and death of Grigoris Lambrakis for sensationalist purposes, but this clinical autopsy of a political murder proves how wrong his critics were.

Director and judge share a similar method, as both painstakingly gather the facts and courageously traverse old political battle-lines. If there is any manipulation going on in the film, then it's to be found precisely in this documentary method, which still has the power to frighten the spectator and stir strong feelings of moral outrage. At a time when military dictatorships of the left and the right were holding much of the world hostage, truth was the most effective weapon available. PB

# THE UNFAITHFUL WIFE

## La Femme infidèle / Stéphane, una moglie infedele

1968 - FRANCE/ITALY - 97 MIN. - MELODRAMA, THRILLER

DIRECTOR CLAUDE CHABROL (*1930)
SCREENPLAY CLAUDE CHABROL DIRECTOR OF PHOTOGRAPHY JEAN RABIER EDITING JACQUES GAILLARD MUSIC PIERRE JANSEN
PRODUCTION ANDRÉ GÉNOVÈS for CINEGAI S. P. A., LES FILMS DE LA BOÉTIE.

STARRING STÉPHANE AUDRAN (Hélène Desvallées), MICHEL BOUQUET (Charles Desvallées), MAURICE RONET (Victor Pegala), MICHEL DUCHAUSSOY (Duval, Police Officer), GUY MARLY (Gobet, Police Officer), SERGE BENTO (Private Detective), Louise Chevalier (Nanny), STÉPHANE DI NAPOLI (Michel Desvallées), Louise Rioton (Mother-in-law), HENRI MARTEAU (Paul).

## *"Do you love me?" "Why do you ask?"*

The title is misleading: *The Unfaithful Wife* is a psychological thriller in which adultery is little more than a side issue. What's more, the story is told from the man's perspective. Rich Parisian lawyer Charles Desvallées (Michel Bouquet) discovers that his wife has been having an affair. For a man whose world consists of strict routines and carefully controlled emotions, it's a catastrophe, so he tracks down his rival, a writer called Victor Pegala (Maurice Ronet), beats him to death and then skillfully conceals the crime from the police and his wife. He's arrested nonetheless, but then long-repressed feelings rise to the surface in a surprising way. Hélène (Stéphane Audran), who had been tormented by the sudden and mysterious disappearance of her lover, doesn't just forgive her husband for killing him: she accepts his crime as the proof of love she has desired for years. The fragile balance of the famous final shot sums up the complexity of the situation. Charles gazes at his wife as he is led away. The camera moves backwards as the couple draw apart, emphasizing the increasing distance between them; but a simultaneous zoom has precisely the opposite effect. A ray of sunshine makes this parting scene seem like a beautiful dream.

What is Claude Chabrol saying here? Does he believe in some form of bourgeois marriage that still admits the possibility of love? Or is the rebirth of love through an act of murder a further proof of the essential culpability of his bourgeois characters? In his middle period above all, Claude Chabrol achieves a precision of expression that forbids any kind of snap judgment (and certainly any form of cynicism). Early on in the film, Charles and Hélène are suffering the silent torments of a marriage stifled by convention. The muted sighs of an unsatisfied wife are audible in every corner of her beautiful country house near Versailles, only Charles can't hear them. He draws back from Hélène's amorous approaches, preferring to end his day by falling asleep in front of a tiny TV. But does the death of passion necessarily mean the end of love?

1

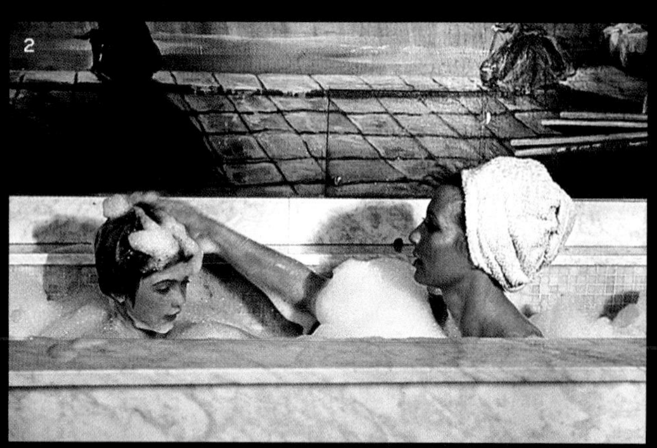

We only ever see Hélène in one scene with Victor; and it seems clea that the affair no longer gives her any real pleasure. The portrayal of the mu der itself is a masterpiece of ambivalence. Charles has gone to his rival house in order to have it out "man to man." Though the *bon vivant* Victor initially shocked, he is lulled into a false sense of security by Charles' jovi manner, and pours him a whisky. Then Victor makes a few careless remark about Hélène, and a glimpse of the tangled bed sheets is enough to inflam Charles' limited imagination. In a fit of rage, he slays a man he need hard have feared as a competitor. It's a crime of passion rather than cold-bloode murder. Only when disposing of the body does Charles display the cool ca culation so typical of the *juste milieu* dissected by Chabrol. He removes a traces of the deed, and after a nerve-wracking drive, he dumps the corpse i

**"The third section of *La femme infidèle* is what makes the film so original and so idiosyncratic. Here, Chabrol plays wonderfully with the ambiguity of feelings. In the spirit that unites the couple in their hour of danger, tenderness, egoism, fear of scandal and the feeling of solidarity peculiar to married couples are all mixed up inextricably."** *Le Monde*

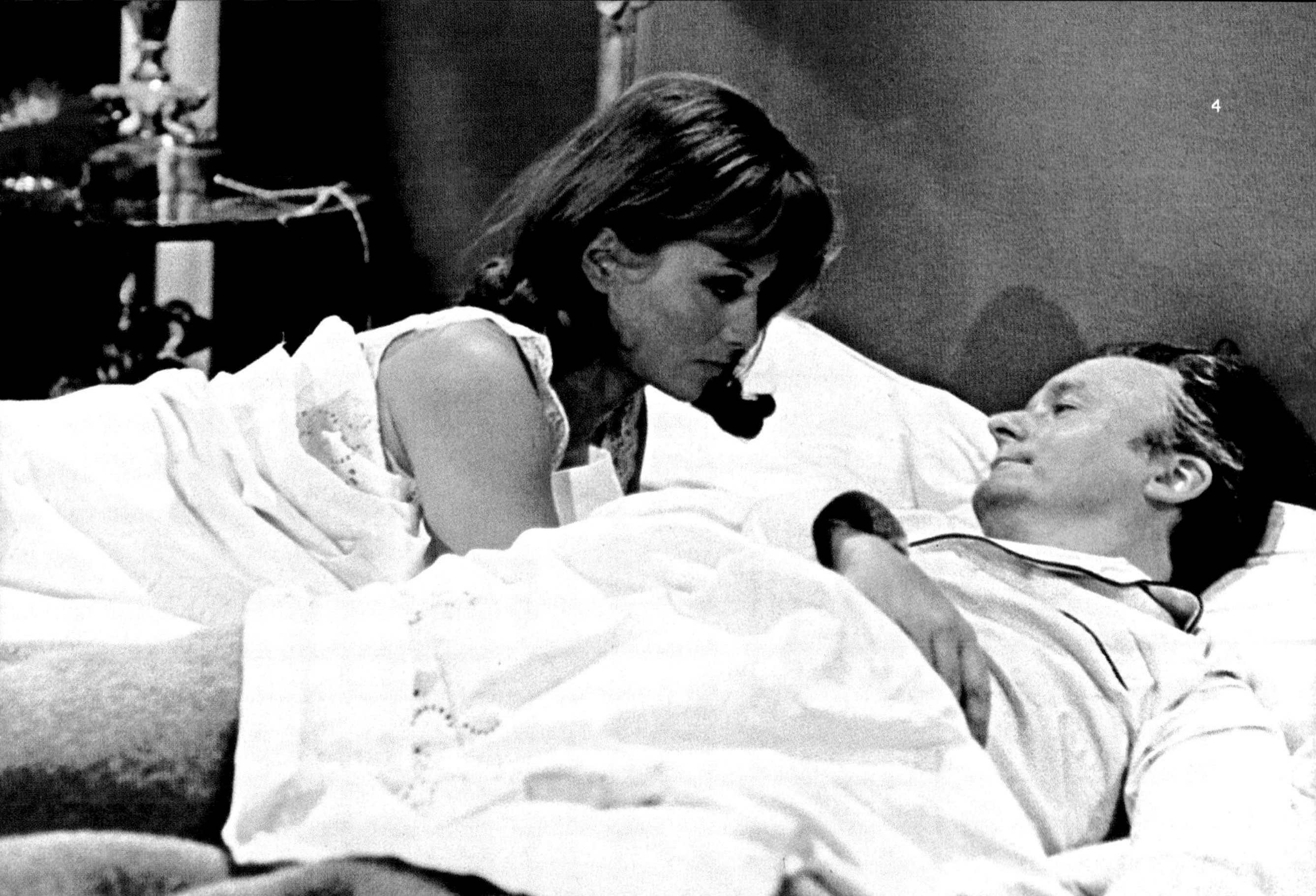

1 Heartache to heartache she stands: In search of a divine sign that her marriage is worth salvaging, Hélène (Stéphane Audran) accepts her husband's crime of passion as proof of his love.

2 Rub a dub dub: You won't find any lovers in this tub – just mommy and her little ducky. Here, Desvallées plays up the guise of everyday normality among the affluent.

3 Marriage interviews: Inspector Duval (Michel Duchaussoy) wants to see how well these two know each other and visits the couple on numerous occasions. However, his incessant questioning can't throw Charles (Michel Bouquet).

4 In bed with boredom: A frustrated housewife demands the attention of her oblivious husband. But he only discovers what a shambles their marriage is in after hiring a private detective. The murder of her lover momentarily sparks the embers of their neglected passion.

a river. The slow submergence of this grisly bundle recalls a similar scene in Hitchcock's *Psycho* (1960). Chabrol never liked to be compared to Hitchcock, but like the English-American master, he too makes the spectator an accomplice to the crime he depicts. But in his calm and almost naturalistic cinematography, Chabrol does maintain a greater distance. We follow the psychological history of a murder, from Charles' first suspicions to his fear of discovery, right up to Hélène's devastating realization that her husband is a killer. Small props acquire major significance, such as the ridiculous TV set, or the lighter that Charles finds in Victor's home (and which had been Charles' third-anniversary present to his wife).

In 2002, Adrian Lyne remade the film as an erotic thriller entitled *Unfaithful* with Diane Lane and Richard Gere in the leading roles. It is no match for the subtle suspense of Chabrol's original. *The Unfaithful Wife* is one of the best films he made, and it marks the beginning of his "Hélène Trilogy," which continued with *Just Before Nightfall* (*Juste avant la nuit*, 1971) and *Ten Days' Wonder* (*La Décade prodigieuse / Dieci incredibili giorni*, 1971). PB

**CLAUDE CHABROL**

In Claude Chabrol's substantial *œuvre*, murder and adultery are the rule rather than the exception. The son of a pharmacist, Chabrol (*1930) made his debut in 1958 with *Le Beau Serge*, a film that helped the *nouvelle vague* achieve its breakthrough in the French cinema. Very quickly, however, he moved away from the naturalistic manner of his contemporaries with a series of pointed, ironical examinations of society's constraints and double standards. After a number of box-office flops and jobs done on commission, he gradually acquired his reputation as "the chronicler of the French bourgeoisie." During this period, the most fruitful of his career, his films were notable for their cool, distant, almost formalistic style. In *Les Biches* (1968), *This Man Must Die* (*Que la bête meure*, 1969) and *The Butcher* (*Le Boucher / Il tagliagole*, 1969/70), the mask of bourgeois normality slips under the pressure of hatred, passion and jealousy. In the process, Chabrol's own moral standpoint became ever harder to identify; indeed, he was eventually accused of being an apologist for the French middle classes he portrayed. His later films never achieved the continuity of this period. *The Hatter's Ghost* (*Les Fantômes du chapelier*, 1982) is another study of a criminal case, while *Betty* (1991) and *La Cérémonie* (1995) are further masterly portraits of women. In 1999, his successful study of small-town life *The Color of Lies* (*Au coeur du mensonge*, 1998) won unanimous praise at the Berlin Film Festival.

# OLIVER!

1968 - GREAT BRITAIN - 153 MIN. - MUSICAL, LITERARY ADAPTATION

**DIRECTOR** CAROL REED (1906–1976)
**SCREENPLAY** VERNON HARRIS, based on LIONEL BART'S musical adaptation of CHARLES DICKENS' novel *OLIVER TWIST*
**DIRECTOR OF PHOTOGRAPHY** OSWALD MORRIS **EDITING** RALPH KEMPLEN **MUSIC** JOHNNY GREEN after compositions by LIONEL BART
**PRODUCTION** JOHN WOOLF for ROMULUS FILMS, WARWICK PRODUCTIONS.

**STARRING** RON MOODY (Fagin), SHANI WALLIS (Nancy), OLIVER REED (Bill Sikes), HARRY SECOMBE (Mr. Bumble), MARK LESTER (Oliver Twist), JACK WILD (The Artful Dodger), HUGH GRIFFITH (The Magistrate), JOSEPH O'CONOR (Mr. Brownlow), PEGGY MOUNT (Mrs. Bumble), LEONARD ROSSITER (Mr. Sowerberry).

**ACADEMY AWARDS 1968** OSCARS for BEST PICTURE (John Woolf), BEST DIRECTOR (Carol Reed), BEST MUSIC (Johnny Green), BEST ART DIRECTION (John Box, Terence Marsh, Vernon Dixon, Ken Muggleston), BEST SOUND (Shepperton Studios), HONORARY OSCAR for ACHIEVEMENT IN CHOREOGRAPHY (Onna White).

## *"Please sir, I want some more!"*

The porridge thickens when Oliver (Mark Lester) draws the shortest straw. Doomed to public humiliation and unbearable torture, this poor runt must make his way to the front of the refectory and impertinently ask Mr. Bumble (Harry Secombe) for a second helping. "More?" screams the outraged orphanage director, and no sooner has the authoritarian uttered this word than he gives the pipsqueak a good "singing" to, casting him out of his institution.

Before Oliver realizes what's going on, he has been sold off to an undertaker. Unfortunately, the boy finds his new home even more atrocious than his previous one. After flying the coop, he crosses paths with a young street urchin and skilled pickpocket who goes by the name of The Artful Dodger (Jack Wild). He takes Oliver under his wing and brings him home to the dilapidated shack where he lives with the evil Fagin (Ron Moody), an elderly crook who uses a gang of children to traffic in stolen goods. These diminutive thieves relieve unsuspecting Londoners of their valuables by day and are rewarded with sausages and a place to sleep by night. Oliver is soon well-versed in the gentle art of picking pockets. But a mishap on The Artful Dodger's part ends in Oliver's wrongful arrest. Afraid the novice will blow the whistle on them during his court appearance, the nefarious Bill Sikes (Oliver Reed), Fagin's partner in crime, comes up with a plan to ensure that the kid will keep his trap shut.

Oliver's journey from the walls of the orphanage to respectable society is accompanied by no less than 14 song and dance numbers. Carol Reed freely adapted Dickens' classic. In fact, the movie sprang from a hit West End and Broadway musical, which painted a rosy ending onto an abridged version

GOD

1 Consider yourself at home: Orphanage director Mr. Bumble (Harry Secombe) believes in providing children in his care with a classical education. Lesson 1 – Spare the rod and spoil the child.

2 Food glorious food: Today's special, sacrificial lamb. Mark Lester as Oliver Twist.

of the novelist's social criticism. Contrary to the book, Fagin and his beloved Dodger do not die on the gallows, but become reformed characters and are thus allowed to partake in the picture's rosy conclusion. Only Sikes – played in the screen version by the director's nephew Oliver Reed – is made to pay for his wickedness with his life.

Reed had an enormous staff at his disposal, which enabled him to flawlessly recreate industrial revolution London circa 1830 on the lot of England's Shepperton Studios. His 350-man team was dubbed the "Box army" in honor of John Box, the set designer who built the film's street expanses and historic squares to scale. The set was simply wondrous. Brick slums, smoky pubs, drafty attics, creaking staircases, and a bustling marketplace all stand in opposition to the replica of the historic Bloomsbury Square, a patrician reserve of stately town houses. The movie's six Oscars are proof that Romulus Films and Warwick Productions made a solid investment by purchasing the rights to the stage musical.

Song, dance and decor emerge as one grand stylistic entity in *Oliver!* The gesticulations and pantomime of the actors are priceless. Colors and costumes are painstakingly matched to underline the characters' individual

3 Petty thief, petty cash: London fence, Fagin (Ron Moody), keeps a stash of valuables that he secretly indulges in when all are sound asleep.

4 A surrogate family: Fagin (Ron Moody) expects his boys to earn or rather steal their keep. The Artful Dodger (Jack Wild) does his part by recruiting and training for the old crook's network of pickpockets.

5 When push comes to shove: Reverse shots emphasize the obstacles that little Oliver has to overcome and his underlying sense of isolation.

**"Vice is what Oliver Twist tells; romance is what Oliver sells in this musical adaptation. And what a musical it is. A contradictory, comic, steaming, rum plum pudding of a film."** *Time*

“If a single word can suggest the essence of *Oliver!* it is vitality. The film seldom flags, and when it does it renews itself almost instantly. The worst letdown is the intermission. How many movies can you say that about?” *Newsweek*

6 Shades of gray and dreary: Nancy (Shani Willis) dreams of finding true love and happiness with Bill Sikes (Oliver Reed), but gets lost in the shuffle.

7 Cast out into the cold: When Oliver challenges Mr. Bumble's philosophies, the child-rearer sells him to the highest bidder.

traits. Nancy (Shani Wallis), ally to the street kids, dons a red dress in the dance scenes, bringing out her fiery nature. Ron Moody is incomparable as the shady Fagin, singing, dancing and sneering with just the right amount of histrionics. Despite being caked in makeup, Moody titillates the audience with sly dance steps and stolen glances. The masterfully executed choreography of the exterior crowd scenes, as well as those in the taverns, is as awe-inspiring as it is whimsical.

The film's energy is further reflected in the stroke of luck that catapults Oliver back into the bourgeois arms of his biological family. The plaintiff drops all charges against the poor little orphan and even takes him home with him for a few days to make amends. It's not long before Oliver's temporary guardian startlingly discovers that the child is the spitting image of his deceased niece. Good thing that the magistrate (Hugh Griffith) who tried Oliver's case isn't the one presiding over family affairs. The stodgy, red-faced upholder of the law blindly commits the boy to hard labor, and is subsequently perturbed to find out that he is innocent. His astonishment speaks volumes: “But sentence has been passed! … Hasn't it?”

SR

**CAROL REED**

He was born out of wedlock to Sir Herbert Beerbohm Tree and May Reed, but you'd never guess Carol Reed originated from anything other than a dignified background. Tall, slender, and always sporting a slicked back hairdo, this British director was the embodiment of elegance. He earned his reputation in film with the postwar drama *The Third Man* (1949), starring Joseph Cotton hot on the heels of penicillin trafficker Harry Lime (Orson Welles). In an atmosphere of perpetual night, *The Third Man* is an elaborately crafted study in shadow and light, a legendary piece of film noir that paints a portrait of the Viennese black market at the end of World War II. Its thrilling chase scenes in labyrinthine sewers are immortalized in the minds of film buffs. Lime's distorted silhouette cast upon the walls of these tunnels – always just a step ahead of his pursuers – is arguably one of the most unforgettable images in cinematic history. It's no wonder that *Oliver's* villain, Bill Sikes, played by Carol Reed's nephew Oliver Reed, appears in a similar shot.

The success of *The Third Man* – which, like many of Reed's other films, is a literary adaptation – caused the audience's expectations of him as well as those he placed upon himself to skyrocket. Boasting thespian beginnings, Reed performed in a celebrated stage troupe headed by Edgar Wallace. It was this prolific author and mystery expert who taught him how to recognize a good story. Shot during the final year of the Second World War, *The True Glory*, a documentary about the Allied landing in Normandy, won Reed international critical acclaim and the 1946 Best Documentary Film Oscar. During the war Reed had served as the head of Army Cinematographic Services, which provided him with an opportunity to direct film. The Brits also gave official credence to his greatness when Queen Elizabeth returned him to his aristocratic stature. Other gems among Reed's films include *Odd Man Out* (1947), *The Fallen Idol*, (1948), *Night Train to Munich* (1940) and *Our Man in Havana* (1959).

# ROSEMARY'S BABY

1968 - USA - 137 MIN. - HORROR FILM, LITERARY ADAPTATION

DIRECTOR ROMAN POLANSKI (*1933)
SCREENPLAY ROMAN POLANSKI, based on the novel of the same name by IRA LEVIN DIRECTOR OF PHOTOGRAPHY WILLIAM A. FRAKER EDITING SAM O'STEHEN MUSIC KRZYSZTOF KOMEDA PRODUCTION WILLIAM CASTLE for PARAMOUNT PICTURES.

STARRING MIA FARROW (Rosemary Woodhouse), JOHN CASSAVETES (Guy Woodhouse), RUTH GORDON (Minnie Castevet), SIDNEY BLACKMER (Roman Castevet), MAURICE EVANS (Hutch), RALPH BELLAMY (Dr. Sapirstein), ANGELA DORIAN (Terry Fionoffrio), PATSY KELLY (Laura-Louise), ELISHA COOK JR. (Mr. Nicklas), CHARLES GRODIN (Dr. Hill), EMMALINE HENRY (Elise Dunstan), WILLIAM CASTLE (Man in the Phone Booth).

ACADEMY AWARDS 1968 OSCAR for BEST SUPPORTING ACTRESS (Ruth Gordon).

## *"He has his father's eyes."*

Neighbors, begone! I will have no more of thee… Rosemary Woodhouse (Mia Farrow) discovers that hellish neighbors can be included in the cost of rent shortly after she and her husband Guy (John Cassavetes) happen upon the Bramford (a building ill-fated in real life and better known as the Dakota, where John Lennon was shot in 1980). The newly-weds, an actor and his homemaker wife, are intrigued by the lovely brownstone, even before their friend Hutch (Maurice Evans) charms them with tales of its illustrious former occupants. Intending to provide the couple with cautionary fatherly counsel, Hutch fills them in on the practices of the eccentric Trent sisters, who are rumored to feast on human children, and Adrian Marcato, America's most prominent Satanist. Concluding that devil worshipers and a coven of witches can't be nearly as frightening as the real estate market in 1960s New York, the Woodhouses decide to move in anyway.

Folklore intrudes on reality when death visits the building. A young woman, who had been living with the Woodhouse's new neighbors, Minnie and Roman Castevet (Ruth Gordon and Sidney Blackmer), inexplicably commits suicide. The incident leaves the elderly couple at a loss for words and without youthful companionship. Despite initial reservations, Guy befriends the charismatic Roman. Soon foreboding shadows are replaced with cheer. Guy's floundering acting career suddenly takes off and Rosemary learns that she is pregnant.

Yet the couple's joy is lined with ill fortune. Not only does a freak accident leave Guy's professional rival blind, but Rosemary learns that she conceived while unconscious. In the first weeks of pregnancy she comes down with what is clearly more than just a case of morning sickness. Dr. Sapirstein (Ralph Bellamy), a renowned gynecologist referred to her by the Castevets,

1

2

1 Breaking and entering: Rosemary's neighbors have invaded her most personal space – her body (Mia Farrow as Rosemary Woodhouse).

2 A sign of the times: It's no wonder so many people are thinking twice about bringing children into this world.

3 Her little bundle of joy: Rosemary discovers that baby Andy takes after his father.

assures her that what she's experiencing isn't out of the ordinary, and that the excruciating cramps will subside in a matter of days – but they don't.

Rosemary's world spirals into a living nightmare. Hutch, who had some pressing news to share with her, unexpectedly falls into a coma and dies. However, he manages to bequeath a book to her that reveals the name Roman Castevet to be an anagram of Steven Marcato, the son of the Bramford's aforementioned Satanist. Rosemary is positive that a conspiracy has been plotted against her and her baby, never suspecting that the baby growing inside her could in fact be the Antichrist himself.

Contrary to Ira Levin's surreal novel, Polanski is intentionally ambiguous about informing the audience as to whether the events are actually taking place or simply the product of a woman's progressively absorbing paranoia. Characteristic of the film's underlying ambivalence is the dream sequence in which Rosemary cries out, "This is no dream! This is really happening!" For in dreams, there is no certainty; and without certainty there can be no indisputable truth.

It was to be the only liberty Polanski took in his adaptation of Levin's novel, given that the director wanted to remain as true as possible to the writ-

**"It may not be for the very young, and perhaps pregnant women should see it at their own risk."** *Motion Picture Herald*

4 How to succeed in business without really trying: Hubby Guy Woodhouse (John Cassavetes) suddenly hears music in the sound of Rosemary's name.

## “Tension is sustained to a degree surpassing Alfred Hitchcock at his best.” *Daily Telegraph*

**IRA LEVIN**

A New York City native (*1929), author, playwright and lyricist Ira Levin is best known in the world of theater. Nonetheless, as the majority of his novels have been adapted for the silver screen (not to mention the several Broadway shows adapted for American television), his work is equally revered by moviegoers. His film career began with *A Kiss Before Dying* (1956, remade in 1991), long before *Rosemary's Baby* saw the light of day. Yet it goes without saying that Roman Polanski's 1967 critical and box-office sensation provided Levin with his Hollywood breakthrough. The 1997-published sequel *Son of Rosemary*, on the other hand, has failed to spark interest in Hollywood.

Film adaptations of Levin's other work have also met with acclaim – albeit from a primarily artistic standpoint. In 1975, *The Stepford Wives* were fully automated for the screen in an electrifying low-budget sci-fi thriller. *The Boys from Brazil* (1978), a spoof on Nazi war movies, wooed audiences with an all-star cast featuring Gregory Peck, Laurence Olivier and James Mason. Phillip Noyce's 1993 film thriller *Sliver* (written for the screen by Joe Eszterhas) met with limited enthusiasm. Nonetheless, the biggest mystery of this acclaimed writer's career is that the novel many consider his masterpiece, an Orwellian vision of the future entitled *The Perfect Day*, has yet to be filmed.

5 Nowhere to run to, Baby. Nowhere to hide: Even a secluded phone booth provides no vestige of hope.

6 Beast feeding: Rosemary and Guy contemplate the mysteries of life over a game of scrabble and some take out.

ten original for his first Hollywood production. Even the symbolic dream sequences are employed as a means of setting up counterpoints between the realistic manner in which the story is presented and its incredible content.

Like the manuscript it is based on, a seemingly self-perpetuating chain of events lures the viewer into the picture and refuses to loosen its grip even after the story's outcome has been made clear. Every sentence, every shot, and every last detail all contribute to the development of the characters and plot. For instance, when Guy and Rosemary play scrabble early on in the picture, Polanski supplies Rosemary with the device she eventually uses to decipher the Marcato anagram.

Ironically, this perfectly streamlined cinematic narrative was the product of a grossly impractical and uneconomical approach to filmmaking. The first edit of the movie was a five-hour monster, containing numerous scenes that, at the time of filming, Polanski was uncertain would make it into the final cut. If the conception was immaculate, then that's just one more miracle to emerge from the mysteries of the editing suite. SH

# THE THOMAS CROWN AFFAIR

1968 - USA - 102 MIN. - CRIME CAPER

DIRECTOR NORMAN JEWISON

SCREENPLAY ALAN R. TRUSTMAN DIRECTOR OF PHOTOGRAPHY HASKELL WEXLER EDITING HAL ASHBY, RALPH E. WINTERS, BYRON "BUZZ" BRANDT MUSIC MICHEL LEGRAND PRODUCTION NORMAN JEWISON for UNITED ARTISTS, MIRISCH, SIMKOE, SOLAR.

STARRING STEVE MCQUEEN (Thomas Crown), FAYE DUNAWAY (Vicky Anderson), PAUL BURKE (Eddy Malone), JACK WESTON (Erwin Weaver), YAPHET KOTTO (Carl), ADDISON POWELL (Abe).

## *"What a funny, dirty little mind."*

A prospect like this would set any director's mind racing. After the success of *In the Heat of the Night* (1967), winner of five Oscars, United Artists handed Norman Jewison a virtual carte blanche, granting him total artistic freedom and control of his next picture. Attorney and screenwriter Alan Trustman's script sweetened the offer to unheard of proportions. By supplying Jewison's team with nothing more than the bare bones of a script, he unintentionally gave them an even scarcer Hollywood commodity – a generous allotment of time.

The plot can be summed up in a few words. Millionaire Thomas Crown (Steve McQueen) is a self-proclaimed enemy of the system. So he's only too willing to mastermind a bank heist and pull strings from behind the scenes while a group of thugs he's never met carry out the job – and rather flawlessly at that. Before long, insurance investigator Vicky Anderson (Faye Dunaway) is on to Crown, but she can't find any evidence to implicate him in the crime. As she moves in for the kill, hunter and prey fall head over heels in love. And right until the bitter end, we're left wondering whether love or a sense of professional duty will carry the day.

While making *The Thomas Crown Affair* Jewison did what any self-respecting artist with a theatrical background would have done – he explored new cinematic avenues. Having recently attended the Montreal film festival, Jewison stumbled upon a new cinematic technique that got his creative juices flowing – the *multiple* or *split screen* effect.

Jewison transformed screen-splitting potential into a novel narrative device. Hence, Thomas Crown's role as the leader of an international crime ring is made clear to the viewer when he appears in a collage juxtaposed against operatives from various corners of the world. Similarly, many purely stylistic sequences were built around the multi-screen concept, some more

1

THE WALL STREET JOURNAL
What's News
ALABAMA

3

effective than others. One need but cite the polo sequence, which today reads like a televised sport cast filmed with a 60s kaleidoscopic lens.

Indeed, Jewison favored style over content in every regard for *The Thomas Crown Affair.* Snappy clichés and flippant one-liners like "money isn't funny" string together otherwise spartan dialog. They're indicative of the film's paean to superficiality. Riding on the coattails of sumptuous Hollywood thrillers like Stanley Donen's *Charade* (1963) and Edward Dmytryk's *Mirage* (1965), Jewison's picture whisks viewers away to an elegant world, populated by jet-setters who divide their time between town and country, sporting events and art auctions. And so it is only natural that the director devotes more energy to versing his audience in the finer points of luxury automobiles and ladies' hats than the inner workings of organized crime.

This makes for a film whose air of grace stands in glaring opposition to the romantic leads' fierce game of cat and mouse. And yet both forces are its lifeblood. For this is far more than style for its own sake. It is a veritable chess game between a "sophisticated, cynical, romantic protester from the upper class" (Jewison), and a cunning insurance investigator who would never allow herself to be intimidated by extortion and kidnapping.

While Faye Dunaway's Vicky fits like a kid glove on an actress revered for her brassy glamour and innate shallowness, Steve McQueen's role is equally mesmerizing for his being cast against type. Sophisticated is probably the last word one would use to describe the midwestern man's man, who acted as his own stuntman in *The Thomas Crown Affair* just as he did in numerous other films. His character is all the more virile for being a real contradiction in terms. The same can be said of the film and its director. SH

4

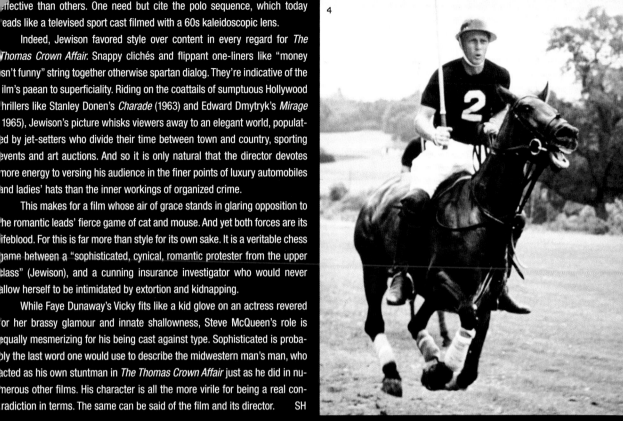

**NORMAN JEWISON** Born 1926 in Toronto, this Canadian writer-director has had a successful career in various show business media, including television, stage, musical theater and film. Although Jewison's films run the gamut of style and genre, the most awe-inspiring thing about them is that they are all connected by one unifying theme – the struggle of the individual against society. Regardless of whether the bigger picture deals with gambling as in *The Cincinnati Kid* (1965), in which a virtual nobody takes on the nation's best card sharps, the inhumanity of racism *In the Heat of the Night* (1967), or the dark side of capitalism as in *Other People's Money* (1991), Jewison's protagonists consistently reject the system. His heroes aren't subversives, but champions of traditional values that stand firm in their breasts. They can be nuns who believe in the right to life like *Agnes of God* (1985), or boxers sentenced to life imprisonment like the *Hurricane* (1999). Closed social communities, such as the one comprised of Italian American immigrants in the heartwarming *Moonstruck* (1987), are the only sanctuary the filmmaker offers from the obligations of society at large. But Jewison is no moralist. He's a stylist, who values form at least as much as content, evidenced in pictures like the *Thomas Crown Affair* (1968) and *Jesus Christ Superstar* (1972). As such, Jewison's social commentary sometimes plays second fiddle to eye candy: *Rollerball* (1974) was proof enough of that.

5

1 It'd be a shame to give all this up: Multimillionaire Thomas Crown (Steve McQueen) puts his entire fortune on the line in the name of vanity and good old-fashioned fun.

2 The king and queen of sensual chess: Following a bit of checkmate, insurance investigator Vicky Anderson (Faye Dunaway) and Thomas Crown get up their strength for the next round in their game of cat and mouse.

3 Let's play something else: The headhunter and detective Eddy Malone (Paul Burke) tire of investigational hopscotch.

4 A sporting chance: Be it polo or sailing, man of leisure Thomas Crown loves a good recreational challenge. But Vicki intends to give him a run for his money.

5 Lovers walk along the shore and leave their footprints in the sand: Where will the winds blow these well-matched opponents?

# BUTCH CASSIDY AND THE SUNDANCE KID

1969 - USA - 110 MIN. - WESTERN

DIRECTOR GEORGE ROY HILL (1921–2002)
SCREENPLAY WILLIAM GOLDMAN DIRECTOR OF PHOTOGRAPHY CONRAD L. HALL EDITING JOHN C. HOWARD, RICHARD C. MEYER
MUSIC BURT BACHARACH PRODUCTION JOHN FOREMAN for CAMPANILE, 20TH CENTURY FOX.

STARRING PAUL NEWMAN (Butch Cassidy), ROBERT REDFORD (Sundance Kid), KATHARINE ROSS (Etta Place), STROTHER MARTIN (Percy Garris), HENRY JONES (Bicycle Salesman), JEFF COREY (Sheriff Bledsoe), GEORGE FURTH (Woodcock), CLORIS LEACHMAN (Agnes), TED CASSIDY (Harvey Logan), KENNETH MARS (Marshal), DONNELLY RHODES (Macon).

ACADEMY AWARDS 1969 OSCARS for BEST ORIGINAL SCREENPLAY (William Goldman), BEST CINEMATOGRAPHY (Conrad L. Hall), BEST MUSIC (Burt Bacharach), BEST SONG: "RAINDROPS KEEP FALLIN' ON MY HEAD" (Music: Burt Bacharach; Lyrics: Hal David).

## *"I've got vision. The rest of the world wears bifocals."*

Up until now, life on the wrong side of the law has been more or less a breeze for notorious outlaws Butch Cassidy and the Sundance Kid (Paul Newman and Robert Redford, respectively). Along with Butch's brains and the Kid's fancy moves, good public relations have been their ticket to success. As we see during a heist on board the Union Pacific, popularity has its privileges. Heck, the engineer nearly greets the bandits with open arms, looking downright pleased to be personally robbed by "Old Butch." There are those, however, who just don't want to go along with the game plan, and Woodcock (George Furth), the train's newly appointed conductor, is one of them. Blocking their path, he leaves the hoodlums with no choice but to dynamite the door. True to form, Butch's first reaction after the blast is to make sure the dazed Woodcock hasn't incurred any injuries – which thankfully he hasn't.

Inspiring more cheer than fear, the tongue-in-cheek title characters in George Roy Hill's tragicomic Western win over most everyone they meet – moviegoers included. There is no show of hands when the sheriff asks for volunteers to hunt these rascals down. Little does he know, they're right under his nose, or rather, he's under theirs. Looking down from the balcony of a nearby brothel, the two bandits get a real kick out of watching the scene below transform from a plea for justice to a sales pitch. The crowd marvels as a traveling salesman gives them their first glimpse of a new-fangled contraption he calls a bicycle. Enthusiastic customers quickly reach for their pocket books, and Butch Cassidy is right there alongside them with a wad of dough.

The next morning he shows up at the house of Kid's girlfriend Etta (Katharine Ross) with his newly acquired purchase. She hops on the handle

1

1 Just like the guy whose feet are too big for his bed: Butch Cassidy (Paul Newman) is the man with the plan – particularly when he needs to find a means to an illegal end.

2 Teacher's pet: Sundance (Robert Redford) tries to get a little extra-credit with young schoolteacher Etta Place (Katharine Ross).

3 Two rowdies and a schoolmarm: Though she had her hopes set high, all Etta has managed to teach these characters is a little sharing among friends.

4 Barnyard burglars: These two foxes are always running from the law, ducking for cover, or checking to see if the coast is clear.

bars and rings the bell of schmaltz as the two of them take a carefree ride to the tune of Burt Bacharach's "Raindrops Keep Fallin' On My Head" – come on, if it's good enough for an Oscar, it's good enough for you! After letting her off, Butch gets a bit carried away with his two-wheeler and lands flat on his fanny in the bull pen. Not to worry, within seconds he's sprung to his feet and is back in the clear.

*Butch Cassidy and the Sundance Kid* may not have been the first picture shot about the two 19th-century Wyoming outlaws, but it's certainly the most memorable, and it quickly became one of the decade's largest grossing hits. Contagiously good fun, William Goldman's script follows the buddies' exploits from their "hole in the wall" hideout to Bolivia, where it is assumed they were eventually gunned down by the military. Even before the film's conclusion, Goldman makes it clear that Butch and Kid's days are numbered, as specially assigned detectives track them down day and night. Yet the charming guns always manage to see the rain cloud's silver lining, with Butch thinking up new half-baked schemes, and Kid game for every one of them. It comes as no surprise that Butch is the one who lands them both way south of the border, where their first move is to learn how to say "hands up" and "this is a robbery" in *español*. At one point, they even attempt to go straight as night patrolmen, but fail miserably: Butch, who's never killed anyone before, jus can't bring himself to shoot vagrants in the line of duty. Needless to say, h quickly sinks into depression following the incident.

Portraying their characters with a boyish, irresistible charm, Paul New man and Robert Redford are undoubtedly the movie's major asset. Butch an Kid do not for a moment see themselves as criminals, remaining blind to th fact that others regard them as a menace to society. Always on the lookou for fun, they pull off increasingly audacious stunts, trying to outdo themselve at every given opportunity.

They uphold this attitude to the bitter end, even when it's clear to th audience that there's no way out. Having been shot at, Butch and Sundanc duck for cover as half the Bolivian army awaits their next move. This, howev er, doesn't stop Butch from dreaming up new plans. They convince eac other that they've survived worse odds and try to make a run for it. The cam era freezes on them and their image is gradually bleached out while th soundtrack explodes with endless gunfire. As such, William Goldman end the movie on a more carefree note. Butch and Sundance remain etched i our memories as optimistic soldiers of fortune, although we know the bloody fate. Hollywood was never grander.

H

5 A bicycle built for two: If it's good enough for Oscar, it's good enough for you.

6 One track minds: Even dynamite can't derail the thoughts of this gruesome twosome. As far as these two guys are concerned, it's capital gains or bust.

7 From bandits to banditos: Try as they might, Butch and Sundance just can't get on the right side of the law. As the saying goes, old habits die hard.

# "The film does wonderful things with mood and atmosphere. The touches are fleeting, but they are there."

*Saturday Review*

**GEORGE ROY HILL (1921–2002)**

Like fellow directors Sidney Lumet, Arthur Penn and John Frankenheimer, George Roy Hill was part of a generation of filmmakers whose career jumpstarted in television. Such displays of talent could not go entirely unnoticed by Hollywood, and dramas like *Delbert Man* (TV 1953; Hollywood 1955) and *Twelve Angry Men* (TV 1954; Hollywood 1957) were adapted for the big screen after debuting on its smaller cousin. Former reporter and actor George Roy Hill's directorial debut came with his film adaptation of Tennessee Williams' *Period of Adjustment* (1962). With *Butch Cassidy and the Sundance Kid,* Hill made it to the big league, maintaining a close friendship with the picture's two leading men, Paul Newman and Robert Redford, for years to come. In 1973, the three of them reunited to work on *The Sting* (1973), for which Hill won the Best Director Oscar. Many of Hill's pictures were based on books, like *The World According to Garp* (1982), a tragicomedy that proved to be another international success. In his memoirs, *Butch Cassidy and the Sundance Kid's* screenwriter William Goldman called George Roy Hill "one of the most underrated filmmakers of the last 30 years."

DIRECTOR TOM GRIES (1922–1977)

SCREENPLAY CLAIR HUFFAKER, TOM GRIES, based on a novel by ROBERT MACLEOD DIRECTOR OF PHOTOGRAPHY CECILIO PANIAGUA EDITING ROBERT SIMPSON MUSIC JERRY GOLDSMITH PRODUCTION MARVIN SCHWARTZ for 20TH CENTURY FOX, MARVIN SCHWARTZ PRODUCTIONS, INC.

STARRING JIM BROWN (Lyedecker), RAQUEL WELCH (Sarita), BURT REYNOLDS (Yaqui Joe Herrera), FERNANDO LAMAS (General Verdugo), DAN O'HERLIHY (Steven Grimes), HANS GUDEGAST A. K. A. ERIC BRAEDEN (Lt. Franz von Klemme), MICHAEL FOREST (Humara), ALDO SAMBRELL (Sgt. Paletes), SOLEDAD MIRANDA (Girl at the Hotel), ALBERTO DALBES (Padre Francisco).

## *"It's not my war, it's not my job."*

In 1970, *Playboy* dedicated a full issue to the "revelation" that Hollywood had started filming sex scenes whose explicit nature would have been unthinkable a mere decade ago. The men's magazine identified the ever-increasing number of big-name stars of both genders to grace the screens in their birthday suits as a new trend, and welcomed the fact that directors and authors were finally exploring age-old taboos like interracial romance. What had recently seemed light years removed from the Hollywood mindset became a focal point of the 1969/1970 cinematic line-up.

*100 Rifles* was to the first picture to cross this line, causing many a head to turn with a love scene that is more than tame by today's standards. Nonetheless, the on-screen intimacy was fired by the hottest sexual cannons of the day: former black pro-football player Jim Brown and 60s light-skinned super vixen Raquel Welch lit up the screen and tripped the media alarm by locking lips. The screenwriters, of course, didn't throw all caution to the wind. Rather than taking a genuine risk and making Welch's character Caucasian (as she was usually marketed to the American audience although she is, in fact, of Bolivian descent), Sarita is a full-fledged Latina. As a "sinner" and violator of the melodramatic code of ethics, the Mexican Sarita is denied a happy ending and doomed to meet a violent end.

Yet until her last breath, it is Raquel Welch who owns the picture. Riding into the project at the height of her popularity, Welch manages to turn Sarita into the patron saint of the oppressed Mexican people. The picture opens with Sarita as the helpless witness of injustice: her father is lynched for the crime of possessing a firearm. Once the scoundrels – the henchmen of the

1

2

3

sinister General Verdugo (Fernando Lamas) – have finished him off they claim Sarita as their own. But it just so happens that the American Sheriff Lyedecker (Jim Brown) arrives in the pueblo of Nogales at about the same time as the bandits. The sheriff has been searching for an Injun with a price on his head named Yaqui Joe (Burt Reynolds). A sly devil himself, Joe has decided to lend a hand in the indigenous people's uprising against the state by rounding up enough cash to supply the "tigres de las rocas" (a.k.a. rock tigers) with 100 rifles.

Sarita manages to get away from her captors and is soon assisting efforts to organize the weapons. After experiencing the cruelties of the military firsthand, Lyedecker joins forces with the two of them, readily becoming the movement's leader. Fighting battles and incurring heavy losses, the valiant guerrillas succeed in attacking a train and Verdugo's military strongholds. The army's German military advisor von Klemme – played by Hans Gudegast (later performing on daytime TV's *The Young and the Restless*, 1973–1980, under the name Eric Braeden) – tries to get out while the going is good. Conversely, the American bureaucrat Grimes (Dan O'Herlihy), who is in charge of developing the railroad and had his sights sets on higher office with Verdugo, switches sides: he welcomes new local official, Yaqui Joe, with open arms. Joe is appointed to take up where Lyedecker leaves off, when the sheriff ultimately decides to return to the States.

Tom Gries' direction of the poorly equipped freedom fighters' foolhardy

**"What may have been inserted for shock purposes is a seduction scene between a white woman and a black man, Raquel Welch and Jim Brown. The action as staged is distasteful as the pair kiss and clinch, and may meet with resistance from certain censorship groups as well as other exhibs."** *Variety*

4

1 Adios muchacha: Last action heroine Sarita (Raquel Welch) fights an impassioned battle in the name of the Yaqui Indians, and dies a martyr.

2 A man with a short fuse: Yaqui Joe (Burt Reynolds) decides he's had enough of life on the wrong side of the tracks and crowns himself king of the road.

3 Make a run for the border, there's a new Sheriff in town: Lyedecker (Jim Brown) helps the indigenous people round up their 100 rifles and ticket to freedom.

4 Resisting arrest: Sarita would charge Lyedecker with assault and battery if we just weren't so damn hunky. The jungle fever was racy enough to create quite an uproar at the time of the picture's release.

5 Cowboys, Indians and Playboy bunnies: Is there really any doubt as to how the West was won in the summer of love?

undertakings is vitalized by a wit and panache usually reserved for pirate movies. Etched in the memories of the picture's fans is the scene in which Sarita uses her womanly charms as a diversion tactic. The skimpily clad beauty walks over to a water tank next to a train line, and sensuously proceeds to shower. Meanwhile, a train transporting weapons and soldiers approaches. The uniformed men enthusiastically wave, cat call and shout obscenities at her. In their ardor, they fail to notice either the embrasures in the water tank or the rebels camouflaged in the surrounding sands. One of the cheekier guys on board jumps off the moving locomotive in the hopes of getting a taste of what Sarita has to offer. He quickly learns his lesson the hard way, when the sexy senorita whips out her weapon and shoots the lecher clear into next Tuesday. Her action, in turn, is the signal to her compadres to open fire and a battle ensues that marks the beginning of the end for Verdugo. The struggle for freedom is not without its casualties, and Sarita will be among them.

HK

**RAQUEL WELCH**

The social revolution of the 1960s fulfilled its promise by proving that a married woman and mother of two could become an international sex symbol.

Marrying high school sweetheart James Welch at age 18, Jo Raquel Tejada (*1940) worked as a waitress, model and weather bunny before moving to Los Angeles in 1963. Her rise to fame was due largely to producer and press agent Patrick Curtis, who made her world famous by marketing her knockout physical attributes. Together, the two of them founded the production company, Curtwell Enterprises. Following Raquel's divorce from James Welch, she married her agent and business partner. She has been married a total of four times to date.

Curtis' publicity efforts met with astounding success. Welch, who had studied acting and ballet as a youngster, even had a bit of acting experience when she signed with 20th Century Fox. From then on she could be seen as skimpily clad set deco in pictures like *Fantastic Voyage* (1966) and *One Million Years B. C.* (1966); she never bared all, but what she didn't show, suggested everything. Welch acted in European productions on the side and gradually began to win more serious roles. Seen in this light, the 1970s were her golden era. She acted opposite Richard Burton in the mystery drama *Bluebeard* (1972) and played Constance de Bonancieux in Richard Lester's *The Four Musketeers* (1974). Since the 1980s, Welch's career has focused on made-for-TV movies and various shows.

# THEY SHOOT HORSES, DON'T THEY?

1969 - USA - 120 MIN. - DRAMA, LITERARY ADAPTATION

DIRECTOR SYDNEY POLLACK (*1934)

SCREENPLAY JAMES POE, ROBERT E. THOMPSON, based on the novel of the same name by HORACE MCCOY
DIRECTOR OF PHOTOGRAPHY PHILIP LATHROP EDITING FREDRIC STEINKAMP MUSIC JOHNNY GREEN PRODUCTION IRWIN WINKLER, ROBERT CHARTOFF for PALOMAR PICTURES, AMERICAN BROADCASTING COMPANIES.

STARRING JANE FONDA (Gloria Beatty), MICHAEL SARRAZIN (Robert Syverton), SUSANNAH YORK (Alice), GIG YOUNG (Rocky), RED BUTTONS (Sailor), BONNIE BEDELIA (Ruby), BRUCE DERN (James), AL LEWIS (Turkey), ROBERT FIELDS (Joel), SEVERN DARDEN (Cecil).

ACADEMY AWARDS 1969 OSCAR for BEST SUPPORTING ACTOR (Gig Young).

## *"There can only be one winner, folks. But isn't that the American way?"*

The kind of torture people were willing to put themselves through during the Depression Era for a few square meals and the chance to win 1,500 dollars is enough to make your jaw drop.

Our story opens in Southern California, where a non-stop, partner-dance marathon is scheduled to take place. Participants are allowed only a ten-minute break every two hours but otherwise the motto is "dance till you drop." Meals, too, must be consumed while moving on the dance floor. The last pair remaining on their feet get to take the prize money home.

As the couples arrive and are "sorted" upon registration, the forces that actually run this production become all too clear. A pregnant woman may participate – she'll be plugged as a "special interest" case. A man with a cough, however, is immediately disqualified – he could be contagious. And so Gloria (Jane Fonda), the cougher's partner, is left without anyone to dance with and must find a substitute. The competition's cynical coordinator and MC, Rocky (Gig Young), supplies her with a young vagrant by the name of Robert (Michael Sarrazin). Soon, the festivities are off to a roaring start as dozens of colorful couples proceed to fill the dance floor. Among them are James and the very pregnant Ruby (Bruce Dern, Bonnie Bedelia), Alice and Joel (Susannah York, Robert Fields), two would-be actors hoping to get discovered, as well as an elderly sailor with a heart-condition (Red Buttons) and his female companion.

Dance, as an art form, embodies grace, beauty and joy. Here, it is none of those things. Instead, it becomes a medium of degradation, a circus in which downtrodden individuals are subjected to Herculean trials solely to entertain the crowd in the bleachers. After some three or four hundred hours, what started off as dancing has deteriorated into something dreadful. Couples listlessly lean against one another. Every so often they dance without their partners, drifting about the dance floor like mindless zombies. But they don't remain that way for long. At the 600 and 1,200 hours mark, everyone

1

2

**"An allegorical, social response to the injuries of the Depression Era, *They Shoot Horses, Don't They?* has managed to survive the late 1960s, unlike so many other films of that period, without appearing the least bit dated."** *Motion Picture Guide*

1 Round and round and round they go: Where Gloria and Robert (Jane Fonda, Michael Sarrazin, center) will stop – nobody knows!

2 Too hot to trot: A footrace takes place at the 600 and 1200-hour marks in the competition. The three couples to come in last bite the dust – and receive no booby prizes.

3 Easy come, easy go: Aspiring actress Alice (Susannah York) hopes to get discovered at the dance marathon, but only ends up losing that which is dear to her – a slinky evening gown.

remaining must compete in a footrace, in which the three slowest couples are eliminated from the marathon. Beyond exhaustion, they look with disoriented eyes as they try to get their bearings on the track, an instance where the reference to horses becomes strikingly clear. As witnessed in the atmospheric images of Robert's remembered childhood near the top of the film, the four-legged animals only need break a leg to be put out of their misery. This event, however, dictates that human beings stay on their feet until they collapse – which is exactly what happens to the sailor character. Director Sydney Pollack and cinematographer Philip Lathrop captured the sense of an eternal rat-race with gripping and majestic images. Lathrop's camera glides through the sea of dancers, circling about them and breathing down their necks. Interestingly enough, it was Pollack who filmed the stunning footrace scene, literally whizzing alongside the action on a pair of roller-skates. Jane Fonda's poignant performance also contributes to the film's excellence. Gloria was arguably the most dramatically demanding role Fonda had taken on to date, and an undoubted shift from the deadpan camp of *Barbarella*, 1968. She was honored with one of the film's nine Academy Award nominations. However, the sole Oscar the movie was recognized with went to supporting actor Gig Young.

*They Shoot Horses, Don't They?* is based on Horace McCoy's novel, first published in 1935. The manuscript passed through many hands in Hollywood – Charlie Chaplin included – before it finally ended up with producer-director Sydney Pollack. At the time of the novel's initial publication, it was widely hailed throughout the literary world, and Jean-Paul Sartre deemed it a masterpiece. Today, the picture's appeal is not so much its allegorical portrait of the Depression Era, but its scathing critique of show business. It does an exemplary job of illustrating the extremes people are prepared to go to when tempted by fame and fortune, and the willingness with which people humiliate themselves in the interests of sensationalism. When the sadistic MC tries to pressure Gloria and Robert into tying the knot on the dance floor for the benefit of the production, is it really all that different from the motivations of modern day reality shows like *Big Brother*, in which everyday people are lured into performing acts that would normally be against their principles?

HJK

**"Pollack turns the marathon into a vulgar, sleazy black microcosm of life in 1932."** *Variety*

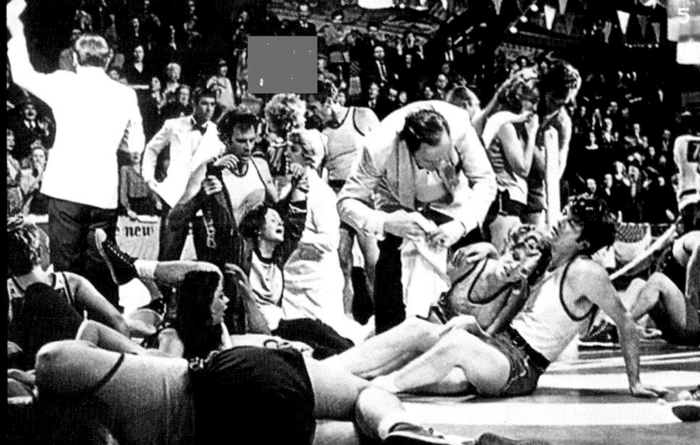

4 And they're off: These guys just can't free themselves from the never-ending rat race.

5 Destined for the glue factory: It's not long before the first tuckered out contestants get trampled and disqualified.

6 All the pretty horses: Why give up when there's still a chance at winning? Robert (3rd from right) switches partners and takes new partner Alice (3rd from left) for a spin round the dance floor.

**GIG YOUNG (1913–1978)**

"Yowser, yowser, yowser!" As master of ceremonies, Rocky's eerie bark is meant to boost the spirits of the dance marathon participants, as they spin around in endless circles. This part proved to be Gig Young's role of a lifetime, and he was awarded his sole Oscar for his performance. Young had been nominated twice before for *Come Fill the Cup* (1951) and *Teacher's Pet* (1958), but as the saying goes – third time lucky. His best supporting actor commendation was, on the one hand, highly indicative of the type of roles that the former student of the Pasadena Community Playhouse played throughout his film career. Yet, on the other, the part for which he received this distinction, that of a cynical emcee, was very much out of character for an actor often cast in light comedies as the charming gentleman with a melancholy veneer. In 1941, the then stage actor was spotted by a Warner Bros. talent scout and immediately signed. He was initially billed under his given name, Byron Barr, until adopting the name of the character he played in *The Gay Sisters* (1942) as his own. Gig Young would appear in more than fifty films over the course of his career, playing alongside stars like Elizabeth Taylor in *The Girl Who Had Everything* (1953), Cary Grant in *That Touch of Mink* (1962) and even Bruce Lee in *Game of Death* (*Si wang you ju*, 1977). *Game of Death*, eerily enough, was Young's final picture. In 1978, he shot his fifth wife, German actress Kim Schmidt, and subsequently turned the gun on himself, taking both their lives.

# PATTON

1969/70 - USA - 170 MIN. - WAR FILM, BIOPIC

DIRECTOR Franklin J. Schaffner (1920–1989)
SCREENPLAY FRANCIS FORD COPPOLA, EDMUND NORTH, based on the reports "Patton: Ordeal and Triumph," by LADISLAS FARAGO and "A Soldier's Story" by OMAR N. BRADLEY DIRECTOR OF PHOTOGRAPHY FRED J. KOENEKAMP EDITING HUGH S. FOWLER MUSIC JERRY GOLDSMITH PRODUCTION FRANK MCCARTHY for 20TH CENTURY FOX.

STARRING GEORGE C. SCOTT (General George S. Patton Jr.), KARL MALDEN (General Omar N. Bradley), PAUL STEVENS (Lieutenant Colonel Charles R. Codman), MICHAEL BATES (Field Marshal Montgomery), ED BINNS (Major General Bedell Smith), LAWRENCE DOBKIN (Colonel Gaston Bell), KARL MICHAEL VOGLER (Field Marshall Erwin Rommel), RICHARD MÜNCH (General Alfred Jodl), SIEGFRIED RAUCH (Captain Oskar Steiger), JOHN DOUCETTE (Major General Lucian K. Truscott), JAMES EDWARDS (Sergeant William George Meeks), FRANK LATIMORE (Lieutenant Colonel Henry Davenport).

ACADEMY AWARDS 1970 OSCARS for BEST PICTURE (Frank McCarthy), BEST DIRECTOR (Franklin J. Schaffner), BEST ACTOR (George C. Scott), BEST SCREENPLAY (Francis Ford Coppola, Edmund H. North), BEST EDITING (Hugh S. Fowler), BEST ART DIRECTION (Urie McCleary, Gil Parrondo, Antonio Mateos, Pierre-Louis Thévenet), and BEST SOUND (Douglas O. Williams, Don J. Bassman).

## *"I feel I'm destined to achieve some great thing. What, I don't know."*

When *Patton* was released in 1970, a large proportion of the movie-going public, and especially its younger members, found World War II considerably less interesting than the Vietnam conflict which was then just entering a further stage of escalation. At a time when more and more people were rejecting – and actively resisting – the war in South-East Asia, a big-budget movie ($12.5 million) focusing on the life and times of the eccentric General George S. Patton Jr. must have seemed like a spectacular commercial misjudgment. Fearing a box-office disaster, the studio added a suffix to the title in a desperate attempt to appeal to a young audience: *Patton – A Salute to a Rebel.* Though several European distributors adopted the altered title, director Franklin J. Schaffner managed to persuade the studio to reconsider their decision. The suffix was dropped for the U.S. market – and plain-and-simple *Patton* was a box-office smash.

*Patton* does without the usual Fox logo and fanfare and begins with a shot from below of an outsize star-spangled banner. The flag, hanging behind a stage, is truly enormous, almost filling the screen. The chatter of the audience subsides as a figure arises from their ranks and heads for the stage. With a face like thunder, General Patton (George C. Scott) addresses the assembled soldiers, and his speech is peppered with expletives. He leaves his listeners in no doubt as to what he thinks of the war, the enemy, an American's duty to the fatherland, and the contempt he feels for the "cowards" in his own ranks. The camera follows his every step. The element he moves in is the Stars and Stripes itself; indeed, he seems almost to melt into it. And whatever the listeners' feelings about the speech, the man himself simply cannot be ignored. *Patton* is not merely a historical drama, but a film that deals directly with its own turbulent times, as this opening speech makes

1

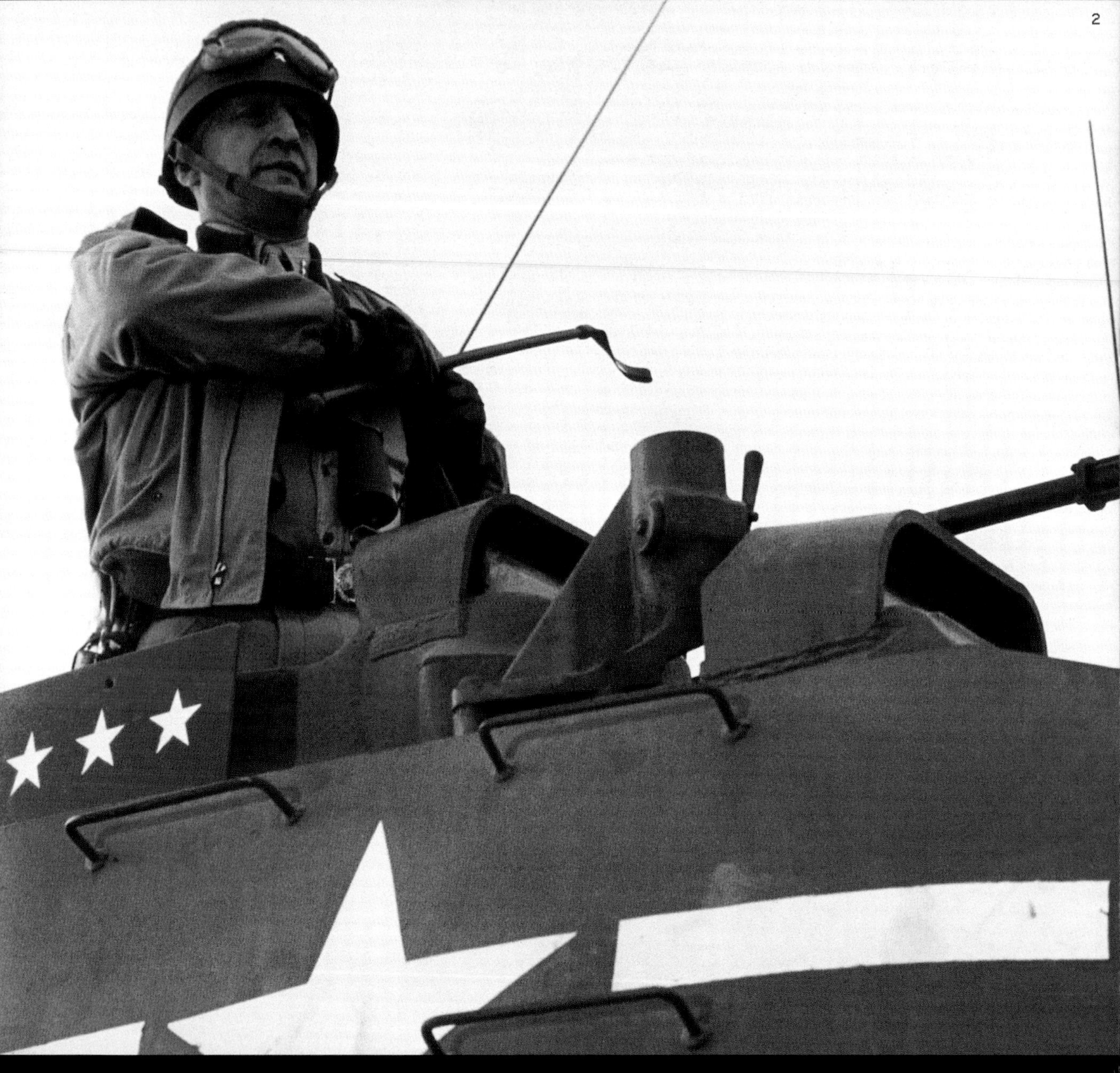

abundantly clear. Only towards the end is the enemy – "the Nazis" – actually named. The preceding sentences, addressed to an audience of soldiers in wartime, were productively, and disturbingly, ambiguous: which war was he talking about? Although the flag obviously appeals to the collective identity of the American public, the scene has an unreal quality that also allows moviegoers to maintain a certain distance. In the two-and-a-half hours that follow this opening speech, *Patton* creates a multi-layered portrait of a figure who was already controversial in his lifetime. The film's account of his career spans the period from the struggle against Rommel in Africa to the end of the war, and concludes shortly before Patton's death in Germany in 1945.

George C. Scott's portrayal of this highly ambivalent character is an exceptional acting achievement. It's a detailed and nuanced performance, and quite riveting to watch. Patton is a bundle of contradictions: a stubborn and implacable commander, a cultivated man of the world, a loyal patriot and an unscrupulous careerist. He believes in reincarnation, he's a Calvinist, and yet he swears like a trooper, non-stop. But besides an Oscar for Scott as Best Actor, *Patton* also marched off with Academy Awards in six other categories, including Best Film and Best Director. And indeed, Franklin J. Schaffner's entire movie is every bit as multi-faceted as its real-life protagonist and its leading actor. Franklin's dynamic wide-screen compositions are as impressive as his meticulously precise rendering of the General's character.

*Patton* moves cautiously across the minefield of public emotions about war and military leadership by presenting a carefully constructed dual image of the controversial General." *Robert Brent Tolpin, History by Hollywood – The Use and Abuse of the American Past*

1 Warmonger and national icon: General George S. Patton Jr. (George C. Scott) runs a tight ship. Scott won a Best Actor Oscar for his depiction of the historical figure and died a legend on September 22nd, 1999.

2 Next stop, Valhalla: Patton rides his tanks into Berlin, where he plans to blow the wolf clear out of his lair. George C. Scott reassumed the role of General Patton for the 1986 TV movie *The Last Days of Patton.*

3 48 stars, but none as patriotic as Patton: Double-edged symbolism is just one of the things that makes *Patton* a cinematic treasure. The film's audience was presented with completely original takes on war, violence and national pride.

Though many episodes in Patton's life have a bizarre touch to them, the film delivers a largely neutral depiction of its hero, so that both supporters and opponents of the hardliner continue to feel confirmed in their view of the man. What's undeniable, however, is that Scott's performance is captivating; and whatever the historical Patton's strengths and weaknesses may have been, it's impossible not to feel some sympathy for the grouchy General as embodied by George C. Scott. Certainly, the film takes care to develop a critical perspective in the early stages, but it's also punctuated by comic scenes in which all critical distance is abandoned. It's hard not to laugh at Patton's indignation when his yellow-bellied bull terrier is panicked by a tiny Chi- visable to avoid spouting insults and curses in the course of an important job interview.

The film's ambivalence becomes particularly clear in the diversity of its perspectives on the war. On the one hand, we're shown the blackened and mutilated corpses of U.S. soldiers on the battlefield – a wholly un-idealized view of what war actually does to the human body. Yet, in stark contrast to this, we have the depiction of Patton's military triumphs. As shown in the last hour of the film, the Allies' grueling Ardennes offensive seems more or less a cakewalk; and the appearance of a few exhausted and poorly-armed U.S. soldiers seems a somewhat perfunctory commentary on a military operation

**FRANKLIN J. SCHAFFNER** Director Franklin J. Schaffner (1920–1989) may have been flattered by the fact that *Patton* (1969/70) was the favorite film of a U.S. President. But he can hardly have been pleased by the rumor that the movie strengthened Nixon in his resolve to bomb Cambodia. Indeed, he insisted repeatedly that *Patton* was intended to be an anti-war film. Like Sidney Lumet and Arthur Penn, Schaffner is a director who learned his trade making live television in the 50s and went on to shape the Hollywood cinema of the 60s. Studio boss Richard Zanuck of 20th Century Fox hired him to make *Planet of the Apes* (1967/68), before entrusting him with *Patton*. Many of the stories Schaffner chose to adapt can be seen as critical commentaries on current affairs. *The Best Man* (1964), based on a work by Gore Vidal, showed politics as a filthy business revolving around money and power. *Planet of the Apes* was a provocative depiction of the hubris of the human race, and it warned of the dangers of nuclear war. Both in form and content, this was an audacious film. It was the fifth movie Schaffner had directed and his second collaboration with Charlton Heston, following *The War Lord* (1965). *Papillon* (1973), starring Steve McQueen und Dustin Hoffman, was an indictment of the arbitrariness and brutality of state power and a defense of the harried and oppressed individual. Shaffner – who had himself served during the Second World War – was awarded an Oscar for *Patton*. The last movie he made was *Welcome Home* (1989), starring Kris Kristofferson, the story of a Vietnam Vet's return to the States. The film's Director of Photography, Fred J. Koenekamp, had been Schaffner's regular cameraman since *Patton*. From 1987 till 1989, Franklin J. Schaffner was President of the Directors' Guild of America. On July 2nd, 1989, he died in Santa Monica, California.

**"I want you to remember, that no bastard ever won a war by dying for his country. He won it by making the other poor dumb bastard die for his country."**

*Film quote: General George S. Patton Jr. (George C. Scott)*

4 Serial killer: Patton lets vanity get the better of him and shoots a newsreel – a. k. a. war propaganda film. His every move hits the German army and his own like a curveball from out of nowhere.

5 A new breed of flying predator: As in so many of his pictures, director Franklin J. Schaffner combines stunning visuals with brilliant character studies.

6 Plowing through land mines: General Bradley (Karl Malden) doesn't just prove his tactical genius on the front, he also can see where Patton intends to steer his career and throws hurdles in his path.

Patton's inexorable onward march is accompanied by the music of Jerry Goldsmith, who composed a stirring musical leitmotif that underscored the General's enthusiasm for the business of war. Here, the music appears to be glorifying Patton, supporting the creation of a mythical hero. At other points in the film, however, Goldsmith's score allows a more critical view of the General and reflects the warring elements in his personality.

The movie's final shots show the General walking across a field. The war is over. We hear Patton's voice, off-camera, describing the triumphal progress of a returning Roman emperor: "A slave stood behind the conqueror, holding a golden crown, and whispering in his ear a warning: that all glory is fleeting." We have just been shown how the war was won, and this "warning" seems to be a critical metaphor for the United States' foreign policy in the quarter-century since the Allied victory. The lines were written by the young Francis Ford Coppola, who had "dodged" the draft in order to avoid serving in Vietnam – and who went on, a decade later, to make *Apocalypse Now* (1979). *Patton* remains ambivalent until the very end. DG

# ZABRISKIE POINT

1969 - USA - 110 MIN. - DRAMA

DIRECTOR MICHELANGELO ANTONIONI (*1912)
SCREENPLAY MICHELANGELO ANTONIONI, FRANCO ROSSETTI, SAM SHEPARD, TONINO GUERRA, CLARE PEPLOE
DIRECTOR OF PHOTOGRAPHY ALFIO CONTINI EDITING MICHELANGELO ANTONIONI, FRANCO ARCALLI MUSIC PINK FLOYD, THE GRATEFUL DEAD, JERRY GARCIA, THE KALEIDOSCOPE PRODUCTION CARLO PONTI for MGM, TRIANON PRODUCTIONS.

STARRING MARK FRECHETTE (Mark), DARIA HALPRIN (Daria), ROD TAYLOR (Lee Allen), PAUL FIX (Café Owner), G. D. SPRADLIN (Businessman), BILL GARAWAY (Morty), KATHLEEN CLEAVER (Kathleen).

## *"I'm willing to die... but not of boredom."*

The Revolution may well be worth the ultimate sacrifice – but does it have to be so deadly dull? Accused of being a bourgeois individualist, Mark (Mark Frechette) drops out of the university circle where black and white students engage in endless discussions about how to beat the Establishment and change the world. Mark attempts to pay the bail for a friend who's been arrested, and is himself taken into custody for no reason. When asked his name, Mark quips: "Karl Marx;" the policeman dutifully writes down: "Carl Marx." Mark is at a demonstration where the cops are laying into the protestors; he pulls a gun out of his boot and shoots a policeman, who crumples to the ground. Mark flees, steals a plane and flies off into the desert. There, he meets Daria (Daria Halprin), who's working for Lee Allen (Rod Taylor), the manager of a company called "Sunnydunes." Allen is planning to open up Death Valley to the property market. Mark and Daria make love at the viewing platform, "Zabriskie Point"...

This thin plotline was apparently enough to persuade the bosses at MGM to grant Italian art-house director Michelangelo Antonioni six million dollars for his first American film. They were hoping to hit the jackpot with the booming youth market. Antonioni's *Blow Up* had been a gripping and stylistically innovative portrait of Swinging London; *Zabriskie Point*, as an expression of the hippie culture of the U. S., was expected to match its success easily. The chaotic and almost universal phenomenon of mass dissent was pruned down to a few simple antitheses: students versus police, Free Love versus authority, the desert versus civilization. Yet the film turned out to be a disaster. Audiences and critics rejected it with remarkable unanimity. MGM went bust even before filming had ended, and the guilty man was quickly found: for not only had Antonioni cast two complete unknowns in the leading roles; he had also made a movie that broke radically with traditional, linear-narrative, storytelling cinema.

1

1 Police interstate: There's no escape from the law, even in the desert.

2 Negative spaces: The university is surrounded and Mark was in the vicinity when a cop was killed. It remains impossible to determine whether he was the one who pulled the trigger as Antonioni's film refuses to distinguish between fact and fiction.

**"What's different about this revolutionary generation is not what the young people want – freedom. Everybody always has wanted that. What's different is the way they go after it. It's a matter of practical application. They know what they want, but they don't know exactly how to reach for it."** *Michelangelo Antonioni*

3 From the mountains to the prairies: In a stolen aircraft, Mark flies Daria over Death Valley.

4 Getting frisked on route 66: Daria attempts to distract the highway patrolman from Mark, but she misinterprets his intentions. The cop has actually been eyeing her from behind his shades all along.

5 Pouty face: After a sordid love affair with her boss, Daria (Daria Halprin) hits the road to get back in touch with nature and finds Mark in the process.

*Zabriskie Point* is an allegorical trip into the silence of Death Valley, a knife in the heart of the American Dream. The promise of freedom held out by the desert has already been crippled by Lee's plans to citify it. In the loneliness of the shimmering red dunes, Mark and Daria live out a sensual utopia. It's a genuine manifestation of the students' dream, but it's over almost before it begins: dopey tourists and violent cops very quickly put an end to it. Mark and Daria's discussions remain abstract, and their revolutionary acts are finally without consequence. It's only the director's authority that gives the film any force at all, and his method is an extravagant aestheticism.

The sex scene is positively surreal, as if the uncontrollable energy of love had shaken Death Valley to the core. To the psychedelic sounds of Pink Floyd, new couples emerge from nowhere, writhing ecstatically in the sand alongside Mark and Daria. Though the scene attempts to express a kind of universal natural harmony, these couples seem strangely and sadly isolated.

The final scene, however, is one of the highpoints of cinematic history – and it, too, functions according to the principle of unexpected multiplication. After Mark has surrendered and been shot by the police, Daria goes back to her boss. His house is located on the side of a mountain in the middle of the

6 Redesigning America: Mark (Mark Frechette) rebels against the police and boredom. A passionate individualist, Mark clashes with the students' movement and escapes to enjoy brief bliss with Daria.

7 Counter culture: Student unrest meets random violence. Now it seems the world's future academics will have more to tackle than just the establishment.

desert. In this heroic edifice, a final meeting on the planned advertising campaign is in full swing. Repelled by the mutterings of these old men, Daria turns away; and in her imagination, the building explodes. But not just once: Antonioni filmed this cataclysm from 17 different viewpoints, and each of these sequences is a tour de force of appalling beauty. The film concludes with the explosion of TV sets and numerous other consumer goods.

While the critics complained mainly about Antonioni's intellectual formalism, activists and politicians of all colors mobilized against the European's attempt to invade their patch. The accusations ranged from fascism to anti-Americanism. Local people sabotaged filming, and the FBI started an investigation into the alleged importation of pornography to California (coals to Newcastle?) Today, despite all its faults and clichés, the film still manages to impress as a European vision of America's counterculture. *Zabriskie Point* is a mesmerizing experience, and perhaps it overwhelmed the charismatic amateur leading man. Mark Frechette died in prison in 1975, under circumstances that have still never been wholly clarified. He had been serving a lengthy jail sentence for bank robbery; and at the time of his arrest, he had described it as a political act. PB

9

8 A capital venture: Lee Allen's (Rod Taylor) Sunny Dunes enterprise believes that untapped profits lie buried in the desert.

9 Just a dreamer or a baby Bin Laden? *Zabriskie Point* embraces controversy and dares to be different.

**REBELLION IN THE MOVIES** The end of the 60s witnessed the displacement of the cinematic underground (from Andy Warhol to Kenneth Anger) by the movies of the so-called counter-culture. The hippie movement – drugs, free love, Anti-Vietnam-War protests, Black Power, and of course music – began to make inroads into the American mainstream. At the very same time, this mainstream cinema was endeavoring to adapt the experimental techniques developed by avant-garde filmmakers such as Godard and Antonioni. Very soon, youth films such as *Skidoo* (1968), *Medium Cool* (1969) and *Easy Rider* (1969) were emerging, along with the rockumentaries *Monterey Pop* (1968) and *Woodstock* (1970). It was notable that two of the biggest flops were ambitious MGM productions – *The Strawberry Statement* (1970) and *Zabriskie Point* (1969) – and it's interesting that both of them have one major feature in common with the cult road movie *Easy Rider*: all three films end with an act of violence that obliterates the protagonists' high ideals. This has often been linked to the excessive violence in Sam Peckinpah's Late Western *The Wild Bunch* (1969), which ushered in a new era in the cinema. Martin Scorsese's *Taxi Driver* (1975) was a kind of farewell to the Revolution: by mowing down the corrupt hippies, Travis Bickle, played by Robert De Niro, became an idol of the coming generation of punks.

# ALICE'S RESTAURANT

1969 - USA - 110 MIN. - TRAGICOMEDY, MUSIC FILM

**DIRECTOR** ARTHUR PENN (*1922)
**SCREENPLAY** ARTHUR PENN, VENABLE HERNDON, based on the ballad of the same name by ARLO GUTHRIE
**DIRECTOR OF PHOTOGRAPHY** MICHAEL NEBBIA **EDITING** DEDE ALLEN **MUSIC** ARLO GUTHRIE **PRODUCTION** HILLARD ELKINS, JOSEPH MANDUKE for FLORIN.

**STARRING** ARLO GUTHRIE (Arlo), PATRICIA QUINN (Alice), JAMES BRODERICK (Ray), MICHAEL MCCLANATHAN (Shelley), GEOFF OUTLAW (Roger), TINA CHEN (Mari-Chan), KATHLEEN DABNEY (Karin), WILLIAM OBANHEIN (Officer Obie), PETER SEEGER (Himself), LEE HAYS (Himself).

## *"Keep America beautiful – cut your hair!"*

Most would agree with Arlo (Arlo Guthrie) that being a deadbeat beats being dead. Every waking moment is a nightmare for him, because one of these days his number will be up and he'll be drafted to Vietnam.

But as they say, knowledge sets you free, and it's certainly true for Arlo. He enrolls in college at a small Montana University, thus exempting himself from an otherwise grim fate – or so he thinks. Upon his arrival at school, it soon becomes evident that the locals don't dig his long flowing hair or hippie ways. It follows that Arlo gets himself into a dispute and is promptly expelled from the institution. He gets word from friends Alice (Patricia Quinn) and Ray (James Broderick) that they have purchased an old church and converted it into a communal style living space where they reside with their entire circle of friends. It sounds like paradise: not only would Arlo find sanctuary, but he would also be surrounded by like-minded pacifists. With this in mind, he heads back east…

With *Alice's Restaurant*, director Arthur Penn (*Bonnie and Clyde*, 1967; *Little Big Man*, 1969) breathes visual depth into the lyrics of folksinger and story protagonist Arlo Guthrie. Guthrie's 18-minute spoken ballad "Alice's Restaurant Massacre" is based on the musician's actual experiences. In the song, we hear of a man who goes to see Alice for Thanksgiving and as a favor takes her trash to the dump. When the dump is closed, he drops it on top of another pile of garbage at the bottom of a ravine. It's not long before the local sheriff finds out, and a major manhunt ensues. Arlo eventually winds up in court and is found guilty. The entire ordeal, ironically, leaves him ineligible for the dreaded draft, as he is now an ex-con in the eyes of the law.

Arthur Penn creates a unique docudrama by integrating many of the song's real-life components in his film adaptation. Arlo, Officer William Obanhein, nicknamed Obie, and folksinger Pete Seeger, all characters in the song, were cast as themselves in Penn's movie. Even the real Alice Brock has a cameo as one of the hippies. Of course, it's impossible to say just how precisely the exposition of *Alice's Restaurant* matches Arlo Guthrie's own experiences, but the film does a first-rate job of capturing the zeitgeist of the late 1960s. The black cloud of the draft hanging over the heads of America's youth; the unkempt manes that met with the wrath of middle class morality; music, drugs and communal life – the film shows it all, as it were ticking off the items on a 1960s checklist. The only item that remains glaringly (and deliberately) absent from the menu in *Alice's Restaurant* is an in-depth depiction of bureaucracy. Decades later, the picture's humor and vitality continue to inspire the imaginations of viewers.

1

1 Reach out and touch faith: Hippie Arlo (Arlo Guthrie) and his girlfriend Mari-Chan (Tina Chen) look toward the future with hopeful eyes.

2 Strummin' to the sounds of peace: Roger (Geoff Outlaw) is as passionate about free love as Arlo is about his music. Illegal dumping lands both of them in court and face to face with heartless bureaucracy.

**ARLO GUTHRIE**

Arlo Guthrie (*1947 in Brooklyn, New York) became an overnight sensation with his 1967 album "Alice's Restaurant." He is the son of legendary folksinger Woody Guthrie (1912–1967), who traveled cross-country as a seasonal laborer and balladeer during the Depression. The songs Woody Guthrie went on to write often dealt with hunger and surviving tough times. Arlo followed in his father's footsteps, becoming a folksinger with a strong social conscience as well as an expert storyteller. *Variety* described one of his concerts as "a night around the campfire with an especially bright and talented counselor." Arlo grew up in the heart of the folk music scene, profiting from the poetic talents of artists like his father Woody and Pete Seeger. Not surprisingly, he could already play the guitar at the age of 6. At 13 he made his stage debut, and he went on a professional tour overseas at 16. His repertoire includes self-composed pieces like the Anti-Nixon "Presidential Rag" (1974) as well as much of his father's work like "This Land Is Your Land." Arlo's biggest and sole number one hit was his rendition of Steve Goodman's wistful train ballad "City of New Orleans" (1972), which Guthrie sang in a raw, nasal style reminiscent of Bob Dylan. Dylan and Woody Guthrie were Arlo's greatest idols. Like many folksingers, Arlo's heyday had come and gone by the end of 1970s. Today, he still tours, often accompanied by his son Abe and his daughter Sarah, who are both musicians and singers.

**"Penn refuses to romanticize his subjects, and as such the film stands as a fair chronicle of the times."** *Motion Picture Guide*

3 Dr. Giggles: Hippie surrogate-father Ray (James Broderick) dreams the impossible dream of having a perfect family.

4 Do not feed the animals: As part of the national beautification project, these peaceful creatures have been given a piece of granola homestead to graze upon. But how much petting and making nice can anyone really take?

Nonetheless, Penn, who received an Oscar nomination in direction for *Alice's Restaurant*, by no means glorifies flower power and free love, and is careful to show the flipside of this romanticized world. One of the commune members suffers a drug overdose, and when her relaxed staff don't take their workload seriously Alice is forced to shut the restaurant she has given her all to open. As such, the group's proclaimed communal spirit ends up getting chipped in the dishwasher.

It's a film that falls easily into two halves. The first part focuses on Arlo, and the second on Alice. Both of them are alone. At the picture's bittersweet conclusion, Alice is left high and dry. Although she has invited all her friends to a sumptuous banquet, attempting to recapture the exuberance of her wedding reception, she still can't save her failing marriage. Her husband Ray always seems to value their co-op over his wife, proving to Alice that communal harmony and a happy marriage do not necessarily go hand in hand.

Arlo, however, exits the film happier than when he entered. He has a girlfriend, and the threat of being sent to Vietnam went out with the trash. No wonder *Look* magazine dubbed *Alice's Restaurant* "an anarchist's success story."

HJK

# EASY RIDER

1969 - USA - 95 min. - ROAD MOVIE

DIRECTOR DENNIS HOPPER (*1936)

SCREENPLAY PETER FONDA, DENNIS HOPPER, TERRY SOUTHERN DIRECTOR OF PHOTOGRAPHY LÁSZLÓ KOVÁCS EDITOR DONN CAMBERN MUSIC STEPPENWOLF, ROGER MCGUINN, THE BYRDS, THE BAND, THE JIMI HENDRIX EXPERIENCE PRODUCTION PETER FONDA for PANDO, RAYBERT PRODUCTIONS, BBS, COLUMBIA PICTURES CORPORATION.

STARRING PETER FONDA (Wyatt), DENNIS HOPPER (Billy), JACK NICHOLSON (George Hanson), LUKE ASKEW (Hitchhiker), LUANA ANDERS (Lisa), SABRINA SCHARF (Sarah), TONI BASIL (Mary), KAREN BLACK (Karen), WARREN FINNERTY (Rancher), ROBERT WALKER JR. (Jack).

## *"This used to be a helluva good country. I can't understand what's gone wrong with it."*

Freedom… and the impossibility of freedom in a country where people are scared to be free. Billy (Dennis Hopper) is sitting at the campfire with the lawyer George Hanson (Jack Nicholson). The legal eagle is no longer perfectly sober, and Billy is a little slow-witted because he's permanently stoned. But George is doing his best to clarify a few matters for Billy: why the motel owner slammed the door on him and his buddy Wyatt (Peter Fonda); why the girl behind the bar in the one-horse town refused to serve them; why the mob and their sheriff chased them out of town instead. The lawyer explains that these people are not scared of Billy personally; they're scared of what he represents: an easy, unforced existence outside of society – a life in which the only things that matters are self-realization and life itself.

Billy and Wyatt ran into the lawyer in a jail cell, where he'd been sleeping off his latest bout with the bottle. Now he's joined them on their motorcycle odyssey, all the way from Los Angeles to Mardi Gras in New Orleans. They cruise down endless empty highways, through stunningly beautiful landscapes, rarely stopping before the sun goes down. Wyatt has spurs on his boots and a star-spangled banner on the back of his leather jacket; Billy wears suede pants, and he sports a Stetson on his long, matted hair. They're two 20th-century cowboys on a quest for space and freedom, chasing an ideal America that disappeared many moons ago.

*Easy Rider* cost only $400,000 to make, but it quickly became one of the cult movies of the 60s. It's a piece of celluloid that evokes an entire generation's outlook on life, a road movie about youth, drugs and the dream of revolution, with a soundtrack as hugely successful as the movie that spawned it. Far from merely accompanying the pictures, songs by The Byrds, The Band and Fraternity of Man provide a running commentary on the film. "Born to Be Wild," Steppenwolf's hymn to freedom, is a programmatic opening number; and Roger McGuinn's cover version of Bob Dylan's "It's Alright Ma (I'm Only Bleeding)" paves the way for the sober and melancholy conclusion. Producer and protagonist Peter Fonda reported that Dylan had refused to allow the original version to be used because he felt the movie offered too little hope. For Wyatt and Billy are ultimately blown out of existence by a reactionary hick with a rifle; they're on their bike and he's in his truck, and he kills them just for the hell of it.

This pessimistic ending casts doubt on the whole freewheelin' on-the-road adventure. In an interview with the German magazine *Filmkritik*, Peter Fonda commented: "We knew there couldn't be any more heroes, yet we still tried to *live* like heroes. This yearning is there in the film – along with the disillusionment." The project began with the simple desire of two real-life friends, Hopper and Fonda, to travel through the country by motorbike, and the end result was this movie. All the various episodes took place on the road, from the visit to a hippie camp in New Mexico to the meeting with a farmer whose entire extended family lived off the land. Like the characters they play, Hopper and Fonda were verbally abused by rednecks – and even threatened with guns – while filming. They also smoked a lot of grass.

In a cemetery in New Orleans, the two protagonists team up with a couple of hookers and embark on an acid trip that turns completely nightmarish. Hopper shoots the drug experience not as a cleansing of the doors of per-

1

2

3

1 Made in the shades: Peter Fonda as the reflective and easy-going Wyatt.

2 Fireside chats: The erratic and eccentric Billy (Dennis Hopper) just loves chewin' the fat – no matter who's listening. It's no coincidence that the film's two main buddies share their first names with legendary cowboys Wyatt Earp and Billy the Kid.

3 The thrill of the open road: Attorney George Hanson (Jack Nicholson) heads down south to New Orleans. Good thing his mom kept his football helmet of his high school glory days intact for him.

**"*Easy Rider* is a Southern term for the whore's old man, not a pimp, but the dude who lives with a chick. Because he's got the easy ride. Well, that's what happened to America, man. Liberty's become a whore, and we're all taking an easy ride."** *Peter Fonda*

**DENNIS HOPPER**

"I'll fuck anything that moves!" As Frank Booth in David Lynch's *Blue Velvet* (1985), he celebrated his unforgettable comeback – as an obscenely violent psychopath horribly dependent on an unnamed gas. Ever since then, Dennis Hopper has embodied the unpredictable, the explosive and the insane. He played variations on these themes in *Red Rock West* (1992) by John Dahl, *Speed* (1994) by Jan de Bont, and *Waterworld* (1995) by Kevin Reynolds and Kevin Costner. All told, Hopper has now appeared in over 100 films, more than 40 of them made in the 90s alone. "I no longer wait to be offered great roles," said Hopper in an interview with the German newspaper *Süddeutsche Zeitung*: "I just work. I make sure I'm always busy, because I love doing what I do."

Dennis Hopper came to Hollywood at the age of 18. Just a year later, after a few TV jobs, he appeared alongside his role model James Dean in Nicholas Ray's *Rebel Without a Cause* (1955) and George Stevens' *Giant* (1956). But Hopper acquired a reputation for being "difficult," and after studying at the Actors' Studio in New York he worked mainly in the theater. In 1969, with *Easy Rider*, he returned to Hollywood as director and protagonist of his own movie. The film's enormous success took its toll on him, however, as he embarked on a wild life marked by excessive drug use. After the failure of *The Last Movie* (1969/71), Hopper disappeared from view for a while, before returning in European films such as Wim Wenders' *The American Friend* (*Der Amerikanische Freund*, 1977) and Roland Klick's *White Star* (1982). He also worked as a photographer and collected artworks, including some important pieces of Pop Art.

Later, he began making his own films again, such as the mesmerizing *Colors* (1988), a police movie set in L. A. But the decisive turning point in his career was undoubtedly *Blue Velvet*. With this film, he began his *third* career, after his successes in the 50s and 60s; and the words of Frank Booth seemed to encapsulate Dennis Hopper's situation yet again: "Let's hit the fuckin' road!"

4 The fall guy: Billy gets pinned with the crime. Is he a victim of circumstance or menace to society?

5 Alien abduction: Hanson gets a first taste of Mary Jane and starts spacing out. Talk of extra-terrestrials who already have the world under their control circulates around the campfire.

6 Road hogs: And hog wild at that. Peter Fonda was already an experienced biker at the time of the shoot – a clue as to why his cycle got more souped up than Dennis Hopper's.

ception, but as a splintering of reality, a kaleidoscope of terror and despair. A short time later, the thoughtful Wyatt comments to Billy: "We're duds." They've reached New Orleans but missed their true goal. A drug deal has brought them several thousand dollars, which Wyatt hides in the tank. It's this money that's supposed to guarantee their freedom. But anyone who wants a free life beyond bourgeois society must break their dependence on its symbols and material values – like that farmer, reaping the fruits of his honest labor, far from the snares of civilization.

Hopper and Fonda seem to feel an almost religious sense of connection to their native country, and this is evoked in gorgeous, panoramic views of the American landscape. In truth, they're in mourning, for they know that the America they revere has long since passed way. If God didn't exist, you'd have to invent him, says Wyatt, as the original duo arrive in New Orleans. George didn't make it with them; in the middle of the night, he was beaten to death by a mob. And in a sudden moment of vision, Wyatt sees his own approaching end.

NM

6

# MIDNIGHT COWBOY

969 - USA - 113 MIN. - DRAMA, LITERARY ADAPTATION

IRECTOR JOHN SCHLESINGER (1926–2003)

CREENPLAY WALDO SALT, based on the novel of the same name by JAMES LEO HERLIHY DIRECTOR OF PHOTOGRAPHY ADAM HOLENDER DITING HUGH A. ROBERTSON MUSIC JOHN BARRY, FLOYD HUDDLESTON, FRED NEIL PRODUCTION JEROME HELLMAN for FLORIN PRODUCTIONS, JEROME HELLMAN PRODUCTIONS.

TARRING DUSTIN HOFFMAN (Enrico Salvatore "Ratso" Rizzo), JON VOIGHT (Joe Buck), SYLVIA MILES (Cass), JOHN MCGIVER Mr. O'Daniel), BRENDA VACCARO (Shirley), BARNARD HUGHES (Towny), RUTH WHITE (Sally Buck), JENNIFER SALT Annie), GILMAN RANKIN (Woodsy Niles), PAUL MORRISSEY (Party Guest), VIVA (Gretel McAlbertson).

CADEMY AWARDS 1969 OSCARS for BEST PICTURE (Jerome Hellman), BEST DIRECTOR (John Schlesinger), and BEST ADAPTED SCREENPLAY (Waldo Salt).

## *"Frankly, you're beginning to smell and for a stud in New York, that's a handicap."*

*Midnight Cowboy* is a portrait of urban life that can also be read as a revisionist Western. For beyond this bittersweet tale of the concrete jungle lies a melancholy ballad that bids adieu to the ideals of the American West. An ode o innocence lost, the movie follows the story of young Joe Buck (Jon Voight), he last urban cowboy, as he tries to hold onto a rapidly disappearing dream n the 1960s. A strapping Texan, Buck has come to the Big Apple to fulfill the sexual fantasies of the city's affluent lonely hearts. What he finds is a world with little need for such services. And soon, after a series of empty encounters with homosexuals, junkies and religious fanatics, he's down and out as a second-rate male prostitute on 42nd Street. Stripped of everything but a ading dream, all that accompanies Buck on his travels is a transistor radio emitting a hollow stream of promises, and a TB-stricken runt in a tattered dress suit known as Rico "Ratso" Rizzo (Dustin Hoffman).

As his dubious name suggests, Ratso is quick to scam the bright-eyed cowboy in the hopes of running off with his money. Mr. Buck however seems oo caught up in his polished appearance to take any notice, preferring instead to steal prideful glances in the mirror before hitting the town. In fact, all the Texan can think about is how his cowboy get-up is sure to be all the rage of the New York penthouse scene. Hearing opportunity knock, the hobbling Ratso appoints himself the kid's manager and sets him up on "dates" with women and men alike – sordid little encounters that slowly but surely rub the shine off the cowboy's illusions.

Ratso and Joe soon become partners in crime, living hand to mouth as small-time crooks and spending most of their waking hours in a squat without even electricity and running water. Their cohabitation is dominated by fantasies of a better life, where they would move to Florida and mingle with the rich and famous. And tragically, the men only realize how much they mean to each other when it is too late. Transcending the picture's wretched ending, their curious love story is a tender message that still strikes a chord with contemporary audiences. Wistfully underscored by "Everybody's Talkin'" (performed by Harry Nilsson), the strength of this paean to friendship lies in John Schlesinger's ingenious visuals and the astonishing talent of the movie's two principle actors. The interaction between a then virtually unknown Jon Voight and his co-star Dustin Hoffman inspires immediat

2

**“This is obviously the sort of film in which people argue endlessly about which of the principals steals it, and the argument is irresistible, if pointless. Both are very good, in different ways. Against Mr. Voight’s unnoticeable acting Mr. Hoffman has a field day with all the fire-works – ugly, crippled eccentric, and dying by degrees, he is always at the very edge of his being, which, as we all know, is a very comfortable place for an actor. He does it very well, but finally I think Mr. Voight has the more difficult part, and carries it off impeccably.”** *The Times*

1 Bridge over troubled waters: Don Quixote and Sancho Pancha are reincarnated in 1960s New York as Joe Buck (Jon Voight) and Rico Salvatore Rizzo (Dustin Hoffman).

2 Cry me a river: Dustin Hoffman made fans see just how sexy a black sheep can be.

3 Pop goes the weasel: Rico ‘Ratso’ Rizzo has killed time long enough and is ready to turn his know-how into a moneymaking scheme as Joe Buck’s manager.

4 Life’s little fetishes: Joe gets to know a couple of gay guys really well and finds out what life in the big bad city is really all about.

5 Back off. I’m contagious: Ratso is the kind of guy who’d think up anything to get out of danger’s path, and so Joe doesn’t realize just how ill he really is.

empathy. Whereas Joe’s unfaltering optimism in a world where raw need overshadows all emotion is the only ray of hope, Ratso’s tenacious pride is no less impressive. No scene encapsulates the nature of their struggle to survive so dramatically as Ratso’s unforgettable outburst when a taxi nearly runs him over in the midday traffic. Screaming “I’m walking here! I’m walking here!” he claims his and Joe’s stake to life with these words of retaliation. This unscripted moment came about when a real New York City cab driver recklessly motored onto the scene and nearly shut down the shoot. Rather than breaking character, Hoffman spontaneously adlibbed an already difficult take.

It is scenes like this that attest to the extraordinary precision of British director John Schlesinger’s gutsy experimental techniques and give the film

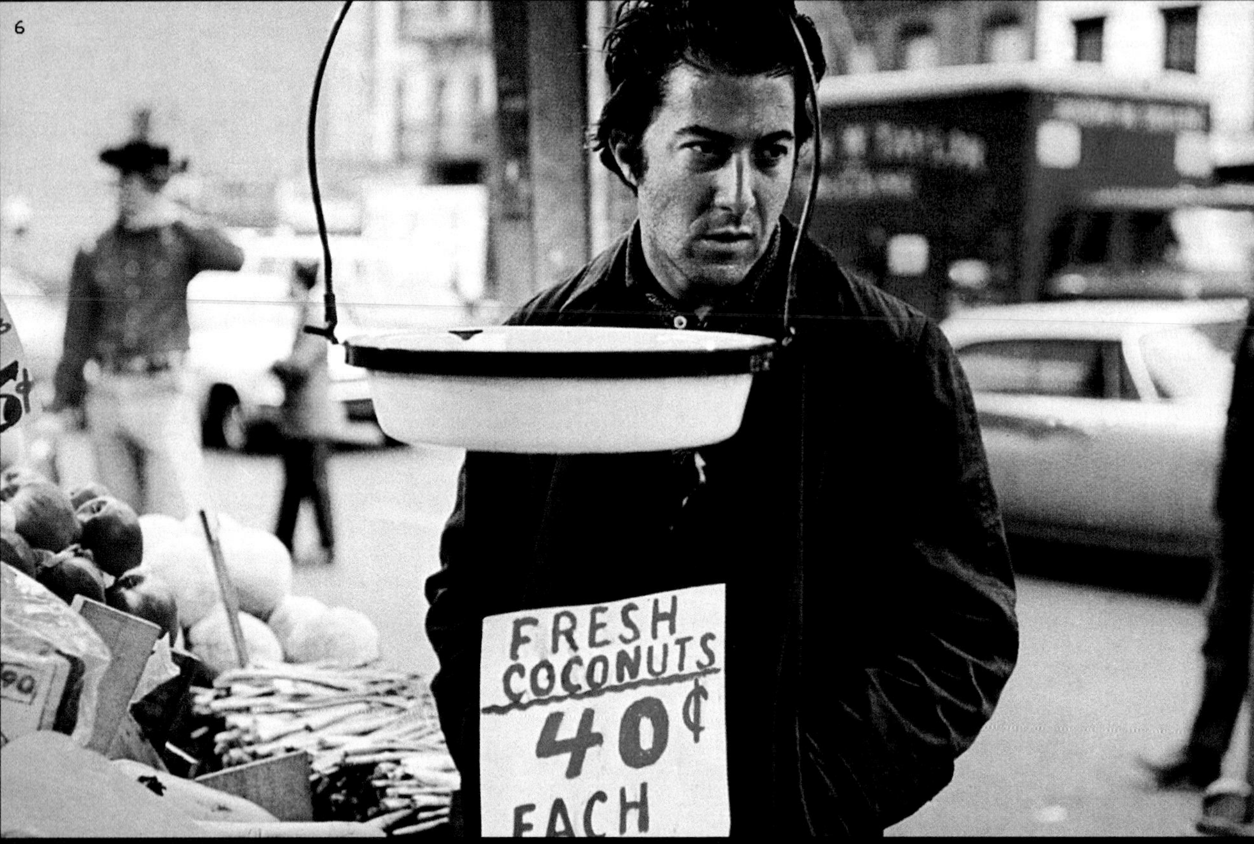


6 Flim flam man: Ratso doesn't want anyone's compassion; he'd much rather have a meal ticket and a cash cow.

7 Hopalong Cassidy: All that's missing to complete this image of American naivety is a broomstick pony. Jon Voight as Joe Buck, the sexy innocent, a role which made the actor an overnight sensation.

such undeniable urban authenticity. Yet somehow *Midnight Cowboy's* nightmarish images accurately capture the darkness and violence of 1969 New York without losing sight of the era's underlying hopefulness. For even though the only remnants of the utopia once promised by flower power and the sexual revolution are the pornography and prostitution beckoning at every corner, Joe Buck goes through life shielded by a diehard innocence.

The cowboy's naive sexuality, played up by his childish misconceptions, is undoubtedly the picture's major riddle. While sex is peddled on the city streets like any other commodity, Joe Buck inexplicably regards physical intimacy and its sale as the most natural thing on earth. No less unsettling are the chilling flashbacks that tell of the Texan's traumatic childhood marked by abuse and rape. But even so, this leaves us far from a psychological diagnosis.

In awarding *Midnight Cowboy* the Oscar for Best Picture, mainstream cinema paid homage to an innovative form of filmmaking that would go on to shape New Hollywood and Indie Cinema. From a contemporary standpoint, it is hard to understand that several of the movie's scenes were considered drastic enough to warrant the X rating usually reserved for pornography.

PB

**DUSTIN HOFFMAN**

Dustin Hoffman (*1937) is among the world's best-known actors and one of the few to gain international acclaim through character roles. His striking features, nasal voice and seeming lack of self-confidence cut him out for difficult parts. A Los Angeles native, he studied music at Santa Monica City College and acting at the Pasadena Playhouse before gaining admission to Lee Strasberg's Actor's Studio in 1958. His big break in Hollywood came at the age of thirty with Mike Nichols' timeless classic *The Graduate* (1967) in which he played Benjamin Braddock, a character ten years his junior. The part brought him his first Oscar nomination.

It took two years and much persistence before the allegedly "difficult" actor delivered his next incomparable performance as the sickly Ratso in *Midnight Cowboy* (1969). It was the beginning of a sterling career, and soon he was cast as a 121-year-old Western pioneer in *Little Big Man* (1970), a title that incidentally became the 5'5" tall actor's nickname. He went on to play a prisoner opposite Steve McQueen in *Papillon* (1973) and claim the stage all for himself as scathing satirist Lenny Bruce in *Lenny* (1974).

A master of disguise, he dazzled audiences in *Tootsie* (1982), one of his few blockbuster romantic comedies, playing an actor who has to dress up like a woman to get work. Hoffman also shone in the political thriller *Marathon Man* (1976) and in the sensitive divorce drama *Kramer vs. Kramer* (1979), which won him his first Oscar. After poignantly portraying an autistic *Rain Man* (1988), his reputation as an insufferable perfectionist started to get the better of him and great roles became more of a rarity. Be that as it may, Hoffman is still a box-office favorite and has continued to impress audiences in recent productions like *Billy Bathgate* (1991), *Outbreak* (1995) and *Wag the Dog* (1997).

# THE WILD BUNCH

1969 - USA - 145 MIN. - WESTERN

DIRECTOR SAM PECKINPAH (1925–1984)
SCREENPLAY WALON GREEN, ROY N. SICKNER, SAM PECKINPAH DIRECTOR OF PHOTOGRAPHY LUCIEN BALLARD EDITING LOU LOMBARDO MUSIC JERRY FIELDING PRODUCTION PHIL FELDMAN for WARNER BROS., SEVEN ARTS.

STARRING WILLIAM HOLDEN (Pike Bishop), ROBERT RYAN (Deke Thornton), ERNEST BORGNINE (Dutch Engstrom), EDMOND O'BRIEN (Sykes), WARREN OATES (Lyle Gorch), BEN JOHNSON (Tector Gorch), JAIME SANCHEZ (Angel), EMILIO FERNÁNDEZ (Mapache), STROTHER MARTIN (Coffer), L. Q. JONES (T. C.), ALBERT DEKKER (Pat Harrigan).

***"We all dream of being a child again, even the worst of us. Perhaps the worst most of all."***

To judge by their faces, the men riding slowly into town have done some serious living. Their path takes them along a railroad line, where some kids are laughing and playing. The men stare at them sullenly as they pass. Only the close-up shows the cruelty of the children's game. While two scorpions struggle in vain to avoid being eaten by a horde of red ants, the kids are using sticks to block the tormented animals' escape route.

Under a tarpaulin, a travelling preacher is fulminating against the evils of drink. A little later, the Temperance Union sets off on a parade, accompanied by a brass band. By this time, Pike Bishop (William Holden) and his men have reached their destination: they're in the wages office of the railroad company, and they're quietly robbing it while holding the customers at gunpoint. Then one of Bishop's men spots the rifles on the roof... There are some pretty rough-looking men positioned all around them, and they're hungry for the bounty on the Wild Bunch's heads. In cold blood, Bishop organizes the breakout. Though the streets are filled with innocent passers-by, the bounty hunters open fire and start shooting wildly into the crowd. Bullets whine, horses whinny, people panic while others die. The bandits know no mercy, but use the crowd and the Temperance parade for cover. Only four members of Bishop's gang survive the massacre, and one of them is so badly wounded that he can't ride a horse. When he asks to be shot, Bishop doesn't hesitate. There is no time for a burial.

These first scenes already contain the essence of Sam Peckinpah's film. Noble heroes like John Wayne or Randolph Scott are nowhere to be found in this Western, and the Law has no claim to moral superiority. The sleazy gunmen hired by railroad boss Harrigan (Albert Dekker) are a bunch of trigger-happy fools and money-grabbers. Only their leader Deke Thornton (Robert Ryan) demonstrates a certain amount of backbone, but even he is driven by self-interest: he's been promised amnesty for his crimes if he manages to hunt down his former friend Pike Bishop.

Peckinpah disposes ruthlessly of the old Western cliché that conflicts

1

1 King of the wild frontier: Pike Bishop (William Holden) isn't going to let renegade leader Mapache pull the wool over anyone else's eyes.

2 Following the leader: Dutch (Ernest Borgnine) has his reservations about Bishop's motives but joins up with him just the same.

3 Let me entertain you: Pike Bishop and Deke Thornton get a rude awakening from their assailants while frequenting a house of ill repute. When Pike leaves him in the lurch, his buddy changes sides quicker than most people change clothes.

4 Always let your conscience be your guide: Demanding the release of their friend Angel, the remaining bunchies head back to Mapache's hideout.

5 White bishop takes black queen – check: Bishop and his men storm Mapache's headquarters, where the dastardly gaucho is being serviced with a smile.

6 Tending to a paper cut: Despite a gaping wound, Bishop refuses to give up the fight against his mighty opponents. But his impassioned battle can only end in defeat.

like these can be solved cleanly, in a heroic dual of individuals. His protagonists and their henchmen are fighting a filthy miniature war. Across the border in Mexico, where the militias of General Mapache (Emilio Fernández) have established a reign of terror, life is even more brutal: soldiers move through Indian villages, raping, torturing and killing – and are hunted in turn by the troops of Pancho Villa. The violence makes no exception of women and children. With unsparing exactness, Peckinpah shows us what bullets are really capable of: he shows us how blood spurts, and how human bodies are torn and tossed around by flying metal. In Peckinpah's vision, the moment of death is extended, as the victims perform a horrible slow-motion dance.

*The Wild Bunch* can only be understood in the context of the late 60s. For the first time, the mass media were bringing uncensored images of warfare

**ERNEST BORGNINE**

He was born Ermes Effron Borgnino in 1917 and in the course of his lengthy career, he got to know every aspect of the acting trade. Ernest Borgnine, as he later became, appeared in provincial theaters, B-movies and prestigious big-budget productions. And just once, in 1956, he stood in front of his peers at the Oscars ceremony, when he received the Academy Award for his performance in Delbert Mann's *Marty* (1955). The quiet butcher Marty was one of the few leading roles Borgnine played, and the film was exceptionally good. But his unmistakeable physiognomy, with gappy teeth, bushy brows and boxer's nose, was never going to make him a matinee idol. Nonetheless, in the 50s and 60s he soon became a familiar face to keen moviegoers.

Borgnine, who spent ten years in the army, gave a rambunctious performance as the sadistic Sergeant Judson in Fred Zinnemann's *From Here to Eternity* (1953). After appearing as the titular hero in the TV series *McHale's Navy* (1962–66), he also co-starred in two well-known movies directed by Robert Aldrich: *The Flight of the Phoenix* (1966) and *The Dirty Dozen* (1967). He also acted in several Westerns and historical epics, as well as turning up in the odd obscure European production. Though he often played the burly bad guy, he was just as memorable playing the rough diamond or the buddy with a heart of gold. Moviegoers liked the warmth and energy he brought to such roles, and when he played Dominic Santini in the TV adventure series *Airwolf* (USA, 1984–86), these qualities won him a whole new generation of fans.

**“Violent, thoughtful and authoritative, it keeps Peckinpah out on his own among the Western directors of his generation.”** *Sight and Sound*

to the attention of the public and it was becoming impossible to ignore the dreadful suffering of civilian populations. Even if some of Peckinpah’s interviews reveal a sneaking sympathy with the doomed desperadoes of his Wild Bunch, he never left us in any doubt that these were ruined men, souls in hell.

Although the film’s outstanding artistic quality was almost universally recognized, its outrageously realistic depiction of violence led to some heated discussions. Peckinpah himself was furious at his producers, who released an allegedly more marketable shortened version of the film without his consent. In some countries, including Germany, further passages were cut, with the result that several different versions were in circulation worldwide. In 1982, a so-called “director’s cut” lasting the originally planned 145 minutes was finally released.

HK

# THE ARISTOCATS

1970 - USA - 78 MIN. - ANIMATED FEATURE

DIRECTOR WOLFGANG REITHERMAN (1909–1985)
SCREENPLAY LARRY CLEMMONS, VANCE GERRY, KEN ANDERSON, FRANK THOMAS, ERIC CLEWORTH, JULIUS SVENDSEN, RALPH WRIGHT, TOM MCGOWAN EDITING TOM ACOSTA MUSIC GEORGE BRUNS PRODUCTION WOLFGANG REITHERMAN, WINSTON HIBLER for WALT DISNEY.

VOICES PHIL HARRIS (J. Thomas O'Malley), EVA GABOR (Duchess), STERLING HOLLOWAY (Roquefort the Mouse), HERMIONE BADDELEY (Madame Adelaide Bonfamille), RODDY MAUDE-ROXBY (Edgar), SCATMAN CROTHERS (Scat Cat), PAT BUTTRAM (Napoleon), GEORGE LINDSEY (Lafayette), MONICA EVANS (Abigail Gabble), CAROLE SHELLEY (Amelia Gabble).

## *"Lay some skin on me, Scat Cat!"*

Class differences are not a uniquely human phenomenon. The feline residents of Madame Adelaide Bonfamille's Paris villa, Duchess and her three kittens Berlioz, Marie and Toulouse, have acquired a taste for the finer things in life. They sleep in a silk-lined basket, their meals do not come out of a can but are personally prepared by Mme. Adelaide's butler – and most unusually for cats – are eaten peacefully as a family, which also includes Roquefort the mouse.

But dark clouds are gathering over this pets' paradise. When the heirless lady of the manor bequeaths her entire estate to her furry little friends, Edgar the Butler devises a scheme to get his own paws on her cash. Soon the cats are singing for their supper alongside the rest of Paris' more mangy down-and-outs. Never having had to fend for themselves, the troop seems destined to meet with a bitter end – until the charming tomcat Thomas O'Malley comes to their aid. O'Malley teaches them to be street smart, and joins forces with Roquefort and a horde of disheveled strays to give the wicked butler the fright of his life.

Following the death of Walt Disney in 1966, his creative team began to mix and match elements that had proven effective in the past. As such, *The Aristocats* emerges to some extent as a hybrid of *Lady and the Tramp* (1955) and *One Hundred and One Dalmatians* (1960). As in these other features, the voices of renowned actors such as Phil Harris (O'Malley) and Eva Gabor (Duchess), contribute significantly to the credibility of the characters.

However, the anthropomorphization of the animal characters was taken to such extremes that they really only resemble cats in their movements. While in *The Jungle Book* (1967), the characteristics of the different species are clearly distinguished, *The Aristocats* are really humans in cats' clothing, who even embody various national stereotypes. Duchess and company have a brief encounter with a gaggle of very British geese and O'Malley's band of caterwaulers includes an Italian, a Russian, and a Siamese cat who bangs out tunes on the piano with a set of chopsticks. The jam session itself, reminiscent of the King Louie dance sequence in the *Jungle Book*, is a clear attempt at integrating a contemporary social agenda into the fabric of the film. Set in Thomas' "penthouse," we witness the cat musicians tripping the psychedelic light fantastic. The visual effect doesn't quite jive with the cats' almost Dixieland sound, but nonetheless makes for one of the film's true highlights.

1

1 Everybody wants to be a cat: Streetwise Thomas O'Malley (right) and his fat-cat friend prove that it don't mean a thing if you ain't got that swing.

2 Insisting upon fancy feast: Edgar the Butler disrespects 24-carat cat owner Madame Adelaide Bonfamille and serves her feline family a little spoiled milk.

3 The cat's meow: The back streets of the French capital provide the perfect hideaway for romance and eavesdropping.

4 Kitty litter: It may sound like caterwauling to the untrained ear, but these sophisticates are just practicing for their next jam session.

5 Love gone astray: Pretty kitty and mother of three, Duchess, loses her heart to a common tomcat, and attempts to teach the puss how to wear designer boots.

# "Dig these cats... and all that Jazz!" *Advert for "Aristocats"*

With historic Paris as its backdrop, *The Aristocats* luxuriates in European flair while maintaining political neutrality. Its location allows the story be situated in the Old World, far removed from American values, thereby permitting a romanticized representation of the class differences between commoners and aristocrats. Furthermore, the setting conveniently reduces the Paris Jazz Boom of the 30s and 40s to a manifestation of local subculture without needing to fear any backlash from the U. S. jazz scene or accusations of perpetuating racial stereotypes. To top it all off, the French metropolis, with its picturesque courtyards and familiar landmarks, gives the American audience an appealing reference point and a ready supply of eye-candy.

Nonetheless, this is a cartoon that makes a habit of flaunting bold contrasts. Hippies and musicians are juxtaposed with regal Parisian streets and images most often found on postcards. The dignified and responsible mother cat crosses paths with a footloose and fancy-free Tom, who is inevitably taken in by the noble Madame Adelaide in the end. Admittedly, it's rather utopian. The comic interludes involving dignified canines Lafayette and Napoleon are meant to take the edge off the sugar, and their boisterous tomfoolery helps bridge the gap that often separates tamer Disney from more savvy Warner Bros productions.

Yet for all its efforts to jump on the contemporary bandwagon, *The Aristocats* falls somewhat short of the mark as a result of its loyalty to wholesome Disney values like fidelity, family and sense of responsibility. Incidental issues that might complicate these matters, such as how Duchess came to be an unwed mother, are left unaddressed. SH

**CARTOONS**

Although experiments in the field of animated multiple-frame illusion were carried out regularly during the 19th century, the age of cartoons really got underway at the beginning of the 20th century. The first cartoon as we more or less know it today was J. Stuart Blackton's *Humorous Phases of Funny Faces* (1906), in which letters, words and faces were animated by means of stop motion photography. At about this time, Frenchman Émile Cohl was breathing life into the "Fantasmagories," while artist Windsor McCay was teaching animated character *Little Nemo* (1911) how to put his best foot forward. McCay soon became the first real star of the cartoon world. His animated film *Gertie the Dinosaur* (1914) ran in nickelodeons of the day, and his *The Sinking of Lusitania* (1918) was the first first-length animated film to appear on the screen. According to Leonard Maltin, the 20s were an era of growth for cartoons, in which animation emerged as art, industry and occupation. Walt Disney dominated the market throughout the 30s and 40s. Truly no other studio shaped the development of cartoons as much as Disney's production company. He brought *Snow White and the Seven Dwarfs* (1937), the first feature-length animated fairy tale, to world audiences as well as the more visionary, though then unprofitable, *Fantasia* (1940) and countless other classics. Fred "Tex" Avery and Chuck Jones emerged on the scene in the 1950s, creating the trademark Warner Bros. cartoon style with *hare*-brained animated shorts – entitled Looney Tunes – and cornered that sector of the market. Nonetheless, the highly expensive and tedious enterprise of full-length animated features remained Disney's domain.

Recent history has witnessed the advent of animated TV series that thrive on satiric black humor and socially critical characters, such as Matt Groening's *Simpsons* (premiered 1989) and Trey Parker and Matt Stone's *South Park* (premiered 1997). On distant shores, the Japanese Anime movement has been gaining speed since the 1970s, presenting the American market with stiff competition. Pictures like *Akira* (1988) and Hayao Miyazaki's *Mononoke-hime* (*Princess Mononoke*, 1997) have taken animation and Hollywood itself by storm. Indeed, the innovations in this sector of the industry have redefined the impact and general direction in which animation is heading.

# CATCH 22

1970 - USA - 122 MIN. - WAR FILM, TRAGICOMEDY, LITERARY ADAPTATION

DIRECTOR MIKE NICHOLS (*1931)

SCREENPLAY BUCK HENRY, based on the novel of the same name by JOSEPH HELLER DIRECTOR OF PHOTOGRAPHY DAVID WATKIN EDITING SAM O'STEEN MUSIC JUNE EDGERTON PRODUCTION JOHN CALLEY, MARTIN RANSOHOFF for PARAMOUNT, FILMWAYS.

STARRING ALAN ARKIN (Captain John Yossarian), MARTIN BALSAM (Colonel Cathcart), RICHARD BENJAMIN (Major Danby), ART GARFUNKEL (Captain Nately), JACK GILFORD (Doc Daneeka), BUCK HENRY (Colonel Korn), ANTHONY PERKINS (Chaplain Tappman), PAULA PRENTISS (Sister Duckett), MARTIN SHEEN (Lieutenant Dobbs), JON VOIGHT (Lieutenant Minderbinder), ORSON WELLES (General Dreedle).

## *"That's some catch, that Catch 22." "It's the best there is!"*

If you want to carry on fighting, you must be crazy. If you don't want to carry on fighting, you're not crazy – and therefore, you have to carry on fighting. "Catch 22" is the name given by the military authorities to the bizarre logic that forces the soldiers at a U.S. airbase in World War II Italy to carry on flying their missions. And when strategically insignificant targets are bombed flat, or when the girls in a Roman whorehouse are suddenly abducted by GIs, it's also "Catch 22." In short: "Catch 22" is the logic of war.

Truth be told, Captain John Yossarian (Alan Arkin), Captain Nately (Art Garfunkel) and their buddies have got a pretty cushy deal. Though they spend their days bombing Italian coastal towns, their leisure hours are free for spaghetti, red wine and beautiful Roman women. But despite such pleasures, Yossarian's had a bellyful of the war, particularly as General Dreedle (Orson Welles) keeps increasing the number of sorties they have to fly before being relieved.

What's more, there's something strange going on: useful things like parachutes and morphine have been disappearing from their kitbags; and instead, the bomber crews are being kitted out with shares in an ominous company called "M & M Enterprises." Behind these initials, and the mysterious disappearances, is none other than Lieutenant Milo Minderbinder (Jon Voight), who's conducting a roaring trade in the soldiers' most vital equipment. Supported by the commanding officer Colonel Cathcart (Martin Balsam) and his general factotum Colonel Korn (Buck Henry), the ubiquitous Milo eventually goes so far as to sell his own airbase to the Germans. Because "What's good for 'M & M Enterprises' will be good for the country" – and if you don't believe that, then let me explain to you about "Catch 22"...

There's something almost nasty about the cockiness with which *Catch 22* ignores all that had hitherto been holy about World War II. It's just totally

1

1 Catching a slight case of insanity: Captain Yossarian (Alan Arkin, in bed) convinces military Chaplan Tappman (Anthony Perkins) that he's flipped his lid to avoid being blown to smithereens.

2 Making quota: General Dreedle (Orson Welles) has no qualms about making a career of sending countless men to their deaths. After all, mincemeat is his favorite dish at the mess hall.

3 Goodnight nurse: Yossarian puts his life on the line and wears his heart on his sleeve with Nurse Duckett (Paula Prentiss).

anti-Hollywood. Even the mundane routine of the airbase has a certain strangely glossy artificiality to it. When the bombers take off, it's a grandiose Cinemascope experience, with the backlit buildings of the airbase silhouetted against a delightfully picturesque background.

Mike Nichols' adaptation of Joseph Heller's best-selling novel is a complex network of allusions, flashbacks and déja-vu. The film is so stylized as to be positively surrealist at times – a radical break with the conventional ambitions of war-film directors to create a veneer of documentary authenticity. It made many American film critics pretty angry. Yet it's precisely this weird intensification of the everyday reality of war – which is, as Oliver Stone pointed out, "mostly pretty boring" – that makes it possible to *see* the cruel absurdity of what's actually going on. The same methods were used, to similar effect, in Robert Altman's military grotesque *M*A*S*H* (1972) and in Coppola's *Apocalypse Now* (1979). Samuel Fuller one remarked that to make a

**"Dr. Strangelove out of *Alice in Wonderland*."** *Daily Mail*

**ANTHONY PERKINS**

Rarely has a character actor been so strongly identified with a single role. For most moviegoers, Anthony Perkins is inseparably associated with Norman Bates, the murderous motel owner in Hitchcock's classic *Psycho* (1960). Yet the artistic basis of his work was and remained the theater. This was where his career began in 1954, in a successful Broadway production called *Tea and Sympathy*, directed by Elia Kazan. Despite some early screen successes, including an Oscar nomination for a supporting role in William Wyler's *Friendly Persuasion* (1956), and the Best Actor award in Cannes for his role as Ingrid Bergmann's young lover in *Goodbye Again* (1961), Perkins would continue to return to the theater. In the cinema, however, he was typecast as the eternal neurotic. And so he was practically predestined to play Josef K. in Orson Welles' Kafka adaptation, *The Trial* (*Le Procès*, 1962). In *Catch 22* (1970), Perkins gave a brilliant performance as the terrified Chaplain Tappman, who is pathetically incapable of offering his soldiers any kind of spiritual support. He returned to the role of Norman Bates three times. Two of these follow-ups, *Psycho II* (1983) and *Psycho III* (1986), were highly watchable movies, even if they couldn't hope to match the original. (Perkins himself directed *Psycho III*.) In Ken Russell's *Crimes of Passion* (1984), he gave his final take on the repressed and traumatized psychopath Norman Bates. For the rest of his career, until his death in 1992, he appeared mainly as a poor imitation of himself in various third-class TV productions.

4 Flying turkeys: With each mission proving more senseless than the last, these bombers will inevitably end up with egg on their faces.

5 Rubber radio room: In an alternate universe, DJ Yossarian has become king of the airwaves thanks to the theme from M*A*S*H, "Suicide is Painless."

6 War hawk: Colonel Cathcart (Martin Balsam) ensures his own safety by putting a price on his men's lives and booking them on a cruise along the river Styx.

7 Bedridden: Mastermind Milo Minderbinder has got the perfect remedy for lunacy. He can just send his afflicted men to one of the many whorehouses in Rome under his control. Note the 'M&M Enterprises' sign.

truthful war film, a director would have to post a sniper behind the cinema screen and tell him to shoot at the audience. Nichols and Altman are content to bombard us with some very black humor.

Nichols also abandons another iron rule of the American war film: that every sacrifice made in wartime must have, and be seen to have, a meaning. For the first time, Nichols shows that even a conflict like the Second World War – which most Americans would agree to have been just and necessary – can also be cruel and unjust. In 1970, it may have been too early for an uncompromising indictment of the Vietnam War; but just look at the dark, symbol-laden finale in Rome, the Fellini-esque images, the Kafka-like situations and the Dostoyevskyan fury. *Catch 22* is an anti-war statement whose validity applies far beyond the particular historical conflict it depicts. SH

# LOVE STORY

1970 - USA - 100 MIN. MELODRAMA, LOVE STORY

DIRECTOR ARTHUR HILLER (1923)
SCREENPLAY ERICH SEGAL, based on his novel of the same name DIRECTOR OF PHOTOGRAPHY DICK KRATINA EDITING ROBERT C. JONES
MUSIC FRANCIS LAI PRODUCTION HOWARD G. MINSKY for PARAMOUNT PICTURES.

STARRING ALI MACGRAW (Jenny Cavalleri), RYAN O'NEAL (Oliver Barrett IV), JOHN MARLEY (Phil Cavalleri), RAY MILLAND (Oliver Barrett III), KATHARINE BALFOUR (Mrs. Barrett), RUSSELL NYPE (Dean Thompson), SYDNEY WALKER (Dr. Shapely), ROBERT MODICA (Dr. Addison), WALKER DANIELS (Ray), TOMMY LEE JONES (Hank).

ACADEMY AWARDS 1970 OSCAR for BEST MUSIC (Francis Lai).

## *"Love means never having to say you're sorry."*

"What can you say about a 25-year-old girl who died? That she was beautiful, and brilliant, that she loved Mozart and Bach. And the Beatles and me." Oliver Barrett (Ryan O'Neal) sits in New York's snow-covered Central Park and mourns the loss of his wife Jenny. Cut to a memory: Jenny (Ali MacGraw) is working the library checkout counter at Radcliffe, the prestigious women's college. Vivacious and argumentative, she's a vision of youth's limitless potential. Oliver, a student at Harvard University, the school's neighboring male counterpart, wants to borrow a book. The two quarrel, agree to go out for a cup of coffee and become a couple. Their relationship, however, is not without its hurdles. Oliver, or more accurately, Oliver Barrett IV, comes from a prominent Boston family and Oliver III (Ray Milland) has no intention of sitting back while his son marries the offspring of some Italian baker from Rhode Island. Despite the objections, the young lovers wed, and Oliver's father all but disowns him. Jenny has, in the meantime, wrapped up her studies, and has to support the couple while Oliver finishes his degree. Struggling and in love, these are nonetheless happy times for the two of them, until the day when Jenny's doctor presents the newlyweds with some shattering news…

*Love Story* is a tale as immortal as its title suggests, and it ranks among Hollywood's most unforgettable boy-meets-girl sagas. Two people, whose feelings for one another overcome the greatest social obstacles, are forced to succumb to the will of Mother Nature. This is melodrama in its purest state. From its framing flashback to Francis Lai's painfully romantic Academy Award-winning score, the narrative makes no secret of this love story's in-

1

The laughter and the tears: She gave him the world, and asked him to brave it without her (Ali MacGraw and Ryan O'Neal in *Love Story*).

2 Woman in love: *Love Story* turned Ali MacGraw into an instant Hollywood sensation. Her character Jenny was received as a modern day Joan of Arc – a woman who'd rather perish than compromise her principles.

evitably tragic end. And yet, the underlying pathos is counteracted by the élan of the couple's fun-loving yet uncompromising relationship. Sarcasm and wit are the currency of regular communication, and Jenny never passes up an opportunity to tease Oliver for being the son of wealthy and influential parents, who have even lent their name to one of the university buildings. On one occasion she remarks: "Hey, I'm having coffee with a real Harvard building. You're Barrett Hall."

The fathers of the two main characters provide the film with two additional poles of opposition. Oliver III is a hard-headed businessman, who prefers the title of "Sir" to "father. " His sole interest in Oliver IV revolves around the latter's professional success. Jenny's father, known to everyone including his daughter as Phil (John Marley), is quite the opposite. A man on his own he embodies compassion, and treats his daughter as an equal. He may disagree with Jenny's decision to not have a church wedding, but he respects her wishes. The father figures emphasize the social conflicts inherent in the lovers' relationship, and the generation conflict effectively provides a second storyline. For besides being a picture about young paramours, it is also one of a son's emancipation from his father.

When the movie hit world screens in 1970, this mélange of romantic anguish and family drama accurately captured the zeitgeist of the youth protest movements and student riots of the late 60s. *Love Story* became an instant international sensation, raking in its entire production costs of 2.26 million dollars within three days of its U. S. premiere. Twelve weeks later, approximately 17 million Americans had seen the film. It received seven Oscar nominations for categories including direction, acting and best picture. Despite these accolades, the only win went to Francis Lai for his score. A sequel, *Oliver's Story*, came and went in 1978. It featured Ryan O'Neal as a young widower, trying to overcome his grief – aided by a woman who was very clearly *not* Ali MacGraw.

HJK

3 Out, out brief candle: Jenny and Oliver's romance is more than a tale full of sound and fury, signifying nothing.

4 Money can't buy everything: Oliver and his bride to be en route to meet Daddy Warbucks. However, Jenny's not the one who'll be left a poor little orphan.

**ALI MACGRAW**

*Love Story* (1970) was not only an international blockbuster, it also marked Ali MacGraw's overnight rise to stardom. Born on April 1st, 1938, MacGraw had appeared in two previous films without generating much buzz. The daughter of visual artists, she was a scholar of art history before landing a job as an editorial staff assistant with *Harper's Bazaar* at the age of 22. This opened the door to a career in modeling, where she rapidly advanced to super model status and was crowned one of *the* faces by the very fashion magazine at which she had once held a desk job. MacGraw was cast in several commercials and debuted on the silver screen shortly thereafter in the 1968 production *A Lovely Way To Die* with Kirk Douglas. That year, she also appeared in Philip Roth's film *Goodbye, Columbus. Love Story* excluded, her most prominent role came with Sam Peckinpah's shoot'em-up action classic *The Getaway*, 1972, in which she plays Steve McQueen's wife. Life soon mirrored art and the leading couple wed, remaining married from 1973–78. Hollywood black sheep Peckinpah cast MacGraw in another of his pictures in 1978, this time as a resolute journalist in the trucker western *Convoy*, co-starring Kris Kristofferson. From there on in, it was a rarity to see Ali MacGraw on the big screen, and her career relocated to television with mini-series like *The Winds of War* (1983) and a recurring role on ABC's *Dynasty*. Nonetheless, this more recent fare hardly compares to her earlier work.

4

# LITTLE BIG MAN

1970 - USA - 147 MIN. - WESTERN, LITERARY ADAPTATION

DIRECTOR Arthur Penn (*1922)

SCREENPLAY CALDER WILLINGHAM, based on the novel of the same name by THOMAS BERGER DIRECTOR OF PHOTOGRAPHY HARRY STRADLING JR. EDITING DEDE ALLEN MUSIC JOHN HAMMOND PRODUCTION STUART MILLAR, ARTHUR PENN for STOCKBRIDGE-HILLER PRODUCTIONS, CINEMA CENTER 100 PRODUCTIONS.

STARRING DUSTIN HOFFMAN (Jack Crabb), FAYE DUNAWAY (Mrs. Pendrake), CHIEF DAN GEORGE (Old Lodge Skins), MARTIN BALSAM (Allardyce T. Merriweather), RICHARD MULLIGAN (General Custer), JEFF COREY (Wild Bill Hickok), AIMY ECCLES (Sunshine), KELLY JEAN PETERS (Olga), CAROLE ANDROSKY (Caroline), ROBERT LITTLE STAR (Little Horse).

## *"It's a good day to die."*

While *Little Big Man's* Allardyce T. Merriweather (Martin Balsam) may be nobody's fool, the miracle elixir salesman spills bits of wisdom like an Elizabethan court jester – and oh how telling they can be. Indeed, it is he who utters the picture's most resonating words, said in passing to the story's hero Jack Crabb (Dustin Hoffman), a white man raised by the Cheyenne. Expressing his "heartfelt" condolences, Merriweather lets Crabb know just how sorry he is that all that time with the Indians has gone to his head, remarking that "Chief Old Lodge Skins gave (him) a sense of moral order in the universe, when there just isn't any." At the time the film was produced, a great number of Americans would have agreed with him. For despite the increasing public insistence on a world order based on moral values, the American government's domestic and foreign policies bent on capital gains – even at the price of internal corruption or racism – were in direct contradiction to all of the "Great Society" doctrines of the late 60s.

It was a time of student riots and minority uprisings, of the equal rights movement and government brutality. And above all, it was the time of the Vietnam War. On the tip of everyone's tongue were issues like the U.S. Army's brutal slaughter of Vietnamese civilians at My Lai (made public while *Little Big Man* was still in production), conscientious objection (draft dodging, the hardliners called it), the fight for minority equal rights, and "free love" – the

**“In the long run, the winning thing about *Little Big Man* is its refusal to toe any line. It mocks the Western myth, as Arthur Penn has done before more seriously in *The Left Handed Gun*. It also has a tendency to gawp at history with something very like awe, while at the same time waxing satirical with a fitful kind of mirth that comes and goes.”** *Films & Filming*

4

1 Little Tomahawk: Being raised by Indians has colored Jack Crabb's (Dustin Hoffman) take on life.

2 Politically neutral: Wild horses couldn't keep Jack away from the action – no matter whose side he happens to be fighting on.

3 Snow job: The American cavalry sweeps across the Cheyenne's land and leaves them to die in the merciless winter.

4 Poke her hontas: The preacher's wife (Faye Dunaway) wants to review the basics of sinning.

5 Cheyenne Viking: Jack braves new territory and boldly goes where no man has gone before. But is he man enough to tackle the needs of his wife and her squaw sisters?

xpression of an attempted break with materialism. Director Arthur Penn and creenwriter Calder Willingham build on a great number of these topics for heir depiction of the Cheyenne in *Little Big Man* (loosely based on Thomas Berger's 1964 novel of the same name). Here, no one thinks less of a man for ot wishing to go to battle for his nation; according to the wise Cheyenne hief (Chief Dan George), individuals not willing to fight should simply stay ome. Nor does anyone seem to be put off by the fact that one such Indian varrior is in the habit of sitting backwards on his horse and saying the opposite of what he means. Then there is a gay Indian who lives among the quaws and is as respected for his choice of lifestyle as the aforementioned acifist. Even free love is an accepted part of the Cheyenne's way of life. Soon fter Jack Crabb marries the young squaw Sunshine (Aimy Eccles), she selfessly entreats him to bed her three unattended sisters in their nuptial eepee; Jack, however, can barely muster up the strength required to satisfy is sister-in-laws.

It is therefore obvious that *Little Big Man* is neither meant to be seen as painstaking reconstruction of the Wild West, nor – contrary to popular beer – a white-washed retelling of a past in which Native Americans are made o look morally superior. The picture is simply an allegory of 1960s society.

The Cheyenne, who define themselves as human beings, stand for the pro ponents of a just, modern utopia – an ideal plagued by the monstrous action of the minions of the State.

For while *Little Big Man* portrays The Red Man with great compassion and a touch of irony, complete with an incident where the Cheyenne go to battle to beat some sense into their opponents, only to be shot and slaughtered, the White Men – whom Jack Crabb all meets twice – are caricatured as morally degenerate or completely neurotic. The preacher's wife, Mrs. Pendrake (Faye Dunaway), who wants to enlighten Jack with the Word of the Lord, turns out to be a bigoted hypocrite up to her chin in sin: when Jack meets her again she is on the payroll at a whorehouse. In the same vein, gunslinger Wild Bill Hickok (Jeff Corey) lets paranoia get the better of him and meets with a dishonorable demise, planting his chin in the toe of some cowboy's boot when he is hit down in a saloon by a crack shot kid. And then, of course, there's General Custer (Richard Mulligan), who takes the screen as a borderline insane, self-righteous narcissist. When, on the brink of the massacre at Little Big Horn, he indifferently gurgles and blabbers some nonsense to his troops about a glob of phlegm caught in his throat, we can't help but be reminded of the mad General Jack D. Ripper (Sterling Hayden) who laun

"One can easily see what attracted Penn to Berger's book: a *déraciné* hero zigzagging his way through America to find a home, the probing into the roots of American violence, and in particular the opportunity to confront the confusion of destructive, White Anglo-Saxon Protestant society with the organic culture of the Cheyenne, who call themselves 'the human beings.'" *Sight and Sound*

6 The soft-spoken carry big sticks: The Cheyenne on the freedom trail.

7 More than he can chew: Jack Crabb's stories about survival on the frontier are often tough to swallow.

ches World War III in Stanley Kubrick's *Dr. Strangelove or: How I Learned to Stop Worrying and Love the Bomb* (1963).

*Little Big Man's* script was written in the literary tradition of the picaresque novel. The pure of heart anti-hero Jack Crabb relies on a bit of luck and healthy opportunism to cross the vast frontiers of time and space. Without batting an eye, he switches sides many times over, leading a ridiculously eventful and unsuccessful life that parodies the classic heroism of the Hollywood Western. A veritable contradiction in terms, Jack is an Indian warrior, the adopted son of a preacher, a gunslinger known as "The Soda Pop Kid," the respectable business colleague of a resolute Swedish wife, a drunkard, a trapper and last but not least a scout for General Custer. It is in this final capacity that he dupes the bloodthirsty warmonger into leading his men to a valley where allied Indian forces are laying in wait. Custer, who has hired Jack to serve as his "negative barometer," follows the scout's instructions to the letter, thinking that he'll dodge any confrontation with the Native Americans by doing so. Needless to say, the general is headed for wholesale disaster. Jack, on the other hand, is the only White Man to come out of Little Big Horn unscathed and smelling like a rose. That, at least, is what he says in the 1950s at the age of 121 in an interview with an aspiring historian (William Hickey). It is a larger than life story preserved for posterity on tape – and as credible as any legend of the wild Wild West.

LP

**REVISIONIST WESTERN** The first Revisionist Western dates back to William A. Wellman's anti-lynch picture *The Ox-Bow Incident* (1943), which put a new slant on a genre notorious for brazenly glorifying the spirit of a frontier pioneered exclusively by Whites. In the 1950s, similar undertakings revamped many of the archetypes prevalent in the Hollywood Western. The films of Anthony Mann and Budd Boetticher, to name but two, consistently feature neurotically flawed, wrathful heroes on the rampage.

Conversely, Native Americans began to emerge as three-dimensional characters in pictures like Delmer Daves' *Broken Arrow* (1950), and were no longer made out to be a mere impediment to the march of U.S. civilization. The critical examination of established Western legends in the 60s and 70s soon paved the way for films that totally ignored the norms of the genre. The Spaghetti Western became known for substituting fair play and golden idealism with cynicism and greed. Director Sam Peckinpah even displayed a taste for having his heroes do the unthinkable and shoot their enemies in the back. Still, the Revisionist Western cannot be categorized by a uniform style or subject: directors either tweak cinematic narratives, focus on an accurate historical portrayal of the period, or use the Wild West as a parable for the Vietnam War, as Robert Aldrich did in *Ulzana's Raid* (1972). But one thing is certain: the once pristine face of the Western acquired indelible scars that blocked any way back to the innocence of yore.

# DEATH IN VENICE
## Morte a Venezia

1970 - ITALY - 135 MIN. - LITERARY ADAPTATION, DRAMA

DIRECTOR LUCHINO VISCONTI (1906–1976)

SCREENPLAY LUCHINO VISCONTI, NICOLA BADALUCCO, based on the novella *DER TOD IN VENEDIG* by THOMAS MANN DIRECTOR OF PHOTOGRAPHY PASQUALE DE SANTIS EDITING RUGGERO MASTROIANNI MUSIC GUSTAV MAHLER PRODUCTION LUCHINO VISCONTI for ALFA CINEMATOGRAFICA.

STARRING DIRK BOGARDE (Gustav von Aschenbach), SILVANA MANGANO (Tadzio's Mother), BJÖRN ANDRESEN (Tadzio), ROMOLO VALLI (Hotel Director), MARK BURNS (Alfred), MARISA BERENSON (Frau von Aschenbach), FRANCO FABRIZI (Hairdresser), ANTONIO APPICELLA (Vagabond), SERGIO GARFAGNOLI (Polish Boy), NORA RICCI (Gouvernante).

## *"Your music is stillborn."*

Venice, in the early 20th century. Gustav von Aschenbach (Dirk Bogarde), an aging German composer, is visiting the city of canals, hoping to recover from a nervous breakdown. He moves into an exclusive hotel facing the beach, where his fellow guests include an aristocratic Polish lady (Silvana Mangano) with her children and servants. Aschenbach immediately notices her son Tadzio (Björn Andresen), a pale, slender boy with long blond hair. Soon, Aschenbach is so fascinated by this beautiful youth that his daily schedule is increasingly dominated by the need to observe him. This obsession leads to a resolve to make contact with the boy – despite the threat posed by the cholera epidemic that is spreading through the city. Aschenbach ultimately succumbs to the disease and dies.

Few film adaptations of literary classics manage to surpass the original. Luchino Visconti's *Death in Venice* is one of the few exceptions, not least because the director refused to be intimidated by Thomas Mann's famous novella. His film version is strikingly different from the book, and he made these changes in order to realize his own cinematic vision.

In the course of his career, Visconti directed opera as well as films, and it shows. The importance of music to *Death in Venice* can be judged by the

1

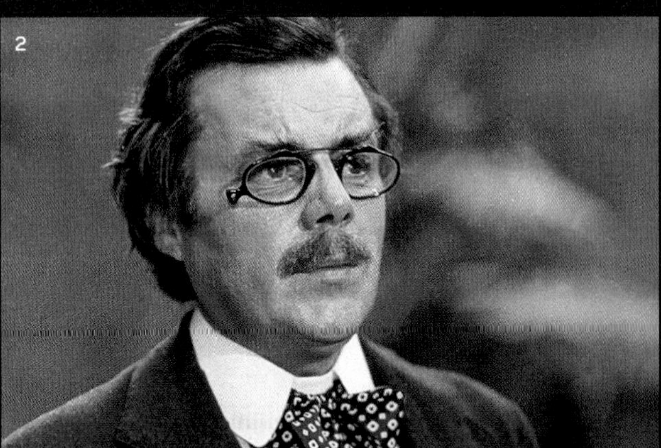


fact that Visconti made Aschenbach a composer; in Mann's novella, Aschenbach was a writer, though the character was in fact based on Gustav Mahler.

Mahler's music is of essential importance to the film. His Fifth Symphony is heard over the opening titles, and it accompanies Aschenbach's arrival in Venice on a steamship emerging into the light of dawn. This musical motif recurs throughout the film, and the elegiac gravity of the piece is mirrored in the almost lethargic rhythm of the images. The drama is contained, and develops, in a series of slow zooms and meticulous tracking shots that capture the morbid and sensual atmosphere of Venice, in the strong but subdued colors of the sultry summer and in the broad Cinemascope format. There is a remarkably serene quality to Visconti's film, strengthening the impact of the music, which is used very sparingly. The film has no narrator, Aschenbach is

**"A film to be savored and one to be enjoyed and studied more than once."** *Variety*

1 Angel of death: Frail aesthete Gustav von Aschenbach is overtaken by youth's fleeting beauty when he lays eyes on Tadzio (Björn Andresen).

2 Music to our ears: The role of composer Gustav von Aschenbach was the crescendo of Dirk Bogarde's acting career.

3 Eternal flame: Much like Visconti, Silvana Mangano's (left) film career rode the wave of post-war Italian neo-realism. She was one of the movement's shining stars.

4 Phoenix from the ashes: Visconti and cameraman Pasquale de Santis masterfully translate Thomas Mann's prose to the screen with sensuous visuals, gliding cinematography and seamless zoom-ins.

3

allowed no internal monologues, and indeed, no one says very much at all. Instead, the camera feels its way around the story discreetly, and Dirk Bogarde's expressive acting does the rest. Thomas Mann's polished descriptions and the fine irony of the text are perfectly translated into a purely visual language. Visconti traces the beginnings of Aschenbach's downfall in a series of flashbacks: the destruction of a happy family, sexual frustration and, above all, failure as an artist. In his ambition to express a pure, absolute beauty through his music, Aschenbach is not merely an anachronism; he is also in fatal rebellion against the claims of the body. When his friend Alfred (Mark Burns) insists on the dual nature of music, Aschenbach resists desperately. These are the moments in which Visconti interrupts the tranquil flow of his narrative and allows the past to erupt into the sluggish present like a feverish memory. The lie that has ruled Aschenbach's life catches up with him in Venice: for in recognizing that Tadzio embodies both perfection *and* sensuality, the noble aesthete is thrown back upon his own physical desire, which is more clearly homosexual in Visconti than in Mann.

By the time Aschenbach realizes what's driving him, it's too late: he's an elderly man with a decaying body. With the bitterest of irony, Visconti shows us how the composer attempts to regain his youth in the hairdresser's salon. At the end of the film, a cadaverous Aschenbach lies slumped in his deckchair on the beach, with black hair-dye trickling down his sweat-soaked face. Tadzio, standing on the shore, turns towards him and points off into the distance: it's a last greeting from an angel of death.

JH

**LUCHINO VISCONTI (1906–1976)**

He was the scion of a noble Italian family, and he described himself as a Marxist – though his politics didn't stop him enjoying the best that life had to offer. The apparently disparate sides of Luchino Visconti's personality left their traces in his filmography. After learning his trade with Jean Renoir, he made his directing debut while Mussolini's Fascist regime was still in power: the naturalistic style of *Obsession* (*Ossessione*, 1943) was the starting point for Italian *neorealismo.* Visconti's *The Earth Trembles* (*La terra trema*, 1948), the story of a fisherman exploited by wholesale merchants, is regarded as one of the masterpieces of the neorealist movement. His sympathy for ordinary people is also evident in later films: see *Rocco and His Brothers* (*Rocco e i suoi fratelli*, 1960), which shows the disintegration of a family that moves from southern Italy to Milan in search of work. With *Senso* (*Senso*, 1954) however, he created the first of the splendidly operatic color films that would dominate his later career. Of these major productions, many critics feel the best was *The Leopard* (*Il gattopardo*, 1963), based on a novel by Giuseppe Tomasi di Lampedusa. This spectacular epic about a family of Sicilian aristocrats in the 19th century won him the Golden Palm at Cannes and made him an international star director. He sustained his reputation with films such as *Death in Venice* (*Morte a Venezia*, 1970) and *Ludwig* (*Le Crépuscule des dieux*, 1972), the latter a biography of the eccentric King of Bavaria. In parallel to his work in the cinema, Visconti was also a successful theater and opera director. The career of Maria Callas was closely linked to his own.

ACADEMY
AWARDS 1961–1970

# 1961 OSCARS

1 Someday, somewhere: A musical finds a new way of winning. In 1961, *West Side Story* sweeps the Oscars, winning legendary Hollywood director Robert Wise an Oscar.

2 Mamma mia: For her performance as one of The Second World War's mothers of courage, glamorous Italian Sophia Loren took home the Best Actress Oscar.

| | |
|---|---|
| **BEST PICTURE** | *West Side Story* (ROBERT WISE) |
| **BEST DIRECTOR** | ROBERT WISE, JEROME ROBBINS for *West Side Story* |
| | |
| **BEST LEADING ACTRESS** | SOPHIA LOREN in *Two Women* |
| **BEST LEADING ACTOR** | MAXIMILIAN SCHELL in *Judgment at Nuremberg* |
| **BEST SUPPORTING ACTRESS** | RITA MORENO in *West Side Story* |
| **BEST SUPPORTING ACTOR** | GEORGE CHAKIRIS in *West Side Story* |
| | |
| **BEST ORIGINAL SCREENPLAY** | WILLIAM INGE for *Splendor In The Grass* |
| **BEST ADAPTED SCREENPLAY** | ABBY MANN for *Judgment at Nuremberg* |
| **BEST FOREIGN LANGUAGE FILM** | *Through a Glass Darkly* (SWEDEN) |
| | |
| **BEST CINEMATOGRAPHY** (black & white) | EUGEN SCHÜFFTAN for *The Hustler* |
| **BEST CINEMATOGRAPHY** (color) | DANIEL L. FAPP for *West Side Story* |
| **BEST ART DIRECTION** (black & white) | HARRY HORNER, GENE CALLAHAN for *The Hustler* |
| **BEST ART DIRECTION** (color) | BORIS LEVEN, VICTOR A. GANGELIN for *West Side Story* |
| **BEST FILM EDITING** | THOMAS STANFORD for *West Side Story* |
| **BEST MUSIC** | HENRY MANCINI for *Breakfast at Tiffany's* |
| **BEST ADAPTED MUSIC** | SAUL CHAPLIN, JOHNNY GREEN, SID RAMIN, IRWIN KOSTAL for *West Side Story* |
| **BEST SONG** | HENRY MANCINI (music), JOHNNY MERCER (text) for "MOON RIVER" in *Breakfast at Tiffany's* |
| **BEST COSTUMES** (black & white) | PIERO GHERARDI for *La Dolce Vita* |
| **BEST COSTUMES** (color) | IRENE SHARAFF for *West Side Story* |
| **BEST VISUAL EFFECTS** | BILL WARRINGTON for *The Guns of Navarone* |
| **BEST SOUND** | FRED HYNES, GORDON SAWYER for *West Side Story* |
| **BEST SOUND EFFECTS EDITING** | CHRIS GREENHAM for *The Guns of Navarone* |

# 1962 OSCARS

3 Atticus Rex: Gregory Peck steps into the role of Finch and defends a sitting duck. He couldn't convince his on-screen jury of his brilliance, but he had no problems convincing Oscar.

4 Epic greatness: David Lean and Sam Spiegel on the set of Lawrence of Arabia, winner of seven Oscars.

**BEST PICTURE** *Lawrence of Arabia* (SAM SPIEGEL)
**BEST DIRECTOR** DAVID LEAN for *Lawrence of Arabia*

**BEST LEADING ACTRESS** ANNE BANCROFT in *The Miracle Worker*
**BEST LEADING ACTOR** GREGORY PECK in *To Kill a Mockingbird*
**BEST SUPPORTING ACTRESS** PATTY DUKE in *The Miracle Worker*
**BEST SUPPORTING ACTOR** ED BEGLEY in *Sweet Bird of Youth*

**BEST ORIGINAL SCREENPLAY** ENNIO DE CONCINI, ALFREDO GIANNETTI, PIETRO GERMI for *Divorce – Italian Style*
**BEST ADAPTED SCREENPLAY** HORTON FOOTE for *To Kill a Mockingbird*
**BEST FOREIGN LANGUAGE FILM** *Les Dimanches de Ville d'Avray* (FRANCE)

**BEST CINEMATOGRAPHY (black & white)** JEAN BOURGOIN, WALTER WOTTITZ for *The Longest Day*
**BEST CINEMATOGRAPHY (color)** FREDDIE YOUNG for *Lawrence of Arabia*
**BEST ART DIRECTION (black & white)** ALEXANDER GOLITZEN, HENRY BUMSTEAD, OLIVER EMERT for *To Kill a Mockingbird*
**BEST ART DIRECTION (color)** JOHN BOX, JOHN STOLL, DARIO SIMONI for *Lawrence of Arabia*
**BEST FILM EDITING** ANNE V. COATES for *Lawrence of Arabia*
**BEST MUSIC** MAURICE JARRE for *Lawrence of Arabia*
**BEST ADAPTED MUSIC** RAY HEINDORF for *Music Man*
**BEST SONG** HENRY MANCINI (music), JOHNNY MERCER (text) for "DAYS OF WINE AND ROSES" in *Days of Wine and Roses*
**BEST COSTUMES (black & white)** NORMA KOCH for *What Ever Happened to Baby Jane?*
**BEST COSTUMES (color)** MARY WILLS for *The Wonderful World of the Brothers Grimm*
**BEST VISUAL EFFECTS** ROBERT MACDONALD for *The Longest Day*
**BEST SOUND** JOHN COX for *Lawrence of Arabia*
**BEST SOUND EFFECTS EDITING** JACQUES MAUMOT for *The Longest Day*

# 1963 OSCARS

1 Samson and Delilah: Oscar-winning director Tony Richardson and his femme fatale Diane Cilento practice the Kama Sutra while filming runaway hit *Tom Jones*.

2 It's a long road to Tipperary: Sidney Poitier becomes the first African American male to receive the Oscar for Best Actor with *Lilies of the Field*.

| | |
|---|---|
| **BEST PICTURE** | *Tom Jones* (TONY RICHARDSON) |
| **BEST DIRECTOR** | TONY RICHARDSON for *Tom Jones* |
| **BEST LEADING ACTRESS** | PATRICIA NEAL in *Hud* |
| **BEST LEADING ACTOR** | SIDNEY POITIER in *Lilien auf dem Felde* |
| **BEST SUPPORTING ACTRESS** | MARGARET RUTHERFORD in *Hotel International* |
| **BEST SUPPORTING ACTOR** | MELVYN DOUGLAS in *Hud* |
| **BEST ORIGINAL SCREENPLAY** | JAMES R. WEBB for *How the West Was Won* |
| **BEST ADAPTED SCREENPLAY** | JOHN OSBORNE for *Tom Jones* |
| **BEST FOREIGN LANGUAGE FILM** | *8 ½* (ITALY) |
| **BEST CINEMATOGRAPHY** (black & white) | JAMES WONG HOWE for *Hud* |
| **BEST CINEMATOGRAPHY** (color) | LEON SHAMROY for *Cleopatra* |
| **BEST ART DIRECTION** (black & white) | GENE CALLAHAN for *America, America* |
| **BEST ART DIRECTION** (color) | JOHN DECUIR, JACK MARTIN SMITH, HILYARD M. BROWN, HERMAN A. BLUMENTHAL, ELVEN WEBB, MAURICE PELLING, BORIS JURAGA, WALTER M. SCOTT, PAUL S. FOX, RAY MOYER for *Cleopatra* |
| **BEST FILM EDITING** | HAROLD F. KRESS for *How the West Was Won* |
| **BEST MUSIC** | JOHN ADDISON for *Tom Jones* |
| **BEST ADAPTED MUSIC** | ANDRÉ PREVIN for *Irma la Douce* |
| **BEST SONG** | JIMMY VAN HEUSEN (music), SAMMY CAHN (text) for "CALL ME IRRESPONSIBLE" in *Papa's Delicate Condition* |
| **BEST COSTUMES** (black & white) | PIERO GHERARDI for *8 ½* |
| **BEST COSTUMES** (color) | IRENE SHARAFF, VITTORIO NINO NOVARESE, RENIÉ for *Cleopatra* |
| **BEST VISUAL EFFECTS** | EMIL KOSA JR. for *Cleopatra* |
| **BEST SOUND** | FRANKLIN MILTON for *How the West Was Won* |
| **BEST SOUND EFFECTS EDITING** | WALTER ELLIOTT for *It's a Mad Mad Mad Mad World* |

# 1964 OSCARS

3 Oscar etiquette: Best Actor recipient Rex Harrison and his pupil Audrey Hepburn celebrate *My Fair Lady's* crowning achievement – a total of eight wins at the 1964 Academy Awards.

4 Using her noggin: Julie Andrews goes from a fair lady of the stage to irresistible screen governess in the timeless classic *Mary Poppins*.

| | |
|---|---|
| **BEST PICTURE** | *My Fair Lady* (JACK L. WARNER) |
| **BEST DIRECTOR** | GEORGE CUKOR for *My Fair Lady* |
| | |
| **BEST LEADING ACTRESS** | JULIE ANDREWS in *Mary Poppins* |
| **BEST LEADING ACTOR** | REX HARRISON in *My Fair Lady* |
| **BEST SUPPORTING ACTRESS** | LILA KEDROVA in *Zorba the Greek* |
| **BEST SUPPORTING ACTOR** | PETER USTINOV in *Topkapi* |
| | |
| **BEST ORIGINAL SCREENPLAY** | S. H. BARNETT, PETER STONE, FRANK TARLOFF for *Father Goose* |
| **BEST ADAPTED SCREENPLAY** | EDWARD ANHALT for *Becket* |
| **BEST FOREIGN LANGUAGE FILM** | *Yesterday, Today and Tomorrow* (ITALY) |
| | |
| **BEST CINEMATOGRAPHY (black & white)** | WALTER LASSALLY for *Zorba the Greek* |
| **BEST CINEMATOGRAPHY (color)** | HARRY STRADLING for *My Fair Lady* |
| **BEST ART DIRECTION (black & white)** | VASSILIS PHOTOPOULOS for *Zorba the Greek* |
| **BEST ART DIRECTION (color)** | GENE ALLEN, CECIL BEATON, GEORGE JAMES HOPKINS for *My Fair Lady* |
| **BEST FILM EDITING** | COTTON WARBURTON for *Mary Poppins* |
| **BEST MUSIC** | RICHARD M. SHERMAN, ROBERT B. SHERMAN for *Mary Poppins* |
| **BEST ADAPTED MUSIC** | ANDRÉ PREVIN for *My Fair Lady* |
| **BEST SONG** | RICHARD M. SHERMAN, ROBERT B. SHERMAN for "CHIM CHIM CHER-EE" in *Mary Poppins* |
| **BEST COSTUMES (black & white)** | DOROTHY JEAKINS for *The Night of the Iguana* |
| **BEST COSTUMES (color)** | CECIL BEATON for *My Fair Lady* |
| **BEST VISUAL EFFECTS** | PETER ELLENSHAW, HAMILTON LUSKE, EUSTACE LYCETT for *Mary Poppins* |
| **BEST SOUND** | GEORGE GROVES for *My Fair Lady* |
| **BEST SOUND EFFECTS EDITING** | NORMAN WANSTALL for *Goldfinger* |

# 1965 OSCARS

1 Double Indemnity: Julie Christie enjoys more critical acclaim in 1965 than any other big-name screen star with a Best Actress Oscar for *Darling* and the many wins of *Doctor Zhivago.*

2 Mother may I? *Patch of Blue's* Shelley Winters earns her second Best Supporting Actress Oscar for yet another brilliant portrayal of an insufferable nag.

**BEST PICTURE** *The Sound of Music* (ROBERT WISE)
**BEST DIRECTOR** ROBERT WISE for *The Sound of Music*

**BEST LEADING ACTRESS** JULIE CHRISTIE in *Darling*
**BEST LEADING ACTOR** LEE MARVIN in *Cat Ballou*
**BEST SUPPORTING ACTRESS** SHELLEY WINTERS in *A Patch of Blue*
**BEST SUPPORTING ACTOR** MARTIN BALSAM in *A Thousand Clowns*

**BEST ORIGINAL SCREENPLAY** FREDERIC RAPHAEL for *Darling*
**BEST ADAPTED SCREENPLAY** ROBERT BOLT for *Doctor Zhivago*
**BEST FOREIGN LANGUAGE FILM** *The Shop on Main Street* (CZECHOSLOVAKIA)

**BEST CINEMATOGRAPHY (black & white)** ERNEST LASZLO for *Ship of Fools*
**BEST CINEMATOGRAPHY (color)** FREDDIE YOUNG for *Doctor Zhivago*
**BEST ART DIRECTION (black & white)** ROBERT CLATWORTHY, JOSEPH KISH for *Ship of Fools*
**BEST ART DIRECTION (color)** JOHN BOX, TERENCE MARSH, DARIO SIMONI for *Doctor Zhivago*
**BEST FILM EDITING** WILLIAM REYNOLDS for *The Sound of Music*
**BEST MUSIC** MAURICE JARRE for *Doctor Zhivago*
**BEST ADAPTED MUSIC** IRWIN KOSTAL for *The Sound of Music*
**BEST SONG** JOHNNY MANDEL (music), PAUL FRANCIS WEBSTER (text) for "THE SHADOW OF YOUR SMILE" in *The Sandpiper*
**BEST COSTUMES (black & white)** JULIE HARRIS for *Darling*
**BEST COSTUMES (color)** PHYLLIS DALTON for *Doctor Zhivago*
**BEST VISUAL EFFECTS** JOHN STEARS for *Thunderball*
**BEST SOUND** JAMES CORCORAN, FRED HYNES for *The Sound of Music*
**BEST SOUND EFFECTS EDITING** TREG BROWN for *The Great Race*

# 1966 OSCARS

3 Letting it all hang out: Best Actress winner Elizabeth Taylor and real-life hubby Richard Burton play a married couple intent on taking their love to the grave.

4 Allies and enemies: King (Robert Shaw) and royal advisor Thomas More (Paul Scofield) prove to be fair-weather friends in *A Man for All Seasons*, the Best Picture winner of 1966.

| | |
|---|---|
| **BEST PICTURE** | *A Man for all Seasons* (FRED ZINNEMANN) |
| **BEST DIRECTOR** | FRED ZINNEMANN for *A Man for all Seasons* |
| **BEST LEADING ACTRESS** | ELIZABETH TAYLOR in *Who's Afraid of Virginia Woolf?* |
| **BEST LEADING ACTOR** | PAUL SCOFIELD in *A Man for all Seasons* |
| **BEST SUPPORTING ACTRESS** | SANDY DENNIS in *Who's Afraid of Virginia Woolf?* |
| **BEST SUPPORTING ACTOR** | WALTER MATTHAU in *The Fortune Cookie* |
| **BEST ORIGINAL SCREENPLAY** | CLAUDE LELOUCH, PIERRE UYTTERHOEVEN for *A Man and a Woman* |
| **BEST ADAPTED SCREENPLAY** | ROBERT BOLT for *A Man for all Seasons* |
| **BEST FOREIGN LANGUAGE FILM** | *A Man and a Woman* (FRANCE) |
| **BEST CINEMATOGRAPHY** (black & white) | HASKELL WEXLER for *Who's Afraid of Virginia Woolf?* |
| **BEST CINEMATOGRAPHY** (color) | TED MOORE for *A Man for all Seasons* |
| **BEST ART DIRECTION** (black & white) | RICHARD SYLBERT, GEORGE JAMES HOPKINS for *Who's Afraid of Virginia Woolf?* |
| **BEST ART DIRECTION** (color) | JACK MARTIN SMITH, DALE HENNESY, WALTER M. SCOTT, STUART A. REISS for *Fantastic Voyage* |
| **BEST FILM EDITING** | FREDRIC STEINKAMP, FRANK SANTILLO, HENRY BERMAN, STU LINDER for *Grand Prix* |
| **BEST MUSIC** | JOHN BARRY for *Born Free* |
| **BEST ADAPTED MUSIC** | KEN THORNE for *A Funny Thing Happened on the Way to the Forum* |
| **BEST SONG** | JOHN BARRY (music), DON BLACK (text) for "BORN FREE" in *Born Free* |
| **BEST COSTUMES** (black & white) | IRENE SHARAFF for *Who's Afraid of Virginia Woolf?* |
| **BEST COSTUMES** (color) | ELIZABETH HAFFENDEN, JOAN BRIDGE for *A Man for all Seasons* |
| **BEST VISUAL EFFECTS** | ART CRUICKSHANK for *Fantastic Voyage* |
| **BEST SOUND** | FRANKLIN MILTON for *Grand Prix* |
| **BEST SOUND EFFECTS EDITING** | GORDON DANIEL for *Grand Prix* |

# 1967 OSCARS

1 Pride and prejudice: Rod Steiger uses his Southern charm to earn himself an Oscar at Sidney Poitier's side in Norman Jewison's *In Heat of the Night.*

2 An affair to remember: Katharine Hepburn takes home one of her four Best Actress Oscars for her role in *Guess Who's Coming to Dinner*. Here, she is pictured with her preferred on and off screen leading man, Spencer Tracy.

| | |
|---|---|
| **BEST PICTURE** | *In the Heat of the Night* (WALTER MIRISCH) |
| **BEST DIRECTOR** | MIKE NICHOLS for *The Graduate* |
| **BEST LEADING ACTRESS** | KATHARINE HEPBURN in *Guess Who's Coming to Dinner* |
| **BEST LEADING ACTOR** | ROD STEIGER in *In the Heat of the Night* |
| **BEST SUPPORTING ACTRESS** | ESTELLE PARSONS in *Bonnie and Clyde* |
| **BEST SUPPORTING ACTOR** | GEORGE KENNEDY in *Cool Hand Luke* |
| **BEST ORIGINAL SCREENPLAY** | WILLIAM ROSE for *Guess Who's Coming to Dinner* |
| **BEST ADAPTED SCREENPLAY** | STIRLING SILLIPHANT for *In the Heat of the Night* |
| **BEST FOREIGN LANGUAGE FILM** | *Closely Watched Trains* (CZECHOSLOVAKIA) |
| **BEST CINEMATOGRAPHY** | BURNETT GUFFEY for *Bonnie and Clyde* |
| **BEST ART DIRECTION** | JOHN TRUSCOTT, EDWARD CARRERE, JOHN BROWN for *Camelot* |
| **BEST FILM EDITING** | HAL ASHBY for *In the Heat of the Night* |
| **BEST MUSIC** | ELMER BERNSTEIN for *Thoroughly Modern Millie* |
| **BEST ADAPTED MUSIC** | ALFRED NEWMAN, KEN DARBY for *Camelot* |
| **BEST SONG** | LESLIE BRICUSSE for "TALK TO THE ANIMALS" in *Doctor Dolittle* |
| **BEST COSTUMES** | JOHN TRUSCOTT for *Camelot* |
| **BEST VISUAL EFFECTS** | L. B. ABBOTT for *Doctor Dolittle* |
| **BEST SOUND** | SAMUEL GOLDWYN STUDIO SOUND DEPARTMENT for *In the Heat of the Night* |
| **BEST SOUND EFFECTS EDITING** | JOHN POYNER for *The Dirty Dozen* |

# 1968 OSCARS

3 Director of the orphanage: Carol Reed is responsible for many a 1940s and 50s cinema classic. In 1968, he claimed his directing Oscar for a heart-warming musical based on Charles Dickens' literary masterpiece *Oliver Twist.*

4 Flowers for Cliff Robertson: The actor goes from mentally retarded to Oscar genius in *Charly.*

| | |
|---|---|
| **BEST PICTURE** | *Oliver!* (JOHN WOOLF) |
| **BEST DIRECTOR** | CAROL REED for *Oliver!* |
| **BEST LEADING ACTRESS** | BARBRA STREISAND in *Funny Girl* / KATHARINE HEPBURN in *The Lion In Winter* |
| **BEST LEADING ACTOR** | CLIFF ROBERTSON in *Charly* |
| **BEST SUPPORTING ACTRESS** | RUTH GORDON in *Rosemary's Baby* |
| **BEST SUPPORTING ACTOR** | JACK ALBERTSON in *The Subject Was Roses* |
| **BEST ORIGINAL SCREENPLAY** | MEL BROOKS for *The Producers* |
| **BEST ADAPTED SCREENPLAY** | JAMES GOLDMAN for *The Lion In Winter* |
| **BEST FOREIGN LANGUAGE FILM** | *Vojna i mir I: Andrei Bolkonsky* (USSR) |
| **BEST CINEMATOGRAPHY** | PASQUALINO DE SANTIS for *Romeo and Juliet* |
| **BEST ART DIRECTION** | JOHN BOX, TERENCE MARSH, VERNON DIXON, KEN MUGGLESTON for *Oliver!* |
| **BEST FILM EDITING** | FRANK P. KELLER for *Bullitt* |
| **BEST MUSIC** | JOHN BARRY for *The Lion In Winter* |
| **BEST MUSIC** (musical) | JOHNNY GREEN for *Oliver!* |
| **BEST SONG** | MICHEL LEGRAND (music), ALAN BERGMAN (text), MARILYN BERGMAN (text) for "THE WINDMILLS OF YOUR MIND" in *The Thomas Crown Affair* |
| **BEST COSTUMES** | DANILO DONATI for *Romeo and Juliet* |
| **BEST VISUAL EFFECTS** | STANLEY KUBRICK for *2001: A Space Odyssey* |
| **BEST SOUND** | SHEPPERTON STUDIO SOUND DEPARTMENT for *Oliver!* |
| **BEST SOUND EFFECTS EDITING** | Not awarded |

# 1969 OSCARS

1 Kiss his grits: Henry Hathaway's *True Grit* won John Wayne the sole Oscar of his legendary career as a Hollywood cowboy.

2 X marks the spot: John Schlesinger's provocative critique on America *Midnight Cowboy* overshadowed the other films at the 1969 Oscars. The picture turned Jon Voigt (left) into a household name as he braved the New York underbelly at the side of Hollywood's favorite son, Dustin Hoffman.

| | |
|---|---|
| **BEST PICTURE** | *Midnight Cowboy* (JEROME HELLMAN) |
| **BEST DIRECTOR** | JOHN SCHLESINGER for *Midnight Cowboy* |
| **BEST LEADING ACTRESS** | MAGGIE SMITH in *The Prime of Miss Jean Brodie* |
| **BEST LEADING ACTOR** | JOHN WAYNE in *True Grit* |
| **BEST SUPPORTING ACTRESS** | GOLDIE HAWN in *Cactus Flower* |
| **BEST SUPPORTING ACTOR** | GIG YOUNG in *They Shoot Horses, Don't They?* |
| **BEST ORIGINAL SCREENPLAY** | WILLIAM GOLDMAN for *Butch Cassidy and the Sundance Kid* |
| **BEST ADAPTED SCREENPLAY** | WALDO SALT for *Midnight Cowboy* |
| **BEST FOREIGN LANGUAGE FILM** | *Z* (FRANCE/ALGERIA) |
| **BEST CINEMATOGRAPHY** | CONRAD L. HALL for *Butch Cassidy and the Sundance Kid* |
| **BEST ART DIRECTION** | JOHN DECUIR, JACK MARTIN SMITH, HERMAN A. BLUMENTHAL, WALTER M. SCOTT, GEORGE JAMES HOPKINS, RAPHAEL BRETTON for *Hello, Dolly!* |
| **BEST FILM EDITING** | FRANÇOISE BONNOT for *Z* |
| **BEST MUSIC** | BURT BACHARACH for *Butch Cassidy and the Sundance Kid* |
| **BEST MUSIC (musical)** | LENNIE HAYTON, LIONEL NEWMAN for *Hello, Dolly!* |
| **BEST SONG** | BURT BACHARACH (music), HAL DAVID (text) for "RAINDROPS KEEP FALLIN' ON MY HEAD" in *Butch Cassidy and the Sundance Kid* |
| **BEST COSTUMES** | MARGARET FURSE for *Anne of the Thousand Days* |
| **BEST VISUAL EFFECTS** | ROBIE ROBINSON for *Marooned* |
| **BEST SOUND** | JACK SOLOMON, MURRAY SPIVACK for *Hello, Dolly!* |
| **BEST SOUND EFFECTS EDITING** | Not awarded |

# 1970 OSCARS

3 Tough sell: George C. Scott wins the Oscar for his performance as the title role in *Patton* – and refuses to accept his Hollywood medal of honor.

4 It brings a tear of joy to my eyes: Sir John Mills proves to be the lucky one after all. His performance as the village idiot in David Lean's *Ryan's Daughter* wins him a Best Supporting Actor Oscar.

| | |
|---|---|
| BEST PICTURE | *Patton* (FRANK MCCARTHY) |
| BEST DIRECTOR | FRANKLIN J. SCHAFFNER for *Patton* |
| BEST LEADING ACTRESS | GLENDA JACKSON in *Women in Love* |
| BEST LEADING ACTOR | GEORGE C. SCOTT in *Patton* |
| BEST SUPPORTING ACTRESS | HELEN HAYES in *Airport* |
| BEST SUPPORTING ACTOR | JOHN MILLS in *Ryan's Daughter* |
| BEST ORIGINAL SCREENPLAY | FRANCIS FORD COPPOLA, EDMUND H. NORTH for *Patton* |
| BEST ADAPTED SCREENPLAY | RING LARDNER JR. for *M*A*S*H* |
| BEST FOREIGN LANGUAGE FILM | *Investigation of a Citizen Above Suspicion* (ITALY) |
| BEST CINEMATOGRAPHY | FREDDIE YOUNG for *Ryan's Daughter* |
| BEST ART DIRECTION | URIE MCCLEARY, GIL PARRONDO, ANTONIO MATEOS, PIERRE-LOUIS THÉVENET for *Patton* |
| BEST FILM EDITING | HUGH S. FOWLER for *Patton* |
| BEST MUSIC | FRANCIS LAI for *Love Story* |
| BEST MUSIC (Song Score) | PAUL MCCARTNEY, JOHN LENNON, GEORGE HARRISON, RINGO STARR for *Let it Be* |
| BEST SONG | FRED KARLIN (music), ROBB ROYER (text), JAMES GRIFFIN (text) for "FOR ALL WE KNOW" in *Lovers And Other Strangers* |
| BEST COSTUMES | VITTORIO NINO NOVARESE for *Cromwell* |
| BEST VISUAL EFFECTS | A. D. FLOWERS, L. B. ABBOTT for *Tora! Tora! Tora!* |
| BEST SOUND | DOUGLAS O. WILLIAMS, DON J. BASSMAN for *Patton* |
| BEST SOUND EFFECTS EDITING | Not awarded |

# INDEX OF FILMS

**English Title** *Original Title*

# INDEX OF FILMS

# GENERAL INDEX

*Production companies are listed in italics; film categories are preceded by a dash; numbers in bold refer to a glossary text.*

# GENERAL INDEX

# GENERAL INDEX

# GENERAL INDEX

# GENERAL INDEX

# GENERAL INDEX

# GENERAL INDEX

# ABOUT THE AUTHORS

*Philipp Bühler* (PB), *1971, studied political science, history and British studies. Film journalist, writing for various regional German publications. Lives in Berlin.

*David Gaertner* (DG), *1978, studied film and art history. Freelances for the German film archives division of the Berlin Film Museum. Lives in Berlin.

*Malte Hagener* (MH), *1971, degree in Literature and Media Studies. Editor and author of numerous academic articles. Lecturer in Film History at Amsterdam University. Lives in Amsterdam and Berlin.

*Steffen Haubner* (SH), *1965, studied Art History and Sociology. Has written many academic and press articles. Collaborator on the science and research section of the *Hamburger Abendblatt*. Lives in Hamburg.

*Jörn Hetebrügge* (JH), *1971, studied German Literature. Author of many academic and press articles. Academic assistant at the Dresden Technical University Art and Music Institute since 2003. Lives in Berlin.

*Harald Keller* (HK), *1958, media journalist, works for national newspapers, essays and book publications on the history of film and television. Lives in Osnabrück.

*Katja Kirste* (KK), *1969, media journalist and academic. Author of numerous publications on film and related subjects. Lives in Munich.

*Heinz-Jürgen Köhler* (HJK), *1963, chief copy editor for *TV Today*. Author of many academic and press articles. Lives in Hamburg.

*Oliver Küch* (OK), *1972, studied English language and British history. Media and computer journalist; author of articles on film and television. Lives in Hamburg.

*Petra Lange-Berndt* (PLB), *1973, studied Art History and German Literature, doctoral candidate at the Department of Art History, University of Hamburg. Has authored numerous academic articles. Lives in Hamburg.

*Nils Meyer* (NM), *1971, studied German Literature and Politics. Has written many articles in various papers and magazines. Academic assistant at the Dresden Technical University Art and Music Institute since 2003. Lives in Dresden.

*Eckhard Pabst* (EP), *1965, film theorist, numerous publications as editor and author. Lives in Rendsburg near Kiel.

*Lars Penning* (LP), *1962, film journalist, works for numerous national newspapers, various articles and books on the history of film. Lives in Berlin.

*Anne Pohl* (APO), *1961, active as a journalist since 1987. Author of numerous academic articles. Lives in Berlin.

*Stephan Reisner* (SR), *1969, studied literature and philosophy in Hanover. Freelance journalist in Berlin, writing for *Edit*, *BELLAtriste*, *Glasklar* and the *Tagesspiegel*. 1st prize, Kritischer Salon-Preis 2001, Hanover; 2nd prize at the 2002 Vienna Studio Awards.

*Burkhard Röwekamp* (BR), *1965, researcher at the Institute for Contemporary German Literature and Media at the Philipps University in Marburg. Has taught numerous courses and published many articles on the aesthetics and theory of contemporary film. Lives in Marburg.

*Eric Stahl* (ES), *1965, studied German language and literature, focusing on communications. Film journalist; cultural editor of *Woman* magazine and freelance writer for other publications. Lives in Berlin.

*Rainer Vowe* (RV), *1954, historian, works for the EU Directorate General XII (audio-visual media) and the Institute for Film and Television Studies at the Ruhr University in Bochum. Numerous articles about the history of cinema and television. Lives in Bochum.

# CREDITS

The publishers would like to thank the distributors, without whom many of these films would never have reached the big screen.

ALAMODE, ALEMANNIA, BUENA VISTA, CINERAMA, COLUMBIA, COLUMBIA-BAVARIA, CONCORDE, FIFIGE, FILMVERLAG / FUTURA, FOX, GLOBUS, INTER-VERLEIH, JUGENDFILM, KINOWELT, KNIPP, KORA, LUPE, MFA, NEUE VISIONEN, PARAMOUNT, PROGRESS, RANK, RING, SONDERFILM ZWICKER, TOBIS, UIP, UNITED ARTISTS, UNIVERSAL, WARNER BROS., WILD UTOPIA.



If, despite our concerted efforts, a distributor has been unintentionally omitted, we apologise and will amend any such errors brought to the attention of the publishers in the next edition.

# ACKNOWLEDGEMENTS

As the editor of this volume, I would like to thank all those who invested so much of their time, knowledge and energy into the making of this book. My special thanks to Thierry Nebois of TASCHEN for his coordination work and truly amazing ability to keep track of everything. Thanks also Birgit Reber and Andy Disl for their ingenious design concept that gives pride of place to the pictures, the true capital of any film book. My thanks to Philipp Berens and Thomas Dupont from defd and *Cinema*, and Hilary Tanner from the British Film Institute and the Bibliothèque du film for their help in accessing the original stills. Then, of course, I am hugely indebted to the authors, whose keen analyses form the backbone of this volume. I would also like to thank Steffen Haubner and David Gaertner for their meticulous technical editing, and Petra Lamers-Schütze, whose commitment and initiative got the project going. And last but not least, Benedikt Taschen, who not only agreed to produce and publish the series, but enthusiastically followed each volume's progress from start to finish. My personal thanks to him and everyone else mentioned here.

# ABOUT THIS BOOK

The 113 films selected for this book represent a decade of cinema. It goes without saying this involved making a number of difficult choices, some of which may be contested. A note also on the stills from some of the earlier films: it is a regrettable but inevitable fact that the older the film, the more difficult it is to obtain images of the required technical quality.
Each film is presented by an essay, and accompanied by a glossary text devoted to one person or a cinematographic term.
An index of films and a general index are provided at the back of the book to ensure optimal access.
As in the preceding volumes, the films are dated according to the year of production, not the year of release.

# IMPRINT

| | |
|---|---|
| **ENDPAPERS / PAGES 1–17** | BREAKFAST AT TIFFANY'S / Blake Edwards |
| **AND PAGES 608–609** | PARAMOUNT PICTURES |
| **PAGE 18** | EDWARD SCISSORHANDS / Tim Burton / 20TH CENTURY FOX |
| **PAGES 417–421, 587–589** | © WALT DISNEY PICTURES |

To stay informed about upcoming TASCHEN titles, please request our magazine at www.taschen.com or write to TASCHEN America, 6671 Sunset Boulevard, Suite 1508, USA-Los Angeles, CA 90028, Fax: +1-323-463.4442. We will be happy to send you a free copy of our magazine which is filled with information about all of our books.


Hohenzollernring 53, D-50672 Köln
**WWW.TASCHEN.COM**

| | |
|---|---|
| **PHOTOGRAPHS** | defd and CINEMA, Hamburg<br>BRITISH FILM INSTITUTE, London<br>BIBLIOTHÈQUE DU FILM (BiFi), Paris |
| **PROJECT MANAGEMENT** | PETRA LAMERS-SCHÜTZE, Cologne |
| **EDITORIAL COORDINATION** | STILISTICO and THIERRY NEBOIS, Cologne |
| **DESIGN** | SENSE/NET, ANDY DISL and BIRGIT REBER, Cologne |
| **TEXTS** | ULRIKE BERGFELD (UB), PHILIPP BÜHLER (PB), DAVID GAERTNER (DG), STEFFEN HAUBNER (SH), JÖRN HETEBRÜGGE (JH), BERTRAM KASCHEK (BK) HARALD KELLER (HK), KATJA KIRSTE (KK), HEINZ-JÜRGEN KÖHLER (HJK), OLIVER KÜCH (OK), PETRA LANGE-BERNDT (PLB), ALEXANDER LINDEN (AL), NILS MEYER (NM), ECKHARD PABST (EB), LARS PENNING (LP), STEPHAN REISNER (SR), ERIC STAHL (ES), RAINER VOWE (RV), ANKA ZIEFER (AZ) |
| **TECHNICAL EDITING** | DAVID GAERTNER, Berlin |
| **ENGLISH TRANSLATION** | PATRICK LANAGAN (introduction and texts), SHAUN SAMSON (texts and captions) for ENGLISH EXPRESS, Berlin |
| **EDITING** | DANIELA KLEIN for ENGLISH EXPRESS, BERLIN and JONATHAN MURPHY, Brussels |
| **PRODUCTION** | UTE WACHENDORF, Cologne |

PRINTED IN SPAIN
ISBN 3–8228–2799–1